God's EPIC Adventure

Changing Our Culture by the Story We Live and Tell

Doug & Gail
Having found your place
in GEA - Play it to the
hilt!
Winn
2009

WINN GRIFFIN

HARMON PRESS

Published by
Harmon Press
Woodinville, WA 98077
http://www.harmonpress.com

ISBN-10: 0-9799076-0-8
ISBN-13: 978-0-9799076-0-9

Library of Congress Control Number: 2007906992

All Scripture quotations, unless otherwise noted, are taken from *Today's New International® Version* TNIV©. Copyright 2001, 2005 by International Bible Society®. All rights reserved worldwide.

"TNIV" and "Today's New International Version" are trademarks registered in the United States Patent and Trademark Office by International Bible Society®.

Cover design by Rich Brimer: TheImageStudio.com

Back Cover Portrait: Sunset Portraits, Everett, WA (SunsetPortraits.com)

Cover: Michelangelo: *The Creation of Adam (The Donnadio)* from the Sistine Chapel, Vatican City.

Graphic art in the Introduction and in Acts 1-4 is copyrighted © 1978 by Winn Griffin. All other graphic art is in the Public Domain.

for
Donna Faith,
wife, mother, teacher, friend
Jason Jonathan,
son, entrepreneur, friend
and
Jeramie Joy,
daughter, giver, friend
JR and Nancy Short,
friends whose generosity made this book possible.

Verses are a convenient way

to look up a reference.

But, that's where their usefulness ends.

Contents

A list of the Acts in God's EPIC Adventure

What someone habitually does, and

the symbols around which they order

their lives, are at least as reliable

an index to their worldview

as the stories they 'officially' tell.

(N.T. Wright. *The New Testament and the People of God*)

Contents

Contents

Introduction

A preface, as to a book.

When we examine how stories work in

relation to other stories, we find that

human beings tell stories

because this is how we perceive,

and indeed relate to, the world.

(N. T. Wright. *The New Testament and the People of God*)

Thanks

Are there any original thoughts? There is nothing new under the sun according to the preacher in Ecclesiastes. I believe that all of us are the product of those who have given input into our lives. I know that such is the case for me. As you will see from the pages that follow, I am indebted to many resources in the material that is presented. To each one that God has called to scholarship and the writing of their findings, I am grateful.

It is apparent to me that first I must acknowledge my family for their continual support while I was writing this project.

To Donna Faith, my wife, from the memorable quote in Jerry McGuire, "you complete me." You are my best friend. Your kindness to allow me to take this journey is without measure. You have been caring and understanding of my time used for study and writing. Your reading of the manuscript many times was an awesome task. I don't know what I would have done without your eagle eye. Thanks, Donna Faith.

To my son Jason, who is flexible in life, who uses his sense of humor to bring comic relief to me in some stressful times. You brought me healing on more than one occasion. Thanks, Jason.

To my daughter, Jeramie Joy, who hounds me to talk to her in several different voices, who laughs and giggles when a voice shows up and talks to her. What voices you say? Matilda, Vern, Scratchnose, and Goofy, to name a few. You are such a delight. Thanks, Jeramie Joy.

To my learning partners who provided an extensive education for me during my second Doctor of Ministry at George Fox University and are truly caring and insightful, friends and colleagues for life: Rick Bartlett, Tony Blair, Jason Clark, Rick Hans, George Hemingway, Nick Howard, Todd Hunter, Randy Jumper, Eric Keck, Mike McNichols, Ken Niles, Craig Oldenburg, Rob Seewald, Rick Shrout, Dwight Spotts, and Dave Wollenburg. Thanks, guys. To the above list I would add Loren Kerns who was always available to help our doctoral cohort journey through the maze of the online world of WebCT and who also added incredible insights.

To my mentors over the years. To Kent Yinger, who drove me to think and reflect and then corrected my thinking and reflection with gracefulness and kindness in those long papers that I wrote. Thanks, Kent.

To Leon@rd Sweet who has taught me to think further outside the box than I was already thinking. Your desire for me to think and reflect with images and text, for me to be all that God wants me to be, will carry me for the rest of my life. Your model for writing books is truly amazing. I hope to follow in your footsteps. Your acrostic EPIC turned my head to title this book: God's EPIC Adventure. I really appreciate that Len agreed to write the Foreword for this book. That is such a blessing. Thanks, Len.

In addition to the present mentors, I would like to mention three more: In my college and seminary career, some of my formation came from Dr. Russ Spittler, now Provost of Vanguard University in Costa Mesa, CA. He taught me to be a critical loyalist. Second, Dr. James Kallas, a Lutheran New Testament specialist, now retired, who demonstrated to me that one could be a scholar and pastor at the same time. Next, to my friend, the late John Wimber, who took me along side of him when I was broken in ministry and helped me find worth in my own calling. Thanks, Russ, James, and John. John is now a part of that "cloud of witnesses" that has passed on to "life after death." I wonder if he can read what I wrote.

To my friend Brian McLaren. I first met Brian in Seattle when he addressed a small group of eager listeners as he told the story of his encounter with a young harp player and how he and she began an email conversation to share about her life's journey. I have followed his "emergent" rise with great interest. I am very thankful that he has taken time to write the Afterword for this book. Thanks, Brian.

To my pastors, Rich and Rose Swetman. They truly are intentional about living in God's EPIC Adventure. They lead an incarnational missional community of faith that is focused on bringing justice locally and globally. Thanks, Rich and Rose.

Finally, to JR and Nancy Short whose generosity has helped this book come to print. They are delightful folks who work continuously in the trenches of God's EPIC Adventure. Thanks, JR and Nancy.

In the Story that we present in this book, we follow the suggested outline of Bishop N. T. Wright and his five-act-play model. I have had the honor of meeting Bishop Wright two times, but on many more occasions than that through his books. Thanks, Dr. Wright.

However, I have taken the liberty to expand the model of Bishop Wright to include more scenes. I take full responsibility for the use and expansion of his framework. Many of his thoughts have influenced the writing of this book. He may or may not like the conclusions that I have come to. I am alone responsible for my own conclusions.

Winn Griffin
Woodinville, WA
October 2007

God's EPIC Adventure

The EPIC in the book's name is a double entendre. Len Sweet has coined the word as an acronym for life's activities: Experiential, Participatory, Image-Rich, and Connectivity. Living in God's Story should certainly be characterized as EPIC. The second meaning of the word used in the poetic world is a literary or dramatic composition that resembles an extended narrative poem celebrating heroic feats. God's Story fits within that characterization. He is the hero of the Story. We should learn to Read Scripture with Both Eyes Open[1] and, in doing so, God's Story Could Be Hazardous to Your Status Quo.[2] So with that in mind, here is the flow of the Story presented in this book.

Prologue

In the Prologue, we will cover four areas: an introduction to Story as a profound way of communicating; the Western world's penchant for minutia and the breaking of the Story into fragments; how Story is an antidote for fragmentation; and the concept of the Kingdom of God as a prism through which we can understand the Story of God.

Setting The Stage

Before we begin Act 1, we look at why it is important to read the Story in the Old Testament. Next, we define the words: Bible, Scripture, and Testament. Then, we will look at some information about the Bible the Storytellers in the New Testament used. Finally, we will overview the background of the first Stories looking at material about the worldview of the ancients and comparing it with the scientific worldview of today.

Act 1. Creation: Creating the Stage On Which the Story Will Be Acted Out

Beginning in Act 1 of the drama (Genesis 1-2) —"there was a time when God spoke all things into existence...." This Act will demonstrate the attitude of Scripture about the Creation narratives and show its polemic use in early Israel as a tract to help her realize that God was serious about not breaking the first stipulation of the Covenant.

Act 2. Separation: From Dependence to Independence

In Act 2 (Genesis 3), we discuss the so called "fall." True humanity became distorted and could no longer see God's image clearly. Humankind, the crown of God's creation, decided to worship what God had created, in order to become more godlike, instead of worshipping the Creator of the universe. This Act will show how the choice of humankind has had an effect on God's creation since the choice was made.

Act 3. Israel: The Called People of God to Be the Light of the World

In Act 3, we will present the Story of Israel (the rest of the Old Testament). God created and called a people, Israel. It was God's desire to have a people that would be the light of the world, to demonstrate what God was like within a pagan society. Israel's vocation, bestowed by a missionary God, occurred with four great events. *First*, the Exodus / Redemption of Israel in which God bought a slave from the slave market. *Second*, the Covenant, a national charter to help Israel to understand how to be the people of God regardless of circumstances, so they could demonstrate what being truly human was all about. *Third*, the Kingdom was where vocation was passed from nation to individual with a forward view toward the coming one who would be "truly human." *Finally*, the Exile/Return from Exile, a time when Israel had all but lost her sense of vocation. This Act is designed to show God's call of Israel to be a "light unto the world."

Act 4. Jesus: The True Human Being

In Act 4, we present the Story of Jesus. His story begins with what is called Second Temple Judaism. This time frame sets the stage for Act 4 and was a significant period in the development of Jewish thinking which influenced the thought world of Jesus' time. During this approximately four-hundred-year period, Israel understood herself as living in exile, waiting for the "promised one" who would bring her freedom. This Interlude is designed as an overview of this period of time in Jewish history.

In the fullness of time, according to Paul in Galatians, Jesus arrived on the scene of human history proclaiming the Kingdom of God in this Present Evil Age. God honored his covenants with Israel and his promises by sending his Son Jesus into the world born truly human, as God intended humanity to be. The Story of Jesus in Act 4 is the apex of God's EPIC Adventure. He called Israel to "Repent and Believe" and stop trying to be God's people via quietist, military means, or compromising ways, and begin living as he would show them to live by his words and works. Jesus came telling the Story in his own words (what it means to be an authentic disciple) and demonstrating the Story with his works (healing the sick, casting out demons, and raising the dead). This Act will help the reader understand the apex of the life and ministry of Jesus.

Act 5. Scene 1-6: The Rest of the Story in The New Testament

In Act 5, Scenes 1-6, we will discuss the rest of the Story that is presented in the New Testament. Act 5, Scenes 1-6 of God's EPIC Adventure is the creation by the Spirit of the church as God's re-created humanity living in community. The church's focus, like Israel before her, is to be the light to the world, empowered by the Holy Spirit who releases his gracelets to accomplish his work. The Story of her struggles to be the people of God are shared in the New Testament's Acts of the Holy Spirit and the rest of the New Testament. This Act will help the reader understand the Story of the New Testament books presented in chronological order.

Act 5. Scene 7: Imagination, Improvisation, and Stories

The opening of Act 5, Scene 7 begins at the end of the first century and has continued until today as you read this book. In this section, we will present the concepts of imagination, improvisation, and share some stories about some folks who are currently endeavoring to live out their lives in God's EPIC Adventure. There are a few clues about how the Story ends (Act 5, Last Scene: Olivet Discourse, 1 & 2 Thessalonians, Revelation, etc.). We conclude by asking the question: When will it end?

Help for Reading

The headings in this book will help you keep on track throughout each Act. There are four major headings. They are as follows:

Heading 1

This heading marks out each of the Acts of the Story.

Heading 2

This heading follows Heading 1 as a major sub-heading of the act.

Heading 3

Heading 3 marks out sub-headings under Heading 2.

Heading 4

Heading 4 is used rarely but supplies information pertaining to Heading 3.

So What?

These sections endeavor to put praxis to the material presented above it.

About Biblical Book

Each book in the Old and New Testament has a brief overview which is marked out by this heading.

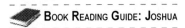 BOOK READING GUIDE: JOSHUA

Each of the books of the Old and New Testament have a separate reading guide which forms the overall StoryLine and are marked by this heading.

Reading the StoryLine

This is a major heading that keeps you abreast of the overall StoryLine in each Testament.

There are visual graphics at the top of each left or right column of the page (see above on this page) that provide a place marker for where you are in the overall StoryLine along with a Learning Objective for that section. These Learning Objectives are listed on the beginning page of each new Act.

In addition, there are special word definitions which are blocked off. When you see something like the following ❖ **sacrificial offerings** ❖ look in the left or right column and you will see an explanation.

Each book also has a basic information block which appears in the left or right column (see next page). This information provides a quick glance at a book's author, age written, aim, audience, etc. In addition, there is also a section in the left or right column called Dictionary Articles (see example in right column above). In each Dictionary Article section, there are articles that are recommended for further study. This is the full note for Dictionary Articles on this page. In the rest of the book, there is an abbreviated one when it appears the first time, and then a shorter one throughout the rest of the Act. Reading these will greatly increase your understanding of a part of the story.

In addition, in the right or left column, there are interactive Question(s). One should not think of these questions as having a final answer. It would be better to see them as conversation starters, which may last three minutes, three hours, three days, three months, three years, or a lifetime. Use them at your own risk.

Covenant

Learning Objective
Understand the Covenant stage of Israel's history.

Dictionary Articles
Read the following Dictionary Articles in *New Bible Dictionary*, Third Edition. D. R. W. Wood, A. R. Millard, J. I. Packer, D. J. Wiseman, and I. Howard Marshall (Editors) InterVarsity Press. 1996.
  Exodus
  Exodus, Book of.,
Search Google for these two online resources: *Easton's Bible Dictionary* and *International Standard Bible Encyclopedia* (ISBE). Easton's is about a century old and ISBE is about seventy-five years old. If you like lots of color pictures, try *The Revell Bible Dictionary* now out of print but still can be ordered from amazon.com.

Sacrificial Offerings:
Origin. The beginnings of sacrifice are found in the primitive ages...

QUESTION
Why are symbols important to use in our gatherings?

Introduction

Covenant

Learning Objective
Understand the Covenant stage of Israel's history.

Genesis 1.1-11.26. TBB. 7-18.

AUTHOR
Unknown, Traditionally Joshua

AGE WRITTEN
Sometime after the Conquest

AIM
To teach the people of God to trust God to give them what he promised.

AUDIENCE
Those who need to understand success of spiritual battles

KEY CONCEPTS
Conquest

KEY LESSONS
The process of learning to obey God

GEOGRAPHY
Israel ⟴ South ⟴ North

Finally, each major reading section is keyed to *The Books of the Bible* (TBB), a newly formatted Bible from International Bible Society using *Today's New International Version*, which has deleted all chapter and verse references to make it easier for you to read and grasp the Story. You may see a reference like:

These early stories in Genesis 1.1-11.26 represent the Hebrew understanding of the Primeval History of the world...

and in the left or right column you will see the text address, TBB, and a page reference.

I trust that the reading and study of *God's EPIC Adventure* will help you locate your own calling to live in his Story as a part of the new humanity that he has created, modeled after Jesus, and that with all your energy, empowered by the Holy Spirit, you live life to its fullest and for the sake of the world. Let it be so!

There are EndNotes in the back of the book for all footnotes found within *God's EPIC Adventure*.

EndNotes

1. N. T. Wright, *The Original Jesus: The Live and Vision of a Revolutionary* (Grand Rapids, MI: William B. Eerdmans Publishing Company, 1996), 105, 124.

2. Leonard I. Sweet, *Out of the Question...Into the Mystery* (Colorado Springs, CO: WaterBrook Press, 2004), 80.

Foreword by Leonard Sweet

A preface or an introductory note, as for a book,
especially by a person other than the author.

If it's not "play," it's not a Jesus Revolution.

(Leonard Sweet: Foreword)

No Table, No Play, No Revolution

The Bible is alive, it speaks to me; it has feet, it runs after me; it has hands, it lays hold of me.

—Martin Luther

The more choices are available to us, the more we seem to be forced to choose between "the Devil and the Deep Blue Sea." When you're reduced to choosing the "lesser of two evils," which means the outcome is still evil, it's time for a revolution.

"Revolution" is one of the words (along with missional, emerging, organic, etc.) that is bandied about to describe what God is up to in these dawning days of the twenty-first century. Two popular but very different books even proclaim the coming "revolution" in their title: George Barna's *Revolution* (2006) and Shane Claiborne's *Irresistible Revolution* (2006). This "revolution" language is pervasive outside the Christian traditions as well, as can be seen in the book by Noah Levine, *Against the Stream: A Buddhist Manual for Spiritual Revolutionaries* (HarperOne, 2007).

What kind of "revolution" are we talking about? And when does a revolution mean mere rotation, and when does it mean true innovation?

Mao Zedong led a cultural revolution in China that cost tens of millions of lives. When asked to explain how this could be, the Chinese dictator shrugged: "A Revolution is not a dinner party."

Sorry, Mao Zedong, but a Jesus Revolution IS a dinner party.

One of the best definitions of the gospel I've ever encountered is this one: "Jesus ate good food with bad people." Goethe, in a famous essay, suggested that Leonardo's "The Last Supper" was written to convey Christ's words "one of you shall betray me." But why not "Take, eat: this is my body?" Why not Christ instituting the eucharist rather than foretelling his betrayal?

A Jesus revolution is a dinner party, the art of play more than work, celebration more than cerebration. Anything artistic involves "play," whether sports or music or video games. You "play" baseball, not "work" baseball. You "play" the piano or violin, not "work" the instrument. You "play" video games on PlayStation3 or listen to music on RealPlayer. Liturgy is not something you "work" at but "play with." If it's not "play," it's not a Jesus Revolution.

The bookends of the Bible are "Eat" and "Drink." God's First Command in the Bible is "Eat Freely" (Genesis 2.16). God's Last Command in the Bible is "Drink Freely" (Revelation 22.17). In the middle: The Table. In his book *God's EPIC Adventure*, Winn Griffin shows how everything in between is a never-ending banquet, not a snack, on which we feast on Him in our hearts with thanksgiving (eucharistia). If the revolution is to mean anything, and if Jesus has anything to do with the revolution, it must "revolve" around that Table. For as Griffin shows in his winsome book, on that Table is spread out a feast that can give life to a dying people and planet.

After reading *God's EPIC Adventure*, I thought of what Mahatma Gandhi said to his Christian friends about their trying to live their life and conduct their "revolutions" without feasting at the Table: "You Christians look after a document containing enough dynamite to blow all civilization to pieces, turn the world upside down, and bring peace to a battle-torn planet. But you treat it as though it is nothing more than a piece of literature."

The Jesus Revolution IS a dinner party. And Griffin's book is an invitation to the party of your life.

Leonard Sweet
Drew University
George Fox University
www.sermons.com

Prologue

An introduction or preface,
especially a poem recited to introduce a play.

Most, if not all, of our reading of Scripture

only reinforces a belief that the Bible is just

a collection of little nuggets that one can choose

from when a small portion is thought to be helpful.

When you finish this session, you should be able to:
◆ Understand the Western world's penchant for minutia and the breaking of the Story into fragments
◆ Know how Story is an antidote for fragmentation
◆ Visualize the Kingdom of God as a prism through which you can understand the Story of God

Our initial focus in this section is to overview three main areas before we start with the overview of the Story of Scripture. First, we will look at the Western world's penchant for breaking the Story into fragments often reducing one's understanding of God to fragments. Then, we will talk about how story is an antidote for fragmentation. Finally, we will preview the concept of the Kingdom of God as a prism through which we can understand the Story of Scripture.

The Bible Says What?
Those Shades Are Cool!
    Where Are We Going!
Houston, "We Have A Problem..."
    A Little Known Problem
    Where Do We Begin?
    A Penchant for Minutia
Foundationalism. How Did We Get to Where We Are?
    From Philosophy to Theology
    A Proper Foundation: Two Answers
Chapters and Verses. An Aid to Foundationalism
Illustrations of the Problem of Reading Fragmentarily
    Summary
Story. The Antidote to Foundationalism
    What Are Stories?
    Story. Bausch's Perspective
        [Thirteen Characteristics of a Good Story]
    Story. Fee and Stuart's Perspective [Scripture's Narrative]
    Story. Brueggemann's Perspective [An Old Testament View]
    Story. Wright's Perspective [Gospel as Story]
    Story. Hays Perspective [Letters as Story]
    Story. Sweet's Perspective [The Importance of Story]
    Story. Peterson's Perspective [A Voice of Reason]
    Story. Corporate America's Perspective [Squirrel Inc.]
    Story. Recent Attempts to Hold the Story Together
        Influenced by a Desire for Improved Reading
        Influenced by Tom Wright's Five Act Play Model
        Influenced by a Biblical Theology Motif
    Story. Other Voices and Perspectives
    Summary
The Kingdom of God
    The Kingdom of God in the Old Testament
        The Lord-Servant Treaty (Ex. 19.2-Num. 10.10)
    The Kingdom of God in the New Testament
    Summary

Praxis and symbol tell us a good deal

about a worldview, but stories are

the most revealing of all.

(N. T. Wright. *The New Testament and the People of God*)

The Bible Says What?

Learning Objective
Understand the Western world's penchant for minutia and the breaking of the Story into fragments.

The Bible has been around for a long time, but not as long as God has. It's been here for several millennia in its literary form and several millennia before that in its oral form.

The Bible is one of the most exciting books in the world to read. However, sometimes it is difficult to read and understand. There are several reasons for this. *First*, the Bible was written to a different culture in a different time frame. People spoke, thought, and lived differently. There were no cars, jets, flat screen TVs, or computers. *Second*, because of the way it is printed—in chapters and verses—we tend to read incomplete portions of Scripture instead of whole stories.[1] *Third*, we don't know where it came from or how it developed. *Fourth*, we overlook the part that man played in God's plan to share his story with us.

Hundreds of hours are devoted to reading and studying the pages of the Bible. I am sure that most followers of Jesus have gone to, or are a part of, an ongoing Bible study. Bible studies come in all shapes and sizes. All colors and sounds. Here's a type of Bible study that I have seen over the years in many churches.

It was bitter cold outside. The temperature was dipping into the low teens as Justin prepared the living room for the weekly meeting of the church's Bible study. He stoked the fire to get it roaring so that the hot ambers would keep the room comfortably warm as the group studied that evening. He could hardly wait for the study to begin.

After the evening meal that all the small group shared together, they gathered in the front room around the cozy fireplace and began to sing some choruses that truly bored Justin and were what his friend Jason called "Jesus is my girlfriend" songs. The melodic line almost caused him to gag and he would often put his finger down his throat while the group was singing, mimicking a gagging action. Of course, no one would see him do such a thing because they all had their eyes closed and looked like they were in some kind of trance.

Soon the musical interlude was over and Mason pulled out his Bible and told everyone to turn to Genesis chapter 1. Justin almost split a gut when someone couldn't find the passage in their Bible and, of course, Trudy had only brought a New Testament to the evening fray.

Mason began by telling everyone that in his considered studies that he was convinced that the earth was no older than 4004 years and that all that Science had discovered had to fit into that time frame, including the dinosaurs.

He began by telling this little eager group that God created the *universe* and by that rendering he meant that creation was recorded in one verse, therefore, creation was a "uni-verse." He challenged others to go look up *universe* in the dictionary to understand what he was talking about. He then took the group on a long expedition through quantum physics.

Next, he told the group about a new generation of Christian scholars and scientists, armed with earned doctorates and a literal view of the Genesis creation narrative. This group hoped to breathe new life into the theory that the earth is thousands, not billions, of years old with a hope that they could finally overcome Darwinism.

Prologue

"I found a new product while surfing the net," he told them with great enthusiasm. "It's called the 'Handy Dandy Evolution Refuter.' I'll give you the web site URL later."

Without skipping a beat, Mason took the group quickly through "seven evidences against evolution." His monotone voice was about to lull Justin to sleep.

Without visiting any of the content in Genesis 1 where the group had been taken, Mason asked them to turn to Genesis 14.10 which reads, "Now the Valley of Siddim was full of tar pits...."

"Even the tar pits were created in full bloom by God," Mason postulated with some glee in his voice. "This was to spoof modern science and trick them into believing that the earth was really older than it really is."

Now turn to Proverbs 16.4a which says, "The Lord hath made all things for himself...."

Mason continued, "In the years that man has been on earth, he has come to believe that the earth is for his own enjoyment, but this verse teaches us that God made the earth for himself."

"And in Habakkuk 3.11, God demonstrates his power to do anything he wants to with what he has created. The Bible tells us that the 'sun and the moon stood still,'" Mason barked out as his voice grew to a fevered pitch.

Justin was thinking, *the Bible says what*, as he raised his hand. His gag reflex was about to turn to a fluid eruption.

Mason responded, "Yes, Justin, do you have a comment?"

"More like a question," Justin replied, wondering if he should really ask it.

"Go for it," said Mason.

"Well, do you think it is wise for us to be trippin' around through all these verses in such a disjunctive fashion to try and understand what God is saying? Why is it so important to prove the theory you have suggested that God created everything 4004 years ago? Would not your supposed theory be better to add the 2000 years or so since the birth of Christ, so wouldn't you really be saying about 6,000 years ago? Even then, what you are doing really makes no sense to me," Justin concluded.

"In fact this reminds me of a story I heard recently about a young minister who was asked to give a Bible Study. Here is what he said:

"There was a man of the Pharisees named Nicodemus who went down to Jericho by night, and fell on stony ground, and the thorns choked him half to death. He said, 'What shall I do? I shall arise and go to my father's house.' And he arose and climbed into a sycamore tree. The next day, Solomon and his wife Gomorrah came by, and they carried him down to the ark for Moses to take care of. As he was going through the Eastern gate of the ark, he caught his hair on a limb, and he hung there for 40 days and 40 nights. And afterwards he was hungered and the ravens came and fed him. The next day the three wise men came and carried him down to Nineveh, and when he got there, he found Delilah sitting on the wall, and he said, 'Chunk her down, boys,' and they said, 'How many times shall we chunk her down, till seven times?' And he said, 'Nay, but until 70 times 7.' And they chunked her down 490 times, and she burst asunder in their midst, and they picked up 12 baskets of the fragments that remained, and they debated whose wife she would be in the resurrection."

The group took a collective sigh as Mason opened his mouth to respond…

Learning Objective
Understand the Western world's penchant for minutia and the breaking of the Story into fragments.

Been there and done that, huh? I have. It is true that as readers of Scripture we read, meditate, and study it in such a fragmentized way. I think there is a solution to this problem. It's story. God has given us a Story to live in and this book is created to give you an overview of that big story of God so that you can discover where you, in the present scene of his story, can become the actor and play the role he has called you to play, and intentionally being focused on being his partner in the redemption of his creation.

So where do we begin our journey?

QUESTIONS
Have you ever attended a Bible Study like the one storied on the left? What are your reflections? What do you think is helpful or harmful about this kind of Bible Study?

Those Shades Are Cool!

It has become fashionable in the West to wear sun shades to protect the eyes. They come in all shapes and sizes and all kinds of colors. It just so happens that as readers of Scripture we all wear some shades of color in our reading glasses. These shades are like our ❖ **presuppositions** ❖ that we bring to the text we are reading. We all have them. Once in a discussion with my father-in-law about Scripture, he announced that he did not have any presuppositions when he read the Gospels. My reply was, "Your presupposition is that you don't have any presuppositions."

Presupposition: To suppose or assume beforehand; take for granted in advance. In our study it stands for root belief you have from which all your other beliefs flow.

We all start somewhere. The starting point will determine the ending point. As an example, on the West Coast of USAmerica, there is a main Interstate highway with the number 5 (I-5 for short). It runs from Blaine, WA, in the North to the Mexican border below Chula Vista, CA, in the South. Let's say you were in Portland, OR, and you wanted to go South to San Francisco, CA. You can't get there on I-5 South. You can go part way, but I-5 doesn't go to San Francisco. Driving South on I-5 from Portland predetermines where you are going. You can't get anywhere else except where I-5 delivers you.

The same is true with our presuppositions. They predetermine before we start where we will end. Assume that you believe that Jesus is returning to rapture the Church before the Tribulation. That is your presupposition, your starting point, and as you read the text of Scripture, you find all sorts of verses that support that presupposition. Such is the flaw of the *Left Behind Series* of books.

QUESTION
Can you list your presuppositions about the Bible?

"So what," you may be saying. "I'm perfectly happy reading Scripture that way because it is the truth that Jesus is coming back before the Tribulation." What if you put on a different color of shades through which you are reading the text of Scripture? What if, instead of collecting verses to prove a point, Scripture is a Story to be lived in for the sake of the world? How would that change your way of reading the text?

In the course of this book, we are going to offer you a different way of reading and thinking about Scripture, a different set of shades, if you please, a different set of presuppositions. My hope is that you will give

Prologue

Learning Objective
Understand the Western world's penchant for minutia and the breaking of the Story into fragments.

time and attention to the way in which you presently read Scripture. If any of the thoughts presented herein find lodging with you and you decide to change some of your presuppositions, well, let's just say that I would be pleased with your transition even though it might be very painful for you to make that move.

Where Are We Going!

In the Prologue, we are going to cover three areas:
1. The Western world's penchant for minutia and the breaking of the Story into fragments
2. How Story is an antidote for this fragmentation
3. The concept of the Kingdom of God as a prism through which we can understand the Story of God.

Houston, "We Have A Problem..."

One of America's finest hours in space flight came when an oxygen tank exploded on Apollo 13. The quote "Houston, we have a problem" is actually a misquote. The actual quote is "Okay, Houston, we've had a problem here." This was a major problem for those on board the *Odyssey*. The crew in space and the crew in Houston had to put their minds together to solve this problem and bring the three astronauts back to earth safely.

It is natural when a problem occurs to to try to find a solution. However, sometimes a bigger problem occurs: we don't know we have a problem. This is the situation with millions of readers of Scripture. We have a problem when we read Scripture and we may not even know it.

A Little Known Problem

The little known problem in Scripture reading is the fragmentized way in which we have come to read it: A little snippet here and a little snippet there, a Bible bit here and a Bible bit there. So, if it is a problem, what do we do about it?

Where Do We Begin?

Word of God: The biblical mode of revelation is the revealing acts of God in history, accompanied by the interpreting prophetic word that explains the divine source and character of the divine acts. Acts and words; God acts and God speaks; and the words explain the deeds. The deeds cannot be understood unless they are accompanied by the divine word. The word would be powerless unless accompanied by the mighty acts of God. Scripture is *words-works* revelation.

One might think of the Bible as a book that demonstrates how God has acted in relationship with his people. According to Dr. George Ladd, the late Professor of New Testament Exegesis and Theology at Fuller Seminary, "Scripture is the ❖ **word of God** ❖ written in the words of men."[2] For him ❖ **acts and words** ❖ are an inseparable unity.[3] God has delivered these acts and words in a variety of literary forms, among them narrative. According to Fee and Stuart, narrative or story comprises about forty percent of the Old Testament.[4] Narrative is the primary genre of the Gospels,[5] and an underlying substructure of the writings of Paul according to Richard Hays.[6]

Acts and Words: God both acts and interprets the meaning of his acts. Scripture is the *works* and *words* of God. This is a *key* concept for understanding Scripture. For us to understand the faithfulness of God, we need to become familiar with how God has acted in faithfulness to his children and what he says those acts mean. *Christ's death* is the act of God. *Christ died for us while we were sinners* is his word of explanation for us.

My argument is that the church's understanding of the Story of God in Scripture is, for the most part, seriously fragmented. Understanding the whole Story is not a concept that is celebrated in the church at the beginning of the twenty-first century.

I have deep concerns for the church moving across a cultural divide, that members on each side of the divide (Modern and Postmodern) have ample opportunity to have a holistic look at the overarching Story of God as it is presented in Scripture. This book is intended to be a challenge to the church to understand what her story is and how to become the people of God living as his recreated humanity, as a light to this Present Evil Age. Knowing the story will help in answering the question: How are the people of God to advance the gospel as they improvise the Story of God for the sake of the world?

One of the primary reasons for not knowing the overarching Story of Scripture is the way readers have come to use Scripture. Individuals and the church have developed the malignant disease of *versitis*[7] (proof texting), which has grown to epidemic proportions. Readers take small fragments (verses) and quote them *ad nauseam* and usually out of context. Scripture is rarely read as a whole complete Story from beginning to end.

Most, if not all, of our reading of Scripture only reinforces a belief that the Bible is just a collection of little nuggets that one can choose from when a small portion is thought to be helpful. It's like using the Bible as an encyclopedia of God's knowledge. When you have a problem, just look up a reference and quote away. Readers of Scripture need to stop memorizing verses of Scripture and then quoting them as proof texts, brutally tearing them from their God-given context and ordering them in a human fashion, as if a reader could do a better job than the Spirit in putting the text together. If followers of Jesus are going to memorize, then they need to memorize the overarching Story and the myriad of stories therein, according to Len Sweet, a current postmodern author.[8] The church and individual readers need to recover the whole Story of Scripture. It is my argument, therefore, that we will never reside in the biblical narrative and make it our way of life if we keep pulling single verses from their context and use them as proof texts to argue our own theological agenda.

In addition to *versitis*, readers have also developed *topicalitis* (a contagious and deadly Bible teaching disorder), and *systematitis* (the art of propositional gathering). *Topicalitis* is best seen in the form of topical preaching and teaching while *systematitis* is extended *topicalitis* in the form of Systematic Theologies. Westerners have developed a penchant for minutia. Is it possible that fragmented teaching produces a fragmented believer who is anemic, listless, and weak with no sense of vocation as a follower and experiencer of God?

These three epidemics are caused by foundationalism, which among Evangelicals has caused too "low" a view of Scripture.[9] Why? Evangelicals have come to believe in the authority of the book that we have made Scripture to be. Evangelicals believe that God somehow has given us the wrong sort of book and it is our job to turn it into the right sort of book by engaging in the fissiparous[10] use of Scripture. How did this happen? To provide a beginning answer we will look at several authors and their discussion about the rise of foundationalism.

A Penchant for Minutia

Foundationalism, as we will see below, has a penchant for minutia which seems to assist readers of Scripture to read it fissiparously. Foundationalism has produced for us the plagues of *versitis*, *topicalitis*, and *systematitis*.

The Bible was designed by God to be heard and read. In the "Welcome" section to the *Contemporary English Version*, its mission is described as being a translation that can be read, heard, and listened to

Prologue

with enjoyment.[11] We must remember that the Bible was first meant to be heard[12] as its stories were told and read later after they were written down. Of course, we in the Western world have a difficult time wrapping our minds around the idea of an *oral Bible*. We think that literacy comes from being able to read *written* works, so if one only had an *oral* work, the person presenting and the people listening would thereby be illiterate. Susan Niditch argues the opposite point of view in her book, *Oral World and Written Word: Ancient Israelite Literature*.[13]

In light of the early Israelites being an oral community, picture the following example in contrast to the story we told earlier about a local Bible Study.

The sun was setting and leaving an array of colors in the western sky. A cool breeze was beginning to take over from the heat of the sun. Jedaiah was stoking the fire to keep it alive for the gathering outside the tent of his father, Shimri. Jedaiah was seventeen years old, a sturdy lad with deep brown eyes.

All day Jedaiah daydreamed about what story Moses might share with his family during the cool of the evening. Would it be the story of Abraham and his journey to Egypt? Maybe it would be about Joseph being sold into slavery in Egypt. Egypt had been a hard life for him and his family. The events over the last few months that had brought them to the foot of Sinai had been breathtaking.

Later after the evening meal, Moses arrived with two of his children. He greeted all who were gathered around the fire and found a comfortable place to sit and enjoy its warmth. The evenings in the desert could get a little chilly. Moses shared a couple of events from his busy day. One was particularly interesting to Jedaiah. Moses spoke of an interaction with a family who had a young son, Boaz, who was awestruck with the daughter of the family just two tents away from his family's tent. Mariah was "drop dead gorgeous," a dazzlingly beautiful, magnificent woman of eighteen years. As Moses relayed the story, Jedaiah fixed his eyes on Hannah with a wry grin on his face.

From the corner of his eye, Moses caught his longing look and said, "Maybe soon, I can return here to the tent of Shimri and have a similar conversation concerning Jedaiah and Hannah." If it had not have been so dark with only the light from the flickering fire, everyone would have seen the flush on the face of Jedaiah.

"Moses," Shimri inquired, "what story did you share with the families of Boaz and Mariah?"

"The same story I am going to share with you tonight," replied Moses.

A solemn hush readied everyone for the story that would fall from the lips of Moses.

"Out of a chaotic time, the voice of Yahweh thundered, 'Light, come into existence,' and in the blink of an eye there was light in the midst of all the chaos."

"You know how dark it is here in the desert just before dawn when most of the family fires have long been extinguished, and over the horizon light appears, a new day dawns. This daily event should always remind us of the creative majesty of Yahweh."

"Remember also that in Egypt we were asked to worship the god of the Sun. Our Egyptian friends would bow each morning and give praise and thanks for the rising of the light globe in the East and many of our people entered into this worship with their Egyptian friends."

"However, the story of Yahweh's creation of all that we see tells us that he is the only God that we are to worship as he has said to us in the first of the stipulations he gave us from the mountain."

Moses paused for a moment and asked, "What are some of the other things that Yahweh created?"

Shimri spoke up and said, "Animals, like the sheep that Jedaiah tends."

"Remember, when we were in Egypt, our friends wanted us to worship at the foot of an idol that looked like a sheep, asking this god to protect our flocks from the harm of the jackals."

Those around the fire gave an affirmative shake of their heads to this recollection.

"Well, the story of creation tells us that there is no sheep god, only the God who created sheep, and when we worship, we should worship him and not what he created."

Shimri was chagrined and his face dropped so that his chin was touching his chest.

"Why the long face, Shimri?" Moses inquired.

"I was one that gave in to the pressure of my Egyptian friends and often bowed to worship the sheep god. I had not heard this story of our Creator God. I only knew the story of the sheep god and the people who worshiped him." Shimri continued, "How can I change my ways to reflect a life ordered by the worship of Yahweh, the Creator of all the animals?"

Moses continued telling the story of God's creative power ending with the creation of humankind. Here again, Moses paused to comment on how in Egypt they were expected to worship the Pharaoh, who was human, as a god, but that God's stipulation in the Covenant he had made with them was that there couldn't be any other gods, including human ones.

"The story of creation," said Moses, "demonstrated that God created humans and gave them authority to be his agents in the world he had created, but humans themselves were not meant to be worshiped as a god."

The chatter went on for almost two hours, but who was counting as long as Jedaiah could see Hannah. Soon the meeting broke up and Moses left with his two sons to return to his tent. Shimri commented on how inspiring it was to hear the creation story.

Jedaiah went to bed that night thinking of how living in the story of creation that Moses told would be when he and Hannah were wed. Being alive in his community and being the light to the world in which he lived truly excited him.

The stories around the campfires of Israel were as much "Bible" for them as the "written" word is a "Bible" for us.

QUESTION
What do you think about the statement: "the stories around the campfires of Israel were as much 'Bible' for them as the 'written' word is a 'Bible' for us?

Prologue

Learning Objective
Understand the Western world's penchant for minutia and the breaking of the Story into fragments.

While the Bible is the bestselling book of all times, it is often the least understood, at least by Americans.[14] In Barna's survey on the Bible he says, "Three-quarters of Americans (75%) believe that the Bible teaches that God helps those who help themselves."

Readers have memorized its fragments, sometimes without knowing it. Although we may not have realized it when we say, "out of the mouth of babes" we are quoting Psalms 8.2. When we describe a person's attitude as being "holier than thou," we are quoting Isaiah 65.5. Some of the greatest speeches in the world have quoted Scripture. One famous line from Abraham Lincoln was, "A house divided against itself cannot stand,"[15] which was a line from the pen of Luke. Parents have told their children to "beware of wolves in sheep's clothing." They are quoting Jesus or misquoting him (Matt. 7.5). While we know some of the classic sayings (verses) of Scripture, we are often still illiterate of its overarching meaning and the power of its Story.

In addition to verse quoting, we story-quote as well. Christians often know lots of stories from Scripture, like the story of creation, Noah and the ark, the tower of Babel, Moses in the bulrushes, the crossing of the Red Sea, the walls of Jericho, etc., yet still do not know how these stories fit into the overarching Story of Scripture.

Readers have focused on the smallest part of Scripture, chapters, verses, and stories and are often content with collecting these fragments in a systematic way and presenting conclusions that may not be the intended meaning of the texts being collected. By doing so, readers become mentally poorer in knowing Scripture's overall meaning.

Some find the Bible a dull read. As I have written elsewhere "the Bible is definitely not a dull book!"

QUESTIONS
Have you ever heard or made this complaint before? If you have heard it or made it yourself, how did you respond to the person who said it or to your own complaint about Scripture being dull?

It is one of the primary ways that God uses to help us know him better and to become more like him for the sake of the world. Our task as readers of HIStory is to understand what God has said. We are too often driven to study the Bible before we have learned to read it well. Study sounds so ominous, so foreboding, and it can be! As followers of Jesus we want to know God, so we jump in and begin our study without having a goal in mind, sometimes without knowing all that study involves. One of our biggest hindrances in our own culture is that we bring good old American foundational presuppositions about topics such as love, grace, mercy, hell, heaven, and many others to our study. America has taught us that "right is might." Therefore, we often study to prove a point rather than hear what God wants to say to us. Instead of topics to prove, God has given us a Story to live within.

God chose to give us his Story through many different authors, media, and centuries. The Story comes through many books written over a 1500-year period with no fewer than forty authors. These individuals included kings, prophets, shepherds, philosophers, the educated, and the unlearned. Each book, like all books, has a beginning, middle, and end. Together they all have historical context and together deliver HIStory.[16]

I once shared the concept of how we read Scripture with an eye to find proof for our arguments with folks with a friend of mine. I challenged him to read for a week with the intention of enjoyment and not with the "hidden" intention of finding proof. The next week he shared with me that for the first time in his adult life, he had enjoyed reading the text of

Scripture as he freed himself from the plague of versitis. Give it a try for yourself and enjoy the refreshment of hearing God's Story with fresh ears as if you were reading it for the first time.

Foundationalism. How Did We Get To Where We Are?

Learning Objective
Understand the Western world's penchant for minutia and the breaking of the Story into fragments.

As culture moves to what is being called the postmodernity ethos, the demise of the modernist approach to knowledge seems to be its causality.[17] This can be seen in the rejection of foundationalism that characterized the Enlightenment ❖ **epistemology**. ❖ In the modern era, a period extending roughly from 1860 to the present, the reading and understanding of Scripture has been deeply influenced by the Enlightenment's nature of the understanding of knowledge that had at its heart the epistemology that is often called foundationalism.[18] The quest of postmodernity is to discover a nonfoundationalist or Postfoundationalist epistemology.[19]

Epistemology: The branch of philosophy that studies the nature of knowledge, its presuppositions and foundations, and its extent and validity.

QUESTION
Have you heard the term "foundationalism" before? Was it presented as positive, negative, or neutral in value?

Grenz and Franke in their book, *Beyond Foundationalism: Shaping Theology in a Postmodern Context*, suggest the following:

> In its broadest sense, foundationalism is merely the acknowledgement of the seemingly obvious observation that not all beliefs we hold (or assertions we formulate) are on the same level, but that some beliefs (or assertions) anchor others. Stated in the opposite manner, certain of our beliefs (or assertions) receive their support from other beliefs (or assertions) that are more "basic" or "foundational." Defined in this manner, nearly every thinker is in some sense a foundationalist.[20]

From a philosophical point of view, the heart of foundationalism is the desire to overcome the uncertainty generated by our human liability to error that leads to so many disagreements. The foundationalist mindset is convinced that the only way to solve this problem is to discover some way of grounding human knowledge on an unconquerable certainty, i.e., the search for absolute truth! Walter Brueggemann, notes, "Descartes' philosophical reflection was an urgent effort to fend off the coming chaos so evident in the world around him."[21]

Using the metaphor of a building, foundationalism advances the argument that like a building, knowledge has to have an irrefutable foundation that consists of a set of unquestioned beliefs. All other knowing proceeds from that foundation. This set of unquestioned beliefs is believed to be universal, context free, and available to anyone. The code of foundationalism reasons that reasoning can only move in one direction—from the bottom up, from the unquestioned beliefs to their logical conclusion.[22]

Foundationalism requires that the foundations of human knowledge be unshakably certain and asserts that the only way of knowing proceeds from *deduction* (such as deducing other truths from the unquestioned beliefs [Descartes]) or *induction* (as deriving truths from sense impression caused by the material world [Locke]).[23]

Grenz and Franke offer a brief overview of the rise of foundationalism.

◆ The quest for a means by which we can justify our claims to knowledge dates to the ancient Greek philosophers.
◆ The quest for a means by which we can justify our claims to knowledge became acute in Western philosophical history in the Enlightenment.

Prologue

Learning Objective
Understand the Western world's penchant for minutia and the breaking of the Story into fragments.

René *Descartes* is often called the father of modern science. He established a new, clear way of thinking about philosophy and science by rejecting all ideas based on assumptions or emotional beliefs and accepting only those ideas which could be proved by or systematically deduced from direct observation. He took as his philosophical starting point the statement *Cogito ergo sum* — "I think, therefore I am." Descartes made major contributions to modern mathematics, especially in developing the Cartesian coordinate system and advancing the theory of equations. <http://www.answers.com/rene_descartes>

♦ The French philosopher ❖ **René Descartes** ❖ is believed to be the father of modern foundationalism because he began his philosophical work by attempting to establish a foundation.

♦ Living in troubled times after the Reformation, Descartes' travels revealed how culturally based and culturally dependent beliefs actually were.

♦ Descartes' response to this situation was to seek to find certainty for a knowing mind.

♦ To accomplish his task, he scrutinized all of his beliefs and assumptions by doubting everything until he arrived at a belief that he could no longer doubt, namely, that he doubted.

♦ This led to his famous dictum, "I think: therefore, I am."

♦ He believed that he had established the foundation of knowledge by the appeal to the mind's own experience of certainty.

♦ From this foundation, he began to construct a new human knowledge edifice.

♦ For him, this new epistemological program yielded knowledge that was certain, culture and tradition free.[24]

Some philosophers, like John Locke, took issue with specific aspects of Descartes' proposal. Locke rejected Descartes' view that our basic beliefs consist of innate ideas from which we deduce other beliefs. He argued that the foundation of human knowledge lies in sense experiences that are observations from the world. His system is known as empiricism.[25] However, most thinkers, despite some disagreements of other particulars, readily adopted Descartes' desire to establish some type of sure foundation for human knowing.[26]

Brueggemann suggests that the outcomes of the work of Descartes are threefold:

♦ "A new model of knowledge grounded in objectivity, and capable of providing a new epistemological security to replace that which was lost in the dissolution of the Medieval worldview."

♦ "The pursuit of 'pure reason,' free of every contingency...."

♦ A "Cartesian masculinization of thought and the flight from the feminine."[27]

From Philosophy to Theology

From the guild of philosophers, the concerns of Descartes spilled over into theology, which became impregnated with a foundationalistic point of view. This led many eighteenth century religious thinkers to two conclusions: *first*, they appealed to the Bible or the church as the foundation one could accept as classical Christian doctrine. *Second*, they embraced the skeptical rationalism that seemed to be the final product of the enlightened mind.[28]

A new cast of theological thinkers in the nineteenth century refused to be boxed in by these two options. These thinkers sought a new foundation on which to construct their theology.

A Proper Foundation: Two Answers

The debate over finding a proper foundation produced two answers. *First*, the bedrock foundation could only be religious experience. While personal in nature, they believed that it was universal. Friedrich Daniel Ernst Schleiermacher, often called the leading nineteenth century theologian of the Protestant church, first voiced this approach to theology.

He maintained that "the essence of religion is an awareness of absolute dependence or the experience of God consciousness."[29] Others of a more conservative bend sought to find a different foundation. As a *second* answer, they concluded that this invulnerable foundation lay in an error-free Bible, which they viewed as the storehouse for all divine revelation. This led to sayings such as the one by Charles Hodge, a Princeton theologian, that the Bible is "free from all error, whether of doctrine, fact, or precept."[30]

The *second* answer bolstered the process of propositional thinking and teaching in the form of systematic theology. Systematic theology took the fragmented view to a larger scale presenting themes without context instead of stories, by thinking it was teaching what the Bible says on any given topic where the "adept theologian claimed that he was only restating in a more systematic form what scripture itself says."[31]

Hodge suggested that just as a natural scientist uncovered the facts pertaining to the natural world, so the theologian brought to light the theological facts found in Scripture by drawing theological propositions from the text and compiling these various facts. With such a foundation, conservative theologians were confident that they could deduce from Scripture the great truths about God or any other category and deliver an objective view of these beliefs.[32]

Just as the legacy of Schleiermacher dominated the liberal project to the present, the foundationalism of Hodge and other nineteenth century conservatives sets the tone for what would become the theological paradigm of Evangelical theology through most of the twentieth century. This "compendium of truths" that can be unlocked through scientific induction came to be the character of American fundamentalism and can be seen in Wayne Grudem's definition of systematic theology as the attempt to determine what the whole Bible teaches about any given topic. Grudem says, "Systematic theology is any study that answers the question, 'What does the whole Bible teach us today?' about any given topic."[33]

A Statement of Faith is an example of this systematic approach. Statements of Faith are attempts at a brief systematic theology (*systematitis*) by breaking the Story into fragmented parts that are held up as "final" beliefs to which one is to ascribe, believing that it has captured all knowable truth on the subject visited. However, I believe that Story is the beginning of belief not the conclusion of belief. The church needs to have restored to her a sense of the "whole" that emphasizes history and story as God's method of revealing himself to her. Could it be that even the early "creeds" like the Apostle's Creed was a shorthand story beginning with God the creator of the universe and ending with everlasting life and not really a "statement of faith" in the sense of what "statements of faith" have become today?

While at odds with each other, those following the legacy of Schleiermacher and those following the legacy of Hodge have one thing in common: they seek to maintain the credibility of Christianity within a culture that glorifies reason and deifies science.[34]

Could it be that the foundation of nonfoundationalism is to believe that there is no foundation? What then of a possible solution? Scripture appears to speak of an objectivity of a future eschatological world that is God's determined will for his creation. How do we proceed toward this

Learning Objective
Understand the Western world's penchant for minutia and the breaking of the Story into fragments;

QUESTIONS
Have you ever been taught that you don't need to know any history, etc., around a Bible passage; all you need to do is just "experience" what the passage says to you?
Can you see where that kind of teaching may have come from?

QUESTIONS
Have you been taught inerrancy, i.e., that the Bible is free from all error?
What did you think about that teaching?
Do you think the Bible is free from error?
If asked could you tell the story of how the church started teaching this "doctrine?"

QUESTION
Have you ever considered the Apostle's Creed to be a "shorthand story" of Scripture?
What do you think about the idea?

Prologue

eschatological world? According to Grenz and Franke, we have a mandate that says that we are to be participants in God's work of constructing a new world that reflects God's own will for his creation, a world which finds its connectedness with Jesus Christ. Where do we find this mandate? We discover it through the Spirit's primary tool: narrative/story. In God's Story, the Spirit's goal is to bring us to view all reality in accordance with God's program for recreation.[35] The redemptive event in which Christians have participated makes each a Story-liver and Storyteller as she or he lives as a newly created being for the sake of the world while telling others the Story by deed and word. Will we know or discover absolute truth? Only in the eschaton will we know truth in its absolute fullness. Until then, we read the Story/stories and live the Story/stories to our fullest capacity with the empowerment of the Spirit.

Chapters And Verses. An Aid To Foundationalism

Chapters and Verses: The books of the Old and New Testaments were divided into chapters from an early time. The Pentateuch was divided by the ancient Hebrews into 54 *parshioth* (sections), one of which was read in the synagogue every Sabbath day (Acts 13:15). These sections were later divided into 669 *sidrim* (sections) of unequal length. The Prophets were divided in the same manner into *haphtaroth* or *passages.*" In the early Latin and Greek versions of the Bible, similar divisions were made. The New Testament books were also divided into portions of various lengths under different names with titles and heads or chapters.

In modern times this ancient example was imitated, and many attempts of the kind were made before the existing division into chapters was fixed. The Latin Bible published by Cardinal Hugo of St. Cher in A.D. 1250 is generally regarded as the first Bible that was divided into our present chapters, although it appears that some of the chapters were fixed as early as A.D. 1059. This division into chapters came gradually to be adopted in the published editions of the Hebrew Bible, with some few variations, and in the Greek Scriptures. The division into verses came in A.D. 1551 when Robert Stephens introduced a Greek New Testament with the inclusion of verses. The first entire English Bible to have verse divisions was the Geneva Bible A.D. 1560.

The modern reader has to read the Story of Scripture through the added distraction of ❖ **chapters and verses.** ❖[36] The reduction of the metanarrative to chapters and verses added in the 1500s became the root for fragmentedly reading Scripture. Chapters and verses are clearly not a part of the metanarrative. The use of chapters and verses diverts the reader's attention from the larger Story by the practice of being encouraged to memorize verses. From our earliest reading experiences, we have learned to read in chapters. Verses, on the other hand, pose a whole different obstacle. Verses are a convenient way to look up a reference. But, that's where their usefulness ends. The addition of verses to the pages of the Bible is the single most harmful barrier to reading and understanding its Story. Most verses are only part of a sentence. To only read them or memorize them has no real meaning. These little groups of words that have been sloganized, placed on banners, greeting cards, and plaques are not God's word when seen, memorized, or printed by themselves apart from their historical context. It is true to say that readers would not read one of their favorite books in this fragmented way.

An Illustration: Psalm 119.11 and 1 Thessalonians 5.22

One might note that the understanding of one Bible verse (Psalm 119.11) has largely been responsible for verse memorization. Its meaning may actually demonstrate that Story, not verses, is a preferred method for memorization. Secondly, the text of 1 Thessalonians 5.22 in the King James Version is often quoted making the author of the text say something that he did not mean to say.

Psalms 119.11

Verses are not helpful when it comes to reading the stories in Scripture. Giving attention to verse breaks would be like reading this sentence:

³I love the sound ⁴of your voice in the springtime.

Then, for some unknown reason we decide to memorize only verse 4, "of your voice in the springtime." After memorizing it, we quote it over and over again hoping it will help the hearer in some moment of need. Doesn't make much sense, does it?

Remember, the books of the Bible were broken down into chapters and verses a long time ago. You may wish to note, however, that the original writers did not write this way, nor did the original readers read this way.

It is unfortunate that we have been taught to memorize and quote verses. We were taught this because of a verse (wouldn't you know) from the book of Psalms.

> I have hidden your word in my heart
> that I might not sin against you (119.11 NIV).

Learning Objective
Understand the Western world's penchant for minutia and the breaking of the Story into fragments.

We have interpreted *word* in this verse as "verse or verses." The context of this verse is vv. 9-16 which form a complete section of the larger poem of Psalm 119. It begins with a question reminiscent of a style of *Wisdom* writings in the Old Testament (Prov. 23.29f.; Ps. 25.12f.). The question posed is: *How can a young man keep his way pure?* The answer is in the second part of the ❖ *parallelism*: ❖ *By living according to your word. Word* can have many meanings in the Old Testament, among them *an event* such as the covenant with Abraham as recorded in Genesis 15.1-21. In 119.9, *word* is the "divine word" that proceeds from the mouth of God as it is in Psalms 17.4 and 33.6. *Word* can indicate:

Parallelism: Hebrew poetry makes use of a literary device called *parallelism*, a thought rhyme in which the second line of a section echoes or reiterates the thought of the first line.

- A particular message as in Jeremiah 7.2, or
- The sum total of God's revealed will as in Deuteronomy 4.2.

In 119.11 the Psalmist says that he has treasured the words of God so that they may determine his actions in life. The word *word* (*imrah*) here is a poetical synonym to the word *word* (*dabar*) in verse 9 and usually means the *Law* in Psalm 119. Law should be understood as instruction rather than a legal prescription.

On one occasion the word *word* means a promise as in 119.140. The followers of God in the Old Testament were taught the stories of God and their meanings. It is in this context that we should render this section of Psalm 119.

To *hide his word in our hearts* is at the very least to hide the stories of how God has acted in faithfulness on behalf of his children throughout the Bible. These action-packed stories should determine how we approach life as a child of God.

QUESTIONS
Have you ever quoted, or should I say, misquoted this verse?
What other verses may you have misquoted?
Can you replace those misquotations with stories?

1 Thessalonians 5.22

The following is an illustration of how quoting memorized verses often causes misquoting the intended contextual meaning of the verse.

The text of 1 Thessalonians 5.22 reads, "Abstain from all appearance of evil" (KJV). This is one of the most misused and abused passages from the King James Version in the New Testament. This was my mother's all time favorite verse that she quoted to me hundreds of times. She quoted it to provide the basis for living a holy life every time she thought that a request to participate in an activity that she deemed as "unholy," was requested by me. She took it completely out of its context when she quoted it. The verse is part of a conclusion that Paul is making in regard to prophecy and should read as follows:

> Do not attempt to put out the fire of the Spirit by treating prophecies with contempt; test every prophecy and act on the good ones while avoiding the bad ones.

Paul is suggesting to the Thessalonians that the things to be avoided are prophecies that have been tested and found not to be from the Spirit. To use this text in any other way is not to use it at all, but to abuse it, thereby making God say something he never intended to say at this point. There

Prologue

are other Scriptures, but not this passage, which urge us to live a holy life and even go to lengths to tell us what evil to avoid, (Gal. 5.19ff. for *evil to avoid* and 5.22ff. for *the Kingdom life to be lived*).

As we will suggest below, if one is going to memorize Scripture, then story memorization might be the choice over verse memorization.

It is almost impossible to find Scripture published without chapters and verses. *The Message* by Eugene Peterson is an exception to the rule and so is *The Books of The Bible* from International Bible Society. Publishers continue to aid the misreading of Scripture by formatting the text of Scripture with the obstacles of chapters and verses, and these additions aid the reader in thinking about the smallest realm rather than the larger realm of the metanarrative.

Sermons are infamous for presenting a topic supported by a few scattered verses. The presentation of sermons in this vein continues to reinforce a fragmented way of thinking about Scripture. Wright suggests that "most churches, even those with well-developed educational programmes, have a long way to go in their teaching of Scripture."[37]

Propositional thinking led to systematic theology which was aided by chapters and verses that served as the basis for the propositions of systematic theology.

Illustrations Of The Problem Of Reading Fragmentarily

There are several ways in which readers of the Old and New Testament have been enticed to read and understand its contents. The implicit idea behind these possible solutions is that knowledge[38] of Scripture is a primary benefit for a believer. The late Stan Grenz has said, "Knowledge is good only when it facilitates a good result — specifically, when it fosters wisdom (or spirituality) in the knower."[39] While knowledge that "fosters wisdom" is a worthy goal, the following solutions do not offer a connected Story of Scripture that holds Scripture together and energizes God's people for mission and orders their life. Rather, these possible solutions may often offer a backdrop from which misreading of Scripture has now become so common that they are accepted by large segments of the church as correct readings.[40] Many of these possible solutions offer stories from within the metanarrative but do not offer any connectors to the metanarrative. Thus, the individual stories become fragments themselves.

One of these ways of reading Scripture is the *Reading the Bible through in a Year* approach. In this approach, there is usually a minimum of three chapters a day to be read in order to reach the goal of finishing the Bible in a year. Often the chapters to be read daily are picked from both the Old and New Testament. What if you read your favorite book in such a fragmented way? What if you read two chapters from the front of the book and a chapter from the middle of the book and then two chapters from the back of the book? How would you ever understand the story presented in the text? To read in such a fashion goes against the continuity of seeing the Story presented in Scripture. If you wouldn't normally read a book that way, then why would you read the Bible that way?

Another offering of the Church to help followers of Jesus is Sunday School. Lessoned materials, offered by the *International Sunday School*

Lessons (ISSL), are often offered in a topical or thematic rather than storied way. ISSL offers denominations a listing of texts that are chosen to cover as much of the Bible "as is fruitful for group study"[41] in a six year cycle. Story is not the driving force of the material.

There are scholarly books such as Old and New Testament introductions, surveys, theologies, and commentaries, which are often written by specialist for specialist and cover lots of content, but still in a disconnected way. Commentaries are usually focused on the smallest part of the text: verses and words. While understanding the text, i.e., its word meanings, historical context, and theological significance, is of great value, it is often done in isolation from the storyline.

Learning Objective
Know how Story is an antidote for fragmentation.

So What?

The rise of propositional thinking in the Enlightenment, aided by the previous addition of chapters and verses in the text of Scripture, has led readers to read the text of Scripture in a fragmented way.

The rise of foundationalism was the result of Descartes' decision, in the midst of culturally based and culturally dependent beliefs, to seek to find certainty for a knowing mind. The concept of foundationalism moved from the philosophical realm to the theological realm and led many eighteenth century religious thinkers to arrive at two conclusions. *First*, the Bible or the church was a sure foundation and *second*, skeptical rationalism was embraced.

Nineteenth century theological thinkers sought a new foundation. Two separate conclusions were drawn: Schleiermacher's "experience of God consciousness" or Hodges' "error free Bible" could be foundational. Hodges' concept led to systematic theology and Scripture's division into chapters and verses aided the foundational mindset along in producing systematic theologies. The systematic theology mindset has influenced a myriad of variations of the Biblical text which has led to fragmentation of the text and away from its Story intent. Educational materials are often built on the smallest fragments of Scripture: verses or sets of verses, topics made up of verses, or individual stories with no tie to the larger Story.

The church and individual reader is presented with a quagmire: fragmentized reading of the text of Scripture. What is the antidote to this problematic situation? Story!

Story. The Antidote To Foundationalism

Learning Objective
Know how Story is an antidote for fragmentation.

Story has become fashionable to write about in the two or so recent decades. William Bausch says in the introduction to his book, *Storytelling*, "We are creatures who think in stories,"[42] but have been trained to think in propositions.[43] Propositional thinking has caused us to reduce the text of Scripture from an overarching Story with many smaller stories to a set of propositions to believe. In the book *Why Narrative?* Stanley Hauerwas states, "In recent years appeals to 'narrative' and to 'story' have been increasingly prominent in scholarly circles, to the delight of some, the consternation of others, and the bewilderment of many. Such appeals have caused delight in that narrative and story appear to provide a cure, if not a panacea, to a variety of Enlightenment illnesses: rationalism, monism, decisionism, objectivism, and other 'isms,'"[44] and one might add fragmentary-ism.

QUESTION
What do yo think of the statement: "We are creatures who think in stories, but have been trained to think in propositions"?

Prologue

It seems that story,[45] not proposition, is the design God picked to call us to our vocation: partnering with him in the redemption of his creation. The Story of Scripture is a continual Story beginning with Creation and moving toward the New Creation, although somewhat chopped up in the way our printed Bibles present the texts to us in its canonical form. It is not my purpose to resolve the question: Does inspiration include the form of canonization that we have in our modern Bibles? The short answer is: the form of the canon is an effort by humans to ratify what the church in the first three centuries thought to be in or out. The overall form of the New Testament is somewhat chronological in sequence, i.e., Gospels (the life and ministry of Jesus); Acts (the life and ministry of the church); Letters (the problems of the church presented in an ad hoc way, listing Paul's letters from largest to smallest with one exception and then the letters not from Paul); finally, Revelation (the consummation of the Kingdom). However, the overall form is not chronological. If that were the case the writings of Paul would have come first. More information on canonical formation can be found in the *Dictionary of New Testament Background*.[46]

We live in the present part of the Story and are connected to the previous episodes of the Story while moving toward its conclusion. Why is story important? To begin to answer that question we shall look at several authors to help us understand the concept of why story is the possible antidote to foundationalism's fragmentized reading of Scripture.

Everyday from the tic of birth to the tock of death[47] we write our own stories, maybe not in print, but nevertheless written in our lives. If they are not saved they will be forever lost.

Once I was creating a TV teaching script for my employer. I was using a computer; this was before personal desktops could be found everywhere. I was using a word processing program that was created by a friend of mine that was used on large computer systems. He had trained me to use the program. I had just added the finishing touch to the script when someone flipped the power off in the office where I was working. In just a flash of the moment, everything that I had created was gone. Stories can be like that.

While our stories may get lost from time to time, God's Story has survived for several millennia for followers of Jesus to read, hear, and see, so we can learn to live within the Story. We may need to learn to apply ourselves to the Story rather than the other way around: applying the Bible to our worldview.[48]

Stories have been around for as long as storytellers have had the ability to engage an audience in getting lost in the tales they are spinning. Our imagination plays a great part in the process of listening to a story. When I was a kid, before TV, I listened every Saturday evening to several radio dramas like *The Shadow*. You could hear the voices, the footsteps, the music, but you had to imagine what the people looked like and what the set looked like as they were playing out this drama. It made for a lively Saturday evening. It seems to me that TV simply spoiled the opportunity to imagine. Watching TV causes us to visually see what someone else imagined and then we take their imagination as reality for the drama being presented. Some believe that storytelling might be the most fundamental way that humans communicate. It just may well be that storytelling is the oldest human communication.

Once on a trip to my birth state, several members of my family got together for an evening. The event quickly turned to storytelling. The youngers wanted to hear stories about the olders and the ones who now are not with us any longer. As I told them story after story, they kept saying, "I never knew that before," or "I never knew mom or grandmother would think or do such a thing." Stories are enlightening to their hearers. They keep the listeners grounded to their roots and teach them things they never knew before.

Stories are powerful. Alister McGrath tells a story in his book *Christian Spirituality.*

> Stories are about finding one's identity, and learning the story of one's own people. This point was brought home to me particularly clearly back in 1990, when I heard an American professor of literature describe how he discovered the importance of learning one's story. This professor, who taught at a leading university in Southern California, was a Kiowa (KAI a wa) Indian, a Native American from the Oklahoma region. He told how he learned the story of his people when he was still a young boy. One day, just after dawn, his father woke him, and took him to the home of an elderly squaw. He left him there, promising to return to collect him that afternoon.
>
> All that day, the squaw told this young boy the story of the Kiowa people. She told him of their origins by the Yellowstone River, and how they then migrated southward. She told him of the many hardships they faced—the wars with other Indian nations and the great blizzards of the winter plains. She told him of the glories of the life of the Kiowa nation—of the great buffalo hunts, the taming of wild horses, and the great skill of the braves as riders. Finally, she told him of the coming of the white man. She told him about the humiliation of their once-proud nation at the hands of the white soldiers, who forced them to move south to Kansas, where they faced starvation and poverty. Her story ended as she told him of their final humiliating confinement within a reservation in Oklahoma.
>
> Shortly before dark his father returned to collect him. His words on leaving the home of the squaw remain firmly planted in my mind. "When I left that house, I was Kiowa." He had learned the story of his people, to which he was heir. He knew what his people had been through. Before he had learned that story, he had been a Kiowa in name only; now he was a Kiowa in reality.[49]

Could it be that when a follower of Jesus hears and understands God's EPIC Adventure,[50] he or she will no longer be a Christian in name only, but will be a Christian in reality, one who lives his or her life in community for the sake of the world? God's EPIC Adventure is a captivating Story, one that is bigger than our small "soap operas" that we so often live in day to day. When we are exposed to this story will we, like the professor in the story, be able to say, "When I finished reading the story, I was a Christian." Before hearing the Story, is it possible that we are only Christian in name only, but after being exposed to God's EPIC Adventure, that we become a Christian in reality?

What Are Stories?

Stories are not a bunch of fragmented stuff that just happens. Stories are moving accounts that are headed for a destination. So when we hear or

Learning Objective
Know how Story is an antidote for fragmentation.

Prologue

Dualism: The view that the world consists of or is explicable as two fundamental entities, such as mind and matter.
Deism: The belief, based solely on reason, in a God who created the universe and then abandoned it, assuming no control over life, exerting no influence on natural phenomena, and giving no supernatural revelation.
Agnosticism: The belief that there can be no proof either that God exists or that God does not exist.
Atheism: The doctrine that there is no God or gods.
<http://www.answers.com>

QUESTIONS
What do you think about the question presented in the paragraph to the right?
So you live in the Story of God or do you apply "short" pieces of the story to parts of your life?

tell a story, it is a whole entity. We need to guard against putting fragments together[51] that produce the creation of a different story and then pass it off as if it were God's story.

The Story of God that Scripture presents is to be told as a challenge to the story of the present world. God's EPIC Adventure is subversive and will subvert the dominant paradigm when told and enacted. The telling and living of this Story challenges the authority of this Present Evil Age. In telling and living God's Story, we are undermining the current worldview of what the world is and offering the world a new worldview. The Story we tell and live is that there is only one God. He is the creator of all that there is. He not only created the world, but he lives within his creation. He is not up there and we are down here (❖ **dualism** ❖). He is not a landlord who made the world and left it to run on its own (❖ **deism** ❖). He is not an absentee landlord (❖ **agnosticism** ❖). He is not absent (❖ **atheism** ❖).[52] This Creator God is transcendent over his creation and is deeply wounded by its fall away from goodness to sinfulness. He was loving enough that he was willing to get his hands dirty, as it were, to bring about its recreation.

The Story of God is about the world that was created by God and functions as an open invitation for all who choose to participate. The hearer can make the Story his or her own by turning away from idols that hinder one from making the Story one's own and worshiping the God who is revealed in this Story.[53]

Knowing the Story is not an end in itself. The Story is there so that the Creator God may be glorified and that his creation may be redeemed. It is our task to be the vehicles through whom this magnificent Story is told and retold, not just in words but also with drama, art, or any form of creative expression. We have been entrusted with a great and wonderful privilege.

What if story, not propositions, is the cause of our actions? What if story, not propositions, gives us our worldview? What if story, not propositions, is at the root of the way we function as human beings? What if we changed our story from one of cultural consumerism, as an example, to God's EPIC Adventure, which provides another view of the world? Wouldn't it follow that we would change how we would relate to the world around us? What if story is the medium through which we develop our hopes and dreams, our joy and anger, our self-expression and fears?

Stories cause us to have emotions (joy, peace, love, fear, etc.). Stories bring ideas to us. We see ourselves in the characters presented in stories. Stories explode our curiosity. Stories are about sending and receiving. Stories include conversation that goes both ways providing interaction. It appears that we could all benefit from the effect of story.

As long as story captures our interest, we have an almost infinite capacity to hear and repeat it. In today's economy, those who market and advertise know the power of story. It seems that story is one of the most powerful and effective tools that we have at our disposal to convey information with which we may engage people. An audience may be immersed in the story that provides them with the information that they need to take an action.

Once while teaching an Old Testament Survey class at the church level, I told the story of Genesis 1.1-2.4a. I provided the background for the writing and then placed the story of Genesis 1 into that background. The background

Learning Objective
Know how Story is an
antidote for fragmentation.

of the story is in the life of Israel, living at the foot of Sinai, being prepared to go to the land promised to their forefathers. They had made Covenant with God in which the first stipulation was that Yahweh was the only God they could worship. The story of Genesis 1 is about God as creator set against all the other formidable gods of the ancient world. In each successive period of creation, two gods were dethroned and Yahweh replaced them. This would have been clear to the Hebrews who were hearing the story. God was serious about being their only God. I ended with a question: "How many gods do we worship today?"

The next time I gathered with that class, one lady brought me a paper that she had handwritten, answering the question I had asked. To her surprise, there were other gods being worshiped in her life that she discovered. God's Story and the interaction with the Spirit brought a new freedom to this person's life. She had improvised within the framework of the Story and gained new light on the gods that were controlling her life.

Story. Bausch's Perspective [Thirteen Characteristics of a Good Story]

In his book *Storytelling, Imagination, and Faith*,[54] William Bausch relates thirteen characteristics of a good story. These story characteristics are:

1. *Stories provoke curiosity and compel repetition.* Good stories are gripping. We want to hear them over and over again.
2. *Stories unite us in a holistic way to nature.* A good story causes us to feel connected to nature and for a believer to the God of creation of nature. That connection makes us have a feeling of holism.
3. *Stories are a bridge to one's culture, one's roots.* We have common stories that evoke our identity to past generations and our roots. We have clan, tribe, culture, family, and individual stories. It is even possible that an outsider can get a glimpse of a culture by looking at its stories.
4. *Stories bind us to the universal, human family.* We are puzzled, especially as believers, to discover that other cultures have similar motifs (like the flood stories in the Bible and in other cultures). These stories could have a binding effect and empower us to understand that we are all part of a universal family, regardless of color, race, or creed.
5. *Stories help us to remember.* The stories we hear and tell remind us of our roots, those things that we share in common, those things that we share in honor, and those things that we share in shame.
6. *Stories use a special language.* Stories use all kinds of language conventions to make the story vivid and memorable.
7. *Stories restore the original power of the word.* Spoken and written words carry great power.
8. *Stories provide escape.* A good story calls us away from the immediate and gives us an opportunity to reenter life. Think of how children forget their hurts by the time a parent finishes a calm and soothing story.
9. *Stories evoke in us right-brain imagination.* The Western world has molded most of us into a left-brain way of thinking. Stories bring about a balance by calling us to use the right side of our brain.
10. *Stories promote healing.* Stories can bring reconciliation and forgiveness.
11. *Every story is our story.* We can identify with something in every story.

QUESTION
What resonates with you
about Bausch's 13 points
concerning story? Why?

Learning Objective
Know how Story is an
antidote for fragmentation.

12. *Stories provide a basis for hope and morality.* Stories call us to the imagination of hope. Reinhold Niebuhr once said, "Nothing that is worth doing can be achieved in a lifetime; therefore we must be saved by hope."

13. *Stories are the basis for ministry.* It is from story that we minister for the sake of the world.[55]

Bausch also suggests that good stories are paradoxical which causes emotions to be stirred. He goes on to say, "We are being asked to learn a language again that resonates with rich metaphor and image. Too long we have been trapped in the perfect square of a stylized laboratory where all things are subject to our measurements."[56] We are invited to learn about God from the stories that he told, not from the propositions that we take from the stories that he told.

Wright takes the position that Evangelicalism's view of Scripture is often a "low view" of Scripture,[57] because we think that somehow the Holy Spirit didn't do as good of a job as he could have done. We treat Scripture as if it were an unsorted Westminster Confession,[58] that we have to take out of the stories the important points to believe, and systematize them.

Story. Fee and Stuart's Perspective [Scripture's Narrative]

The genre of literature that dominates the landscape of Scripture is narrative. There are some captivating as well as some shocking narratives. In many cases, we have been taught about the human characters within these narratives and how to discover ourselves in those characters. Who hasn't tried, like Abraham, to help God bring a promise to its conclusion well before its time and in another way than it would naturally occur?

These stories, whose plots and characters are so intriguing, allow us in a powerful way to see God at work with his people. The Old Testament makes up seventy-five percent of Scripture and forty percent of its material is narrative.[59] There are many kinds of narratives in the Old Testament. As readers, we must understand the characteristic of Old and New Testament narratives as a first step toward becoming a competent reader of the Story which Scripture presents.

A Two-Story House

Fee and Stuart present a metaphor of a three-story house. I have modified it to a two-story metaphor with a foundation/substratum (does that make me a foundationalist?). What Fee and Stuart call the first floor; I call the house foundation or substratum.

QUESTION
How does the illustration of a
"two-story house" help or
hinder your thinking about
reading the text of Scripture?
Explain either way.

Think of Old Testament narratives as a two-story (no pun intended) building. The house has a foundation that is the big picture of God's acts in his world—creation, the fall and its effects, sin and its power, redemption, and the coming of the Kingdom in Jesus. This foundation is the overall Story of God's salvation history of humankind. The *first* floor centers on Israel—the Old Testament people of God. Its Story begins in Genesis 11.27 with the call of Abraham. It continues with the promise to Abraham to give him a land and a people and the rise of a nation beginning with the Exodus; the giving of the Covenant and the working out of that Covenant in the life of Israel; the rise of the United Kingdom and the Divided Kingdom and their restoration after the exile. The *second* floor contains several hundred individual narratives. Each narrative on

Learning Objective
Know how Story is an antidote for fragmentation.

this floor goes to make up the whole of the narrative of the *first floor*, Israel's history, and, finally, the foundation narrative, HIStory.[60]

We spend most of our time reading the stories on the *second floor*. To really grasp their intentional meaning, we must give due attention to the *first floor* story and the *substratum* of the house.

What Narratives Are Not

In order to understand what narratives are and how to read them, it is helpful to observe what narratives are not. Fee and Stuart present a summary:[61] *First*, they are *not* stories about people who lived in an ancient age. They are stories about what God did to and through these people. *Second*, they are *not* stories filled with allegory or hidden meaning. *Third*, they are *not* always direct in their teaching. *Fourth*, they do *not* always have a specific moral of their own.

Next, they present some targets to shoot at when reading narratives.[62] *First*, they do *not* directly teach a doctrine. They illustrate doctrine that is taught elsewhere in Scripture. *Second*, they record what happened, *not* what should or could have happened; therefore, not every narrative has a moral. *Third*, the actions of the characters in the narratives are *not* necessarily the correct actions to imitate. Most characters are *not* hero models to follow. *Fourth*, the story does *not* usually tell us if the actions were good or bad. We are left to make up our minds based on what God has taught in the teaching parts of Scripture. *Fifth*, these stories are incomplete and selective. Not every detail or even all needed details are given. What does appear in the story is what the inspired author thought important for the reader to know.

The narrative is not written to answer theological questions. *First*, narratives may teach by stating something clearly, which should be the action of the reader, or by implying something without actually saying it. *Second*, God is the hero of all of the biblical narratives. In the final analysis, they demonstrate how he has acted in relationship to his people. By that we can know how he will act on our behalf.

Narratives according to Fee and Stuart are not written for the reader to become a monkey-see-monkey-do person. Remember, no biblical narrative was written especially for a person living today. The narrative concerning Joseph is about Joseph and demonstrates how God worked through him. We can learn a great deal from narratives, but we should never assume that God expects us to do exactly the same things that the Bible characters did. Otherwise, we would have to live part of our lives as sinners following characters that sin and become righteous when they show signs of righteousness. Our task is to learn from these narratives how God has acted concerning his children, not to do everything that was done in each one of them.

Narratives demonstrate and illustrate God's acts among men.[63] Why do we find things in narratives that are not there? Here are some possible reasons: *First*, we wrongly expect that everything in Scripture applies directly to each part of our lives. *Second*, we are desperate for information from God that will help us through some problem or situation. *Third*, we are impatient and want answers now from a specific verse in a specific chapter in a specific book in Scripture.

Fee and Stuart suggest that being selective by combining verses

Prologue

Learning Objective
Know how Story is an
antidote for fragmentation.

contextually that are not connected naturally and allegorizing them is not helpful.[64] The authors suggest: *First*, do not practice *selectivity*: Do not pick and choose specific words and phrases to concentrate on while ignoring the overall context of the passage. *Second*, Do not combine verses contextually not connected: Do not combine a verse from here and a verse from there and a part of a verse from yet a third place and place them together as God's word for a situation.

The problem of "selectivity" is addressed by Richard Hays under the concept of intertextuality, which is the "imbedding of fragments of an earlier text within a later one...."[65] Kent Yinger sees "intertextual play" found in "all strata of the OT" which helps us have a "better understanding" of concepts like "grace and works" in the New Testament.[66] What Paul and others may be doing when they quote a text from the Old Testament (remember, the Old Testament was not yet canonized and certainly not versified at this time in history) is simply drawing attention to the whole story from which the text is being quoted. A present analogy would be the use of "keywords" in a search engine such as Google to find the larger context in which those words are recorded. It just might be that we have taken our propensity to proof text and projected it back on Paul and other writers of the New Testament.

Story. Brueggemann's Perspective [An Old Testament View]

Brueggemann, in his book *The Creative Word*, focuses on the Torah as he declares the following five beliefs about story.

Story is concrete

Biblical stories are about particular persons in particular times and places.[67]

Story is open-ended in its telling

Brueggemann believes that the community of Israel was not interested in a static meaning or flat memories for Israel's new generation. Rather, she was concerned about creating a context, evoking a perception, forming a frame of reference that went beyond and did not depend on any particular version or nuance of any particular narrative. The storyteller requires fidelity, however, by knowing the boundaries of form and plot and characters.[68] Brueggemann appears to be saying that the boundaries are literary and he remains unclear about any historical boundaries.

Story in Israel was intended for the practice of imagination

Brueggemann believes that the listener has as much freedom as the speaker in deciding what is happening in a story.[69] He says:

> ...there is no straight-line communication of data from speaker to listener. There is an open field of speech between the parties that admits to many alternative postures. This means that the listener has nearly as much freedom as the speaker in deciding what is happening. The listener is expected to work as resiliently as the teller. The communication between the two parties is a bonding around images, metaphors, and symbols that are never flattened to coercive instruction. Israel has enormous confidence in its narrative speech, sure that the images and metaphors will work their own way, will reach the listener at the point of his or her experience, and will function with a claiming authority. Such communication is shared practice of the secret which

Learning Objective
Know how Story is an
antidote for fragmentation.

evokes imagination. It includes the listener in the secret, thus forcing the awareness of an insider. And it serves to draw a line on the other side of the listener, distancing the listener from all the outsiders who do not know the secret. That is, once the secret is known, it cannot be not known. The telling of the secret evokes imaginative work in the listener. Thus the practice of imagination moves, on the one hand, with liberation. The listener has freedom to hear and decide, and is expected to decide. On the other hand, however, the story moves with authority to claim people for the inside. The authority that moves through it is not only the authority of the teller, but also the authority of the story. Israel's imagination is liberated and liberating. That does not mean unlimited and undisciplined, as though anything goes. The imagination of Israel is circumscribed by the scope of the stories about which there is consensus. Israel has a covenant with its tongue that the evoking of imagination does not move outside this consensus. We shall see that in the other parts of Israel's canon, there is a breaking beyond this consensus. For the Torah, however, it is enough to accept the consensus and to move around in it fully. It is the consensus on which stories are based that defines the arena for free imagination.

If Brueggemann is saying, and it is unclear to me, that there is no historical setting behind the story, then I would disagree. I am not yet convinced that history and grammar are to be given up in our quest to hear the meaning of a story. Surely, the storytellers told their stories within a context with a purpose in mind, and the collectors of these stories, via inscripturating, then place them in a certain order for a purpose. The author(s) of the Pentateuch did not start with the story of the Exodus, as important as it was, but placed it in its context for some purpose. I often wonder if those who espouse a "reading from in front" of the text would allow those reading their text to make of it what they will. I think not!

Stories in Israel are characteristically experiential

By experiential, Brueggemann does not mean personalized or privatized in the immediate time frame. Rather, he speaks of stories that were the public experience of Israel, a notion that is not easy in a culture beset by narcissistic individualism and subjectivity.

For Israel the personal immediate experience was not adequate for life. Some community shapes perception and governs personal experience. To speak of personal experience that is private is to be deceived. "As there is no 'presuppositionless exegesis' of the text, so there is no 'presuppositionless experience' of life." For Israel these stories were "a counter experience, a subversive alternative to an imperial consensus. Every time Israel told one of its stories, it meant an assault on and refutation of other stories." This point is well lost in the Western Church. "We have become gently benign, as though our stories were simply casual alternatives to some others that are also worthy of consideration. ...For Israel their stories meant to dismantle alternative worlds as well as to construct new ones for the listening community."[70]

QUESTION
What resonates with you
about Brueggemann's
thoughts concerning stories
in the Old Testament?

Story in Israel is the bottom line

Israel had confidence in its stories, in and of themselves. Israel understood them not as instruments of something else, but as castings of reality. Israel's epistemological message was that they trusted the stories.

Prologue

Learning Objective
Know how Story is an antidote for fragmentation.

Here stories were posited "to build a counter community, one that was counter to the oppression of Egypt, counter to the seduction of Canaan, counter to every cultural alternative and ever-imperial pretense." Brueggemann asks: "Can we risk these stories?" His answer: "The answer is known only when we decide if we want to subvert the imperial consciousness and offer a genuine alternative to the dominant forms of power, value, and knowledge."[71]

It is difficult to get a handle on Brueggemann's belief about the historical background from the above references about story. However, in a more recent book, *A Theological Introduction to the Old Testament*, written with three others, the quartet is frank about their belief about a historical backdrop in reading the text, in their case, the Old Testament. They state:

> There is increasing recognition that interpretation now takes place in a postmodern context, one in which the previously settled assumptions of the modern world have become unsettled and must, therefore, be reassessed. One of those assumptions, closely allied with the claims of historical criticism, was that history was the primary category for assessing the truth claims of the biblical text and the reality assumed to "stand behind" the text. In our view, the search for a historical reality behind the text sometimes did violence to the imaginative and rhetorical integrity of the text itself.[72]

Brueggemann points out in his book, *The Bible Makes Sense*, that the historical emphasis has waned.[73]

At this point, I am still persuaded that history and grammar cannot be totally laid aside in favor of one's own imagination. What do we mean by Historical-Grammatical? It is the study of history and grammar surrounding the biblical account/Story. Each biblical document must be studied in its own context that includes language, types of literature, historical background, geographical conditions, and the life setting of the people, in order to discover that meaning.

It is my opinion that there is an interaction between the Old Testament and its ancientness, the New Testament and its first centuriness, and the church and me in all its twenty-first centuriness, when I hear its stories. How do I understand the Story? By using all the tools of historical exegesis to enable me to hear the words of the Old and New Testaments' writers and writings as their first readers and hearers might have read and heard them, catching the full meaning intended by the writers, but always with an ear open for the unexpected word of God through the writers of the Old and New Testaments, challenging my own twenty-first centuriness and all its presuppositions and perceptions. William Lane captures this idea well in the introduction to his commentary on Mark.[74]

QUESTIONS
Do you think that the authors of Scripture intended to say something to the audience to which he or she was writing? Why or why not?

The fifteen contributors to *The Art of Reading Scripture* set a core of nine affirmations when interpreting Scripture. The fourth of the affirmations is as follows:

> Texts of Scripture do not have a single meaning limited to the intent of the original author. In accord with Jewish and Christian traditions, we affirm that Scripture has multiple complex senses given by God, the author of the whole drama.[75]

While the authors do not reject historical investigation of biblical texts, they suggest that it should be used in "stimulating the church to undertake new imaginative readings of the texts."[76] This is a move away from authorial intent and debatable. Fee and Stuart hold that, "a text cannot mean what it never could have meant to its author or his or her readers."[77] If words had an "original intent"[78] then how do the meanings of those words change their meanings to a different audience? Would not that cause God to be saying one thing at one time and possibly something completely different at another time? If one loses the sense of the author's intent, then it seems that a text can mean, and usually does, anything the reader wishes to say it means.

Learning Objective
Know how Story is an antidote for fragmentation.

Story. Wright's Perspective [Gospels as Story]

Tom Wright suggests that the writers of the Gospels collected useful and interesting material about Jesus and strung the material together in "what looks for all the world like a continuous narrative, a story."[79]

In the Gospels, according to Wright, it was no surprise that Jesus told and retold the Story of Israel as a part of his work.[80] He advances an argument in five stages: *First*, the announcement of the Kingdom by Jesus is best understood as evoking the Story of Israel and her identity. *Second*, the Story summoned Israel to follow Jesus in a new way of being the true people of God. *Third*, the Story included a climactic ending. There would be judgment and vindication. *Fourth*, the Story generated a new structure for Israel which put Jesus in conflict with others who had alternative agendas. *Fifth*, the retelling of the Story included a battle behind the rival agenda conflicts in which a real enemy was being faced.[81] Wright seems to see the Gospels as the collection of stories about Jesus within a Story of Jesus.

QUESTION
How does Wright's five-part summary help or hinder your understanding of story?

Wright works out his theology within the framework of critical realism.[82] Critical realism "is a way of describing the process of 'knowing' that acknowledges the *reality of the thing known, as something other that the knower* (hence 'realism'), while also fully acknowledging that the only access we have to this reality lies along the spiraling path of *appropriate dialogue or conversation between the knower and the thing known* (hence 'critical')."

In the first of his proposed six-volume project on the subject "Christian Origins and the Question of God," which is *The New Testament and the People of God*, Wright sees Story as an important ingredient in understanding the larger Story presented in the New Testament. He says:

> The New Testament, I suggest, must be read so as to be understood, read within appropriate context, within an acoustic which will allow its full overtones to be heard. It must be read with as little distortion as possible, and with as much sensitivity as possible to its different levels of meaning. It must be read so that the stories, and the Story which it tells, can be heard as stories, not as rambling ways of declaring unstoried 'ideas'. It must be read without the assumption that we already know what it is going to say, and without the arrogance that assumes that 'we'—whichever group that might be—already have ancestral rights over this or that passage, book, or writer. And for full appropriateness, it must be read in such a way as to set in motion the drama which it suggests. [83]

He tackles the question of what might be called a pure postmodern reading of Scripture's Story in which there seems to be a lack of need to see the historical by stating:

Prologue

Learning Objective
Know how Story is an
antidote for fragmentation.

While history and theology work at their stormy relationship, there is always a danger, particularly in postmodernism, that literary study will get on by itself, without impinging on, or being affected by either of the others [history or theology]. The more we move toward a climate in which 'my reading of the text' is what matters, the less pressure there will be to anchor the text in its own historical context or to integrate a wider 'message' of the text with other messages, producing an overall theological statement or synthesis. (Bracketed material by present writer.)[84]

RESPONSE
Ponder the paragraph to the
right and then respond.

We are, in fact, drawn irresistibly into the world of a *story*—and a story, moreover, which, like the modern 'short story,' invites us to share its world as much by what it does not say as by what it does. The questions posed are: How open is the story to new ways of being read? Or, what would count as a correct reading, and how important is it to try to achieve a correct reading? One might be left with the reality that there should be a distinction between things that can and must be right and things that must be left open to conversation.[85]

Wright suggests, "What we need, then, is a theory of reading which, at the reader/text stage, will do justice both to the fact that the reader is a particular human being and to the fact that the text is an entity on its own, not a plastic substance to be moulded to the reader's whim."[86] To Wright's last statement, I would whole-heartedly agree.

Gordon Fee says that if one reads the stories of Scripture from "in front" of them taking no care of what lies "behind them," then one will read the stories from "over" the text having control of what the text says to them. If, however, one reads the stories of Scripture from "in front" of the text while giving due attention to what lies "behind" the text, then one will learn to live "under" what the text says.[87]

Wright argues in *Scripture and the Authority of God* "neither for a variety of modernism, nor for a return to pre-modernism, nor yet for a capitulation to postmodernism," but for what he hopes is "a way through this entire mess and muddle and forward into a way of living in and for God's world...,[88] which sees story as the vehicle.[89] Wright goes on to argue for a "totally contextual" reading of the Story and a fully "incarnational" reading of the Story.[90]

Story. Hays' Perspective [Letters as Story]

We have certainly been taught that the writings of Paul and other New Testament letters are to be understood didactically, as intended to convey instruction to the reader. But as Richard Hays points out in his book, *The Faith of Jesus Christ: The Narrative Substructure of Galatians 2:1-4:11,* there is a narrative/story substructure to Paul's writings. Hays undergirded his belief in the Story-structure of Paul by showing that while we have not thought of Paul as a storyteller, his use of narrative is very important.[91]

QUESTION
What do you think about
Hays' "story-shaped"
character in Paul's writings?

Hays, who was educated at Yale in the '70s, was influenced by Hans Frei who contended in *The Eclipse of Biblical Narrative* that biblical criticism had gone astray by failing to grasp the narrative sense of Scripture. This prepared the way for Hays' dissertation and then his book entitled *The Faith of Jesus Christ,* which is a discussion of the phrase "faith of Jesus Christ" as being a *subjective* or an *objective* genitive in the original Greek language, but argues that this is set within a narrative framework. It would be fair to say that Hays believes that there is a "story-shaped" character to Paul's writings.[92]

Story. Sweet's Perspective [The Importance of Story]

Len Sweet[93] was the mentor of the *Leadership in Emerging Culture Doctor of Ministry* program at George Fox University when I did my second Doctor of Ministry. As the seismic writer of *SoulTsunami*, he says that "every kid in the world knows these four words:...'Tell Me A Story.'"[94] He believes that story came to be a negative word in the modern world. To be a "storyteller" was one of the worst things you could call a person, but in the postmodern world storytellers hold the future in their hands, especially those who use all the "basic media forms: print, software, audio, and video."[95] He suggests that the life of Jesus was neither essay, doctrine, nor sermon, but was "a story."[96] For Sweet the "Christian message is not a timeless set of moral principles or a code of metaphysics. The Christian message is a story...."[97] His favorite definition for preachers is "story doctors"[98]

In *AQUAchurch*, he speaks about two kinds of stories: "rut stories" and "river stories." A "rut story" limits us and locks us in place by keeping us stuck in "old tracks and trajectories." On the other hand, a "river story" moves us forward. These stories "add life-giving software (accumulated memories and learning) to the brain's hardware (billions of neurons)." He believes that the greatest "river story" is the Story of Jesus.[99] He further suggests that we do not discover "the Way, the Truth and the Life by memorizing verses and mastering facts."[100]

QUESTIONS
How does the definition for preachers as "story doctors" strike you?
What do you think about Sweet's "rut" and "river" metaphors?
Where are your color crayons?

In *Summoned to Lead*, Sweet says, "'Telling stories' used to be a euphemism for lying. No more. Story is crucial in communication." He quotes John Raymond as distinguishing between "tradition-stories, map-stories, and vision-stories."[101] Sweet suggests that we need all of these kinds of stories.[102]

Finally, in *Out of the Question... Into the Mystery*, Sweet suggests (as we have suggested above) that we should:

1. "Memorize and live out its stories."
2. "Fall in love with a new passage every day."
3. "Take it to bed with you."
4. "Talk to it and hear it talk to you as you wrestle with the text."
5. "Become a fifth gospel, a third testament."[103]

He suggests that the Story of God is not yet finished that God has framed, "but that we are invited to have a hand in coloring."[104]

Story. Peterson's Perspective [A Voice of Reason]

For Eugene Peterson, story is the heart of language. He suggests that we need to present the story with some definition added and let the Holy Spirit help the hearer figure the story out without becoming impatient. By "some definition" I understood Peterson to mean "historical setting." Peterson senses that the biggest fault of those who teach is that they don't trust their students to really have the capacity to learn. He believes that one needs to understand the context from which the story is being taught and that the reader of the story needs to be aware of the "big picture" of the Story.

Prologue

Learning Objective
Know how Story is an
antidote for fragmentation.

For Peterson, "story is an act of verbal hospitality." He insists, "We live in a world improvised of story." Words provide a form of currency used to provide information. To be *schooled* is primarily to accumulate information. Motivational speech runs a close second to the accumulation of information. While both are important, they are impersonal. In them there is no discovery, no relationship, and no personal attentiveness. For it to be personal, we need story and storytellers.[105]

Story. Corporate America's Perspective [Squirrel Inc.]

Squirrel Inc. is sub-titled "A Fable of Leadership through Storytelling." Its author is a well-known consultant for corporate America. His thesis is that "you can use the magic of narrative to lead...." He believes that you can transform change in an organization with six different kinds of stories that impact work and personal life.[106] It is intriguing to see that those outside the church are picking up on what the church has had from its beginning, but somehow got sidetracked over the past years as outside sources influenced the church instead of the church influencing the outside sources. While storytelling in cultures has never been dead, it has somewhat been diminished in the church in favor of the fragmentation of the Enlightenment.

Story. Recent Attempts to Hold the Story Together

Influenced by a Desire for Improved Reading.

Fee and Stuart, authors of the book *How To Read The Bible For All Its Worth*, have added the volume *How to Read the Bible Book by Book* to help the reader of Scripture find his or her way through the morass of books. The authors provide an overview of the biblical Story in an attempt to set a grid through which to read their work.[107] They provide an introduction to each of the major sections of Scripture with information that puts this section into the overall Story, as well as a short section at the end of each book which attempts to place the book's content into the overall Story. The downside: each book is still read independently of the other. There seems to be no attempt to put the books into the storyline. As an example, at the end of the section on Hosea one reads: "The book of Hosea, which burns with the fire of God's love for his people, reminds us that the God of the biblical story judges unfaithfulness, even as he lays out hope beyond judgment."[108]

Also, influenced by the desire for improved reading is *The Books of The Bible*. This new edition of *Today's New International Version* is a groundbreaking new presentation of the Scriptures designed to accurately reflect the biblical authors' intentions. This edition comes without any additives, i.e., the publishers have removed chapter and verse numberings from the text entirely. Blank line spacing is used as the text separator into units designed by the author with the goal to encourage meaningful units to be read in their entirety.

Influenced by Tom Wright's Five-Act-Play Model

Only recently, influenced by Tom Wright's Shakespeare's five-act-play model, has anyone produced a theological Story including both the Old and New Testaments.

The Drama of Scripture: Finding Our Place in the Biblical Story believes that every "part of the Bible — each event, book, character, command, prophecy, and poem — must be understood in the context of

Learning Objective
Know how Story is an
antidote for fragmentation.

the *one* storyline.[109] Bartholomew and Goheen follow Wright's five-act-play model stretching it into six acts and an interlude (Second Temple Judaism) borrowing from Wright the idea of Scripture as a drama.[110] This is an excellent book for those in college and was written with "first-year university students in mind."[111] The beauty of this book is that even the beginner will be able to grasp the Story of Scripture as an unfolding coherent story. In addition, they have added value through a website with downloadable information.[112]

Influenced by a Biblical Theology Motif

The Story of Israel: A Biblical Theology from InterVarsity Press states its purpose as "integrating the biblical Story into a coherent whole."[113] There are overtones of N. T. Wright in this book, but it is not written within the framework of the five-act-play model. Rather, the authors (there are six of them) look at each major section of the Old and New Testaments with the prayer that the book "will become an important tool of study for students, professors and ministers as well as for informed laity as they come to understand their own faith in light of the fulfillment of Israel's story in Jesus the Messiah."[114]

This volume appears to be a much more technical work than *The Drama of Scripture* mentioned above. As an example, in the Introduction the authors define Biblical Theology (the sub-title of their book) and then propose a question: "Can We Have a Biblical Theology?" In the answer section, words like *Heilsgeschichte* and *Religionsgeschichte* are used. While a translation of these words is provided, this sort of writing has a voice that is elevated beyond what the average attender of church might understand or even be able to pronounce for that matter.[115] The authors conclude that story may "qualify to be characterized as biblical theology in its own right" and suggest that Wright's *The New Testament and the People of God* may suggest such even though Wright may not, in fact, condone such a conclusion.[116] While *Drama* appears to retell the story, this book appears to work out a biblical theological view working to make a cohesive work of the Old and New Testament with all its unity and disunity problems.

The three books mentioned above are overt solutions to provide an overarching story over against the systematic fragmentation of the Enlightenment's foundationalism. Fee and Stuart's *Book by Book* makes a gallant attempt but falls short of putting the book by book reading into a storyline. *The Story of Israel* is well suited for an advanced study of story with a biblical theology motif. *Drama* is the closest to the book you are now reading.

The basic differences between this book and the books mentioned above are: *First*, I am providing a basic background of how we find ourselves in our present position of reading Scripture in a fragmentized way. *Second*, In the Acts to come, I will stress the gluing theme of Covenant in the Old Testament and Kingdom of God in the New Testament, which appear to be two ways of saying the same thing: the rule of God has invaded this Present Evil Age. *Third*, I will offer a chronology of both the Old and New Testaments as a storyline for reading the Story. *Finally*, I will provide some thoughts in Act 5 Scene 7 about how we as actors in this great drama can "improvise" in our part of the play.

Intr
Key

sweet. "color"

Prologue

Learning Objective
Know how Story is an antidote for fragmentation.

Story. Other Voices and Perspectives

There are other voices and perspectives that should be heard from, but the limitations here do not permit an interaction with them. Some of these are Hans Frei,[117] Paul Ricoeur,[118] and Stanley Hauerwas.[119] Hauerwas has a rather novel thought in his book, *Unleashing the Scripture*, where he states, "The Bible is not and should not be accessible to merely anyone, but rather it should only be made available to those who have undergone the hard discipline of existing as part of God's people."[120] I'm not exactly sure what "hard discipline of existing as part of God's people" really means. I rather think that followers of Jesus should give due attention to understanding God's EPIC Adventure and this book is given to helping that become real in the lives of those followers.

So What?

The antidote to foundationalism's fragmented reading of Scripture is Story. We can recognize this in the following ways. While we are creatures who think in stories, we have been trained to think in propositions. Stories are powerful and can place us within its reality as demonstrated by the story of the Kiowa professor. Different characteristics of story give us a language that resonates with rich metaphor and image and, if accepted, would lead us away from a low view of Scripture that is rearranged as if it were an unsorted Westminster Confession. Narrative is the genre of literature that dominates the landscape of Scripture. Narratives in the Old Testament are concrete and cast reality. The Old Testament Story is the ingredient that leads to an understanding of the continuing Story presented in the New Testament. The story of Jesus is not an essay but a story. The letters of the New Testament have a substructure which is story. Corporate America is turning to story as a way of teaching leadership. There have been three recent attempts to demonstrate that God has a Story that is presented in the Bible beginning in Genesis and ending in Revelation. Scriptures are now being printed without chapters and verses to help readers grasp the Story without all the additives. This present book is an attempt to give its readers a guide to help comprehend God's EPIC Adventure and to learn to live within its story and living therein as God's new humanity for the sake of the world.

The Kingdom Of God

Learning Objective
Visualize the Kingdom of God as a prism through which you can understand the Story of God.

Scripture tells a single overarching narrative from Genesis to Revelation.[121] The Story is held together in Old and New Testaments by the concept of the Kingdom of God, i.e., the Lord-Servant Treaty concept in the Old Testament in which God is Lord/Ruler and Kingdom of God in the New Testament where God is Lord/Ruler.

The Kingdom of God in the Old Testament

The Old Testament has fallen out of fancy with the modern reader of Scripture, except when one wants to proof text some special section of it. From the beginning of the Old Testament, God is pictured as king.[122] Picture language, i.e., metaphor and other literary devices, was the currency of the Hebrew storytellers and writers to help their listeners and readers grasp the Story.

From where did this notion about the Kingdom of God come? The

Kingdom of God concept is rooted in the Old Testament and is certainly broader than the specific term.[123] The term, however, does not even appear in the Old Testament.[124] Ladd writes, "While the idiom 'the Kingdom of God' does not occur in the Old Testament, the idea is found through the prophets." He concludes after viewing several Old Testament references that "this leads to the conclusion that while God is the King, he must also become king, i.e., he must manifest his kingship in the world of men and nations."[125] To comprehend this concept, we might need to look in the Old Testament for the idea even though the term Kingdom does not appear.

Learning Objective
Visualize the Kingdom of God as a prism through which you can understand the Story of God.

QUESTION
Can you see the Kingdom of God in the OT?

The article "King, Kingship" in the *Dictionary of Biblical Imagery* says that king and kingship are common words in Scripture and goes on to give a brief overview of the Kingdom concept in the Old Testament.[126]

Arthur Glasser in his book *Announcing the Kingdom* suggests that the Old Testament sees God as King over the Kingdom he created.[127]

The Old Testament presents the Kingdom in the context of Jewish messianic expectation and eschatology. The Old Testament people believed that God would deliver them, which was their hope for the future. This deliverance is what Wright calls the "return from exile," a central theme along with restoration that Israel believed herself to be acting out.[128] Israel reached its apex during the rule of Kings David and Solomon. From that point forward, Israel began to descend as a nation. At the death of Solomon, the Kingdom was divided into two Kingdoms with their own kings and governments. This division set in place a longing among the Jews for God to restore to them their past blessings. There were two ways which the Kingdom began to be understood according to James Kallas: the Davidic and the Danielic/Apocalyptic Concept.

The Davidic Concept of the Kingdom. Israel's hope was that God would send a king like David. Israel's focus was militaristic and geographic. Israel wanted a nationalistic kingdom to return.

The ❖ Apocalyptic ❖ Concept of the Kingdom. In the Second Temple Period (ca. 400 B.C. - A.D. 135)[129] hope did not diminish; it only assumed a new language with a modified meaning. The prophets hoped for a nationalistic kingdom, while the hope of the Apocalyptic writers was for a heavenly kingdom which would end this Present Evil Age.[130]

Apocalyptic. Writings that contained prophetic or symbolic visions, especially of the imminent destruction of the world and the salvation of the righteous.

The Lord-Servant Treaty (Exodus 19.2-Numbers 10.10)

This section of the Pentateuch is self-contained and describes some of the teachings that Israel needed on their way to the Promised Land. It covers the period from Israel's arrival at Mt. Sinai (Ex. 19.2) to their departure (Num. 10.10). The time period is about one year in the life of Israel.

The Covenant

The Mosaic Covenant was given to a redeemed people essentially in the form of an elaborate oath[131] often called a Lord-Servant (Suzerain-Vassal) Treaty.[132] The Covenant (Law) was not (as has been thought and taught) a way in which Israel could become God's children. Israel was to have no other God. They were to worship no idols. The Covenant was a way in which these redeemed people could relate to God and to each other and demonstrate to the world what being the people of God was really like. He was their Lord (ruler), they were his people through whom his light was to

Prologue

Learning Objective
Visualize the Kingdom of God as a prism through which you can understand the Story of God.

be seen. The Lordship of God over his people is the same idea as the Kingdom (Lordship/Ruler) over his people in the New Testament.

Redemption/Exodus came first, then the Covenant (Law). The *law* was never intended to be a system of legal observances by which you could earn God's acceptance, if you obeyed them. The Commandments are the stipulations of the *Covenant relationship* which is rooted in *grace!* They are *basic statements* on the *quality of life* that must characterize those who belong to God. All of Scripture knows only one way of salvation…*the grace of God*. God reveals his redemptive purpose always based on grace, not on man's ability to obligate God to save him because he has kept the law.[133] Alas, they turned the windows of their lighthouse into mirrors.[134] We will return to this concept in Act 3: Israel.

The Kingdom of God in the New Testament

Kingdom of God: The Kingdom of God is the *Rule of God* on earth. Jesus brought the future rule of God into the present. We now live in the presence of the future.

Central to the ministry of Jesus was the concept of the ❖ **Kingdom of God**.❖[135] The authors of the Synoptic Gospels fill their books teaching this concept. It seems like they had so much material about the Kingdom that they often summarized the teachings. The beginning of the Gospel of Mark is a great illustration. Mark 1.14-15 reads: "After John was put in prison, Jesus went into Galilee, proclaiming the good news of God. 'The time has come,' he said. 'The kingdom of God has come near. Repent and believe the good news!'" His brief summary told his readers what Jesus *did* and *said* during his ministry.

Tom Wright suggests that the phrase "repent and believe" should not be understood in some Pelagian way[136] but rather from its own historical context. Josephus uses the same phrase in describing an incident which took place in Galilee around A.D. 66. Josephus had traveled to Galilee to help with sorting out its factionalism. He met with a bandit named Jesus (there are 21 people by that name in the index of Josephus) who was plotting against the life of Josephus. After foiling the plot, Josephus told the bandit that he should "repent and believe" in Josephus. What was Josephus saying? He was telling the bandit that he should give up his way of living and trust Josephus for a better way of living.[137] It seems that the phrase used by Josephus could not mean anything less coming from the mouth of Jesus.

James Kallas suggests in his book *Jesus and the Power of Satan* that Jesus never explained the Kingdom because the people to whom he was speaking knew what it meant or thought they knew what it meant.[138]

Matthew summarized the Kingdom as Mark did. He succinctly shows the ministry of Jesus in 4.23 and 9.35 as it centered on the Kingdom. Jesus also summarized the message of the Kingdom when he gave instructions to his twelve disciples (Matt. 10.1ff.). The gospel of the Kingdom is the only gospel that he instructed his disciples to preach. When Luke recorded the sending of the seventy disciples (Luke 10.1ff.), Jesus used similar language. The term Kingdom was frequently on the lips of Jesus. His *works* were designed to demonstrate how to enter the Kingdom (Matt. 5.20; 7.21). His *words* authenticated that the Kingdom was present in his ministry (Matt. 12.28). His *parables* informed us about the mysteries of the Kingdom (Matt. 13.11). His *prayers* modeled for his disciples the desire of his heart, which was that the Kingdom would come to earth (Matt. 6.10). His *death, resurrection, and ascension* made us the instruments of the Kingdom (Acts 1.8). His *second coming* promised the consummation of the Kingdom for his children (Matt. 25.31, 34).

One particular brand of popular theology in USAmerica called dispensationalism holds a distinctive concern that the Kingdom of Heaven as mentioned in Matthew means a future millennial kingdom. Rather, the Kingdom of Heaven in Matthew and Kingdom of God language in the other Synoptic Gospels are simply equivalent phrases. The equivalence of the two expressions is indicated by their content, context, and interchangeability in the Gospels.[139]

Learning Objective
Visualize the Kingdom of God as a prism through which you can understand the Story of God.

John the Baptist proclaimed that there was one coming in which the Age of the Spirit would come. The words of Jesus in Mark clearly denote that the Kingdom had arrived[140] with Jesus. The *words* and *works* of Jesus form a unity in which the Kingdom of God is spoken about and demonstrated. In Jesus we have the presence of the future. Jesus has brought the rule of God from the future into the present.

The Age to Come (Kingdom of God)

Exodus | Judgment/Captivity | First Coming of Jesus | CHURCH AGE | Second Coming of Jesus | The Age to Come

The Present Evil Age (kingdom of Satan)
Ladd. *A Theology of the New Testament, Revised.* p. 67

The Present Evil Age | The Age To Come

The church lives in the shaded area.
Kallas, *The Satanward View: A Study in Pauline Theology.* p. 80

We then live in *the presence of the future*, an expression often used by the late Dr. George Ladd to express Kingdom reality and the name of one of his books.[141] He often said that the church is *between the times*; she lives between the inauguration and the consummation of the Kingdom,[142] which Wright agrees with.[143]

To understand the Kingdom of God is to understand the theme from which the ministry of Jesus and the writings of the New Testament flow. We live in the *presence of the future*, the "now but-not-yet." When we view any passage of Scripture in the New Testament, we must put on our Kingdom of God glasses and ask questions of that passage with that set of presuppositions.

Narrative is powerful and life-changing and the retelling of the narrative by the earliest preachers was good news that carried power to change people effectively bringing them under the rule (kingdom) of God.

The Covenant theme and the Kingdom theme are part of the gluiness that holds the Story together in the Old and New Testaments.

So What?

The problem of fragmentized reading can be addressed by learning to read and comprehend the Story of Scripture using the gluiness of the Covenant and Kingdom. We have learned:
- ◆ Narrative comprises a large percentage of the Old Testament, the Gospels, and is the substructure of the Letters of Paul.
- ◆ Scripture tells an overarching story from Genesis to Revelation.
- ◆ The concept of the Kingdom is broader than the specific term, which is not mentioned in the Old Testament, but can be seen in the Covenant that was made between God and Israel.
- ◆ The Lordship of God over his people in the Mosaic Covenant of the Old Testament is the same idea as the Kingdom (Lordship/Ruler) over his people in the New Testament.

Prologue

◆ The metanarrative of Scripture is held together by the concept of the Kingdom of God (the Lord-Servant Treaty concept in the Old Testament in which God is Lord/Ruler and Kingdom of God in the New Testament where God is Lord/Ruler).

◆ Central to the ministry of Jesus was the concept of the Kingdom of God.

◆ The concept of the Kingdom is the undercurrent of all the writings of the New Testament as demonstrated in the example of Matthew, Paul, John, and the other writers of New Testament books.

Setting the Stage

The arena where God's EPIC Adventure is played out.

It is true that all worldviews are

at the deepest level shorthand

formulae to express stories,

this is particularly clear in the case of Judaism.

(N. T. Wright. *The New Testament and the People of God*)

When you finish this session, you should be able to:

- ◆ Understand why it is important to read the Story of the Old Testament

- ◆ Comprehend Bible, Scripture, and Testament as a way of referring to Story

- ◆ Know about the translation that the New Testament Storytellers used

- ◆ Visualize the backdrop of the first Stories in the overarching Story

Our initial focus in this section is the beginning stage on which God set his Story. First, we will look at why it is important to read the Story in the Old Testament. Next, we define the word: Bible, Scripture, and Testament. Then, we will look at some information about the Bible the Storytellers of the New Testament used. Finally, we will overview the background of the first stories looking at material about the worldview of the ancients and comparing it with the scientific worldview of today.

The Book You Always Meant To Read.
Bible, Scripture, and Testament
    Bible
    Scripture
    Testament
The Old Testament
    The Septuagint (A Greek Translation)
BackStory of Genesis 1.1-2.4a
    Back in Time
    Questions Galore
    Ancient Worldview Beliefs about gods
    Why We May Read The Way We Do
    The Modern god of Science
    Not gods at all
    A Final Thought

In place of a complete Old Testament,

we have devised in contemporary Christianity

our very own "folk Bible."

This "folk Bible" often leaves out

most of the Old Testament...

The Book You Always Meant To Read

Learning Objective
Understand why it is
important to read the Story of
the Old Testament.

According to Margueritte Harmon Bro, the Old Testament is the book you always meant to read,[1] but never really got around to reading it. In my experience, for the most part, people are not reading the Old Testament, or much of the New Testament, for that matter. They read their favorite stories, they sometimes read in Psalms or Proverbs for devotions. Each year Christians make New Year's commitments to read the Bible through. They jet through Genesis, take an excursion through Exodus, and have their last gasp in Leviticus. Leviticus has been the burial place of *many* New Year's resolutions. The Old Testament remains the book you always wanted to read and understand, but never did.

Walter Brueggemann suggests that "the Bible is a strange book that is put together in an odd way." He goes on to suggest that it will not do to read the Old Testament from cover to cover and it is *not* much better to read it chronologically because of the dating of the material.[2] While this may be a difficulty, the chronological approach appears to have greater value than reading it from cover to cover, usually with the rather senseless reading of a few chapters of the Old Testament interspersed with a few chapters from the New Testament, or reading it in is Canonical order.

The place to begin to understand the Story is with its *primal narrative*, according to Brueggemann who followed the thought of Gerhard von Rad, an Old Testament specialist writing in the middle of last century. Then one moves to its expanded narrative, derivative narrative, then including the literature of institutionalization, of mature theological reflection, and finally of instruction and vocation.[3] Wow! that sounds like a lifetime of reading.

So What?

In contemporary Christianity, the Old Testament is neglected more than the New Testament. Because of the popularized slogan that "we live under grace, not under law," the readers of Scripture do not understand that God operated by grace in both testaments in his dealings with humankind. We will discuss this concept more anon. This presupposition often leads the reader to ignore the Old Testament because it appears to have no practical value.

In place of a complete Old Testament, we have devised in contemporary Christianity our very own "folk Bible." This "folk Bible" often leaves out most of the Old Testament, but usually includes Genesis, most of the narrative material through Esther, Psalms, an occasional Proverb, the "messiah" parts of the Prophets, and for those bent to only see the future everywhere, there are additional sections of the Prophets added which would support their view. Verses and phrases are often ripped out of context. The difficulty with originating a "folk Bible" is that we have less of a Story than what we should have. One can tell when one has a "folk Bible" when the contents are challenged and responses like, "Don't confuse me with so many facts!" becomes the outcry. In our culture, popularized writing about the Old Testament often minimizes the value of the whole by focusing over and over again on certain parts, thus, the complete picture of the Old Testament is lost.

A helpful clue for understanding the whole Story is that each reader of

Setting the Stage

Learning Objective
Understand why it is important to read the Story of the Old Testament.

Scripture should endeavor to find a translation that offers a friendly language handshake so that the reader can understand the text and begin moving toward living in its Story. There are many such texts sold in bookstores. You can see Appendix 1 for a brief overview of several Bible translations. My recommendation is *The Books of The Bible*, which is published by International Bible Society and is printed without any additives, i.e., chapters and verses, so the reader can enjoy the Story without human-included material. (See http://www.thebooksofthebible.info for more information).

We now turn briefly to some terms with which you may or may not be familiar to clarify and orient you to the terms Scripture uses of itself.

Bible, Scripture, and Testament

Learning Objective
Comprehend Bible, Scripture, and Testament as a way of referring to Story.

Have you ever wondered how the Bible speaks about itself? There are three terms that are often used to speak about God's Story.

Bible

First, the word *bible* comes from the Greek word *biblos*. *Biblos* could best be originally defined as *any kind of written document*.[4] It initially meant a document that was written on papyrus, a kind of ancient paper made from an Egyptian plant. The Greeks renamed an ancient Phoenician port with the name Byblos. It was a world-renowned city that was famous for working with written material on papyrus. The citizens of Byblos were forerunners in the development of writing and originated one of the first alphabets. When in later centuries the codex—a book that has folding pages—was invented, the term *biblos* persisted and came to be the standard word for book. The word *bible* then simply means a book. The term has been used since the fourth century to denote the Christian Scriptures.[5]

Biblia is used in the Old Testament Septuagint (the Greek translation of the Old Testament often marked by the Roman number LXX, see below for fuller discussion.) The word *biblia* is used in the Apocrypha with the meaning *scriptures* (Dan. 9.2[6]; 1 Maccabees 1.56; 3.48; 12.9[7]). The Apocrypha is noted here from an orthodox Protestant position. These books are useful as a window into how the Jewish mind viewed certain ideas during Second Temple Judaism (formally called the Intertestamental Period). With the arrival of the fifth century A.D., the church fathers had applied the term *biblia* to the whole of Christian Scriptures.

Scripture

The terms Scripture, Scriptures, or Holy Scriptures are terms used by the writers of the New Testament to denote the Old Testament.[8] The following are a few examples of where Scripture uses these terms:
- Scripture: Acts 8.32; Galatians 3.22
- Scriptures: Matthew 21.42; 22.29; Luke 24.32; John 5.39; Acts 18.24
- Holy Scriptures: Romans 1.2; 2 Timothy 3.15

Testament

The terms Old Testament and New Testament have been used since the close of the second century. The word *testament* which is used to describe both divisions of the Bible comes from the Latin *testamentum* or *diatheke* in the Greek language and often means *covenant* rather than *testament*. Thus, the Old Testament books are those associated with the old covenant and the New Testament books are the ones associated with the new covenant.[9] The Old Testament is a collection of thirty-nine books while the New Testament is a collection of twenty-seven books.

Learning Objective
Comprehend Bible, Scripture, and Testament as a way of referring to Story.

So What?

It is important to remember that the only Scripture that Jesus and the New Testament church had was the Old Testament. That should give us pause about the way in which we often treat the Old Testament as unimportant as compared to the New Testament.

The Old Testament

The Bible, Old and New Testaments, is the bestselling book of all times.[10] Its message is considered to be so vital to humankind that it has been translated into hundreds of different languages. The Jews, Muslims, and Christians find their beginnings in the Old Testament.

Learning Objective
Know about the translation that the New Testament Storytellers used.

The term Old Testament is a distinct Christian use of the term. The Jews have come to call their Scripture *Tanakh* (the sacred book of Judaism, consisting of the Torah, the Prophets, and the Writings; see below for a brief discussion).

Many stories in the Old Testament were first told around the warmth of camp fires, among family and friends. Later, they were written down, most likely as separate stories. About the time of David (about 3,000 years ago), people started to put these stories into larger collections that today we call books. This process of collection took a lot of time and the whole of the Hebrew Scripture was not assembled for many years.

In the Protestant wing of Christianity, the thirty-nine books of the Old Testament are divided into four categories: The Pentateuch, Historical Writings, Poetical Writings, and Prophetical Writings. These writings were written to disclose the Covenant God of Israel as he revealed himself and demonstrate how he acted toward his children and what those acts mean. They make known the Covenant God of Israel with whom he chose to have a special relationship. These thirty-nine books were written by many different authors over many years. The Jewish breakdown of their Bible is different from the Protestant one. It contains three parts: the Torah, the Prophets, and the Writings. We do not know when they were first assembled into one volume that we call the Old Testament. However, we do know that the first five books, often called the *Pentateuch* or the Law, were accepted as inspired or canonized between 450-300 B.C. The *Prophets* were received around 200 B.C. and the *Writings* were accepted sometime in the first century B.C.[11]

Jesus was aware of this three-fold Hebrew ❖ **canon** ❖ (Luke 24.44). The text of the Old Testament was written in Hebrew on scrolls—long strips of paper—called papyri. Jesus read from such a scroll at the synagogue in Nazareth (Luke 4.16-17).

Some argue that the ❖ **Hebrew Bible** ❖ was complete by the beginning of the first century A.D. and was accepted by Jews in Jamnia in the mid '90s. Christian scholars have often posited the idea that the canonization of the Hebrew Bible occurred because of the non-inclusion of the

Canon: From the Greek *canon* which means a level or a ruler used by a cabinet maker. The word is used figuratively as a standard or rule of conduct or belief, or a list or catalog of things that may or may not be done. It came to mean a list of books of the Bible and was first used by Athanasius in the fourth century.

The *Hebrew Bible* is arranged in three sections: the Torah, which we know as the Pentateuch (Genesis to Deuteronomy); the Prophets, which are in two parts, the Former Prophets (Joshua, Judges, 1 & 2 Samuel, 1 & 2 Kings) and the Latter Prophets (Isaiah, Jeremiah, Ezekiel and Hosea to Malachi); and the Writings (Psalms, Proverbs, Job, Song of Songs, Ruth, Lamentations, Ecclesiastes, Esther, Daniel, Ezra, Nehemiah, and 1 & 2 Chronicles).

Setting the Stage

Learning Objective
Know about the translation that the New Testament Storytellers used.

Apocrypha: A group of religious writings that developed during the Intertestamental Period–the 400-year period between the Old and New Testament–and had its roots in Old Testament prophecy.

Second Temple Judaism (515 B.C - A.D. 70): The Temple that Solomon built, also known as the First Temple, was destroyed in 586 B.C. when the Jews were exiled into the Babylonian Captivity. The Romans destroyed Jerusalem and its Second Temple that was the reconstructed Temple in Jerusalem which stood between 515 B.C. and A.D. 70.

❖ **Apocrypha** ❖ into the Old Testament by Jews. The most that can be said is that at Jamnia the Jews discussed the authority of the Hebrew Scriptures.[12]

Israel had faith in and relationship with God before there were any inspired books to represent her faith and relationship. In other words, the worship of God came before Scripture, which should be ever present in our minds lest we find ourselves reversing the order and worshiping Scripture before we worship God. Scripture is the primary tool which God uses to express how he will act toward his children in many and varied life situations. Scripture is a means to an end. Scripture is not an end in itself. One must remember that the God of Scripture is more important than the words of Scripture which disclose him to us.

The Septuagint (A Greek Translation)

In the stretch of time called ❖ **Second Temple Judaism,** ❖ the Greek language became the language of choice for much of the Mediterranean world. Some of the Jews, fleeing the Northern Kingdom's occupation by Assyria, moved to North Africa. During this period of time, the Old Testament was translated into the Greek language. The Greek version was called the Septuagint (often designated LXX, which is the Roman numeral for seventy). There was an ancient tradition which believed that seventy elders went to Mount Sinai with Moses. Based on that tradition, it was only fitting that seventy elders should be responsible for translating the Old Testament into the Greek language. The first books to be translated were the Pentateuch at about 250 B.C. Pentateuch comes from two Greek words which together can be defined as "five books." The remaining books of the Old Testament were completed by 100 B.C. In addition to what was later received by the Jews as authoritative, there were additional books which are called the Apocrypha by Protestants. It is believed that the Septuagint had wide circulation during the first century A.D. It can be noted that the authors of the New Testament often quoted from the LXX instead of the Hebrew texts of the Old Testament (see Hebrews 2.6-8).

The Old Testament provides the historical background so that we can understand the New Testament. The New Testament contains hundreds of references or allusions, often called echoes, to the Old Testament. Jesus and the writers of the New Testament books constantly referred to it in their teachings. It was the only Scripture that the New Testament church had.

So What?

Scripture is not silent about itself, but it does not speak of itself often. This might give us pause about the amount of time that we spend defending certain views about Scripture. What if we spent as much time relating to the ultimate author of the stories in Scripture by living in those stories? How would that change our lives?

BackStory of Genesis 1.1-2.4a

Genesis 1.1-2.4a. TBB. 7-8.

Why do we study background? Why don't we just read the text of Scripture and hear what it says? These kinds of questions are often asked of those teaching Scripture, who persist in sharing what sometimes seems to be boring to the students who are listening. These questions are not really difficult to answer. We study background because it puts us in touch with the people for whom the stories were first told. God did not let his storytellers tell stories in a vacuum. The stories were placed in a real time history and told to real human beings.[13] To understand the background of those first hearers/readers will help us understand what God was saying to them and by extension what God is saying to us. This means that it would be helpful to place the early stories in Genesis in a possible historical context.

Learning Objective
Visualize the backdrop of the first Stories in the overarching Story.

Back in Time

Time is a difficult idea to comprehend. It is fair to say that our time, the beginning of the twenty-first century, is much different from the time at the beginning of the twentieth century. Even fifty years ago in time, ideas, concepts, lifestyles, and gas prices were different. Push back further to the stories found in the beginning of Scripture and it is difficult for us to get our arms around and embrace how much different things would have been.

The beginning stories in Genesis 1.1-11.26 were passed along through generations. The story in Genesis 1.1-2.4a was originally addressed to Israel at Mt. Sinai.[14] Remember, Israel had just been delivered from slavery in Egypt by the hand of God. Egypt, like all societies around it, was polytheistic. Polytheism was a belief system in the ancient world that there were many gods to be worshiped. Most societies believed there to be a pantheon of gods who were responsible for the creation of the world. Israel was not immune from knowing, believing, and practicing polytheism.

Genesis 1.1-11.26. TBB. 7-18.

In Egypt, Israel was exposed to the belief that the Pharaoh was himself a god. At the foot of Sinai, a newly redeemed people heard from an inspired Moses the story that the God who had secured their freedom by delivering them from the bondage of Egypt, the God who had made Covenant with them, was the only true God and was the creator of the universe.

They had left Egypt, a polytheistic society, and were traveling toward Palestine, a polytheistic society. The story of Genesis 1.1-2.4a was told in this context to help them understand the first of the commandments of the Covenant, "You can only have one God."

To understand the creation story the way these first listeners would have understood it is to hear it against a backdrop of polytheism. God wanted his newly redeemed people to understand that he was their true God and they could have no other gods.

To understand the history will cause the Story to come alive to you as you read it and it reads you.

Questions Galore

When you were a child you were full of questions. Why is this orange? Why doesn't orange rhyme with something? Why was the leaf green and now it is orange? Where did I come from? Where did that big light in the sky come from? What are all those little lights in the sky at night? Why is sister's nose so big? What's this, mommy?

Questions lead to some kind of answer. The answers are colored with the presuppositions of the society in which the questions are being asked. In the ancient world, they also asked questions about things like: Where

Setting the Stage

did the world come from? The answers were colored by the beliefs of the ancients. There were many stories about the creation of the world being created by many gods. More than anything else, the ancient Hebrew needed to understand that there was only one God. The prevalent cultural belief about deity in their day was that there were many gods. The idea that there was only one God and it was he who created the world is what separates the Old Testament faith from its ancient Near Eastern counterparts.

Ancient Worldview Beliefs about gods

In ancient Egypt, from where the Hebrews had been recently rescued by God, there were five cities, each of which had an account of how the world, the gods, and humankind came into being. Each of these stories was designed to authenticate that creation began in the specific city and that the gods of that city were the supreme gods. The stories vary in telling, but they have this in common: each portrayed creation as a process of birth from single gods or male-female god couples. These gods materialized in such items as air, moisture, earth, sky, sun, and moon.

Another ancient worldview found in the story in Babylon was called *Enuma Elish* that was written to demonstrate how Marduk became the chief god of Babylon. Here is a summary of that story.[15]

In the beginning there were two gods, Apsu and Tiamat, who represented the fresh waters (male) and marine waters (female). They cohabited and produced a second generation of divine beings. Soon Apsu was suffering from insomnia because the young deities were making so much noise; he just could not get to sleep. He wanted to kill the noisy upstarts, despite the protest of his spouse, Tiamat. But before he managed to do that, Ea, the god of wisdom and magic, put Apsu to sleep under a magic spell and killed him.

Not to be outdone, wife Tiamat plotted revenge on her husband's killer and those who aided the killing. Her first move was to take a second husband, whose name was Kingu. Then, she raised an army for her retaliation plans.

At this point the gods appealed to the god Marduk to save them. He happily accepted the challenge, on the condition that if he were victorious over Tiamat, they would make him chief of all gods.

The confrontation between Tiamat and Marduk ended in a blazing victory for Marduk. He captured Tiamat's followers and made them his slaves. Then, he cut the corpse of Tiamat in half, creating heaven from one half of it and the earth from the other half. He ordered the earlier supporters of Tiamat to take care of the world.

Shortly thereafter, Marduk conceived another plan. He had Kingu killed and arranged for Ea to make man out of his blood.

This ancient story goes on to tell that man's lot is to be burdened with the toil of the gods.

Why We May Read The Way We Do

When you open your Bible to the first story (Genesis 1.1-2.4a), your natural tendency is to think of it as a treatise about how God created the earth. This was *not* the driving question of the day among the Hebrews as it has become in our day.

The Scopes Trial in the 1920s turned American popular theology on its heels when John Thomas Scopes, a high school teacher, was charged with violating Tennessee state law by teaching the theory of evolution.

An early spokesman for the cause of Biblical Creation was William Jennings Bryan (1860-1925). Bryan believed that the moral decay in America during his lifetime was the result of the teaching of evolution. The idea of evolution was argued in many arenas, but it wasn't until 1925 that the most famous of the platforms of argumentation, the Scopes Trial, set the standard. In the early part of the twentieth century, religious leaders became fearful of the rise of the teaching about evolution. They believed that Christians should only believe in a literal reading of the Genesis account of creation. This literalness, they believed, would keep believers from losing their faith.

Because of the Scopes Trial, American popular theology has come to believe that it must stand against evolution. What we have settled for is a popular theology (disguised as the only correct theology) of Creation Science. The term has become a household name especially among homeschooling parents. Creation Science, or Creationism as it is sometimes called, is the result of a response to Charles Darwin's book *Origin of the Species* (1859) and the Scopes Trial.

Several years back, I was asked by a homeschool mom to call a homeschool co-op that was looking for a teacher to teach a class on the Bible. In the phone interview, I was asked if I believed in a literal six day creation as recorded in Genesis. I said, "no, I didn't," and the conversation ended within seconds without a question of how I might have presented the material in Genesis 1. Creationism was the litmus test. It was like the interviewer was saying, "This is what we believe that our children should believe and we don't want anyone telling them anything different." I wonder how this plays out when children come face to face with other thinking when they enter their college days.

In today's climate, it's difficult to speak about the creation story of Genesis 1.1-2.4a in any other way than a "literal" way, because of the Scopes Trial. To teach the first chapter of Genesis in any other way than the Creation Science version positioned against secular science will not pass the litmus test of popular theology. It is my opinion that popular theology about this story so misses the point that we must stop, refocus ourselves, and ask some serious questions about the conclusions we have come to believe. Some questions that are important to ask would be: What did the first storyteller, Moses, mean when he told this story to the children of Israel at the foot of Sinai, and what might they have understood by the story being told? It is within the framework of these two questions that the story comes alive with meaning. Outside this framework the story can be twisted like a wax nose, as Martin Luther[16] once said of Scripture, and can be molded into saying and teaching anything one wants to teach.

Our task, then, is to help you as a reader of Scripture to grasp the meaning of Act 1 of Scripture's Grand Narrative, so you can tell it and retell it, and even find yourself in the Story.

Arguing about Creation as a scientific fact or certainty is not the point of the first story in the Bible. The story is theological. It is not scientific. This often comes as a jolt to those who have been formed by the

Setting the Stage

Learning Objective
Visualize the backdrop of the first Stories in the overarching Story.

Enlightenment project of the last three hundred years and have come to revere science as the enemy of Christianity.

The Modern god of Science

Modern science and the first chapter of Genesis are answering different questions. Science wants to know the answer to one question: "How did this happen?" The story in Genesis is interested in answering the question: "Who created the world?" Science has become a god of the modern world that tempts us to believe that "how" is the only valid question to be asked. The beginning stories in Genesis were not written to handle the issues that were raised by twentieth and twenty-first century science. It was told and written by an ancient to handle the issues of his day. As an example: the ancient worldview believed that humankind was simply an afterthought that the gods were not happy about. In contrast to this ancient belief, the storyteller of the creation narrative asserts that humankind (man), male and female, was the goal of God's creation. The ancient author goes about deconstructing the polytheistic belief system and replacing it with a monotheistic one. It is our task as modern readers to concentrate on the scene into which this bit of storytelling came and not waste time trying to solve some scientific issue that is foreign to the purpose of the story.

Not gods at all

The first teller of this story, Moses, and the first hearers of this story, Israel in the wilderness, were not privy to Darwin's theory or modern science. It was not part of their mindset. One might reason that if it were not part of the original storyteller's mindset and it had meaning for the first hearer, who also did not have a scientific mindset, then we might need to look in another direction for the meaning of the story of creation.

Alas, we return to our original thought: The ancient Hebrews needed to understand that there was only one God and not many gods. They needed to realize that other so-called gods that were being worshiped at that time and thought to be creative forces were in reality not gods at all.

We, then, might see the need for understanding the historical context of a text by this brief exercise of looking at the BackStory of Genesis 1.1-2.4a. We will take a closer look at this passage in Act 1.

A Final Thought

If there had been public schools among the ancient Hebrews in the wilderness, the burning question of debate would have surrounded monotheism (one God) and polytheism (many gods). Questions surely would not have been around creation and evolution, which is an issue that Americans, who now live thousands of years later in the midst of a scientific worldview, might imagine it to be.

So What?

A misreading of the beginning of the story may lead us down a different path which may not be useful in learning to live within God's Story. As we will see later, the idea of serving many gods is still alive here at the beginning of the twenty-first century. It is important, then, to orient ourselves to what the intent of the first story in Scripture, and many others as well, may have been and how our lives are affected by them.

QUESTIONS
What surprises you about the polytheistic background of Genesis 1-11?
Why do you think that we are so scientific-oriented even when it comes to reading and understanding an ancient document that was written to a people before science?
How much do you think the Scopes Trial has influenced the reading and understanding of the first story of Scripture?

Dictionary Articles

Read the following Dictionary Articles in *New Bible Dictionary*, Third Edition. D. R. W. Wood, A. R. Millard, J. I. Packer, D. J. Wiseman, and I. Howard Marshall (Editors), InterVarsity Press. 1996.
  Genesis
  Mt. Sinai
  Egypt
  Polytheism
  Pharaoh
  Moses
Search Google for the following terms.
  Scopes Trial
  William Jennings Bryan
  Creation Science

Act 1

Creating the Stage On Which the Story Will Be Acted Out

Genesis 1.1-2.4a...is a

small treatise...against polytheism.

When you finish this session, you should be able to:

◆ Understand some of the images used for God in Scripture like God as Creator
◆ Know the three major names of God used in the Old Testament
◆ Understand the first two verses of Genesis 1
◆ Comprehend that there is only one God to serve
◆ Visualize how the different creation containers speak of God's order

Our initial focus in this lesson is to overview God as Creator and look at other images that are used to help us understand God in this first Story. Then, we will look at the three names of God and the different variants of those names. Next, we will begin the Story of Genesis 1 viewing the creation of God and its meaning for the People of God. Then, we will examine how the first of the ten commandments is the backdrop for Genesis 1.3-24a. Finally, we will overview the six creative containers and the day God rested.

Act 1: Creating the Stage On Which the Story Will Be Acted Out

God as Creator
Other Images of God in Genesis 1
  God as Deliverer
  God is Communicator (a speaking God)
  God is One Who Brings Order
  God is a Builder of Community
The Names of God
  El
  Yahweh
  Adonai
The Story Begins. When God Began to Create: Genesis 1.1-2
  God Calls a People
  In the Beginning: Genesis 1.1-2. An Examination
    Summary
Only One God. Genesis 1.3-2.4a: An Examination
  Pass the Splenda®
  A Present Quandary
  BackStory
The Six Containers of Creation. Genesis 1.3-2.4a: An Overview
The Six Creative Acts of Creation: Genesis 1.3-2.4a: An Examination
  Creative Container (Day One): Genesis 1.3-5
  Creative Container (Day Two): Genesis 1.6-8
  Creative Container (Day Three): Genesis 1.9-13
  Creative Container (Day Four): Genesis 1.14-19
  Creative Container (Day Five): Genesis 1.20-23
  Creative Container (Day Six): Genesis 1.24-31
  Note
  Vegetarian?
Was God Tired?
  Creative Container (Day Seven): Genesis 2.1-4a
A Word About Numbers

In the ancient world, there was

a constant struggle between order and chaos.

The forces of nature were personalized

as divine beings.

Act 1: Creating the Stage On Which the Story Will Be Acted Out

Ancestral stories are a heritage of humankind. They are told and told again by generations of storytellers. These narratives come from families, tribes, and national collections of stories.[1] The Hebrew story begins with the story of Abraham (Gen. 12), but the Bible Story begins with the creation of the universe by God (Gen. 1).

These early stories in Genesis 1.1-11.26 represent the Hebrew understanding of the Primeval History of the world,[2] a preface to ❖ **salvation history** ❖ which addresses the origin of the world, humankind, and sin.[3] These stories were told with a pre-science worldview and should be thought about within that worldview and not used to try to prove a modern form of creationism. The ancient's view of God was not laden with scientific presuppositions. They were not dominated by explaining "how" the world came into existence or "how" long it had existed. These stories of creation began to be told to early Israel by Moses at the foot of Mt. Sinai during their eleven-month stay to help them understand what it meant to be the people of one God.[4]

The teller of this story, usually understood to be Moses, and the listeners to this story had a completely different view of God than we do living in the Western world some millennia later.[5] From their recent experience, the people to whom this story was told knew God as their *redeemer,*[6] the God who had brought them "...out of Egypt, out of the land of slavery" (Ex. 20.2).

The ancient world was a world of polytheism, which is the belief in many separate and distinct deities or gods. The many deities were believed to be personal and distinguished from the creation. World religions today are overwhelmingly polytheistic with the exception of Judaism, Christianity, and Islam.

The ancient worldview included two divine beings, a male and female god. The male (Apsu) and female (Tiamat) gods were believed to be the father and mother of all gods. In due course they mated and had children who were also gods. In time, as in most families, quarrel broke out between children and their father. The male/father god (Apsu) was slain, which led to war between the mother (Tiamat) and her children. Tiamat was pictured as a monster. One of her children was Marduk, the god of Babylonia. He was believed to be the creator of the universe and of humankind, the god of light and life, and the ruler of destinies. He rose to such eminence that he claimed fifty titles. Eventually, he was called simply Bel, meaning "Lord." (Isa. 46.1, Jer. 50.2, 51.44). In their family fight, Marduk slays the mother god and from her body creates the world: the earth, sky, sun, moon, and stars.

In the ancient world, there was a constant struggle between order and chaos. The forces of nature were personalized as divine beings. The planets were deities and ruled the course of human affairs. Astrology was developed as early as 3000 B.C.[7] Astrology is still around today in the popular form of horoscopes, and, often, Christians live in the story it presents instead of the Story the Bible presents, a subtle form of ❖ **henotheism.** ❖

When the first hearers of this story in Genesis 1.1-2.4a listened to this story presented by Moses, they were well aware of this worldview. The

Learning Objective
Understand some of the images used for God in Scripture like God as Creator.

Genesis 1.1-11.26. TBB. 7-18.

Salvation History views the historical events of God's saving acts in history which has its climax in the incarnation of Jesus and finds its completion in the consummation of the Kingdom.

Henotheism. The worship of one god without excluding the possibility of other gods.

Act 1

Primeval

Learning Objective
Understand some of the images used for God in Scripture like God as Creator.

Genesis 1.1-2.4a. TBB. 7-8.

story Moses told them has been called an *anti-polytheistic tract*, a literary piece whose thesis was to stand against polytheism.[8] In the case of Israel, this story was useful to help her have a firm belief in God when entering into the Promised Land where the religious belief system of the people was polytheistic.

Genesis 1.1-2.4a, as a whole story, is a small treatise, then, against polytheism. As previously acknowledged, we have seen the rise of Creation Science, which is an effort to give scientific proof for the account of the creation of the universe. We must remember that the first chapters of Genesis predate science.[9] These chapters have no interest in discussing science, teaching science, nor entering into any argumentation about scientific assumptions. This opening story, as well as the rest of the Story, are theological in scope and nature. Their only intent is to teach us about who God is, not what he did or how he did it.[10] The crucial teaching of this section of Scripture centers on polytheism versus monotheism. That was the burning need of their day and time. Hearing it as the first people may have heard and recited it would be very different from the way certain American groups, thousands of years later in the middle of a scientific age, might think and speak about it.

We should observe that all the elements that were created by God from *light* to *humans* were believed by the ancients to be gods. God's purpose in the telling of this story to his children was to let his newly redeemed people, whom he had just rescued from the land of Egypt, know that he was the *only* God they should worship.[11] The story is a perfect illustration of the first commandment: "You shall have no other gods besides me" (Ex. 20.2). Nothing has really changed; we still live in a pagan society. We are surrounded with many gods and many evangelists of those gods offering us to come to their feet and worship. Shall we worship the god of power, the god of culture, the god of sex, the god of communications, or will we worship the Creator God who has called us to bring his redemption to his created world?

God as Creator

At the beginning of the Story we are introduced to God who is the main character of the whole Story. We are also introduced to the other character, humankind, represented by Adam and Eve. No definition of God is offered in these opening verses. Unlike the pagan cosmology, Genesis displays no interest in the question of God's origin. This story demonstrates that God's nature finds expression through his acts, not through philosophical or scientific hypotheses.

The opening sentence of Scripture confesses that God is Creator. In addition to Genesis, Isaiah understood God as the creator of the "heavens and the earth" (Isa. 40.28; 42.5; 45.18). In the New Testament, Mark and John understood the same thing (Mark 13.19; Rev. 10.6). Isaiah, Malachi, and Mark understood God as the creator of humans along with Genesis (Gen. 1.27; 5.2; Isa. 45.12; Mal. 2.10; Mark 10.6). Paul and John tell us that God created "all things" (Eph. 3.9; Col. 1.16; Rev. 4.11). The existence of the world and human existence is explained by God as Creator. We can see this in the following three illustrations:

1. **God is our source**. God is sovereign over all. No other power can be coequal with him. The biblical picture of God is that of a good Creator whose creative word is powerful and wise (Jer. 10.12;

Prov. 3.19), who created all things good (Gen. 1.31). As creator over all, he is the only one who can be worshipped. Idolatry in any form is prohibited.

2. **God's creation is dependent**. Dependence suggests relationship. God created humankind with freedom and intelligence that could be used either to affirm or deny relationship with him. Adam and Eve rebelled against that relationship. God has provided a way in Jesus to reenter relationship with him. The choice is ultimately ours.

3. **God is in control**. While our experience may not validate that God is in control, Scripture suggests otherwise. Revelation 4 suggests that while the world may appear to be sitting on the brink of catastrophe, God has ultimate and perfect control, and that should lead us to comfort and peace.

Learning Objective
Understand some of the images used for God in Scripture like God as Creator.

So What?

God as creator establishes for us the following about his character: he is a good God who created everything good; he is our source because he created us to be dependent on him; he is in total control, even though life often looks out of control.

As God has created, his creation may also create. Everything that is needed in order to create is available, but not everything has been created that will be created. This limitlessness of creation is due to God's creativeness.

Other Images of God in Genesis 1

God as Deliverer

Another act that demonstrates God's character was his act of the deliverance of Israel in the Exodus. This act of deliverance became part of the central core of Israel's faith. It embraces the themes of *escape* and *safety*. The humbling of Egypt and the establishment of the Covenant at Sinai demonstrated the character of liberty by which God makes people free. Annually the celebration of the Passover is the commemoration of Israel's deliverance from the grips of bondage in Egypt. In this vein, Psalms 105-107 celebrated the God who delivered Israel. The deliverance of Israel from Egypt by God establishes the true nature of all deliverance activity. God did not free this group from bondage merely to provide relief from a disastrous situation or for them to pursue their former way of life. He delivered them so they could be free to serve him and him alone. Deliverance is the act of being changed from serving one master to serving another master. This concept is essential to the Covenant given to Moses at Mt. Sinai and is still an abiding concept of spirituality today.

God is Communicator (a speaking God)

Throughout the story of Genesis 1.2-2.4a, the author portrays God as a speaking God. His speech brings the world into existence. God still speaks today. Some believe that he only talks through the pages of Scripture. That's just nonsense. While he does communicate with his children through the stories we find in Scripture, that is not the only way that he intends to communicate with us. Again, the rational side of us becomes very mistrusting of people who contend that they hear from God. Why is hearing from God directly so surprising to us? We believe and often try to persuade others to believe that God does not change. Then, we sometimes

Act 1

Primeval

Learning Objective
Understand some of the images used for God in Scripture like God as Creator.

send a mixed message by saying that he has changed in the area of communication. That he no longer speaks directly. That he has only chosen to speak to us through the Bible. Nowhere in Scripture does God stop talking to his children. He has not stopped talking to us today. We might want to get our antennas fixed so we can tune in to what he is saying.

God is One Who Brings Order

Until one can hear that chaos is good, order cannot happen. It is, after all, out of chaos that God created. Things haven't changed much, if at all. God does like to bring order, but we must not be tempted to think of order in some enlightened rational manner. Order does not necessarily mean that everything must be neatly fitted in a row, a column, or in a circle. There are hundreds of shapes that are orderly. As an example, there is a game called "Shape to Shape: Creative Pattern Puzzle." There are fourteen puzzle pieces and sixty different images with over 25,000 ways to arrange the pieces inside the puzzle frame. Humankind needs to have order, but the sand box that God has designed for us is much larger than we want to admit or even play in. Let him bring order, but don't be surprised if his order in no way fits your conception of order.

God is a Builder of Community

In 1624, John Donne wrote in *Devotions*, "No man is an island, entire of itself; every man is a piece of the continent...."[12] He caught a glimpse of the fact that deep in the breast of humankind lies a desire to be a part of a community. God created it to be so. Our cultural selective value of individualism runs counter to what God created us to be a part of. This is why there is so much tension and frustration in today's society. We seek what we were not created to be. This story tells us that humankind will only achieve its highest potential when it gives in to God's creative forces and separates itself from the culture's selective position.

So What?

There is not any situation that you can find yourself involved in, whether by your own hand or by the hand of others, from which God is not capable of delivering you.

The Names of God

In the Old Testament, names were not mere labels. A name represented an identification, but it also represented an identity.[13] The *first* of the three names for God that we will look at is El. The word in itself suggests authority[14] and is found in several compound forms.

El

- ◆ **El Shaddai**. The *God who is strong, stable, and permanent.* The most common name used for God in the period of the Patriarchs. The name suggests permanence, stability, and strength. It is often translated *God Almighty*, as in Genesis 17.1 (TNIV). We need to understand that in a time when we are weak, unstable, and fleeting that God is strong. This will bring peace and comfort to our day-to-day lives. We can praise him for his strength, his stability, and his permanence.
- ◆ **El Elyon**. *God Most High.* This name suggests that God is the Supreme Being (Gen. 14.18; Num. 24.16). In a day of red tape

Act 1

Primeval

Learning Objective
Know the three major names
of God used in the Old
Testament.

where there are many echelons of people and grief to wade through in order to talk to a decision maker, we have instant access to God, the highest decision maker of all. We can praise him because we have access to the Supreme Being in the universe.

- **El Olam.** *God the eternal or everlasting one* (Gen. 21.33: Eternal God). In this name, God is seen as the everlasting one or the God of eternity. He is unaffected by the passing of time. When life seems to be in constant change, we can lean on the everlasting, unchanging arm of God. We can praise him because he does not change with time.

  I grew up listening and singing Southern Gospel music. One of the songs that I remember my mom and dad singing was "Leaning on the Everlasting Arms." The authors of this song caught the essence of El Olam in their creation. You can hear it on the Net.[15] Go ahead and listen and give yourself a treat.

- **Elohim.** *God is the creator of the universe.* Elohim is the subject of the first sentence in the Story of God (Gen. 1.1).[16] With this name, the ancient Hebrew understood God as the absolute Lord over all his creation. There is not anything in our life with God over which he is not in control. We can praise him for the universe that he has created.

Yahweh

A *second* name attributed to God is Yahweh. In our English Bibles it is translated Jehovah. This name revealed God as a personal God. Yahweh became so significant in Israel that the scribes would avoid pronouncing it. With the Exodus, Yahweh assumed a specifically redemptive role in the mind of the children of Israel. His mighty acts were saving acts. In his deliverance at the Sea of Reeds, Yahweh had shaped the forces of nature to serve the ends of grace, thus bringing his power to bear on the nation in a time of historic emergency and crisis. There are seven compound names that use the name Jehovah. For the most part, all seven have been mistaken for names of God, when in fact all are not.

- **Jehovah-jireh.** *God has provided.* Abraham gave this name to the *place* on Mount Moriah where God supplied a substitute for Isaac (Gen. 22.13-14). The place was remembered by the action of God— he provided the need of Abraham. God provides for our needs whether they are great or small. We need to turn to him for both. We can praise God for the things he has provided. For an interesting interpretation of this story see Len Sweet's *Out Of The Question... Into the Mystery.*[17]

- **Jehovah-rapha.** *God who heals.* This is a name God used of himself (Exodus 15.26). God told Moses that he was the Lord who heals. Because God heals, we should turn to him first when any dimension of our life needs to be healed. We can praise God for the times he has healed us, physically, emotionally, spiritually, financially, and socially.

- **Jehovah-nissi.** *God is my banner.* Moses erected an altar to commemorate the defeat of the Amalekites (Exodus 17.8-15). The altar's name revealed the assurance that God was the one who gave the Israelites strength to win the victory. God's desire is to bring us victory over the areas of life in which we seem to be continually bound. We can praise him for all the success he brings to our lives.

Primeval

Learning Objective
Know the three major names
of God used in the Old
Testament.

◆ **Jehovah-shalom**. *God of Peace.* Another name for an altar—this time given by Gideon (Judges 6.24). It is usually translated, "the Lord is peace." God brings peace and harmony to our lives, not like the world offers, not a reduction in the circumstances, but peace in the midst of life's problems. We can praise God for all the times of peace in the midst of turmoil and stress.

◆ **Jehovah-ra'ah**. *God our Shepherd.* David calls God his shepherd as a metaphorical way of describing some of the characteristics of God (Psalm 23). This is a name ascribed to God. God is a provider. As a shepherd he provides rest, refreshment, restoration, freedom from fear, protection, care, more than enough, and security. We can praise him for feeding us and protecting us.

◆ **Jehovah-tsidkenu** (tsid-kay'-noo). *God our righteousness.* Jeremiah is the only person who used this name (Jeremiah 23.6). It is the name of the future king who would bring the rule of God to earth— translated "The Lord our righteousness." Jesus came as the one who demonstrated the righteousness of God and calls us to walk in the right paths that he has set before us. We can praise God for his righteousness.

◆ **Jehovah-shammah**. *God is present.* Ezekiel uses this term to describe the restored city of Jerusalem (Ezekiel 48.35). It is translated, "the Lord is there present." Regardless of how we think or feel about where God is in proximity to our life, whether we think he is near or far away, he is always present. In fact, in Jesus, we are in him and he is in us. We can praise God that he is always present with us.

Only two of the Jehovah compound names are really names attributed to God (Jehovah-rapha and Jehovah ra'ah). One is a future name of a Davidic king (Jehovah-tsidkenu). The remaining are names of *places* where God interacted with his people in a special way.

Adonai

A *third* and final name is Adonai. It is usually translated as *the sovereign one* (Exodus 23.17). It means God has dominion and authority.

So What?

The names of God demonstrate the character of God. If we want to know him seriously, we must understand his character. Too often we are too frivolous with the name of God, thereby demonstrating that we do not take him seriously. Remember, God wants us to take him seriously. There are many other ways that God has been named in the Old Testament which tell us something about his character. In fact, there are 152 designations, descriptive titles, and figures of speech for God. See Appendix 2 for a partial list.

We need to understand how and what we think about God. Here are some reasons why it is important to know and understand who God is. Knowing God:

◆ directly affects our response to pain and hardship
◆ gives us the strength to stand firm when we are attacked or tested
◆ intensifies our worship and praise
◆ determines our lifestyle and philosophy of life
◆ provides meaning and significance to our relationships

- gives us stability
- gives us a desire to be like him (Jer. 9.24)
- reveals the truth about us (Isa. 6.1-2)
- helps make us stronger and more secure (Dan. 11.31)
- introduces us to the eternal dimension of life (John 17.3)

Primeval

Learning Objective
Know the three major names
of God used in the Old
Testament.

Remember, this is only a small opening to the vast amount of biblical material about who God is. Read his Story and look for his acts. In understanding them, you will become better acquainted with who God is and how he will act in your life situations.

We have looked at a brief overview of God as an introduction to his Story. Now we can turn to Act 1 and begin the process of grasping what it means to live in his Story.

The Story Begins. When God Began to Create: Genesis 1.1-2

Genesis 1.1-2. TBB. 7.

Learning Objective
Understand the first two
verses of Genesis 1.

Morning has broken
    Like the first morning,
Blackbird has spoken
    Like the first bird.
Praise for the singing!
    Praise for the morning!
Praise for them, springing
    Fresh from the Word!

So says the hymn by Eleanor Farjeon.[18] These words catch the essence of the beginning story of Scripture that affirms that God's creation came "fresh from his word."

So the first story begins. This little tract (Gen 1.1-2.4a) presents God as the creator of his universe. The Story of God begins with a picture of God's creation, perfect in every manner. There was a time when God spoke the world into existence: the creation of light distinguished from darkness, dry land from chaos, a perfect home for perfect humans to live in and enjoy each other and their relation with God. These first beings were the crown of his creation, created to bear his image, made in his own likeness, creatures with whom he could communicate and they, in turn, could delight in his favor and presence, creatures who as created beings were created to be dependent on their creator for their very existence in the world. They were charged by God to populate and have authority over his creation and continually reflect his glory. After he spoke all this into existence, he rested.

We live in an era that is different from the era in which this story first appeared. Because of our culture, we ask different questions from what the ancients would have asked. We want to know how God created. We want to know if the *big bang theory* is a possibility. We want to know how life began on earth. We want to know if there is life anywhere else in the universe. We are beginning to ask if God created and gave us the power to create, is cloning humans okay?

The story of creation presented in Genesis 1.1-2.4a is not equipped to answer such questions. As we have pointed out previously, this story is not a scientific treatise. Rather, it is a theological work presented in a narrative or story form.

Rather than trying to figure out with scientific certainness what a text means, we should be interested in the theological meaning it carries. An

Act 1

Primeval

Learning Objective
Understand the first two
verses of Genesis 1.

illustration is in order: The dawn of the very first day created by God carries an expectation of a dawn of a new age. In the beginning of the Story, God created out of chaos and set Adam and Eve in Eden to till and keep it. At the end of the Story, God will again create out of chaos a new Eden, peopled by a new creation. These *theological allusions* are important to begin to see and comprehend as you read God's EPIC Adventure.

God Calls a People

Into the ancient world of polytheism, God called his people to be monotheistic (believing only in him).[19] When Israel was delivered from their bondage in polytheistic Egypt and journeyed toward polytheistic Canaan, God began the long process of training them to relate to him and not to all the other gods that were believed to be at hand. It is difficult for our Western mind to grasp that almost everything in their ancient's culture was thought to be divine. There was a sun god, a moon god, a light god, a darkness god, a sky god, a sea god, male gods, female gods, and the list goes on and on. Israel was faced with learning and relating to the one and only God, the creator of the universe in which they lived and moved. That was not easy then and seemingly it is no easier today.

As Israel camped at the foot of Mt. Sinai, they could not shake the polytheism of Egypt. They were headed into the land that God had promised which was filled and fueled by the worship of many gods. Israel needed a clear word about who God was. On their journey, they had witnessed God's power and judgment. It is not difficult to picture the family meetings at night as they sat around their campfires as the story of creation was told and retold. In simple rhythmic form, they learned about their God and how he was different from the many gods of the land they were to inherit.

With impact and power, they learned that God spoke and the world came into existence! The world was not itself divine. The great lights in the heavens were not deities. God and God alone was deity. He had created all that there was. Genesis 1.1-2.4a rehearses these great acts. From nothing to a beautiful world filled with his creation, Genesis rings out a clear message: God is creator!

In the Beginning. Genesis 1.1-2: An Examination

The first word in the text of Genesis is *re' shiyth* (pronounced ray-sheeth). It is translated in most versions as *in the beginning. In the beginning* is not just a simple reflection of temporal time. It announced the setting in motion of a series of events. The phrase is pregnant with the end. The creative acts of God recorded here set history in motion determining its flow toward a specific end. It could be translated, *when God began to create.*

This simple sounding phrase, *in the beginning*, is really not that simple. We must note that it is not the beginning of everything because God predates this beginning. Because our dialogue partner is often science and not theology, we just try too hard to prove something out of nothing. Could it be possible that *beginning* is no more than the "beginning of our story as a human race"? We often try to define the English translated word without thinking about the Hebrew word from which we are translating.[20] Our English word *beginning* indicates the beginning of something. However, with closer examination, we might discover that the

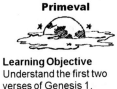

Learning Objective
Understand the first two verses of Genesis 1.

Hebrew usage might not carry the same implication. A great concern that we should hold in tension is our propensity to think in our own cultural and linguistic categories when trying to interpret words in Scripture. Make no mistake about it. We are all interpreting, even those of us that often boast that we are only reading the "plain meaning" of the text. The so-called "plain meaning" of the text is also an interpretation and usually an interpretation of the English words only. We shouldn't be shocked by our tendencies to read within our categories; after all, they are often the only categories that we know.[21] A simple exegesis of the English word *beginning* will not do in trying to understand what the storyteller meant.

While *re'shiyth* (ray-sheeth) may refer to the beginning of something, it can have other meanings. It can mean an initial period or duration of time rather than a specific point in time. In Jeremiah 28.1, the prophet speaks about the beginning (*re'shiyth*, ray-sheeth) period of Zedekiah's kingship. This was a period of time, not a point in time.[22]

It may then be well to translate Genesis 1.1 as: "In the beginning when God created the heavens and the earth, the earth was a formless void…(*New Revised Standard Version*, NRSV). Thus "in the beginning" does not point to a point in time in which there was nothing and God began to create, but rather, a period of creative time that encompasses the six days of creation. The ❖ **TANAKH** ❖ (the Jewish Bible) suggests a rendering of Genesis 1.1 as: "When God began to create…."[23] One may conclude that the text is not suggesting that anything was created in 1.1, but that the verse is an introduction and summary of what follows. The period of time indicated by the first sentence in Genesis is the events discussed in the first story (1.1-2.4a).

TANAKH. This word is derived from the Hebrew letters of its three components: Torah (the Pentateuch), Nevi'im (the Prophets, former and latter), and Ketuvim (the Writings).

Again and again, we must remind ourselves that understanding words in the Hebrew Bible is different than understanding the translated English words. Most all translations use the word *created* to translate the Hebrew word *bara* (pronounced baw-raw). *Bara* appears forty-eight times in the Hebrew Bible, and in all its uses, God is the subject, thus *bara* is a divine activity. However, what is created is diverse: Jerusalem (Isa. 65.18); people groups (Ezek. 21.30), things like wind, fire, darkness, etc. (Ex. 34.10, Num. 16.30). *Bara* is not the creation of material by manufacturing.[24] It does not appear in a context where material is mentioned. Manufacturing is not the issue. *Bara's* essence concerns itself with the creation of the cosmos [universe; heavens and earth is a ❖ **merism** (merismus), ❖ together they represent the entirety of the created cosmos] and suggests that this initial period of beginning was a time when God gives roles and functions to his creation. It is true that Scripture later supports the idea that God created matter from nothing (Col. 1.16-17; Heb. 11.3), but this is not the idea being forwarded by the storyteller of Genesis 1.

Merism is a figure of speech by which a single thing is referred to by a conventional phrase that enumerates several of its parts, or which lists several synonyms for the same thing. As an example, when we mean to say that someone searched thoroughly, everywhere, we often say that someone *searched high and low*.

It is more likely that the storyteller's concern was much like other storytellers of the ancient world, where the greatest exercise of power was not that a god created something out of nothing, but rather the amount of power that the gods had in fixing the destinies, i.e., the fixing of roles and functions. Again, the dialog partner is not science, how God created the universe, but it is polytheism. Against that dialog partner, the storyteller affirms that it is the Hebrew God who has the exclusive authority to create roles and functions to his cosmos.

Act 1

Primeval

Learning Objective
Understand the first two verses of Genesis 1.

Hendiadys is the use of two independent words that are connected by the word "and" which express a single concept such as grace and favor for gracious favor.

Israel's needs at the foot of Sinai were many. Among them was their need to understand their calling in the world that God had created. They needed to understand that God was a God of order, and that by his power he could bring clarity to their function with the chaos of their own world. For them, the beginning of the story was a clear word of order in a foggy world of chaos.

There is no grammatical tradition that supports the supposed Gap Theory (that the creation of verse 1 was destroyed and a new creation occurred in verse 2). The next phrase "formless and empty" (TNIV) is a ❖ **hendiadys.** ❖ Verse 2 pictures God during a period of time bringing order out of chaos. James Barr suggests: "Genesis is interested in an organized world, as against a chaotic world, and not in the metaphysical sense of something against nothing."[25] In this phrase, one might see an allusion to the historical experience of Israel coming out of bondage in which God begins to work his creative purpose through them.[26]

In the ancient world, chaos was a concern. The gods of the ancient were pictured as holding back the forces of chaos. The storyteller of Genesis tells his listeners that the God of Israel did not hold back chaos; he created order from the disorder of chaos. From the wasteland of chaos, God spoke and order came into being.

The next phrase "darkness was over the surface of the deep," continues the description of the chaotic state into which God spoke. There is nothing malicious about the chaos;[27] it may just imply that God had not yet begun his work. Because *darkness* or *surface of the deep* is not personified as in other ancient creation accounts (i.e. Enuma Elish), it may be the storyteller's way of saying at the beginning that these are not gods, as they were feared to be in other ancient cultures.

The next phrase to consider is: "and the Spirit of God was hovering over the waters." What could that mean? In order to understand what this phrase means, we must ask: What may it have meant to the original audience? Certainly, we must realize that there was communication taking place from God to the storyteller (author) to the audience. What we don't want to do is to see quickly a reference to the Holy Spirit as the third member of the Trinity, which would run the risk of superimposing a Trinitarian concept on Genesis 1 that is not necessarily present.[28] The same word in Hebrew (*ruah*) can be translated "wind," a meteorological phenomenon or a metaphysical entity "spirit." It is not all that easy to determine which usage of the Hebrew word the author intended.[29]

QUESTIONS
How does this picture of Genesis 1.1-2 differ from what you may have encountered before? What struggles does it present to you? How does a "period of time" versus "a point in time" clarify how God works in the life of your faith community and your personal life?
In what ways does God want to bring order to the chaos of your faith community and your own personal chaos? When is the last time that you remember being visited in your faith community by the power of God to create order and functionality?

The text of the Hebrew Bible is concerned with convincing the people of God that there was only one God. This is the purpose of Genesis 1.1-2.4a. So God did not provide them a confusing message with a bit of Trinitarian complexity. It is generally attested that the ancient Israelites did not know about the Trinity, a fact that remains current today. When we accept this, it becomes apparent that we must look elsewhere for the authoritative communication of "spirit of God." It is clear in the Hebrew Bible that "spirit of God" was an extension of God's power, not a separate entity. The meaning of "spirit" was understood, for example, like the metaphor "the hand of the Lord." We are not saying that the Holy Spirit is an "it" rather than a "he." We are suggesting that the text here is not a direct reference to the Holy Spirit in the mind of the Hebrew storyteller. The "spirit" here is an extension of the power of God in the work of creation.[30]

Finally, let's look at "hovering." This word only occurs one other time in the Hebrew Bible (Deut. 32.11). There it is a picture of a mother bird "hovering" over her nest. This could be a picture of fertility based on the way a mother bird keeps her eggs warm during gestation, in which case it would point to the power of God to bring about his creation. One commentator translates the verse using the word *circulated*: "The earth was nonfunctional, primordial, watery darkness prevailed, and a supernatural wind that was permeated with the power of God circulated over the service of the waters."[31]

Learning Objective
Understand the first two verses of Genesis 1.

So What?

These interpretative conclusions presented here may be new to you. Not to fear. It is clear that the ancient people who first received this word were different than we are today. Our approach to the text, then, is based on trying to familiarize ourselves with what the text may be addressing to the first hearer/reader rather than letting our present culture dictate the questions that are answered by the text. We cannot feel free to transform the text into a scientific query. If we as interpreters are free to transform the text into answering questions that the text does not answer, then we may strip the text of transforming our lives.

This text sets up the remaining part of the story of God's creation as presented by the storyteller in Genesis 1.1-2.4a. It works as the beginning framework for the whole Story of God of which Genesis 1.1-2.4a is the beginning. These thoughts will frame our continuing discussion about the Story presented in Scripture. Genesis 1.1-2.4a demonstrates that God works in periods of time to create order by his power.

Dictionary Articles
Read the following Dictionary Articles in *New Bible Dictionary*, Third Edition. D. R. W. Wood, A. R. Millard, J. I. Packer, D. J. Wiseman, and I. Howard Marshall (Editors), InterVarsity Press. 1996.
  Gap Theory
  Egypt
  Sinai

Only One God. Genesis 1.3-2.4a. An Examination

Pass the Splenda®

We have substitutes for almost everything today. Substitute sugar like Splenda® and substitute fat are two that come to mind. We are a generation not unlike any other generation; we love to substitute something lesser for something more. We are no different than ancient Judaism in this manner. Its biggest substitute was other gods for Yahweh.

Learning Objective
Comprehend that there is only one God to serve.

Genesis 1.3-2.4a. TBB. 7-8.

We live in the Western world today with a delusion that our world is somehow "Christian" or somehow neutral when it comes to other gods. Nothing could be further from the truth. Our society is as thoroughly pagan as the ancient world was pagan. There are idols galore. But, we think that because we don't have some molded image sitting on our mantel that we bow down and worship, that we don't have any idols to be rid of. When we begin to worship anything that God has created instead of the God who created it, we are in jeopardy of worshipping an idol.

A Present Quandary

Remember, the point of Genesis 1.1-2.4a is that there is only one God to be worshipped. Yahweh is it! As a new nation, just delivered from the land of Egypt, the Jews were in great need to understand that the God of their forefathers who had delivered them was, in fact, the only God that they should worship.

Those thoughts are not usually in our mind when we open Scripture to its first pages and begin to read the story of Creation in Genesis 1.1-2.4a. We are more apt to think that we are to discover *how* God created the

Dictionary Articles
Read the following Dictionary Articles in *New Bible Dictionary*, Third Edition.
  Idols
  Idolatry

Act 1

Primeval

Learning Objective
Comprehend that there is only one God to serve.

earth. All in all, this was not the driving question among the Hebrews as it is in our own day.

The Scopes Trial (see Setting the Stage) in a previous generation, and century, for that matter, turned twentieth-century Christians into a war with science. Darwin became its chief dialogical partner. So against what Darwin taught, Christians reached out into the Bible to combat it. Making Genesis 1.1-2.4a an argument against Darwinism and teaching it as a scientific fact was not and is not the focus of this first story of Scripture. The first storyteller, Moses, and the hearers of the story, Israel in the wilderness, did not have privy to Darwin's theory. His theory was not part of their mindset.

We get caught in a quagmire between our need to have meaning and what it meant to the first teller of the story and his listeners. Since science and especially Darwin were not a part of the original storyteller or listener's mindset, we must look elsewhere for the meaning of the story.

With a plurality of gods to worship, God's intention through Moses was to let his children know that he was the creator of the world in which they lived, and the gods that they would be called on to worship were not really gods at all. The idea that there was only one God and it was he who created the world is what separates the Old Testament faith from its ancient Near Eastern counterparts.[32]

BackStory

Let's be reminded again and possibly again later. In a time far, far, away, much different from ours, the children of God (Israel) were surrounded with a lifestyle of polytheism. Polytheism was a belief system in the ancient world that there were many gods to be worshipped. The ancient world believed that there was a pantheon of gods who were responsible for the creation of the world. Israel lived among these ancient beliefs.

God had recently delivered Israel from a land with plentiful gods, including the belief that the Pharaoh was himself a god. The Hebrews sat at the foot of Mt. Sinai, a newly redeemed people of God. At Mt. Sinai, God, through his servant Moses, gave them instructions that would turn their heads toward him and away from polytheism.

Their destination, the land of promise, was also overrunning with polytheism. So there they sat having been delivered from a land filled with polytheism, headed to a land filled with a belief in many gods.

It was during this period of time that Moses first revealed the creation account that we read in Genesis 1.1-2.4a. Thus, to understand Genesis the way these first people would have heard it is to hear it against a backdrop of polytheism. God was strongly urging his newly redeemed children to understand that there was really only one God that they were to serve. He had even given them a Covenant stipulation to that effect (Exodus 20.2a).

Learning Objective
Visualize how the different creation containers speak of God's order.

Genesis 1.1-2.4a. TBB. 7-8.

The Six Containers of Creation. Genesis 1.3-2.4a: An Overview

Let's begin this section by viewing the overall structure of 1.3-2.4a. To convey meaning to an audience, biblical storytellers and writers used certain structural schemes that helped them communicate the message they were delivering. In the creation story there is such a structure. The storyteller constructed his story in seven parts that correspond to the six

creative containers of creation, called *days* in the text, and one creative
container of rest. In the first six time periods, God orders his world out of
chaos. The structure is as follows:

Learning Objective
Visualize how the different
creation containers speak of
God's order.

Forming		Filling	
Day 1	Light (and darkness)	Day 4	Light Holders: (sun and moon)
Day 2	Sky and Sea	Day 5	Fish and Birds
Day 3	Earth and Vegetation	Day 6	Animals and Humankind
		Day 7 Rest[33]	

God's creation in the first three creative containers accommodated
what was to be created in the last three containers.

Each of the first six creative containers has the same internal structural
design. Each container is like a creative chant.

1. And God said (an introduction to each container of creation)
2. Let there be (the creative word)
3. And it was so (the fulfillment of the creative word)
4. God called (Name giving)
5. And God saw that it was good (a divine commendation)
6. And there was evening, and there was morning ... (Conclusion of
   container)[34]

It is not difficult to see that by its structure this story would rehearse
for Israel that their God was a God who brought perceivable order out of
chaos. Of course, God's order was in contrast to the gods of the ancient
mind, who did things haphazardly or as an afterthought.

The Six Creative Acts of Creation: Genesis 1.3-2.4a: An Examination

Creative Container (Day One): Genesis 1.3-5

And God said destroyed the primeval cosmic silence and signaled the
birth of a new order. *God said* means that God thought or willed and
signified that he is wholly independent of his creation. In each of the
creative containers, God dismissed two gods within polytheism.[35] The
intent of the storyteller of this little story is to demonstrate that God is the
creator even of those things that their society may have thought to be
gods. So, on this first day, the gods of light and darkness are dismissed.
God called placed him in the position of power over the object that was
named. In the ancient world, the one who gave a name had power over the
object named. What about time? Should the twenty-four hour days of
creation be taken literally? One might ask how there could be a day of
twenty-four hours before the sun and moon were present to determine
days, which did not occur until Day Four. John Walton suggests that the
essence of creation on day one is simply to be understood as the creation
of time.[36]

Creative Container (Day Two): Genesis 1.6-8

In the second container of creation, God dismissed two more gods of
the ancient world, the gods of sky and sea. Remember that the intent of
the author is to present his material to be recited for ease of remembrance,
as well as training the Israelites that monotheism, not polytheism, was
their inheritance.

Act 1

Primeval

Learning Objective
Visualize how the different creation containers speak of God's order.

Creative Container (Day Three): Genesis 1.9-13

In the third creation container, the earth gods and gods of vegetation were booted. Hesiod was a contemporary writer with Homer. In his *Theogony*, he writes about the generation of the gods. The family tree of the gods was: *In the beginning was Chaos alone [Hesiod Theogony 1.115], but shortly thereafter came Gaia (Earth) who bore Uranus (Sky) for covering and to father the fifty-headed Hecatonchires, the Cyclopes, and the twelve Titans.*[37] In the 1960s James Lovelock, a British chemist specializing in the atmospheric sciences, revived the old primeval goddess Gaia, suggesting that the earth is alive, a living organism. This suggests that the earth is able to self-regulate essential characteristics of its environment, such as the average temperature, the salinity of the oceans, and the mixture of gases (such as oxygen and carbon dioxide) in the atmosphere.[38] Earth god worship is alive and well.

Creative Container (Day Four): Genesis 1.14-19

The sun, moon, and star gods are now dismissed. We should take note that the author did not call these gods by their names. They are reduced to the natural reality, simply referred to as the *greater* and *lesser* lights. To speak the name of the god was to give it its divine authority. By referring to their natural reality, he removed the ancient claim of divinity to these heavenly bodies.

Creative Container (Day Five): Genesis 1.20-23

The fifth day of creation brought the dismissal of the fish and fowl gods.

Creative Container (Day Six): Genesis 1.24-31

The last repository of creation disposed of human male and female gods such as pharaohs, kings, and heroes who were believed to be gods. God created man (*adam*) male and female. God created *man* in his image. This phrase may indicate that God created humankind to be a community. While our culture places a high value on individualism, the ancient Hebrew culture was being trained to place a high value on community. The community theme continues in the New Testament with the many metaphors for the Church, like the Body of Christ. Even after the rebellion of humankind, Scripture can still say that *man* is in God's image (Gen. 9.6).

Genesis 1.28 makes it clear that God intended Adam and Eve to have children in their sinless state. He commanded them to be fruitful and increase. God invented human sexuality within the framework of marriage (see Gen. 2) for both procreation and enjoyment. Sexual expression is a joyful affirmation of a married couple's intimacy. What God had created and said was very good, pleased him. We could substitute the words *exceedingly good* as an appropriate picture for the evaluation of humankind. In each creative container (day) of creation, another set of gods was smashed and in their place was a pronounced creation of the one and only God.

Note: Gen 1.26. The Creation of Humankind (male and female)

Four things could be noted about the passage in which the creation of humankind is told.

1. Humankind is made in the image of God. In the ancient world, an image was believed to carry the essence of that which it

Act 1

Primeval

Learning Objective
Visualize how the different creation containers speak of God's order.

represented.[39] An idol image of a deity was used in the worship of that deity because it contained the deity's essence, not because it looked the same as the deity. The deity's work was believed to be accomplished through the idol. It is through the image of God (his community) that he intends to accomplish his work in the world. Also, in this passage, the word *us* refers to the angels in the heavenly council (Psalm 82.1; 89.7) that made up the community in which God was the creator.

2. Traditionally, New Testament believers have thought the *us* of this passage to refer to the Trinity. While this is a possible fuller interpretation with New Testament in hand, it was not the primary meaning of the words from the mouth of Moses. It seems his intent was to declare that Israel, like God, needed to be concerned about being in community, because that was the purpose of God for creating male and female as a community, to bear his essence and to do his work in the world he had created.

3. The community that God created was to be his representative on earth to "rule…over all the earth." The concept of *rule* may be a command to become the agent of God's Kingdom in the world for the sake of the world.

4. The male and female creation created by God as a community would produce community. They were to be "fruitful and increase in number." Sexual intimacy plays an important part in God's created plan. In the ancient world, there was worry about the population growth. The ancients told of their gods preparing plagues, famines, floods, miscarriages, etc., to curb human growth. The God of Israel, however, wanted them to understand that growth was to be seen as a blessing, not something to be blotted out. Sex is to be seen as an important part of God's good creation (Gen 1.31).

So What?

In the Creation narrative, we discover that the creation of humankind, male and female, was a creation of community which told Israel the importance of being the people of God. Community is not just a loosely knit group of people who believe the same thing about certain issues. It is not a group of individualized individuals who gather in a building and do certain religious activities on a regular basis, or small groups that provide occasions for individuals to focus on themselves in the presence of others. Community is a tightly knit group of people on mission, sent by a redeeming God as his conduits for bringing his world back to him. Its vocation is to find the pain of the rebellious world and bring the church/community there to begin the process of redemption.

Vegetarian?

While, in this story, food was primarily plants and fruit, the intent of the story is not to teach that in creation God intended everyone to be vegetarian. Its only meaning is that God provided them with food. In Mesopotamian mythology, the gods created mankind to provide them with food, while the creation story demonstrates that, in fact, it is the other way around. It is God who feeds humankind.

Act 1

Learning Objective
Visualize how the different creation containers speak of God's order.

QUESTIONS
How many of the twelve polytheistic gods do you still serve?

SUGGESTION
Create something that helps you explain visually one of the creative acts of God.

Was God Tired?

Creative Container (Day Seven): Genesis 2.1-4a

On this day, God rested. Surely, we do not think that the God of the universe grew tired and needed a day off. In the culture of the day, the people would often act out what they wanted the gods to do. God simply reverses this action and models for his children what he would like them to do. Remember, the ancient mindset was dominated by many gods. As an illustration: When the ancient celebrated a new year, the making merry was to keep the gods awake, so the gods would have sexual intercourse, so that a good harvest would occur at harvest time. Ancient humankind demonstrated this for the gods during their feast. This same idea can be seen in the American Indian Rain Dance in which water is poured on the ground during the dance to demonstrate what is being requested from the gods.[40] Creative container (day) seven is another blast against polytheism and a victory for monotheism.

A Word About Numbers

Numbers (not the book of Numbers) in Scripture are often quality instead of quantity. In this story against polytheism, this is true. There are two sets of gods disposed of each day, which totals twelve, a number of completion for the ancient Hebrew. The story has seven parts. Seven is another number of completion and perfection. What might this have meant for them? The creation of God is *perfect* and *complete*. He and only he was the creator. It could certainly have the same meaning for us all these thousands of years later.

So, we conclude Act 1 in which we have visited the stage created by God on which the rest of the Story will be played out. We now turn our attention to Act 2. Separation: From Dependence to Independence.

Act 2

Separation: From Dependence to Independence (Gen. 2.4b-11.26)

The purpose of the second creation story

(2.4b-25) was to answer the question:

How did sin enter into the world

that God had created?

When you finish this section, you should be able to:

♦ Understand second Creation narrative and its corresponding Rebellion Story
♦ See some of the beginning metaphors used to describe Yahweh
♦ Comprehend that work is not part of the curse
♦ Understand the value of community
♦ Comprehend that the serpent is not Satan in this story
♦ Understand the consequences of "she took and ate"
♦ Begin understanding of God as missional
♦ Comprehend that disobedience to God's command brings judgment
♦ Begin to understand separation from God

Our initial focus is to get an overview of Creation and Rebellion. Then, we provide some background for Act 2 along with some guidelines about the Story. Next, we will visit each of the seven scenes within this act. Then, we will share some thoughts about Separation or what is often called the Fall. Finally, we will summarize the Primeval Story of Genesis 1.1-11.26.

Act 2: Separation: From Dependence to Independence (Gen. 2.4b-11.26)
　　Creation and Rebellion: An Overview
　　BackStory
　　Some Guidelines about the Story
　　Some Observations
　　Scene 1: Creation (Gen. 2.4b-17)
　　　What to Look For?
　　　Genesis 2.4b-7
　　　Genesis 2.8-17
　　Scene 2: Home Alone (Genesis 2.18-25)
　　　So What?
　　Scene 3: Chatting with the Crafty Serpent (Genesis 3.1-5)
　　　Time Travel
　　　Interlude: The Five Scenes of Genesis 3.1-24
　　　Genesis 3.1-5
　　Scene 4: She Took and Ate (Genesis 3.6-7)
　　　So What?
　　Scene 5: Hide and Seek (Genesis 3.8-13)
　　Scene 6: Disobedience Payback (Genesis 3.14-24)
　　　Genesis 3.15-16
　　　Genesis 3.17-19
　　　Genesis 3.20-21
　　Scene 7: Banishment from the Garden (Genesis 3.22-24)
　　Some Thoughts about the Fall
　　The Primeval Story: A Summary with
　　　Scenes 8-14 (Genesis 1.1-11.26)

It should be noted that the story does not tell us

that the woman tried to tempt the man.

She simply gave him some of the fruit

and he chose to eat it.

Act 2. Separation: From Dependence to Independence (Gen. 2.4b-11.26)

Primeval

Learning Objective
Understand second Creation narrative and its corresponding Rebellion Story.

Genesis 2.4b-11.26. TBB. 7-18.

Primeval: Belonging to the first or earliest age or ages

The focus of the first creation story (Gen. 1.1-2.4a) was to provide Israel with an understanding within her background that there was only one God to be worshiped and he had created the world in which they lived. The purpose of the second creation story (2.4b-25) was to answer the question: How did sin enter into the world that God had created? This second story is not a standalone story as was the creation story at 1.1-2.4a. It has two parts: creation and separation. Act Two has 14 scenes and continues to Genesis 11.26 which is the end of the ❖ **Primeval Narrative**. ❖ The importance of this Act is to grasp what went wrong with God's creation and what its earliest results were.

Creation and Rebellion: An Overview

In the first garden, true humanity was lost, a garden with all the first humans' needs were met and a daily conversation with God occurred in the cool of the day. What could be better? What went wrong? Act 2 of God's Story is the story of the deconstruction of God's gloriously created world by the failure of Adam and Eve.

The second creation story found in Genesis tells the story (Creation of Adam and Eve: Gen 2.4b-25) which falls into seven scenes (2.4b-3.24) in which the listener/reader is taken through the creation story in a different fashion. The order of creation is totally inverted. It is written in a mirror-image style, where the first scene is matched by the seventh, the second scene is matched by the sixth, and the third scene is matched by the fifth. It is a "masterpiece of ❖ **chiastic** ❖ writing."[1] The story opens and closes with God as the sole actor (Scene 1: 2.5-17) to God as the sole actor (Scene 7: 3.22-24) in these scenes. It is built like a sandwich. This story tells of God's good creation corrupted by the rebellion of humankind.

Chiastic. A chiastic arrangement refers to an inverted parallelism or sequence of words or ideas in a phrase or clause, sentence, paragraph, chapter, or an entire literary work. This was an often-used literary form in Hebrew poetry. It was used in both writing and speaking.

Humankind's rebellious story (Gen 3.1-24) is told by the storyteller at the beginning of the book of Genesis. The result of this story is the conflict out of which the rest of the Story of God is told. This dark story of humankind tells of a time when the created beings, created to be dependent on God, decided to challenge God in their desire to be more godlike. The choice of independence over dependence is the plot in which the story proceeds. Male and female were created to be dependent and find their ultimate meaning in their creator. The choice to rebel sets up a long and ferocious battle between God and his creation. The rebellion caused humankind to blame God for their fallen state. True humanity became distorted and could no longer see the divine image of itself having lost the divine presence of God. In its place, humankind set up parodies of that which was real by creating other images to bow their knee to. Fellowship with God was lost.[2] Humankind became alienated from God; loneliness and brokenness were the result. The world plays out this act of the great story on a daily basis.

Genesis 3 offers a paradigm of sin, a model of what happens when humankind chooses to disobey God. The story illustrates for us what constitutes sin and what the consequences of sin are. The essence of humankind's first sin was his and her disobedience to God's command and the consequences were toil, pain, alienation from God, and death. Sin is a serious matter.[3]

Act 2

Primeval

Learning Objective
Understand second Creation narrative and its corresponding Rebellion Story.

Today, this story is usually told to show how the Fall occurred, to identify the serpent as Satan, and to teach about the first blood sacrifice (the provision of skin to replace the fig leaf is believed to have only come from God sacrificing an animal). One thing is clear: in the first two chapters and the last two chapters of the Bible, Satan is not present in the story.[4] Scripture begins and ends without a mention of him. The main thrust of the story is to demonstrate the care and concern of God for his children, even when they disobey him. In this story, Scripture offers an important and unique insight: Humankind's desire to be other than what God had created them to be caused them to deconstruct into what they became, fallen and in need of repair. They had broken the only command that God had given them. The bond of trust between the Creator and his creation had been broken. Our first parents knew they were naked. They discovered their vulnerability by trying to become something they were not.

All the world's ills and evils come from this one selfish act. The world that was given to them to be their perfect garden became a wilderness full of sweat, thorns, and thistles. One wrong deed and separation occurred. When did they know this? When God came calling, "Adam, where are you?" God, the missionary, was looking for his broken children, broken and hiding. This is the story in a nutshell. Humankind hides. God is like Francis Thompson's *hound of heaven* sniffing us out to redeem us. This story runs straight through the Bible and becomes our vocation. The "rebellion" story demonstrated to Israel that any transgression of God's Covenant stipulations would bring severe consequences. The storyteller shares that God takes freedom seriously. To play outside of the set boundaries is to be bound.

These two chapters establish the parameters from which the rest of the Story proceeds. We will spend a disproportionate amount of time on this material for that reason.

BackStory

As a reminder, Moses told these stories in Genesis 1.1-11.26 against the backdrop of polytheism. His job was to lead Israel on their way to the Promised Land. The second backdrop was the Covenant given to Israel at Mt. Sinai. It was Moses' job to assist Israel to understand that the community they were created to be would work well within the Covenant stipulations that God had made with them. Some have suggested that in the mind of Moses (as well as one can know another's mind, especially an ancient mind), there may have been an intention of providing them with a new mindset, i.e., God-approved meaningful work. They no longer needed to make bricks for some mindless deity of another country (Egypt, in this case). It may also have been his intent to embrace the boundaries that would be imposed on them by God, because therein true freedom is discovered. Lastly, he may have wanted them to fathom that marriage was an honorable quest and that God approved of them using their intelligence once they had entered the land promised to their forefather Abraham.

Some Guidelines about the Story

Remember, this story was first an oral presentation, carried on orally for generations. So, the Genesis 2 storyteller conveyed to his listeners what transpired within God's creation as told in Genesis 1.1-2.4a.[5] The heart of the story steers those first listeners to believe in the creation of human life by God. Humankind was no whim of some drunken deity. Humankind was not created to be the slave of some aroused deity, awakening after a long sleep. A thoughtful God, who had the interest of his creation in his heart, created humankind. The storyteller gives his audience a peek of what life was like in this perfect garden of peace. Here are some insights to ponder as you proceed.

Primeval

Learning Objective
Understand second Creation narrative and its corresponding Rebellion Story.

- ◆ Look for the developing relationship between God and man
- ◆ Observe the relationship of man within the environment that he was created to live
- ◆ Notice the interpersonal relationship within the first human community

Before humankind made the decision to disobey the one prohibition (read stipulation) that God had laid down, there were three flawless relationships revealed by the storyteller.

- ◆ **Call/Vocation**. The first created being was given meaningful vocation to accomplish. He was to till and keep the garden.
- ◆ **Community**. Male and female (the first human community) found delight in the presence of God without any fear or shame.
- ◆ **Covenant**. There was a relationship that was established between God and the first male and female and between the first male and female.[6]

The story we are covering in this Act has several parts: the first part is Genesis 2.4b-25 and the second part is 3.1-24 with concluding scenes ending with Genesis 11.26. The complete story of creation and rebellion, told in 2.4b-3.24, is masterfully told around seven scenes as seen in the list below. Each scene has a number along with the text address, whether it is narrative or dialog, and who the characters in the scene are.

1	2.5-17	Narrative	God is the main character, man present but passive
2	2.18-25	Narrative	God is the main character, man has a minor role, the woman and animals are passive
3	3.1-5	Dialogue	The snake and woman
4	3.6-7	Narrative	The man and woman
5	3.8-13	Dialogue	God, man, and woman
6	3.14-21	Narrative	God is the main character, man has a minor role, woman and snake are passive
7	3.22-24	Narrative	God is the main character, man is passive

Some Observations

- ◆ The first and seventh scenes are similar to each other.
- ◆ The only actor is God. Man is there, but he is not an active character.
- ◆ Several phrases, *on the east, tree of life, garden of Eden, till, and guard* are found only in these scenes.
- ◆ An inversion occurs. Man is made from dust and placed in the garden in scene one and man is driven out of the garden to go back to dust from which he was taken in scene seven.
- ◆ Scenes two and six are played out with all four characters of the story present. God is the main character (as he is through all the stories of the Bible). All the action within the scene took place within

Act 2

Primeval

Learning Objective
Understand second Creation narrative and its corresponding Rebellion Story.

the garden. Both scenes two and six are concerned to present humankind in relationship with all of creation.

- ◆ The scenes that include dialog are the third and fifth scenes. They tell about the fruit of the tree, the prohibition, and its consequences.
- ◆ Finally, the middle scene (4) demonstrated the human characters alone. Neither God nor the serpent was present. It seems that God may well trust us after all![7]

To understand narrative stories, we must remember a basic presupposition: Discover what it wants to say by remembering that it was a story that was originally told orally. It appears that the intention of Moses and other storytellers through the ages was to share with their readers some basic impressions about the Creator God who had delivered them from Egypt.

Some have taught that the focus of this story is about the creation of the woman and the origin of love between male and female. Others have wanted to press the importance of the consummation of marriage. Still others see the whole story as two parts about crime and punishment within the community of which the family is the basic unit.

More than a few have wanted to visit the comparisons between the living space of the garden that God had prepared for these first human parents and the living space of the land that God had prepared for Israel.

Genesis 1.1-2.4a says little about how God created humankind: male and female. But it does say something about the authority of God given to humankind. This story in Genesis 2 underscores that humankind, male and female, are under authority. It tells of the first harmonious community and meaningful work.

The second part of the story (Genesis 3) points toward the restoration of human life after its failure. The storyteller contends that all gifts of humankind come from the hand of God. There is a wonderful flow to the story. Adam and Eve, in an indescribable setting, are working, eating, playing, enjoying the bounty of God, and visiting with him daily. It is almost overwhelming, given our present circumstances, to fathom the inexplicable generosity of God.

Genesis 2.4b-17. TBB. 8-9.

Learning Objective
See some of the beginning metaphors used to describe Yahweh,

Scene 1: Creation (Genesis 2.4b-17)

What to Look For?

The function of the first part of this Story was to equip the newly redeemed children of Israel by helping them to comprehend that God was serious about the Covenant he had made with them at Mt. Sinai. As you read this story, you will see the name "Lord God." This name is the covenant-making name for God that would have been well understood by Israel. This story urged Israel to grasp that the God who created the world was the very same God who had rescued them from their bondage in Egypt and who had made Covenant with them.

In the garden there was a clear abundance for Adam and Eve. They could consume at will with only one prohibition, a stipulation, if you please. It is not too difficult to see the lucid implications of keeping the Covenant stipulations. Adam and Eve had the abundance of the garden that was freely theirs. God would bless Israel if they kept the stipulations given to them at Sinai. Adam and Eve were told not to eat of a specific

Act 2

Primeval

Learning Objective
See some of the beginning metaphors used to describe Yahweh.

tree. If they did, they would die. Israel was told that God would curse them if they broke the stipulations of the Covenant.

It is crucial and important to hear this story through the ears of the children of Israel at Mt. Sinai. It is helpful to think "in the garden," as an allusion to "in the promised land" and see the parallels for God's newly redeemed people.[8]

Genesis 2.4b-7

The story begins (2.4b) by pointing out that there was no life, growth, rain, or anyone to cultivate the soil. Against that background, God formed the first man. In Genesis 1, the authorial emphasis is on one majestic God, not many gods, who speaks and creation takes place. The emphasis in 2.4b-7 is more personal. The context turns from the galaxy to the garden.

What is significant in the following verses (2.4b-5, 7-9, 15-16, 18-19, 21-22) is the repeated emphasis of the phrase "the LORD God." What one might deduce from this recurring phrase is: that the sovereign Creator God of Genesis 1 was also the covenant-making Yahweh (LORD) of Genesis 2. It was important for this newly formed people of God to understand that the God who made Covenant with them was the one who formed humankind by a special design.

Yahweh, which is translated LORD in our story, is the name that is commonly connected with the covenant relationship between the Hebrews and God. Elohim, which is translated God in our story, is comprehended by the Hebrews as the creator of the universe.[9] When the two names are combined in a story as they are in this one, the emphasis of each name is in play. The hearer would understand that the Covenant God and the Creator God were in fact the same God. The first humans, according to this story, had a relationship with the same God that they, the Israelites, had. God was both Israel's Covenant partner and her creator.

The storyteller prepares his listeners for the creation of the first human being. There is language of cultivation ("work the ground") that anticipates the work of caring for the garden, which would be Adam's work. Work was not a part of the latter curse after the rebellion. God's work in creating human life involved fashioning the first man "from the dust" and breathing life[10] into him. In our text, the word "formed"[11] is a word that described an artist. God is pictured like a potter[12] who was shaping an earthen vessel from clay. Not only is there a picture of God as a potter but God as an animator as he breathed life into this first human creation. This work of God is given in highly ❖ **anthropomorphic** ❖ terms. God is pictured as an artisan who sculpts humankind.

Anthropomorphic:
Described or thought of as having a human form or human attribute.

So What?

When they first heard this story, Israel was journeying toward a land that God had promised. It may well have suggested that the land God had promised Abraham would also be productive because of God's Covenant with them.[13]

Genesis 2.8-17

The mythological stories of the ancient Near East gods are often presented as living in a garden full of fertile herbage, abundant water, and beautiful stones.[14] In our story, God does not live in the garden he created. The garden is pictured as the place where he meets and fellowships with

Act 2

Primeval

Learning Objective
See some of the beginning metaphors used to describe Yahweh,

his creation. In literature, Eden has been identified with "paradise." This is a Persian loan word that meant *a royal park*. It should be noted that while God does not take up permanent residence in the garden, the garden is an archetypal sanctuary that prefigures the tabernacle of later Jewish history. Water, trees, gold, gems, and cherubim adorned the later tabernacle (Ex. 25.17) and the temple (1 Kings 7; Ezek. 41-47). These symbols suggest that what was most important about the garden was that God was present therein. In the cool of the day he would walk and talk with Adam and Eve (3.8).

Two trees are crucial to the narrative presented by the storyteller. Dietrich Bonhoeffer has correctly observed that the middle of Adam's life was not for himself but was for the very presence of God. The tree of knowledge as prohibition signified that man's limitation as a creature is in the middle of his existence, not on the edge.[15] Man's pursuit of eternal life given by the gods was a common storyline of Near Eastern folklore. However, in each story the human fell short of achieving eternal life. The Gilgamesh Epic shows the hero finding a plant that would produce eternal life only to have the plant stolen by a great water serpent.[16]

After all the speculation about the meaning of the "tree of knowledge," we should note that in the story of this first human couple, they broke covenant with God.[17] This was surely a lesson here for the Hebrews at Sinai who had just received the Covenant from God.

The trees that were created by God in this garden produced fruit that was edible. The two trees in the story have produced an endless amount of discussion. When we read "of good and evil," we're reading a merism[18] (a theory that holds that the whole can be explained through the nature or functioning of its parts). This clever use of a figure of speech told the listener that the things that protect life and destroy life would be experienced in the forbidden fruit if it were eaten.

On one hand, the tree that is forbidden by God for Adam to eat is called the "tree of the knowledge of good and evil"[19] and is mentioned only two times in the story (2.9, 17). In the next story in Genesis (chapter 3), this tree is mentioned seven times but never by the same name that it is called in the story we are studying (2.4b-25). On the other hand, the "tree of life" is known in several other places in Scripture (Prov. 3:18; 11:30; 13:12; 15:4; Rev. 2:7; 22:2, 14-19).

We may suggest that the tree named "the knowledge of good and evil" did not produce knowledge of good and evil but rather produced death when eaten. The prohibition not to eat was the necessary boundary to the freedom with which God had entrusted Adam. To say *no* to God's command is to say *no* to life. To say *no* to God's boundaries is to become bound. To say *yes* to his boundaries is to remain free.

The "knowledge of good and evil" means the ability and power to determine what is "good" and what is "evil." This knowledge is God's prerogative alone. He never delegated moral autonomy to any of his created beings.

The flow of the narrative is interrupted by giving some details about the rivers that ran through the garden.[20] Trying to discover the exact location of Eden is impossible, given the only information we have is in Genesis 2.4-10. The rivers were not mentioned as locators, but as a picture of the abundance given by God to his creation.[21]

The narrative ending at verse eight is now picked up in verse fifteen. God took the man that he created and placed him in the garden to take care of the garden by working in it.[22] To "work it" means to cultivate the soil (2.5, 3.23). In a religious sense, this kind of work is used as a "service" to God (Num. 3.7-8). In a similar fashion to "take care of it" means to do the work of "guarding it". This word is commonly used in legal texts for observing religious commands and duties (Lev. 18.5) and is also used for the Levitical responsibility of guarding the tabernacle from intruders (Num. 1.53).[23] Here, again, the storyteller may be making an interplay between the tabernacle and Eden.

Learning Objective
See some of the beginning metaphors used to describe Yahweh,

Work is a gift from God. It is not a condition that is cursed. Work came before sin.[24] In the Mesopotamian accounts of humankind, humans were created for the sole purpose of working to supply food for the lazy gods. In contrast to these ancient stories, God provides for his creation, not vise-versa. Part of that provision was honorable and meaningful work. Eden was not a paradise in which humankind could pass his or her time being idle with uninterrupted bliss, where there were no demands on his or her daily schedule.[25]

Learning Objective
Comprehend that work is not part of the curse.

The story continues by rehearsing the bountiful provisions of God for humankind.[26] Humankind could eat of any tree that was desirable. "Free to eat" is a strong affirmation that indicates the provision of God for the first couple was plentiful and to be enjoyed liberally by them.[27] All earthly goods and pleasures were at man's disposal, except this one tree that was forbidden.

There was only one prohibition. Human life, along with the entire natural world, also had its boundaries. The command here is like the commandments given through Moses in the Covenant stipulations. God addresses the first man personally (*thou* in KJV, *you* in NIV). Without prohibition, freedom does not have any meaning.[28]

The boundary that was given to the first couple was given in only one command. "You must not eat," is set in the form of the Covenant stipulations given by God through Moses. The command has a curse attached. This also is a characteristic of the Lord-Servant Treaty (we will look at this concept later). The death sentence demonstrated God's seriousness about accessing the tree. The verse is not concerned with the immediate execution of the death penalty but with ultimate death.[29] It could be translated "you are doomed to die." Some believe that the withholding of death from the first human couple is an indication of God's grace on them.[30]

So What?

The primary lesson in this scene is related to the people of God under Moses. God prepared humankind with a specific design and gave them the capacity for moral responsibility. He set them in the Garden to be obedient servants, warning that before them was life or death, depending on whether they obeyed the commandment. Deuteronomy 28 sets forth for Israel all the instructions parallel to the motifs of Genesis 2:8-17: obedience to the commandments of God results in life and blessing, while disobedience will result in death.

Learning Objective
Understand the value of community.

 Scene 2: Home Alone (Genesis 2.18-25)

Genesis 2.18-25. TBB. 9.

There is no equal in the literature of the ancient Near East to the creation

Act 2

of woman found in our story.[31] An elevated view of woman was not widely held in the ancient civilizations and Israel failed at times to give proper recognition to honor women. This account of the act of creating a woman demonstrates that God very much intended woman to be equally as important as her counterpart.[32]

For the first time in our story the storyteller suggests that there is something that is "not good." In a search for companionship man could not find a corresponding companion. The text demonstrates that God does not create woman because man complained about his situation. Man did not offer God any grievance about his circumstances. It is God alone (the hero of all stories in the Bible) who makes the judgment about the improperness of man being in solitude.[33] God did not consult his creation on this matter. God evaluates and rectifies the situation. The remedy is to provide a helper who is not inferior or superior, but equal.

We may point out here that isolation (individualism) is not a high value for human beings. Community was the solution that God created. The focus of the story was to establish the equality of personhood. The term "helper" defined the role that the woman would play. The word means to "help in the sense of aid and support." There is nothing in the word or in the context of the garden story that would suggest that the woman is a lesser person because her role differs from man.[34]

She was created to help the male achieve the divine commission to "be fruitful and increase in number." What the male lacked, the female possessed. The woman made it possible for the man to achieve the blessing that he otherwise could not achieve alone and the man made it possible for the woman to achieve the blessing that she would not achieve alone.[35] The words "matching him," is found only here. It is to express the notion of complementarity and not identity. It is the mutual support that is provided by companionship.[36] The creation of humankind, male and female, is egalitarian.

In 2.19-20a God is introduced by the storyteller as sort of a divine zookeeper. As he created the animals, he brought each one to Adam who had been given the task of naming them.[37] The storyteller helps us to see the obedience of this first human as he followed through with the task that was given to him. The names of the animals are not disclosed.[38] The giving of names does not suggest that Adam had authority over the animals that he named or Eve, as has sometimes been espoused.

The storyteller now tells his readers that God created the woman from the side of man (2.21). In the creation narrative tradition of Israel's neighbors, there was no separate account of a woman being created. God created two human beings that would bear his image. One was a male and the other was a female (1.25-26.). The first story said nothing about how God created male and female or when he created them (simultaneously or sequentially). This text says that God made a woman from the side (*sela*) of man. In almost all the translations, "rib" instead of "side" is preferred by the translators. The passage says that the woman was created from a non-designated part of the body of the man rather than from one of his organs or from a portion of his bony tissue.[39] This was certainly not a modern operation complete with scars. God puts Adam to sleep and when he awakes he receives another gift from God.

In verse 22, the storyteller suggests that God "built" the woman. "Built" is used only here and in Amos 9.5-6 in the Hebrew Bible.[40] It is a

word that is used of the creative activity of God. Two metaphors are striking here: God as potter (when working with clay/dust) and God as builder (when working with body tissue). Eve becomes the first creation that was created from another living being. Eve was not taken from Adam, only the raw material to make her was taken.[41]

To this point in the story, only God has had a speaking part. When Adam names the animals, there is no recorded speech from him.[42] For the first time in Scripture (v. 23), the first human speaks. He spoke in reflection to the gift presented to him by his friend, God. The words he spoke indicate that he immediately recognized that she was made of the same stuff of which he was made. A good translation of verse 23 might be: "At last, here is one of my own kind."[43] The phrase "bone of my bone and flesh of my flesh," could be understood as a covenant statement of loyalty.[44] It might serve as the biblical counterpart to our modern marriage ceremony that states: "...in weakness (flesh) and in strength (bone)," which means that circumstances will not alter the loyalty and commitment of the one to the other.

The storyteller introduced the origin of family, the underlying institution of the ancient Hebrew life. It is by no accident that the covenant language of the Old Testament between Israel and God is husband and wife. The present story should not be viewed as a paradigm for all man-woman relationships in society. It is about husband-wife relationships. To apply this story universally to other social contexts, such as government, education, or commerce, would make it say more than the storyteller intended. This story simply does not address these institutions as important as they may be. The most that the reader/hearer can understand is that the couple was equal to each other but different from each other. Exactness and sameness are not identical.[45]

"For this reason" (v. 24) is not an explanation of the previous words in the text. The phrase describes the outcome of God's charge for the human family to "be fruitful and increase in number." Marriage and family are the paradigm for carrying out these instructions given to the first couple by the Creator God.[46]

There are some insights about marriage offered from this passage. First, marriage is monogamous. It is a covenant relationship shared by male and female. Second, it is clearly heterosexual. Sexual identity was instrumental in defining marriage. An abolishment of sexual boundaries would have threatened the identity of this foundational community. Without proper sexual identity limits, a family would cease to exist. Thus, adultery and promiscuity overstep the boundaries of another's household. Incest resulted in muddled lines of family relationship. Homosexuality could not produce "be fruitful and increase in number." Sexual relations with animals were detested because that reversed the separation between God's created creatures.[47]

We must constantly remind ourselves that in the Old Testament marriage is a metaphor for the relationship between God and Israel.

To leave a father and mother in the ancient world and cling (be united) to one's wife would mean to sever a loyalty to one entity and commence one's loyalty to another entity. This story can also be understood as a call to Israel to leave the other gods and cling to her one God: Yahweh-Elohim. What may be said about this verse is that marriage is a covenant rather than an ad-hoc, temporary, or expedient substitute for something else.[48]

- And Image f God. N.T. Wright

Act 2

Primeval

Learning Objective
Understand the value of community.

When the first couple is joined in covenant, they become one flesh. The storyteller has not let us in on any information about procreating roles in this story. While this verse may have to do with sexual union (the most often interpretation of the verse), it rather has to do with solidarity of union.[49] It is a rather nonwestern way of doing math: two equals one.

The conclusion to our present story (v. 25) explains that nakedness was not a shameful condition in the first human family. How utterly appropriate! The idea of "felt no shame," would indicate that it was simply a normal condition. The idea of nakedness might be transitional for the next story in which the storyteller has a play-on-words in the Hebrew language between naked and crafty, which describes the nature of the serpent.[50]

So What?

Verses 20-24 examine the idea of companionship within marriage. It is fair to note that the husband and the wife were created to complement each other. The words "suitable helper" (2.20b) could be better translated "a helper matching him that supplied what he lacked." Diversity complements each other in a community. It seems to me that there is often too much focus on every believer being a clone where every believer must think alike, talk alike, believe alike, etc. This would be boring and would not fit the pattern of God creating diversity.

The union between husband and wife should be understood as permanent. One must note the text says that God created only one Eve for Adam, not several Eves, or even another Adam or several Adams. This would have taught the Israelites that God disapproved of polygamy (Lev. 18.18; Deut 17.17) and homosexual practice (Lev. 18.22). The man was to leave his father and mother (neither of which Adam had, one might note) and cleave to his wife. Elsewhere in the Old Testament these terms are covenant terms. When Israel forsook God's covenant, she "left" him. When Israel was obedient to God's covenant, she "cleaved" to him. Already in Genesis 2.24, the Israelites are learning that from the beginning, marriage was a covenant. The language of the storyteller is covenant language.

We can now continue to the second part of this story for which the Act is named: the separation of humankind from God, a move from dependence to independence.

Learning Objective
Comprehend that the serpent is not Satan in this story.

Genesis 3.1-5. TBB. 9.

Scene 3: Chatting with the Crafty Serpent (Genesis 3.1-5)

Genesis 3.1-24 is the second part of Act 2 and is comprised of five subscenes. The popular version of this story offers answers to two questions[51] such as: How did the rebellion of humankind occur, or is the serpent as Satan, or what did the first blood sacrifices mean (i.e., the provision of skin to replace the fig leaf is believed to have come from God by sacrificing an animal)?

It would be great for the Western reader if the stories of Scripture answered every question that we could conceive of and bring to the text to be answered. The text was not built by God to answer all of our questions. These scenes in the saga of Genesis have raised some interesting questions for which the storyteller, Moses, and the ultimate storyteller, God, simply do not share the answers. It often strikes me as strange that we want answers where God doesn't give them. So, in our rebellious fallen condition, we often force answers onto texts that the text is not trying to answer for the questions that we are asking. We force the answers as "the truth of Scripture." How abusive is that? Fallen humankind telling God that we know better what we need than he does or have found an answer that he didn't provide. Sound familiar? It seems that the key to these scenes is: the care and concern of the Creator God for his creation, even when they disobey him.

Here is a teaser thought: There is no detailed account about who the serpent in this story really is. There is one thing for sure: The storyteller does not identify him as Satan, as so much of our popular theology and thought does. If he really is the fallen angel who is God's great antagonist, the storyteller, Moses, and the ultimate storyteller, God, do not reveal this to these first listeners/readers.[52]

Many readers and interpreters of Genesis 3 have supposed that its original purpose was etiological. ❖ **Etiology** ❖ is the study of causes or origins. So we have read this as an attempt to answer the question: How did evil come into the world, or why is there enmity between real snakes and humans?[53]

There is no reason for asking etiological questions of this text. The storyteller and the resulting text do not explain the origin of the serpent other that it was a creation of God (Genesis 2.19), nor does this story explain the origin of evil. The story only explains where evil did *not* come from.

Evil was not in the genes of God's created humankind. Sin was not the consequences of some "divine" trap set by God. Little is said in the Hebrew Bible (Old Testament) about the source of evil and the Hebrew Bible never attributes evil as coming from the hand of God.[54] God is not responsible for the sin of the first humans nor can he be blamed for the serpent's deceit.

Time Travel

With polytheism as his dialogue partner, Moses most probably told this story to the Israelites as they sat at Mt. Sinai. Remember, they had left a polytheistic society in Egypt, and were journeying toward a polytheistic society in Canaan. They must be taught that there is but one God, that he is the one who had delivered them from Egypt and was moving them toward the land he had promised their forefathers.

This is where the tale of the serpent comes into the picture. In the ancient world of this time, the serpent was believed to be divine and was often worshiped because of his ability to bring health, fertility, immortality, and wisdom. It is likely that the storyteller was giving Israel yet another reason to worship the one and only God, and not any other god.

An interpretation of Genesis 3, other than one based on Creationism and Satan as the serpent, can be tough territory for Evangelicals. So let's listen to the text against the background into which it was originally given and hear what the text is saying, even if it runs counter to what we have "always been taught."

Interlude: The Five Scenes of Genesis 3.1-24

The story in Scene 1 and 2 (Gen. 2.4b-25) demonstrated a loving God

Primeval

Learning Objective
Understand the value of community.

QUESTIONS
How does viewing God in different roles help you get a better grasp of who he is?
If art was important to God, why has it become so unimportant to the Western Church?
What do you think about the concept of the wholeness of man rather than some foreign Greek dualism of the anthropology of man?
How much of your thinking life is filled with Greek dualism?
How does Greek dualism cause you to view God?
How does the concept of worker with God inform your beliefs?
How does your concept of freedom register with the following concept of freedom as presented in this story? Freedom is only found within the boundary of rules. When you break the rules and think you are free, you are actually bound.
Why do you think that many believers suffer with the illness of "fear of not enough," when God is the God of "enough"?
How does the subject of "equality" between male and female cause so much "heat" in conversations between believers?
How does one Adam and one Eve fly in the face of today's popular sexuality?
Why does the subject of "nakedness" cause believers to run for cover?

Etiology is the study of causes or origins.

Genesis 3.1-24. TBB. 9-11.

Act 2

Learning Objective
Comprehend that the serpent is not Satan in this story.

and an obedient creation. The story is about to change in Scenes 3-6, (Gen. 3.1-24) which are about how humankind decided to disobey God and the consequence of such a decision.

The following is a quick overview of the five scenes in Genesis 3.1-24. The narrative section of Genesis 3.6-8 is bookended by two exchanges of dialogue that involve the four actors in this account (God, Adam, Eve, and the serpent).

- ◆ The first bookend is the dialogue between the serpent and the woman (Scene 3: Gen. 3.1-5), the present scene we are in.
- ◆ The second bookend is the hide and seek scene (Scene 5: Gen. 3.9-13)

Scene 6 (Gen. 3.20-21) of the story is about man's reaction, the naming of Eve, and the skin garments.

Scene 7, (Gen. 3.22-25), the final scene, is a divine monologue (God is talking to himself) that determines the couples' expulsion and the execution of the decision.[55]

The former story (Scenes 1 and 2: Genesis 2.4b-25) is the near background for understanding the snake's challenge of the first human couple. In the previous story, we were told about the life of this first couple in the garden. The description by the storyteller demonstrates to the hearer of the story what will be lost by the human couple because of a poor decision. Without the previous story (Gen. 2.4b-25), we would simply have no way of knowing what was lost by the bite taken from the fruit.

Genesis 3.1-5

In Genesis 3.1, the Hebrew word for "subtle" is *arum*. The word sounds like the Hebrew word for "naked" (*arumim*) as in the last verse of Genesis 2 (2.25). This is most likely a literary way of connecting the last story (Genesis 2.4b-25) with our present story (Genesis 3.1-24).[56]

This part of our story opens by the sudden appearance of the serpent.[57] There are five views that are usually held about the serpent that appear in the story of Genesis 3:

1. The serpent is disguised. It is really Satan who is the real tempter. It is Satan who is cursed in Genesis 3.15. This is the popular understanding of who Satan is and is the long-standing explanation from early Christian and Jewish commentators, but has been mostly abandoned by Evangelical exegesis.[58]
2. The serpent is purely symbolical.
3. The serpent is a mythological character.
4. The serpent is an animal that is particularly clever. Its ability to speak is a characteristic of the story. (Remember, we have speaking animals in many stories today.)
5. The serpent is seen as an important character given the evidence from ancient Near Eastern literature and art. Some folks think that serpents were important because of their poison that was a threat to life or because of their lidless eyes. In the Gilgamesh story, Gilgamesh is cheated out of being perpetually young when a serpent consumes a magical plant that Gilgamesh had retrieved from the bottom of the sea. In other ancient stories, the serpent is cursed to crawl on its stomach.[59]

There are two things that can be noted about the serpent: first, he was crafty and, second, God made him. First, the storyteller told his listeners

that the snake was a "crafty" character. This word would alert the hearer that they should be very suspicious of the words of the serpent and examine them very carefully.[60] The term "more subtle" (KJV) or "crafty" is used in the Hebrew Bible both positively and negatively. The term introduces a certain amount of ambiguity into the story. "Crafty" in this text is an indecisive term, but most likely it means something like "astute" or "clever."[61] There is a clear anti-polytheistic theme that can be noted in the fact that God made the serpent, the serpent was not a god itself. There is no enmity suggested by the text between God and the serpent.

Second, we are told that God is the creator of the serpent.[62] "God had made" the serpent among the beasts of the field (Genesis 2.19) and everything created by God was "good." It seems likely that the serpent represents a being that has corrupted its own good purpose, not one that God created as corrupt from the start. This should dispel any belief about a rival dualism[63] (the concept that the world is ruled by the antagonistic forces of good and evil), since God created the serpent. Even though God is identified as creator of the serpent, there is no attempt by the storyteller to give an explanation of the origin of evil. Looking for an explanation of the origin of evil is a preoccupation with the Western mindset. It's almost as if we believe that if we could figure its origin out, then we could do better at controlling it.

There is no explanation in the text about how the serpent was able to speak.[64] This would help the listener to be more focused on what the serpent said rather than trying to find out who the serpent is.[65] As the serpent was among the "good" animals that God had created, there was no reason why the woman should suspect the serpent's deception, other than by listening to what the serpent spoke.[66]

First, the serpent used the tactic of causing doubt in the mind of the woman. He did this through asking questions and generating misrepresentations. He wanted her to believe that God was sinister. In fact, he wanted her to think that God was abusing her. The serpent did not gainsay what God had said in a direct fashion. Rather, he questioned the motivation of God with his wry "did God really say?"[67] He was not asking Eve a question, but rather distorting a fact. So, his tactic was to deny the truthfulness of what God had spoken. The serpent did not ask allegiance from Eve. He indirectly suggested that she shift her commitment from doing what God requested, to doing what she wanted to do. He suggested that disobedience would not really bring any disadvantages, but, rather, would bring an advantage to the first couple, "you will be like God."

Next, the serpent used the name God rather than the covenant name Lord that is so characteristic of the previous story. Lastly, the serpent reworked the command of God by:

- Adding the negative "not" to the word "any" which made the expression appear to be an absolute prohibition.
- The serpent omitted the word "freely."
- The serpent placed "from any tree" at the end of the sentence rather than at the beginning (see 2.16). This would be understood as robbing God's command of the nuance of liberality.[68]

In the mouth of the serpent the words of divine command by God were revised.[69] The serpent did this for his own purpose, which incidentally, is not stated. One might ask why the serpent directed his remarks toward the

Act 2

Primeval

Learning Objective
Comprehend that the
serpent is not Satan in this
story.

QUESTIONS
What in our disobedience
makes us think that we can
hide from God?
How does answering a
question that is not asked
avert attention away from
your present situation?
What have we been taught
about God's character that
when we disobey we believe
that God is going to be angry
and judgmental? Try to
discover God as one who
receives confession rather
than first handing out
condemnation.
What about the story of the
disobedience of Adam and
Eve makes us want to take
the props of the story and
make them literal?
How does this approach
damage the text and the
meaning of the text for the
first hearer?
Could it be that the "rule" of
a husband over a wife is a
characteristic of the fall, but
in the redemption of Jesus
that this has been removed?
(One must note that the
story is about a husband and
wife, not men and women in
general, thus it is a fallacy to
think that this story teaches
male domination over
females.)
Where is your garden?

woman. The text is clear: The serpent talked to the woman and the man at the same time. The "you" in "you shall not eat," you shall not touch lest you die," "you will not die," "when you eat of it you shall be," are all plural. The woman does act as the spokesperson for this first dynamic duo when she says, "we may eat." In the course of interpretation, it is often the woman who is chastised as being the weaker more vulnerable sex. However, it is just as proper to understand this text as the woman being aggressive, intelligent, and sensitive.[70]

The question of the serpent is an attempt to create an impression in the mind of the couple that God is a spiteful, mean, obsessively jealous, and self-protective God. Adam and Eve were lured by the prospect of instant pleasure.[71] Let me point out that Israel could have used this insight at Ai. Throughout Scripture, the essence of sin is to put human judgment above divine command. The woman now on the defensive begins to defend God and clarify his position, as if that is ever our job to do. The serpent's picture of God was to suggest a change in God from a caring provider to a cruel oppressor.

We can detect from Genesis 3.2-3 six things that went wrong in Eve's conversation.

1. Eve's first mistake may have been to respond to the question of the serpent. All questions do not deserve answers. Misrepresenting what God had actually said compounded her mistake. Eve was drawn into another possible interpretation of what God had commanded. She was being asked to live in a different story than the one she was created to live in.
2. Eve omitted "any" and "freely" which would place a prohibition in the context of God being a generous provider. At this point in the story, she was thinking collectively with her husband by responding "we may eat."
3. Eve identified the tree according to its location rather than to its significance.
4. Eve referred to God with the same language as the serpent used. Neither called him Lord.
5. Eve added the phrase "you must not touch it," which may make the prohibition even more stringent than God intended it to be.
6. Finally, Eve failed to capture the urgency of the death threat given by God.[72]

Even though these alterations of God's command are slight, they may suggest that Eve was moving slightly away from God toward the thinking of the serpent. The generosity of God was not being given its full value. God was being painted as somewhat harsh with a suggestion that even "a touch" of the fruit could be lethal.[73]

The snake's reply in verses 4-5 helps us understand why the snake was called "crafty."[74] He questioned the motivation of God. In the Wisdom Literature tradition, the adversary often argues the same case, i.e., a concern about God's motivation (see Job 1.2-11; 2.4-5). The argument is somewhat like the following: God is not gracious or good. He is illusive and self-centered and he wants to prevent his creation from achieving all that they could become.[75] God holds his creation back. The temptation of the serpent was to place before the couple the possibility of being more than they were and more than God intended them to be. Sounds vaguely familiar, huh? Some things really never change.

The storyteller may be using the "uncertainty about God" idea to propose that the couple cannot trust God. A question comes to mind: What do we do when we are tempted?"[76]

The serpent made three counterclaims:

1. Surely, if they ate, they would not die.
2. Instead of death, their eyes would be opened. ("Eyes opened" is often a metaphor that suggests one has gained a newfound awareness that was not previously possessed).
3. Finally, the first couple would gain what belonged to God. They would know "good and evil."[77]

Learning Objective
Comprehend that the serpent is not Satan in this story.

In the larger context of the present story, the serpent's words are true and false. The words will prove true in that the couple would not immediately die physically. It was also true that their eyes were opened. However, the half-truths of the serpent concealed a falsehood and led the couple to expect something different than what they received. The words of the serpent came true, but in a very different way than the way the first couple expected it to be true.[78]

In this text, there are two possible meanings for the phrase "you shall die:" *physical* or *natural* death. In the worship of the Hebrews, true life was experienced when one went into the sanctuary (where they believed that God lived) to worship him. To be expelled from the encampment, like lepers were, was to enter the realm of death. In the same way, the couple died on the day they ate the fruit of the tree. They no longer were able to have a daily conversation with God in the comfort of the garden, nor enjoy the bounteous provision of the garden, nor eat of the tree of life. Instead, the first couple was driven out of the garden to toil for their food, suffer, and eventually return to the dust from which they were taken. Adam lived to the ripe old age of 930 years.[79]

When autonomy displaces submission and obedience in a person, that finite individual attempts to rise above the limitations imposed on him by his creator. The end results will be separation from God.

So What?

Clearly the serpent is not the main character, but his craftiness is still on the prowl amidst those following God. Listening to his realm can be lethal as it was in the case of the first couple whose story is presented in this Act. What may be a main theme here is obedience. The need for the children of Israel to hear about obedience in light of the Covenant they had made with God was paramount. Obedience, as we shall see later in the Story, is not a set of laws to be ruthlessly followed, but the kind act of a loving God, not a capricious God, whose greatest desire for his creation is to return them to their former state of glory and majesty where continual communion with humankind can be unhindered by their independence.

Scene 4: She Took and Ate (Genesis 3.6-7)

This scene is composed of the fatal steps which are described in a series of consecutive clauses that suggest the rapidity of the action of Eve:

- "she saw"
- "she took"
- "she gave"

Learning Objective
Understand the consequences of "she took and ate."

Genesis 3.6-7. TBB. 9.

Act 2

Primeval

Learning Objective
Understand the consequences of "she took and ate."

- "he ate"
- "good to eat"
- "delight to the eyes"
- "giving insight"
- "eyes opened"
- "knowing they were nude"[80]
- "hiding in the trees."

The forbidden tree has three commendable virtues:

- It was physically appealing because it was good for food.
- It was aesthetically pleasing because it was pleasing to the eyes.
- It was transforming because it was desirable for acquiring wisdom.[81]

The text literally reads: *When the woman saw that the tree ... was desirable in order to become wise.* Here is the texture of being covetous: an attitude that says I see something that I want that I don't presently have, and if I only had it I would be happy.[82] This text reveals a shadow of the tenth commandment where one might add the idea of not only wanting what another has but wishing that the other person didn't have the possession at all.

The apple has often been labeled as the forbidden fruit. However, the text does not reveal such information. It may be that the fruit received its name from the Latin *malus* "evil," and *malum* "apple," a close sound alike.[83]

It should be noted that the story does not tell us that the woman tried to tempt the man. She simply gave him some of the fruit and he chose to eat it. Adam did not challenge or raise a question, he simply eats.[84]

Breaking God's commandment "not to eat" carried with it a consequence. Nothing has changed in God's economy. The same "rapid-fire" style of words suggested the severity of making the choice to "eat." What happened?

1. Their eyes opened.
2. They realized they were naked.
3. They sewed fig leaves.
4. They made a covering.[85]

The plural "they" demonstrates that this first dynamic duo experienced the result of eating the forbidden fruit simultaneously. But, instead of knowing good and evil, the first couple knew that they were naked.[86] This was hardly the "special knowledge" that they had hoped for. What had been a healthy relationship between the male and female in the garden had now turned into something unpleasant and filled with shame. They immediately knew the consequences of committing sin. Their first response: cover it up. Gardengate precedes Watergate (and all other "gates"), but the same response is apparent.

The cover up was accomplished by sewing a few fig leaves together. The storyteller is unclear why the man and woman chose fig leaves. Some have suggested that it was because of their size. The aprons (loincloths) may suggest the skimpiness of their own act to cover themselves.[87] A curious question could be asked: Was the couple hiding themselves from each other or from God?

So What?

She "took and ate" was an act of rebellion of humankind against a loving and gracious God. Jesus "took and ate" removes the curses of the fall on God's creation, now but not yet, as we continue to live within God's EPIC Adventure.

It is always important to apply what you have learned. Pause at this point and ask for the help of the Holy Spirit to meditate on and put into practice some or all of what you have encountered thus far in this story.

Scene 5: Hide and Seek (Genesis 3.8-13)

Scene 5 (Gen. 3.8-13) is an inquest by God. The actors are addressed in the opposite order to their appearance in the preceding scene (present scene: man, woman, snake; preceding scene: snake, woman, man). In this section the sins of the various characters are summoned for them. There is a certain kind of gentleness about the questions. The Creator God is now pictured as the missionary God who was seeking the disobedient and fallen. The storyteller reverts back to the term "Lord God" as a hint that God was still man's covenant partner as well as his creator and judge.

As this scene opens, Adam and Eve heard the thunder (the word translated *sound* is often connected with thunder in the Old Testament)[88] of the Lord moving about in the garden in the wind of the storm (cool of the day).

The description of God "walking" in the garden is anthropomorphic and suggests that he enjoyed fellowship between himself and our first parents. "In the cool of the day," or "the breezy time of the afternoon," or "at the time of the evening breeze" forms a picture of comfort and relaxation.[89] It was toward sundown that the first couple heard God walking in the garden.

"Walked with God" is an expression that was a favorite of the storyteller in Genesis. It pictured the righteous conduct of the Israelite heroes like Enoch, Noah, and Abraham.[90] When the first couple heard God, they hid in fear. They did not anticipate a cordial time of fellowship with their Creator Friend. The couple who had previously hid their nakedness from each other by making aprons of fig leaves were now attempting to hide themselves from God in the trees of the garden. The storyteller does not comment on exactly how one can camouflage him or herself with trees and escape detection by God.[91]

God begins the conversation with a question (v. 9): Where are you? We may note that God was not ignorant of where Adam and Eve were; he was simply drawing them out of their hiding. The phrase "the Lord God called" in verse 9 would have been understood by the Hebrews at Sinai as an enraged suzerain who was calling his covenant partner for an explanation of his or her acts.[92] The storyteller exposes the couple as somewhat naïve and childish in their game of hide and seek. If God had asked, "Why are you hiding?" instead of "Where are you?" his question would have drawn attention to the uselessness and lunacy of the couples' attempt to hide from their maker.[93] God's question is directed only to the man even though both were hiding. As a parent might know where his children are hiding, and calls out for them with the line from the movie *The Shining*, "Come out, come out, where ever you are."[94] God was

Learning Objective
Understand the consequences of "she took and ate."

Learning Objective
Begin understanding of God as missional.

Genesis 3.8-13. TBB. 9-10.

Act 2

offering a way for them to show themselves. We can assume that this is what happened here, because the couple emerged from their hiding place. They replied, because they understood God's question as an invitation to come out and explain their behavior.

Verse 10 depicts Adam as not willing to tell a lie to his Creator. He comments only on his behavior, "I hid myself," not on the behavior of the woman.[95] The answer Adam provided to God does not answer the question God asked but answers another question: "Why are you hiding?" This seems characteristic of fallen humankind. We seem to answer questions that are not being asked in order to avert attention away from our situation.

The next two questions (v. 11) in the conversation are not those of a primitive questioner. The formation of the questions suggests that God, the detective, is prodding his creation to confess their guilt.[96] The response of Adam produces a further inquiry from God. The first question, "Who told you that you were naked?" may sound somewhat strange to the reader/hearer. Being naked is not something about which one is ignorant, but rather than pausing to give Adam an opportunity to answer, God asked a second question. "Have you eaten from the tree that I commanded you not to eat from?" This question is a prosecutor's question. We may note that God did not charge the man with transgression but rather allowed him to acknowledge his disobedience. The question urges the man to confess rather than condemning the man.[97]

Adam's response (v. 12) demonstrates the two things he did wrong: first, he hid as we saw in verse 10 and, second, he blamed his spouse and God for his present predicament. She received the full force of his blame along with God, who is faulted for giving the woman to Adam in the first place. The effects of sin could not be more observable: Adam turned against his companion and is alienated from his all-caring Creator. She was a mistake and God was mistaken for putting her in Adam's life. By shifting the blame, Adam may have hoped to evade being accountable for his autonomous actions.[98] People are often given to justifying their own poor conduct by pointing to the fate and sometimes the mate they believe God has given them in life.

God now turns his attention to the woman (v .13) and asked her to explain by questioning her actions. Adam's partner who was blessed to tend to the garden with him was now a partner in his crime. She responded no differently than Adam. She shifted the blame to the serpent. While she shifted the blame to the serpent, she does not blame God as Adam did instead by saying something like, "the serpent whom you made and the man to whom you gave me." She openly admitted that she was duped.[99] The serpent presented an enchanting proposal and she bought it hook, line, and sinker. What the first couple had in common was their refusal to accept responsibility for their actions. Some things appear to stay the same.

So What?

Ever noticed that we often play the same game of "hide and seek" that the first couple played with God? His greatest desire is to have relationship with humankind. Our greatest problem is that we are hiding when he comes calling, often because, like the first couple, we have broken the parameters of the Story he wants us to live in. Could it be that we are living in another story, one full of anti-Story lifestyles? Could it be that we live there because we have never had a clear picture of what God's EPIC Adventure really is?

Scene 6: Disobedience Payback (Genesis 3.14-19)

The interrogation of Adam, Eve, and the serpent was designed to bring them to confession, not to gain information about what they had done.

This scene describes the judgment oracle of God assigning judgment to the serpent first (vv. 14-15), the woman second (v. 16), and finally the man (vv. 17-19). The order of the narration of the sin and the sinner is the reverse of the order in which each comes under God's judgment. The sin of the man (vv. 9-11), the sin of the woman (v. 12), and the sin of the serpent (v. 13) are a ❖ **chiastic** ❖ arrangement with the judgment of the serpent (vv. 14-15), the judgment of the woman (v. 16) and the judgment of the man (vv. 17-19).[100] It looks like the following:

Sin of man
   Sin of woman
      Sin of serpent
      Judgment of serpent
   Judgment of woman
Judgment of man

In each judgment citation, the punishment will match the nature of the crime. Each oracle consists of a penalty that is followed by an account of their actions and the consequences. The serpent is not given an opportunity to reply.

- ◆ The serpent's penalty is disgrace (14a) and the consequence is that he will be defeated by the woman's seed.
- ◆ The woman's penalty is birthing children in pain (16a) and the consequence is conflict with her husband (16b).
- ◆ The man's penalty is painful toil of the cursed ground (17-18) and the consequence is conflict in his agricultural life.[101]

There are only words of condemnation for the serpent. The couple receive God's careful concern and provision even in the middle of their discipline. It is important to note that curses were uttered against the serpent and the ground, but not against the couple.[102]

The first occurrence of a divine curse (v. 14) appears in the curse of the serpent. The root of the word *curse*, which is used here, appears fifty-five times in the Old Testament, mostly in the Pentateuch with eight of the occurrences happening in Genesis. It is also in Deuteronomy 27-28 in the list of blessings and curses of the Covenant. The idea of curse would be of particular interest to the Hebrews at Sinai as they had just received the Lord-Servant treaty with its blessings and curses.

The punishment of the serpent has three segments: The serpent is:

1. consigned to crawl on its belly
2. given a diet of dust
3. ultimately destroyed by the seed of the woman.[103]

The eating of dust is a common reference to personal humiliation found elsewhere in Scripture (Micah 7.17; Ps. 72.9; Isa. 49.23).[104] This is not to say that snakes live on dust. It is obvious that snakes do not eat dust and no ancient writers believed that they did.[105]

Primeval

Learning Objective
Begin understanding of God as missional.

Learning Objective
Comprehend that disobedience to God's command brings judgment.

Genesis 3.14-19. TBB. 10.

Chiastic. A chiastic arrangement refers to an inverted parallelism or sequence of words or ideas in a phrase or clause, sentence, paragraph, chapter, or an entire literary work. This was an often-used literary form in Hebrew poetry. It was used in both writing and speaking.

Primeval

Learning Objective
Comprehend that
disobedience to God's
command brings judgment.

Etiology is the study of
causes or origins.

One should note that eating was a part of the temptation offered to the woman as well as a claim that she would not die. Yet the serpent is cursed to eat and to die. The very things they were tempted with were the punishments given to the serpent as punishment. We might give pause to consider how God's punishment works.

It is fruitless to see in this particular verse an ❖ **etiology** ❖ for why snakes no longer walk on legs or why they lost their legs. If a change in locomotion is what occurred and the story is told to help the hearer to understand that purpose, then to be consistent one must also allow the decree to eat dust to be a change in the snake's diet. The writer clearly intends crawling on the belly and eating dust to carry symbolic recognition.[106] The end result: the snake will never improve its stature. It will bear the curse all the days of its life.

As Israel first heard this, it was a word of comfort. They were being told that as they moved forward to conquer the land, they would have both victories and defeats. This story prepared them for such events that would happen in their future.

Genesis 3.15-16

We have arrived at one of the most crucial texts in Scripture. There are those who interpret the *fall* in two categories:

1. Those who understand the text as messianic.
2. Those who do not.[107]

There are at least three difficult issues that await those who try to interpret this part of the Story:

1. What does the verb, which describes what the seed of the woman and the seed of the serpent do to each other, mean?
2. Who or what is the "offspring"?
3. Who is identified as "it," who will crush the head of the serpent?[108]

Other than that, no problem!

So let's dig in. The final destruction of the serpent will come at the hands of the woman's descendant. We must note that the hostility between the snake and the woman's seed is clearly instigated by God. The serpent helped in undoing the woman and in turn the woman will ultimately undo the serpent. The serpent has a life expectancy that will come to a violent end.[109]

There are three observations to make. First, let's look at the verb *crush/strike* (*sup*). "It will sup your head and you will sup its heel."[110] In such close quarters, it seems likely that the word should be translated by the same English word in both places. There is no evidence from the Hebrew text to support a different reading. The TNIV translates the first *sup* as *crush* and the second *sup* as *strike*.[111] This translation creates the appearance that the lick struck against the serpent's head is fatal because its head is crushed. The lick unleashed by the serpent against the woman's seed is not deadly, only painful. The seed just comes away with a bruised heel. Such a shift in the translation is manufactured by the translation and places on the text a focus that is not naturally there. The comparison is between the it (*he* TNIV) and *you*, as well as the head and heel.[112]

The precedent for translating *sup* in two different ways comes from the ❖ **Vulgate**. ❖ The Vulgate used a Latin word which meant "to crush,

Vulgate: The Latin edition or translation of the Bible made by Saint Jerome at the end of the fourth century A.D., now used in a revised form as the Roman Catholic authorized version.

Act 2

Primeval

Learning Objective
Comprehend that
disobedience to God's
command brings judgment.

grind, bruise" for the first occurrence, but used another Latin word which means "to lie in wait, to lie in ambush, to watch" for the second occurrence. The Septuagint (LXX), on the other hand, chose to translate both occurrences of *sup* by *tereo* (to watch, guard).[113]

Second, let's observe the word "offspring" or "seed." The hostility ordained by God is to take place between the seed of the serpent and the seed of the woman. In the vast majority of cases where seed (*zera*) appears, it refers to an individual child, a near offspring rather than a remote offspring. However, in a number of passages seed is a collective noun referring to a distant offspring or a large group of offsprings (Gen 9.9; 12.7; 13.16; 15.5, 13, 18; 16.10; 17.7-10, 12, 21.12; 22.17-18). In these passages a term like "posterity or offspring" would capture the collective sense of seed.[114]

Finally, we can look at the word "it". The question is whether one translates the "it" as "he, she, or it." The TNIV opts out for "he." The ancient versions give various alternatives. The Vulgate suggests "she." (go figure!). The LXX has *autos* (he) even though the antecedent is *spermatos*, which is neuter in Greek. The LXX would appear to have had a messianic understanding of the verse. It emphasizes the "he-ness" of the woman's seed, not the seed's "it-ness" or "they-ness" in some collective sense.[115] The independent personal pronoun (*hu*) in Hebrew appears more than 100 times in the Old Testament, but only here does the LXX translate it with autos (he). The ❖ **Targums**, ❖ Jewish ❖ **Pseudepigrapha**, ❖ and later rabbinic commentators, however, generally viewed the seed as collective for humankind. Christian interpreters are mixed:

- ◆ ❖ **Paul** ❖ identified Christ as the *seed* intended in the covenant blessing to Abraham (Gal. 3.16).

- ◆ ❖ **Justin** v and ❖ **Irenaeus** ❖ by making a parallel with Eve, interpreted the woman of Genesis 3.15 to be the virgin Mary.

- ◆ Greek Fathers, such as ❖ **Chrysostom,** ❖ viewed Genesis 3.15 as a picture of the struggle between Satan and humanity.

Others interpreted *seed* as the church.

- ◆ The Latin Fathers, such as ❖ **Augustine** ❖ with others, allegorized or moralized the verse, designating it as a collective use.

- ◆ ❖ **Ambrose** ❖ first quoted Genesis 3.15 as not "her seed" but "the woman's seed."

- ◆ ❖ **Luther** ❖ took "her seed" as reference to both general humanity and specifically to Christ.

- ◆ ❖ **Calvin** ❖ applied it as a collective, not to all humanity, but rather to the church under the headship of Christ, which would prove victorious (quoting Rom. 16.20).[116]

Targums. Any of several Aramaic explanatory translations or paraphrasings of the Hebrew Scriptures.

Pseudepigrapha. A body of texts written between 200 B.C. and A.D. 200 and spuriously ascribed to various prophets and kings of Hebrew Scriptures.

Paul identified Christ as the *seed* intended in the covenant blessing to Abraham (Gal. 3.16).

Justin. (around A.D. 100-165) Greek theologian who founded a school of Christian philosophy at Rome and wrote the *Apology* and the *Dialogue.*

Irenaeus. (around A.D. 125–202) A Greek theologian, Bishop of Lyons, and one of the Fathers of the Church.

As Patriarch of Constantinople (from A.D. 398) whose eloquent sermons earned him the name **Chrysostom** which means "golden-mouthed." His oratory against corruption eventually led to his death.

Augustine (around 396) became Bishop of Hippo. His sermons and writings gained fame, notably his Confessions and the treatise City of God. His notions of God's grace, free will, and Original Sin had a great influence on Christian theology.

Ambrose was a writer, composer, and bishop of Milan (374–397) who imposed orthodoxy on the early Christian Church.

Luther. German theologian and leader of the Reformation. His opposition to the wealth and corruption of the papacy and his belief that salvation would be granted on the basis of faith alone rather than by works caused his excommunication from the Catholic Church (1521). Luther confirmed the Augsburg Confession in 1530, effectively establishing the Lutheran Church.

Calvin. one of the fathers of the Reformed branch of Protestant Christianity. Born to a Roman Catholic family of means, Calvin was schooled in Latin, Hebrew, Greek, philosophy, and law in Paris, Orleans and Bourges. Around 1533, he had what he later described as "conversion" and by 1534, religion had become foremost in his writing and work. He sympathized with the Protestant sentiments sweeping Europe since Martin Luther's appearance on the scene. In Basel in 1536, Calvin published Institutes of the Christian Religion, a six-chapter catechism that grew to 80 chapters by its final edition in 1559. It is widely regarded as the clearest, most systematic treatise of the Reformation. Calvin's most famous and controversial doctrine is that God chooses to save some people and not others, a notion known as "election" or "predestination."

Act 2

Primeval

Learning Objective
Comprehend that
disobedience to God's
command brings judgment.

Israel at Sinai might understand this phrase as "from time to time you will lose battles, but the ultimate victory will be yours." For the Hebrews who had just left the captivity in Egypt, hostility began with a purge of Hebrew children from which Moses was delivered. It climaxes with God's tenth plague against the house of Pharaoh and the Egyptian's firstborn.

In the present text (16) there are penalties announced against the serpent and the man while there is no "curse" that relates to the woman's suffering. There is an abundance of controversy in regards to the interpretation of this text. It is almost as famous as the text above.[117] There are five basic interpretations of Genesis 3.16.[118]

The penalty given to the woman impacted her in two ways: pain in childbirth and being ruled over by her husband.

Hendiadys is the use of two independent words that are connected by the word "and" which express a single concept such as grace and favor for gracious favor.

First, the "painful labor" literally "your pain and your childbearing." This couplet is to be understood as a ❖ **hendiadys**. ❖ Her punishment is her hope. She will live to birth children. While it signals hope, it also is a continual reminder of sin and the woman's part in it.[119]

Second, her sin damages her relationship with her husband. The Hebrew word for "desire" appears two more times in the Old Testament (Gen. 4.7; Song of Songs 7.10). The meaning of "desire" in this text has no clear meaning. "Desire" has been explained in the following ways:

◆ As sexual desire based on the passage in the Song of Songs (7.10) and the reference to giving birth in Genesis 3.16.
◆ As emotional or economic reliance on her husband.
◆ Is not part of the judgment on the woman only a description of the natural outcome of sin.[120]

Genesis 4.17 is a close companion to our text here at 3.16 and may have something to say about its meaning. In Genesis 4, "sin" is like an animal that, when stirred up, will assault Cain. Sin's "desire" is to overcome Cain and Cain's responsibility is to exercise "rule" or "mastery" over sin. "Desire" and "rule" are closely related in Genesis 3.16 just like they are in Genesis 4.17. The woman's "desire" is to overcome him while he "rules" over her. This is the result of their rebellion. We should not understand the words "he will rule over you" as an instruction to impose control over the woman any more than Genesis 3.16a is an exhortation for the woman to suffer as much pain as she can while giving birth. It is misguided to interpret this text to find in it defense for the absolute rule of the male.[121]

There is a close relationship in the first chapter of Genesis where we are told that the "larger light" will "rule" over the day and the "smaller" light will "rule over the night. The word "rule" there (Gen. 1.16-17) is in the same family as the word "rule" here. This may provide us another picture of what it means to "rule" over. The basic concept is not *power* but *giver* of light and life. The word is more inclined to bear the mark of "giving to" rather than "power over."

Genesis 3.17-19

The final judgment is given to the man (3.17-19). It is more lengthy than the preceding judgments. The ground was cursed on his account.

Under his care in the garden the ground provided delightful growth but will now produce a dreaded harvest of thorns and thistles, an image of great toil with little results as it turns to a source of pain as man wearily ekes out his existence. This would surely be a constant reminder of his sin.

While the word "adam" has been used through this story and translated as "man," it appears that we may have the first instance of Adam being used as the man's name in this text.[122]

Five times in this text eating is mentioned.[123] Man's offense consisted of eating what God forbid and his punishment is to sweat for what he will now eat. Sweat is metaphorical for all the frustration that will now go along with working the ground for his food. It is not work that is the punishment for his sin against God. It is the toil that lies behind the preparation of his labor to produce food for his family which is a constant reminder of his judgment. It is made more painful when it is set against what was lost in the garden.

How do you spell "relief" for all this toil? "DEATH!" There is not anything about retirement in Scripture. Death was exactly what God had forewarned and what the serpent had denied. Death is the reversal of man's God-given state of being a living being. This reversal is the deterioration of the body that will return to the dust from which it was taken.

Genesis 3.20-21

Subsequent to their sin, these first humans experienced the penalty for their disobedience. Their ease with one another is shattered, for they cover their nakedness. Their communion with God is broken, and they hide from the one who created them in his image. Their grasp of truth is weakened as they blame others for what they each have done. Fractures in friendship, fellowship, and integrity are all causalities of sin. Sin begins with mistrust of God and includes a craving for what harms one's self. Sin neglects revelation of truth and ultimately concludes in destruction.

Two events signal the continuing hope for the couple following the pronouncement of judgment:

1. **Adam names his wife Eve.** The name means *living* and is traditionally rendered Eve. Her name is sparse in the pages of Scripture (Gen. 4.1; 2 Cor. 11.3; 1 Tim. 2.13). Adam explains why she is named Eve: She is the mother of all human life.
2. **God's provision of animal skins for garments.** The text does not specifically say that an animal was slain, but the inference would be such for those living in a time when animal sacrifice was a way of life. Many images in the garden are an allusion to the Tabernacle which paints a theological picture of renewed union with God. Having said such, one must remember that the text is silent, and to say more than the text is to say more than God revealed in the text. It appears that God simply leaves some things unsaid in a shroud of mystery.

These two events suggest that the couple will weather their storm because God intervened.[124]

So What?

The Christian tradition has referred to Genesis 3.15 as the first *protevangelium* or *protoevangelion*.[125] Historically, interpreters have

Learning Objective
Comprehend that disobedience to God's command brings judgment.

QUESTIONS
What in our disobedience makes us think that we can hide from God?
How does answering a question that is not asked avert attention away from your present situation?
What have we been taught about God's character that when we disobey we believe that God is going to be angry and judgmental? Try to discover God as one who receives confession rather than first handing out condemnation.
What about the story of the disobedience of Adam and Eve makes us want to take the props of the story and make them literal?
How does this approach damage the text and the meaning of the text for the first hearer?
Could it be that the "rule" of a husband over a wife is a characteristic of the fall, but in the redemption of Jesus that this has been removed? (One must note that the story is about a husband and wife, not men and women in general, thus it is a fallacy to think that this story teaches male domination over females.)
Where is your garden?

Dictionary Articles
Read the following Dictionary Articles in *New Bible Dictionary*, Third Edition. D. R. W. Wood, A. R. Millard, J. I. Packer, D. J. Wiseman, and I. Howard Marshall (Editors), InterVarsity Press. 1996.
  Adam
  Bible
  Egypt
  Eve
  Genesis
  Hebrew Poetry
  Mt. Sinai
  Polytheism
  Septuagint
  Vulgate

Act 2

Primeval

Learning Objective
Comprehend that
disobedience to God's
command brings judgment.

Learning Objective
Begin to understand
separation from God.

Genesis 3.22-24. TBB. 10.

come to different conclusions about whether "her seed" refers to an individual or a collective community. While a messianic interpretation may be justified in the light of subsequent revelation in the New Testament, it would perhaps be misguided to suggest that this was the narrator's own understanding for the first hearer.

 Scene 7: Banishment from the Garden (Genesis 3.22-24)

Finally, God banished Adam and Eve from Eden and restricts their reentry. This is the seventh and final scene and it matches the first. In Scene 1 the garden was planted for man. He was allowed to eat of the tree of life. His job was to till and guard the garden. The storyteller goes into great detail to describe the lushness of the garden so the reader/hearer understands the garden as man's perfect home where he enjoyed peace with his Creator.

In Scene 7, man is expelled from the garden. He no longer will have access to the tree of life. Instead of Adam and Eve guarding the garden, an armed cherubim is stationed there to keep them out. Adam was appointed to till the garden, but now will till the cursed land outside the garden instead.[126]

The exile of Adam and Eve from the garden is decisive, definitive, and swift. This passage continues to share the imagery of the Tabernacle by allusion. The cherubim (3.24) at the "east side" of the garden parallels the direction the Tabernacle and Temple were entered. Entrance to Eden's garden was guarded by the cherubim who are known from the Old Testament as winged, composite beings associated with the presence of God (Ps. 18.10). Their golden images formed the covering of the ark (Ex. 25.18-22) and decorated the curtains of the holy of holies (Ex. 26.1, 31; 36.8, 35).[127]

These features in the story combine to suggest that the Garden of Eden was a type of sanctuary where God was uniquely present in all his life-giving power. The Tabernacle was now the garden for the Hebrews. It was the presence of God that man forfeited when he ate the fruit.

So What?

Banishment is not a pretty word, but the allusions presented in this scene offer the followers of God hope that banishment is not forever. If the Tabernacle was the new Garden for Israel, what might be the new Garden in the new creation for the followers of Jesus?

Some Thoughts about The Fall

The events of Genesis 3, often called "the Fall," have given rise to the doctrine of "original sin" in Christian theology. The Old Testament has little to say about this first couple after Genesis 5. The prophets who would come later often used the story of Sodom and Gomorrah to picture the aftermath of disobedience, never once using the garden story as an analogy. The story reader must await the books of Romans (chapter 5) and First Corinthians (chapter 15) to hear a discussion of Adam.

The creation provided humankind the capacity to make her or his own independent choices. This story implies that a choice should not be made with the self-interest of the chooser in mind. On the other hand, choices should be made within the grid of the directives of God. Freedom is not a characteristic of being autonomous. The couple's choice to become free ultimately led to them being bound. True freedom lies within the boundaries of living in God's EPIC Adventure.

The Primeval Story: A Summary (Genesis 1.1-11.26)

Primeval

Learning Objective
Begin to understand
separation from God.

Genesis 1.1-11.26. TBB. 7-18.

Here is a succinct remembrance of the whole of the first eleven chapters of Genesis. We only detailed the first three chapters. The remaining scenes are left for you to flesh out for yourself.

Act 1: 1.1-2.4a

An anti-polytheistic tract told to Israel after the redemption from Egypt to help illustrate God's seriousness about only worshiping him.

Act 2 (Gen 2.4b-11.26)

- ◆ Scene 1: Creation (Gen. 2.4b-17)
- ◆ Scene 2: Home Alone (Genesis 2.18-25)
- ◆ Scene 3: Chatting with the Crafty Serpent (Genesis 3.1-5)
- ◆ Scene 4: She Took and Ate (Genesis 3.6-7)
- ◆ Scene 5: Hide and Seek (Genesis 3.8-13)
- ◆ Scene 6: Disobedience Payback (Genesis 3.14-24)
- ◆ Scene 7: Banishment from the Garden (Genesis 3.22-24)
- ◆ Scene 8: The Killing Fields (Gen. 4.1-26)
- ◆ Scene 9: The genealogy of Adam's descendants (Gen.5.1-32)
- ◆ Scene 10: The story of the sons of God and the daughters of men (6.1-4)
- ◆ Scene 11: The story of Noah and the flood which describes why God caused the flood (Gen. 6.5-9.28)
- ◆ Scene 12: The Table of Nations which emphasizes the repopulation of the earth after the Flood (Gen 10.1-32)
- ◆ Scene 13: The story of Babel (Gen. 11.1-9)
- ◆ Scene 14: The genealogy of Shem (11.10-26)[128]

At Genesis 11.27-32, we find the story of Terah. This begins the long Patriarchal section which begins Act 3 to which we now turn our attention. Act 3 is the longest part of God's EPIC Adventure which we have entitled: Act 3. Israel: The Called People of God to Be the Light of the World.

When autonomy displaces submission and

obedience in a person, that finite individual

attempts to rise above the limitations

imposed on him by his creator.

Act 3

Israel: The Called People of God
to Be the Light of the World

The third act covers almost two millennia

with hundreds of sub stories and scenes

that tell how God set about

redeeming and restoring his creation.

When you finish this session, you should be able to:

Learning Objectives

- ◆ Understand each of the major sections of the Old Testament
- ◆ Comprehend the vocation of Israel
- ◆ Understand the Patriarchal stage of Israel's history
- ◆ Comprehend God as being missional
- ◆ Understand the Covenant stage of Israel's history
- ◆ See Israel's journey to the land promised to them by God
- ◆ Understand the Conquest stage of Israel's history
- ◆ Comprehend the Judges stage of Israel's history
- ◆ See the United Kingdom stage of Israel's history
- ◆ Understand the Divided Kingdom stage of Israel's history
- ◆ Comprehend the Exile stage of Israel's history
- ◆ Understand the Restoration stage of Israel's history

The story of the Old Testament is long, and often, only one's favorite parts are read. This lesson will take you through the Old Testament section by section. First, you will look at the vocation of Israel. Then, you will see each of the stages of Israel's history; Patriarchal, Exodus, Covenant, Conquest, Judges, United and Divided Kingdom, Exile, and Restoration.

Preview of Act 3

Act 3: Israel: Called to Be His People
   The Vocation of Israel
   Scene 1. Patriarchal Stage: The Beginning of Israel
   (Genesis 11.27-50.26)
      About Genesis: The Book of Beginnings
         Abraham and Sarah. The Promises of God
         (Gen. 11.27-20.18)
         Isaac and Rebekah. Strife Between Brothers
         (Gen. 21.1-27.40)
         Jacob. Exile and God's Protection and Blessing
         (Gen. 27.41-37.1)
         Joseph. Relationship with Brothers
         (Gen. 37.2-50.26)
   Scene 2. The Exodus: The Missionary God (Exodus 1.1-19.2)
      About Exodus: The Book of Deliverance
         Exodus from Egypt (Ex. 1.1-13.16)
         Journey into the Wilderness (Ex. 13.17-19.1)
   Scene 3. The Covenant Stage: Lord-Servant Treaty
        (Exodus 19.2-Numbers 10.10)
     The Covenant (Ex. 20.1-24.18)
     About Leviticus: The Book of Holiness
   Scene 4. Journey to the Promised Land (Numbers 10.11-Deuteronomy 34.12)
      About Numbers: The Wilderness Years
      About Deuteronomy: The Covenant Restated
   An Interlude. Job: A Theodic Protest (Job 1-42)
      About Job: Why Is There Human Suffering?
   Scene 5. The Conquest Stage (Joshua 1-24)
      About Joshua: The Book of Conquest

Outline of Act 3

Act 3

Act 3. Israel: The Called People of God to Be the Light of the World

Learning Objective
Understand each of the major sections of the Old Testament.

At this point, an observation might be helpful. The reader may observe that there was a lot of written material in Act 2. Act 3 will cover the rest of the books of the Old Testament with a little over twice as much written material presented. However, the amount of material given to each Act does not equal the importance of each Act. If that were true, there would be much more material for Act 3 than presently written in this book. After all, it was the only Scripture that Jesus, Peter, Paul, and the church in the New Testament had. It was the only Scripture that the first three centuries of the church had as they wrestled with all the texts looking for entrance into the New Testament. I might add, Act 3 is the part of the Story which most current followers of Jesus spend the smallest amount of time reading and considering, except for their favorite parts.

The presentation of the material in this Act is to allow you an opportunity as a reader of the Old Testament Story to read it chronologically and, hopefully, as a reader you can get a sense of reading it as a story. The storyline covers all thirty-nine books of the Protestant version of the Old Testament with the exclusion of the first eleven chapters of Genesis. The storyline is preserved from Genesis 11.27 to the end of Ezra-Nehemiah while the rest of the Old Testament material is placed within this storyline in a mixture of introductory and theological material. While it has many characters and many subplots, it carries the Story forward to its climax in Jesus in Act 4.

The main thread that carries the Story forward from Exodus is the Mosiac Covenant, so keep your eye out for that thread as you read through the text of the Old Testament using the material in this book as a roadmap for your reading and learning journey. As we have mentioned before, this book is also keyed to *The Books of The Bible* to help you read along in the Story.

The Vocation of Israel

Learning Objective
Comprehend the vocation of Israel.

The third act covers almost two millennia[1] with hundreds of sub stories and scenes that tell how God set about redeeming and restoring his creation.[2] Gordon Fee and Douglas Stuart in their book *How to Read the Bible for All Its Worth* say that the Bible contains more narrative than it does any other literary type.[3] God's desire for his creation to be recreated is told in the Story of Israel, the people of God in the Old Testament, and is primarily narrative in its formation.

The Story Begins

As a missionary God, Yahweh chose a man from Ur whose name was Abram and made a covenant with him. God promised him a *people* and a *land* in which the people would live and fulfill their vocation as the light to the world. Israel's election by God was for the following purpose as recorded at Genesis 12.1-3:

> The LORD had said to Abram, "Leave your country, your people and your father's household and go to the land I will show you.

> "I will make you into a great nation
>   and I will bless you;
> I will make your name great,
>   and you will be a blessing.

Act 3

I will bless those who bless you,
> and whoever curses you I will curse;
and all peoples on earth
> will be blessed through you." (Gen. 12.1-3. NIV)

Gerhard von Rad, an Old Testament specialist, sees this initial promise of God to Abraham as functioning as the hinge and connecting point to bring together the history of the nations in Genesis 1.1-11.26 and the history of Israel in all the stories that follow.[4] This initial promise is to be carried and embodied by Israel to counter and nullify the curse of Genesis 3. The people of God (Israel in the Old Testament) were "blessed to be a blessing" for the sake of the world.[5]

Reading the StoryLine

A little proverb says, "A picture is worth a thousand words." On the following page is a chart: *Old Testament Book Chronology and Timeline*, which provides you with an overview of the Old Testament. The small graphics that appear in this chart will appear on each page, top upper left and right, to keep you adjusted to what part of the Story you are in currently. As you can see, the Patriarchal graphic appears on this page to the left. From time to time throughout this book, you will see the above heading, *Reading the StoryLine*, which also intends to keep you abreast of where you are reading in the overall Story.

 Scene 1. Patriarchal Stage: The Beginning of Israel

About Genesis: The Book of Beginnings

Patriarchal

Learning Objective
Understand the Patriarchal stage of Israel's history.

BOOK
Genesis
AUTHOR
Traditionally Moses
AGE WRITTEN
Sometime after the Exodus
AUDIENCE
Those who need to have a firm foundation
AIM
To teach the people of God in the wilderness that God had chosen them.
KEY CONCEPTS
Beginnings, Blessings, Family
KEY CONCEPTS
God delights in beginnings and blessings
GEOGRAPHY
Ur ☉ Canaan ☉ Egypt

Genesis 11.27-50.26.
TBB. 18-71.

Genesis is a book of Beginnings. The *toledoth formula*, translated "This is the account of the heavens and the earth" (2.4), which appears ten times in Genesis and signals the beginning, survival, and continuity of God's plan for creation in spite of the ravages of human sin.[6] The second section of Genesis (11.27-50.26) presents the tradition of the earliest ancestors of Israel. There are four generational accounts for the beginning of the community that became Israel. The stories include:

- Abraham and Sarah (11.27-20.18)
- Isaac and Rebekah (21.1-27.40)
- Jacob and Rachel (27.41-37.1)
- Joseph (37.2-50.26)

The first three stories have a lot in common and focus on family relationships, acquiring land, obtaining a wife, and producing the sons who may become heirs.[7]

Abraham and Sarah. The Promises of God (Genesis 11.27-20.18)

The stories of Abraham and Sarah focus on acquiring an heir to God's promise with a subplot that involves Abraham's nephew, Lot.[8] The covenant with Abraham (15.7-21) was ratified in a solemn, mysterious ceremony[9] and signified that the promise of land would come to pass. If Abraham was going to have descendants, they needed to live somewhere.

The story of God's promises to Abraham set against Abraham's circumstances is a demonstration of how the storyteller tells stories in the Patriarchal section of Genesis. The circumstances of Abraham are clearly set out in the ending section of Genesis 11 and in the first verses of Genesis 12 (an unfortunate break in the storyline).

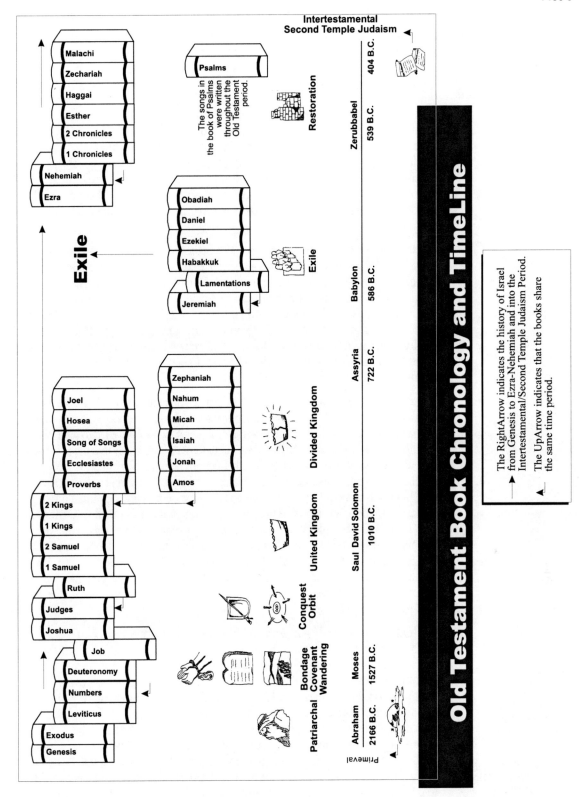

Old Testament Book Chronology and TimeLine

The RightArrow indicates the history of Israel from Genesis to Ezra-Nehemiah and into the Intertestamental/Second Temple Judaism Period.

The UpArrow indicates that the books share the same time period.

Act 3

Patriarchal

Learning Objective
Understand the Patriarchal
stage of Israel's history.

As you read these stories, you can see the contrast as the storyteller provides his theological imprint in the stories. Abraham is told that he is going to be a great nation (12.2). This was God's promise to him. On the other hand, Sarah was barren (11.30), which displays Abraham's circumstances. In Genesis 12.6-7, the storyteller provides this contrast: Abram passed through the land that God had promised and the land was occupied by the Canaanites (man's circumstances). At Shechem, God's promise was that he was going to give Abraham the land. There are many paradoxes within this story which the author wishes for his hearers/ readers to encounter; one is: regardless of man's circumstance, the promises of God will come true. It didn't matter that the Canaanites occupied the land. God was still going to give the land to Abraham and his descendants. So what if Sarah was barren! God's promise of a child was still going to be a reality.

Here is every person's dilemma. We attempt to help God bring about his promises in another time frame other that God's own time frame. So Abraham goes to work to help God out! Sound familiar? The first solution of Abraham to the problem of Sarah's barrenness was to purchase a slave to be his heir. In Genesis 15.2-3, we read, "But Abram said, 'Sovereign LORD, what can you give me since I remain childless and the one who will inherit my estate is Eliezer of Damascus?' And Abram said, 'You have given me no children; so a servant in my household will be my heir.'"

Adopting an heir into a childless family was an ancient custom. If parents did not have any male children, they could purchase a slave and upon the death of the husband, the slave would become the rightful heir.[10] So Abram tried to alter his circumstances by partaking in this ancient custom. Abram knew that the promise depended on having a child to be his heir. Because he remained childless, he purchased an heir to alter his circumstances. God said, "This man will not be your heir, but a son coming from your own body will be your heir. Look up at the heavens and count the stars—if indeed you can count them. So shall your offspring be" (15.4-5). God would have none of Abraham's plan. He told Abram that the servant would not be the heir. He showed Abram the stars and talked about how one could not number them and told him that the rightful heir was to be born to Sarah. God's plan was to bless him by giving him a nation and a land on which the nation would live. Abram tried his best to help God by altering his circumstances. God refused his help.

QUESTIONS
What does this teach us about how Abraham responded to God, how God responded to Abraham, how Abraham responded to his fellowman?

What does this teach us about responding to God, God responding to us, and our response to our fellowman?

Next is the story of Hagar and Ishmael. Sarah grew weary of remaining barren even though there was a promise of a child which had not yet been fulfilled. So she offered her maidservant Hagar to her husband as a solution to the problem (16.1-16). This story is formed from another custom of the day.[11] Here Abram's wife is trying to alter his circumstances. At Genesis 21.1-2, we read, "Now the LORD was gracious to Sarah as he had said, and the LORD did for Sarah what he had promised. Sarah became pregnant and bore a son to Abraham in his old age, at the very time God had promised him." Again, God would not allow any interference in his plan. Abraham and Sarah may have tried to live in another story, but it was not God's Story. His ideal for them was to live in the Story he had prepared for them to live in, not one of their own creation.

Finally, we are told in Genesis 21.1ff. that God fulfilled his promise. The text suggests that when old age appeared to make it impossible, God

Patriarchal

Learning Objective
Understand the Patriarchal
stage of Israel's history.

brought it to pass.[12] When Abraham and Sarah had exhausted the story they created, God came and presented them with his Story.

In each of the stories of the four great figures of Chapters 12-50, Abraham, Isaac, Jacob, and Joseph, you should look for these three things: 1) The circumstances of humankind compared with the promises of God, 2) The faith and righteousness of the characters, and 3) Their covenant relationship with God.

The beginning of the family promise was fulfilled with the birth of Isaac to Abraham and Sarah, but the promise of the land was to await many generations till the time of Joshua. It appears that not all of God's promises to us may actually occur during our lifetime.

These stories allow Israel to understand that their circumstances, too often ominous, are only their circumstances, which they are not to confuse with God's promises.

So What?

There are often delays, or what seems to us as delays, in the fulfillment of the promises of God to us. One can see this being worked out in this story. These stories are a perfect example of living in another story. Abraham chose to live in a cultural story that was accessible to him. God, however, had a different Story for Abraham and Sarah to live in. It might be well if we allowed God full reign in our lives as we live in his Story. While others may have meant events in our lives for bad, God can work them out for the good in our life. At least that was true of Joseph, as the last story in Genesis shares with us.

Reading the StoryLine

Here is the storyline for the Abraham and Sarah stories.

- ☐ The Journey to Canaan and Egypt (Promise of Descendants and Land): Genesis 11.27-12.20
- ☐ Abraham and Lot (Separation and Rescue): Genesis 13.1-14.24
- ☐ The Promise of God to Abraham: Gen. 15.1-21
- ☐ Hagar and Ishmael: Genesis 16.1-16
- ☐ God's covenant with Abraham (Name changed, circumcision instituted, promise of a son given again, Abraham and Ishmael circumcised): Genesis 17.1-27
- ☐ The Promise of God for a Son (Sarah laughs): Genesis 18.1-15
- ☐ Abraham, Lot, Sodom and Gomorrah: Genesis 18.16-19.38
- ☐ Abraham and Abimelech (Abraham lies about Sarah in Gerar. God protects her): Genesis 20.1-18

Genesis 11.27-21.18.
TBB. 18-28.

Isaac and Rebekah. Strife Between Brothers (Genesis 21.1-27.40)

There are two other aspects of theology that one can discern in the stories in the last part of Genesis. The *first* has to do with faith and righteousness. The *second* with covenant relationship.[13]

There are several short episodic stories in the account of Isaac. Finally, after many years of waiting, the promise of an heir is fulfilled, but not without some difficulties along the way. There is an intermingling of stories including Hagar and Ishmael and the oft told story of God directing Abraham to sacrifice Isaac, the promised heir.

Act 3

Patriarchal

Learning Objective
Understand the Patriarchal stage of Israel's history.

QUESTION
When the events of your life seemed out of whack, how many times have you seen God.?

Genesis 21.1-27.40.
TBB. 28-38.

Reading the StoryLine

Here is the storyline to the Isaac and Jacob stories.

- The Birth of Isaac: Genesis 21.1-7
- Hagar and Ishmael: Genesis 21.8-21
- The Treaty at Beersheba: Genesis 21.22-34
- Abraham Offers Isaac to God: Genesis 22.1-19
- The Sons of Nahor: Genesis 22.20-24
- Sarah's Death: Genesis 23.1-20
- Isaac and Rebekah: Genesis 24.1-67
- Abraham Dies: Genesis 25.1-10
- Ishmael's Sons: Genesis 25.12-18
- Jacob and Esau's Birth: Genesis 25.19-34
- Strife over Abraham's Wells: Genesis 26.1-33
- God Chooses Jacob: Genesis 26.34-27.40

Jacob. Exile and God's Protection and Blessing (Genesis 27.41-37.1)

The primary plot within the Jacob story is between Jacob and Esau, whose birthright is stolen, whereupon Jacob flees his father's house to escape Esau's anger. The story moves along with the search for a spouse for Jacob, which is told in the Jacob-Laban story. Once Jacob's family is established, the story of Jacob and Esau resumes in which the two brothers meet again (33.1-16).[14]

In the story of Jacob, we discover the difficulty of trusting in the promises of God, especially when they have been given to a previous generation. Jacob's grandfather, Abraham, had been called a righteous man (15.6). As conceived in the present era, *righteousness* is seen as conformity to a set of moral values and codes. However, from a biblical perspective, righteousness is understood as faithfulness to a relationship.[15] A righteous, person was one who was faithful to the claims of all of his relationships. This does not mean that a righteous person does not conform to a set of values and codes, but that she or he can conform because of her or his faithfulness in relationship. In short, one does not keep a set of moral values to become righteous, but righteousness occurs because of the faithfulness of a relationship and the end result is that one will cherish keeping the moral values. This story would be so relevant to the children of Israel and their Covenant relationship with God. They knew well that the Covenant stipulations that they were keeping did not make them the children of God, but that they could work toward keeping those stipulations because of their relationship with God. We will discuss this concept later in the stories provided in Exodus.

This story in Genesis presents us with the picture of Jacob as a worldly man, full of cunning, an independent man. He was a deceiver from his birth (25.26 TNIV footnote). He was scheming and crafty just like his mother (27.5-17, 41-45). He worked for twenty years for his uncle Laban and was himself deceived. The story is full of plots where each character is trying to get the best of the other.

But God refused to let Jacob live this way forever. At the Jabbok River, Jacob met his match. It was not until later that Jacob knew who his opponent was who brought to him a divine visitation. It was only by God's actions that Jacob, the deceiver, became Israel, the "Prevailer"[16] (Gen. 32.28).

Patriarchal

Learning Objective
Understand the Patriarchal
stage of Israel's history.

Reconciliation with his brother Esau followed this dynamic encounter with God (33.1-11). Other changes also occurred in Jacob's life. He realized his own need as well as his family's need to turn to God. The overt action which pictures this transformation is the story of his command to throw away all the foreign gods (35.2-5). Idols are a continual plague in the story of Israel and this story surely made sense to these early Israelites in light of the first stipulation of the Covenant. The stories of Jacob, after the encounter with God, describe a person who was no longer self-reliant, but one who had been mastered by God.

So What?

Righteousness and change! They appear to be different subjects. In fact, they go hand in hand. Remember, righteousness is being faithful to a relationship. If a person chooses not to be faithful, God will continually pursue that person to give every opportunity for change.

Reading the StoryLine

Here is the continuation of the storyline to the Isaac and Jacob stories.

Genesis 27.41-37.1.
TBB. 38-51.

- Jacob Flees to Laban: Genesis 27.41-28.9
- Jacob's Dream at Bethel: Genesis 28.10-22
- Jacob's Marriage: Genesis 29.1-30.24
- Jacob's First Scheme: Genesis 30.25-43
- Jacob and Laban: Genesis 31.1-55
- Jacob Prepares to Meet Esau, wrestles with God, meets Esau: Genesis 32.1-33.20
- Dinah and the Shechemites: Genesis 34.1-31
- Returning to Bethel: Genesis 35.1-15
- The Death of Rachel and Isaac: Genesis 35.16-29
  [A second account of Esau: Genesis 36.1-37.1]

Joseph. Relationship with Brothers (Genesis 37.2-50.26)

All the family relationships are depicted at the beginning of the Joseph stories (Gen. 37.2-4) and the story deteriorates from there, but ends in the reconciliation of Joseph and his brothers. The Jacob and Joseph stories are stories of family reconciliation.[17]

In the story of Joseph, God is seen as the one who is in control of the events of a person's life, in this case for the sake of the family. While Joseph was arrogant and got himself in a fix with his brothers, and while they made poor choices about how to solve their family problem, God used all of those events in the life of Joseph to fulfill his purpose so the end of the story says, "But Joseph said to them, 'Don't be afraid. Am I in the place of God? You intended to harm me, but God intended it for good to accomplish what is now being done, the saving of many lives. So then, don't be afraid. I will provide for you and your children.' And he reassured them and spoke kindly to them."

Dictionary Articles
Read the following
Dictionary Articles in *New Bible Dictionary*, Third Edition.
  Genesis
  Archaeology, I, II, III
  God
  God, names of
  Eden, Garden of
  Spirit, Holy Spirit, I, II
  Creation
  Fall
  Sin
  Flood
  Babel
  Abraham
  Isaac
  Jacob
  Joseph

So What?

Sometimes being in the wrong place at the wrong time or being in the right place at the right time is not the issue. God overrules the wicked intentions of men and women in order to save his people. While this theme runs through the Old Testament, it is explicit in the story of Joseph.

Act 3

Patriarchal

Learning Objective
Understand the Patriarchal
stage of Israel's history.

Genesis 11.27-50.26.
TBB. 51-71.

Reading the StoryLine

Here is the storyline to the Joseph stories.

- Joseph the Dreamer (sold by his brothers): Genesis 37.2-36
- Judah and Tamar: Genesis 38.1-30
- The Wife of Potiphar: Genesis 39.1-23
- Joseph Interprets Dreams: Genesis 40.1-41.57
- The Brothers of Joseph Journey to Egypt: Genesis 42.1-47.12
- Joseph Ascends in Egypt: Genesis 47.13-31
- Manasseh, Ephraim: Genesis 48.1-22
- Jacob Blesses his Sons and Dies: Genesis 49.1-50.14
- Joseph Reassures his brothers and dies: Genesis 50.15-26

What began as life with God in the Garden ends with lying in a "coffin in Egypt" (50.26). What a contrast! So the narrative of Genesis ends with the descendants of Abraham living in Egypt, and the story continues in the opening section of Exodus some 400 years later.

 Scene 2. The Exodus: The Missionary God (Exodus 1.1-19.2)

About Exodus: The Book of Deliverance

The story of the Exodus[18] is central to God's EPIC Adventure and is theological in nature.[19] Exodus tells the salvation history Story of Israel.[20] The book marked the birth[21] of the nation of Israel. Exodus is the dynamic story of God's deliverance of Israel from the bondage in which they lived in Egypt. This redemption story is seen as the greatest act of God's salvation in the Old Testament.[22] The God who created the world is now pictured as the God who delivers,[23] a missionary God who went after his people to rescue them. The deliverance of Israel from bondage in Egypt should give folk theologians, who skip from the creation story to the story of Jesus, pause. This story is important in Israel's Gospel.[24]

When Israel arrived in Egypt, they were honored guests and Joseph was second in command. Some 400 years later, they had been demoted to slaves and were ruled by a Pharaoh[25] who did not know about their beginnings. A lack of history can be a cruel thing. The task set before Israel was to keep its identity intact and its belief in God vital while living in an alien culture. Sounds familiar, huh? Polytheism was the order of the day. The Pharaoh himself was regarded as a god. If you chose not to worship him, it was considered treason. The children of Israel had to maintain their own faith in an invisible God with no ceremonies and no priests. How do people, who for all appearances look like victims instead of victors, keep on believing? They could have become polytheistic, which some did (3.13). They could have become ❖ **henotheistic**. ❖ They could have chosen to be ❖ **monotheistic** ❖ while living in Goshen. No doubt there were individual Israelites in all of these categories when Moses, a central figure in the story as told in Exodus through Deuteronomy,[26] came on the scene.

Exodus tells about the birth of Israel by three definitive acts of God on their behalf. The *first* act was God's deliverance of Israel from the oppressive bondage of the Egyptians. Israel looked back on this deliverance as a time when God redeemed her, as he came into the slave market (Egypt) and bought a slave (Israel) in order to make her his own

Bondage

Learning Objective
Comprehend God as being
missional.

BOOK
Exodus
AUTHOR
Traditionally Moses
AGE WRITTEN
After the Exodus
AUDIENCE
Those who are new
believers
AIM
To remind Israel of the
power of God
KEY CONCEPTS
Redemption/Covenant
KEY LESSONS
God redeems, makes
covenant, and provides a
place for worship
GEOGRAPHY
Egypt ❂ Wilderness

Exodus 1.1-19.2. TBB. 77-98.

Henotheism: Belief in one
god without denying the
existence of others.

Monotheism: The belief
that there is only one God.

special people: a kingdom of priests and a holy nation (19.6). In the *second* act, he called delivered Israel into Covenant relationship with him using an ancient Near Eastern treaty form, a Lord-Servant Treaty. God gave Israel a national charter (the law or Torah) that gave Israel a way, regardless of circumstances, to function as a people who could show the rest of humanity what being human was all about.[27] In the *third* act within Exodus, he summoned Israel to crown him as their king in the building and placement of the Tabernacle.

The book of Exodus introduces five important theological points, three of which appear in this scene and two in the Covenant Stage scene that follows.

1. Yahweh is seen as the personal Covenant name of God: the *I Am*[28] who is there and acts for his people. He is the God of Abraham, the God of Isaac, and the God of Jacob (3.6, 15-16). God is true to the promises he made in the past. He separates himself from all other so-called gods who are powerless to save those who follow them.[29]

2. The acts of God reveal his character. God:

   ◆ preserves Israel through Joseph (1.1-7), while Pharaohs may come and go, God remains to preserve his people even in their bondage 1.8-2.20
   ◆ rescues 6.6
   ◆ saves 14.30
   ◆ guides 15.13
   ◆ provides 16.4, 8
   ◆ disciplines and forgives 32.1-34.35.

3. The concept of Passover was God's act of rescue and deliverance for his captive and oppressed children.

The Exodus story has two parts. They are:

Exodus from Egypt (Exodus 1.1-13.16)

The story of Exodus begins with Israel in captivity where they had slipped from prestige under Joseph to poverty under the current Pharaoh. Moses' birth, with miraculous events surrounding it,[30] came during a desperate time when the Pharaoh was trying to curb the growing size of Israel,[31] with a form of genocide.[32] Moses tried to help but was banished for his efforts. During his banishment, God called him to go back to Egypt and lead Israel from bondage to freedom. Moses' effort to negotiate deliverance with eight requests made to Pharaoh was blocked by Pharaoh who hardens his heart.[33] As a response, God sent ten plagues[34] on the land of Egypt of which the final vertex was the death of the firstborn sons of Egypt. Passover finds its roots in this act of God.

- -

Reading the StoryLine

- -

Here is the storyline for the Exodus stories.

- Israel Oppressed and the Birth of Moses: Exodus 1.1-2.10
- Moses Leaves Israel: Exodus 2.11-25
- Moses meets God in the Burning Bush: Exodus 3.1-4.17
- Moses Returns to Egypt: Exodus 4.18-31
- Moses and Pharaoh: Exodus 5.1-7.13
- Plagues in Egypt: Exodus 7.14-11.10
- The Passover and Redemption: Exodus 12.1-13.16

Exodus 1.1-13.16. TBB. 77-91.

Act 3

Journey into the Wilderness (Ex. 13.17-19.1)

Pharaoh relented and allowed Israel to leave, only to follow them to the Sea of Reeds where God's act of redemption brought safety to Israel as they traveled into the wilderness. The wilderness was "an environment of acute risk and deep jeopardy." As a geographical location, Walter Brueggemann says "the term refers to the area traversed by Israel between Egypt (slavery) and the Promised Land (and secure well-being)." The term also may signify an area without visible evidence of life-sustaining resources such as water, bread, or meat.[35]

Reading the StoryLine

Here is the storyline to the wilderness stories.
- ⬚ Departure from Egypt: Exodus 13.17-15.21
- ⬚ Water, Manna, and Quail: Exodus 15.22-17.7
- ⬚ Amalekites and Arrival: Exodus 17.8-19.1

Exodus13.17-19.1.TBB.77-98.

 Scene 3. The Covenant Stage: Lord-Servant Treaty (Exodus 19.2-Numbers 10.10)

This section of the Pentateuch is self-contained and describes some of the teachings that Israel needed on their way to the Promised Land. It covers the period from Israel's arrival at Mt. Sinai (Ex. 19.2) to their departure (Num. 10.10). The time period is about one year in the life of Israel. The following overview may help in seeing the flow of this scene.

Reading the StoryLine

Covenant

Learning Objective
Understand the Covenant stage of Israel's history.

Here is the storyline to the Covenant stories.
- ⬚ Theophany on Sinai: Exodus 19.2-20.21
  [10 commandments Exodus 20.1-17]
- ⬚ God has no form: Exodus 20.22-24.11
  [judicial laws: Exodus 21.1-23.33]
- ⬚ Instructions for building the Tabernacle and dedicating priests: Exodus 24.12-34.28
  [laws given: Exodus 25.1-31.18]
- ⬚ Tabernacle building: Exodus 34.29-40.28
  [laws followed: Exodus 35.1-40.33]
- ⬚ Regulations about Sacrifices: Leviticus 1.1-10.20
  [laws of sacrifice: Leviticus 1.1-9.24]
- ⬚ Regulations about Purity: Leviticus 11.1-18.30
- ⬚ Holiness Laws and Marching Orders: Leviticus 19.1-Numbers 10.10
  [holiness laws: Leviticus 19.1-Numbers 9.14]
  [marching orders: Numbers. 9.15-10.10]

Exodus 19.2-Numbers 10.10. TBB. 98-176.

The Covenant: (Exodus. 20.1-24.18)

The giving of the Covenant provided a format to have relationship with God based on his act of mercy in deliverance. The Covenant was given to a redeemed people essentially in the form of an elaborate oath[36] often called a Lord-Servant (Suzerain-Vassal) Treaty.[37] God had demonstrated his salvation love to Israel in the historical act of her deliverance from the hands of her Egyptian oppressors. The Covenant (Law) was not (as has been thought and taught) a way in which Israel could become God's children. The Covenant was a way in which these redeemed people could relate to God and to each other and demonstrate to the world what being the people of God was really like. It was a Covenant to assist them in being light bearers to the world. They were to have no other God. They were to worship no idols.

Redemption/Exodus came first, then the Covenant (Law). The *law* was never intended to be a system of legal observances by which you could earn God's acceptance, if you obeyed them. The Commandments are the stipulations of the *Covenant relationship* which are rooted in *grace!* They are *basic statements* on the *quality of life* that must characterize those who belong to God. All of Scripture knows only one way of salvation and that is *the grace of God.* God reveals his redemptive purpose always based on grace, not on man's ability to obligate God to save him because he has kept the law.[38] Alas, they turned the windows of their lighthouse into mirrors.[39] We will ask later in Act 5 if Paul was a Lutheran. The Law/Grace perspective may be Luther's input, not Paul's.

Stipulations: The Ten Commandments (Exodus 20.1-17)

Some of the most famous words in the Old Testament, called the Ten Commandments, are found in Exodus 20.1-17. These commandments are significant in that by obeying them Israel will "remain the people of God."[40] They are listed as follows with the first four focusing on a relationship with God and the last six focusing on relationship with others.

- *No other gods:* God's uniqueness and supremacy
- *No graven images:* God's concern for proper worship
- *Not taking name in vain:* The dignity/power of God's name and being
- *Keep Sabbath holy:* God's claim to His creatures' time, his concern for re-creation
- *Honor parents:* Recognition of legitimate authority
- *No murder:* Reverence for life; human right to live; unauthorized or premeditated killing
- *No adultery:* The sanctity of marriage, the home, human sexuality
- *No stealing:* Respect for property
- *No false witness:* Respect for reputation; good name; honesty
- *Avoid coveting:* Contentment

The Tabernacle. God in their Midst (Exodus 25.1-40.28)

Brueggemann says that "hosting the Holy One is not a small, trivial, or casual undertaking. And therefore the practice of symmetry, order, discipline, and beauty is essential to the reality of God's presence in Israel."[41] In chapters 25-31, God shows Moses the plan, material, and the designs for building the Tabernacle. He carries out his assignment in minutest detail. The Tabernacle performed double duty: It was a visible symbol that God's presence was with them, that each person had equal access to him, and it provided Israel a place to worship and make atonement for their breaking of the Covenant stipulations.[42]

Exodus is pivotal to the promises in the past to Abraham, Isaac, Jacob, and Joseph, and to the fulfillment of those promises in the future.

So What?

The Tabernacle is important because it provides a living picture of worshiping God. God gave Israel an optical object lesson to demonstrate his Kingship. It was the building and placement of the Tabernacle within Israel. The Tabernacle, set in the midst of his children, painted a picture

Act 3

Covenant

Learning Objective
Understand the Covenant stage of Israel's history.

BOOK
Leviticus
AUTHOR
Traditionally Moses
AGE WRITTEN
Sometime after the Exodus
AUDIENCE
Those who are redeemed and need to understand their uniqueness
AIM
To call God's people to be holy and distinct when they enter the land of promise
KEY CONCEPTS
Holiness
KEY LESSONS
To be holy is not an option, it is a command.
GEOGRAPHY
Wilderness

Sacrificial Offerings:
Origin. The beginnings of sacrifice are found in the primitive ages of man and among all the nations of antiquity. Cain and Abel offered sacrifices to God (Gen. 4.3-4)— Cain "of the fruit of the ground" and Abel "of the firstlings of his flock and of their fat portions." Noah expressed his gratitude for deliverance from the Flood by presenting burnt offerings unto the Lord (Gen. 8.20).

Fundamental Idea. The fundamental idea of sacrifices may be gathered partly from their designation and partly from their nature. At the beginning, sacrifices were spontaneous expressions of reverence and gratitude that man felt toward God. It became a substitution to pay for sin by the offering of life (usual metaphor: blood) to secure a continuance of God's favor and mercy.

well-known in the ancient Near East. God in the midst of his children, easily accessible to all his children, was in the Near East tradition that the center of the camp was the place for the King's tent. The picture was easily identifiable to the ancient mindset.

The design of the Tabernacle provided an insight that God was to be understood as a holy God. The inner shrine demonstrated the holiness of God. It was called *a dwelling place* showing God co-dwelling with his people. It was *a tent of meeting* displaying that God does meet his people and reveal himself to them. It was *a tent of testimony*—a reminder that within it was the Covenant that regulated the life of Israel. One moved ever closer to the presence of God going from the outside to the inside. Allegorical attempts have been made to place special meaning on each color, each piece of material, and each fixture in the Tabernacle. This is a carryover from the early church fathers and seems misguided.

About Leviticus: The Book of Holiness

The book of Leviticus encourages the people of God to center their lives around God. It describes how his people are to respond to the presence of God in the midst of their camp. It provides instructions from God about worship and daily living.

Leviticus took its name from the Septuagint (LXX). The duties of the Levitical priesthood are discussed even though the Levites are unmentioned in the book. Because it is often looked upon as a rule book,[43] it often gives the modern reader difficulty. One must always remember that the instructions in Leviticus were given to a redeemed people. It is not a book of works. It is a book for maintenance of relationship with God.

The System of Sacrifices

The first few chapters of Leviticus provide instructions about the
❖ **sacrificial offerings**[44] ❖ that were given to God. The *first* was called *The Burnt Offering.* It was made to atone for sin. It was the only sacrifice in which the whole animal was burnt—a visual of the need for total dedication. The *second* was *The Cereal or Meal Offering.* It was made to secure or retain good will, often an accompaniment to the burnt or peace offering. The *third* was *The Peace Offering.* It was made to render thanks to God. It reestablished fellowship between the sinner and God. It could be a thank offering, a vow offering, or a freewill offering. The *fourth* was *The Sin Offering.* It was made to atone for a specific sin. It allowed the offending person to receive forgiveness. When offense against God had occurred, this offering was given. The *fifth* offering was *The Guilt or Trespass Offering.* It was made to atone for sin and required restitution. This was offered after an offense toward some social transgression including person or property.

The modern reader is often repulsed by the amount of shed blood which is written about in this book. The *shedding of blood* or the violent death of a sacrifice is the idea which finds its completeness in Jesus. Without an understanding of Leviticus, the death of Jesus would remain a riddle. The sacrificial system was a daily occurrence in the life of Israel. It was a daily reminder of how sin cuts a person off from God.

The Worship Calendar

Israel's yearly calendar for worship included: Sabbath, Passover, Firstfruits, The Feast of Weeks or Pentecost, The Feast of Trumpets, The Day of Atonement, The Feast of Tabernacles, The Sabbatical Year, and the Year of Jubilee. What if Christian churches found the meaning of Israel's worship calendar and added them to their worship cycle? What would that be like?

So What?

Behind all the laws and rituals in Leviticus is the central theme of the holiness of God (11.45; 18.2, 4, 5; 19.2-4, 10; 20.7; 20.26).[45] To be *holy* meant *to be set apart* for a special purpose. This was Israel's job. God had set them aside for his purpose of bringing a blessing to all nations, to be a light to the world, to be a guide for what it meant to be truly human. Leviticus sets up the guidelines for living in his Story and returning to his Story when a community or an individual fails. There were four things set apart as holy for Israel:

1. The Tabernacle as a place to worship God
2. The rituals as a means to worship God
3. The priests as facilitators to help worship God
4. The Sabbath, feasts, Sabbatical, and Jubilee years as times to worship God

Israel could walk with God through their participation in the sacrificial system established by God. These sacrifices rendered a person holy because he or she accepted the atoning benefits of the sacrificed animal.

 ### Scene 4. Journey to the Promised Land (Numbers 10.11–Deuteronomy 34.12)

The storyline picks back up at Numbers 10.11 as Israel leaves Sinai on their journey toward the land God had promised them.

About Numbers: The Wilderness Years

In the Wilderness was the name of the book of Numbers for the Jew. The name Numbers is derived from the two instances in the book in which two censuses are recorded, which were the gathering of Israel's army (1, 26). The first numbering occurred as they entered Canaan; the second was nearly forty years later. The number offered in the text was the number of males over twenty years of age who were eligible for military duty. There is an open debate over the numbers provided in the book of Numbers.[46] However one solves the problem, the point remains that there was a considerable increase in the number of Abraham's descendants which entered Egypt some four hundred years before, as recorded at the conclusion of the book of Genesis, and the number given in this book. The importance of the book is that it provides the narrative transition from the generation that left Egypt and rebelled against God after crossing the Sea of Reeds and the new generation who are on their way to the land that God promised.[47] Numbers is yet another recital, not unlike Joshua 24, which we will visit later, of the acts of God, a complex story of "unfaithfulness, rebellion, apostasy, and frustration, set against the background of God's faithfulness, presence, provision and forbearance."[48]

Covenant

Learning Objective
Understand the Covenant stage of Israel's history.

QUESTIONS
How do the past feasts inform your present worship of God? Should followers of Jesus celebrate the Jewish feasts?

BOOK
Numbers
AUTHOR
Traditionally Moses
AGE WRITTEN
Sometime after the Exodus
AUDIENCE
Those who need to understand how to follow God.
AIM
To teach that God will judge his children when they disobey.
KEY CONCEPTS
Wandering
KEY LESSONS
Obedience will bring blessing, disobedience will bring judgment.
GEOGRAPHY
Wilderness
Kadesh-barnea
Moab

Numbers 10.11-Deuteronomy 34.12. TBB. 176-256.

Act 3

Covenant

Learning Objective
Understand the Covenant stage of Israel's history.

So What?

The book of Numbers demonstrates that in the face of rebellion, God still keeps his promises and provides for his children. He had made Covenant with them and he was faithful to that Covenant. We can see both the grace and judgment of God in this book, as God continued to woo Israel to have relationship with him. God judged a generation because they rejected his equipment to conquer the land (10.11-36), because of their constant desire to go back to Egypt (11.1-35). They rejected the leadership of Moses (12.1-15), who God had chosen to lead them to the land. They ultimately rejected the conquest of the promised land (12.16-14.45). These actions caused Israel to wander in the desert (15.1-22.1) until the disbelieving generation was dead.

In addition to these failures, there were other external and internal obstacles: the external threat of the curses of Balaam (22.2-24.25) and the internal threat of Israel's idolatry and immorality (25.1-18). There will always be external and internal obstacles which try to distract us from continuing to live in God's EPIC Adventure.

About Deuteronomy: The Covenant Restated

Deuteronomy is the fifth book of the Pentateuch and the most influential.[49] The name in our Bible means "second law." The Law was first given to Moses at Mt. Sinai and recorded in Exodus. Deuteronomy is the second record of the Law given to a new generation so that they could hear and commit to it. It is a collection of sermons by Moses which were given to Israel before his death.

Forty years before, Moses had led a generation of Israelite slaves out of Egypt. That generation disobeyed God on route to the land of promise and died in the wilderness. Now on the banks of the Jordan, Moses presented this new generation an opportunity to make Covenant with God and receive his blessings.

Deuteronomy follows the outline of a Lord-Servant Treaty:[50]

The Preamble 1.1-5: This section sets the context of the treaty.

The Historical Prologue 1.6-3.29: The history of God and his people are discussed in this section.

Stipulations

Basic Stipulations 4.1-40; 5.1-11.32: The basic stipulations which govern the relationship between God and Israel are stated.

Detailed Stipulations 12.1-26.19: Specific stipulations are explained.

Instructions about Reading 27.1-26: This section states how often the treaty should be read to the people as a reminder of their relationship with God.

Blessings 28.1-14: The blessings, which occur when the stipulations are kept, are given.

Curses 28.15-68: The curses, which occur when the stipulations are broken, are stated.

Provision for Continuing Treaty 31.1-34.12: A review and summary of the treaty is supplied.

God is powerful in the eyes of this new generation (6.4; 35.10; 14, 17). His power demonstrated in the Exodus suggested that the future of Israel was secure. The narrative has moved along from the creation of the earth

BOOK
Deuteronomy

AUTHOR
Traditionally Moses

AGE WRITTEN
Sometime after the Exodus

AUDIENCE
Those who are about to face a spiritual challenge

AIM
To help a second generation understand how not to make the same mistakes as their fathers and mothers.

KEY CONCEPTS
Restatement of the Covenant

KEY LESSONS
We obey because we are God's child, not in order to become his child.

GEOGRAPHY
Moab

(Gen. 1) to the conquest of the land (to follow in Joshua).[51] God, the creator of all lands, was about to fulfill the promise of the land given so many generations before to their forefather Abraham. This new generation was called to be loyal to the Covenant given to their fathers at Mount Sinai.

It is a warm and touching book in which we see and hear Moses for the last time. His great legacy outlasted the pages that tell of his last instructions and life events.

Covenant

Learning Objective
Understand the Covenant
stage of Israel's history.

Reading the StoryLine

Here is the storyline for the stories of Israel's journey to the Land of Promise.

Wilderness Journey: Numbers 10.11-21.20

Numbers 10.11-Deuteronomy
34.12. TBB. 176-256.

- Leaving Sinai and Complaining: Numbers 10.11-11.35
- God's Punishment of Miriam and Aaron: Numbers 12.1-16
- Kadesh Rebellion: Numbers 13.1-14.45
  [Regulations: Numbers 15.1-36]
- Korah's Revolt: Numbers 15.37-16.50
- Aaron: Numbers 17.1-18.32
- The Red Heifer: Numbers 19.1-22
- Kadesh Rebellion: Numbers 20.1-21
- Aaron's Death, Complaining, Arrival at Moab: Numbers 20.22-21.20

Victory in Moab: Numbers 21.21-Deut. 3.29

- From Sihon to Og: Numbers 21.21-Deut. 3.29
  [Obey God: Deuteronomy 4-11 An Exhortation to Israel to obey God]
  [Various Stipulations: Deuteronomy 12-26 Stipulations to keep in the new land]

Moses' Final Words: Deuteronomy 27-34

- Moses gives final instructions: Deuteronomy 29.1-29
- Turn to the Lord: Deuteronomy 30.1-20
- Joshua and the twelve tribes: Deuteronomy 31.1-33.29
- The Death of Moses: Deuteronomy 34.1-12

So What?

Deuteronomy demonstrates what living in God's Story (Covenant life with God) is like. The Covenant was grounded in the love of God. It was never meant to be taken as a way in which the nation or an individual could enter into God's Story. God had moved in a historical act and delivered his children from their bondage into freedom. If they would continue to live in his Story, i.e., keep his commands, things would go well with them. If not, Deuteronomy 28.15ff. tells that part of the story.

Deuteronomy also provides the concept that new generations have to hear the same story told in a different way.[52]

A READING GUIDE FOR THE PENTATEUCH

The following reading guide is designed to help you read through the Pentateuch by understanding which sections are narrative and which sections are instruction. This does not infer that there is no teaching value in the narrative sections. It is only a guide to help you see the flow of the Story and, thereby, have a clearer pattern by which to read.

Act 3

Covenant

Learning Objective
Understand the Covenant
stage of Israel's history.

Dictionary Articles
Read the following
Dictionary Articles in *New
Bible Dictionary.*
  Exodus
  Exodus, Book of
  Egypt
  Moses
  Law, I
  Tabernacle
  Leviticus, Book of
  Worship
  Sacrifice and Offering, I
  Atonement, Day of
  Numbers, Book of
  Wilderness of Wandering
  Deuteronomy, Book of

Narrative
  Ur: Genesis 11.27-32
Narrative
  Haran: Genesis 12.1-3
Narrative
  Canaan: Genesis 12-50 (Abraham, Isaac, Jacob, Joseph)
Narrative
  Egypt: Exodus 1.1-19.1 (The Exodus)
Instruction
  Mt. Sinai
    Fellowship With God: Exodus 19.2-24.18 (Covenant)
    Worship Of God: Exodus 25-40 (Tabernacle)
    Way To God: Leviticus 1-17
    Walking With God: Leviticus 18-27
    Taught By Moses: Numbers 1.1-10.10
Narrative
  Kadesh-barnea
    Wandering: Numbers 10.11-21.35
    On to Moab: Numbers 22.1-36.13 (Preparation for Conquest)
Instruction
  At Moab
    The Giving Of The Second Law: Deuteronomy

An Interlude. Job: A Theodic Protest (Job 1-42)

About Job: Why Is There Human Suffering?

In the Protestant canonical form of Scripture, Job is listed in the Poetry Books. We have included it here at the end of Deuteronomy because of its contrast with Deuteronomic thought. Job is a part of the tradition of Wisdom Literature (see below) in the Old Testament. It is the antithesis of the Covenant. Could it be that Job balances out the Covenant and begins to answer the question of why do righteous people suffer?[53]

The book of Job is a literary showpiece that asks the haunting question about the meaning of human suffering and makes suggestions concerning how those who suffer should conduct themselves when misfortune descends mercilessly upon them. The book is a dialogue between Job and three of his friends. Its purpose is to help its reader understand that life is not always fair.

Job was a righteous man (1.1) who was tested and lost everything. His loss was seen by his wife and friends as a curse from God because of sin. Job does not view his circumstances the same way as do his wife and friends. With some passion about his unfair treatment, he complains and protests to God. The main purpose of the book is to affirm the sovereignty of God. No solution suitable for the Western mind is provided concerning suffering except that suffering is a sovereign gift from God, given for his purposes, on whom he chooses to bestow it. This is somewhat of a foreign thought to the mind of modern humankind. The following two important concepts are useful to help you in your journey through Job.

Wisdom Literature

Wisdom Literature is often the most unfamiliar genre of literature to the modern reader of Scripture. Wisdom for the Old Testament person

Job

BOOK
Job
AUTHOR
Unknown
AGE WRITTEN
Unknown (Possibly during
the Patriarchal Period)
AUDIENCE
Those who are going
through suffering for
no apparent reason.
AIM
To provide wisdom for the
times
when trials in life appear.
KEY CONCEPT
The Sovereignty of God
KEY LESSONS
The proper response to
God during times of
suffering is worship.
GEOGRAPHY
Unknown

was the discipline of applying to his or her life the truth that experience had taught. Wisdom occurred when an Old Testament person thought and acted according to the truth as he or she had learned it through their own experience.

Old Testament Wisdom Literature does not touch all areas of life, only selected ones. This genre is made up of three Old Testament books: Job, Proverbs, and Ecclesiastes with additional individual Psalms (19, 37, 73, 104, 107, 147, 148). Proverbs dealt with everyday life from family and social relationships to business affairs. Ecclesiastes considered the ultimate value of life and concluded that without a relationship with God, life is meaningless. Job demonstrates that suffering is a divine gift given from God. The New Testament representative of this genre of literature is James.

Satan

The word *satan* without the definite article in the Old Testament is a general word that can be defined as adversary or opponent (Num. 22.22; 1 Sam. 29.4; 1 Kings 11.14). When the definite article is used with the word, it becomes a proper name (Job 1-2; Zech. 3.1-2). The one exception to the above is 1 Chronicles 21.1 where the proper name appears without the definite article. It is only when you open the pages of the New Testament that the full understanding of an evil and personal devil is developed. We have read this character back into the story of creation and other stories as well. The theology of *satan* is undeveloped in the Old Testament. The New Testament describes Satan with various terms such as: slanderer, accuser, enemy, one who leads astray, the father of lies, the god of this age, a murderer, the tempter, etc. The various names provide the New Testament reader with some indication of the character of Satan. He is a personal being in cosmic conflict with the Kingdom of God.

So What?

There are at least three theological points to be considered in Job.

God's Freedom

Everyone in Job, including Job, was awestruck by God's freedom. God was not bound by human agendas or human concepts of him. He can work within the bounds of Deuteronomic Code or transcend those concepts as he does in the book of Job. In short, God can be God and do what he wants to when he wants to.

Suffering

The book of Job examines the premise of retribution represented by Eliphaz, Bildad, and Zophar which is: If you sin, then you will suffer. Scripture does work on that premise with the Deuteronomic Code. But these friends go beyond the generally true proposition that sin leads to suffering. They reversed the cause and effect to reach a belief that said, "If you suffer, then you have sinned." For them all suffering was explained by sin. It was the telltale sign: Job was suffering, therefore he had sinned. The book of Job is the corrective against this type of faulty reasoning. Job does not explain all the reasons for suffering in the world; it does, however, reject the reasoning that all suffering is caused by sin. One could say that living in the wrong story often causes one useless suffering.

Act 3

Job

The reader of Job must be struck with the understanding that God will work to bring about good through suffering. Job did not suffer in silence. He argued with his friends and complained to God constantly. Through all of this, Job remained loyal to God. One in the midst of suffering can surely be strengthened by Job. Complaining to God in suffering is not a sign of weakness on the complainer's part. As a matter of fact, complaining was a part of the worship of Israel, both as a community and as an individual.

Satan's Testing

Here is an early attempt to understand evil. There is every indication that the *satan's* intentions are harmful. He is the representative of conflict and ill will. He has a purpose in mind which is contrary to God's, and his desires are hostile to Job's welfare. In Job, there is an anticipation of Satan in the New Testament Story, but it is not full blown in the Old Testament.

Job's Placement in the Story

Some scholars think that Job is a book reflecting the patriarchal period.[54] Its presence in the canon has not been debated, but its location has. The LXX placed it at the end of the Old Testament following Ecclesiastes, while the ❖ Syriac Bible ❖ inserts the book between the Pentateuch and Joshua[55] as we have followed here.

BOOK READING GUIDE: JOB

Here is a reading guide to the Job story.

📖 **Job Tested 1.1-2.13**
Job was introduced as having a wonderful relationship with God and as a wealthy man. He was described by God as blameless and upright (1.1). God granted permission for Satan to test Job. He lost his material goods and family. His wife told him to curse God and die. These two chapters were written in a narrative style.

📖 **Oration of Friends 3.1-42.6**
The friends of Job come to comfort him in his loss. Elphaz accused him of having hidden guilt. Zophar accused him of lying and being a hypocrite. Bildad reminded Job about the punishment of those who are wicked. Job responded to each man. Elihu gave a number of speeches and God responded. These chapters were written in Hebrew Poetry which must be kept in mind when reading.

📖 **Blessed More Than Beginning 42.7-17**
God was faithful to Job and gave him a new family and his material goods were restored. This section, like the first, was written in a narrative style.

Syriac Bible. Often called the Peshitta, it was the standard Bible of the Syriac-speaking churches by the early fifth century.

Job 1-42. TBB. 1197-1254.

Dictionary Articles
Read the following Dictionary Articles in *New Bible Dictionary.*
　Wisdom Literature
　Job
　Job, Book of

Conquest

Scene 5. The Conquest Stage (Joshua 1-24)

About Joshua: The Book of Conquest

Moses' death marks a transition from Deuteronomy to Joshua.[56] The closing scenes of Deuteronomy found Israel encamped in the Plains of Moab waiting for God's command to enter the land he had promised.

Scholars believe that the conquest began about 1240 B.C. (the late date[57] of the conquering of Canaan). It is also held that the stories in Joshua were written during Samuel's lifetime (ca. 1045 B.C.). Joshua was born in Egypt during the captivity period of the Jews. Moses chose him as a potential leader during the Exodus and wandering period. Chosen as one of the twelve spies sent from Kadesh-barnea to investigate Canaan, he was one of two which gave a favorable report.

On the way to the land promised to Israel by God, a whole generation spent their life in the wilderness between Sinai and Canaan.[58] Wilderness does not have a negative image in the Old Testament. It is a place that provides pasturage for sheep but doesn't support much human life. It is a place you go if you want to be alone.[59] Joshua is more than a shift of leadership to a younger from an older. It is a leap from the Torah to the first book of the Former Prophets, which is a group of books that are preoccupied with the giving and inhabiting of the land.[60]

When the book was written,[61] Israel was living in a period of success and prosperity, at rest in the land which God had given them. The writing of the book allowed God to keep alive the memories of what he had accomplished for them in their past. Past events made it quite clear that Israel was prone to forget the saving acts of God during times of prosperity.

A Short Excursus: War

What occurred in Joshua was a continuation of the salvation history which began in Genesis 11.27 at the call of Abraham. Deuteronomy provided the concepts under which Israel was to engage in battle in a holy war (Deut. 7.1-26; 20.1-20, 21.10-14; 25.17-19). The book of Joshua demonstrated in action the concepts of holy war in the conquest of Jericho and Ai.[62] As in all the Old Testament, we find God breaking into history to bring his rule, a Kingdom motif. It is easy to believe that God created all the world. What is difficult for the Westerner is to believe that God can choose to give a certain piece of land to his chosen people. The point of the sovereignty of God is missed. The promised land was a land taken over by those who had given themselves to false gods. The Kingdom of God was advancing. God's Kingdom would ultimately disinherit anyone who opposed its advancement. The conquest of Canaan was God's holy war carried out by his chosen people at a specific time in salvation history. The mission to conquer Canaan should be understood as a limited mission for God's people. War, on the other hand, for the sake of taking something by means of force which cannot be gained by a normal relationship, has been and still remains the curse of fallen humankind.

There are many people who oppose Scripture because of the Old Testament's portrayal of war and slaughter (Joshua 6.21). They ask, "How can God who is pictured as love send his people into war with others of his creation?" We must keep at least two ideas in mind when

Learning Objective
Understand the Conquest stage of Israel's history.

BOOK
Joshua

AUTHOR
Unknown, Traditionally Joshua

AGE WRITTEN
Sometime after the Conquest

AIM
To teach the people of God to trust God to give them what he promised.

AUDIENCE
Those who need to understand success of spiritual battles

KEY CONCEPTS
Orbit

KEY LESSONS
The process of learning to obey God

GEOGRAPHY
Israel ✪ South ✪ North

Act 3

Conquest

Learning Objective
Understand the Conquest stage of Israel's history.

dealing with this subject. *First*, God gave these nations many years, hundreds actually, to repent (Gen. 15.16-21). They snubbed God and refused to turn from their obscene ways. A review of Leviticus 18 will demonstrate what their lifestyle and religious worship included. Any person falling short of God's divine plan could be rescued because of their faith. Rahab, in Joshua, serves as a model of God's willingness to redeem those outside the chosen race. *Second*, the city of Jericho had been forewarned (Joshua 2.8-13). We simply do not understand the bigger picture of God as he carries out his divine purpose for salvation in the history of humankind. It does appear that he sometimes uses war to chasten and even destroy those who choose to forget him. He may have used this avenue to punish the wicked nations for their sins while at the same time protecting his people from their evil ways.

Reading the StoryLine

Joshua 1-24. TBB. 261-289.

This book tells the story of the conquest of the land under the leadership of Joshua.[63]

- Joshua becomes Israel's Leader: Joshua 1.1-18
- Rahab hides spies: Joshua 2.1-24
- Crossing into the Promised Land: Joshua 3.1-5.12
- Walls of Jericho fall down: Joshua 5.13-6.27
- Achan's Sin: Joshua 7.1-8.29
- Covenant and Deception: Joshua 8.30-9.27
- War in Canaan: Joshua 10.1-11.23
  [List of conquered kings: Joshua 12.1-24]
- God's challenge to Joshua: Joshua 13.1-7
  [Allocation of Land: Joshua 13.8-22.34]
- Me and my house: Joshua 23.1-24.33

So What?

The book of Joshua provides evidence that God is serious about the Covenant he made with Israel. A way of thinking about this is that God is serious about Israel living in the Story he was creating for them. When Israel lives in the Story, obeys the Covenant, God blesses them with victory at Jericho (Joshua 5-6). When they choose to rebel and disobey, i.e., live in a different story of their own choosing, he brings them defeat at Ai (Joshua 7-8).

The renewal of Covenant by Joshua at the end of the book demonstrates the continuing need for Israel to have relationship with their God (24.1ff.). The book of Joshua is a positive account of how the Covenant works, with minor exceptions like Ai. At the conclusion of the book, Joshua recites for Israel what God had done and then calls them to recommitment based on the actions of a loving Covenant God.

Orbit

Learning Objective
Comprehend the Judges stage of Israel's history.

Scene 6. The Judges Stage (Judges 1-24; Ruth 1-4)

The word which is often translated *judge* in the Old Testament does not always have a clear meaning. It conjures a picture in this present century of a person seated behind an elevated desk wearing a black robe swinging a gavel. On each occasion in the book of Judges, as Israel broke Covenant stipulations, God raised up a judge, not a legal expert, but a charismatic military leader who was empowered by God to fight against an enemy.

Orbit

Learning Objective
Comprehend the Judges
stage of Israel's history.

BOOK
Judges
AUTHOR
Unknown, Traditionally
Joshua
AGE WRITTEN
Sometime after the
Conquest
AIM
To teach the people of
God to trust God to give
them what he promised.
AUDIENCE
Those who need to
understand
success of spiritual battles
KEY CONCEPTS
Conquest
KEY LESSONS
The process of learning to
obey God
GEOGRAPHY
Israel ⊕ South ⊕ North

About Judges: A Dark Period of History

Judges describes the occupation of the Promised Land as undertaken by individual tribes or sometimes one tribe working with another[64] and includes the interval of time when the tribes of Israel, having entered the Promised Land, are learning to live together as well as living with their neighbors while in the midst of hostile nations on their borders.[65] We must think of Israel during this period of time as a loosely bound group of tribes which were held together by the Covenant made with God. It was a theocracy. God was king. The first part of Judges pictures a cycle through which the tribes would *orbit* as they broke Covenant with God. The phrase "did evil in the eyes of the Lord" might be understood as a technical phrase which means "breaking Covenant." Several of the dates of the Judges overlap[66] because often more than one tribe would be in the cycle at the same time. What the book of Judges presents for its readers is a concept that was developing in the history of Israel about what would happen to them if they did not keep the stipulations of the Covenant.[67]

There is a pattern to Israel's failures that appears several times:

O pposition to God
R etribution of God
B eseechment to God
I mpartation of Deliverance by God
T ranquility with God

So What?

Judges may be a demonstration of what occurs when there is no recital and recommitment in each generation as seen at the end of Joshua (Joshua 24). Each generation must remember what God has done and recommit to his faithfulness. It also points toward the concept that when one lives in God's EPIC Adventure, i.e., keeps his Covenant, God is pleased. When one chooses a different story to live in, well, things can get out of hand.

Reading the StoryLine

Judges 1-24. TBB: 291-319.

📖 **Introduction 1.1-2.10**
This segment describes Israel immediately after Joshua's death.

📖 **The Judges 2.11-16.31**
These chapters comprise the main body of the book, which gives its reader the exposé of Israel as they cycle through their *orbit* pattern. Twelve Judges are recognized in this section, but only six stories are told in some detail.

Othniel 3.7-11: Othniel was the first to be called to the position of judge in approximately 1200 B.C. God gave him victory over Mesopotamia.

Ehud 3.12-30: Ehud rose to leadership about 1170 B.C. as a leader in Transjordan and Central Palestine. God gave him victory over Eglon of Moab.

Shamagar 3.31: Shamagar became leader in 1150 B.C. in the Palestine Plain. God gave him victory over the Philistines.

Deborah with Barak 4.1-5.31: Deborah and Barak's leadership occurred around 1125 B.C. in Central Palestine and Galilee. God gave them victory over Jabin and Sisera. Attention should be drawn that even in an ancient patriarchal

Act 3

Orbit

Learning Objective
Comprehend the Judges
stage of Israel's history.

society, God selected a woman to conquer an enemy. The song of Deborah recorded in Judges is one of the oldest ancient worship pieces in the Old Testament.

Gideon 6.1-8.35: Gideon was leader around 1100 B.C. in Transjordan and Central Palestine. God gave him victory over the Midianites and Amalekites.

Abimelech 9.1-57: Some scholars do not consider Abimelech a judge but the first shadow of kingship.

Tola 10.1-2: Tola was leader in Central Palestine. There are only two verses which describe the rule of Tola. Beyond this brief mention, we know nothing else about him.

Jair 10.3-5: Jair was the leader in Transjordan. Only three verses tell of his judgeship.

Jephthan 10.6-12.7: Jephthan was leader in Transjordan about 1070 B.C. God gave him victory over the Ammonites.

Ibzan 12.8-10: Ibzan was leader in Southern Palestine. He is only known by these three verses recorded about him.

Elon 12.11-12: Elon was leader of Northern Palestine. Only two verses give information about his leadership.

Abdon 12.13-15: Abdon was the leader in Central Palestine with only three verses given about his rule.

Samson 13.1-16.31: Samson is probably the best known of all the Old Testament judges. His rule was in the plain of the Philistines about 1070 B.C. God gave him victory over the Philistines at the cost of his life.

Appendix 17.1-21.25

The stories told in this segment of Judges are tales which occurred during the time the judges were ruling. Israel had abandoned the Covenant relationship with God as the stories in this section note. The book closes with the sad picture that "everyone did as he saw fit." Without the recital and recommitment of their forefathers, they doomed themselves to disaster.

About Ruth: Doing What Is Right in Dark Times

The book of Ruth is a part of the Scrolls under the section called The Writings in the Hebrew Bible. The first words of Ruth invite the reader to read it in association with the Judges.[68] The story of Ruth is about an Israelite family who moves from Israel to Moab. All the males in the family die leaving the mother and two daughters-in-law. Ruth, one daughter-in-law, follows her mother-in-law, Naomi, back to Israel. This action in the story demonstrates the welcoming of those who are not Israelites into the Covenant.[69] In the story, she meets and marries Boaz and becomes a direct ancestor of King David (Ruth 4.17b).

So What?

The story demonstrates that in the midst of the darkest part of Israel's history (Judges), individual families can make a choice to keep the Covenant, i.e., live in God's Story rather than break the Covenant, that is live in another story of one's own choosing. It is a contrast between two stories.

BOOK
Ruth
AUTHOR
Unknown, Rabbinic
Tradition: Samuel
AGE WRITTEN
During the United
Kingdom
AIM
To demonstrate how God
is faithful to those who are
faithful in the midst of an
unfaithful society
AUDIENCE
Those who need a positive
role model of
the faithfulness of God
KEY CONCEPT
Salvation History
KEY LESSONS
God blesses faithfulness

One strong theological perception which the story of Ruth conveys is the perception of God as one who gives guidance to his people. In this little story, guidance is not viewed through the often supernatural means of which other Old Testament books are full. Such things as dreams, angelic visitations, visions, prophets, and voices from heaven are not seen. God works behind the scenes through the ordinary events of history.

Learning Objective
Comprehend the Judges stage of Israel's history.

 BOOK READING GUIDE: RUTH

This is a reading guide for the book of Ruth.

Ruth 1-4. TBB. 321-327.

📖 **Resolve of Ruth 1.1-22**
In the period of the judges, Elimelech, a Jew, migrates to another country with Naomi, his wife, and their two sons. His sons marry foreign women. Both he and his sons die. Naomi decides to return to her homeland, and Ruth, one of her daughters-in-law, determined to return with her mother-in-law. A story of true conversion.

📖 **Utility of Ruth 2.1-23**
Ruth worked daily in the fields of Boaz. Boaz demonstrated kindness to Ruth by leaving the corners of his fields for her to harvest.

📖 **Tenderness of Boaz 3.1-18**
Naomi planned for Ruth to find fulfillment in life through the Deuteronomic law called *levirate marriage*.

📖 **Husband and Wife 4.1-22**
Ruth and Boaz are married. The lineage of David continued through their marriage with the birth of their son Obed.

Dictionary Articles
Read the following Dictionary Articles in *New Bible Dictionary*.
Joshua
Joshua, Book of
Jericho
Promised Land
Canaan, Canaanites
Judges, Judges, Book of
War, I, II, III
Ruth, Ruth, Book of

An Excursus: Psalms

About Psalms: Israel's Worship Book

Psalms is Israel at worship with their God. The Psalms were lyrical poems which were probably set to music. It is the best-loved book of the Old Testament. While Moses was one of the earliest Psalm writers (Psalm 90), the Historical Books of the next scene are where most of the psalms may have come into existence as Israel was at worship in the Temple. So, we take a brief break from the Story to share some information about the Psalms.

The title *Psalms* comes from the title of the book in the Septuagint and means *songs*. Psalms, in its completed form, has five separate books, which may have reminded the reader of the five books of Moses. It has been suggested that Psalms 1 and 2 serve as an introduction, while Psalms 146-150 serve as a conclusion. Each of the sections or five books ends with a psalm that completes the overall book while Psalm 150 concludes the whole book of Psalms.

These 150 psalms were written over a 600 year period. There are seventy-three (73) psalms that are ascribed to David, thirty (30) which were written by other authors like Solomon, Asaph, Korah, and fifty (50) which are anonymous.[70]

C. S. Lewis once said, "The Psalms must be read as poems; as lyrics, with all the licenses and all the formalities, the hyperboles, the emotional rather than the logical connections, which are proper to lyric poetry."[71] Psalms as lyric poems were sung by Israel. The thoughts and feelings of a single writer are being expressed. Four characteristics of lyric poetry should be noted:

Psalms

BOOK
Psalms
AUTHOR
David, Solomon, Asaph, Moses and Anonymous
AGE WRITTEN
From Moses to the end of the OT period
AUDIENCE
Those who need to experience God, whether traumatized or jubilant.
AIM
To provide the worship music for God's children
KEY CONCEPTS
Worship
KEY LESSONS
The God-given ability to worship God during times of peace and prosperity.

Act 3

◆ **Musical:** Lyric poems were sung with the accompaniment of a musical instrument like a lyre.
◆ **Personal:** Lyric poems were spoken to God in the first person.
◆ **Emotional:** Lyric poems used emotive and vivid descriptive words to evoke feelings in the hearer. Some feelings expressed were praise, awe, joy, adoration, depression, and sorrow.
◆ **Brief:** Lyric poems were short and were usually the development of a controlling metaphor such as "The Lord is my shepherd," in Psalm 23.

There are several different kinds of Psalms that have been identified by scholarship. Here is a beginning list: Individual Complaint, Community Complaint; Wisdom, Salvation History, Celebration, and Trust. Knowing about them often helps the reader understand the intent of the psalm better.

So What?

The Psalms were lyric pictures of the relationship of Israel and God. As Israel used psalms in worship, they were provided a profound understanding of their faith. There were summaries of their history (78, 105-106, 136), instructions in piety (1, 119), creation celebrations (8, 9, 104), knowledge of God's judgment (103), and awareness of rulership over all nations (2, 110). The Psalms were also declarations of relationship between Israel and her Lord. Intimacy and awe were combined in her relationship. Through them one learns what God's salvation in its fullness can mean to God's people. The book of Psalms presents a model of intimacy with God. They relate how biblical people related to God in their life experiences.

BOOK READING GUIDE: PSALMS

The Psalter in its final form is divided into five books. They are:

Psalms 1-150. TBB. 923-1094.

Psalms of Adoration 1-41
Primarily written by David, the psalms in this first book consist of his personal experience as the King of Israel. Psalm 1 is an introduction to this collection.

Songs of Admonition 42-72
The psalms in the second book are an anthology written by the Sons of Korah (42-49), David (51-72), and Asaph (50).

Arias of Neglect 73-89
Because there is some reference to the destruction of Jerusalem, some of the psalms in this book may have come from the exile period.

Lyrics of Submission 90-106
The last two books are a collection of miscellaneous poems. They most likely were compiled during the Restoration Period.

Melodies of Excellence 107-150
The last section includes several post-exile psalms in addition to fifteen psalms by David and one by Solomon.

Dictionary Articles
Read the following Dictionary Articles in *New Bible Dictionary*.
Psalms, Book of

United Kingdom

Learning Objective
See the United Kingdom stage of Israel's history.

 ## Scene 7. United Kingdom Stage (1 Samuel 1.1-1 Kings 11.43)

As we enter this part of the Story, we must pause and gain perspective on Israel as the people of God living as a light to the world. At this point in the Story, Israel was not a nation in the sense of having a central government or a standing army. They were a large group of people in smaller tribal groups, a loose confederacy of tribes whose only unity was that they worshiped one God who had called them to be lights to the world and celebrated together on an annual basis. Each tribe was independent of the other tribes but interdependent as children of Abraham. There was no organization of any sort within the tribes. There was no gulf between the rich and the poor. There was no lower, middle, or upper class. There was no ruler; therefore, there were no subjects. God was the ruler and the tribes covenanted to him to be his loyal servants. The Ark of the Covenant, which was the hub for the tribes, moved from place to place finally coming to rest at Shiloh. The association of tribes was a brotherhood/sisterhood, a fellowship that shared a similar interest, their Covenant with God to be his people for the sake of the world.[72] What if the church followed that pattern? How would that change how we operate in the world for its sake?

About the Book of Samuel: Samuel, Saul, and David

The Book of Samuel (1 and 2 Samuel) is one book and is the third element of the Former Prophets.[73] With the translation of the Septuagint (LXX) the two books were separated. It is a book that transitions the story of God's people from a loosely knit[74] group of tribes to the beginning of nationhood, from theocracy to monarchy.[75] It moves from the period of the judges to a monarchy that was hereditary and covers the story of three individuals. First, Samuel, who was Israel's last Judge; then Saul, Israel's first King; and last, David, the founder of a dynasty that would last for three centuries.

So What?

The Kingdom of Israel was God's Kingdom (I Samuel 12.1-25). To have a kingdom meant to have a king and the success of the king was dependent on his obedience to God. The failure of Saul to obey God led to his rejection as king. The repentance for sin by David led to the establishment of the line of David forever. Obedience to the Covenant stipulations continued to dominate the storyline in Samuel. Saul disobeyed, he found God's wrath; David obeyed, he found God's grace. The Davidic covenant is central to these two books. God promised David that his descendants would rule over an everlasting kingdom (7.12-16).

About Kings: United and Divided Kingdom

The Book of Kings (1 and 2 Kings) is also one book and is the fourth element of the Former Prophets.[76] Its stories include Solomon, the split of Israel into the Northern and Southern Kingdoms, the kings of both kingdoms, several prophets within the storyline, and then some of the written prophets who are not in the narrative storyline.

Several hundred years of Jewish history is recorded in the books of 1 and 2 Kings. The beginning chapters record yet another transition: from David to Solomon. Solomon becomes known for his wisdom and Israel believes she sits on the pinnacle of her history. But at the death of Solomon, Israel divides back into the Northern and Southern Kingdoms which were a part of their history prior to and during the life of King Saul. Ten tribes composed the Northern Kingdom which was referred to as Israel. Two tribes composed the Southern Kingdom which was called Judah. The official split came in 931 B.C. Israel, the Northern Kingdom, only lasted for 209 years, from 931 B.C. to 722 B.C. The Southern Kingdom lasted 345 years, from 931 B.C. to 586 B.C. There were twenty kings in each of the kingdoms over their active years. The kings of the

BOOK
Samuel
AUTHORS
Samuel, Nathan, Gad
AGE WRITTEN
During the Divided Kingdom
AIM
To demonstrate that God chooses leaders
AUDIENCE
Anyone living in a time of trouble who wants to understand how God works in history
KEY CONCEPTS
Transition
KEY LESSONS
Learning to live in the pressure of transitions
GEOGRAPHY
Israel

BOOK
KIngs
AUTHOR
Rabbinic Tradition: Jeremiah
AGE WRITTEN
Sometime during the Exile
AIM
To provide an explanation to Israel for why they were in Exile
AUDIENCE
To those who have sinned and are experiencing the discipline of God
KEY CONCEPTS
United Kingdom, Divided Kingdom, The Exile
KEY LESSONS
Life should be ruled by the King, not by a committee
GEOGRAPHY
Israel ⟴ Northern and Southern Kingdoms

Act 3

United Kingdom

Learning Objective
See the United Kingdom
stage of Israel's history.

North were not in the lineage of David, whereas all the kings of the South were in David's lineage. Judah was held captive for 46 years from 586 B.C. to 538 B.C. This period is called the Exile. The period called Restoration occurred when Judah was allowed to return from captivity by the decree of Cyrus of the Persian Empire. This period only lasted for 135 years from 538 B.C. to 404 B.C. There were approximately 400 years of time which lapsed before the birth of Jesus in 5 or 4 B.C. Second Temple Judaism is another way of referring to this period, i.e., the period when the second temple stood (following Solomon's first temple): 515 B.C. – A.D. 70.

Should Israel have a king like all the other nations? In one sense, the choice to have a king was rebellion against God. In another sense, a king was a gift from a loving God to keep his wayward people from going totally astray.[77]

So What?

Israel's vocation, to be God's means of blessing the whole world, was passed from the nation to an individual in this section of the Story. This is the profound move by God to move toward the coming king who would become what Israel failed to become: the light of the world.

The keeping of Covenant or living in God's EPIC Adventure finds a continued central place in Kings, as we read the story of Solomon and the last of the United Kingdom and witness the pitiful story of the Divided Kingdom, both North and South.

The habitual breaking of the Covenant caused the Northern Kingdom to go completely out of existence. The Southern Kingdom only lasted a few years longer, but because of God's promise to David, it was not only taken into captivity but restored. However, restoration was only for a brief time.

The disasters, which struck the Northern and Southern Kingdoms, are not an indication that God had forsaken Israel and Judah in a time of need. Rather, it was evidence that God was faithful to the Covenant he had made with Israel which gave promise of both blessings and curses. First and Second Kings is a prophetic interpretation of how each of the kings affected the spiritual decline of Israel. The theological perspective provided by the author cautioned against idolatry and encouraged commitment (1 Kings 8.33-34; 14.14-16).

Reading the StoryLine

Below is an outline of the storyline within this section with additional material noted within the storyline, which includes the placement of some of the Psalms of David. No attempt has been made to place all the Psalms in chronological order in this Act.

Samuel (1 Samuel 1-7)

Samuel may be the greatest Old Testament figure in the storyline since Moses. He plays a central role in the significant transition from tribalness to monarchy. He was regarded as the last judge of Israel and the first prophet of Israel (3.20). He was the conduit through which the establishment of the kingship occurred, although at odds with the people of Israel who wanted to have a human king. He was able to shape Israel's future while still clinging to and insisting on their ancient Covenant practices.[78] He was never corrupted by the power he possessed (12.2-4).

Reading the StoryLine

Here is the storyline to the Samuel stories.

- ☐ The Birth of Samuel (Hannah's Prayer): 1 Samuel 1.1-2.11
- ☐ The Wicked Sons of Eli: 1 Samuel 2.12-36
- ☐ The Call of Samuel by God: 1 Samuel 3.1-4.1a
- ☐ The Ark is Lost: 1 Samuel 4.1b-7.2a
- ☐ Samuel Rules: 1 Samuel 7.2b-17

1 Samuel 1.1-7.17.
TBB.331-338.

Saul (1 Samuel 8-15)

Human king or God as king was a quandary for the Israelites at the conclusion of the period of the judges. The issue was met with mixed emotions. The desire to have a king and a request for such by Israel was in some way a rejection of the rule of God over Israel.[79]

Saul is introduced in 1 Samuel as a handsome youth who was taller than his peers. Saul's (from the tribe of Benjamin, 1 Sam. 10.21) ascent to kingship was accomplished in stages, each of which increased his stature with the people. He was anointed by Samuel in response to God's command after the two had met, while Saul was tracking his father's stray asses. The invasion of the Ammonites put Saul's charismatic gifts to the test, and, finally, Samuel proclaimed him king.[80] Years of influence and authority caused his character to corrode. He was an extremely jealous man who overreacted in decision situations. His kingship fell into disrepute by the end of his life. He resorted to consulting a *witch* and finally committed suicide.

Reading The StoryLine

Here is the storyline to the Saul stories.

- ☐ Saul Becomes King: 1 Samuel 8.1-11.15
- ☐ Samuel says Goodbye: 1 Samuel 12.1-25
- ☐ The Philistines: 1 Samuel 13.1-14.52
- ☐ God Rejects Saul: 1 Samuel 15.1-35

1 Samuel 8.1-15.35.
TBB.338-348.

David (1 Samuel 16.1-1 Kings 2.12)

The story of David is narrated in three sections. *First*, David's ascent to king is told in 1 Samuel 16.1-2 Samuel 5.10. *Second*, David's exercise of king was told in 2 Samuel 5.11-24.25. *Finally*, David's transfer of kingship was told in 1 Kings 1.1-2.46.[81]

His story looks much brighter by contrast with Saul's. He was the youngest son of Jesse of Bethlehem. David's early life of being a shepherd formed his character of strength and courage. He spent many hours soothing the troubled mind of Saul with his gifted musical talents. He was fearless in his battle as the giant slayer. He was the choice of God to replace Saul as the king of Israel.

After the death of Saul, David moved his family to Hebron in Judea and was there crowned king of Judah while Ishbosheth, the son of Saul, was made king of Israel, a finalization of a situation that had long

Act 3

United Kingdom

Learning Objective
See the United Kingdom stage of Israel's history.

existed. Israel and Judah are separate states. After about two years of fighting, Ishbosheth was assassinated, Israel moved to join David, and they anointed him king over all Israel. His life as king succumbed to the political pressures of the day and often he broke Covenant with God. David's contrite spirit and his ability to repent set him apart as a man who had a heart like God.

David's kingship focused on centralization of Israel with two programs. *First,* a census of the people was taken, most likely for taxes and compulsory enrollment of personnel for military service. *Second,* the building of the Temple was planned. The first was accomplished and the latter awaited Solomon. David's domestic problems are well recorded in these stories, and in spite of his sub-humanness or fallenness, God made an everlasting covenant with him (1 Sam. 7).[82]

Reading the StoryLine

Here is the storyline to the David stories.

1 Samuel 1.1-1 Kings 2.12.
TBB.348-403.

☐ David anointed and serves Saul: 1 Samuel 16.1-23
☐ David and Goliath: 1 Samuel 17.1-58
☐ David on the Run (Success and Jealousy): 1 Samuel 18.1-27.12
   [Psalm 11: Possibly set against Samuel 18.8-19.7]
   [Psalm 7: Possibly set against Samuel 18.10-24]
   [Psalm 59: Prayer of David for God's strength as Saul chased him 1 Samuel 19.10-11]
   [Psalm 57: When David had fled from Saul into the cave 1 Samuel 21]
   [Psalm 142: When David had fled from Saul into the cave 1 Samuel 21]
   [Psalm 34: Set against 1 Samuel 21]
   [Psalm 56: Set against 1 Samuel 21.10-15]
   [Psalm 17: Possibly set against 1 Samuel 23.25ff.]
☐ Saul and the spirit of Samuel (the witch at Endor): 1 Samuel 28.1-25
☐ Saul and his sons die: 1 Samuel 29.1-31.13
☐ David, Saul's Killer, Laments: 2 Samuel 1.1-27
☐ David the King of Judah: 2 Samuel 2.1-4.12
☐ David the King of Israel (Philistines and dancing before God: 2 Samuel 5.1-6.23)
   [Psalm 24: Set against 2 Samuel 6 (the restoration of the ark)]
   [Psalm 68: Set against 2 Samuel 6.12-16]
☐ God's covenant with David and his response: 2 Samuel 7.1-29
   [Psalm 2: Rooted in 2 Samuel 7, the promise to David of a supreme name]
☐ David the Warrior: 2 Samuel 8.1-10.19
☐ David and Bathsheba: 2 Samuel 11.1-27
☐ Nathan's Rebuke of David's Sin: 2 Samuel 12.1-31
   [Psalm 51: David's Repentance of the Bathsheba Affair]
☐ The Consequences of David's Sin: 2 Samuel 13.1-20.26
   [Psalm 3: Set against 2 Samuel 15.13-17.24]
   [Psalm 4: Set against David's fleeing from Absalom]
   [Psalm 5: Set against David's fleeing from Absalom]
   [Psalm 6: Set against David's fleeing from Absalom]
   [Psalm 63: Set against David's fleeing from Absalom]
☐ David's Rule Ends: 2 Samuel 21.1-1 Kings 2.12

Solomon (1 Kings 2.13-11.43)

Solomon developed the empire that his father David created. His rule was an era of unparalleled economic and political prosperity. Offered a choice of gifts by God, Solomon wanted a wise and discerning mind to help him in his responsibilities as king. His most lasting and influential legacy was the Jerusalem ❖ **Temple**. ❖ He was astute administratively with a keen finesse toward diplomacy.

History smiled on this period of time with a combination of wealth, centralized government, and relief from enemy attacks which helped complete the Temple project. His foreign policy was mainly based on friendly alliances secured by political marriages. His wives were political trophies from many different nations who served many different gods. He had 700 wives and 300 concubines. He chose to continually break the stipulations of the Covenant, i.e., live in a different story of his own choosing.

He had a formidable army who were the first to use chariotry effectively. He was a trade genius. In his embrace of the religions of his wives, he forsook his Covenant heritage and lost his way as the guardian of Israel's faith.[83]

Learning Objective
See the United Kingdom stage of Israel's history.

Temple. The people of the ancient world believed that deities were attached to specific locations, so they built temples to house their gods. Because the God of Israel did not need a place to be housed which Solomon realized, he built a Temple with a different purpose. The Temple of Solomon was a meeting place between man and God. His Temple was the first of the Jewish Temples. Solomon's Temple was destroyed by the Babylonians and lay in ruins until Ezra and Nehemiah returned to the land in the Restoration Period to rebuild it. When it was built, it was approximately twice the size of the portable Tabernacle which was constructed by the Jews under the guidance of Moses. About 180,000 workers were needed to complete the task of building the Temple. In today's economy, it would have cost several billion dollars.

1 Kings 2.13-11.43.
TBB.403-419.

Reading the StoryLine

Here is the storyline to the Solomon stories.

▢ Solomon Becomes King: 1 Kings 2.13-46
▢ Solomon's Wisdom: 1 Kings 3.1-28
   [Government Overview: 1 Kings 4.1-28]
   [The Wisdom of Solomon: 1 Kings 4.29-34]
▢ The Temple for God: 1 Kings 5.1-9.9
   [Other Activities of Solomon: 1 Kings 9.10-28]
▢ The Queen of Sheba and Great Wealth: 1 Kings 10.1-29
▢ Solomon Breaks Covenant (marriage to foreign women): 1 Kings 11.1-43

[**Proverbs**: A collection of practical bits of Wisdom by Solomon and others.]

About Proverbs: The Book of Wisdom

The title of this book comes from the Hebrew text which is at the beginning of this book: "The proverbs of Solomon, son of David, king of Israel" (1.1). The Hebrew word which is translated *proverb* is *mashal* which usually means *a comparison* or *a likeness*.[84] It is a statement that shows the real nature of one thing by comparing it with something else.

The wisdom of the Proverbs is directed toward helping individuals to live a responsible and productive life on a day-to-day basis. Written as short pithy sayings, these proverbs do not say everything about a certain subject. They rather point a reader toward the wisdom of the truth. Taking these little wisdom sayings with a wooden literalness rather than as guidelines for shaping your daily behavior will cause you to err in gaining the intended wisdom they harness. They must be taken on their own terms. Proverbs was finalized somewhere in the fifth century.[85] Over the centuries, they have provided the reader with godly wisdom about basic patterns for living life. Genuine wisdom is knowing when one of these clever little proverbs is usable in your present circumstance.

BOOK
Proverbs
AUTHOR
Solomon and Company
AGE WRITTEN
During the OT Period
AUDIENCE
Everyone who needs wisdom to avoid the pitfalls of life.
AIM
To provide practical living skills
KEY CONCEPTS
Wisdom
KEY LESSONS
Knowing how to avoid the traps of life and live successfully
GEOGRAPHY
Israel

Act 3

United Kingdom

Learning Objective
See the United Kingdom
stage of Israel's history.

These assembled sage sayings aim at producing wise and good people who know how to live well and work effectively in God's Story.

___

So What?

Proverbs chapters 1-9 is the prism through which we can understand the pithy sayings of 10-31. The contrast between Wisdom and Folly is skillfully drawn in the first nine chapters. The key to the metaphors of Wisdom and Folly is given at 9.3 and 14 with the phrase "highest point of the city." In the ancient Near East, the god of the city lived at the highest point in the city. Both Wisdom and Folly try to gain the attention of naive young men who are walking on the path of life to come and be intimate with them. To be intimate with a god was to worship him or her. The question that is proposed in Proverbs is: Will you follow Wisdom (Yahweh) or Folly (Baal)?

The beginning of the section of small pithy sayings (10.1) illustrates the point. If children bring joy to their parents, then they are wise. With the prism of Proverbs 1-9, that means that they have demonstrated by their behavior that they have embraced wisdom, which means they have committed themselves to God. If, however, children bring grief to their parents, then their behavior suggests that they have turned their allegiance to Folly and decided to follow a pagan deity, thus breaking the first Covenant stipulation.

Once we pass the proverbs through this prism, we can recognize that they are deeply theological. As a matter of fact, they are a matter of life or death.

 BOOK READING GUIDE: PROVERBS

Proverbs 1-31. TBB. 1123-1175.

☐ **Wisdom Should Be Sought 1.1-9.18**
The book begins with an encouragement for the hearers to seek wisdom. Written in a style in which a teacher shares wisdom with a student, this segment is the longest sustained part of Proverbs. In reality, the section is dealing with a father encouraging his son to seek and gain wisdom in his life. Wisdom and Folly are contrasted in this section. Folly is characterized by such items as violent crime (1.1-19), sexual impurity (2.16-19), promises or pledges that are given carelessly (6.1-5), laziness (6.6-11), and dishonesty (6.12-15).

☐ **Instructions of Solomon 10.1-22.16**
Written mostly in antithetic parallelism, there are about 375 short pithy sayings without topical grouping.

☐ **Sayings of the Wise 22.17-24.34**
If you want to be happy, here is a list of things to avoid in life.

☐ **Dictums of Solomon 25.1-29.27**
A selection of proverbs from the hand of Solomon.

☐ **Oracles of Agur and Lemuel 30.1-31.9**
The wisdom of Agur and Lemuel is dispensed.

☐ **Model Wife 31.10-31**
A godly wife and mother are praised by her family.

[The **Song of Songs**: May or may not be by Solomon, A poetic portrayal of the romantic relationship between a young man and a young woman. The book is also found in The Writings/Scrolls.]

About Song of Songs: Romantic Love

The Hebrew text gives us the title The Song of Songs, which pertains to Solomon (1.1). The expression is like *the holy of holies*, or vanity of vanities. It is a superlative and means *the finest song.*

Its interpretative history is intriguing. It has been read and understood in many different ways over the centuries. Very few, if any, would have interpreted the book as God's sex manual within marriage during the Middle Ages. To do so could have caused excommunication. Today it is most commonly interpreted as a look at the erotic passion of a married heterosexual couple, a celebration of sexual passion between spouses. One might ask: Why is such a book in the canon? Scholars suggest that the Song is a drama which pictures Solomon falling in love with a young woman who he met while traveling in disguise. He later returns as King Solomon and takes her to Jerusalem to be married. The TNIV shares this view and breaks the book into poetic speech sections between the bride and her lover.

Sex in Solomon

Sexual relationships were an integral part of worship in the ancient world. Worshipers would have sexual intercourse with the temple prostitutes of the local god who was being worshiped. Baal religion taught its followers that sexual relationship with a cultic prostitute would secure fertility for crops and humans. The Song of Songs stands in this tradition. It declares that sexual union is a God-given gift to humankind and should be experienced in the sanctity of a heterosexual marriage relationship. As an illustration: Man and woman are physically different and attractive to each other. This idea is clearly perceptible throughout the book. The husband uses explicit language to describe the physical beauty of his bride (4.1-7; 7.1-9). He describes her beginning with her eyes, to her hair, her teeth, lips, cheeks, neck, breasts, and genitalia. Chapter 7, verses 1-9 pictures the wife from her feet to her head. The Song clearly illustrates that God created sex as a gift for his male and female creation to enjoy each other within marriage.

So What?

The Song of Songs does not appear to be an allegorical or typological message through which one can view God. It does, however, appear to be a bold presentation on the wholesome and biblical balance of the extremes of sexual excess and asceticism. Sex has an essential goodness, and the rightness of physical love is God's basic desire for his creation as practiced within the prescribed framework of the marriage of male and female.

Society and the church have often perverted human sexuality. It is important in the church to be reminded that sex in marriage is a God-given gift. Perversion of sex usually comes in two forms. *First*, society makes sex an idol. Sex becomes a major obsession. No matter what kind of sex: homosexual, adulterous, or heterosexual, our society promotes the idea that without some type of sexual stimulation, there is only boredom to life. Sex has become an idol. God has been rejected and the void in lives is filled with sexual relationships. *Second*, the church perverts sexuality by making it unclean or taboo. The bias against the body, as if it were bad by itself, causes parts of the church to proclaim that sexuality

---

BOOK
Song of Songs
AUTHOR
Traditionally Solomon
AGE WRITTEN
Unknown
AUDIENCE
Those who misunderstand
the value of sexual
relationships in marriage.
AIM
To celebrate the gift of
love and sex in marriage.
KEY CONCEPTS
Intimacy
KEY LESSONS
Learning to become
intimate
with one's spouse.
GEOGRAPHY
Israel

Act 3

United Kingdom

Learning Objective
See the United Kingdom stage of Israel's history.

is base or wicked even within the confines of marriage. This view often says that a marriage without sexual pleasure is more spiritual than one with sexual pleasure.

The inclusion of the Song in Scripture is an inspired corrective to the perversion of sexuality. It demands that we take God's view of sex as being wholesome, good, and pleasurable. The Song redeems the story of the Garden of Eden, where love went astray. It is the picture of the restoration of human love in its pre-rebellion bliss. Man and woman were both naked and they felt no shame (Gen. 2.25).

While God is never mentioned by name in the Song, the book teaches by inference, using the marriage metaphor, that God and Israel have a marriage covenant which promises exclusive allegiance to God and does not allow Israel to commit adultery against God by sleeping with other gods.

📖 BOOK READING GUIDE: SONG OF SONGS

Song of Songs 1-8.
TBB. 1109-1119.

- 📄 Bride and Bridegroom 1.1-2.7
  Mutual affection of two impassioned lovers is presented.
- 📄 Rapturous Praise 2.8-3.5
  The bride acknowledges the praise of her bridegroom and his love toward her.
- 📄 Intimate Moments 3.6-5.1
  The marriage pictured.
- 📄 Departure of the Bridegroom 5.2-7.9
  The bride searches for her bridegroom and finds him.
- 📄 Everlasting Communion 7.10-8.14
  The love and devotion of the couple is acknowledged.

[**Ecclesiastes**: Addresses the issue of the meaning of Life: may or may not be by Solomon.]

BOOK
Ecclesiastes
AUTHOR
Traditionally Solomon
AGE WRITTEN
During the Late
United Kingdom
AUDIENCE
Those who are searching
for life's meaning
AIM
To help understand the
meaning of life
KEY CONCEPTS
The Vanity of Life
without God
KEY LESSONS
Life without God is futile
while life with God
is freedom.
GEOGRAPHY
Israel

About Ecclesiastes: There is Hope in God

Ecclesiastes is a book in the Wisdom Literature genre that struggles with questions about the meaning of life. The name comes from the Septuagint and usually means *a teacher* of *an assembly*. Its Hebrew counterpart means *preacher*. Solomon was traditionally accepted as its author, but since the time of Luther it has been dated much later than Solomon.[86] It is thought that Solomon was the model to demonstrate for the writer of the book of a life of wisdom. His conclusion: Life without a relationship with God is meaningless. Within the book, the author demonstrates how wisdom, pleasure, hard work, popularity, wealth, and fame fail to bring lasting satisfaction.[87]

So What?

The book of Ecclesiastes clearly captures the despair of a world without God. In the very areas where the Teacher of Ecclesiastes felt most oppressed, those living in God's Story can experience deep significance and restoration. The book's last two verses (12.13-14) reveal the heart of the author. God is faithful to his Covenant, his Story.[88]

BOOK READING GUIDE: ECCLESIASTES

◻ Vanity of Human Wisdom 1.1-2.26
The author describes the vanity of all human effort and experience.
◻ Aimlessness of Life 3.1-5.20
It is normal to have disappointments during your life.
◻ Inadequacy of Wealth 6.1-8.17
Earthly goods and treasures will not secure satisfaction in your life.
◻ Nuisances Left to God 9.1-12.14
The injustices of life will adequately be dealt with by God.

Scene 8. Divided Kingdom Stage (1 Kings 12.1-2 Kings 25.30)

The Story continues with the death of Solomon, which brought on the beginning of the end for Israel as a nation and as God's light to the world. At his death, the United Kingdom, built by David and Solomon, disintegrated into two separate nations again. The Northern Kingdom existed as an independent nation for about two hundred years before being carried off into captivity by Assyria. Judah survived for about 340 years before her own captivity at the hands of Babylon.[89]

The Northern Kingdom had twenty kings, all of them portrayed as "doing evil in the eyes of the Lord," which became code words for breaking the stipulations of the Covenant. During this period, there were several prophets like Elijah and Elisha.

Almost all cultures in the ancient world produced individuals who were believed to speak to humankind on behalf of a deity. Israel was no exception. Prophecy in Israel had its beginnings early in Israel's history with Moses, but reached its zenith during preexilic, exilic, and postexilic periods.[90] According to Fee and Stuart, the prophets were Covenant enforcement mediators announcing the positive and negative enforcement of the Covenant to Israel, reminding Israel that keeping the Covenant brought blessing and breaking the stipulations of the Covenant brought punishment.[91]

Learning Objective
See the United Kingdom stage of Israel's history.

Ecclesiastes 1-12.
TBB. 1179-1193.

Dictionary Articles
Read the following Dictionary Articles in *New Bible Dictionary*.
Samuel,
Samuel, Books of,
Kings, Books of,
Saul, 3,
Jerusalem,
David,
Solomon,
Proverbs, Book of,
Song of Solomon,
Ecclesiastes, Book of,
Temple, I, II, III, IV

Learning Objective
Understand the Divided Kingdom stage of Israel's history.

Reading the StoryLine

Here is the storyline to the Kings stories.

Northern Kingdom (1st Seven Kings): 1 Kings 12.1-16.34

◻ Rehoboam, Jeroboam, and the splitting of the Kingdom: 1 Kings 12.1-24
◻ Jeroboam (N):[92] 1 Kings 12.25-14.20
[Three Judean Kings [Jeroboam, Abijah, Asa (S):[93] 1 Kings 14.21-15.24]
◻ Nadab, Baasha, Elah, Zimri, Omri, Ahab (N): 1 Kings 15.25-16.34

Elijah Stories: 1 Kings 17.1-2 Kings 2.12a

◻ Elijah and Ahab: 1 Kings 17.1-18.46
◻ God encourages Elijah: 1 Kings 19.1-21
[Attack of Samaria: 1 Kings 10.1-43]
◻ Naboth's vineyard: 1 Kings 21.1-29
[Israel and Aram at war: 1 Kings 22.1-40]
◻ Jehoshaphat: 1 Kings 22.41-50
[Psalm 83: Set against the reign of Jehoshaphat (2 Chronicles 20)]
◻ Elijah and Ahaziah: 1 Kings 22.51-2 Kings 1.18
◻ Elijah goes to heaven: 2 Kings 2.1-12a

1 Kings 12.1-2 Kings 12.21.
TBB. 419-453.

Act 3

Divided Kingdom

Learning Objective
Understand the Divided Kingdom stage of Israel's history.

Elisha Stories: 2 Kings 2.12b-8.6

- ❑ The Company of Prophets: 2 Kings 2.12b-18
- ❑ Water, Mocking, Water, Poison, Loaves: 2 Kings 2.19-4.44
- ❑ Naaman Healed: 2 Kings 5.1-27
- ❑ Axhead, Blinding, Provision, Healing: 2 Kings 6.1-8.6

More Kings: 2 Kings 8.7-13.35

- ❑ Elisha and Hazael: 2 Kings 8.7-15
- ❑ Jehoram and Ahaziah (S): 2 Kings 8.16-29
- ❑ Jehu and the Death of Jezebel and Ahab (N): 2 Kings 9.1-10.36
- ❑ Joash (S): 2 Kings 11.1-12.21

[**Joel** (S) Prophecy against Judah: Joel 1.1-3.21]

Prophets: Reminders of God's Covenant Story

It should be remembered that the prophets of Israel and Judah were the Covenant enforcement mediators for God. They were not social reformers or innovative thinkers. They had a message from God to his people and they were determined to give it. They came from a narrow period of Jewish history: Amos about 760 B.C. to Malachi about 460 B.C., about 300 years total. This historical period is characterized by political, economic, social and military agitation, Covenant unfaithfulness, and shifts in population.

About Joel: A Prophecy of Judgment

The book of Joel does not tell us much about its namesake or indicate any historical person that would help date the book. Jerusalem had not been destroyed and the enemies of Judah are from before the Exile. The catalyst for delivering his message is a locust plague, which he compared to a human army advancing on Judah.[94]

So What?

Two areas in Joel are important to the Story. The *first* is the Day of the Lord. The popular idea was conceived as a time when God would come and fight Israel's enemies like in the day of Joshua. This popular idea was suggested with phrases like "the day of the wrath of the Lord" from Ezekiel 7.19, "that day" from Isaiah 2.11, and "the day of the Lord" as used by Isaiah, Jeremiah, Ezekiel, Joel, Amos, Obadiah, and Zechariah. However, Joel gave a new meaning and spoke of it as God's coming to judge his own people. It was understood as a period of time, not a twenty-four hour day. Some of the words of the prophets were fulfilled in events like the fall of Jerusalem in 587 B.C., but also have a future fulfillment like the coming of Jesus, the outpouring of the Holy Spirit, the return of Jesus, and the final judgment. This *day* is seen by the prophets as close and the hearers should prepare for it without hesitation.[95]

The *second* significant concept is the coming of the Spirit. The Old Testament shows a movement toward the fulfillment of the experience of the Holy Spirit on the day of Pentecost. The second verse of the Old Testament shows the Spirit as hovering over the waters waiting to create. In the wilderness, Eldad and Medad prophesy. Some did not understand and came to Moses and reported what the two men were prophesying. Joshua wanted Moses to stop them, but Moses responded, "I wish that all

BOOK
Joel
AUTHOR
Joel
AGE WRITTEN
Unknown
AUDIENCE
Those who have suffered a misfortune
and did not realize that it was a judgment of God
AIM
To demonstrate to Judah that God will judge his own children
if they will not repent.
KEY CONCEPTS
The Day of the Lord (Judgment)
KEY LESSONS
Repentance is easier than being stripped by God.
GEOGRAPHY
Judah

the Lord's people were prophets and that the Lord would put his Spirit on them!" (Num. 11.26-30). Joel prophesies in his day that God was going to pour out his Spirit on all people (2.28). Peter's sermon on the day of Pentecost reported that the prophecy of Joel was fulfilled that day (Acts 2.16ff).[96]

Divided Kingdom

Learning Objective
Understand the Divided Kingdom stage of Israel's history.

Joel 1-3. TBB. 905-912.

📕 BOOK READING GUIDE: JOEL

Here is a reading guide to the book of Joel.

📖 Judgment of Locusts 1.1-2.11
The invasion of Assyria in the future is seen by Joel as an invasion of locusts. He called it the Day of the Lord.

📖 Outcry for Repentance 2.12-17
Joel's call for repentance.

📖 Effusion of the Spirit 2.18-32
A prophetic picture of the outpouring of the Holy Spirit.

📖 Lord's Day of Judgment 3.1-21
God's final triumph in the Day of the Lord.

QUESTION
Could it be that a way to prophesy in the current culture is the way the book of Joel prophesies: by telling a story?

We now continue the main storyline.

Reading the StoryLine

Continued storyline to the Kings stories.

📖 Jehoahez and Jehoash (N): 2 Kings 13.1-25

2 Kings 13.1-25. TBB. 453-454.

[**Jonah** (N) Prophecy to Nineveh]

About Jonah: God's Grace

The book of Jonah contains one of the most unforgettable stories in the Old Testament. Most folks only remember the internal story of the big fish swallowing Jonah. This book is unlike other prophetic books in which the prophet preaches the message to his hearers. The book is a narrative and the preaching of Jonah is recorded in one verse (3.4).[97] Scholarship has viewed Jonah in four different ways: historical, mythological, parabolic, and allegorical.[98]

BOOK
Jonah
AUTHOR
Unknown
AGE WRITTEN
Sometime after the Exile
AUDIENCE
Those who do not believe that God cares about any other ethnic group but their own.
AIM
To teach God's people that God cares about all mankind.
KEY CONCEPTS
Mercy and Compassion
KEY LESSONS
Obedience is better than running.
GEOGRAPHY
Israel ✈ toward Tarshish (probably Spain)
✈ Nineveh
via a great fish

Historical

This view believes that Jonah is a factual account of a historical incident. The story does mention historical places which give this view support. Jews acknowledge Jonah as a historical account. Objections which have been raised are: Nineveh's size and the king's name are from a later historical period and there is no other historical record of the conversion of Nineveh.

Mythological

Myths attempt to stage truth about the experiences of humans as they interact with gods and offer a result in a form that looks historical. There is some mythic language or ideas within the story, but this view is not currently favored.

Parabolic

This view suggests that this is a story of a prejudiced Jew who believed that God could love only Jews and did not care for other nations.

Act 3

Divided Kingdom

Learning Objective
Understand the Divided Kingdom stage of Israel's history.

It is a parable that suggests that God does care for others who are not of Jewish descent. The primary objection to this view is that parables in the Old Testament are usually told and then interpreted. Interpretation does not occur in Jonah.

Allegorical

Some have interpreted Jonah from an allegorical position seeing the characters like the dove as Israel. The fleeing of Jonah from Nineveh is seen as Israel's movement away from God and his Covenant. The sailors are seen as nations, while the storm is the judgment of God. The big fish swallowing Jonah is understood as Israel being absorbed by the influence of surrounding nations.

So how should we interpret this story? How does one struggle with the big fish story? From the group of books called the Minor Prophets, Jesus only referred to Jonah. Conservative scholarship takes this point of reference to imply that Jonah was a historical person and the story a literal fact of history. One must give due consideration to the words of Jesus.

Good people can see things differently! It seems that despite the interpretative view that one takes, the message is essentially the same: The King of the universe cares about every person he has created. Prejudice will not terminate God's goals. He will forgive those who repent.

So What?

Jonah was among those who believed that God was limited to the land where his people lived. He tried to remove himself from the presence of God by fleeing from Israel (1.3). In addition, the concept of prejudice can be seen as Jonah did not want to bring any message of deliverance to those who he felt had no part in the blessings of God. The one concept which prevails in Jonah is the universality of God and his redemptive purpose. The role of Israel as mediator is based on the Covenant concept. Here we have a case of anti-gentileism which God had to break in Jonah. Like other places in the Old Testament, God shows himself ready to accept and deal with any and all people.

 **BOOK READING GUIDE: JONAH**

Here is a reading guide for Jonah.

Jonah 1-4. TBB. 483-485.

- ☐ **Flight from God 1.1-17**
  God called his prophet Jonah to go to Nineveh. Not only did Jonah decide not to go to Nineveh, he went in the opposite direction from Nineveh. During a storm at sea, Jonah was cast overboard and is swallowed by a great fish.
- ☐ **In the Fish 2.1-10**
  From inside the great fish, Jonah cried out to God and the fish regurgitated him.
- ☐ **Second Call by God 3.1-10**
  Jonah was called a second time by God. He responded and went to Nineveh. Nineveh repented.
- ☐ **His Complaint to God 4.1-11**
  Jonah did not like the result of his proclamation and became angry with God.

We now return to the Old Testament storyline.

Reading the StoryLine

Northern Kingdom (final years): 2 Kings 14.1-29

- Amaziah (S): 2 Kings 14.1-22
- Jeroboam II (N) 2 Kings 14.23-29

[**Amos** (N) A prophecy against Israel: Amos 1.1-9.15]

About Amos: Justice in Society

When Jeroboam II was King of Israel, the Northern Kingdom rivaled the affluence of the United Kingdom. Because of her prosperity, Israel became socially corrupt. They worshiped Baal in drunkenness, violence, sexual perversion, and idol worship. The mirror which reflected the social decay was the treatment of the poor within Israel. The rich were determined to destroy the poor. Into this historical context, Amos emerged with a blunt message from God. Israel had been measured by God's plumb line and they did not measure up. If they did not repent and return to their Covenant with God, they would be taken into captivity. Amos was at a disadvantage. He was from the Southern Kingdom, a shepherd or possibly a breeder of herds[99] and tree keeper. The hearers of his message accused him of rebellion because of his message and maybe because of where he was from.

So What?

The corruption of society can often be sparked by looking at what the society is openly practicing. In Jeroboam's Israel, idol worship which included all kinds of perversions pointed to Israel's decay. Israel was not living in God's Story and God was not happy with their propensity to live outside of his Covenant. The message of Amos was that social injustice, which was the result of their wayward lifestyle, would bring punishment on the wrongdoers. Prolonged living in a story of one's choosing does eventually have serious consequences.

BOOK READING GUIDE: AMOS

Here is a reading guide for Amos.

- **A**ccount of Nations Judgment 1.1-2.16
  The doom of Syria, Philistia, Tyre, Edom, Ammon, and Moab is prophesied. Then the wrath of God would fall on Israel.
- **M**essages of Israel's Judgment 3.1-6.14
  Amos detailed the judgments Israel would face. These judgments would occur because the rich, while living in extravagance, were oppressing the poor. Idol worship was rampant.
- **O**ptic View of Fate 7.1-9.10
  Amos presents Israel's fate in five visions of locusts, fire, plumb line, late summer fruit, and a smitten temple.
- **S**alvation Assured 9.11-15
  Messianic blessing is promised.

Divided Kingdom

Learning Objective
Understand the Divided Kingdom stage of Israel's history.
2 Kings 14.1-29. TBB. 455-456.

BOOK
Amos
AUTHOR
Amos
AGE WRITTEN
Sometime between 760-750 B.C.
AIM
To teach that God will not stand for blatant sin among his people.
AUDIENCE
Those who believe that their peace and prosperity are because of their own endeavors.
KEY CONCEPTS
Measured for Justice
KEY LESSONS
Righteousness is measured by our responsibility to act justly toward the oppressed, not because of our religious merit.
GEOGRAPHY
Israel

Amos 1-9. TBB. 489-504.

Act 3

Divided Kingdom

Learning Objective
Understand the Divided Kingdom stage of Israel's history.

2 Kings 15.1-16.20.
TBB. 456-459.

BOOK
Isaiah
AUTHOR
Traditionally Isaiah
AGE WRITTEN
Sometime during the Divided Kingdom
AUDIENCE
Those who have extremely difficult problems
AIM
To condemn sin and call for repentance (1-39) To provide hope for those under the judgment of God (40-66)
KEY CONCEPTS
The grace of God
KEY LESSONS
Receiving Salvation by grace
GEOGRAPHY
🌐 Judah

Reading the StoryLine

The storyline continues.

- Uzziah (S): 2 Kings 15.1-7
- Zechariah, Shallum, Menahem, Pekahiah, Pekah (N): 2 Kings 15.8-31
- Jotham and Ahaz (S): 2 Kings 15.32-16.20

[Isaiah and Micah (S) Prophecies against Judah]

About Isaiah: Promised Salvation

Isaiah's name means *Jehovah is Salvation*. The book of Isaiah presents a collection of visions and prophecies which belonged to different segments of the life of Isaiah. The book contains both prose and poetry with poetry more dominant than prose. Isaiah is a book of "sheer grandeur,"[100] and second in size only to Psalms. His prophetic ministry was to the Southern Kingdom. Four kings reigned during his ministry: Uzziah, Jotham, Ahaz, and Hezekiah. He was born during the reign of Uzziah and his call to prophetic ministry came at Uzziah's death (740 B.C.).

During the reign of Hezekiah, Assyria was making ready to capture the Northern Kingdom (722 B.C.). Judah would be next. King Hezekiah (2 Kings 19.5-7; Isa. 37.6-7) prayed and Isaiah told the officials of the King that God would spare them from the Assyrians. Because they continued to break Covenant with God, the Southern Kingdom was not spared forever. They were finally captured by Babylon. The message of Isaiah reflects the scope of the judgment and salvation of God. His major theme is God's salvation imparted because God is a gracious God.

There is an ongoing discussion among scholars about who wrote this lengthy book. Few still hold to the view that Isaiah wrote the complete book. Some accept two books (1-39 and 40-66). Others see three books breaking the last section into two (40-55 and 56-66). While disagreement about who the author is abounds, it seems clear that the book suggests that God provides salvation and completely controls his creation.[101]

So What?

Isaiah's name "Jehovah is Salvation" may partly explain his interest in salvation. The word *salvation* appears eighteen times in Isaiah out of the seventy-seven times in the Old Testament. Salvation is personal (12.2) as well as corporate (37.35). The idea of corporate salvation is mostly foreign in the first part of the twenty-first-century. While the nudge of postmodernism is pushing the church toward focusing on otherness, we are still caught up in the individualness of salvation. What if the church asked the question: Can a local expression of the church be "saved?" How would that change the way we view sin and corruption?

The metaphorical concept of God as Father has a rich heritage in Isaiah. Father is just one of hundreds of metaphors that is used for God in the Old Testament. I give an overview of this concept in Appendix 7. In addition, the concept of the Servant Songs is also important from Isaiah. There is an overview of this concept in Appendix 8.

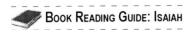 BOOK READING GUIDE: ISAIAH

Here is a reading guide for Isaiah.

☐ **Grace and Judgment 1.1-6.13**
Four sermons urge the hearers of Isaiah to repent and be forgiven of their Covenant breaking. He spoke to Judah about her future and her need to become Covenant disciplined. After a parable story about a vineyard, he prophesies about an invasion. The section concludes with the story of his personal call by God.

☐ **Redeemer Promised 7.1-12.6**
Another four sermons are recorded in this section. For Ahaz's benefit, a sign in the birth of Immanuel is given. He spoke about a future deliverer, Samaria's doom, and a false empire's judgment.

☐ **Accounts of National Judgment 13.1-23.18**
A prophetic word about ten nations which will be destroyed. They were: Babylon, Assyria, Philistia, Moab, Damascus (Syria), Egypt, Edom, Arabia, Israel, and Tyre.

☐ **Certainty of Judgment 24.1-27.13**
Four more sermons by Isaiah are recorded. He spoke about universal judgment, deliverance, rejoicing, and the punishment of oppressors.

☐ **Inhabitants of Jerusalem Warned 28.1-33.24**
Five more sermons are recorded in this section. Isaiah spoke about scoffers, judgment of those who wanted to deceive God, confidence in man versus confidence in God, deliverance, and the triumph of God. Jerusalem will be destroyed, but God will restore it.

☐ **Opposition Destroyed 34.1-35.10**
Two additional sermons are recorded: the destruction of the Gentiles and the redemption of God.

☐ **Usurping by Babylon Foretold 36.1-39.8**
Babylon's captivity is foretold.

☐ **Salvation through Servant 40.1-66.24**
The God of faithfulness will deliver his people through his servant, the prince of peace.

About Micah: Do What The Lord Requires

Micah's name means *who is like God* and nothing personal is known about him. His book dates from the days of King Hezekiah and discusses the sins of Samaria, the capital city of the Northern Kingdom, and Jerusalem, the Southern Kingdom's capital. Micah was contemporary with Isaiah in Judah and Hosea in Israel. His message was very similar to the message of Isaiah. He was convinced that Judah was heading for disaster because of her leader's lifestyle of idol worship.[102]

So What?

Micah shows God as continuing to be a Covenant God who is faithful to bless or punish. He reminds his people that God desires loyalty and that they were showing their disloyalty. He renounced the rulers, religious leaders, false prophets, pilfering, abuse of the poor, corruption in business, and fraudulent religion.

One of the most moving passages in Micah, which demonstrates the heart of a longing God to have his children live in his Story, is 6.6-8:

Learning Objective
Understand the Divided Kingdom stage of Israel's history.

Isaiah 1-66. TBB. 547-669.

BOOK
Micah
AUTHOR
Micah
AGE WRITTEN
Sometime during the Divided Kingdom
AUDIENCE
Those who believe that they have no responsibility to change the society around them.
AIM
To teach the necessity of living a daily righteous life.
KEY CONCEPTS
Controversy
KEY LESSONS
The by-product of saving faith is social reform and practical holiness.
GEOGRAPHY
✪ Judah

Act 3

Divided Kingdom

Learning Objective
Understand the Divided Kingdom stage of Israel's history.

With what shall I come before the LORD
  and bow down before the exalted God?
Shall I come before him with burnt offerings,
  with calves a year old?
Will the LORD be pleased with thousands of rams,
  with ten thousand rivers of oil?
Shall I offer my firstborn for my transgression,
  the fruit of my body for the sin of my soul?
He has shown all you people what is good.
  And what does the LORD require of you?
To act justly and to love mercy
  and to walk humbly with your God.

BOOK READING GUIDE: MICAH

Here is a reading guide for Micah.

Micah 1-7. TBB. 529-541.

☐ **Message of Judgment 1.1-16**
Micah pictures the judgment on the Northern and Southern Kingdoms.

☐ **Informed of Sins 2.1-3.12**
Sins are recited and judgment is predicted.

☐ **Coming Kingdom 4.1-5.15**
The necessary condition for the Kingdom of God to be fulfilled is pictured. The triumph of the remnant is given.

☐ **Altercation with God 6.1-16**
The Northern Kingdom is petitioned for repentance. A failure on their part would bring crop failure.

☐ **Hope of Mercy 7.1-20**
Micah tells the people of God about their need to confess their sins so they can see the mercy of God which follows repentance.

We continue with the main storyline.

2 Kings 17.1-41. TBB. 459-461.

Reading the StoryLine

☐ Hoshea (fall of Northern Kingdom): 2 Kings 17.1-41

[**Hosea** (N) A prophecy against Israel (N): Hosea 1.1-14.9]

About Hosea: A Faithless Wife

Hosea stands first in the collection of the prophetic books in the Hebrew Bible called "The Twelve." This book is part of the Minor Prophets in the Protestant Bible.

Born during the reign of Jeroboam II, Hosea was one of two prophets who spoke to the Northern Kingdom. He was a contemporary to Isaiah and Micah from the Southern Kingdom. Prosperity was still the order of the day during the life and ministry of Hosea. Economic and commercial development was at an all time high and Israel was in a religious mess.

Israel had misplaced her focus on being a model of a Godly society, a light to the world, and followed the surrounding nations into their immorality. In short, one might say that Israel switched stories. Worship of false gods, usually thought to be male or female, was worship. Sexual intercourse with cultic prostitutes was high worship and was modeled for the gods, to stimulate them and suggest how these gods should make their

BOOK
Hosea

AUTHOR
Hosea

AGE WRITTEN
At the end of the Northern Kingdom just before its fall.

AIM
To teach Israel that they were in covenant with God and they should be faithful to it or suffer the consequences.

AUDIENCE
Those who have turned away from God and do not recognize the consequences of their decision.

KEY CONCEPTS
Return

KEY LESSONS
God's love is sometimes tough.

GEOGRAPHY
✪ Israel

land fertile. Orgies and other erotic practices were an integral part of the religion of the era. In Israel, these foreign ideas were incorporated into the worship of God.

Divided Kingdom

Learning Objective
Understand the Divided Kingdom stage of Israel's history.

Hosea stepped into this situation and used his own personal tragedy with his wife Gomer to illustrate the relationship of Israel to God. Scholars are divided between two opinions concerning Hosea and Gomer's relationship.[103] One opinion holds that Gomer was not a prostitute when she married Hosea and then became unfaithful. The other opinion believes that she was a prostitute when they married and returned to her trade. Regardless of one's position about Hosea and Gomer, the point remains clear. Gomer was married and then became unfaithful in the marital relationship. She and Hosea were reunited and restored. This crystal-clear picture demonstrates how Israel had become a harlot in God's eyes by worshiping other gods, the breaking of the first stipulation of the Covenant, but that she could be fully restored by repentance. Hosea lived the message he delivered. This makes his book unique in Old Testament prophetic literature.

So What?

The cardinal sin of Israel was infidelity to God. She continually lived in the wrong story. Hosea was called to live with a wife who was a prostitute. This allows him to feel the anguish of God over his unfaithful people and presents a picture of God experiencing a conflict of emotions, torn between his love for an unfaithful Israel and his own righteousness in judgment. In this emotional conflict, God's righteous judgment finally prevails (13.9-16). What if God called us to experience his pain, how would that change the way we see his creation?

When Gomer as a married woman gave herself to others, Hosea went after her to restore her. This pictures the heart of God toward his children who had constantly disobeyed his Covenant, living in a different story than God had prepared for them. He is truly a missionary God.

BOOK READING GUIDE: HOSEA

Here is a reading guide for Hosea.

Hosea 1-14. TBB. 507-526.

☐ **Hosea Marries 1.1-2.1**
Hosea and Gomer are married and have three children.
☐ **Adultery of Gomer 2.2-23**
Gomer commits adultery and is judged.
☐ **Reunion of Hosea and Gomer 3.1-5**
Gomer is restored to Hosea.
☐ **Lascivious Israel 4.1-7.16**
Israel's adultery is revealed. If she repents, she will be restored to God.
☐ **Outcry of Judgment 8.1-10.15**
God passed sentence on Israel.
☐ **The Love of God 11.1-14.9**
God demonstrated his tenderness to Israel.

Southern Kingdom: The Final Years (2 Kings 18.1-25.30)

☐ Hezekiah (S): 2 Kings 18.1-20.21
[Psalm 75: Set against 2 Kings 18-19]
[Psalm 76: Set against 2 Kings 18-19]
☐ Manasseh: 2 Kings 21.1-18
☐ Amon (S): 2 Kings 21.19-26

2 Kings 18.1-21.26.
TBB. 461-467.

Act 3

Divided Kingdom

Learning Objective
Understand the Divided Kingdom stage of Israel's history.

BOOK
Nahum
AUTHOR
Nahum
AGE WRITTEN
Sometime after Assyria destroyed Samaria
AUDIENCE
Those who are undergoing persecution.
AIM
To pronounce judgment of a nation who opposed Israel.
KEY CONCEPTS
Retribution
KEY LESSONS
The patience of God does not
mean he is impotent
GEOGRAPHY
 Judah and Nineveh

Nahum 1-3. TBB. 683-688.

BOOK
Zephaniah
AUTHOR
Zephaniah
AGE WRITTEN
Immediately before the Exile
AUDIENCE
Those who have repeatedly ignored the warning signs of God's judgment.
AIM
To give Judah a warning of the impending destruction of evil.
KEY CONCEPTS
The judgment of God
KEY LESSONS
God is in control regardless of contrary appearances.
GEOGRAPHY
 Judah

[Nahum and Zephaniah (S) Prophecies against Judah]

About Nahum: Woe To Nineveh!

Nahum, whose name means *compassion,* was the second prophet to give a message to Nineveh, a very stern message of judgment about its destruction. Nothing is known about the author who wrote the most pictorial poetry in the Old Testament.[104]

So What?

God is righteous and he will bring judgment on those who are the enemies of his people. He is pictured by Nahum as a Divine Warrior ready to do battle on behalf of his children. Nahum's prophecy is a reaction to the suffering of God's children at the hand of the Assyrians. Acute suffering calls for acute punishment—"an eye for an eye." The point of Nahum is that even those who are instruments of God's judgment are themselves not exempt from his judgment.

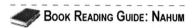

BOOK READING GUIDE: NAHUM

This is a reading guide for Nahum.

- **Majesty of God 1.1-15**
  God is pictured in all his majesty and power. He will punish his enemies and restore his children.
- **Attack on Nineveh 2.1-13**
  Nineveh's siege is given.
- **Destruction Reasons Given 3.1-19**
  The sins of Nineveh are described.

About Zephaniah: Destruction and Deliverance

It was during the rule of King Josiah that Zephaniah prophesied. The prophecies of Zephaniah are usually dated during the period of 640 to 622 B.C. His message was simple but forthright. If you break Covenant, God will judge you. Judah was full of sin and the Day of the Lord awaited them.

So What?

Zephaniah interprets the Covenant and demonstrates that Judah's judgments were not final. God would show his love and mercy through the restoration of a remnant. God's judgment is not only judgment of the wicked, but a vindication of the righteous.

The concept of the remnant of God's people, which would survive the judgments of God brought on his unrepentant people, is seen many times in the Old Testament prophets. The prophets believed that there was going to be a small group of people within Israel and Judah that God would raise up after his judgment to become the people of God he intended them to be. Zephaniah uses *remnant* on three occasions in his book (Zeph. 2.7, 9; 3.13).

📖 BOOK READING GUIDE: ZEPHANIAH

This is a reading guide for Zephaniah.

▢ Sin of Judah Judged 1.1-2.3
  The Day of the Lord will come.
▢ Ire of God 2.4-3.7
  God will judge the surrounding nations.
▢ Nations Destroyed 3.8-12
  While the nations will be judged, the remnant will survive.

We now continue the main storyline.

Learning Objective
Understand the Divided
Kingdom stage of Israel's
history.

Zephaniah 1-3. TBB. 673-679.

Reading the StoryLine

Continuing the storyline of the kings.

▢ Josiah, Jehoahaz, Johoiakim, Jehoiachin (S): 2 Kings 22.1-24.17

2 Kings 22.1-25.30.
TBB. 467-473.

  [**Jeremiah (S)** Prophecies against Judah]

▢ Zedekiah (S): 2 Kings 24.18-25.30
  [Psalm 74: Set against the events of 2 Kings 24-25]
  [**Jeremiah and Ezekiel (S)** Prophecies against Judah]

About Jeremiah: Judgment is Executed

Jehovah Establishes is the meaning of the name Jeremiah. The
impending judgment on Judah because of their sin of idolatry is the main
theme of his book. He ministered during the final years of the Southern
Kingdom about 100 years after Isaiah. Babylon had become a world
power and its existence put Judah at risk. As with other prophets,
Jeremiah railed against idolatry, immorality, while at the same time
providing hope for his listeners during the time frame of the destruction
of Jerusalem. His career as a prophet spanned four decades. His book is
not in chronological order, but he continues in the tradition of prophets
before him by being a Covenant enforcement mediator, preaching
adherence to the Mosaic Story for the people of God. Somewhere after
the barrage on Jerusalem, Jeremiah was taken into exile in Egypt.

By modern standards, Jeremiah's mental health would have been
thought to be pathological, with acts of motionless periods, no mourning
over the death of his wife, and engagement in some really quirky
conduct.[105]

BOOK
Jeremiah
AUTHOR
Baruch: Jeremiah's
amanuensis
AGE WRITTEN
Immediately before and
after the Exile
AUDIENCE
Those who are persistent
in their rebellion to the
point that the discipline of
God cannot be reversed.
AIM
To teach God's people
how
to accept his judgment.
KEY CONCEPTS
Divine Discipline
KEY LESSONS
Without repentance God
will break us so that he
can remake us.
GEOGRAPHY
🌐 Judah and Egypt

So What?

Jeremiah is noted for his writing about the New Covenant (Jer. 31).
This New Covenant is designed to meet the specific needs that made it
necessary.

1 It will arise in the future and move toward uniting all the tribes of
   Israel (31).
2 It is more personal than a marriage vow (32); shows Israel's breaking
   of this vow.
3 It would be written on the hearts of people, the place from which
   their sinfulness spreads (33).
4 There will be no need to provide instruction about this Covenant (34).

Divided Kingdom

Learning Objective
Understand the Divided Kingdom stage of Israel's history.

Jeremiah 1-52. TBB. 699-801.

5 The Covenant will never come to an end (v. 35-37).

6. It would result in a fuller knowledge of God and it would carry full forgiveness (v. 34).[106]

This New Covenant does not abolish the old, but supplies the motivation and spiritual resources to help keep the stipulations and have an obedient relationship with God.

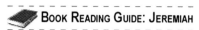

BOOK READING GUIDE: JEREMIAH

This is a reading guide for Jeremiah.

☐ Judgment on Immorality 1.1-20.18
Jeremiah is called to his prophetic ministry and prophesies about the fall of Jerusalem. He told a parable about a potter and his clay, which demonstrated how Jerusalem would be broken.

☐ Usurping of Israel 21.1-39.18
Israel is called to repentance by Jeremiah and warned against listening to false prophets. He informs Israel about a vision of two baskets of figs and prophesies the coming of their seventy-year captivity, the fall of Babylon, and the destruction of their Temple. He promised Judah that God would return them from captivity and give them a new Covenant. He described the attack on Jerusalem and his own imprisonment.

☐ Detoured to Egypt 40.1-45.5
Jeremiah prophesied in Egypt after his abduction.

☐ Guilt of Nations 46.1-51.64
Jeremiah prophesied the fate of Egypt, Philistia, Moab, Ammon, Edom, Damascus (Syria), Arabia, Hazor, Elam, and Babylon.

☐ End of Jerusalem 52.1-34
Jerusalem's downfall is given in great detail.

BOOK
Ezekiel
AUTHOR
Traditionally Ezekiel
AGE WRITTEN
After the fall of Jerusalem
AUDIENCE
Those who are stubborn and need to hear more than one way about the judgment of God.
AIM
To explain why the presence of God was departing from Judah and a promise that it would return.
KEY CONCEPTS
Optical Learning
KEY LESSONS
Stop disobeying God or learning to follow him the hard way.
GEOGRAPHY
✦ Judah

About Ezekiel: A Messenger to the Captives

The name Ezekiel means *God is Strong*. He was from a family of priests. His ministry can be divided into two segments. First, in Jerusalem which ends with its destruction in 587 B.C., he prophesied about the soon coming devastation of Jerusalem because her people had a habit of life of breaking God's Covenant. This segment of his ministry is in tandem with the death of his wife which is recorded in chapter 24. Second, about two years after the fall of Jerusalem, he continued his prophetic ministry in Babylon with a message that emphasized the comfort and care of God.

Visual Prophecy

Ezekiel is best known for prophecy by symbolic action. He is not alone with such visual prophetic media: Isaiah went naked and barefoot for three years. Jeremiah demonstrated God and Judah's relationship with a potter and clay metaphor. In his creativity, God allowed his prophets to speak using different media, a sure sign that the Story can be told using different presentation forms.

Visual Prophecy: Ezekiel made a picture of Jerusalem on a tile and mimicked a siege against it (4.1-3).
Meaning: Jerusalem would be overthrown by a foreign power.
Visual Prophecy: Ezekiel lies on his left side for several hours a day for 390 days and then on his right size for several hours a day for forty days (4.4-6).

Divided Kingdom

Learning Objective
Understand the Divided Kingdom stage of Israel's history.

Meaning: An illustration of the iniquity of Judah and Israel.
Visual Prophecy: Measured out food and water (4.9-11).
Meaning: An example of the insufficiency of food and water during the coming siege on both the Northern and Southern Kingdoms.
Visual Prophecy: Cut his hair and divided it into three equal parts. He burned one-third. He struck one-third with a sword. He scattered one-third to the wind (5.1-4; 12).
Meaning: This was an illustration of the three ways Judah would be handled in its capture. One third of the people would be burned. One third of the people would be killed by the violence of a sword. One third would be carried away to Babylon.
Visual Prophecy: Ezekiel was instructed to dig a hole in his house and carry his household goods into the street.
Meaning: The breaking down of the walls of Jerusalem and the carrying away of its inhabitants was the intended meaning.

The death of Ezekiel's wife is seen by some as a visual prophecy of the death of Judah.[107]

___

So What?

Ezekiel quotes a current proverb (18:1-4):

The word of the LORD came to me:

"What do you people mean by quoting this proverb about the land of Israel:

"'The parents eat sour grapes,
and the children's teeth are set on edge'?

"As surely as I live, declares the Sovereign LORD, you will no longer quote this proverb in Israel.

For everyone belongs to me, the parent as well as the child—both alike belong to me. The one who sins is the one who will die."

This disclaimer of personal responsibility was rejected by Ezekiel as no longer valid. Individuals within the community were responsible for their own sin of breaking the Covenant. One of the most famous stories in Ezekiel is the Valley of the Dry Bones (37). Here is a prophecy underlined by a belief in resurrection, that Israel will be reestablished and restored, a foreshadowing of the coming Messianic Kingdom.

- -
 Book Reading Guide: Ezekiel
- -

This is a reading guide for Ezekiel.

☐ **Optic Call of Ezekiel 1.1-3.27**
God called Ezekiel. Ezekiel had a vision of God.

☐ **Pronouncement of Judgments 4.1-24.27**
Ezekiel pictured the destruction of Jerusalem by word and symbolic act. He spoke about Jerusalem becoming a harlot and that God would judge her regardless of her belief that God would not punish his own people. He gives three parables to demonstrate that Judah's view of God's punishment of his own was false.

☐ **Trouble for Nations 25.1-32.32**
Ezekiel delivered his message that Ammon, Moab, Philistia, Tyre, Sidon, and Egypt will fall.

Ezekiel 1-48. TBB. 813-878.

Act 3

Divided Kingdom

Learning Objective
Understand the Divided Kingdom stage of Israel's history.

BOOK
Habakkuk

AUTHOR
Habakkuk

AGE WRITTEN
Immediately before the Exile

AUDIENCE
Those who need to understand that God's inactivity does not mean God's abandonment.

AIM
To explain the inactivity of God in the face of suffering.

KEY CONCEPTS
Faith

KEY LESSONS
Learning to trust God when it's bright, as well as when it's night.

GEOGRAPHY
Judah

Habakkuk 1-3. TBB. 691-696.

⬚ Israel Restored 33.1-39.29
God will give new life to Judah is indicated by the vision of the dry bones that come to life. Judah recognized the mercy of God.

⬚ Clear Vision of a New Temple 40.1-48.35
Ezekiel has a clear vision of the new temple and how God would fill it with his glory.

Reading the StoryLine

[Habakkuk (S) The just live because of the Faithfulness of God]

About Habakkuk: Living by God's Faithfulness

Habakkuk was written to handle the same problem as Job and Psalm 73. The ancient Israelite could constantly ask: In view of the Covenant, why do righteous people suffer? Remember, keeping the Covenant stipulations brings blessings, while breaking the Covenant stipulations brings curses. The question of a righteous person who found him or herself suffering could be, why? The book of Habakkuk begins doubting that there is any justice in the world for the righteous, but ends in faith that there is justice in God.

So What?

Habakkuk answers the question, How can a righteous God allow faithless men to be victorious? In view of the Covenant, which suggests that only those who broke the stipulations of God would receive judgment, why do those who are righteous suffer? Another way of saying this is: Why does it look like those living in another story are blessed while those who live in God's Story fall on hard times? As usual, God's concern is with our relationship with him, not our need to know information. Habakkuk 2 answers the question by telling how the unrighteous will suffer.

1. They are never satisfied even when they seem to prosper (2.4-5).
2. The wicked create the hostility that will destroy them (2.6-8).
3. The wicked will never be secure (2.9-11).
4. The accomplishments of the wicked will not last (2.12-14).
5. The things the wicked do determine the way they will be treated (2.15-17).

On the other hand, the just live because of the faithfulness of God (2.4).[108]

BOOK READING GUIDE: HABAKKUK

This is a reading guide for Habakkuk.

⬚ First Question of Habakkuk 1.1-4
Why does wrong go unchecked?

⬚ Answer by God 1.5-11
God will check wrong and use whatever he wishes as his scourge.

⬚ Interrogation by Habakkuk 1.12-2.1
Why will God permit a wicked nation to triumph over his nation?

⬚ The Answer by God 2.2-20
God punishes the wicked for their sins of greed, covetousness, cruelty, and idolatry.

⬚ Habakkuk's Prayer for Mercy 3.1-19
Habakkuk's faith is revealed as he prays for renewal.

The Captivity period of Israel's history is not covered by any one book. However, during this period, there are prophecies from the Exile in Jeremiah and Ezekiel (S).

Scene 9. The Exile Stage

The exile of Israel (both the Northern and Southern Kingdoms) provided a sharp blow on their nationalism. They had all but lost their vocation, blessing the nations by being the light to the world. For hundreds of years, even after their return to Jerusalem, they saw themselves as being in exile. The presence of God did not return to his Temple as they returned to their homeland.[109] This thought of "exile" is central to the Second Temple Judaism period.

Reading the StoryLine

[**Lamentations**: A eulogy of mourning of the fall of Jerusalem in 586 B.C.]

[**Daniel:** A narrative and apocalyptic story within Second Temple Judaism]

About Lamentations: A Sad Song about Jerusalem

Lamentations is made up of five mournful poems. They lament over the destruction of Jerusalem. The first four poems form an ❖ **acrostic** ❖ based on the Hebrew alphabet. In these four poems, there are twenty-two thought rhymes. Each of the thought rhymes begins with a word whose initial consonant is one of the twenty-two Hebrew characters. The third poem has a triple alphabetical arrangement. The fifth poem is not an acrostic even though it has twenty-two thought rhymes. To mark the anniversary of the destruction of the Temple in Jerusalem in 587 B.C., these poems are still read today in Jewish synagogues. The author presents sobering and dramatic pictures in this book. It suggests that God does have patience with his children, but it will eventually run out.[110]

So What?

The book of Lamentations struggles with the question of corporate suffering not unlike Job struggles with the question of individual suffering. The one difference is that Job's suffering is not caused by sin. Lamentations is a theology of the emotions. It was an aid to help the people of Judah process emotionally the destruction of their home and learn to confess their sin. Confession leads to recovered hope.

BOOK READING GUIDE: LAMENTATIONS

This is a reading guide for Lamentations.
- **D**esolation of Jerusalem 1.1-22
  Because of her sin, God forsakes Jerusalem.
- **I**niquity Judged 2.1-22
  Jerusalem's sin is judged by God.
- **R**epentance of Jerusalem 3.1-66
  God's mercy still ignites faith in the author even though he has suffered being pulverized and thrashed to the crossroads of hopelessness..

BOOK
Lamentations
AUTHOR
Traditionally Jeremiah
AGE WRITTEN
The destruction of Jerusalem
AUDIENCE
Those who are suffering because of the judgment of God.
AIM
To weep over loss because of sin and judgment
KEY CONCEPTS
The Lament over Jerusalem
KEY LESSONS
Mourning comes before morning.
GEOGRAPHY
Jerusalem

Lamentations 1-5.
TBB.1091-1105.

Act 3

Exile

Learning Objective
Comprehend the Exile stages of Israel's history.

Apocalyptic. Apocalyptic Literature is literature which is composed of dreams and visions. There are five features which historically mark most examples of Apocalyptic Literature. They are: visionary experience, the use of ancient names as authors, dualistic, symbolic language, and hope and encouragement. Revelation in the New Testament is the best known book in this genre of literature in Scripture.

AUTHOR
Daniel
AUTHOR
Traditionally Daniel
AGE WRITTEN
During the Exile
Others ascribe it to the Intertestamental Period
(164 B.C.)
AUDIENCE
Those who are weary under persecution.
AIM
To demonstrate the ability of God to judge world powers
and deliver his children.
KEY CONCEPTS
Understanding God's actions
KEY LESSONS
Do what is right regardless of the cost and God will guide you
no matter what the crisis.
GEOGRAPHY
🌐 Babylon (?)

Daniel 1-12. TBB. 1393-1410.

📖 Glory of Zion Contrasted 4.1-22
The author contrasted the past with the present. Present evil will occur because of the continued sins of Judah.
📖 Entreaty for God's Mercy 5.1-22
The prophet appealed to God for mercy.

About Daniel: Dreams and Visions

In the Protestant Bible's Major Prophets section, Daniel appears last. In the Hebrew Bible it is found in the section called The Writings and is a form of ❖ **Apocalyptic** ❖ writing.[111] Daniel was one of the youths that was taken into captivity by the Babylonians.

In the first six chapters, there are six stories. These stories are some of the best known among Christians. Daniel was uprooted from his homeland and educated in a foreign society. Even so, he remained faithful to God. At the right place and at the right time, he interpreted the King of Babylon's dreams when no one else could.

The second six chapters of Daniel are part of a genre of literature called Apocalyptic Literature. It begins with a vision of four beasts: a lion, a bear, a leopard, and a monster. The book has an Aramaic language section (2.4b-7.29), while the rest is written in Hebrew. Because these chapters are Apocalyptic, some scholars have placed them in 165 B.C.[112] Regardless of the time period of its writing, the supernaturalism is still believable. One of its major messages is: God is faithful regardless of the story his children find themselves living in.

Walter Brueggemann says that the book of Daniel is among the most peculiar and most difficult books in the Old Testament, an expression of faith voiced in genres that are unusual in Old Testament rhetoric.[113] The book is divided into two parts: a section of narratives which give an account of the way Daniel exercised influence in the kingdom of Nebuchadnezzar. The last section is a series of visions and are presented in Apocalyptic form.[114] There is ongoing discussion about the date of the book of Daniel. Some believe that it faithfully relates to the end of the sixth century B.C., while others think that 164 B.C. is the correct date.[115]

So What?

Daniel was intended to proclaim to every reader who chose to believe that in their time of persecution, God was in charge and ruled over them. God rewards those who remain faithful by continuing to live in his Story during trying times.

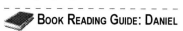

BOOK READING GUIDE: DANIEL

This is a reading guide of Daniel.
📖 Daniel's Faith 1.1-21
Daniel rises to power in Babylon.
📖 Answer to King's Dream 2.1-49
No one but Daniel can interpret the king's dream. Daniel disclosed information about four world powers and the Kingdom of God. He received a promotion.
📖 Nebuchadnezzar's Golden Image 3.1-30
The three Hebrew children refuse to bow their knee and worship the golden image which was built. They are thrown into a fiery furnace and then delivered by God without even a singe.

Exile

Learning Objective
Comprehend the Exile
stages of Israel's history.

⌐ Interpretation of King's Dream 4.1-37
Daniel interprets another dream of Nebuchadnezzar.

⌐ Events at Belshazzar's Feast 5.1-30
In an arrogant fit, Belshazzar misused the Holy Vessels. During a
feast, a human finger appeared and wrote a message on the banquet
wall which was interpreted by Daniel. The interpretation of the
dream told about Belshazzar's judgment.

⌐ Lion's Den 6.1-28
King Darius is persuaded to formulate a decree that no one could
pray to the Hebrew God. Daniel continued his custom of prayer, was
brought to the King, judged and thrown in a den of lions. God
delivers him and King Darius testified about the sovereignty of God.

⌐ Son of Man 7.1-28
Daniel has a vision about four beasts: the lion, bear, leopard, and
beast. Often interpreted as: the lion of Babylon, the bear of Medo-
Persia, the leopard of Greece, and the beast of Rome.

⌐ Dream about a Ram 8.1-27
Daniel has a vision of a ram and a goat.

⌐ Record of Seventy Weeks 9.1-27
The vision of the seventy weeks is conveyed.

⌐ Encouragement of Daniel 10.1-11.1
Daniel asked questions that were answered by an angel.

⌐ Antiochus and Prototribulation 11.2-45
The historical period of Antiochus is cited. This period is often seen
as somewhat typical of the final tribulation at the close of the age.
Prototribulation is understood like prototype, the prototype being the
original or model on which something is based or formed. Thus, a
prototribulation was the prototype of the final tribulation.

⌐ Master Stroke of God 12.1-13
The final triumph of the people of God is specified.

Reading the StoryLine

[**Obadiah** (Exile Prophet) Edom's mistreatment of Judeans during
the Babylonian destruction of Jerusalem]

About Obadiah: The Judgment of Edom

The name Obadiah means *the servant of the Lord*. Thirteen men in the
Old Testament are named Obadiah. There are no insights from his book,
which is the shortest in the Old Testament, to help us understand who he
was. The date of the book is also difficult to determine. Some scholars
believe that its message was likely given after the captivity of Judah by
Babylon. The message of Obadiah was given to Edom who were
descendants of Esau. Edom had not acted kindly toward their kin in
Judah. They had plundered Judah and enjoyed the fruit of their victories.
Because of these actions, God would judge them and their treasures
would be ravaged. Obadiah uses the familiar term: the *Day of the Lord* to
indicate that God would judge. This short prophecy was intended to help
Judah see the dangers of becoming nationally arrogant.[116] The Edomites
were finally destroyed in the fifth century by the Arabs. Herod the Great,
in the New Testament, was a descendant of the Edomites.

BOOK
Obadiah
AUTHOR
Unknown
AGE WRITTEN
Unknown
AUDIENCE
Those who have chosen
not to respond to
the message of God.
AIM
To announce judgment on
Edom
KEY CONCEPTS
Judgment
KEY LESSONS
God will reward you in
the same fashion you
reward others.
GEOGRAPHY
♦ Edom

Act 3

Exile

Learning Objective
Comprehend the Exile stages of Israel's history.

Obadiah. TBB. 807-809.

Dictionary Articles
Read the following Dictionary Articles in *New Bible Dictionary*.
Prophecy, I, II, III, IV
Joel, Joel, Book of
Jonah, Jonah, Book of
Amos, Amos, Book of
Isaiah, Isaiah, Book of
The Servant Songs
Micah, Micah, Books of
Hosea, Hosea, Book of
Nahum, Nahum, Book of
Jeremiah, Jeremiah, Book of
Ezekiel, Ezekiel, Book of
Habakkuk, Habakkuk, Book of
Lamentations, Book of
Daniel, Daniel, Book of
Obadiah, Obadiah, Book of

Restoration

Learning Objective
Understand the Restoration stage of Israel's history.

BOOK
Ezra-Nehemiah
AUTHOR
Traditionally Ezra
AGE WRITTEN
Sometime after the Exile
AIM
To encourage Jews who were returning to Jerusalem to re-establish their nation.
AUDIENCE
Those who desire to learn how to be restored to the favor of God and those who are doing the work of God and are facing opposition and are having limited results.
KEY CONCEPTS
Rebuilding Security and Worship
KEY LESSONS
Recommitment and Completing a Mission
GEOGRAPHY
⊕ Jerusalem

So What?

Obadiah demonstrates God as the ruler of all nations who gives people and nations freedom to make choices, but also holds them responsible for the choices they make.

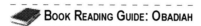 **BOOK READING GUIDE: OBADIAH**

This is a reading guide for Obadiah.

🗐 **B**ad News for Edom 1-7
Edom received the news that she had wronged her brother Judah.
🗐 **A**loofness of Edom 8-14
Obadiah exposed the sins of Edom.
🗐 **D**ay of the Lord 15-21
Edom was judged.

 Scene 10. The Restoration Stage (Ezra; Nehemiah; Esther)

The geographic return from Exile in Babylon did not fare well as the returning Jews anticipated a new dawn of nationalism. Instead, the nationhood faced a crisis which threatened its existence. Into this period, God provided two leaders, Ezra and Nehemiah, to nurture the nation back to health. The book of Ezra-Nehemiah is part of The Writings.

The book of Esther also appears in The Writings in the Scrolls section of the Tanakh. Its story is set in Susa, the winter capital of Persia. The book never uses the word God,[117] but his presence is implicit within the book.

About Ezra-Nehemiah: Return and Rebuild

These two books, one book in the Jewish Bible, continue the history of the Jews during the Restoration Period, which covers 536 B.C., when the Jews began to return to Jerusalem, to 458 B.C. when Ezra returned to bring the reforms needed for this new generation of Jews.

Nehemiah was a cup bearer to *Artaxerxes*, the King of Persia (Neh 1.11; 2.1). He returned to Jerusalem about twelve years after Ezra. Nehemiah had secured permission for the King to return to Jerusalem and restore its walls which provided security and safety for those living in the city.

So What?

Ezra

The book of Ezra plays a significant role in emphasizing the teaching of the Mosaic Covenant. This led Israel in a spiritual awakening and resulted in a Covenant renewal. Ezra reads the Law and calls for commitment to it. Repentance occurs. One must understand that the Law was not being read to people who need to reform, but was read to the people of God who were in Covenant with him. The continuation of God's care on their behalf was due to their commitment to his Covenant.

Nehemiah

Nehemiah ties together three theological themes: Scripture, worship, and community. Scripture, the Covenant, was read, interpreted, and applied in the life of the community (8.1-18). Worship was a direct result of teaching Scripture (8.11-18). It was the community working together that provided the rebuilding of the walls for protection and the temple for worship.

Reading the StoryLine

Learning Objective
Understand the Restoration stage of Israel's history.

Ezra-Nehemiah.
TBB.1341-1372.

The order of the material in Ezra-Nehemiah is somewhat confused. It may be clearer to rearrange the text as follows:

- Ezra 1.1-4.5; 4.24-6.22; 4.6-23
- Nehemiah 1.1-7.3; 11.2-13.31; 9.38-10.39
- Ezra 7.1-10.44
- Nehemiah 8.1-9.37
- Nehemiah 7.6-73 duplicates Ezra 2.1-70
- Zerubbabel Returns and Temple Building Begins: Ezra 1.1-4-23
- Prophets Encouragement: Ezra 5.1-12

[**Haggai** and **Zechariah** (Restoration Prophets) Prophecies about building the Temple]

About Haggai: Rebuilding The Temple

Haggai is the first of the Restoration prophets: Haggai, Zechariah, and Malachi. The people of God returned to their land with high hopes of rising again to the pinnacle of nationalism as they were during the days of David. It did not occur. Haggai gave four prophetic messages to these Restoration people. Because of the name Darius in Haggai 1.1, it is possible to convert these ancient dates to our modern calendar with great precision. When Israel arrived back in their land, they made an effort to rebuild the Temple, but when opposition came, a degree of indifference arose which brought the work to a halt. Haggai's clear call to these returning people was to get the Temple rebuilt and by 516 B.C. it had been rebuilt.

BOOK
Haggai
AUTHOR
Haggai
AGE WRITTEN
During the Restoration Period
AUDIENCE
Those who get sidetracked from
God's projects by the pursuit
for personal prosperity.
AIM
To challenge the returning people to finish the Temple rebuilding project.
KEY CONCEPTS
Temple
KEY LESSONS
God's work should always come first.
GEOGRAPHY
✈ Jerusalem

So What?

There are four oracles[118] that are important to the Story in Haggai. They are:

Oracle #1: Rebuild the Temple

The slowness of the rebuilding of the Temple and Israel's worship is attributed as the cause for the poverty and misfortunes of the struggling community. God calls them *this people* instead of *his people,* thus showing his displeasure with them. The usual response of Israel to the message of the prophets was scoffing and hostility. In this case, the people recognized that what Haggai was saying was right and responded with obedience. The Temple was started twenty-three days later on September 21, 520 B.C. (1.15).

Oracle #2: The Glory of the Temple

Haggai provided a message of encouragement to Israel and assured them that the glory of this Second Temple would far outshine the glory of the former Temple (2.6-9).

Act 3

Restoration

Learning Objective
Understand the Restoration stage of Israel's history.

Haggai 1-2. TBB. 885-886.

Oracle #3: Becoming Holy

Haggai's message was to help clean up a misconception that working on the Temple would make one holy. Holiness did not come by work. He also had to encourage them that time away from their farms during the middle of the growing season to work on the Temple did not mean a poor harvest but a great harvest.

Oracle #4: Not Now But Later

Zerubbabel was not to be the Davidic king that would help Judah overthrow foreign domination, but his leadership would point toward an eschatological day when God would send one in the line of David.

📖 BOOK READING GUIDE: HAGGAI

This is a reading guide for Haggai.

- ☐ **Call to Rebuild Temple (August 29, 520 B.C.) 1.1-15**
  Haggai's first message was about the neglect of the people for the Temple which resulted in poverty.
- ☐ **Assurance of God's Presence (October 17, 520 B.C.) 2.1-9**
  Zerubbabel and Joshua received word in Haggai's second message that God was with them.
- ☐ **Loyalty and Blessing (December 18, 520 B.C.) 2.10-19**
  Loyalty to God will bring blessing was the third message of Haggai.
- ☐ **Love For Zerubbabel (December 18, 520 B.C.) 2.20-23**
  Haggai's fourth message gave God's choice for leader: Zerubbabel.

About Zechariah: Apocalyptic Visions

Zechariah was a contemporary of Haggai and prophesied during approximately the same time frame. He presented eight prophecies to the Restoration people. Conflict had caused indifference among the returned captives of Judah. Zechariah was to encourage these returned people of God.

BOOK
Zechariah
AUTHOR
Zechariah
AGE WRITTEN
During the Restoration Period
AUDIENCE
Those who are unaware that God is ready to forgive and to restore.
AIM
To motivate the returning Jews to finish the Temple.
KEY CONCEPTS
Restoration
KEY LESSONS
Restoration is based on repentance.
GEOGRAPHY
📍 Jerusalem

So What?

Zechariah is Apocalyptic prophecy, much like the end of Daniel and the New Testament book of Revelation. It is full of symbolic prophecies.[119] It must be read with glasses that can see the symbols when being interpreted. The message of hope is of more value than the placement of visions into a time frame. The eight prophecies that are listed below were very symbolic.

1. **The horseman among the myrtle trees:** This oracle suggested that Israel would receive special care from God.
2. **Four horns and four smiths:** A prophetic word that told Israel that the enemies that stood against the rebuilding of the temple would not succeed.
3. **Measuring line:** God will defend Israel even when she outgrows her present walls.
4. **Joshua, symbol of priestly nation:** He is given charge of the Temple after his sins are cleansed.
5. **Lampstand and two olive trees:** God will continue to bless his people through their leaders.
6. **Flying scroll:** When the Temple is rebuilt and the people rededicate themselves to the Covenant, God will purify their land.

7. **The bushel of iniquity back to Babylon:** God will forgive his people, but he will allow them to be carried back to Babylon.
8. **Four chariots of divine judgment:** The protection of God will cover his people.

God uses all kinds of ways to tell his Story. It is helpful when we broaden our perspective on the various ways in which we live and tell his Story.

Learning Objective
Understand the Restoration stage of Israel's history.

![book icon] BOOK READING GUIDE: ZECHARIAH

This is a reading guide for Haggai.

☐ Veer Back to God 1.1-6
God calls for the nations to repent.
☐ Impartation of Eight Visions 1.7-6.15
The eight visions of Zechariah.
    1. The horseman among the myrtle trees
    2. Four horns and four smiths
    3. Measuring line
    4. Joshua, symbol of priestly nation
    5. Lampstand and two olive trees
    6. Flying scroll
    7. The bushel of iniquity back to Babylon
    8. Four chariots of divine judgment
☐ Sincere Piety 7.1-8.23
The purpose of fasting is questioned and an answer is given.
☐ Installation of King 9.1-11.17
A king and his program is declared, but he is rejected.
☐ Opposition to Israel Completed 12.1-13.6
Israel's final victories are presented.
☐ Nations Subjected to King 13.7-14.21
God will subject other nations to his holiness.

Zechariah 1-14. TBB. 891-902.

We continue reading the main storyline.

Reading the StoryLine

Continuing the storyline of Ezra-Nehemiah

☐ Temple Completed: Ezra 3.1-6.22
☐ Ezra Returns: Ezra 7.1-8.36
☐ [List of people: Ezra 7.27-8.14]
☐ Ezra's deals with intermarriage: Ezra 9.1-10.44

Ezra-Nehemiah.
TBB. 1341-1372.

Nehemiah

☐ Nehemiah's Return: Nehemiah 1.1-2.20
☐ Rebuilding Walls, Opposition, Plot: Nehemiah 3.1-4.23
☐ Helping Poor, Plot, Opposition, Walls Completed: Nehemiah 5.1-7.3
☐ [List of returnees; Nehemiah 7.4-73]
☐ Ezra assembles people, Reforms: Nehemiah 8.1-10.39
☐ [List of names: Nehemiah 11.1-36]
☐ Nehemiah assembles People, Reforms: Nehemiah 12.27-13.31

[**Malachi** (Restoration Prophet) Prophecies about robbing God]

Act 3

Restoration

Learning Objective
Understand the Restoration stage of Israel's history.

BOOK
Malachi

AUTHOR
Malachi

AGE WRITTEN
During the Restoration Period

AUDIENCE
Those who think they are spiritual.

AIM
To call Judah from its spiritual apathy.

KEY CONCEPTS
The Kingdom to Come

KEY LESSONS
Superficial religious practices will bring curses on those who participate.

GEOGRAPHY
⊕ Jerusalem

Malachi 1-4. TBB. 915-918.

About Malachi: Robbing God

Malachi stands at the conclusion of the Old Testament books as well as being the last prophet of the Restoration Period. With his book, the last prophet in the Story of the Old Testament concludes. The Restoration Period gave way to the continuation of Second Temple Judaism which lasted until the fall of Jerusalem in A.D. 70.

Malachi means *my messenger*. While Malachi is the messenger, God is the speaker. Its central message is: God is always in control regardless of what the outward circumstances may look like. The last few words of the book share a promise that looks toward the continuing Story in the New Testament and the coming of Jesus as Messiah.

So What?

The prophetic period closes with a message which is unfinished, looking forward to the coming Messiah and his forerunner, which suggestion is unique to Malachi. He calls the forerunner "my messenger" (3.1) and Elijah. One must turn to Act 4 of the Story to see John the Baptist as the fulfillment of this forerunner.

The exile was not the end and the return was not the beginning of the New Age to come. Malachi provides six ideas around which our relationship with God exists:

1. An awareness of God's love (1.1-5).
2. An honoring of God's actions (1.6-2.9)
3. A faithfulness in our social relationships (2.10-16).
4. A fear and reverence of God which is expressed in our commitment to justice. (2.17-37)
5. Serving God with our material resources. (3.6-14)
6. Meeting with others to talk about God (3.15-18)

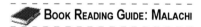

Book Reading Guide: Malachi

This is a reading guide for Malachi.

☐ Love for Israel 1.1-5
God demonstrates his love to Israel in the fall of Edom.
☐ Appeal to the Priests 1.6-2.16
God spoke to the sins of the priesthood and gave them warning.
☐ Salvation Coming 2.17-4.3
Salvation is coming in the person of a Messiah. The sins of Judah are reviewed and Malachi teaches about the difference between good and evil.
☐ The King is Coming 4.4-6
Obedience is commanded. Elijah is pictured as coming before the promised Messiah.

Reading the StoryLine

[**The Book of Chronicles**: A retelling spin of the story of 1 & 2 Kings for the sake of the people of the restoration.]

[**Esther**: The Queen of Persia]

About Chronicles: Learning from History

In the Jewish Bible, 1 & 2 Chronicles are one book. They record the same period of Jewish history as 1 & 2 Kings. The Hebrew name for this book was "The Words of the Days," that is, the events of the times. In the Septuagint, the book was called "The Things Omitted," that is, omitted from the books of Samuel and Kings. In the *Vulgate* translation, Jerome suggested that the work be called "a chronicle of the whole divine history." It is from the Vulgate that the English title Chronicles comes.

It appears, from the language, style, method of writing, interest, and general point of view, that 1 & 2 Chronicles and Ezra-Nehemiah were written as a continuous work by the same author.[120]

Written during the Restoration Period of Israel's history, the Chronicler chose his material to fit his purpose. Written for the Southern Kingdom after her return to the land from captivity in Babylon, the chronicler traces the family trees which led to David. This new generation of Jews needed to be grounded in its history. They needed to know how to reestablish worship as they rebuilt their temple. They needed to know how to keep themselves from repeating the errors of the past. They needed to know the faithfulness of God to his Covenant.

Family Histories: Genealogies

Family histories, like the one in 1 Chronicles 1-9, were common. There are about two dozen of these family histories in the Old Testament. The family histories of the Old Testament are not like modern family histories. They include only important people, not everyone who descended from the original person.

So What?

Here the Chronicler's desire is to tell the story of the first building of the Temple with all its structure and personnel. His purpose is to help those who have returned from exile to be encouraged to rebuild the Temple, while not making the mistakes of their forefathers.

The use of the writer of the genealogies, from Adam to the restoration after the exile in Babylon, demonstrates that God had a continuity of purpose for Israel from the beginning. The Chronicler demonstrates that God's selection of Israel and his Covenant with them was the basis on which they could worship God. It also suggests that there is more than one way to tell this story. This is a shorter view of the overall story than the one beginning in Genesis 11.27 and ending at the conclusion of Nehemiah. The message is the same. The form is different. This should provide hope that we have freedom to tell the Story in many different genres, while being careful not to tell a completely different story.

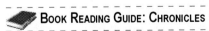 BOOK READING GUIDE: CHRONICLES

This is a reading guide for 1 and 2 Chronicles.

- Lineage 1 Chronicles 1-9
  The genealogies from Adam to David are listed.
- Envisioned Temple by David 1 Chronicles 10-29
  Saul's death is recorded and the reign of David is presented. The ark is seen as essential to the worship of Israel as David made preparation to build the Temple. Before the Temple is built, David dies.

Act 3

Restoration

Learning Objective
Understand the Restoration stage of Israel's history.

BOOK
Chronicles
AUTHOR
Unknown, Traditionally Ezra
AGE WRITTEN
Sometime after the Exile
AIM
To help those in exile not to make the mistakes of their parents
AUDIENCE
Anyone who has been disciplined by God in order for them to understand that God still has a plan for their life.
KEY CONCEPT
History viewed from a positive perspective
KEY LESSONS
Success is never final. Failure is nevr final.
KEY LESSONS
⊕ Israel

Chronicles. TBB. 1259-1341.

Act 3

Restoration

Learning Objective
Understand the Restoration stage of Israel's history.

BOOK
Esther
AUTHOR
Unknown
Ascribed to Mordecai by Clement of Alexandria
Ascribed to Ezra by St. Augustine
AGE WRITTEN
Sometime after the Exile
AIM
To teach that God will protect his children regardless of their geographic placement
AUDIENCE
God's people living as a persecuted minority
KEY CONCEPTS
Care of God
KEY LESSONS
God has a window of opportunity for you to go through.
GEOGRAPHY
Persia

☐ Vision Completed by Solomon 2 Chronicles 1-9
The building of the Temple and the wealth of King Solomon is recounted.
☐ Impairment of Temple 2 Chronicles 10-36
The Kingdom divides into the Northern and Southern Kingdoms and the story of the Southern Kingdom is presented from the break with the North to the captivity by Babylon. Prophecy about the return from captivity is shared.

About Esther: The Providential Care of God

The name of the book is taken from its heroine's non-Jewish name, Esther (perhaps from a Persian word meaning *star* or from the name of the Akkadian goddess Ishtar). Her name in Hebrew is given in 2.7 as *Hadassah* which means *myrtle*. The book of Esther is somewhat unusual as compared with other books in the Old Testament. It has been regarded by some as the only secular book in Scripture. Nowhere does it mention God, prayer, or corporate worship. The author is said to be more nationalistic than religious. But that makes a line between nationalism and religious where there was not a line in Jewish history.

Esther is set in the Ezra-Nehemiah period. Not every Jew returned to the homeland under Ezra-Nehemiah. Some chose to continue to live in a foreign country. Most lived in the major population areas and were very prosperous. Esther's story centers around a plot by Haman to annihilate the Jews living under the rule of *Xerxes*, King of Persia.

The Feast Of Purim

The Feast of Purim came into existence because the plot of Haman was discovered and abolished. This feast is still celebrated today on March 13-15 each year. During its celebration, Esther is read in the synagogues. When the name of Haman is read, the congregation boos because of his desire to annihilate the Jews. The name of the feast comes from the words *casting lots*.[121]

So What?

The attempt to exterminate Jews, called genocide, has occurred at least three times in history. The first full-scale attempt is recorded here at the hand of Haman. Later, others would attempt with the same result. This is a hatred of God's people (John 15.18) and it is certainly satanic in its source. It is the constant attempt to defeat God in his redemptive purpose.

The book of Esther demonstrates that God is ultimately in charge of human events. It is not from a random set of circumstances that Esther becomes Queen of Persia at this specific time in Jewish history. Nothing in God's world happens by chance. There are no coincidences.

The Feast of Purim finds its birth in Esther. It is a yearly celebration which commemorated the deliverance of the Jews through Esther and Mordecai. What if the church invented a "feast" or celebration of the acts of God in their midst as a way of living in and telling his Story?

Restoration

BOOK READING GUIDE: ESTHER

This is a reading guide for Esther.

☐ Choice of Esther 1.1-2.23
Vashti, King Xerxes wife and queen, is removed for her refusal to obey the King. Esther, the adopted daughter of Mordecai becomes Queen. Mordecai hears and reports the plot of Haman to execute the Jews.

☐ Arrogance of Haman 3.1-4.17
Haman plots to wipe out the Jews in revenge. Mordecai asked Esther for help.

☐ Request of Esther 5.1-7.10
Esther, even though it is against the law of the land, intervenes and appealed to the King for the Jews to be delivered. Haman is hanged on the gallows which had been prepared by Haman for Mordecai.

☐ Elevation of Mordecai 8.1-10.3
Mordecai inherits Haman's house and the feast of Purim is established.

Conclusion of Act 3

Putting the overarching story of the Old Testament together has its challenges. As an example, not all of the Psalms or Proverbs are listed in this chronological reading order. However, these events in Act 3 provide the understanding of Israel's vocation as it was in the day of Jesus. The Covenant was not a work-righteousness pact. The King was the representative of the whole people of Israel. The drama was not over. When Jesus arrived on the scene, he came proclaiming the Kingdom of God, which was the good news that God would restore Israel from exile.

We now enter Act 4. We begin with the period which is called Second Temple Judaism, which was the world into which Jesus and the writings of the New Testament came. Then, we will cover the birth, life, death, resurrection, and ascension of Jesus.

Learning Objective
Understand the Restoration stage of Israel's history.

Esther 1-10. TBB. 1381-1389.

Dictionary Articles
Read the following Dictionary Articles in *New Bible Dictionary*, Third Edition. D. R. W. Wood, A. R. Millard, J. I. Packer, D. J. Wiseman, and I. Howard Marshall (Editors), InterVarsity Press. 1996.
Ezra, Book of
Ezra
Nehemiah
Nehemiah, Book of
Zerubbabel
Haggai
Haggai, Book of
Zechariah
Zechariah, Book of
Malachi
Malachi, Book of
Chronicles, Books of
Esther
Esther, Book of

When Jesus arrived on the scene,

he came proclaiming the Kingdom of God,

which was the good news that God

would restore Israel from exile.

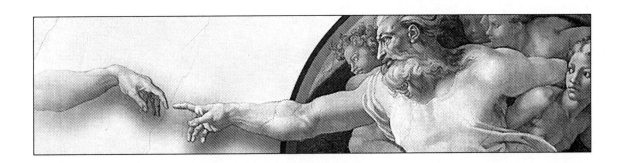

Act 4

Jesus: The True Human Being

Jesus is the central character around which

the Story of God's Kingdom

comes to its climax in what appears

to be the middle of the Story.

When you finish this session, you should be able to:

◆ Understand the Second Temple Period and how it bears on the New Testament
◆ Comprehend the Story of Jesus
◆ Understand Kingdom works of Jesus
◆ Comprehend the Kingdom words of Jesus

In this lesson, we begin with an overview of the Second Temple Period. Then, we look at ways the Story of Jesus could be told and make a choice. Next, we look at the life of Jesus using birth, life, death, resurrection, and ascension as an outline. Then, we share about the Kingdom works of Jesus. Then, we look at the Kingdom words of Jesus..

Act 4: Jesus
  Scene 1. Second Temple Judaism (587 B.C. to A.D. 70)
    The World Into Which The New Testament Came
      The Alexandrian Period (332–301 B.C.)
      The Egyptian Period (Ptolemaic: 301–198 B.C.)
      The Syrian Period (Seleucid: 198–167 B.C.)
      The Maccabean Period (167–63 B.C.)
    The Roman Period (63 B.C. –)
    The Rise of the Major Jewish Parties in the Second Temple Period
      Pharisees
      Sadducees
      Essenes
    The Symbols of Judaism in the Second Temple Period
      The Temple
      The Land
      The Torah
      Racial Identity
    The Literature of Judaism in the Second Temple Period
      Apocrypha
      Apocalyptic
    Telling the Kingdom Story
    The Christ Event
    Kingdom of God: Old Testament
      The Davidic and Apocalyptic Concept of the Kingdom
      The Davidic Concept of the Kingdom.
      The Apocalyptic Concept of the Kingdom.
  Scene 2. The Birth of Jesus: God Becomes Man
    How Did This Happen?
  Scene 3. The Life of Jesus
    Kingdom Proclamation
      Kingdom of God: Two Ages
      Kingdom of God: Two Views
    Kingdom Interpretation: Its Problem
      Kingdom: Realm or Kingdom Rule?
      Kingdom: War with Satan

Act 4

Act 4: Jesus

We begin Act 4 with the continuing Story coming from the Old Testament Restoration period. Turn on your TV to almost any news channel, ABC, CBS, NBC, CNN, FOXNews, etc., and most likely you will see a story about the Middle East that involves Israel. It seems that tensions in that region run high on a daily basis. In reality, this is not any different than during the period of time between Malachi, the last book in the time frame of Ezra-Nehemiah in the Old Testament and the continuing of the Story in the New Testament.[1] This period has often been called the Intertestamental Period with a time frame of about 400 years (404 – 6/4 B.C.). In recent years, the name and time frame has been changed. It is now referred to as Second Temple Judaism and the dates are usually set as 587 B.C. to A.D. 70.[2]

Learning Objective
Understand the Second Temple Period and how it bears on the New Testament.

 ## Scene 1. Second Temple Judaism (587 B.C. to A.D. 70)

We will cover four areas in this scene. First, we will look at the world into which the New Testament came.[3] Next, we will take a peek at the major Jewish parties that came out of this period. Then, we will give a brief overview of the symbols of Judaism that survived. Finally, we will mention some of the literature that arose from this period.

The World Into Which The New Testament Came

There are four important periods during the time span which is referred to as the Intertestamental Period, now referred to as Second Temple Judaism. To know something about each of them is useful in one's reading or studying of the Story in the New Testament.

The last period of the Old Testament (Ezra-Nehemiah) could rightly be called the Persian Period. It was during this time that the Temple in Jerusalem was destroyed and the land of the Southern Kingdom was conquered. Two important symbols of the nation Israel were in ruins. The following story draws a picture of the cultural movement within Israel beginning with the Alexandrian Period. To some extent, the Jews never returned from exile in their theological outlook. This concept plays itself out in the continuing Story.

The Alexandrian Period (332-301 B.C.)

This period was one of the most dramatic periods to emerge in history. Alexander the Great, as he is referred to, began making the known world of his time conform to the Greek culture. His father Philip was known by the title "man of war." This environment gave Alexander the platform from which he determined to conquer the world. His tutor philosophically was Aristotle, who provided him with the ambition to make the whole world Greek.

The coming of Alexander to Israel exposed the Jewish people to Hellenization. During this period of time, the Middle East became unified culturally. What this meant was that this process began to break down the highly valued distinctiveness of the Jews. Homer became the holy book and Platonic philosophy and its dualism became the lifestyle of this region. For almost 300 years before the life of Jesus, the Greek language was everyone's second language and second culture.[4]

Act 4

Alexander died in 323 B.C. and the empire he had accumulated was divided among four of his generals. When the air had cleared, the Jewish community in Palestine had become a part of the Egyptian Kingdom ruled by Ptolemy.

The Egyptian Period (Ptolemaic: 301–198 B.C.)

Very little about the Jewish community is known from this period. This was a period of peaceful Hellenization, the continuance of Alexander's dream of making the world conform to Greek philosophy, socially, mentally, and architecturally. The Jews were allowed to worship God in the way of their ancestors with no attempt to interfere, but the Jews were exposed to the Greek way of life through festivals, games, visits to amphitheaters, and public baths.

The capital of the Egyptian Kingdom was Alexandria, designed by Alexander and his architect, which grew fast into a leading Hellenistic center for culture and commerce. During this period of time, the Old Testament books were translated into Greek by a group of Jewish men. This production is called the Septuagint and is often referred to in written material by the symbol "LXX." The control of the Jewish community and Palestine lasted for approximately 100 years at which time the ownership of Palestine moved from the Egyptians to the Syrians.

The Syrian Period (Seleucid: 198–167 B.C.)

The defeat of Egypt by Antiochus III, who is often called Antiochus the Great, began a long and heated period of Jewish history. The new governmental ownership was greeted with positive support at the beginning. There was a degree of harmony under the new regime. This was all to end when the successor of Antiochus the Great rose to power. The empire was in decline because of a Roman victory over Antiochus the Great when Antiochus Epiphanes began to reign. The Jewish community would face some of its darkest hours in its bitter fight for life. There was an internal quarrel over leadership in the Jewish community. The high priest, Onias III, was in Antioch of Syria when Antiochus Epiphanes came to the throne. He sought help from the new ruler in the conflict. Jason, Onias' brother, saw this as an opening to seize the high priest's position and offered money to the new king. In addition, he offered to cooperate with the new king's desire to spread the Greek culture among the Jews. His offer was accepted and Onias was overthrown.

Jason was an ardent pursuer of performing his promise. He planned to turn Jerusalem into a Greek city. He built gymnasiums and racetracks in which the Jewish boys would exercise and race in the nude, which was the Greek custom. The races and events were opened by invocations to pagan gods. Jewish priests often attended these events. Greek theaters were built. Greek dress was adopted and there was a surgical operation developed to remove the marks of circumcision.[5] The Jews would exchange their Hebrew names for Greek ones. Some Jews opposed the paganization of their culture. Soon a party arose which was called the Hasidim or pious ones. They stood in the mainstream of Jewish tradition and resisted the Greek culturalization of the Jews.

The high priest question was not completely settled during this period. Menelaus, who was not even a part of the high priest's family, offered to replace Jason by offering the government a higher bribe. He incurred the hatred of the Jewish people by arranging for the assassination of Onias

III, who exposed the fact that Menelaus had stolen from the Temple treasury to pay off his bribe.

When Antiochus saw that his kingdom was being strongly established, he decided to invade Egypt and expand it. He had initial success in his venture. While returning home to Antioch, he stopped in Jerusalem and stripped the Temple of most of the items of value to the Jews. He was in deep financial difficulty and needed help to support his expansion plans. He finally met defeat in Egypt by the hand of Rome. At this point, the Jews felt the overwhelming expression of the wrath of Antiochus Epiphanes.

The rumor in Jerusalem was that Antiochus Epiphanes had been killed in Egypt. This news reached Jason who was living on the Eastern side of the Jordan. He returned to Jerusalem and seized control of the high priest's position. When Antiochus heard this, he became enraged and responded to the revolt by Jason by sending an army to Jerusalem to reinstate Menelaus. These dark hours will never be forgotten by the Jewish people. Apollonius came to Jerusalem with an army of thousands of soldiers. He plundered the city and killed many of its people, taking others, mainly women and children, captive.

Antiochus decided that he would no longer tolerate the piety of the Jews who had refused to accept the culture he presented to them. It became a capital offense to observe the Sabbath, celebrate any Jewish festival, or possess any copies of Old Testament scrolls. As many Old Testament scrolls as could be found were destroyed. Pagan sacrifice became compulsory. In the Temple, the altar of God was profaned,[6] and an altar to Zeus was erected. Unclean animals were sacrificed in the Temple, and sacred prostitution was practiced there. Many Jews supported this change, supposing that Judaism could survive and continue to function.

The Maccabean Period (167–63 B.C.)

This action by Antiochus led to a full-scale rebellion among the pious Jews. It is often referred to as the Maccabean Revolt. In the village of Modin outside of Jerusalem, a royal agent of Antiochus Epiphanes arrived to encourage the leader of the community to perform a sacrifice of swine. Mattathias, a priest, refused. Another Jew stepped forward to oblige the royal agent. Mattathias killed him and the royal agent. He demolished the altar which had been set up and fled to the mountains with five of his sons and other sympathizers. The revolt had begun!

The name Maccabean was a nickname, which meant "hammer," given to Judas, the son of Mattathias. Judas led successful guerrilla warfare until he finally defeated Syria. The Jews ultimately regained their religious freedom. They reestablished Temple worship by a rededication of their Temple. Today, this celebration is called ❖ **Hanukkah.** ❖ They took Palestine back and expelled the Syrian troops from Jerusalem.

Independence came in 161 B.C., two years after Antiochus Epiphanes' death. Judas was killed and was succeeded by his borther Jonathan. He began rebuilding and assumed the high priest's position. The next leader was Simon who gained recognition of Jewish independence and renewed a treaty with Rome. He was proclaimed as "The Great High Priest and Commander and Leader of the Jews" (1 Maccabees 13.42). He took leadership in religious, political, as well as military areas. Internal strife and ambition for power controlled the years from 142-137 B.C.

Learning Objective
Understand the Second Temple Period and how it bears on the New Testament.

Hanukkah is an eight-day festival beginning on the 25th day of Kislev, commemorating the victory in 165 B.C. of the Maccabees over Antiochus Epiphanes (215–164 B.C.) and the rededication of the Temple at Jerusalem. Also, called *Feast of Dedication, Feast of Lights.*

Act 4

Learning Objective
Understand the Second
Temple Period and how it
bears on the New
Testament.

QUESTIONS
Does history impede or help
you better understand the
text of Scripture?

Dictionary Articles
Read the following
Dictionary Articles in *New
Bible Dictionary*, Third
Edition. D. R. W. Wood, A.
R. Millard, J. I. Packer, D. J.
Wiseman, and I. Howard
Marshall (Editors),
InterVarsity Press. 1996.
  Alexander the Great
  Egypt
  Maccabees
  Roman Empire

The Roman Period (63 B.C. –)

Rome was founded in the eighth century B.C. It was formed as a republican form of government in the fifth century B.C. Rome ended a 200 year war with Carthage in 146 B.C. and began its conquest of the Mediterranean basin by Pompey while Julius Caesar was in Gaul (Spain) bringing it under Roman rule. Augustus became emperor after the defeat of Antony and Cleopatra. For approximately 200 years, there was peace in the Roman Empire. It is often called the Pax Romana. It was broken only two times, A.D. 70 and A.D. 135; both times the Jews were at the center of the conflict.

The kind of government which lies behind the New Testament story was set up by Augustus. The Roman administration was a provincial system of government. There were two forms. The first was called Senatorial. The leader was called a proconsul and he was appointed by the Roman Senate for a term of one year and was answerable to them. Paul converted some of these governmental officials on his first church planting mission (Acts 13.4-12). The second form was called Imperial. Its leader was called a proprietor. He was appointed by the Emperor and answerable to him. He could exercise civil and military authority and did so by means of a standing army. This is the kind of province in which the Jewish community in Palestine lived at the coming of Jesus.

The Roman government had learned over the years what was workable in governing people that they conquered. In the case of Palestine, they allowed a local native to be a vassal ruler. The first ruler was Herod the Great who ruled from 37 to 4 B.C. It was during his kingship that Jesus was born (either 6 or 4 B.C.). Herod was a scheming, jealous, and cruel man. He had two wives and at least three sons killed during his reign. Augustus once said, "It was better to be Herod's pig than Herod's son." In the Greek language, there is a play on words between "pig" and "son." It was under the rule of Herod the Great that the infants were slaughtered when the wise men returned home without reporting to him.

The Jewish people did not receive Herod kindly. He sought to gain their loyalty by a massive building project. The one he is most noted for is the beautification of the Temple in Jerusalem. This project lasted over a long period of time and in the ancient world a short proverb arose, "Who has not seen the Temple of Herod has seen nothing beautiful." In his cruelty, he commanded a number of leading Jews to die at his death, so that there would be mourning. The decree died with Herod.

His dynasty consisted of three sons who lacked their father's ambition. They ruled separate parts of Palestine. Archelaus ruled Judea, Samaria, Idumea; Herod Philip ruled Ituraea (Caesarea Philippi); Herod Antipas ruled Galilee and Perea. It was the latter that John rebuked in Mark 6.17-29, and Jesus called "the fox" in Luke 13.32. Archelaus misruled and was banished by Augustus. It was this same misrule that caused Joseph and Mary to settle in Nazareth (Matt. 2.21-23). After the removal of Archelaus, Roman governors ruled: Pontius Pilate was the judge of Jesus and Felix and Festus heard Paul's case in Acts 23-26. Herod Agrippa I was the grandson of Herod the Great and was the Herod mentioned along with Festus in Acts 23-26.

The everyday life of the Jewish community was ruled by the Jewish priesthood and the Sanhedrin. It was into this environment and time that

Learning Objective
Understand the Second Temple Period and how it bears on the New Testament.

Jesus was born. Paul calls it the fullness of time (Galatians). The stage was set and the greatest event of human history was ready to unfold. It was the apex and climax of God's Story.

So What?

From the time the Babylonians destroyed the Temple (ca. 587 B.C.) and took the land, the Jews awaited the time when they would once again worship in their Temple and take back the land that God had given them. There was tension within Israel during their return caused by the faith they had and the facts they could see on a daily basis.[7] Their exile from their homeland and their return during the Ezra–Nehemiah period still did not free them to be their own masters moving forward. They were still controlled by the Persians, then Alexander the Great and the Greek influence, then Egypt followed by Syria, and finally by Rome.

They had been Hellenized, even though there were some pockets of following the ways of Yahweh. Their dilemma was to discover how, if at all, they were to remain distinct from the alien culture they were living in. Which story would they choose: assimilate or acquiesce?

When Antiochus desecrated the Temple in 167 B.C., some Jews who would hold on to the beliefs of their forefathers found martyrdom rather than assimilation. Others, who escaped, formed a belief that God would vindicate his people and himself, along with his land and Covenant, if they would just remain faithful to his faithfulness.[8]

The concept of "assimilate or acquiesce" is being faced today in light of the cultural shift from modernity to postmodernity. What will the Church do?

The Rise of the Major Jewish Parties in the Second Temple Period

The major religious parties of the ongoing Story are the Pharisees, who were about 6,000 strong who may have been birthed from the Hasidim;[9] the Sadducees, who were about 20,000 strong; and the Essenes, who may also have come from the more devout sector of the Hasidim,[10] were about 4,000 strong.[11] The Pharisees have received mounds of bad press over the years as the legalist religious party who would work their way into a relationship with God. This view has been made somewhat popular by the writings of Martin Luther. One specialist has written, "Martin Luther, Reformer, is charged with misreading Paul the apostle, confusing the latter's first-century controversies with his own idiosyncratic and sixteenth century concerns, thereby distorting for centuries the understanding of Paul held alike by undiscerning scholars, unsuspecting preachers, and the masses that know not the law."[12] Other recent scholars like Sanders, Wright,[13] and Dunn have all taken an opposing view to Luther. These writers write under the rubric of "The New Perspective on Paul," a phase originated by Dunn.[14] See Appendix 11 for a discussion of this topic.

Pharisees

The Pharisees were a party who were spiritual descendants of the Hasidim,[15] that originated in the time of Antiochus Epiphanes who revolted against his Hellenization program. They were a group of pious Jews who entered the Maccabean revolt. Josephus suggested that they first appeared during the reign of ❖ **John Hyrcanus.** ❖

John Hyrcanus. A Hasmonean (Maccabean) leader of the 2nd century B.C. Apparently the name "Hyrcanus" was taken by him as a regal name upon his rise to power. He was the son of Simon Maccabee and hence the nephew of Judah Maccabee and the other Maccabees, whose story is told in the ❖ **Deuterocanonical** ❖ books of 1 Maccabees and 2 Maccabees.

Deuterocanonical Books. The Deuterocanonical books are the books that the Roman Catholic and Eastern Orthodox churches include in their Old Testament that were not part of the Hebrew Bible. The word *Deuterocanonical* comes from the Greek meaning *second canon*. These books were accepted by theologians in 1548 at the Council of Trent.

Act 4

Learning Objective
Understand the Second Temple Period and how it bears on the New Testament.

Hasmonean. This group was established under Simon Maccabees about twenty years after his brother Judah defeated the Syrian army in 165 B.C. They were the ruling dynasty from 140 to 37 B.C.

Philo was an Alexandrian Jewish philosopher who was known for his pioneering attempt to interpret the Hebrew Scriptures in the terms of Platonic philosophy.

Pliny was a Roman, a military officer who was a historian. He is most known for his only extant work, a thirty-seven-volume *Natural History* that served as the basis for scientific knowledge for centuries. Using mostly Greek sources and his own vivid imagination, Pliny wrote his works in Latin.

The Dead Sea Scrolls are the papyrus scrolls and scroll fragments that were discovered between 1947 and 1960 at sites along the Dead Sea, dating from the last two centuries B.C.. These scrolls contained many passages from the Hebrew Bible. They are very useful in reconstructing the compiling of the Hebrew Bible as well as understanding Jewish culture in the era immediately preceding the birth of Jesus.

When one talks about the Pharisees in the popular world of Bible readers, they are often seen as the thought police of Judaism, the legalists who were interested in piety. While they did concern themselves with private and ritual purity, they were never the legalist thought police that they have often been portrayed as.[16] While they began as a political and religious group during the Maccabean period, they were the most powerful under the ❖ **Hasmoneans**. ❖ They aspired to free Israel from pagan practices.[17] One might say that they were one of several options presented to the ancient Jew to be the people of God for the sake of the world.

Sadducees

The only sources for understanding the Sadducees come from the New Testament and Josephus.[18] Their origins are not completely understood, although the name "Sadducee" has been associated with endeavors to determine the group's origin which include a link with Zadok the founder of a prominent priestly family.[19] They have been understood as a religious group of conservative priests who were in the Jewish aristocracy and were a political party. The Sadducees were understood by Josephus as one of the three groups of Jewish philosophy.[20] The only issue on which all our sources agree is that the Sadducees rejected beliefs in the afterlife, resurrection, and a post-mortem judgment. The party was bound to the Temple and its traditions, so when the Temple was destroyed in A.D. 70, they passed out of existence.[21]

Essenes

The Essenes were a small Jewish sect that originated during the Second Century B.C. Josephus gives a longer account of this group than the other two with ❖ **Philo** ❖ and ❖ **Pliny** ❖ adding to the mix. They were a monastic group who may have broken away from the Hasidim because they wished to be more rigorous in the following of the Torah. It was tough to get into the group. One had to wait a year to meet with others in the group. After two years, they were admitted if they passed the test of character. Upon entering, they gave up all their possessions.[22]

Isolated theologically, this group lived at Qumran on the Northwest shore of the Dead Sea which also isolated them from Israel geographically. They believed themselves to be the "Sons of Light," while everyone else, all Israel and all pagans, were the "Sons of Darkness." This group may be best known today because of the discovery of the ❖ **Dead Sea Scrolls**. ❖

While other religious groups during this time believed that God would act on their behalf somewhere in the future, the Essenes believed that God had already begun to act in history to bring about his purposes in secret through them to bring Israel back from Exile.[23]

The Symbols of Judaism in the Second Temple Period

Symbols are powerful[24] as I found out as a young minister when I was pastoring my first church. I removed the altar bench from the front of the sanctuary to give more room for the front of the small auditorium and folks were not happy and that is an understatement.

Symbols bring one's worldview into a seeable and concrete reality. The Old Testament Story had four such symbols: Temple, Land, Torah, and Racial Identity.[25]

The Temple

Jewish national life was focused on the Temple. While there were schools that taught the Torah and synagogues in other parts of Palestine, which gained significance because of their relationship with the Temple, they in no way replaced the centrality of the Temple. For the Jews of this period as before, God lived in and ruled from the Temple where he provided forgiveness for them and restored them to fellowship with him. The Temple was the place where reintegration into community life occurred after defilement.

Learning Objective
Understand the Second Temple Period and how it bears on the New Testament.

The Temple was not just the religious center for the Jews. It was a combination of religion, nationhood, and government, along with the financial and economic being included. The Temple in Jerusalem controlled the city, as compared to a city like Corinth which had many small temples dotting the cityscape. It became controversial during the Jesus time frame that a half-breed king named Herod had rebuilt the Temple. This action brought resentment because, in the Jewish mind, only a proper successor of Solomon could actually rebuild the edifice.

The Temple was the heart of Judaism in a metaphorical sense and was seen as the place from which the healing and restoring presence of the Covenant God resided.

The Land

In the mind of the Jewish people, the Land did not take a backseat to other symbols. The Land was God's and he had given it to the Jews as a place to be the light of the world, for the sake of the world. No one except the rightful owner had the right to rule the Land, not the Romans, the Greeks, the Persians, the Babylonians, nor the Assyrians.

As a symbol, it was the place where the Jewish people grew their agricultural products that gave them daily life. It was Eden again, the new garden of God, given for the new humanity.[26] During this time period, the Land lay in waste because of the heavy taxation of the oppressors. In addition, it was being defiled with the building of institutions foreign to the Story of God. Pagan schools, temples, and gymnasia were built as a visual sign of the conquerors who were idol worshippers.

Temple and Land were alike in that each had been possessed again by those that had returned from Babylon's captivity, but only partially.[27] Jews lived on their land and had their Temple but still lived in Exile.

The Torah

Torah was the Covenant lease of Israel who had been chosen by God to be the light to the world demonstrating who God really was. Torah and Temple as well as Torah and Land were bonded together. In the former, the Torah regulated what happened in the Temple and the Temple was the focal point in which the Torah was observed. In the latter, the Torah offered the promise of the Land and the details of how the blessing of the Land would remain. One must stop and note that the very reason that the previous occupiers of the Land had been chased out was because of their immorality and idolatry. God would surely do the same again to those that defiled the Land by not practicing the Torah.

The Pharisees began to teach that one could practice without the need of the Temple. One may find an illustration herein about worldviews. "A symbol that loses touch with either story or praxis becomes worthless."[28]

Act 4

Learning Objective
Understand the Second Temple Period and how it bears on the New Testament.

QUESTIONS
What are your thoughts on these symbols: Temple, Land, Torah, and Racial Identity?

Racial Identity

Who was a real Jew became a hotly debated item with those who returned from Babylon's captivity. As the returnees told and retold the story of their ancestors (like the book of Chronicles), they were reminded over and over what calamities came upon Israel when they disobeyed God's Covenant. During their captivity interracial marriage with captors was understood as a slide toward paganism, becoming the focal point of the ministry of Ezra. Unless one could figure out who was a true Jew, how could they continue as the people of God? This focus, during the restoration period on this issue, survived and moved forward, and the covenant markers of the Jewish people, like circumcision, were seen as a true boundary marker of being a true Jew. Racial identity was understood as a symbol of being the "seed" of Abraham's promise given by their Covenant God.[29]

So What?

Symbols are often the currency of telling stories. In an image-rich society in which we now live, we need to become as good in our exegesis of images and symbols as we do in our exegesis of words, which are in themselves symbols carrying certain ideas.

The Literature of Judaism in the Second Temple Period

Two lists of literature are found in this period that continue the story of Israel. They are called the Apocrypha and the Pseudepigrapha. The Apocryphal books are broken down as follows followed by a list of the Pseudepigrapha.

Apocrypha

Deuterocanonical Books. The Deuterocanonical books are the books that the Roman Catholic and Eastern Orthodox churches include in their Old Testament that were not part of the Hebrew Bible. The word *Deuterocanonical* comes from the Greek meaning *second canon*. These books were accepted by theologians in 1548 at the Council of Trent.

The Protestant church rejected these books based on ideas that disagree with Protestant doctrine, such as purgatory, masses for the dead, good works earn merit with God. The Roman Catholic Church accepted twelve of these fifteen books as ❖ **Deuterocanonical** ❖ at the Council of Trent in 1546 in response to reformers. The Eastern Orthodox Church accepted all but 2 Esdras as canonical.

Apocalyptic

Only one Apocryphal book falls into this genre. Apocalyptic works were highly cryptic in their language. They were written in a code of sorts so that only the receiver could understand the message.

> **2 Esdras** tells its readers that while times may be bad now, there is a new time coming when the righteous will be saved and all evil banished.

This type of literature was usually written to comfort the reader in the midst of trouble.

Devotional Literature

Dictionary Articles
Read the following Dictionary Articles in *New Bible Dictionary*.
  Pharisees
  Sadducees
  Essenes
  Philo
  Dead Sea Scrolls
  Temple

There are two pieces of Apocryphal Literature in this genre. These pieces demonstrate an unusually high piety.

> **Baruch** instructs Jews to celebrate feasts and confess sins even during times of agony.
> **The Prayer of Manasseh** gives a pattern for prayer to God. These books intend to keep the reader's eyes directed toward God through praise and prayer.

History

There are two histories and one interpretation of history within this genre.

   ☐ **1 Esdras** that covers the same history as 2 Chronicles, Ezra, and Nehemiah.
   ☐ **1 Maccabees** that covers the history from 175 B.C. - 134 B.C.
   ☐ **2 Maccabees** is an interpretation of parts of the history of 175 B.C. - 134 B.C.

     These histories have some inconsistencies in them, but they were used by the historian Josephus in his writings about the history of this period.

Learning Objective
Understand the Second Temple Period and how it bears on the New Testament.

Moralistic Novels

     There are six selections that fall within this genre. These stories or additions to an existing canonical book were oral tales in which morality or virtue was extolled so that the readers could benefit in their daily lives.

   ☐ **Tobit** teaches devotion and obedience to God.
   ☐ **Judith** teaches that no circumstance is beyond the intervention of God.
   ☐ **The Letter of Jeremiah** exhorts the reader not to worship idols.
   ☐ **The Song of the Three Hebrew Children** enlivens hope in God's deliverance.
   ☐ **Susanna** exhorts the reader to live with virtue in spite of the evil circumstances around.
   ☐ **Bel and the Dragon** shows how to challenge evil that is contrary to the revealed plan of God.
   ☐ **Additions to Esther** These additions are not a narrative by themselves. They are inserted into the text of the Book of Esther at selected points. While the Book of Esther does not mention God by name, these additions have many references to God.

     The hope of the authors of these pieces of literature was to exhibit behavior that, when copied, could bring the same result in life as that of the hero of the story.

Wisdom

     There are two pieces of Apocryphal Literature in this genre. This wisdom literature is like the Wisdom Literature in the canonical Scripture. This genre of literature is the most unfamiliar to today's Bible readers. You could define "wisdom" as the discipline of applying to one's life the truth that experience teaches. Wisdom is personal and not theoretical or abstract. Wisdom exists when people think or act according to the truth as they have learned through their own experience.

   ☐ **The Wisdom of Solomon** was written to protect the Jews in Egypt from the danger of falling into skepticism and idolatry.
   ☐ **Ecclesiasticus** was the oral traditions that were used to teach young men to live piously.

     These two books are often held as being the more important books in the Apocrypha.

Pseudepigrapha

     The word pseudepigrapha means "false authorship." It may be better to understand these as books which were written using well-known ancient figures' names as the authors. Today, one might call it a "pen name" or pseudonym used by a writer. These books are called Apocrypha by the

Learning Objective
Understand the Second Temple Period and how it bears on the New Testament.

QUESTIONS
Have you ever read any of these books as background to the Story of the New Testament? If not, why not?

Dictionary Articles
Read the following Dictionary Articles in *New Bible Dictionary*.
  Apocrypha
  Pseudepigrapha

Roman Catholic Church while the Eastern Orthodox accepts Third and Fourth Maccabees as canonical.

- 1 Enoch (Ethiopic Apocalypse of Enoch)
- 2 Enoch (Slavonic Book of the Secrets of Enoch)
- 4 Baruch (a.k.a. Paraleipomena Jeremiou)
- Adam and Eve, The Books of
- Ahikar, The Story of
- Apocalypse of Abraham
- Apocalypse of Adam
- Apocalypse of Moses
- Joseph and Aseneth
- Jubilees, The Book of
- Letter of Aristeas
- Martyrdom of Isaiah
- Paraleipomena Jeremiou (a.k.a. 4 Baruch)
- Psalms of Solomon
- Pseudo-Phoclides
- Revelation of Esdras
- Second Treatise of the Great Seth
- Sibylline Oracles
- Testament of Abraham
- Testament of Job
- Testament of Solomon
- Testaments of the Twelve Patriarchs

So What?

These books give us a window into the way folks in Second Temple Judaism thought about ideas and concepts of their day. As an illustration, it would be like an archeologist finding a *Left Behind* book about two thousand years from now in A.D. 4007 and the scholars reading the text say, "So, there was a group of folks at the beginning of the twenty-first century that thought that Jesus was going to return within days. Obviously, they were wrong because here we are some two thousand years later. However, it's interesting to note what some of them believed during that period of time."

So What?

At loss for a Kingdom, the people of Israel were ripe for the message of a young Jewish man who came preaching "the Kingdom of God is at hand." We continue with the remaining part of Act 4 and investigate Jesus and his message of the Kingdom.

Telling the Jesus Story

The Kingdom of God is about the Creator God putting things to right that had taken a serious turn in the Garden story. Jesus is the central character around which the Story of God's Kingdom comes to its climax[30] in what appears to be the middle of the Story.[31]

There are several ways to venture into the material about Jesus. One is to tell his life story as a biography. The difficulty with that approach is that it has to work really hard to harmonize the four Gospels that try to fit every detail of the life of Jesus into one story. There have been many harmonies of the Gospels written.[32] All seem to miss a basic point, each of

Learning Objective
Comprehend the Story of Jesus.

the Gospel writers had their own reasons for writing their particular Gospels, and putting them together in a harmony destroys the shades of meaning that each author worked to produce for his audience.[33] Another difficulty is the double tier of interpretation: What did Jesus mean by what he said and what did the authors mean by what Jesus said?[34]

Second, one could use the primary theological backdrop of the life ministry of Jesus, which was and still is the Kingdom of God, and tell his Story from that point of view.

The late George Ladd approached the concept of the Kingdom of God from a "framework of salvation."[35] Salvation History, known in theological writings as *Heilsgeschichte*,[36] is a record of the saving acts of the Creator God of humankind. His approach was a "biblical theology" perspective. "Biblical theology is that discipline which sets forth the message of the books of the Bible in their historical setting."[37]

James Kallas (a little known Lutheran scholar) would also be considered a proponent of biblical theology. According to James Kallas, the story of the Kingdom is told as a war between the Kingdom of God and the kingdom of Satan and God's victory over it,[38] a motif stressed by Kallas but not completely left out by Ladd or Tom Wright.

Tom Wright, the present Bishop of Durham, suggests that when Jesus was proclaiming the Kingdom, he was "deliberately evoking the entire story-line that he and his hearers knew quite well" and "that he was retelling this familiar story in such a way as to subvert and redirect its normal plot."[39] Wright would also stand in the biblical theology arena. According to Wright the story of the Kingdom is told in four stages:

- ◆ **Invitation**: a call to repent and believe the good news
- ◆ **Welcome**: everyone was a potential participant and the ones who most benefited were the poor and sinners
- ◆ **Challenge**: having heard the call of Jesus, followers become actors living as the renewed people of God
- ◆ **Summons**: to follow Jesus and work in his mission[40]

QUESTION
How do Tom Wright's four stages: Invitation, Welcome, Challenge, and Summons, help you have a better grasp on the Story of the Kingdom?

I was introduced to Ladd at Fuller Seminary and Kallas at Fuller and California Graduate School of Theology, where I took courses from both. I have listened and read Wright for about six years now, meeting him on two occasions. I am convinced that their basic thesis is correct.

Other readings of the Kingdom of God might include creation, covenant, salvation history, etc. Some might suggest[41] that these readings are in fact different meanings. I prefer to understand them as different angles through which the story is being viewed. As an illustration: one story comes through a prism and many hues of color result. Each hue is different and is only part of the whole of the original light. So it is with the Story of the Kingdom. The Story told from Genesis to Revelation is God's Story and it is theological. However, different readings of the Story present one of the many colored hues of the Story, so it is with the Kingdom of God. In Act 4, there will be a mixing of the thoughts of these three New Testament specialists, with some emphasis given to Kallas and his war motif. One must remember that there is no one correct way to tell this Story, but one has to choose to tell it some way. I have chosen to relay this Story within a rubric that is sometimes called "The Christ Event."[42]

Act 4

Learning Objective
Comprehend the Story of Jesus.

Dictionary Articles
Read the following Dictionary Articles in *New Bible Dictionary*.
  Jesus Christ

The Christ Event

Most believers know a lot of the stories which occurred in the life of Jesus. Few have had the opportunity to think about how those stories fit into his life. When we are making friends with others, we often want to know certain facts about the person we are befriending. We might want to know where he or she was born, who her or his parents were, or what some of the notable events were which occurred in his or her life.

There are many stories in the New Testament that share some of those details for readers, but there was only "one event" which comprised the life of Jesus. The event of Jesus coming to earth was the turning point in the salvation history of humankind, the climax of the Story of God. This event was made up of five important and inseparable parts: *The Virgin Birth,*[43] *The Sinless Life, The Crucifixion, The Resurrection,* and *The Ascension.* Each of these parts are important and dependent upon each other. Each part holds its own significance in the Christ-Event. No part can be left out. No part has more importance than any other part. It is with this "outline" that we will frame the Story of Jesus. I have chosen this outline because it is a natural outline of the Story of Jesus. He was born, lived, died, was resurrected, and then ascended.

It is common knowledge that the four Gospels in Scripture all tell the Story of Jesus but in quite different ways. Mark, usually understood as the earliest Gospel to be written, begins with the story of Jesus being baptized by John and reminds his readers that John was the one whom the Story of the Old Testament pointed toward who would prepare a way for the coming Messiah. The Gospel of Matthew begins with a genealogy that demonstrates that the ministry of Jesus is grounded in the Old Testament Story reaching back to Abraham. Luke, on the other hand, takes the Story back to Adam which may suggest that Jesus' Story encompasses all of humankind. Finally, John gives his readers a "pre creation" view of Jesus as the eternal Logos. They each have a specific purpose in mind in which they tell their story. The glue that holds the Gospels together is the telling of the Kingdom Story of Jesus.

Kingdom of God: Old Testament

Before we start with Act 4 Scene 1, let's review the Kingdom in the Old Testament. From the beginning of the Old Testament, God is pictured as king.[44] Picture language, i.e., metaphor and other literary devices, was the currency of the Hebrew storytellers and writers to help their listeners and readers grasp the Story.

The Kingdom of God concept is rooted in the Old Testament and is certainly broader than the specific term.[45] The term does not even appear in the Old Testament.[46] Ladd writes, "While the idiom 'the Kingdom of God' does not occur in the Old Testament, the idea is found through the prophets." He concludes after viewing several Old Testament references that "this leads to the conclusion that while God is the King, he must also become king, i.e., he must manifest his kingship in the world of men and nations."[47] To comprehend this concept, we might need to look in the Old Testament for the idea even though the term Kingdom does not appear.

The *Dictionary of Biblical Imagery* suggests that king and kingship are common words in Scripture.[48] Arthur Glasser, in his book *Announcing the Kingdom,* suggests that the Old Testament sees God as King over the Kingdom he created.[49]

The Old Testament presents the Kingdom in the context of Jewish messianic expectation and eschatology. It believed that God would deliver them, which was their hope for the future. This deliverance is what Wright calls the "return from exile," a central theme along with restoration that Israel believed herself to be acting out.[50] Israel reached its apex during the rule of King David and Solomon. From that point forward, Israel began to descend. At the death of Solomon, the Kingdom divided again into two Kingdoms with their own kings and governments. This division set in place a longing among the Jews for God to restore to them their past blessings.

The Davidic and Apocalyptic Concept of the Kingdom

There were two ways which the Kingdom began to be understood during the Second Temple period according to Kallas: the Davidic and the Danielic/Apocalyptic Concept.

The Davidic Concept of the Kingdom.

Israel's hope was that God would send a king like David. Israel's focus was militaristic and geographic. Israel wanted a nationalistic kingdom to return. The prophets of the Old Testament began using a phrase "the day of the Lord," which was a two-sided belief system including restoration and judgment. Israel believed that the "day of the Lord" was a time when Israel would be fully restored (Amos 9; Isa. 11; Zech. 8.4-8). The nations would be judged (Amos 1). The message of Amos came to pass when the Northern Kingdom virtually ceased to exist after the Assyrian invasion. When the Southern Kingdom went into exile, the hope remained and glittered again during the Restoration Period when Zerubbabel, a descendant of David, became king. This hope is reflected in Psalm 126. The Davidic hope for a military and political power emerged again during the time of Zerubbabel. Judah hoped that the descendant of David was the one to return them to the glory of David's rule. Haggai and Zechariah mirrored the expectation which surrounded Zerubbabel. But when his kingship failed, hope began to wane.

Once again during the Maccabean revolt, these old nationalistic aspirations had a revival. However, the rise of a Davidic king, an anointed one to bring them to political power with military might, did not occur. When you turn to the pages of the New Testament, there is a remnant of those who still believed that God would restore a nationalistic kingdom to Israel (John 6; Acts 1). The Kingdom of God was thought to be a Kingdom of this world which would be peopled by the Jews. There was nothing spiritual or future about it. The Kingdom was a dream of Jewish nationalism for the present.

The Apocalyptic Concept of the Kingdom.

The second view arose during a part of Second Temple Judaism sometimes called the Intertestamental Period (404 - 6 B.C.). During this period, there arose a new kind of writing within Judaism called Apocalyptic Literature and the term Kingdom of God came into popular usage. Hope did not diminish; it only assumed a new language with a modified meaning. The prophets hoped for a nationalistic kingdom, while the hope of the Apocalyptic writers was for a heavenly kingdom which would end this Present Evil Age. A new world would break into the present world and bring the rule of God. This view developed a belief that Satan dominated this Present Evil Age;[51] it was under his rule. When

Act 4

Antiochus Epiphanes unleashed his persecution on Israel (175-164 B.C.), this view began to flourish. This horrific deluge of evil could only be the result of a cosmic conflict. Evil was winning. Good was losing. The demonic and sickness were in control. It was here that the Jews' consciousness of evil spirits began to develop. The books of the Intertestamental Period give us a window to view the beliefs of the people in a specific period of time. In *First Enoch* 54.3-6, Satan is pictured as the ruler of a kingdom of evil with many followers, the demons. The book of *Jubilees* 23.29 suggests a golden age to come in which God himself would usher in his kingdom reversing the evils of Satan. Good would triumph, healing would occur, the demonic would be defeated.[52]

Scene 2. The Birth of Jesus: God Becomes Man

By all accounts, Jesus was born in Bethlehem approximately 6 or 4 B.C. Some two years later, because of the murderous attitude of Herod, Joseph moved the family to Egypt. There are spotted accounts of the early life of Jesus in the Gospels. His ministry began in the year A.D. 28 or 29 and he was killed by Jewish and Roman hands in the year A.D. 30 or 33. You might pause to note that using the outside numbers of birth and death that the numeric age of Jesus at death was approximately 38 years of age.

The Bible presents the Virgin Birth of Jesus as a real event with no apologies. Jesus is seen as being born of human flesh from a normal human mother who was a virgin who became pregnant by the miracle given by the Spirit.

For Matthew, the Spirit may have put new light on an Old Testament text from Isaiah which says, "Therefore the Lord himself will give you a sign: The virgin (young woman) will conceive and give birth to a son, and will call him Immanuel (God with us)" (Isa. 7.14).[53] The original hearer of Isaiah's words would not have had a concept for what Matthew applies to the passage. This passage is the focus of many heated debates. In its own context, Ahaz, a King of Judah, needed comfort. God gave it to him in time and space by a birth of a child named Immanuel. This concrete act of God provided Ahaz with the faith to believe what the name implied, i.e., that God was surely with him. That may have been the original meaning to the first hearers. But, the Holy Spirit sheds new light into the pen of Matthew that this also applied to the birth of Jesus (Matthew 1.23).

Luke, on the other hand, tells the story of the birth of Jesus, in his first chapter (Luke 1.26-38), as announced by an angel to Mary. There is no mention of the Isaiah passage. James Dunn suggests that a better phrase for virgin birth is "virginal conception.[54] He gives a brief summary of this issue in his book, *Jesus Remembered*.[55] "What the core traditions affirm (Matthew and Luke) is that Jesus' birth was special — 'from the Holy Spirit' (Matt. 1.20), by the power of the Holy Spirit (Luke 1.35)."[56] The insights gained from these two Gospel passages demonstrate "how the earliest Christian thinking developed" about the birth of Jesus.[57]

I would suggest that importance should not be given to the number of times something is mentioned in Scripture. This is a difficult thought for the Westerner to grasp because for her or him the higher the number, the more important it seems to be. It may just be that the virgin birth is the anchor that holds "The Christ Event" together.

Jesus' birth is the incarnation of God into humankind, a picture of the Tabernacle in flesh. The birth of Jesus, announced by an angelic choir to

a group of lowly shepherds, may be a possible allusion to the outcast state of Israel at that moment in her history. This motley group received the news that a savior was born, the Messiah for whom Israel had been waiting. When Jesus was eight days old, as per custom, he was taken to be circumcised, a sure sign that he was entering the Covenant community. About two years later, a visit from the Magi may be another allusion that his Story included all humankind, those inside and outside the Covenant people of God. After the visit of the Magi, a move to Egypt was prompted by the Holy Spirit. Returning to Nazareth several years later, Jesus grew up with his brothers and sisters. Very little is known of the years between his return to Nazareth and the beginning of his public ministry except for the small story of being left behind in Jerusalem where he was found chatting with the elders (Luke 2.49).

How Did This Happen?

How could the changeless God become a man? This is an interesting question about which the Western mind speculates. The idea of God becoming a man has perplexed the Greek mindset for a long time. How is it that what *is* one essence can become another essence that it is not? Believers are faced with somewhat the same problem. How could God, the creator of the world, become a baby? There are all kinds of answers and positions on this question. Some believe that God never really changed into an actual man. Others believe in the true humanity of Jesus, but deny he was truly the eternal Second Person of the Trinity. Still others defend the position that he was a God-Man, all God and all Man at the same time. The following is representative of some of the views over the centuries.

Docetism. This was an opinion especially associated with the Gnostics that Jesus had no human body and only appeared to have died on the cross. This group believed that Jesus living in a physical body could not be real. Therefore, he was a mirage, a dream, an appearance. God, in their estimation, would be contaminated by partaking of humanity.[58]

Unitarians. This group is a form of Christianity that denies the doctrine of the Trinity, believing that God exists only in one person. Jesus, as the best of men, was adopted to a divine status at a certain point, like his baptism. After that point, he could be called divine.[59]

Arianism & Jehovah's Witnesses. Jesus was more than a man, he was an angel of high rank. He left that position to become a mere man. After his death, he was given a higher status than before. He is never God, only the highest representation of Jehovah.[60]

Reinhold Niebuhr. Jesus was fully human. He had a sinful nature. Even though Jesus sinned, he is the finest symbol of divine love that has ever been revealed to mankind.[61]

Karl Barth. Jesus was fully human including a sinful nature, even though he never sinned. God acted in the world through him incognito.[62]

Orthodox Christianity. Jesus is the Second Person of the Trinity and shares in all the divine attributes. His divine attributes were not taken from him at the incarnation. In becoming flesh, he added to his divine characteristics the essentially human attributes which did not include a sinful nature or actual sin. The properties of the divine and human

Learning Objective
Comprehend the Story of Jesus.

QUESTION
In what way is it difficult for you to believe that Jesus lived in a human body?

Act 4

Learning Objective
Comprehend the Story of Jesus.

natures did not combine to form a third nature, and he did not become two separate persons. Jesus was one person with two natures, divine and human.[63]

So What?

Taking these stories at face value and regarding the Virgin Birth as a historical fact will result in certain consequences. Among the most obvious is that it strongly suggests that one who does accept it, believes miracles are possible. If one believes in the Virgin Birth of Jesus, it should not be too difficult to believe that God can and still performs other miracles in his world today.

 ## Scene 3. The Life of Jesus

Kingdom Proclamation

In the days when Jesus lived, Israel was in a great bit of trouble. The pagan Romans were in control and the leadership of Israel had compromised with Rome. During this period, a number of revolutionary groups arose led by a professing prophet-messiah. The vision of these prophet-messiahs was greater than just overthrowing the Romans. They hoped that this would be the time when God would at last come and set his people free from their exile by bringing justice and peace. There were many such groups and prophets fifty years on either side of the life of Jesus. Usually, the blade of Rome shortened their life.[64]

One such group gathered around a strange person living in the wilderness called John. His tactics were different than the other revolutionaries. He was baptizing people in the Jordan River as a re-enactment of Israel as the people of God going through the Jordan River into the Promised Land. Baptism was a symbol of the Exodus, a symbol of rescue, of salvation, and of a new start for the people of God. Baptism was a symbol that Israel had at last come home from exile, and that God would soon be king of the earth, and evil would finally be defeated.[65]

The people of Israel would resonate with such a symbolic act. After all, they were being taxed to death and driven off their land, not to mention that they were irate about the polluting of their culture by the pagan Romans. In the crowds that swarm to the desert to hear this strange fellow was Jesus, the cousin of John. After Jesus was baptized and driven into the wilderness to be attacked by Satan, he came preaching the gospel of the Kingdom of God village by village in both his words and works (summarized by Mark in 1.14-15). The first part of Mark 1.14 summed up the entire narrative of Israel's new exodus, her final return from exile.[66] Jesus told his listeners that the Kingdom of God was happening right before their eyes in his ministry. It is no wonder that they followed him and hung on his words.

Act 4, then, is the proclamation of the Kingdom of God and was the final act in God's triumph over the powers of evil and suffering in a *now* but *not yet* system of thought.

The question is: What might Jesus have meant when he came proclaiming the Kingdom of God? Another way of thinking about this is to ask what the average first century Galilean living in a small village heard when this young prophet Jesus came visiting his or her town and announced that God was becoming king of his people and that he was doing it in this young prophet's own ministry. In order to converse here, we must think our way back into someone else's world and try to grasp what they may have thought. If we do not know what the contemporaries of Jesus were thinking, it will be impossible to understand what Jesus meant.[67]

There are two points that can help us toward an understanding of Jesus and his message of the Kingdom. *First*, Jesus believed that the Creator God's purpose from the beginning was to deal through Israel with the problem within his creation caused by Adam. Not by looking at Israel as an example under the rule of God, but as the means through which God would save the world. *Second*, the vocation of Israel would be accomplished in the history of Israel in a final act in which Israel herself would be saved, and the Covenant God would bring his love and justice to the world which would in turn produce the renewal of his creation.[68]

In Israel during the lifetime of Jesus, there were three different options for *being the people of God* that were practiced. *First*, the Quietist of Qumran. They practiced: Separate yourself from the wicked world and wait for God. *Second*, the Herodian Compromisers. They practiced: Buy into the present political climate, get along with your political bosses (Herod) the best you can, and hope for the best. *Third*, the Zealots: They believed that you should sharpen your swords, fight a holy war, and God would fight on your side.[69]

Jesus, on the other hand, selected twelve disciples (Mark 3.13-19) which was seen as a symbol of the gathering of the twelve tribes of Israel for a new start at truly being the people of God for the sake of the world.

However, the Kingdom-initiated message that Jesus came proclaiming was that there was a new way of being the people of God. The boundary markers which had become mirrors in their lighthouse were to be broken and the windows reset. In God's continuing missionary work, he sent Jesus into the world to demonstrate what the true image of God was really like.

Jesus came preaching that the Kingdom of God was near. This message of the Kingdom was the *only* message that Jesus preached. The gospel of the Kingdom was the only gospel that he instructed his disciples to preach. [70] We must continually ask ourselves the question: What message are we really preaching?

Central to the ministry of Jesus was the concept of the Kingdom of God.[71] The authors of the Synoptic Gospels filled their books teaching this concept. It seems like they had so much teaching about the Kingdom that they often summarized the material. The beginning of the Gospel of Mark is a great illustration. Mark 1.14-15 reads: *After John was put in prison, Jesus went into Galilee, proclaiming the good news of God. "The time has come," he said. "The kingdom of God has come near. Repent and believe the good news!"* His brief summary told his reader what Jesus *did* and *said* during his ministry.

If you went to the streets today or within the corridors of the church and asked what Jesus meant by "repent and believe," you would most likely hear that he meant "Give up your private sins (most likely sexual, alcohol, and drug abuse) by accepting Jesus and gain some "inner peace" by believing a body of dogma and joining the local church at the corner of walk and don't walk so you can go to heaven when you die."

Learning Objective
Comprehend the Story of Jesus.

QUESTION
What do you hear and think when you read the phrase "proclaiming the Kingdom"?

A DOABLE POLL
Next time you are attending a church meeting, ask your neighbors sitting around you what they think the phrase "repent and believe," means.

Act 4

Learning Objective
Comprehend the Story of Jesus.

Wright suggests that the phrase "repent and believe" should not be understood in some Pelagian way[72] but rather from its own historical context. Josephus uses the same phrase in describing an incident which took place in Galilee around A.D. 66. Josephus had traveled to Galilee to help with sorting out its factionalism. He met with a bandit named Jesus (there are 21 people by that name in the index of Josephus) who was plotting against the life of Josephus. After foiling the plot, Josephus told the bandit that he should "repent and believe" in Josephus. What was Josephus saying? He was telling the bandit that he should give up his way of living and trust Josephus for a better way of living.[73] It seems that the phrase used by Josephus could not mean anything less coming from the mouth of Jesus. So, to the ears of the first century hearer it would mean "Give up your agendas for how to be Israel and trust Jesus for a new way of being Israel." This message was not a message to sinners but was a message for Israel and the Church for their misguided way of being the people of God.[74]

The Story that Jesus told was an adjustment from the story that Israel was living. Peace and justice would surely come, but not as many believed through a military conquest of the Romans. The message of Jesus was that the rule of Rome would be broken, but that it wouldn't look like what the people of Israel had thought it would look like. Somehow in the life of Jesus, God would bring his people out of exile and make them into the true humans that the fall of Adam had destroyed.[75]

The message of Jesus was about being in the Kingdom. We, on the other hand, have turned his message into a personal privatized religious quest to get to heaven. The story of Jesus is not about saying a prayer so that you can go to heaven when you die and in the meantime be kept safe from all harm in the world. However, this is the story in which much of the church is presently living.

Kallas suggests in his book *Jesus and the Power of Satan* that Jesus never explained the Kingdom because the people to whom he was speaking knew what it meant or thought they knew what it meant.[76]

Jesus accomplished his Kingdom preaching by his *works* and his *words* that enacted and explained the Kingdom. Jesus was the true image of God through which redemption and restoration of God's creation would take place. Jesus came to be for the world what Israel had failed to be. He has made it possible for us to be restored into the image of God, to become truly human. Becoming truly human is not an end in itself. Our restoration into a truly human being is for the sake of the world. Our vocation then is to be the agents of God's kingdom bringing his restoration to his world.[77]

Matthew summarized and succinctly showed the ministry of Jesus in 4.23 and 9.35 as it centered on the Kingdom. Jesus also summarized the message of the Kingdom when he gave instructions to his twelve disciples (Matt. 10.1ff.). When Luke recorded the sending of the seventy disciples (Luke 12.1ff.), Jesus used similar language.

The term *Kingdom* was frequently on the lips of Jesus. His *words* were designed to demonstrate for us how to enter the Kingdom (Matt. 5.20; 7.21). His *works* authenticated that the Kingdom was present in his ministry (Matt. 12.28). His *parables* (stories) informed us about the mysteries of the Kingdom (Matt. 13.11). His *prayers* modeled for his disciples his desire that the Kingdom would fill the earth (Matt. 6.10). His

death, resurrection, and *ascension* made us the agents of the Kingdom
(Acts 1.8). His *second coming* promises the consummation of the
Kingdom for his children (Matt. 25.31, 34).

In Kingdom thought, the charge for the people of God, being for the
sake of the world, is to live *now* in the way it will be appropriate *then*.
The future has invaded the present and we live in the tension between the
first coming of the Kingdom and the *consummation* of the Kingdom.
Jesus sought to give his followers a new vision of their identity so that it
would transform their behavior. We must ask what it means to become a
follower of Jesus, to take up his agenda, and to allow our praxis to be
generated by the Story that he told and lived. Isolated individuals seeking
to cultivate a private spirituality cannot carry out this Story. We need to
ask ourselves how our church communities might become the authentic
"cells" of followers that Jesus sought to birth.

John the Baptist proclaimed that there was one coming in which the
Age of the Spirit would come. The words of Jesus in Mark clearly denote
that the Kingdom had arrived[78] with Jesus. The *words* and *works* of Jesus
form a unity in which the Kingdom of God is spoken about and
demonstrated. In Jesus, we have the presence of the future. Jesus has
brought the rule of God from the future into the present.[79]

We live then in *the presence of the future,* an expression often used by
Ladd to express Kingdom reality.[80] He often said that the church is
between the times; she lives between the inauguration and the
consummation of the Kingdom.[81]

Kingdom of God: Two Ages

In his public ministry, Jesus came announcing to Israel that the long
awaited Kingdom was being birthed but that it did not look like what was
expected.[82] The *key* for comprehending the New Testament is to
understand the overlapping of the two ages.[83] In the Synoptics, the
Kingdom or Rule of God is the future blessing that belongs to the age to
come (Mark 10.23-30). In the mission of Jesus, the Kingdom had come
among humankind (Matt. 12.28). In John, eternal life is the *life* of the age
to come (John 12.25) although Jesus' eternal life has come to humankind
as a present existence (1 John 5.13).

The gift of the Spirit is a future ❖ (**eschatological**) ❖ gift now available
in the present. Two metaphors used of the Spirit in Scripture are *aparche*
(ah-par-kay) and *arrabon* (are-a-bone). The *first,* firstfruits (*aparche,*
Rom. 8.23), indicated the actual beginning of the harvest. It is not a
promise or hope of harvest. It was harvest which was already being
experienced. The *second,* (*arrabon,* Eph. 1.14), tells us that the Spirit was
the down payment of a future inheritance—an inheritance which begins in
the present, but is not completed until a future time.

Eschatological. Broadly, a
belief concerning the
ultimate or final things, such
as death, the destiny of
humanity, the Second
Coming, or the Last
Judgment.

In Galatians, this same future–in–the–present scheme is seen in regard to
the Spirit. Galatians 1.4 sets the tone for Paul's outlook in Galatians. We are
rescued from this Present Evil Age. We are not removed from it, but in
anticipation of the age to come, we are *freed* from the Present Evil Age.

In Jesus, the age to come has broken into the Present Evil Age in order
to rescue us from the power of the god of this world (2 Cor. 4). There is
an overlapping of the two ages. The old age remains and believers and
unbelievers can fall to its power. For Paul (Gal. 3.1-5), the Spirit is
received now, even though he is also the blessing of the age to come.

Act 4

Learning Objective
Comprehend the Story of Jesus.

QUESTION
Which of these two views do you pay more attention to when you are reading the Gospels? Why?

Kingdom of God: Two Views

According to Kallas, there are two ways in which the material of the New Testament concerning the Kingdom can be viewed: first, the Satanward view and second, the Godward view.

Satanward View

The Satanward view, a term coined by Kallas, is meant to demonstrate that Christians should take Satan seriously as God's enemy. It is a joint work of the Father and the Son linked together. Together they are in conflict with evil external forces. The ministry work of Jesus as seen in the New Testament is aimed at Satan; it is Satanward and takes seriously the idea that Jesus came to earth to wage war against Satan.

Godward View

The second way in which the material of the New Testament can be seen is called by Kallas the Godward view. The work of Jesus is not aimed at an external foe, but seen as a transaction between Father and Son. It is to God that Jesus offers himself for sinful humanity. The work of Jesus is aimed at God. It is Godward. In this view, the mission of Jesus was to bring us salvation and return us to fellowship with God, what Tom Wright refers to as vindication and a return from Exile.

Which View Is Correct?

With a postmodern mindset, the answer would be *both* the Godward *and* Satanward views are legitimate. Biblical truth is often found in holding what appears to be the contradictory in harmony with each other. Holding such tensions together is the Hebrew bent toward dialectic.[84] According to Kallas, the following approximate percentages are found:

- The contents of the Synoptics and Paul are eighty percent Satanward and twenty percent Godward
- The contents of John, Hebrews, Revelation are eighty percent Godward and twenty percent Satanward

Both ways of interpretation are helpful. It is beneficial to grasp that biblical truth can never be discerned by choosing one truth over another. Both truths must be held in tension. "When the two are separated," states Kallas, "it is not that one has half a truth, but that one has no truth, but distortion." If Kallas is correct, the higher percentages do not mean that they are more important, but that the authors of these materials wanted to stress their point of view.

To accurately understand the Kingdom of God, we must be committed to the Satanward view of Scripture as well as the Godward view. Within the Satanward view, the Church is seen as *the army of God* which continues the cleanup mission until the return of the King. In the Godward view, the Church is seen as the *functioning body* of the King left on earth to minister redemption to those outside and care to those inside the body.[85]

Is it possible that not taking this Satanward motif seriously has caused an undo balance on the Godward view and left Kingdom theology rather one-sided?[86]

Kingdom Interpretation: Its Problem

In history, the Kingdom of God has been interpreted many ways from Augustine to the Reformer's view that the church and the Kingdom were

the same; to the old liberal view of Harnack; to the eschatological view of
J. Weiss; to Schweitzer's belief that the entire career of Jesus should be
seen from an eschatological point of view; to Dodd's "realized
eschatology;" to Kümmel's "eschatology in process of realization" view;
to the dispensational view that the Old Testament prophecies to Israel
must be literally fulfilled and their sharp distinguishing between the
Kingdom of God and the Kingdom of Heaven; to Ladd's view of the
Kingdom as God's kingly rule "now but not yet;" to Wright's view that it
was the Jewish expectation of the saving sovereignty of the Covenant
God, exercised in the vindication of Israel and the overthrow of her
enemies.[87]

Kingdom: Realm or Kingdom Rule?

What does *basileia tou theou* (Kingdom of God) mean? A way to view
the idea of Kingdom is found in its dictionary definition: "The reign or
rule a king has over his subjects." This definition is closer to the primary
meaning of the Hebrew and Greek words than the concept of realm. In
Hebrew, the word for Kingdom is *malkût* (mal-coot). The Greek word is
basileia (bah-see-lay-a).[88] Scholars are not agreed about the definition.[89]
Their discussion centers around Realm and Rule. The late G. B. Caird, a
British theologian adds yet a third consideration when he said, "It is
fortunate that the Greek *basileia* is an ambiguous term which
comprehends the three possible senses: sovereignty, reign, and realm.[90]
Sovereignty, however, may just be a synonym for rule. The Kingdom as
realm is normally understood as a realm over which a king rules.[91] A
modern day example of this idea was the United Kingdom which was
made up of many nations: Great Britain, Scotland, Ireland, Wales, etc.
People live in the Kingdom (a place) and are subjects of the King or
Queen who exercises his or her authority over his or her subjects. Rule-
Reign usually means rule that a king has over his subjects.[92] Tom Wright,
a New Testament specialist, says, "the word kingdom does not mean the
area over which the king rules but the fact that a king rules, not a realm
but the sovereign rule over the realm which the king exercises. Rule not
realm is a good shorthand way of saying kingdom."[93] Ben Witherington,
also a New Testament specialist, says, "In the future sayings Jesus speaks
about entering while Paul speaks about inheriting the *basileia*. Both Jesus
and Paul envision a realm on earth where there will be transformed human
conditions."[94]

Kingdom: War With Satan

When one opens the pages of the New Testament, you may be struck
by the apparent war in which Jesus is immediately engaged. In his book
The Real Satan, Kallas says, "A war is going on! Cosmic war! Jesus is
the divine invader sent by God to shatter the strengths of Satan. In that
light, the whole ministry of Jesus unrolls. Jesus has one purpose—to
defeat Satan. He takes seriously the strength of the enemy."[95]

It is fair to ask the question: What did Jesus do in his ministry? Mark's
Gospel makes it clear that the mission of Jesus was to destroy the activity
of Satan in the world. He gave his hearers an optical illustration of the
Kingdom in his ministry of healing the sick and casting out demons. Jesus
and Satan were in a cosmic conflict that was being played out in the battle
for ownership and rule in the lives of men and women. In like manner,
other battles were afoot: hunger (John 6), natural catastrophes (Mark 4),
sickness and death (Luke 7).[96]

Act 4

Learning Objective
Comprehend the Story of Jesus.

QUESTIONS
What is the ministry into which God has called you to participate?
Is it fair to say that all followers of Jesus are ministers? Why or why not?

Matthew's Gospel (12.22-31) clearly demonstrates that the war between Jesus and Satan is not a civil war within a kingdom. Rather, it is a battle between the Kingdom of God and the kingdom of Satan. The strong man, Satan, is bound (*deo*: to bind–a metaphorical term indicating the curbing of power) so the strong man's house (Satan's kingdom) may be plundered. The power is curbed, but not rendered completely powerless (Matt. 16.23; Mark 8.33; Luke 22.3).[97]

Jesus won the war, but there are battles still left to be fought. Jesus gave his disciples the mission of continuing to bring the Rule of God into the world in their lives and proclamation (Luke 10.8-9). In their preaching and miracles, Jesus saw Satan's defeat (Luke 10.18). The last words of Jesus to his disciples when he left (Acts 1.1-8) demonstrate that he would empower his disciples to continue in the cleanup of the war.

An illustration from Oscar Cullman's book *Christ and Time* will help us understand this concept of cleanup. He shares a story from World War II's D-day and V-day. D-day was June 6, 1944, a day that the result of the war was decided. However, the war did not officially conclude until May 7-8, 1945, on V-day.[98] Between these two dates, almost a year, there were still battles being fought and allied lives being lost. In fact, more lives were lost during this period than any other period during the war. Even though the battles went on, the war had been decided. So it was with Jesus. The earth was his. In his birth, life, death, resurrection, and ascension, God had overthrown Satan. God planted his flag in the form of a cross, and Jesus said, "It is finished." The war is over, but the aftermath still continues and will until the return of Jesus.

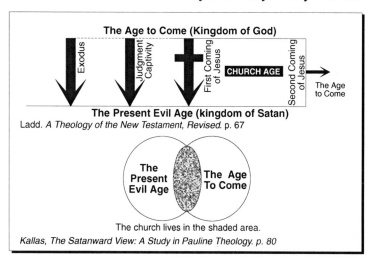

Ladd. *A Theology of the New Testament, Revised.* p. 67

The church lives in the shaded area.
Kallas, The Satanward View: A Study in Pauline Theology. p. 80

The essence of the Kingdom of God is understandable by thinking about "the Age to Come" invading "This Present Evil Age." The graphic above suggests that the Kingdom of God was in the Old Testament as well as the New Testament. The top graphic demonstrates that the Kingdom can be seen in events like the Exodus and Israel's captivity in Babylon. God acted in kingly power to deliver and judge his children. The Kingdom came into history once-and-for-all in the person and works of Jesus. The second graphic gives a different perspective of the same idea showing the present status of the church as she lives in a time where the Kingdom of God has come into the Present Evil Age and both ages continue in tandem.

To understand the Kingdom of God is to understand the theme from which the ministry of Jesus and the writings of the New Testament flow. We live in the presence of the future, the "now but- not-yet." When we view any passage of Scripture in the New Testament, we must put on our Kingdom of God glasses and ask questions of that passage with that set of presuppositions.

The Works and Words of Jesus

John writes in his Gospel a very revealing sentence. Jesus tells his audience that "...the Son can do nothing by himself; he can do only what he sees his Father doing, because whatever the Father does the Son also does" (John 5.19). This has been used to suggest that Jesus was constantly watching to see if God the Father was doing something and then he would join his hand to it.[99] While this may have some validity, it seems that there is more here than this interpretation provides. It could

very well mean that Jesus, who is the only one among them to have ever seen the Father, has seen what the Father has been doing since creation and does the same things that the Father does. If this is the case, to understand Jesus, we must understand his works.

The Works of Jesus: An Assault on the Kingdom of Satan

Learning Objective
Comprehend the Story of Jesus.

Dictionary Articles
Read the following Dictionary Articles in *New Bible Dictionary*.
    Kingdom of God

There is an indispensable relationship between the *words* of Jesus and the *works* of Jesus. His preaching and teaching ministry and his miracles are in essence the same thing. [100] Some have suggested that the miracles of Jesus were no more than a form of great advertising. They heightened interest in the message of Jesus, often startling men and women into paying attention to his message. Others have suggested that the miracles are rewards for having faith. When a person has gained enough faith, then a miracle can occur. The words of Jesus in the Gospels, *Go your way, your faith has made you whole*, could validate this kind of a meaning. However, there are other places where miracles occurred in which an individual did not have a personal faith response. Certainly the widow's son who was resuscitated would certainly fit this category. It would be hard to press a meaning that the dead man's faith brought him back to life.

Yet another reason offered for the miracles of Jesus is that he had compassion on people in need. Certainly we are shown his compassion in the Gospels (the widow's son, Mark 6.34ff.; the feeding of the five thousand, Matthew 14.21ff.). However, it must be pointed out that Jesus did not heal everyone that he passed. He left many sick and hungry, more people than he healed and fed, even though the impression of the Synoptics is that "he healed all who were brought to him."

If miracles were rewards for people's faith, then it follows that one left unhealed who has genuine faith might deduce that his or her faith is insufficient. If miracles are evidence of the compassion of Jesus, the unhealed person might come to believe that in his or her case Jesus has no compassion. We must look elsewhere to discover the purpose of the *works* of Jesus.

Remember, the *words* and *works* of Jesus are identical.[101] There is no difference between them. The works have the exact same meaning as the words. The *words* of Jesus announce that the Kingdom of God is at hand. The *works* of Jesus demonstrate what the Kingdom of God is like. His preaching, teaching, parable telling, and healing ministry were announcements of the fact that the Kingdom had arrived and the Rule of God would destroy the rule of Satan. One might say that these works not only demonstrate the Kingdom, they are themselves the inbreaking of the Kingdom.

The New Testament believes that while Satan is not in control of the world, he does have limited power and authority. The ills and woes of mankind originate with him. Suffering, tragedy, and pain are not punishments of an angry God. They are the result of living in a fallen world and are sometimes a direct attack of the kingdom of Satan.

The miracles of Jesus are attacks on Satan and his demonic forces, to reverse the stronghold of Satan, and demonstrate the Kingdom of God. Jesus both announced the Kingdom with his *words* and carved out an arena in which the Kingdom invaded the rule of Satan with his *works*.

Act 4

Learning Objective
Comprehend the Story of Jesus.

We can see the miracle ministry of Jesus in five different areas: expelling demons, curing diseases, dealing with nature, dispensing hunger, and overcoming death. Let's take them one at a time.

The Works of Jesus over Demons

It seems apparent that the arrival of the Kingdom in the ministry of Jesus is simultaneous with, dependent on, and manifested in the throwing out of demons from people's lives in his ministry.[102]

When Jesus expelled a demon from a person, it was a direct attack on Satan. At the beginning of the ministry of Jesus (Mark 1.15), Jesus withstood the attacks of the enemy in the wilderness and demonstrated that one area of nature in the presence of Jesus had been restored. The wild beasts were with him but did not harm him (Mark 1.13). When Jesus left the wilderness, he came to preach that the Rule of God was present in the synagogue of Capernaum. No sooner than he had opened his mouth, the demonic forces attacked. One can only surmise that he may have been teaching about the Kingdom. A demon recognized Jesus (*I know who you are—the Holy one of God*), and the demon knew that Jesus had come to destroy him.

Jesus *rebuked* the demon and told him to *be silent* (Mark 1.25). The two Greek words here are very strong. "Rebuke" can be defined as *to scold, denounce, censure in order to bring an action to an end*. "Be silent" can be defined as to *muzzle, strangle, or tie shut*. Jesus lashed out at the demon, denounced him, choked him off, and set the man who was demonized free. It is not only Satan, the strong man of Mark 3.27, who alone is to be bound. It is his co-workers who would also be attacked, strangled, choked, and destroyed.

When Jesus delivered the young boy with a dumb spirit (Matt. 17.18; Mark 9.25; Luke 9.42), he used the same word *rebuke*. Driving out demons and the smashing of the ruling grip of Satan on the stolen world was proof and fulfillment that the Kingdom which Jesus had announced had arrived. The Kingdom will arrive in its fullness on a worldwide basis at the Second Coming of Jesus.

Until that future moment, the battles go on, even though the decisive battle has been won by Jesus on the cross. The call of the army of God is to rout out Satan and his demonic friends.

The Works of Jesus over Disease

A second arena in which Jesus attacked the rule of Satan was disease. The mindset of those living in the first century was that sickness was a work of Satan, a heavy weapon of his demonic force. Sickness and disease were ways in which Satan ruled the world. When Jesus healed those who were sick, he was in the act of pushing back the kingdom of Satan. In healing, Jesus not only attacked the demons, he attacked their work. He undid their damage.

Peter's Mother-in-Law Mark 1.29–31 and Luke 4.28–39

Jesus *rebuked* the fever when he healed Peter's mother-in-law. The same language that he used on the demon in Luke 13 is used here. Since words are clues to our thoughts, it is my conclusion that Jesus used the same word in addressing the fever that he did when addressing the demon because he saw a lethal unity between sickness and Satan. He spoke to the fever directly and told it to stop.

The Crippled Woman: Luke 13.10–17

The mindset of the medical world is that sickness is always caused by physical factors. Jesus, however, ascribed sickness directly or indirectly to the perversity of Satan. He pointed to a little old lady, bent like a horseshoe for eighteen years, and claimed that her physical infirmity was caused by the power of Satan (Luke 13.16). One might want to note that Dr. Luke's worldview was different from today's medical worldview. (This is not an argument saying that the ancient world's medicine was superior, only that one doctor saw sickness from a different perspective.)

We who are living with a Western mindset often see crippling diseases as the will of God in a person's life; or that we will understand it better when we get to heaven. Western theology does not make room for satanic intervention in illness. This was not so with Jesus. On many occasions, he looked at a sick person and called his or her infirmity the work of the devil, not the will of God (Luke 13.11-16). This passage is loaded with profound theological significance. One might note that the woman had a *spirit of infirmity,* translated in the TNIV as *crippled by a spirit.* The doctor confirmed the idea that illness can be inflicted by a supernatural force. Luke equated this *spirit of infirmity* with Satan, the one who stood behind the twisting and binding. Jesus attacked the demonic host when he healed this sick woman.

In *Essentials of Demonology,* Edward Langton says, "Special demons came to be associated with particular forms of disease or sickness. Certain diseases were held to be caused by particular demons."[103] We are not to get carried away with this bit of knowledge and do as an acquaintance of mine once did and cast the *spirit of bark* out of his dog. However, we should take the words of Luke seriously and understand that sickness can and is often tied to the supernatural realm.

Demons and Disease Tied Together: The Demonized Boy: Matthew 17.14

Matthew tied sickness and demons together in his story of the demonized boy. Mark only shared that the boy was demonized. Matthew added the information that the boy's condition was epilepsy. Jesus rebuked the demon by attacking his works and the boy was cured.

The Scourging of the Enemy

The words *disease* and *suffering* in the following passages do not communicate the force of the original language.

- ◆ For he had healed many, so that those with **diseases** were pushing forward to touch him (Mark 3:10).
- ◆ Immediately her bleeding stopped and she felt in her body that she was freed from her **suffering** (Mark 5:29).
- ◆ He said to her, "Daughter, your faith has healed you. Go in peace and be freed from your **suffering**" (Mark 5:34).

The original word here is "martix" which is defined as a *whip* or a *lash*. It is the same word which is translated as *scourging* in Acts 22.24 and Hebrews 11.36. It appears that *whip* is closer to the meaning in these passages as in Mark 3.10; 5.29 and 34. The idea is that sickness can be viewed as being whipped by the enemy.

Act 4

Learning Objective
Comprehend the Story of Jesus.

The whips, scourges, and lashes inflicted by the evil one were not ordinary diseases which the Western mindset often accepts as ordinary experiences—fevers, cancers, and heart problems—Jesus considered these the result of satanic oppression. Satan uses a spiritual whip to inflict pain on humans. Sickness is not a part of the Story of God for his creation. Satan rules his captured realm by causing suffering and agony in the world. Jesus, on the other hand, came to take the whip off the backs of those enslaved by Satan (Luke 7.21).

Are You the One?

When John the Baptist received a report that Jesus was healing people, he sent his disciples to question Jesus. When his disciples found Jesus, they asked, "Are you the one who was to come or should we expect someone else?" Jesus responded by "curing many who had diseases, sickness, and evil spirits" (Luke 7.18-21). In this verse the word "sickness" means *lash* or *whip*. One should note that in this context the word is used with disease and evil spirits.

Later when John was in prison, he sent word to Jesus asking for assurance that Jesus was indeed the one to bring the Kingdom. Jesus replied to John by first performing a healing and then sending his disciples back with this word, "Go tell John what you have seen and heard" (John 7.22). Jesus summarized his ministry by talking about what had been seen, his works, and what had been heard, his words.

He told John that the blind receive their sight, the lame walk, lepers are cleansed, the deaf hear, the dead are raised, and the poor have the good news preached to them. What *good news*? Satan's power was being broken by the ministry of Jesus. How do the poor know this message? The blind were being healed. The lame began to walk. The lepers were made clean. The deaf could hear. The dead were alive. The Kingdom/Rule of God was invading the kingdom of Satan.

Sickness. The View from Today!

Today's Westerner still has difficulty in believing that sickness can be a work of Satan. They rather see this belief as medieval, superstitious, and totally incredible in an enlightened age. The ancient world is seen as immature and adolescent in its belief that sickness could be caused by the demonic. For the Westerner to accept sickness as demonic is to have a primitive animistic mindset. The Western medical community is persuaded that sickness is caused by viruses and germs, not because of the demonic. While it is certainly true that viruses and germs cause sickness, it is my contention that they are not the only cause. They may even be included in the realm of the demonic. In the Western worldview, the belief that sickness can be the direct work of Satan is ridiculed, scorned, and rejected. The biblical mindset is quite the opposite.

Take Two Aspirin and Call Me Tomorrow

What is the first thing we do when we get a headache or a fever? Do we pray or go to the medicine closet for two aspirin? If it is the latter, does that say that we see sickness or disease as physical in origin and not theological?

It is not the point of this discussion to disdain medical technology or the medical practice of doctors. Every time we have a throbbing toothache we should not automatically cry that Satan is stabbing us in our molars.

We can acknowledge the value of modern medicine and still have a biblical belief and practice, which understands that Satan can be the cause of physical suffering.

We believe we have become profound because we can isolate a death-dealing virus and give it a Greek or Latin name, a virus that destroys children, wipes away our hopes, and ravages our loved ones. There is an element of mysterious and malignant evil in sickness. When Jesus encountered it, he did not philosophize about it; he did not do a psychological study on it; he did not theologize about it; and he did not explain it in medical terms. He simply healed the disease. Oh, to be like Jesus!

Learning Objective
Comprehend the Story of Jesus.

The Works of Jesus over Nature

Demonic forces play havoc in the lives of mankind through demonization and sickness. They also indirectly exert their perverted influence by causing nature to run amuck. This may be a key to understanding the nature miracles.

The Storm at Sea Mark 4.25–41

Often this story is used to posit a meaning of the ability of Jesus to bring inward harmony. "As the winds and the waves of life begin to sink your boat, Jesus is there to speak, 'peace, be still!'" While it is true that Jesus can bring peace into a stormy life, this is not the primary interest of Mark in telling this story. Rather, he wanted to demonstrate for his readers that the ministry of Jesus was in conflict with nature itself.

According to Paul (Rom. 8.21), the forces of evil hold creation in *bondage and decay*. In the beginning when God created, he gave humans dominion over all things. When Jesus and his disciples were in the boat, Satan was attempting to take that dominion away. The twelve, in fear, cry, "Master, we perish!"

They woke Jesus and immediately he rebuked the wind. The word which Mark used for *rebuke* is the same word spoken to the demonized man in the synagogue and to the fever of Peter's mother-in-law. Jesus spoke to the storm and told the sea to "be quiet." Again the same word was used by Jesus as the one he spoke to the demonic in the synagogue. He simply scolds the sea in the same way he did the demon.

It can be reasoned that the same words are used by Jesus in dealing with demons and sickness that he used in dealing with the storm at sea, because he saw them as having the same cause. In rebuking the storm, Jesus attacked the person of the demon. In healing the mother-in-law and bringing the sea into compliance, he attacked the work of the demon.

The Works of Jesus over Hunger

Hunger was also believed to be the work of the devil. Before the fall of humankind, there was an abundance of food to eat, just for the taking. Later becasue of humankind's rebellion in the Garden, when Satan's rule became the controlling rule, picking up where humankind has left off, the abundance went away. Man had to toil to gain his food. The harmony of the Garden had turned to the disharmony of sweating to gain food. Abundance changed to deprivation and feasting to famine and hunger. Mark saw famine as one of the signs of the Devil's increased resistance in his fight to retain stolen property. It appears that Paul has the same view (Rom. 8.35).

Act 4

Learning Objective
Comprehend the Story of Jesus.

The nature miracles can all be viewed from the perspective of the Kingdom of God at war with the rule of Satan. In the nature miracles, the strongest attacks of Jesus against Satan are demonstrated. In nature, the work of Satan stands in all its malignancy, exposed in all its perverse, starving, crippling, destroying forces of evil which crush humankind at every turn.

The Fig Tree Cursed: Mark 11.12–14

One of the most difficult passages in the Gospel of Mark is the story of Jesus cursing the fig tree. At first sight, it appears to be the only negative miracle, a miracle of destruction, recorded in the ministry of Jesus. In the Intertestamental literature, there is a recurring theme that Satan had revolted against God. He had become God's enemy. He had stolen the world and the world had taken on the effects of this great sin against God. Nature was believed to be corrupt as observed in simple things like worms in fruit, famines, storms at sea, and the refusal of trees to bear fruit, all evidences of a world which had gone berserk.

The most usual interpretation of this passage is to understand the fig tree as a symbol of the Jewish leadership of the day which was barren and unfruitful. Jesus rejected the barren leadership of the Jewish priests and Pharisees. There is nothing in the reading of the text that demands such an interpretation. We must learn to take the worldview of Jesus seriously. Jesus was hungry (v. 12). He went to the fig tree to find something to eat. The tree had no fruit, therefore, it had no right to exist (Luke 13.6-9). In the Kingdom of God there is no right season for fruit bearing. Trees under the rule of Satan may promise one thing and deliver another and, therefore, receive the curse of death for not bearing. All that was barren, fruitless, or enslaving would be no more in the Kingdom of God. The fruitless, worthless demonic was being rooted out and destroyed. Both the storm at sea and the nonbearing fig tree have a common link. Both were demon-inspired perversions of a God-created function. In the Kingdom of God, this will be reversed.

The malignancy of the rule of Satan will be neutralized and the bounty of the world will be restored. Luke took this position when he told the story of Peter fishing all night with nothing to show for his efforts. When Jesus went along with Peter, they caught more fish than his boat could hold. In the Garden humankind had been given dominion of all things. In the fall, that God-given right was forfeited. The Kingdom of God restored what the rule of Satan came to violate.

The Works of Jesus over Death

Death was the last bastion of rule for Satan. It was his most powerful and feared weapon. It was thought to be final! For those who suffered famine, there was hope that they would live to eat again. For those who suffered sickness, there was hope that they would be cured. But, for those who died, all hope was gone. The grave wrote *final* over all the hopes of humankind. It was in the arena of death that Jesus broke the back of Satan. The miracles of resuscitation are important aspects of the Kingdom ministry of Jesus. There are three specific accounts (Mark 5.21-24, 35-43; Luke 7.11-17; John 11.38-44), a report (Matt. 10.5), and one general account (Matt. 27.51-53) of raising the dead in the Gospels. We will look at one account

The Daughter of Jairus Mark 5.21–24; 35–43

Jairus was the ruler of the local synagogue. He had been faced with the illness of his twelve-year-old daughter. He sought Jesus for help. On the way to the home of Jairus, Jesus paused and healed a woman who had been hemorrhaging for as long as Jairus' daughter had been alive. As Jairus, Jesus, and his disciples were coming to Jairus' home, he was greeted with the tragic news that his daughter had died. The pause for compassion to the hemorrhaging woman had been costly. The servants told Jairus that there was no longer any need for Jesus. Death had shattered all the aspirations and optimism of Jairus' family. His girl was dead. It was final!

Learning Objective
Comprehend the Story of Jesus.

One difficulty we have as Westerners some 2,000 years after the stories of Scripture is the two millenniums of Christian tradition. We stand on the positive side of Easter. We no longer see death with the same eyes that the people before the Resurrection of Jesus saw death. We see death as a door to the hereafter, an entrance into the presence of a loving parent with whom we will have fellowship forever. Struggle for a moment to let your Christian understanding of death be temporarily suspended. Think of death as it was before the Resurrection of Jesus. It was final. No hope, for life itself had gone. Stand for a moment in the graveyard of the ancient past and see a father bury his only daughter of twelve, dead before life had had its fullest expression. Comprehend the agonizing note of finality wrapped in the shrouds of death as you adjust to the cold hard fact that your only daughter was gone with no promise of ever seeing her again. Feel the emptiness, the void, the hollow, vacant feeling that Jairus must have felt when he heard the thundering word that his daughter was dead. *Dead* must have struck his ears like the blow of a hammer. She's dead; don't trouble the teacher any longer. Depression was already setting in.

Jesus, on the other hand, had a different view. He began to change the atmosphere around him. He sent everyone outside the girl's room except his small team and her mother and father. He spoke to the dead, lifeless body and life came rushing back like a torrent of water. Victory had been snatched from the jaws of defeat. Death had been conquered by the Rule of God. Jesus had come into the enemy's camp and snatched death from his hands and abolished his greatest weapon.

Jesus was on the attack. Out to plunder the strong man's house. He drove out demons; stilled storms; healed the sick; cursed the unfruitful; fed the hungry; and threw death back into the pit. The victory over the grave was the final blow. It was a foretaste of the ultimate stroke of victory when Jesus was raised from the dead by the powerful rule of God.

The writers of the Gospels do not present Jesus as some kind of victim being led to slaughter. He was the conquering one who submitted to the Cross so he could ascend to the throne. The death of Jesus was not the end. Satan may have thought he had won, but he had not. The death of Jesus was only a means to his final victory over Satan, his resurrection. We should note that Jesus never announced his death without announcing his resurrection (Matt. 16.21; 17.22-23; 20.17-19; Mark 8.31ff.; Luke 9.22).

The cosmic overtones of war and judgment are all there in the Cross: darkness at a strange hour, rocks splitting, an earthquake, people coming out of the graveyards. The war had been fought and Satan had lost. The

Act 4

Resurrection of Jesus assures, confirms, and completes the victory of the Kingdom of God over the kingdom of Satan. It is for this very reason that the Resurrection is at the very heart of the message of the early Church. It was the final authoritative announcement that God had won the battle and the firstfruits of the Age to Come had arrived. Paul insisted that there was no Christianity apart from the Resurrection (1 Cor. 15.14, 17). It was a decisive event in history. If Jesus had not been brought back from the tomb, Satan would have indeed been stronger than God.

Death has been somewhat romanticized in Western Christianity. It is often seen as a sweet release provided by a loving Father who gently calls us home to be with him. Not so with the early Christians! They saw death as an enemy, a work of Satan to destroy them. Paul told the Corinthians that death was the last enemy to be destroyed (1 Cor. 15.26). It was last chronologically and last because it was the most powerful stronghold of Satan. The author of Hebrews sums it up: *through death he might destroy him who has the power of death, that is, the devil* (Heb. 2.14).

The Kingdom ministry of Jesus can plainly be seen in his words and works. His ministry over demons, sickness, nature, and death are models for his followers to pursue. The Kingdom of God is more than a theology to establish; it is a life to be lived.

So What?

So let's summarize the Kingdom from Ladd, Kallas, and Wright's points of view. George Ladd's central thesis is that the Kingdom of God is the redemptive Reign of God dynamically active to establish his Rule among men, and that this Kingdom, which will appear as an apocalyptic act at the end of the age, has already come into human history in the person and mission of Jesus to overcome evil, to deliver everyone from its power, and to bring them into the blessing of God's Reign. Willis in his book *The Kingdom of God in 20ᵗʰ-Century Interpretation* says "…Ladd's work did not itself achieve the place or have the impact that he had hoped.[104] While his works are in the "Bibliography" of Wright's *Jesus and the Victory of God*,[105] he is only referenced three times in the "Index of Modern Authors,"[106] Of course, this is only one set of data about the contention by Willis. Ladd's revised *Theology* presents another picture.[107]

Kallas contends that those who read his books will most likely take issue with his belief that you can't understand the Kingdom without understanding the war with Satan.[108] A second contention is a literal reading of the works of Satan in which one in the present century would expect the identical expression of demonology as was portrayed in the narrative stories of Jesus. While not denying that expressions of demonology may be the same, he has suggested in a personal conversation that alcoholism is a form of demonization in today's world. There are others I'm sure.

QUESTIONS
Which of the works of Jesus have you participated in since you became a follower of Jesus?
If you have not participated in any of them, why not?
If you have not participated in all of them, why not?

Tom Wright's work talks about the Kingdom in relationship to Second Temple Judaism and the Jewish hope to be returned from exile and become the people of God in his world. He says in *Jesus and the Victory of God*:

> But Israel would return, humbled and redeemed: sins would be forgiven, the Covenant renewed, the Temple rebuilt, and the dead raised. What her god had done for her in the exodus – always the

crucial backdrop for Jewish expectations – he would at last do again, even more gloriously. YHWH would finally become king, and would do for Israel, in covenant love, what the prophets had foretold.[109]

In the footnote to the above cited piece, he says:

Anyone who supposes that all these things had happened by the time of Jesus, or that any devout Jews of the period would have imagined that they had, has simply not learned to think historically.[110]

Some have entered the conversation with Wright about his way of thinking theologically as seen in *Jesus & the Restoration of Israel* edited by Carey C. Newman. In Wright's response, he notes:

As one of my heroes, Ernst Käsemann, once said, "In scholarship as in life, no one can possess truth except by constantly learning it afresh; and no one can learn it afresh without listening to the people who are his companions on the search for the truth. Community does not necessarily mean agreement."[111]

Finally, although only mentioned in passing, the concept of "salvation history" (*Heilsgeschichte*) seems to be the conversation partner of Ladd,[112] and to some degree Kallas, but there is no mention of the subject in Wright's works that I am aware of with the exception of three references in *The Climax of the Covenant*.[113]

The Words of Jesus

Jesus has been remembered as a teacher because his teaching was so memorable both in style and in content.[114] He was God's "eschatological emissary and representative"[115] of the Kingdom. We must remember that the preaching and teaching ministry and miracles of Jesus are in essence the same thing. We have demonstrated that his *works* ministry can be understood in relationship to the Kingdom of God, which rule he had come to bring to humankind. His teaching must be understood with this same framework.[116] What he taught tells us a lot about what he believed, which helps us not only to believe, but to "know" him better, to have a deeper relationship with him. If we know what was important to him, these things can become important to us. When we know what he taught, we can proceed toward a richer relationship with him.

Jesus' Methods of Teaching

Here are some of the methods Jesus used and some of the material he taught. He could be regarded as a "literary genius."[117] He used unforgettable *quips*, a phrase that would tend to lodge in one's mind and stay there even when one tries to forget. He said things like:

◆ For those who exalt themselves will be humbled, and those who humble themselves will be exalted. (Matt. 23.12).
◆ Then he said to them, "Watch out! Be on your guard against all kinds of greed; life does not consist in an abundance of possessions" (Luke 12.15).
◆ Jesus replied, "No one who puts a hand to the plow and looks back is fit for service in the kingdom of God" (Luke 9.62).
◆ For whoever wants to save their life will lose it, but whoever loses their life for me will find it (Matt. 16.25).
◆ What good will it be for you to gain the whole world, yet forfeit your soul? Or what can you give in exchange for your soul? (Matt. 16.26)

Act 4

Learning Objective
Comprehend the Story of Jesus.

Jesus often used phrases which refused to be forgotten. The first hearer had to figure out what the meaning of these sayings were. To respond to these pithy little sayings of Jesus often meant that the hearer had to change a perspective in his or her life or to say it another way, the hearer had to change the story they were living in.

Second, Jesus used *thought-provoking paradoxes*.[118] He said things which sounded incredible to the mind. It set the hearer to think about and wrestle with the haunting suspicion that the thought was somehow true. These little thought-provokers are riddled throughout Matthew's presentation of the Sermon on the Mount (Matt. 5.1-16). Blessed are the poor, blessed are the hungry, blessed are the sorrowful, blessed are the persecuted. These bluntly contradicted the standard of their world and ours as well. Success in life is not thought of as found among the poor, the hungry, the sorrowful, and the persecuted. These little sayings turned the meaning of life upside down. They reversed the accepted wisdom of his day and ours as well. When he says, "Unless a man becomes like a little child, he cannot enter the Kingdom of Heaven," the standard in the world for greatness and prestige are annihilated. These thought-provoking statements are valuable because of their power to disturb the person who has heard them long after other things are forgotten. Jesus loved to disturb the comfortableness of men and women. His words drove them to rethink what they thought and experience again what life really was all about. These thought-provoking paradoxes presented new perspectives on old thought patterns. They provide the same impact on the reader today!

Third, Jesus used *hyperbole*.[119] Often men and women need a shock treatment to dislodge them from their hard-line beliefs if they are to come to the truth. He would say things that would shake them from their lethargy. Jesus told his listeners, "If your right eye causes you to sin, gouge it out and throw it away. It is better for you to lose one part of your body than for your whole body to be thrown into hell. And if your right hand causes you to sin, cut it off and throw it away. It is better for you to lose one part of your body than for your whole body to go into hell" (Matt. 5.29-30). This is a shocking statement. Literalness is forbidden because passionate hyperbole is in use. On another occasion he said, "If anyone comes to me and does not hate his father and mother, his wife and children, his brothers and sisters—yes, even his own life—he cannot be my disciple. And anyone who does not carry his cross and follow me cannot be my disciple" (Luke 14.26-27). Jesus did not hesitate to say the most startling things in order to stab at the minds of his listeners, so that they would hear and respond to his message.

Fourth, Jesus used *humor*. Our reserved religious mindset usually has a difficult time thinking of Jesus as having a good old belly laugh with his friends. Most all of our artistic renderings show a somber Jesus. In Matthew 7.1-5 Jesus drew a word picture of a man who had a log in his eye while he was trying to extract a speck of dust from the eye of someone else. While the first audience would have seen the humor in this saying, they were left with the gravity of its truth long after the laughter left. Other sayings like, "You blind guides! You strain out a gnat but swallow a camel" (Matt. 23.24), and "You are like whitewashed tombs" (Matt. 23.27) are all humorous sayings which Jesus used within his culture to get his message home.

Finally, Jesus used *parables*. He has been called a parabolist.[120] Using

parables in that day was the fine art of storytelling. To teach in parables was to teach in pictures. Most folks think in pictures. Few of us are capable of grasping abstract truth, a notable form of teaching in the Western world. Most of us need truth to become concrete before it can be intelligible. We can try to define beauty with many words, but when we point to a person and say, "This person is beautiful," the abstract becomes clear. Parables do not tell the person a truth as much as help the person discover the truth. A parable tells a person to put on another set of glasses. It suggests that one looks at the information from a different perspective. The individual hearing the parable is left to draw his or her own conclusions and to make his or her own deductions. Truth which is told and memorized is quickly forgotten. Truth which is discovered will last a lifetime. The great value of parables does not impose truth on a person; it places a person in a position to realize truth.

Jesus' parables broke into the world of first-century Judaism cracking open ways of understanding God's Kingdom and creating hermeneutical space for fresh insight in which people could image different ways of thinking, praying, and living.[121] The telling of stories by Jesus can be understood as one of the ways that the Kingdom breaks into the world.[122]

Here are two illustrations of his parable teaching. First, the parable of the sower/seed and second, the parable of the friend at midnight.

The Parable of the Sower (An Illustration)

Ladd, Kallas, and Wright all write about the "Parable of the Sower." I think their understanding of this parable demonstrates their differing views of the Kingdom while at the same time holding to the root idea of the Kingdom being the Rule of God.

George Ladd says, "The Kingdom has come into the world to be received by some and rejected by others."[123] There is in the parable a diversity of response to the proclamation of the word concerning the Kingdom. First, the path demonstrates that Satan robs the seed before the plowman can turn it into the soil to take root, demonstrating Satan's antagonism. Next, the rocky soil represents those who reject the word of the Kingdom because of the world with its tribulation and persecution. The thorns are the symbol of those who reject it because of the world with its cares and riches. Lastly, the good soil denotes those who accept and produce. Jesus is the sower. The seed is the good news that God's Rule has come now. Satan will rob some. Some will reject and others will accept the present Rulership of God into their lives.

Ladd argued that "We do not discover (in the New Testament) the idea of Satan attacking the Kingdom of God or exercising his power against the Kingdom itself. He can only wage his war against the sons of the Kingdom…God is the aggressor; Satan is on the defensive."[124] By saying that Satan does not war directly on the Kingdom, (he cannot ascend to heaven and attack God directly) this does not imply that Satan does not attack the people of the Kingdom. He does attack and with great effectiveness when we are unaware of his methods. Ladd also stated, "God's rule makes its way with great force and keen enthusiasts lay hold on it, that is, want to share in it…. God was acting mightily in his own mission; and became the dynamic power of the Kingdom which has invaded the world; men are to respond with a radical reaction." Jesus used violent language to demonstrate that the presence of the Kingdom demands radical reaction (Matt. 10.34; Mark 9.43; Luke 14.26).[125]

Dictionary Articles
Read the following Dictionary Articles in *New Bible Dictionary*.
Parable

Act 4

Learning Objective
Comprehend the Story of Jesus.

James Kallas sees the activity of Satan in the Parable of the Sower as an enemy of the Kingdom. He places this in what he calls the Satanward View[126] of the Synoptic material. In short, that means that this material takes Satan very seriously as the enemy of Jesus and the Kingdom of God.

Tom Wright sees the Parable of the Sower as a retelling of the Story of Israel, particularly the return from exile, with a paradoxical conclusion and it tells the story of Jesus' ministry as the fulfillment of that larger Story, with a paradoxical outcome using "apocalyptic" imagery and structure which evoked the retellings of Israel's story. For Wright, it is a "Kingdom Announcement" parable.

The parable claimed that Israel's history had reached its great climatic moment in the work of Jesus himself. The end of the exile was at hand; the time of lost seed was passing away, and the time of fruit had dawned; the Covenant was to be renewed; YHWH himself was returning to his people, to "sow" his word in their midst, as he promised and so restore their fortunes at last. The parable of the sower tells the Story of the kingdom.[127]

The Friend at Midnight (Luke 11.5-8)

There are three distinct teachings on prayer in Luke 11.1-13. First, Jesus teaches his disciples a model prayer (11.1-4). Second, he shares a parable often called the friend at midnight (11.5-8). Third, he tells yet another parable concerning prayer which is often placed as a part of the first parable, but seems best to be seen as a different parable because it carries a different meaning.

This parable's interpretation turns on the translation of the word *anaideia* (ah nay day ah). When it is properly understood, the parable makes sense, and has a different meaning from that usually seen in popular interpretations.

The parable opens with a question expecting an emphatic negative answer. The question can be paraphrased: Can you imagine having a guest and going to a neighbor to borrow bread, and the neighbor offering several ridiculous excuses about a locked door and sleeping children? The listener from the ancient Middle East would respond, "No, I cannot imagine such a thing!"[128]

Contemporary exegetical literature has many references to the idea of traveling in Israel by night as being preferred because of the heat. This is true in certain desert areas, but it was not customary in Palestine. A friend arriving at midnight was unusual.

When a friend did arrive unexpectedly, he was not simply a guest of the individual at whose house he had come to; he was a guest of the whole community. When the host went to his neighbor and asked for bread, he was only asking the sleeping neighbor to fulfill his duty as a part of the community to the unexpected guest of the whole village.

With this background in mind, verse 7 should become clearer. In verses 5 through 7 we have the question, as we stated above, which expects the negative answer. Jesus is saying, "Can you imagine having a friend and going to him with the request to help you entertain a guest, and then he offers silly excuses about sleeping and a barred door?"[129] "No!," would be the reply.

As we also stated, the significance of the passage turns on the meaning of the word *anaideia* in verse 8. The word usually means *shamelessness* (a negative quality), but it is translated in most Bibles today by *persistence* (a positive quality).[130] The negative meaning of the Greek word certainly raises a problem in the interpretation. Is it shameless for a follower of Jesus to make a request to God in prayer? Undoubtedly not! To make sense of the parable, the Church apparently felt it necessary to turn this negative word into a positive word, and by the twelfth century, the shift had occurred.

What then is the solution? Another translation of the word is possible. It could be translated *avoidance of shame*.[131] Most people read this parable and think that the sleeper finally gave in to the persistence of the host who was making the request. This may be an unfortunate reading of the text. The qualities of verse 8 are the qualities of the sleeper, not the host. If the sleeper refused the request of anything so humble as a loaf of bread, the host would continue his rounds, cursing the stinginess of the sleeper who would not get up even to fulfill his duty. The story would be all over the village by morning. The sleeper would be met with cries of shame everywhere he went. Keep in mind if he had not given the bread, he would have brought shame on the entire community as well as himself. Therefore, because of his desire for the *avoidance of shame*, he would rise and grant whatever the borrower asked.

What does this teach us, if it does not teach us persistence in prayer? I believe it can teach us two things. First, it teaches us something about the character of the Creator God, the Ruler of the Kingdom. He will answer prayer because of his integrity. Everything was against the host getting his request answered. It was night. His neighbor was in bed. His children were asleep. This made the request awkward but not impossible. Therefore, because of the neighbor's integrity—his *avoidance of shame*—he graciously replied. Our cultural presuppositions in the twenty-first century tend to make us uneasy about seeing the preservation of honor as a virtue that is appropriate to God. Given the importance of this concept in the Eastern value system, it would be surprising if Jesus did not use such a quality as a prime virtue for the Father.

Second, this parable teaches us that we can be assured of an answer. If you are confident that you will have your needs met when you go to a neighbor in the night, how much more should you be able to trust God for supplying an answer to your need! Because the supplying of an unexpected guest's need was a matter of community honor, it had to be met by community resources. God has committed himself to us as family and has obligated himself to meet our needs. The parable, then, teaches that God is a God of honor, and that humankind can have complete assurance that their prayers will be heard.[132] The parable of the Friend at Midnight reveals that God is an honorable God who will protect his integrity as the ruler of his Kingdom by answering the prayers of a community of faith as well as individual petitions.

In addition to the above methods of teaching, Jesus used proverbs, poetry, questions, discourses, quotations, symbols, and examples as methods of teaching.[133]

QUESTION
How does God "avoiding shame" strike you? Why?

Kingdom Discourse: The Lord's Prayer (Matthew 6.1-15)

Matthew presents several large discourse sections of the teaching of

Act 4

Learning Objective
Comprehend the Story of Jesus.

QUESTION
What parts of the interpretation of the "friend at midnight" causes you pause? Why?

Jesus in his book.[134] Here is one of the more famous discourses as Jesus teaches his disciples about prayer.

Remember, the basic background of the teaching of Jesus that we are working on is that of the invasion of God's rule into the kingdom of Satan. This provides an adequate key for understanding what Jesus is teaching.

Jesus taught his disciples about acts of righteousness and the place they should be accomplished (1-4). The place for doing acts of righteousness is in secret, not in public. The pattern for prayer is the same. Jesus said, *Do not be like the play actors when you pray...this is how you should pray...* (5, 9). The address is not a put-down of prayer, but a put-down of the showboating style of prayer which would call attention to the one praying!

There are two sets of petitions in what is often called the Lord's Prayer. Actually, it is a model for the disciples to use in their prayers not necessarily a prayer to be memorized and prayed verbatim as we have so often been taught to do. The first set, petitions one and two, are concerned with the establishment of God's purpose on a cosmic scale. The second set, composed of the last three petitions, regards the personal needs of the disciples. All five petitions are imperatives. Remember, the basic background of the teaching of Jesus is that of the invasion of God's rule into the kingdom of Satan. This provides an adequate key for understanding what Jesus is teaching.

The *first* petition is the hallowing of God's name, which means not only reverence and honor given to God, but also to glorify him by obeying his commands.

Let your name be hallowed: We can speak to God about allowing us to act in such a manner that his reputation is not slandered.

The *second* petition is that God's Kingdom would come and be practiced on earth as it is in heaven. At some point in past time, Satan was cast out of heaven along with a host of beings, most likely not before the creation of the world. The war which arose in heaven had been cast down to earth. Jesus was teaching his disciples and us to ask the Father: "Just as you have expelled Satan from heaven, establishing your rule there, that you continue to bring about that same rule on earth." Everything was now all right in heaven, Satan was cast out—now he is to be pursued on earth.

Let your kingdom come, your will be done: We can pray for God's Rule in our life, work, children, family, and recreation.

The *third* petition comes in verse 11. *Give us today our daily bread...* This unfortunately is an inadequate translation. It could better read, *...Give us today the bread of tomorrow....* Hunger is a work of Satan. Jesus took the work of Satan seriously. He requested the Father to bring to his people today some of the abundance of God's rule from tomorrow.

Give us today the bread of tomorrow: We can pray for the specifics which we need in our lives. We can pray for spiritual, emotional, physical, financial, and social needs.

The *fourth* petition is *...forgive us our debts as we have forgiven our debtors.* This is a prayer for the forgiveness of sins. This petition has a condition attached to it. Matthew 6.14-15 makes this petition clear. These words do not mean that our forgiveness of others earns us the right to be

forgiven. The words mean that God forgives only the penitent, and one of the chief evidences of penitence is a forgiving spirit.

Forgive us our sins: This is the arena to pray for forgiveness of our sins.

The *fifth* petition is *...And lead us not into temptation, but deliver us from evil.* Here again a better translation could be: *Do not let us succumb to the attack of the evil one, but deliver us from the evil one and his attacks.* Jesus was giving instruction to his disciples on how to pray when Satan comes to attack because Satan was surely going to attack them in their ministry.

Do not let us succumb to the attack of the evil one: Stand against the attack of the evil one.

The entire prayer of Jesus is based on his conviction that this present world is under the control of the evil one.[135] The praying of the disciples in this fashion was one more tool in their arsenal.

Kingdom Symbols

Symbols are powerful. As a young man in my first pastorate, I made the mistake of removing some altar benches which were located at the front of the tiny chapel to, of all places, the men's dressing room in the gymnasium. I did so because the choir was tripping over them every Sunday morning coming off the stage. What followed was not a pretty sight. If only I had recognized the power of symbols to arouse passion and put it to positive use.

Jesus used symbols in his teaching because they do arouse passion in the hearer. Jesus often attacked the standard symbols of the Second Temple period.[136] The Sabbath was a day set apart by the Covenant to keep holy (Ex. 20.8-11). Jesus simply ignored what the time honored Sabbath had become. Luke tells two Sabbath-conflict stories (Luke 13.10-17; 14.1-6). The Sabbath was surely a day for healing to take place. By healing on the Sabbath, Jesus may have been indicating that the long-awaited Sabbath day was breaking into the world through his ministry. One might note that this is the same story that we covered under the *Works of Jesus over Disease* section above, which was viewed with the motif of the war with Satan. So here, in addition to that motif, Jesus takes the occasion to do his teaching, both words and works, by using a symbol that would surely get the attention of his audience.

Food is another symbol that raised passion among the Jews (Mark 7 and Matthew 15). Food laws were thought to mark off the Jews from their pagan neighbors. In this controversy Jesus gave a cryptic saying in public and then a fuller explanation in private to his disciples. Can one imagine what turmoil would have occurred if Jesus had said in public that the time-honored food laws which marked out the Jews were now insufficient? The breaking in of the Kingdom in the ministry of Jesus was meant to be understood as God's rule taking back what had been lost.

Family and Land were also important to the Jews of this period. We looked at the concept of Land earlier. Land was tied up with the original promise to Abraham of both a Land and a People. The Jews never understood themselves as an association who had volunteered to live together in a geographic place and share common customs. Israel believed

QUESTION
Have you ever thought of the Lord's Prayer as a prayer to model prayer versus a prayer to be memorized and repeated?

Dictionary Articles
Read the following Dictionary Articles in *New Bible Dictionary.*
    Prayer
    Lord's Prayer, The

that she existed because the Covenant God had chosen her to be his people
and given her a place to live out their Covenant relationship. To tell the
Jews to choose to leave family (Matt. 8.21-22) to inherit the Kingdom was
calling on them to be loosed from the tribalness of their ancestors who had
chosen to live in another story offered to them by their cosmic foe. He was
intending them to understand that his Kingdom plot was the development
of an alternative family.[137]

The Temple during the life of Jesus was the symbol around which
everything Jewish centered. It is fair to say that the Temple was the center
of the national and political life of Israel. After all, it was believed that it
was where the God who had created the universe actually lived. For Jesus
to suggest that the Temple had lost its pristine function and would be
abolished would certainly cause one's eyebrows to rise. Israel's vocation
had turned in on herself and the symbol that represented her to the world
must be destroyed.

Another symbol, the Torah was Israel's sacred Covenant with God: it was
the guide for their daily life as the people of God. In Jesus' teaching for the
new people of the Kingdom, the Torah was being redefined.

The above symbols are only a thumbnail sketch of the symbolic
teaching of Jesus. If the reader is interested, Tom Wright gives a full
treatment of symbols in *Jesus and the Victory of God*,[138] and a concise
treatment in *The Challenge of Jesus*.[139]

One may conclude that all of the teaching of Jesus may be read
through the war motif because the real enemy was never Rome but the
evil one.[140]

Kingdom Message

The people who Jesus taught were familiar with their own history and
heritage. These people shared a fundamental knowledge about who God was
by understanding the pictures of God as presented in the Story of their Bible,
the Old Testament. Jesus taught with the motive of bringing fresh insights
with his communication. There are several recurring themes which Jesus used
in his teaching. Here are a few:

Being Intimate With God

QUESTIONS
Why are symbols important
to use in our gatherings?
Does your church use
symbols in its weekly
worship? If not, why not?

The term most used by Jesus to demonstrate this new intimate
relationship was "father." The Old Testament understood God as "father"
of the nation of Israel in the sense that he was the Creator of the nation
(Deut. 32.6). Jesus, however, takes this concept beyond the Old
Testament concept. This intimate relationship would bring freedom to
those who love the Son. To say *Abba* to God was to use the warm,
familiar term used in everyday life in the family. This was entirely new for
the Jew. This unheard of use of the familiar term demonstrated the unique
relationship of Jesus to God. It showed his attitude of trust and obedience
toward God. We should not jump to the belief that God is Father just
because Jesus addressed God as Father. This is one of the many
metaphors used of God to help his creation understand and identify with
him. So why the Father metaphor?

First, everyone has a father and a mother. For the most part everyone
knows who their mother is. However, not everyone knows who his or her
father is. This is caught correctly by Margaret Turnbull when she said,
"No man is responsible for his father. That is entirely his mother's

affair."[141] This possible broken relationship between father and child provides a basis for humankind to know God in a way that we may not have ever been able to experience on a human plane with a human father.

Second, the metaphor of Father is one that crosses time and culture. Not everyone has a King, not everyone understands Rock, not everyone comprehends Shepherd, or any of the other hundred plus metaphors for God.[142] Nor can all people identify with these metaphors in a personal way. God chose lots of ways to reveal himself so that humankind could have an intimate relationship. The primary one in the New Testament is Father. One must remember that God is not a man, but spirit. Scripture uses language of condescension to help us understand and relate to God. He is a personal spirit with which those who have become his children can be intimate. While the term is not used, God is also revealed as Mother.

It is the need of our culture to understand the Fatherhood of God because of the number of broken relationships between fathers and children, which might affect our understanding of what a true father is like. The parenting aspect of God is often misunderstood. He wants us to experience the freedom to be his children and enter into the intimate relationship with him that awaits us. To know and understand him as Father is of great value.

Experiencing The Kingdom of God

The Jews had longed for the establishment of God's Kingdom on earth. In the ministry of Jesus, this long awaited event was taking place. Jesus announced that in his ministry, "The Kingdom of God is near." Remember, the Kingdom is his rule and reign on earth. It is occurring "now" but will not have its fulfillment until a future time. We the church live between the times. Jesus told Nicodemus (John 3) that the entry point of having God's rule was to be "born from above." Alas, we will discuss this metaphor in another Act.

Knowing The Freedom of Being Ethical

The ethical teaching of Jesus mirrored those of the Old Testament. The teaching of Jesus was found by his contemporaries to be somewhat novel because of the new approach to the issue of ethics. The Pharisees approached ethics from a stringent point of view. The ancient Hebrew was called to live life according to a specific set of stipulations. However, how ethical you were in any situation of life was measured by your conformity to a set of rules, regardless of whether the rules came from the Law or from tradition.

Jesus attacked this approach to living. The rules often led the leaders and followers in Judaism to ignore human need, which often kept them from doing good deeds as the story in Matthew 12.1-14 makes clear. Rules had become an end in themselves.

The teaching of Jesus called for the replacement of ethics based on rules with ethics based on love found in the rule of God. An ethic based on love does not do away with the rules; it only focuses the attention on the motive behind the rule. In Matthew 5, Jesus shifts attention from murder to the anger which led to murder. In addition, he transferred from adultery to the lustful attitude of the person who commits adultery (Matt. 5.21-30). These acts of anger and murder are part of this Present Evil Age. The teaching of Jesus around these, shows his concern for men and

Learning Objective
Comprehend the Story of Jesus.

QUESTION
Can you get beyond thinking of God as a male?

women to move beyond the evil of this age to the rule of the Age to Come. You can't get there from here without the love of the Age to Come abiding in your life on a continual basis.

So What?

The teaching ministry of Jesus has often been seen as simple "moral principles" to apply to our lives. When his teaching is viewed the same as his works, they take on a whole different dimension. Instead of principles to apply to one's life, his teaching can be understood as the Kingdom Story in which a follower and a community of followers can enter into and begin to live with a focus of doing his works for the sake of the world.

Scene 4. The Death of Jesus

Death-Crucifixion

The turning point in the ministry of Jesus came at Caesarea Philippi.[143] Peter gained supernatural understanding of who Jesus was and Jesus accepted this confession and began to tell his disciples that he was going to die in Jerusalem (Mark 8.27-31). This didn't set well with them. When he arrived in Jerusalem, he cleansed the Temple. This action, on the part of Jesus, caused great turmoil among the Jewish leaders. In effect, he had judged their way of being God's people as non-effective in the eyes of God. This action on the part of Jesus drove the Jews to make decisions about what they were going to do about this ever-popular teacher. His doom was sealed. Jesus was going to die.

Schweitzer. A French philosopher, physician, and musician who spent much of his life at a missionary hospital in present-day Gabon. Schweitzer was a noted organist and wrote many theological works. He won the 1952 Nobel Peace Prize. His book *The Quest of the Historical Jesus* portrayed Jesus as a Jewish apocalyptic preacher who belonged to the first century Judaism but has hardly any application for the modern person.

Albert ❖ **Schweitzer** ❖ suggested that one could divide this story about Jesus into two groups, those who believe that Jesus went to Jerusalem to work and those who believe that Jesus went to Jerusalem to die.[144]

The night he was betrayed, he instituted an ordinance which the Church calls the Lord's Supper, a symbol of the New Covenant, which would be sealed by his violent death not many hours later. The Lord's Supper said two specific things: *first*, it was the remembrance of leaving Egypt. For the first century Jew, it spoke of the return of Israel from exile, the beginning of a New Exodus, which was the renewal of the Covenant spoken about by the Old Testament prophets. *Second*, the meal brought to a climax the Kingdom story of Jesus. It was symbolic that the New Exodus was happening in the ministry of Jesus.[145]

The symbols of bread and cup also spoke about his death. The unleavened bread, a symbol of the urgency of the Exodus, and the cup would be understood as his coming death which would affect the renewal of the Covenant, an echo of Exodus 24.8.[146]

So Jesus went to Jerusalem to die. There in those last days he enacted two symbolic actions which captured his agenda. The *first* was in the Temple where his actions suggested that the present system was corrupt, contumacious, and ripe for judgment. *Second*, in the upper room, his actions suggested that the Exodus from exile would occur from his death, and that would be how Satan and evil would be defeated. The death of Jesus would result in the Creator God becoming King of all the earth.[147] In the Crucifixion, God drove a cross into the ground and claimed what was rightfully his.

Jesus was arrested in the Garden of Gethsemane and tried before the
Sanhedrin, Herod Antipas, and finally Pontius Pilate. Pilate condemned
him to death on the political charge that Jesus had claimed to be the
Messiah (Mark 15.26). Jesus was led away to be killed by the Roman
execution called Crucifixion. Because Rome was the ruler of the land
during this time frame, it would likely be by Roman crucifixion. Wright
says:

> Crucifixion was a powerful symbol through the Roman world. It
> was not just a means of liquidating undesirables, it did so with the
> maximum degradation and humiliation. It said, loud and clear: we
> are in charge here; you are our property; we can do what we like
> with you. It insisted, coldly and brutally, on the absolute sovereignty
> of Rome, and of Caesar. It told an implicit story, of the uselessness
> of rebel recalcitrance and the ruthlessness of imperial power. It said,
> in particular: this is what happens to rebel leaders. Crucifixion was
> a symbolic act with clear and frightening meaning.[148]

On a hill called Golgotha (Mark 15.22), Jesus died between two
revolutionaries (Matt. 27.38). God saw the good in the humans that he had
created and in Jesus who was willing to die for them. Again, we notice that
the cosmic overtones of war and judgment are all there in the Cross: darkness
at a strange hour, rocks splitting, an earthquake, people coming out of the
graveyards. The war had been fought and Satan had lost.

In the Garden, recorded in Act 2, humankind chose to disobey God and
death was the result. In Act 4, on the Cross, God dealt with this rebellion
once and for all through the *violent death* of Jesus. The Cross was the
decisive blow to the enemy. It brought salvation and freedom to
humankind who were enslaved by their sin and rebellion and freed
humankind to become the people that God had intended humans to be,
now but not yet. It set about putting to rights the whole Creation of God.

So What?

Tomes have been written on the subject of the death of Jesus. As an
example Raymond Brown's *The Death of the Messiah*[149] which is two
volumes (Vol. 1 is 912 pages and Vol. 2 is 752 pages). You may have
thought this book is long. The amount of material printed about the death
of Jesus can be overwhelming. The point of Jesus' death was to bring
redemption for the rebellion in the Garden. It was the ultimate victory of
God coming back into full ownership of his creation, now, but not yet.

Scene 5. The Resurrection of Jesus

Up From the Grave

Readers of the Story may be surprised that the Gospels say very little
about the Resurrection of Jesus.[150] They end their stories about Jesus with
an empty tomb and stories of his appearing (Mark does not share the
latter.) There simply are no extended sections about the Resurrection. One
must wait for other writers, primarily Paul, to get a grasp of the meaning
of the Resurrection.

The writers of the Gospels do not present Jesus as some kind of victim
being led to slaughter. He was the conquering one who submitted to the
Cross so he could ascend to the throne. The death of Jesus was not an end.
Satan may have thought he had won, but he did not. As we have

suggested before, Jesus never announced his death without announcing his resurrection (Matt. 16.21; 17.22-23; 20.17-19; Mark 8.31ff.; Luke 9.22). The death of Jesus was only a means to his final victory over Satan, which was his Resurrection. Resurrection was something new. There had never been such an event in the life of the Jews. After the Resurrection, Jesus is depicted as having a human body with properties that are somewhat unusual. Others had come back to life, but Jesus had gone through death and come out on the other side.[151]

Resurrection assumes death. Jesus frequently said that he was going to die and be resurrected. Mark records three times that he forecasted his death (Mark 8.31; 9.30; 10.33). Remember, death has been somewhat romanticized in Western Christianity. It is often seen as a sweet release provided by a loving Father who gently calls us home to be with him. The early followers of Jesus did not see it that way. Instead, they saw death as an enemy, a work of Satan to destroy them. Paul told the Corinthians that death was the last enemy to be destroyed (1 Cor. 15.26). It was last in order of time of occurrence because it was the most powerful stronghold that Satan had. Be reminded again that Hebrews sums it up: *through death he might destroy him who has the power of death, that is, the devil* (Heb. 2.14).

The resurrected Christ was seen by his disciples, his brother, Paul, and about 500 brothers and sisters (John 21.1-23; 1 Cor. 15.3-8). Paul's decisive teaching on the resurrection of Jesus in 1 Corinthians 15 may suggest that the church had a problem understanding the significance of this part of the Story. Paul makes it clear by his statement in 1 Cor. 15.12-17 that without the resurrection, our faith is useless.

The allusions in the Gospels, especially John, are worth commenting on. The beginning of John's Gospel is certainly an allusion to Genesis 1. It is also a book about the New Creation in Jesus. At the conclusion of his book (chapter 20), Jesus told his readers that the Resurrection was "on the first day of the week" (20.1, 19). On the sixth day in the original creation, humankind (adam/man) was created. In the last week of Jesus' life, on the sixth day, Pilate announced: "Behold the man!" On the seventh day of the original creation, God rested. On the seventh day, Jesus rested in the tomb. The day of Resurrection was the beginning of the New Creation,[152] a new gardener in a new garden.

So What?

Like the Sadducees of old, the denial of a bodily-resurrection is often impossible for the modern to accept.[153] So to close off this section, let me share the conclusion of a sermon delivered by Tom Wright to The Falls Church congregation in Falls Church, VA, on November 11, 2001.[154]

> Denying the resurrection is a necessary part of the Enlightenment worldview. The Enlightenment split off God from the world and denied that God could or would act in the world. That's the culture we've been living in for the last 200 years, that denial. God was upstairs and we were downstairs. Christian faith enables you (Enlightenment allows it) to enjoy a private spiritual relationship upstairs with God, but that couldn't and shouldn't affect how the world runs. God was banished upstairs and we humans, we in northwestern Europe, we in America, would get on with running the downstairs world the way we wanted to.

The denial of bodily resurrection in the scholarship and popular writing of the last 200 years has gone hand-in-glove with the political position of the contemporary Sadducees. "We are in power. We run this world. And we aren't going to allow any messages of revolution of a new world order of Jesus to disturb our privileged position." When, as a New Testament scholar, I fight day by day the battle with the skepticism that dogs my own discipline, I have come to believe that that is part of a larger, cultural battle. It isn't just a battle with Enlightenment philosophy at one level; it's a battle with the whole Enlightenment package — culture, politics, the lot.

This leads to the necessary application of all this to our own day and situation. With the resurrection of Jesus, God created a new world and sent Jesus' followers off to announce it to the world. If you go to the resurrection chapters in Luke 24, or in Matthew, or Mark, or John, and say, "What do the evangelists think this stuff means; why are we telling this story?" The answer is not, "Jesus is risen again, therefore, we can go to heaven when we die and be with him." It's interesting they never say that, those resurrection chapters. Rather, they say, "Jesus is risen from the dead. Therefore, God's new creation has begun, and you are commissioned to go off and make it happen." That's the emphasis. And it's a new world of justice and freedom; it's the exodus world, the return-from-exile world, the world where Jesus already reigns as Lord, it's the world with good news for all, especially, as in the New Testament, for the poor.

As we move into a new century, with all the contradictions of post-modernity swirling around us, and now the sense of living in a dangerous and scary world with the forces of violence and hatred suddenly unleashed in our midst, we have to ask: What might God's new world look like? Start with Easter and what dreams will come? What are we, the privileged ones, doing to help implement God's victory over evil, over death, over poverty, over slavery? Where in the world today is the "exodus" as God listens to the cry of the slaves who cannot help themselves and is assuring them that he is the God of Abraham, Isaac and Jacob?

There are many, many different answers that could be given to that question. There is just one that I want to highlight that we can't ignore. The majority of our fellow Christians in this world, indeed the majority of our fellow Episcopalians in this world, live in countries where the burden of debt is so great that it is crippling them and enslaving them, just as surely as Israel was enslaved in Egypt. If we believe in God's new world, in the world that began at Easter, the world where Jesus brings new hope, we cannot turn our backs on them. I know this is only one example among many. I know there are many debates and difficult questions to ask about how we do debt remission and all that. I'm aware of those debates. But we cannot content ourselves with telling stories about how it's impossible to do anything about the plight of those enslaved by massive and unpayable debt. Or, if we do, we must look in the mirror and realize who we're starting to look like. We are starting to look like the Sadducees who were reduced to telling stories to show how impossible it was to believe in the coming of God's new world.

Act 4

Learning Objective
Comprehend the Story of Jesus.

QUESTION
What are your impressions of Tom Wright's sermon?

But we are here today, on Sunday, the resurrection day, to celebrate and proclaim to the world the fact that Jesus Christ is risen from the dead. We live by this truth and we shall die by this truth. We comfort each other by this truth and we are stirred to love and devotion and service by this truth. Let us therefore settle it in our minds and hearts that we will allow the truth of the resurrection to propel us to be true revolutionaries. Not the cheap and easy kind of revolutionary, those who want to use violence to overthrow the present order and simply turn it upside down and replace it with one of their own. No, we've had plenty of those and it doesn't work. No, we are like Jesus and, in his love and power to be double revolutionaries, celebrating his victory over death and sin, and finding through prayer and politics and Bible study and campaigning and love and fellowship and celebration and truth—finding the way to bring that victory to birth, both in the dark corners of our own private and personal lives and in the dark corners of God's suffering world.

So What?

Remember, Jesus was on the attack, out to plunder the strong man's house. He drove out demons; stilled storms; healed the sick; cursed the unfruitful; fed the hungry; and threw death back into the pit. His victory over the grave was the final blow. It was a foretaste of the ultimate stroke of victory when Jesus was raised from the dead by the powerful Rule of God. It was an integral part of the Story.[155]

Dictionary Articles
Read the following Dictionary Articles in *New Bible Dictionary*, Third Edition. D. R. W. Wood, A. R. Millard, J. I. Packer, D. J. Wiseman, and I. Howard Marshall (Editors), InterVarsity Press. 1996.
Resurrection

The Resurrection of Jesus assures, confirms, and completes the victory of the Kingdom of God over the kingdom of Satan.[156] It is for this very reason that the Resurrection is at the very heart of the message of the early Church. It was the final authoritative announcement that God had won the battle and the firstfruits of the Age to Come had arrived. Paul insisted that there was no Christianity apart from the Resurrection (1 Cor. 15.14, 17). It was a decisive event in history. If Jesus had not been brought back from the tomb, Satan would have indeed been understood as stronger than God.

Scene 6. The Ascension of Jesus

Ascension

The ascension of Jesus may be regarded as "the cessation of the resurrection appearances of Jesus," with the exception of his appearance to Paul.[157] As conqueror of death, Jesus became the first fruits[158] among his people. Peter speaks of his ascension (1 Pet. 3.18-22) suggesting that Jesus ascended with a brief stop to announce his victory to imprisoned spirits (19) and ended his ascension at God's right hand with everything in submission to him (22).

Resurrection without ascension would leave many essential aspects of Jesus' ministry unaccounted for. One of the most important ministries of the ascended Jesus is that of intercession. The work of mediation between God and man depended on the entrance of Jesus into heaven (Rom. 8.31-34). Another ministry of Jesus by virtue of his ascension is the bestowing of the gift of the Spirit. Pentecost could not have come without the ascension.

So What?

The ascension of Jesus is a fitting climax to the "Christ Event." The enemy is defeated and bound, all be it, with a long rope, but defeated nevertheless and Jesus sits in a place of authority with everything in submission to him.

Recap

The Kingdom ministry of Jesus can plainly be seen in his *words* and *works*. His ministry over demons, sickness, nature, and death are models for his followers to pursue. The Kingdom of God is more than a theology to establish; it is a *perspective* about life to be lived. In his ministry, Jesus revealed what God is like. He was the living, walking proof that God was working in the lives of his creation. To understand how Jesus acted is to understand how he will act in the lives of his followers and how his followers are to act in the lives of others.

Two things can be said about Act 4. *First*, the Story of Jesus can be viewed through glasses that take Satan seriously. *Second*, while Satan is strong, Jesus is stronger. The "Christ Event" was the final victory in the war.[159] It seems reasonable to say that the idea of the Kingdom is prominent in the Story of Scripture, both Old and New Testaments. It may well be the grounding presupposition by which one can move forward in understanding God's EPIC Adventure.

If Wright is correct and Jesus came to be the king that the Jews were looking for and he came to do for Israel what Israel was unable to do for herself, i.e., become the true human and show a way forward of what it meant to be the "people of God," living under the rule of God, then certainly that impacts how one would live in that Story today.

This Act only scratches the surface of the theology of the Kingdom of God. As an example, it does not address a Pauline or Johannine view of the Kingdom of God. It does not discuss a practical hermeneutic which begins to answer the question: "So What?" It does not converse about the Spirit's part in the Kingdom. It only infers that it is God's Rule brought to the fore by Jesus. It does not address the ongoing mission of the church empowered by the Spirit to continue bringing the Kingdom into this Present Evil Age.

However, may we pray with Jesus,

"your Kingdom come,
your will be done,
    on earth as it is in heaven"

Or as Peterson says in *The Message*:

"Set the world right;
Do what's best—
    as above, so below."

We now turn to Act 5 Scenes 1-6 in which we will look at all the books of the New Testament in a proposed chronological order.

There is an indispensable relationship between

the *words* of Jesus and the *works* of Jesus.

His preaching and teaching ministry and

his miracles are in essence the same thing.

Act 5: Scenes 1-6

The Rest of the Story in the New Testament

The Gospels, Acts, and Letters of the New Testament (Romans-Revelation) play a critical role in defining how God's people are to live in this Present Evil Age and what their focus is to be.

Act 5: Scenes 1-6. The Rest of the Story in the New Testament

When you finish this session, you should be able to:

- ◆ Comprehend that Paul may not have been a Lutheran
- ◆ Understand who Paul was
- ◆ Comprehend what letters were
- ◆ Understand the chronological presentation of the Story in the New

In this lesson, we begin with an overview of the Second Temple Period. Then, we look at ways the Story of Jesus could be told and make a choice. Next, we look at the life of Jesus using birth, life, death, resurrection, and ascension as an outline. Then, we share about the Kingdom works of

Act 5: The Rest of the Story in the New Testament
  Introduction 1: Was Paul a Lutheran before Luther?
  Introduction 2: Paul. Who Was He?
  Introduction 3: Letters
  Act 5 Scene 1: The Story Begins (A.D. 34-45)
    A Chronological Reading of the New Testament Story
    What Happened After the Resurrection?
    A Quick Look At Acts
    Where to Begin?
  Act 5 Scene 2. The First Church Planting Mission: Acts 13-14
    About Galatians: Christian Freedom
    About James: The Wisdom of God
  Act 5 Scene 3. The Second Church Planting Mission: Acts 15.36-18.22
    About 1 Thessalonians: He is Coming
    About 2 Thessalonians: The Day of the Lord
  Act 5 Scene 4. The Third Church Planting Mission: Acts 18.23-21.17
(A.D. 52-57)
    About 1 Corinthians: Problem Solving
    About 2 Corinthians: Reconciliation
    About Romans: God's Righteousness
  Act 5 Scene 5. The Journey Continues (A.D. '60s)
    About Mark: An Evangelistic Tract
    About Philemon: An Appeal For Forgiveness
    About Colossians: How to Deal With Cults
    About Ephesians: The Church
    About Luke: A Defense of the Gospel of Jesus
    About Acts: A Defense of the Ministry of Paul
    About Philippians: Joy Comes When Unity Abides
    About 1 Timothy: Pastoring A Second Generation Church
    About Titus: Pastoring a First Generation Church
    About 2 Timothy: Passing the Torch!
    About 1 Peter: What to Do When The Hard Time Comes
    About 2 Peter: What Do You Mean He's Not Coming?
    About Matthew: How To Teach New Converts
    About Hebrews: A First Century Sermon

Act 5 Scene 6. The Journey Continues (A.D. '70-'90s)
  About Jude: Combat Ready! Author: Jude
  About John: So That You May Continue To Believe
  About 1 John: Belief Problems With A New Generation
  About 2 John: Undesirable Guest
  About 3 John: Church Discipline Is Important
  About Revelation: A Book Of Comfort

Act 5: The Rest of the Story in the New Testament

In this Act, we read about the continuing creation of a newly redeemed people of God, the church, who have the same function that Israel had as the people of God, i.e., to be the light for the world to see God. As the church developed in the first century (Acts), she faced problems in being the light to the world. The Gospels, Acts, and Letters of the New Testament (Romans-Revelation) play a critical role in defining how God's people are to live in this Present Evil Age and what their focus is to be.

The canonical presentation of the Gospels (Matthew, Mark, Luke, and John) followed by the Acts of the Holy Spirit and then Romans through Revelation does not necessarily present the Story in the way in which these books may have originated. As an example, Paul's letters are arranged in order of their size from Romans to Philemon.[1] Thus, in Act 5, we are going to present the Story in a chronological fashion.

Before we take a quick tour through the Book of Acts to set up the more detailed story of the chronology of the Story in the New Testament, we are going to provide three introductions. The first introduction is to discover if Paul was an early Lutheran in his teaching or if there is validity in what is called the "New Perspective on Paul." The second introduction will be an overview of Paul. The third will cover letters as a genre of literature.

Why are the introductions important at the beginning of Act 5? First, if the standard view of reading Paul (the Lutheran view) is held, then the ad hoc material of Paul would be read one way. If, on the other hand, there is another valid way of reading Paul, then the results of reading him in that way would be different. Second, Paul is the central writer and thinker of the New Testament Story, so it is important to have an introductory view of him as well as his letters. Letters were the conventional way he used to convey his material, so a limited look at that genre of literature is also valuable in understanding how the Story proceeds. A letter for him could be thought of somewhat like and email for us. We sit down at a computer and write in an ad hoc way. So did Paul, but without the computer.

Introduction 1: Was Paul a Lutheran before Luther?

The Lutheran reading of Paul has ruled the reading of his books for centuries until recently. For the most part, we have been offered a set of "Luther glasses" through which we read the writings of Paul in the New Testament. Luther understood the Pharisees as legalists and saw Paul as calling for a non-legalist position in following Jesus. In this short excursion, we will evaluate this Lutheran claim and also look at the theological position that is being offered to replace the Lutheran reading. Knowing about his dispute with the Roman Catholic Church of his day and possibly making a decision about it may help you as a reader of the New Testament Story see things quite differently.

Learning Objective
Comprehend that Paul may not have been a Lutheran.

Here is a decision for you to make: Is Paul's message a "Lutheran" version of the Old Testament Story as reflected in the Lutheran reading of Paul (legalism or meritorious works could not lead to justification), or is it a "new Perspective on Paul" which suggests that justification is about

Act 5: Scenes 1-6

Learning Objective
Comprehend that Paul may not have been a Lutheran.

Learning Objective
Understand who Paul was.

exclusivism and inclusivism as reflected in Tom Wright, James D. G. Dunn, and others?

In any writing about Paul, one should remember that his books were ad hoc letters, not theological discourses. They were designed to help local communities of faith solve concrete problems that they faced. The result is that they are not presentations which serve as a vehicle for ordered and complete thought on a subject.[2]

Lutheran and Exclusive/Inclusive Reading

The reformation leader, Martin Luther, has been charged with reading Paul wrongly by confusing some of the first century controversies with his own quirky concerns in the sixteenth century. For centuries, then, this misreading of Paul has distorted the understanding of his writings "by undiscerning scholars, unsuspecting preachers, and the masses that know not the law."[3]

Against this reading is the so called "new perspective on Paul" that first appeared in the writings of N. T. Wright, following E. P. Sander's *Paul and Palestinian Judaism* in 1977, a book that suggested that the belief that Paul was arguing against Rabbinic "legalism" was a misunderstanding of Paul's thought and Judaism.[4] The phrase was "christened"[5] by James D. G. Dunn in his article "The New Perspective on Paul" which is found in his book, *Jesus, Paul, and the Law*.[6]

We may summarize in general terms that the "Lutheran" view of Paul is a "legalism/law and grace" or "works righteousness" argument while the "new perspective on Paul" is an "exclusivism to inclusivism" argument.

There have been millions (who knows really) of words spilt in ink and voices chatting about Paul's theology. Students of Paul find it difficult to keep up with all the latest developments in Pauline study.[7] For a brief survey of this topic see Appendix 11.

So What?

If it is correct that the hermeneutical error of Luther's charge that Judaism and Roman Catholicism meritorious works are the same, and I think that the evidence suggests that it is, then the church has labored under a false impression of legalism for almost four centuries. In a recent class that I taught, I suggested that this might be the case. Every member of the class had only been exposed to the view that legalism was what was meant by "under the law." If, on the other hand, the "new perspective on Paul" as heralded by Dunn, Wright and others is correct, and at this moment in my theological journey I think they are on to something and am leaning in their direction, then boundary markers as a social enclosure to prohibit different races from sitting at table with each other can probably be found in many churches of many stripes, Lutheran or otherwise. Ways that have been constructed to keep people from becoming the people of God have cropped up alongside "works to do" to become the people of God. The church needs to become open versus closed and the "new perspective on Paul" which holds out inclusivism over exclusivism could be a blessing to the church to bring that to pass.

Introduction 2: Paul. Who Was He?

Perhaps a corner in the chutzpah hall of fame should be reserved for those of us who write about Paul. We are, after all, hardly less liable than other mortals to misconstrue the thinking of our spouses; that of our teenage offspring we have long since despaired of divining. We, too, contend daily with the impenetrable *other*ness of our contemporaries: any forgetfulness of our limitations incurs prompt and painful refutation. The study of the ancients, on the other hand, allows a good deal of scope for our pretensions and, best of all, immunity from instant rebuttal — and we have certainly milked its potential to the fullest. Given a first-century apostle a few of whose letters we have read, we make bold to distinguish what he said from what he really thought, and even to pontificate on why he thought the way we think he did. Indeed, as the assumptions that governed Paul's thinking become more and more remote from our own, the assurance with which we pronounce on the direction and deficiencies of his reasoning seems only to increase. Isn't America wonderful?[8]

I remind myself of this quote as I begin to make some brief comments about Paul and, as we proceed, his letters. It's a sobering thought.

Notwithstanding Jesus, Paul is the greatest figure in the Story of Christianity.[9] Christianity found its "first and most vivid voice"[10] in Paul. There is little information about Paul from his birth to his appearance in the book of Acts as the persecutor of the Church. What is known about him is mainly drawn from his self-portraits in his documents (Gal. 1.13ff.; Rom. 9.1; Phil. 3.5). His birth place was Tarsus (Acts 16.27; 21.29; 22.25ff.). Tarsus was a commercial city, and a center of learning. It was there he became acquainted with various Greek philosophies and religious cults. He was raised by his mother (Acts 22.3) and later moved to Jerusalem for his education that he received from Gamaliel (Gal. 1.13ff.).

While in Jerusalem, he was given authority to direct the persecution of this new cult of Christians. He was officially sanctioned by the Sanhedrin to go to Damascus and bring bound to Jerusalem any Christians that he found.

His conversion on the road to Damascus was a rather sudden jolt to Paul, as well as to his friends in Judaism. After three years of instructions from the Lord and teaching in the synagogue in Damascus, he made his first post-conversion trip to Jerusalem after a close escape with his life from Damascus (Acts 9.23; 2 Cor. 22.32). He had a brief stay in Jerusalem with the disciples who were in continuing fear of him even after three years.

Paul's Importance

While the central character in the New Testament is Jesus, the central writer and thinker is Paul.[11] There are at least three reasons that Paul is important in the framework of the New Testament. First, the *literary reasons*.[12] He wrote over fifty percent of the New Testament books, thirteen by count, although some are disputed as to being written by him.[13] Luke, the convert of Paul, wrote about thirty percent of the New Testament books. Between these two men, eighty percent of the New Testament came into existence. A focused reader can see many similarities between Paul and Luke. As an example: Luke's genealogy leads to a Second Adam. Paul writes about a Second Adam (1 Cor. 15.45).

The second reason Paul is important is *historical–geographical*. Paul brought the gospel to Europe for the first time on his second mission.[14]

Act 5: Scenes 1-6

Two thousand (2,000) years of Western culture have been influenced because of his ministry. The literature, art, and music of Western culture, in particular, are deeply indebted to biblical themes, motifs, and images.

The third reason: Since half of the New Testament books are written by Paul, then half of the New Testament is *Pauline Theology*. Every reformer from Augustine to Luther to Barth has known and used Paul to bring about reformation.[15]

Paul's Cultural Background

Tarsus was a seaport and cultural city. As a seaport city, it was a commercial city. Paul was not a country boy. However, Jesus was a rural boy and his language indicates such. Paul's language was from city life. Being from the city gave him a perspective about the gospel that God would use to spread his Story throughout the European world. His attitudes were broader than the narrow attitudes of rural Palestine. However, when Paul spoke, he meant the same thing that Jesus meant when he spoke. A different audience demanded different terminology.[16] He did not come from Rome, as an example, which would have given him more of a political attitude. His rearing in Tarsus made him open to commercial life and exposed him to thinking through the implications of the message of Jesus for his world. He was a tentmaker by trade.

As a cultural city, Tarsus had a Greek Stoic University. It was a center of intellectual life. Strabo emphasized the native interest in learning in Tarsus, where the schools were full of local students (XIV.673-4). Many of the Tarsian philosophers went to teach in Rome. The Stoics taught that one can achieve freedom and tranquility only by becoming insensitive to material comforts and external fortune and by dedicating oneself to a life of reason and virtue.[17]

Paul the Greek, Roman, and Hebrew

Paul was a functional member of three cultures: Greek, Roman, and Hebrew, which all influenced his life. He knew the language, culture, and heartbeat of the *Greek* people. He was at home in the Greek culture with its language, customs, and thought. He quoted the Greek poets with ease (Acts 17.28; Titus 1.12).

He was a citizen of Rome with all its rights and privileges. Citizenship was important in the ancient Roman world (Acts 16.17ff.). One could win or pay for citizenship. It is believed that Paul's was paid for by his family. Roman citizenship gave him full access to the whole Roman Empire.

Finally, He was a Hebrew with its language, customs, and thought forms. He claimed that he excelled as a Hebrew (Gal. 1.14). The implications: He spoke the language of the day in the culture of his day with a distinct Hebraic flavor. He was a Hebrew thinker, which is important for the Westerner to understand when reading Paul. Greeks typically think through the ear gate (word definitions) while Hebrews think through the eye gate (word pictures). After his conversion, Paul began the process of subverting each of these three areas that overlapped to make up the culture to which he took the gospel.

As a reader of the Story, we have to realize that we have been given a Hebrew book, but we often read it with a Greek mind. Simply stated, a Hebrew mindset often expressed truth in terms of opposites. One discovers the truth of the matter by holding the two opposites together in tension. A Greek mindset is not dialectical, it is logical. When we find two opposites, as we read with a Greek mind, we tend to favor one and dismiss the other. As an example, the sovereignty of God and the freedom of humankind. Which is right? From a Hebrew perspective, both are.

So What?

To be a proclaimer of the Gospel in the ancient world one might need to know the Hebrew Scriptures, and be a Roman citizen to travel, and have access to the Greek culture for communication. Like Paul, your own background perfectly prepares you for the ministry that God has for you.

Paul's Church Planting Pattern: Acts 13.13-52

Synagogue: A Ready–Made Audience: Acts 13.15

When Paul began his travels to spread the gospel, he would stop in at a local synagogue because he knew the Jews were looking for the Messiah. He had a ready-made theological audience. In the ancient world when Jewish travelers would go to synagogue, they were often asked to speak and bring the congregants up-to-date on what was happening in other parts of the world they had traveled through. They functioned like a news broadcaster functions today. This situation made it practical to speak to the Jews about the message of Christ.

Received and Preached: Acts 13.16b

One must remember, these were Jews living within the boundary markers of the Jewish faith where the Deuteronomic Code was a way of life. From the Covenant, they believed that good folks received good stuff and evil folks received evil stuff. So when the congregants of a synagogue would hear that the long awaited Messiah had arrived in Jesus of Nazareth, they were exuberant, but when they heard he had been crucified, they did not respond well (Gal. 3.13 from Deut. 21.23). They reasoned that if Jesus hung on a cross, he must have been evil. If he was evil, he could not be the Messiah because the Messiah was a good gift that would come from God. This would cause the congregants of the synagogue to rise up and send Paul packing, often driving him out of town.

Gentiles Converted: Acts 13.48

Paul would then turn his message to the Gentiles among the synagogues. There were two kinds of Gentile converts: those that were "God fearers" and those that had been circumcised. Paul would often draw them with the good news of Jesus, effectively stealing converts from the Jewish faith.

Increased Hostility: Acts 13.50

The result of this pattern was an increased hostility toward Paul and he would leave town.[18]

Introduction 3: Letters

Letters Were Actual Letters

Twenty-one of the New Testament books are letters (exceptions: the four Gospels, Acts, and Revelation). However, Revelation contains the seven letters to the seven churches. Acts contains the letter sent by the

Council of Jerusalem to the churches of Asia Minor (15.23-29) and the letter sent by Claudius Lysias to Felix (23.26-30). See the graphic on the next page to help you view the contents of the New Testament in a chronological fashion.

The correspondence of Paul and other writers in the New Testament were written in the genre of letters. This was a common way of communicating in the ancient world. One must remember that during this time frame, the culture was primarily oral. Letters served mainly as a surrogate for oral communication. Because the literacy rate was about twenty percent, the letters had to be read aloud for the whole community of faith to receive benefit. We might want to think of letters as part of a larger ongoing conversation between its author and recipient.[19] As with the Old Testament Covenant, God chose forms that were current through which to communicate, a lesson churches stuck in yesteryear might want to consider. Letters were written on papyri and then rolled up into a scroll and there are general things one should observe about them. At the very top of the document was the author's name, followed by the person or place to whom it was written, then a greeting was given. The leading paragraphs in a letter were the most important with "chit chat" left to the end of the scroll.

Here is an example of an ancient letter that follows this pattern.

> Isias to her brother Hephaestion greeting. If you are well and other things are going right, it would accord with the prayer which I make continually to the gods. I myself and the child and all the household are in good health and think of you always. When I received your letter from Horus, in which you announce that you are in detention in the Serapeum at Memphis, for the news that you are well I straightway thanked the gods, but about your not coming home, when all the others who had been secluded there have come, I am ill-pleased, because after having piloted myself and your child through such bad times and been driven to every extremity owing to the price of corn I thought that not at least, with you at home, I should enjoy some rest, whereas you have not even thought of coming home nor given any regard to our circumstances, remembering how I was in want of everything while you were still here, not to mention this long lapse of time and these critical days, during which you have sent us nothing. As, moreover, Horus who delivered the letter has brought news of your having been released from detention, I am thoroughly ill-pleased. Notwithstanding, as your mother also is annoyed, for her sake as well as for mine please return to the city, if nothing more pressing holds you back. You will do me a favor by taking care of your bodily health. Goodbye[20]

Letters Were Occasional

These first century letters arose from and were intended for a specific occasion. In the case of the New Testament letters, they were to solve unique church problems. Usually the letters were to solve some kind of behavior that needed correcting, a belief error which needed to be set to right, or some misunderstanding which needed further discussion. In the letters, we have the answers; what we do not have are the questions. We must, as interpreters, try to reconstruct the original *occasion* of the letter

Reading the StoryLine

The graphic below can help you keep atuned with where you are reading.

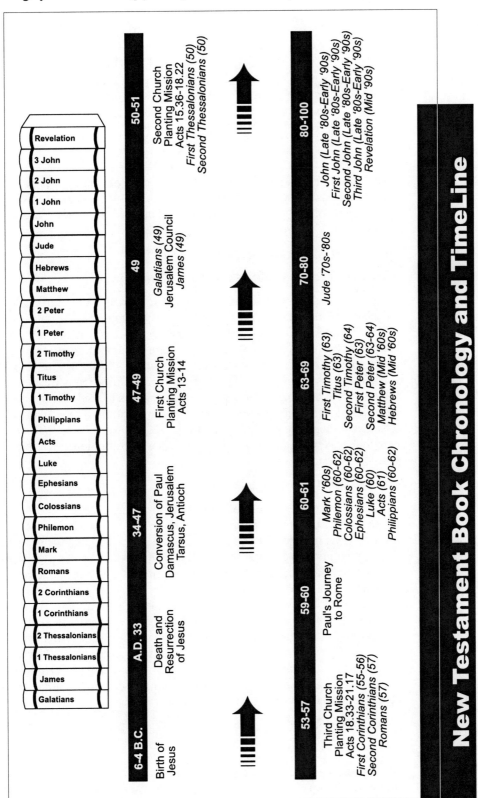

New Testament Book Chronology and TimeLine

Book list		
Revelation		
3 John		
2 John		
1 John		
John		
Jude		
Hebrews		
Matthew		
2 Peter		
1 Peter		
2 Timothy		
Titus		
1 Timothy		
Philippians		
Acts		
Luke		
Ephesians		
Colossians		
Philemon		
Mark		
Romans		
2 Corinthians		
1 Corinthians		
2 Thessalonians		
1 Thessalonians		
James		
Galatians		

6-4 B.C.
Birth of Jesus

A.D. 33
Death and Resurrection of Jesus

34-47
Conversion of Paul
Damascus, Jerusalem
Tarsus, Antioch

47-49
First Church Planting Mission
Acts 13-14

49
Galatians (49)
Jerusalem Council
James (49)

50-51
Second Church Planting Mission
Acts 15.36-18.22
First Thessalonians (50)
Second Thessalonians (50)

53-57
Third Church Planting Mission
Acts 18.33-21.17
First Corinthians (55-56)
Second Corinthians (57)
Romans (57)

59-60
Paul's Journey to Rome

60-61
Mark ('60s)
Philemon (60-62)
Colossians (60-62)
Ephesians (60-62)
Luke (60)
Acts (61)
Philippians (60-62)

63-69
First Timothy (63)
Titus (63)
Second Timothy (64)
First Peter (63)
Second Peter (63-64)
Matthew (Mid '60s)
Hebrews (Mid '60s)

70-80
Jude '70s-'80s

80-100
John (Late '80s-Early '90s)
First John (Late '80s-Early '90s)
Second John (Late '80s-Early '90s)
Third John (Late '80s-Early '90s)
Revelation (Mid '90s)

Act 5: Scenes 1-6

Letters

Learning Objective
Understand the chronological presentation of the Story in the New Testament.

as close as possible. It was theology being written because of the problem(s) which faced the author. It is theology at the service of a specific need.[21] One might call letters problem-solving literature.[22]

Why Letters?

In the case of Paul, he would start a church (Rome excluded) and leave, sometimes run out of town. After a period of time, problems would occur in the newly planted community of faith to which he would respond. He responded in one of the following ways. He would go back to the church himself, if possible, or he would send someone else like Timothy or Titus. In some cases, he would send a letter (often through dictation as in Rom. 16.22).

So What?

It may be fair to say that if there had been no problems in the early church, there would have been no New Testament. It is also fair to say that current forms of communication should be used to communicate the Gospel.

 Act 5 Scene 1: The Story Begins (A.D. 34-45)

A Chronological Reading of the New Testament Story

I use the word "a" instead of "the" because there is more than one way that scholars have dated the books in the New Testament. The dating of the New Testament Books is disputed as is the place of writing and identification of authors.[23] I am using the dating and authorship from Robert Gundry's *A Survey of the New Testament, 4th Edition*[24] as a guide for such matters in this Act. May it be said that inspiration is far more important than date and authorship. As long as it is agreed that the books of the New Testament are canon, then one can afford to disagree on secondary issues. The presentation of this Act is to serve as a reading guide for the New Testament as it is presented in chronological versus canonical order.

What Happened After the Resurrection?

The Gospels end the Story of Jesus with his appearances to the disciples. Luke picks up the Story in the book of Acts to which we now turn for a brief overview. Luke takes his readers on a quick tour of three decades beginning in Jerusalem and ending in Rome. There is plenty of action from the ascension, to a stoning, to a blinding, to earthquakes, jailbreaks, and shipwrecks. Acts is divided in several ways.[25] I have chosen to break it down in what seems like a more natural way, the summary statements of Luke[26] using SPIRIT as an acrostic. It is a good idea that when one reads Acts, they should read it together in sequence with Luke. They were, after all, written as a two volume work. The

Acts

Learning Objective
Understand the chronological presentation of the Story in the New Testament.

Acts 1-28. TBB. 1463-1501.

separation of Luke and Acts in our own canonical setting of Scripture is unfortunate, at least, and horrible, at best, for any coherent reading of the Story as presented by Luke.

A Quick Look At Acts

Spirit Arrives in Jerusalem 1.1-6.7

Luke begins his second volume with the story of the arrival of the Holy Spirit in Jerusalem on the Day of Pentecost. The Spirit's advent came first to a few faithful followers of Jesus in the upper room and then to thousands as a

result of the preaching of Peter. This first section of Acts is packed with the stories of supernatural intervention by the Spirit and concludes with a summary statement at 6.7, which says that the word of God was spreading and there was an increase in disciples.

Proclamation in Judea-Samaria 6.8-9.31

Trouble lifted its ugly head and because of the persecution of Stephen, the church moved outward from Jerusalem into Judea and Samaria. This is the first movement of the church outside of the safety of Jerusalem. The story of Saul (later he took the name Paul) and his conversion is told in this section. Saul asked for and received permission to travel from Jerusalem to arrest those who were following Jesus. He was struck blind while on his way to Damascus and several days later recovered his sight. The section also ends with a second summary about the growth of the church in the geographic area of Judea and Samaria.

Inclusion of Gentiles 9.32-12.24

Gentiles were not highly valued by the Jews. For the first time the Church was faced with their inclusion into God's work in the world. To demonstrate this move of the Holy Spirit into Gentile territory, Luke tells the story of the conversion of Cornelius under the ministry of Peter, the devout Jew, and how the church at Antioch developed in Gentile territory with Gentile growth. Another summary statement ends this section of Acts, which also concludes that the Church is continually growing (12.24).

Received Gospel in Asia Minor and Europe 12.25-16.5

Paul now becomes the main character of the rest of Acts story. In this section, Luke told the story of Paul's first missionary trip. He and Barnabas left Antioch and traveled through Cyprus and the cities of Galatia. They had great success on this journey which lasted about two years. Included in this section is the story of the meeting of the Church at Jerusalem to decide about a problem statement which had been posed by the Jews: "Unless you are circumcised, according to the custom taught by Moses, you cannot be saved" (15.1). The Church council settled the question favoring Paul's position on circumcision, i.e., one does not have to be circumcised in order to be a follower of Jesus. He was sent out with a letter of recommendation to other churches about the conclusions reached by the Jerusalem council. Paul began his second trip to plant churches in Gentile areas. Luke concludes this segment with another summary statement about the growth of the church (16.5).

Involvement of Gospel in Asia Minor and Europe 16.6-19.20

Paul continued his second mission trip. He received a vision from God to travel and minister in Macedonia. His travels took him to Philippi, Thessalonica, Berea, Athens, and Corinth. After eighteen months of ministering in Corinth, he left and returned to Jerusalem. Again, as was his custom, Luke closed this part of Acts with a summary statement (19.20).

Trials – Appeal – Rome 19.21-28.31

Paul's final mission trip concludes. After traveling to Ephesus, Macedonia, and Greece, Paul returned to Jerusalem where he was arrested and put on trial before the Sanhedrin. A plot developed to assassinate him, but was spoiled by a relative. He was sent to Caesarea to be tried before Felix, Festus, and Agrippa. Paul makes a request to go to Rome for his

Learning Objective
Understand the chronological presentation of the Story in the New Testament.

Act 5: Scenes 1-6

Acts

Learning Objective
Understand the chronological presentation of the Story in the New Testament.

Acts 9.1-12.24. TBB. 1474-1479.

trial and it is granted. On his journey to Rome, he suffers his fourth shipwreck. Luke ends the Story of Acts with Paul preaching the Kingdom of God without hindrance in Rome.

Reading the StoryLine: Where to Begin?

The above overview is to familiarize you with the content of Acts. The following scenes will not specifically follow the acrostic account provided above. We now begin our chronological look at the Story using Acts as a guide. We begin in Acts 9.1-19a where we find Saul, the converted Jew, preaching in Damascus and Arabia for three years. After his conversion and because of his preaching, he had escaped from Damascus via a basket lowered over the walls and traveled back to Jerusalem. He had left Jerusalem several years before, looking for those who were following the man named Jesus in order to imprison them.

In Acts 9.19b-30, Luke told his readers that Saul traveled to Jerusalem where he was to be formally introduced to the church there. This caused a certain dilemma among folks in Jerusalem. Because of his prior actions of arresting followers of Jesus, his new found friends, those who were following Jesus, did not trust him. While, on the other hand, his old friends who had commissioned him wanted to kill him.

The believers in Jerusalem discovered the plot to kill Saul, so they took him to Caesarea and sent him off to Tarsus, his place of birth, for the next few years. Nothing is written about Saul during these years, but there are some clues that we will see later that may suggest what he did in Tarsus.

The church at Antioch of Syria had begun with those who had left Jerusalem because of Stephen's stoning. Barnabas had traveled there to take an account of what was going on. He discovered that there was some help needed for this fledging church, the first outside the city of Jerusalem. So he traveled to Tarsus to find Paul to come and help him there along with others in the church at Antioch (Acts 11.19-26).

In the next part of the Story (Acts 11.27-30), Barnabas and Saul were assigned to take a famine relief offering to Jerusalem to help those in the church who were being ravished by the famine (Acts 11.30). On their return, they brought John Mark back to Antioch with them (Acts 12.24).

We now begin a journey through the books of the New Testament in a proposed chronology. Each book will be overviewed. Reading through the New Testament in this fashion will give you a different perspective of the Story of the New Testament. So let's begin.

Acts 12.25-14.28.
TBB. 1479-1482.

Act 5 Scene 2. The First Church Planting Mission (Acts 12.25-14.28, A.D. 46-49)

Reading the StoryLine: The First Church Planting Mission

Barnabas and Saul were commissioned (Acts 12.25-14.28) by the Spirit and sent out by the church at Antioch to take the message of Jesus to other cities. They left Antioch and went to Seleucia where they boarded a ship for Cyprus. They sailed to Salamis and journeyed across Cyprus to Paphos. During this leg of the trip, the missionary duo met BarJesus (Elymas) who became blind, the proconsul Sergius Paulus became a follower of Jesus. After this event, Saul changed his name to Paul in honor of his first Gentile convert. From Paphos they traveled to Perga where John Mark left them to return to Jerusalem.

From Perga they went to Pisidian Antioch, followed by Iconium, Lystra, and Derbe. During this part of their journey, Paul healed a cripple in Lystra, which resulted in Barnabas and Paul being worshiped as gods. Paul was stoned and dragged outside of the city. But the new converts prayed for him and he got up and went back into Lystra, then on to Derbe.

Learning Objective
Understand the chronological presentation of the Story in the New Testament.

From Derbe they retraced their steps to Lystra, Iconium, and Pisidian Antioch. Along the way they strengthened the new converts. From Pisidian Antioch they returned to Attalia and sailed back to Antioch in Syria. Back in the church in Antioch they gave a report of all that God had accomplished on their trip. This amazing journey took approximately three years and covered about 1,250 miles.

During the time that Paul was in Antioch giving his report, he wrote the book of Galatians. There are two theories about the writing of Galatians: a Northern Theory and a Southern Theory.[27] The following material takes the Southern Theory as the correct one to follow.

About Galatians: Christian Freedom

Galatians is the first of Paul's letters.[28] After returning from his mission trip to South Galatia, he wrote to the churches that he had planted. After he departed from this area, a group of Jewish agitators, who believed that you had to add the boundary markers of circumcision, food laws, and calendar events, arrived in Galatia and began to preach their gospel. When Paul discovered that this group had followed his ministry and tried to destroy it with a distorted gospel, he became rather heated and wrote Galatians. Two problems caused this situation. First, Gentiles had accepted Jesus but not Judaism. Second, Jews who had accepted the Jesus Story did not know what to do about having table fellowship with Gentiles.[29] Paul's intention was to recover anyone who had been lost because of the false teaching about conversion and to keep others from accepting the teaching of these Jewish missionaries.

Galatians, contrary to a long tradition, does not address the question about how someone becomes a follower of Jesus or obtains a relationship with God. The problem addressed by Paul was not how people came to be in relationship with the Creator God but who they could eat with.[30]

Did this letter solve the problem in the Galatian churches? One could suggest that because Paul did not have to write them again, although he did visit them again, that it did what it was supposed to do. But, more than likely, the mixture of Jews and Gentiles did not happen overnight. It was a long difficult struggle. The problem of judaizing, i.e., what pagans do to become Jews,[31] stands behind other writings of Paul like Romans and Philippians.[32]

Some Beginning Theological Thoughts

The intent in each of these sections, listed under each of the books below, is to help the reader to begin thinking about the Story in theological ways. Thinking theologically could be understood as "thinking God's thoughts behind him." Everyone is a theologian! There seems to be a hostility to the idea of being a theologian. That was the case in my own personal story. My mother told me, more times than I would like to

BOOK
Galatians
AUTHOR
Paul
AGE WRITTEN
A.D. 49
After
First Church Planting
Mission
FROM
Antioch in Syria
TO
Christians in South
Galatia
PROBLEM
Jesus PLUS Gospel
AUDIENCE
Those who add
cultural practice to
Christianity
GEOGRAPHY
South Galatia

Learning Objective
Understand the chronological presentation of the Story in the New Testament.

remember, that what I needed was "kneeology" not "theology." Of course, both are needed. So, these sections are the beginning practical phase of thinking theologically about some of the content within a book of Scripture within the Story of God. Let me recommend a wonderful book by the late Stan Grenz and his co-author Roger Olson called: *Who Needs Theology?* There the authors talk about defining theology and defending theology and how professional theologians and lay theologians need each other.[33]

Justification

Tom Wright says,

> Many people, including many supposedly 'Pauline' Christians, would say, off the cuff, that the heart of Paul's teaching is 'justification by faith'. What many such people understand as the meaning of this phrase is something like this. People are always trying to pull themselves up by their own moral bootstraps. They try to save themselves by their own efforts; to make themselves good enough for God, or for heaven. This doesn't work; one can only be saved by the sheer unmerited grace of God, appropriated not by good works but by faith. This account of justification owes a good deal both to the controversy between Pelagius and Augustine in the early fifth century and to that between Erasmus and Luther in the early sixteenth century.

And Wright continues,

> 'Justification' in the first century was not about how someone might establish a relationship with God. It was about God's eschatological definition, both future and present, of who was, in fact, a member of his people. In Sanders' terms, it was not so much about 'getting in', or indeed about 'staying in', as about 'how you could tell who was in'. In standard Christian theological language, it wasn't so much about soteriology as about ecclesiology; not so much about salvation as about the church.[34]

In addition to justification, Paul uses other metaphors to describe the nature of God's act, namely, redemption, reconciliation, and salvation.[35]

Faith alone in Christ will set the sinner in a right relationship with God (2.1-16.21). This has been the rallying cry for reformers through the ages. Paul wanted the converts at Galatia to understand that the liberty that came in Jesus was not a license to do what they wanted, when they wanted (5.13). The freedom which Christ brought to a believer was a quality of life that causes the believer to care and enter into a life of service in the new community (5.22-6.10). He taught them that they, as the church, were a direct descendant of Abraham and because of that they should be united (3.16ff.). Because of Jesus there were now no differences which had formerly brought separation. The church was made up of Jews, Gentiles, men, women, slaves, and free. Table fellowship, which included all these groups fellowshiping together, was a true sign of justification. In this new community, the church, there was no difference between these groups because they were all one in Jesus (3.27-29).

QUESTION
If Paul's idea of the church was diversity, then how come there is so much uniformity in churches?

Works of the Flesh and Fruit of the Spirit

Works of the Flesh (5.19-21)

In chapter five, Paul talks about two different lifestyles. The works of the

flesh which represent the lifestyle (habits of life) of this Present Evil Age, and the fruit of the Spirit which represents the lifestyle of the Age to Come lived out now as the new humanity of God is supposed to express itself.[36] The following is the list with short definitions.

Learning Objective
Understand the chronological presentation of the Story in the New Testament.

Sexual Sins

◆ **Sexual Immorality.** Sexual intercourse outside the marriage relationship.

◆ **Impurity.** A general word for any immoral activity that shuts a person off from God's presence.

◆ **Debauchery.** The lack of restraint. A love for sin that is so reckless that the one sinning has ceased to care what God or man thinks of his or her actions. There is no attempt to hide sin, it is committed in the open.

Religious Sins

◆ **Idolatry.** The worship of gods which humankind has made. It is the sin in which material things have replaced God. One worships what is created versus worshiping the Creator.

◆ **Witchcraft.** The use of drugs for magical purposes to bring spells.

Relational Sins

◆ **Hatred.** An attitude of total hostility toward humankind. It is the attitude that puts up barriers and is ready to fight immediately.

◆ **Discord.** An attitude that leads to contentions and quarreling.

◆ **Jealousy.** The desire to have what someone else has.

◆ **Fits of Rage.** An uncontrolled burst of temper which flames quickly and dies quickly.

◆ **Selfish Ambition.** The attitude of self-seeking with no concept of serving others.

◆ **Dissensions.** The attitude of disagreement that leads to division.

◆ **Factions.** A self-willed opinion that leads to divisions. It ends in disliking a person's views as well as disliking the person who holds the view.

◆ **Envy.** This is not the attitude that desires something that someone else has. It is the attitude that begrudges that someone else has anything at all.

Sensual Sins

◆ **Drunkenness.** Habitual intoxication.

◆ **Orgies.** Sexual orgies.

Fruit of the Spirit (5.2-23)

The *fruit of the Spirit* are the habits of life of the Age to Come which has invaded this age in the life and ministry of Jesus. It is the way in which the new humanity lives out their calling in this Present Evil Age.

◆ **Love:** The action that seeks the best and highest potential for others—even if the person seeks the worst for us.

◆ **Joy:** The delight that comes from experiencing God's work in our lives that is not material.

◆ **Peace:** The calm that everything is okay because it is in God's hands.

◆ **Patience:** The gentle tolerance of others. It is patience in dealing with people, not things or events.

Act 5: Scenes 1-6

Letters

Learning Objective
Understand the chronological presentation of the Story in the New Testament.

- ◆ **Kindness:** Treating others the way God treats us.
- ◆ **Goodness:** Doing good deeds for those within the community of believers.
- ◆ **Faithfulness:** Being reliable
- ◆ **Gentleness:** The balance between excessive anger and excessive patience. The quality of a person who is always angry at the right time and never angry at the wrong time.
- ◆ **Self-Control:** This is allowing the Spirit to control one's life rather than a person trying to control her or his own life.

So What?

The *So What* sections in Act 5 take on a more personal form of some stories intermingled with comments than the previous *So What* sections.

The idea of living in the Story vs. applying part of the Story to one's life is a paradigm switch for most readers. As an actor, finding your part to play in God's EPIC Adventure, is a different mindset. Sermons and Bible study books mainly focus on helping us apply Scripture to our lives. Picture taking something in from the outside and trying to make it fit as a way of understanding application. Rather, than application, think of the Story as something that you have the privilege to "live in." By this, I mean that you are not taking something and putting it into your life, you are taking your life and putting it into something. The *So What?* sections moving forward are developed to help you begin to think about what part of the role, as actor in this great drama, you are playing. Think of the Story as a great light moving through a prism with many different hues of light coming through on the other side. The great light is you as the actor, the many and varied colors are provided by the different books in the New Testament Story. Use *theomagination*, by which I mean, let God stimulate your imagination as to how you play out the color hue from each part of the Story.

Galatians is about learning to be with others that are unlike you. Having table fellowship is a way of breaking down the walls between different groups. Recently our community of faith started having a brunch for the neighborhood that is on a monthly basis. On two occasions, I sat at a table with two folks that were completely unlike me and listened to them for over an hour. I did not purpose to preach the gospel to them, only listen to where the gospel might find acceptance in their life. I listened to see what the community of faith or me personally could do to help the person in their daily life. Just being with others sometimes is all that God might wish for us to do. So, look for someone in your community that is not like you, find a way of fellowshipping with them, and begin living in the Story of God's reconciliation.

Of course, table fellowship is not the only hue of light in Galatians. As you read the text, look for these hues of light that call you to live differently in this Present Evil Age.

- -
 **BOOK READING GUIDE: GALATIANS**
- -

Galatians 1-6. TBB. 1551-1556.

This expanded reading guide and the ones that follow for each book are intended to help you as a reader as you read the text of Scripture. These guides are not supposed to replace the reading of Scripture. As you read the text, become an actor, travel companion, community of faith member, or another character in the Story. Use *theomigination*, that is the imagination that sees and does things from God's perspective.

Opening Thoughts 1.1-5

Faithfulness to One Gospel: An Autobiography 1.6-2.21

Paul asserted that his authority as an apostle comes directly from God because his gospel came directly from a revelation of Jesus Christ at his conversion. He was not inferior to the Jerusalem apostles because his ministry has been performed with the power of God.

Faithfulness to One Gospel: A Rebuke 3.1-4.31

Paul demonstrated to the Galatians that it was not by adding the boundary markers that they become true followers of Jesus. It was because of the death of Jesus on the cross that one's salvation has been secured. We have become his heir, thus forfeiting our status as slaves.

Faithfulness to One Gospel: A Request 5.1-6.10

We can stop living a lifestyle according to this Present Evil Age, because of the power of the Holy Spirit in our lives. Instead, our lives should be Spirit-controlled and lived out according to the Age to Come, demonstrated by the fruit of the Spirit in our lives, as the church and as individuals.

Closing Thoughts 6.11-18

Reading the StoryLine: The Jerusalem Council. Acts 15

When Paul and Barnabas finished delivering their report to the church at Antioch, they went to Jerusalem. In Acts 15, Luke shares the story of the church debate with Paul over his Gentile ministry and decides in favor of putting their hands on what looked to them like what the Spirit was doing.

Sometime after the debate, James,[37] the leader of the Jerusalem church and brother of Jesus,[38] wrote a book to Christians everywhere with a focus on sharing with them God's wisdom about their new humanity.

About James: The Wisdom of God

The book of James is the New Testament equivalent of the Old Testament Wisdom books.[39] Its recipients are in question. The phrase "to the twelve tribes scattered among the nations" (James 1.1) could be understood as a metaphor (see 1 Peter 1.1) or to Jewish believers who lived outside of Palestine.[40]

It is a collection of proverbial sayings and stories in the form of ❖ **aphorisms.** ❖ James uses about sixty imperatives in his book. An imperative in the Greek language offers the reader/listener a place to make a decision. There is a similarity between James and the Sermon on the Mount in the Gospels (James 1.2 cp. Matthew 5.10-12; James 1.5-7 cp. Matthew 5.48). Some of the sayings in James have a resemblance to the wisdom found in Ecclesiasticus in the Apocrypha.

There has been a lot of discussion between New Testament specialists about the apparent conflict between James and Paul over justification.[41]

Learning Objective
Understand the chronological presentation of the Story in the New Testament.

Dictionary Articles
Read the following Dictionary Articles in *New Bible Dictionary*, Third Edition. D. R. W. Wood, A. R. Millard, J. I. Packer, D. J. Wiseman, and I. Howard Marshall (Editors), InterVarsity Press. 1996.
  Galatians
  Galatians, Epistle to the
  Justification / Faith

Acts 15.1-35. TBB. 1482-1484.

BOOK
James
AUTHOR
James, half brother of Jesus
AGE WRITTEN
A.D. 49
FROM
Jerusalem
TO
Christians Everywhere
PROBLEM
Too Little Wisdom
AUDIENCE
Those who feel that they do not have to serve in the church
GEOGRAPHY
🜨 Jerusalem

Aphorisms. *Tersely phrased* statements of a truth or opinion.

Letters

Learning Objective
Understand the
chronological presentation of
the Story in the New
Testament.

These disputes are rooted in the misconception that James was speaking about "works" as a way of gaining salvation, which could in fact cause some difficulty, if James meant by "works" what Luther meant by works (see discussion above, 221-222). In fact, Luther was so distraught that James was in the canon that he called it an "epistle of straw."[42] Even though their language may overlap, "they are addressing different issues without reference to each other."[43]

Some Beginning Theological Thoughts

Wisdom Literature

Wisdom Literature is the literature which describes the applying of truth to one's life in the light of experience. James is the New Testament representation of this kind of Literature. Ecclesiastes, Proverbs, and Job are pieces of Wisdom Literature in the Old Testament along with Psalms 37 and 73.

We often say that we need the wisdom of God. We quote our favorite passages of Scripture thinking that provides wisdom for us. We must remember that these sayings in James are not simply Christian Proverbs to be used to get anything we think we need. There are several areas of wisdom which James discusses. We should be aware of all of them. There is wisdom:

- regarding attacks: 1.2, 12-27
- to control one's tongue: 3.1-12
- of this age and the age to come: 3.13-18
- to submit to God: 4.1-10
- not to slander one another: 4.11-12
- not to boast: 4.13-17
- on the treatment of the poor: 5.1-12

The Wisdom of This Age and The Age To Come: 3.13-18

Let's take a closer look at the second item in the list above, controlling one's tongue. James begins with a comparison. *First*, there is earthly wisdom (3.13-16). The word *earthly* only appears six times in the New Testament. It has the usual meaning of *being godless in source and sphere*. Earthly wisdom is the wisdom which is played out in the habits of life in this world, i.e., what Paul called the works of the flesh in Galatians. James clarified by telling his readers that this wisdom is *unspiritual*. This means that the origin is not from the Spirit. *Earthly wisdom* is from the devil. This means that it proceeds from or is inspired by demons. Thus, earthly wisdom is natural wisdom which is bent on things of this Present Evil Age. It does not come from the Spirit, but has its source in demons.

Second, there is the wisdom of the age to come (3.13–18). James describes the wisdom of the Age to Come as:

- **Pure.** Not being polluted by the values of this Present Evil Age
- **Peace-Loving.** Freedom from strife with others and an inward peace
- **Considerate.** Being fair, generous rather than rigid, and exacting, i.e., reasonable
- **Submissive.** Yielding to persuasion: This only appears here in the New Testament. It is the opposite of disobedient. As Jesus obeyed

the Father and only did what he saw him doing, such should be the attitude and lifestyle of a Christ follower.

◆ **Full of Mercy–Good Fruit.** The believer should demonstrate mercy rather than venom, and, thus produce good fruit.

◆ **Impartial.** This word appears only here in the New Testament and means single-minded.

◆ **Sincere.** To be sincere is the opposite of being a hypocrite.

Works

When faced with the attitude to dismiss works as unnecessary for Christ followers, James needs to be heard as he was during the time of Wesley. James exhorted followers of Jesus to demonstrate by their works that they were justified. If one were to ask Paul: How are we justified before God? He would answer: By faith! If one were to ask James: How are we justified before man? He might answer: By works! If one were to ask James: How do I know that you are justified? He might well reply: By works!

So What?

James is full of the wisdom of God for the new humanity in God's EPIC Adventure to begin to live within. Remember, there are more hues of light coming through the prism than you can grasp on any one reading of the text. Which age will you live in? Which values will your new humanity choose to live out of?

 BOOK READING GUIDE: JAMES

Introduction 1.1

True Religion 1.2-18

True religion comes from the strength that one receives from overcoming the attacks that come in life.

True Worship 1.19-27

True worship comes from being a doer of the word. Keeping the tongue bridled is a sure sign that worship has occurred.

True Faith 2.1-26

True faith is demonstrated by the good works in one's life. One cannot work into a position of faith by doing good works. One does good works because of faith in Jesus and his acceptance.

True Wisdom 3.1-5.20

True wisdom is the experience of the Age to Come in the Present Evil Age of our life. It is peaceable, gentle, full of mercy, and good fruit.

 Act 5 Scene 3. The Second Church Planting Mission (Acts 15.36-18.18a, A.D. 49/50-51)

Reading the StoryLine: The Second Church Planting Mission

From Jerusalem, after the council of Acts 15, Paul and Barnabas returned to Antioch. There they had a quarrel about John Mark going on another mission trip with them (Acts 15.36ff). Barnabas wanted to take

---

Letters

Learning Objective
Understand the chronological presentation of the Story in the New Testament.

QUESTION
How has the concept of grace caused you to lie back and not do the works of ministry that God has called you to do?

James 1-5. TBB. 1687-1691.

Dictionary Articles
Read the following Dictionary Articles in *New Bible Dictionary*.
James
James, Epistle of

Acts 15.36-18.18a.
TBB. 1482-1487.

Letters

Learning Objective
Understand the chronological presentation of the Story in the New Testament.

QUESTION
How do you think Paul's ministry in Athens affected his ministry in Corinth? What would a church that you planted look like if you only stayed there for three weeks and then moved on?

BOOK
1 Thessalonians
AUTHOR
Paul
AGE WRITTEN
A.D. 50
During
Second Church Planting
Trip
FROM
Corinth
TO
Christians in Thessalonica
PROBLEM
The Pattern for Church Life and Correction of Misunderstanding about the Second Coming
AUDIENCE
Those who are concerned about understanding the Second Coming of Jesus
GEOGRAPHY
✈ Corinth and Thessalonica

Mark with them, perhaps to give him another chance after he had deserted them on their first journey. Paul would have nothing to do with the idea. The argument was settled by Barnabas taking Mark and going to Cyprus while Paul took Silas and went through Syria and Cilicia headed West. Paul revisited the cities of Derbe, Lystra, Iconium, and Pisidian Antioch and added Timothy to his team (Acts 16.1ff.).

From the Galatian cities, they traveled to Troas. In Troas, Paul had a vision (Acts 16.9ff.); a man from Macedonia told him to come there to help. Luke was added to the team. Luke gives us a clue about this in the writing of Acts by changing the first personal pronoun to include himself. The group left and journeyed to Philippi where Lydia was converted, a demonized girl was delivered, Paul and Silas were jailed, and the jailer was converted (Acts 16.11-40). Then, the team moved on to Thessalonica for a short three week stay. During that time, a mob assaulted the home where Paul was staying causing the team to pack up and leave (Acts 17.1-9). The next stop was the city of Berea where the dwellers searched the Scriptures daily to see if what Paul was teaching them was correct (Acts 17.10-15).

Finally, Paul came to Athens. He preached on Mars Hill about the unknown god. Timothy and Silas, who had been sent on a task, returned and rejoined Paul. Timothy was sent back to Thessalonica while Silas was sent elsewhere. Finally, Paul was laughed out of Athens (Acts 17-16.34).

Paul moved south to Corinth (Acts 18.1-18a) where he met Aquila and Priscilla and worked his trade of tentmaker in the marketplace. Timothy and Silas rejoined him. After teaching for a while in the synagogue in Corinth, he moved his teaching ministry from the synagogue next door to the house of Titius Justus. Crispus, the synagogue ruler, was converted. Paul had a vision and was told to stay in Corinth and not to worry about the suffering he was experiencing. The Jews became outraged and took him to Gallio to be tried, but Gallio refused to condemn Paul. Paul and his team remained in Corinth for eighteen months.

While in Corinth, Paul wrote First and Second Thessalonians.

About 1 Thessalonians: He Is Coming

Paul received word from Timothy and Silas while in Corinth that the Thessalonians church was being persecuted by the local synagogue. Paul had only been able to stay with this new church for three to four weeks. That did not give him very much time to establish a firm foundation for these new believers. Apparently, Paul had taught them about the Second Coming of Jesus[44] because there was some misunderstanding and questions that had arisen about this theme. He wrote the church to encourage them during their time of persecution and to answer the two questions which they had raised.

A note of explanation. Sometimes you can read what answers are being given and deduce what the questions may have been. Think of it as listening to one side of a phone conversation and trying to figure out what the other side is saying. It is with that scenario that we proceed. After Paul congratulates the Thessalonian believers (chapter 1), he turned to answer the two questions[45] that may have precipitated the writing of the letter.

Some Beginning Theological Thoughts

Questions about the Second Coming

Letters

Learning Objective
Understand the
chronological presentation of
the Story in the New
Testament.

It is interesting to observe that when this church needed valid information to help them continue in their journey, they did not hesitate to ask the person who was foundational in their spiritual formation.

The first question was: *What happens to those who die before the return of Christ?* Paul must have taught about the Second Coming while in Thessalonica, and after he left, some of the new believers died. Death before the Second Coming may have been viewed as chastisement for sin, or even a loss of one's salvation.[46] This may have sparked the question above. Paul's answer is in 4.13-18.

A second question was: *When will Christ return?* It is an often asked question even today. There had not been enough time with this congregation during his stay with them to allow Paul to teach fully on this subject. So, he answered the above question in 5.1-11.

Second Coming

There are three words in the New Testament used for the event of the Second Coming. They are:

◆ *parousia* translated by *presence* in 1 Thessalonians 3.13
◆ *apokalypsis* translated by *revealed* in 2 Thessalonians 1.7; and
◆ *epiphaneia* translated by *coming* in 2 Thessalonians 2.8.

This event will be the personal and visible coming of the same Jesus who departed at the beginning of the Acts Story (Acts 1.11) and will be observed by everyone on earth. The coming of Jesus will indicate the closure of all things as they are and the beginning of the fullness of the future. His coming is the consummation of the Kingdom. The time of this event was unknown. Within scholarship, there are those who differ from the classic position found in early church creeds such as the Apostles' and Nicene Creeds. They believe that the coming of Jesus will occur in two parts: the first, a secret coming to gather believers; the second, a coming for everyone to see at the same time. This second one occurs seven years later than the first event. This position is widely held within a system of belief called pretribulational dispensationalism and can be found in the Scofield Reference Bible and updated by what is being called Progressive Dispensationalism,[47] and has been read by millions in the *Left Behind Series*. You may note for the reading of the material in this book that I believe that this view of the end is simply wrongheaded.

Paul gives emphasis to the Second Coming in each of the five chapters of First Thessalonians.

1. The safety of the believers at the second coming (1.10)
2. The reward for believers at his coming (2.19-20)
3. The character of believers at his return (3.13)
4. The reunion of family and loved ones at the coming of Jesus (4.13-18)
5. The living of a holy life until he returns (5.23)

The key for a lot of modern eschatology about the Second Coming is the word *rapture*. The word *rapture* does not appear in Scripture. Popular thinking and writing has replaced the words *caught up* by the word *rapture*. There are three points of view on when the rapture will occur: Pretribulation, Midtribulation, and Posttribulation.[48] The Midtribulational

Letters

Learning Objective
Understand the chronological presentation of the Story in the New Testament.

view is the newest of the views. The pretribulational position is a little over 150 years old. The posttribulational position appears to be the view of the writers of the New Testament, but this is all debatable.

So What?

Currently, we remain at a high water mark in our society concerning the Second Coming. The most popular theory of the last 150 years still holds sway in millions of lives. Living in a different understanding of this Story will cause different responses to the world that you live in. As an example, thinking that Jesus will cause you to escape this world in a moment, may cause you to make decisions that you might make differently if you thought you were going to live well into your '90s. How would thinking about the Second Coming differently change the way you respond to needs around you?

 BOOK READING GUIDE: 1 THESSALONIANS

1 Thessalonians 1-5. TBB. 1507-1510.

Introduction 1.1

In Suffering Become Imitators 1.2-10

Paul suggested that the life of a believer will have suffering.

Imitation of Paul's Ministry 2.1-4.12

As the church continued in ministry, they should look at Paul's ministry as a model.

Instruction about the Second Coming 4.13-5.24

Paul answered the two questions the church had about the Second Coming.

Conclusion 5.25-28

BOOK
2 Thessalonians
AUTHOR
Paul
AGE WRITTEN
A.D. 50 During
Second Church Planting
Trip
FROM
Corinth
TO
Christians in Thessalonica
PROBLEM
Suffering and
the Second Coming
AUDIENCE
Those who are concerned
about understanding the
Second Coming of Jesus
GEOGRAPHY
🌐 Corinth and
Thessalonica

About 2 Thessalonians: The Day of the Lord

This second letter to the church at Thessalonica arrived only weeks after the first letter from Paul.[49] After the first letter was delivered to the church at Thessalonica, the courier returned with more concerns from the Thessalonian community to which Paul responded.

Some Beginning Theological Thoughts

Rebellion and the Man of Lawlessness

The day of the Lord—the Second Coming of Jesus—would not occur until the restrainer appeared. This is a very debated subject within 2 Thessalonians.[50] Paul did not intend his readers or us to take these events in some chronological order.

Rebellion

The word is *apostasy* and has been translated by some Dispensational Theologians as *departing*.[51] There is no support for such a translation in ancient literature. The word usually means outright opposition to God. This is not a *falling away* as has often been suggested as much as it is *apathy* toward God and his authority (1 Tim. 4.1).

The Man Of Lawlessness Revealed (2.1-4)

The phrase *man of lawlessness*, is usually understood as referring to the Antichrist. Here is an interesting thought. If 2 Thessalonians 2.1

means the *rapture* of the saints before the tribulation as stated by John Walvoord in *The Rapture Question*[52] and in verse 2, *the day of the Lord* is the Second Coming of Jesus, and the rebellion and man of lawlessness are revealed during the tribulation when the church has already been raptured, then Paul is telling the Thessalonians something they did not really need to know because they would already be taken in the rapture.

Learning Objective
Understand the chronological presentation of the Story in the New Testament.

Obviously, he was telling them something that they should observe had not happened so they may be calmed about the reports which they had received. Paul leaves his readers with a description of the character of the Antichrist. The spirit of Antichrist is always here (1 John 4.3). At the conclusion of this Present Evil Age, all evil will be embodied into one human being—the Antichrist. He will arrogate to himself all authority both secular and sacred. He will demand total submission including worship. His character is lawless. His destiny is to be doomed to destruction. His activity will be to set himself up against God. I do not believe that Paul was referring to a rebuilt Temple in this passage. The Temple had not yet been destroyed and the word he used is not the whole temple but the innermost shrine. He used this word later in his book to the Corinthians to mean the church (1 Cor. 3.16ff.). The phrase "setting himself up in the temple," was a metaphorical way of expressing defiance to God by the Antichrist.

QUESTION
What does Paul tell the readers of these two books to do with the information about the Second Coming?

Holding Him Back

This person of Antichrist will not be revealed until a *restraining* influence is out of the way. In verse 5, Paul reminds his readers that he has told them all this before. Verse 6 warrants an understanding that they knew what the restraining influence was. The question is: Can we? Paul's vagueness should make everyone hesitant to use this part of Scripture as proof of their particular brand of eschatology. There are several views set forth as to the meaning of the restraining influence:

◆ The Roman Empire and its Emperor:

The early church fathers may have held this view. The restraining influence is referred to as a "what" in verse 6, as well as a "he" in verse 7.

◆ Human Government:

This view comes from the one above. When human government fails in its effort to restrain rebellion, the Antichrist will step in and begin to rule.

◆ The Holy Spirit

Most who hold to a pretribulational rapture theory believe this as the correct view. The Holy Spirit will no longer be active in the world because the believers have been taken out.

◆ The Church

This is akin to the Holy Spirit view above. When the church has been raptured, then the Antichrist can be revealed. It often amuses me as to how much time some teachers spend trying to figure out who the Antichrist is, while at the same time holding to the view that they are not going to be here when he arrives. My question is: So what difference does it make who it is, if you are not going to be here?

There are grave difficulties which attend these last two positions. In

Act 5: Scenes 1-6

Letters

Learning Objective
Understand the chronological presentation of the Story in the New Testament.

fact, they teach a regression back to Old Testament times. They deny the power and fullness of the Holy Spirit and the church. It is a matter of biblical record that the greater the activity of Satan, the greater the activity of the Holy Spirit—there is no theology of reduction in the New Testament.

If the Holy Spirit is the restraining influence as he fills the church, then here is an interesting situation. Within the pre-tribulation rapture theory, it is taught that there will be 144,000 Jews to evangelize in seven years without the presence of the Holy Spirit. Thought: *What the church has been unable to do in centuries with the presence of the Holy Spirit, these Jews will do in seven years without the presence of the Holy Spirit.*

One cannot know for sure what this passage really means. I do believe that whatever it means, that the church will be around to see its full revelation.

The coming of the lawless one has the power of Satan behind him (9a). This power was displayed in all kinds of counterfeit miracles, signs and wonders (9b). The power of the lawless one will result in the seduction of the wicked (10). Here is an interesting thought: *God uses the very evil that men and Satan produce for working out his own purpose in the lives of people who have been seduced* (11-12).

God had chosen from the beginning the process he would use for salvation. Notice the idea of Trinity in verse 13—Lord, God, Spirit. This must have been the accepted view. Paul encouraged these believers to stand firm. Standing firm means to get a firm grip by holding to the teaching he has given them concerning the Second Coming, both orally in person and written in his letters. He concluded the chapter with a prayer that God would provide for the followers of Jesus eternal encouragement and hope which will in turn strengthen everyone in every task that is done and every word that is uttered.

So What?

As with the church at Thessalonica, a part of the church in today's society is slightly skewed toward an overabundance of wrongheaded information about the Second Coming of Jesus. The second part of this book often overshadows the first part which is about suffering. We have been provided with a story in the church that says when we become a believer, everything will turn around for us. If bad things happen to us, it is because we have done bad things and an angry God looks for punishment. So suffering is seen as something that happens because of something we do, a sort of quid pro quo or tit-for-tat theology. How would we live differently if we believed that the suffering that becomes a part of our life was because of the age we lived in and that God will vindicate our suffering? How would we live in that Story?

 BOOK READING GUIDE: 2 THESSALONIANS

2 Thessalonians 1-3. TBB. 1513-1515.

Introduction 1.1-2

Encouragement During Suffering 1.3-12

Paul told the Thessalonians that they would be vindicated for their suffering.

Enlightenment about Christ's Return 2.1-17

The Day of the Lord had not yet arrived. When others try to persuade you by means of letters, prophetic words, etc., that the Day has arrived, don't believe it!

Exhortation to Steadfastness 3.1-15

Paul asked the church to pray for him and keep the community disciplined.

Conclusion 3.16-18

Letters

Learning Objective
Understand the chronological presentation of the Story in the New Testament.

Dictionary Articles
Read the following Dictionary Articles in *New Bible Dictionary*.
 Thessalonica
 Thessalonians, Epistles to the
 Suffering
 Eschatology

Reading the StoryLine: End of Second Church Planting Mission

Eighteen months after Paul began his ministry at Corinth, he left for Jerusalem. On his way, he visited Ephesus. After a short stop in Jerusalem, he went to Antioch of Syria. This was the conclusion of his Second Church Planting Mission, which took approximately four years.

Act 5 Scene 4. The Third Church Planting Mission (Acts 18.18b-21.14, A.D. 52-57)

After staying in Antioch for a short period of time, Paul began his Third Church Planting Mission. He left Antioch and traveled back through Cilicia, the cities of Galatia and Phrygia, and returned to Ephesus. Upon arrival in Ephesus, he began working with the church, which had been started by Aquila and Priscilla, and a group of disciples of John the Baptist who had received the Spirit.

Acts 18.18b-21.16.
TBB. 1487-1491.

About 1 Corinthians: Problem Solving

Remember, Paul evangelized Corinth during the Second Church Planting Mission (Acts 18:1-18a). His second journey brought him to Ephesus. During his time in Ephesus, Paul preached in the School of Tyrannus for two years and three months about four hours a day. The seven sons of Sceva were delivered and there was a book burning of many sorcery books. This caused a riot which was led by Demetrius the silversmith on behalf of the goddess Artemis/Diana.

Sometime during the last part of his trip that brought him back to Ephesus, he received a message that there were some problems back in Corinth. He wrote a letter to the church during this time period, which he referred to in 1 Corinthians 5.9, in which he commanded disassociation from professing Christians who lived immorally. Moffat suggests the following about the church at Corinth, "the church was in the world as it had to be, but the world was in the church as it ought not to be."[53] Some scholars believe that 2 Corinthians 6:14-7:1 is a fragment of the *lost letter* which was inserted in 2 Corinthians when Paul's Letters were collected and published[54] to which Paul is pointing in his reference to writing to them a former letter. What we call 1 Corinthians is not the letter to which Paul was pointing in the text of 1 Corinthians 5.9.

New Testament literature is best understood as problem-solving literature.[55] This is certainly true of the Corinthian correspondence. We may reconstruct the writing of 1 Corinthians in the following way. *First*, a group from Corinth, called Chloe's people, visited Paul and asked for his guidance about a problem of unity in the church at Corinth (1 Cor. 1.11). Second, before he could send his message back to them, three other folks from the Corinthian church, Stephanas, Fortunatus, and Achaicus,

BOOK
1 Corinthians
AUTHOR
Paul
AGE WRITTEN
A.D. 55-56 - During
3rd Church Planting Trip
FROM
Ephesus
TO
Christians at Corinth
PROBLEM
Divisions,
A specific case of
Immorality,
Lawsuits,
Immorality in general,
Marriage,
Food
Public Worship:
Veiling of women,
Lord's Supper
Spiritual Gifts
Resurrection,
Collections
Apollos
AUDIENCE
Believers who have church and individual problems which need to be solved
GEOGRAPHY
 Ephesus and Corinth

Act 5: Scenes 1-6

Letters

Learning Objective
Understand the chronological presentation of the Story in the New Testament.

(1 Cor. 15.15-18) arrived bringing a letter asking Paul for his guidance in some other problems the church was also facing. The response to those problems is found in 7.1-16.24. Finally, they also brought him news of three current problems which also needed attention. The response to this oral material is found in 5.1-6.20. The visit and letter disclosed twelve problems within the church to which Paul responded to their questions and gave his response to Timothy to deliver back to the Corinthian church. This response is our 1 Corinthians.

Some Beginning Theological Thoughts

The theology of 1 Corinthians is found in the solutions that Paul provided to the problems the church was having. Here is part of the list:

Spirituality

For the Corinthians, spirituality was determining that in human nature the spirit had greater value than the body.[56]

Unity

Unity is the quality of having the same passion. This was not the case in Corinth (1 Cor. 1.11-12). In the pages of Scripture, unity is never organizational, but rather an expression of love and consideration of other believers because we are all a part of one family. It is not uniformity or the sharing of one opinion on a matter. It is the God-given ability to put aside differences because of a shared common goal. Jesus prayed that the believers have unity so that the world may see the love of God. Paul wanted the Corinthians to experience this kind of unity.

Sex

The New Testament writers are not embarrassed by human sexuality. In 1 Cor. 7.5, Paul told married couples that sex is very important within their marriage relationship. This passage is set in the context of the Corinthians' belief that a married man should not have sexual relations with his wife (7.1). Couples are told that they are not to deprive each other of sex, except for a limited time for prayer. Young widows and virgins who have strong sexual desires should not hesitate to marry (1 Cor. 7.36-40).

Idols

For Paul, idolatry serves as a contact with the demonic (1 Cor. 10.20). Paul wanted his readers to understand that any supernatural aid offered through an idol was demonic in nature.

Spiritual Gifts

There are two ways gifts are understood: constituted and spontaneous. Those who believe that the gifts are constituted believe that you can discover and then develop your gift. Those who believe that the gifts are spontaneous believe that each believer is eligible for God to use him or her at any time to deliver a gift to another. It may be argued that the first of these options was not what Paul had in mind when he was writing to the Corinthians. One should also remember that lists in the New Testament are representative, not all inclusive. There are surely more gifts of the Spirit than Paul provides in any of his lists and there are more gifts of the Spirit than the sum total of all gifts listed in all of Paul's and other's lists.

One of the most revered passages recorded in Scripture is 1 Corinthians 13. It is used often at weddings to help define love. One must understand, however, that its context is between chapters twelve and fourteen which has to do with the misuse of gifts of the Spirit. Without doubt, the major concern of Paul in this chapter was to identify love as the lubricant to be used when Spiritual Gifts were in operation.

Learning Objective
Understand the chronological presentation of the Story in the New Testament.

Tongues

In Scripture, there seems to be a difference between the Gift of Tongues as presented by Paul in 1 Corinthians 12-13 and speaking in tongues. They are often confused as being the same. Most likely they are not! It appears that the Gift of Tongues is used in a public worship setting, the speaker is speaking to God (1 Cor. 13.2), and the interpretation would then be a Godward speech. The term *Praying in the Spirit* may be thought of as a technical phrase in the New Testament whose meaning includes praying in tongues.[57] Today this concept is often referred to as one's prayer language.

Giving

The 1 Corinthian 15.1-3 passage gives the reader insight into part of Paul's theology of giving. Here it indicates that regular systematic giving should be nurtured. The New Testament does not teach *tithe* as a form of giving. Well, neither does the Old Testament where tithe is Israel's taxation system. Generous giving is a reflection of believers' new covenant relationship with God through Jesus.

Resurrection

Bodily resurrection was a concept foreign to Greek thought. Paul suggests that the resurrected body will have continuity with the present body, but be suited to the conditions of eternal life. For Paul, Resurrection life is life after life after death.

So What?

The Corinthian church was into everything and everything seemed to be into them. Life was syncretistic. Life in the world moving from modernity to postmodernity (or whatever it will be called) offers syncretism. How would you as an actor in this time and space find a way to live a non-syncretistic life? 1 Corinthians may help you solve that problem.

 BOOK READING GUIDE: 1 CORINTHIANS

Introduction 1.1-3

Admonition Concerning Divisions 1.4-4.21

1 Corinthians 1-16.
TBB. 1519-1534.

Chloe's people brought a report of disunity within the church at Corinth. Four different men were being chosen by congregants as their leader. They were Paul, Apollos, Peter, and Christ. Paul responds in this first section by suggesting that their activity of choosing sides was a sure sign of their immaturity.

Activities Denounced 5.1-6.20

Three men (16.17) arrived from Corinth and informed Paul via letter of their concerns about the church. In addition to the set of problems in

Letters

Learning Objective
Understand the chronological presentation of the Story in the New Testament.

the letter they brought to Paul, these three Corinthians inform Paul that there are other concerns which were not recorded in their hand-delivered letter. They are:

1. A specific case of immorality in which a member was sleeping with his stepmother.

2. Members were trying to resolve lawsuits outside the confines of the church.

3. Immorality in general, idolaters, adulterers, male prostitution and homosexuality, thieves, greed, drunkards, slanderers, and swindlers.

Answers to Corinthian Questions 7.1-16.9

There are seven specific questions to which the Corinthians wanted Paul to give them a response:

1. Marriage Activities

2. Food which had been offered to idols

3. The length of women's hair

4. The Lord's Supper

5. Spiritual Gifts

6. Misconceptions about the Resurrection

7. Receiving an Offering

   Conclusion 16.10-24

BOOK
2 Corinthians
AUTHOR
Paul
AGE WRITTEN
A.D. 57 - During
3rd Church Planting Trip
FROM
Macedonia (Philippi)
TO
Christians at Corinth
PROBLEM
Reconciliation
AUDIENCE
Any believer who needs to know the process of reconciliation
GEOGRAPHY
✈ Macedonia and Corinth

About 2 Corinthians: Reconciliation

After writing First Corinthians, Paul made a quick, painful visit to Corinth (2 Cor. 2:1, 12:14; 13:1-2) in an effort to straighten out the problems in the church at Corinth. He was not successful.

The Letter of Discipline: 2 Corinthians 10-13

Upon his return to Ephesus, he sends another letter (2 Corinthians 2:3ff.) in which he commanded the Corinthians to discipline his leading opponent in the Church. Some feel that this letter is preserved in part at 2 Corinthians 10-13.[58] Paul left Ephesus and anxiously awaited Titus at Troas and then in Macedonia.

The Letter of Reconciliation: 2 Corinthians 1-9

Titus arrives with the news that the Church has disciplined Paul's opponent and that most of the Corinthians had submitted to Paul's authority. Paul then wrote 2 Corinthians from Macedonia (still on his Third Church Planting Trip) in response to the favorable report of Titus. Some here feel that what Paul wrote here was 2 Corinthians 1-9, with the exception of 6.14 -7.1.[59]

The Traditional View

The traditional view is that Paul wrote this second letter to the Corinthians within the year of the first letter. After sending his first letter, Paul went to Troas expecting to meet Titus and learn about the effect of the solutions he had written to the church. Titus was not there so he continued to Macedonia. He found Titus and received the information he desired. There was good news and bad news. Many of the Corinthian believers had corrected their conduct and beliefs, but some of them still opposed the authority of Paul and his teaching. So he wrote this second letter to defend his motives, authority, and ministry while he was with them.

Some Beginning Theological Thoughts

Reconciliation

The root idea of reconciliation is a change of attitude or relationship. Reconciliation is necessary between two parties where something or someone has disrupted fellowship, which causes one or both parties to become hostile toward each other. In theological terms, sin alienated humankind from God. Sin broke relationship and became an obstacle between humankind and God. Reconciliation was initiated by God and accomplished in the work of Jesus (2 Cor. 5.19).

Offerings

Paul was taking up an offering for the church at Jerusalem which would demonstrate his primary message that in the church there is neither Jew nor Greek. (2 Cor. 8.1-9.15) This passage suggests the wisdom of generous giving to benefit others.

Apostolic Credentials

In 2 Corinthians 1.1-13.13, Paul talks about his extensive sufferings, special revelation from God, and miracle working powers. In this book comes the famous "thorn in the flesh" passage. There are many suggestions as to what the thorn is: epilepsy, eye disease, malaria, leprosy, migraine headaches, depression, stammering, and false teachers. What ever it was, it was painful to Paul.

So What?

The Corinthian church could be any church on the corner of walk and don't walk in America today, or, for that matter, other cities in the world. Well, at least any Pentecostal or Charismatic church. This church and its modern equivalent was filled with theological, ethical, social, and personal problems, as well as libertines (everything is permitted) and sexual ascetics (don't have sexual intercourse with your wife). What a mess! How should we handle such problems in the church today? Did the instructions in the Corinthian correspondence provide solutions to the problems the church faced? In one sense we can answer that question by saying, "Yes, it did!" at least for that generation. But history gives us more insight into the church at Corinth. At the end of the first century, approximately fifty years later, ❖ **Clement of Rome** ❖ responded to a letter written to him from the church at Corinth revealing that the church was struggling with some of the same problems then that it had struggled with during Paul's ministry.[60] One might suggest from this information that a second generation group can not rely solely on the behavior of their forefathers. A second generation group and all groups following must find their own way through the problems within their community of faith.

Clement of Rome was one of the Apostolic Fathers and the author of the First Epistle to the Corinthians (ca. A.D. 96) .You can read the complete text online at: <http://www.earlychristianwritings.com/1clement.html>

"The parents have eaten sour grapes
and the children's teeth are set on edge."

So the prophet Ezekiel said to Israel (Ezek. 18.2), inferring that a new generation cannot blame the previous generation for problems, but must take responsibility for the problems themselves. So, in every generation, these letters may provide many ways to improvise solutions to these same problems in today's church.

Letters

Learning Objective
Understand the chronological presentation of the Story in the New Testament.

2 Corinthians 1-13.
TBB. 1539-1548.

Dictionary Articles
Read the following Dictionary Articles in *New Bible Dictionary*.
  Corinth
  Corinthians, Epistles to the
  Marriage
  Spiritual Gifts
  Lord's Supper
  Resurrection
  Body of Christ

Acts 20.1-6. TBB. 1489-1490.

BOOK
Romans
AUTHOR
Paul
AGE WRITTEN
A.D. 57
During 3rd
Church Planting Trip
FROM
Corinth
TO
Christians at Rome
PROBLEM
Justification by Faith
Acceptability:
To demonstrate that he was not the cause of trouble in the towns in which he had ministered.
AUDIENCE
To those who need to understand that God has created a new humanity by the death of Jesus.
GEOGRAPHY
☽ Corinth and Rome

 **BOOK READING GUIDE: 2 CORINTHIANS**

Introduction 1.1-2

Devoted Majority 1.3-7.16

Paul wrote to reconcile with his church. He defended his ministry to the church.

Deliverance for Jerusalem Saints 8.1-9.15

Paul gave the church at Corinth instructions about meeting the financial needs of the church at Jerusalem.

Disobedient Minority 10.1-13.10

Opponents to the ministry of Paul attacked his ministry. He defends himself. The tone of Paul in this letter is much harder than the first chapters of this book which are much softer.

Conclusion 13.11-14

Reading the StoryLine: Leaving Ephesus and Traveling to Corinth

After writing the Corinthian correspondence, Paul left Ephesus to return to Corinth via Macedonia. There he met Titus who shared that the Corinthian church had finally taken care of the discipline problem within the church. He continued his trip to Corinth and from there in a more peaceful time of his ministry, he wrote the book of Romans.

About Romans: God's Righteousness

Till this moment in Paul's writing career, he had written to churches that he had planted. Now, he was going to write to a church that he had not founded nor had he ever visited. In the moments of peace after solving the Corinthian problems, Paul wrote his view of the Christian faith and how to live within its Story as he had come to understand it at this point in his life.

The book of Romans has had tremendous influence through the years having influenced significant figures like Augustine, Martin Luther, John Wesley, and Karl Barth as well as all those who have been blessed because of them.[61] It has been suggested that the book has multiple purposes: *first*, a missionary and public relations purpose. Every place Paul had gone to minister, unrest had broken out because of what he preached. It would be insane for him to go to the seat of the Roman government and cause unrest for the believers in Rome. After all, it had been less than a decade since the emperor Claudius had issued an edict which expelled Jews including Jewish Christians, though later they were allowed to return.[62] So he wrote to assure the Roman church that his intentions were to bring a balanced Gospel and to move on from their midst to minister in Spain (Rom. 15.24).

Second, Romans can be understood as having an apologetic purpose. Therein, Paul wanted to defend the gospel he had come to understand. Finally, Romans has a pastoral purpose which shares Paul's thinking about how God has broken the barriers between Gentiles and Jews so that a full on rupture between Jewish and Gentile Christians could be avoided.[63]

Some Beginning Theological Thoughts

The Covenant God

As we suggested at the beginning of this Act, a Lutheran reading of Paul, in this case Romans, may not be an adequate reading. Rather, a reading that takes seriously the Covenant God's faithfulness and justice might be more appropriate. The faithfulness of the Covenant God in his justice, love, and reliability are major insights of Romans. This church, and the church of the ages, needs to know what God has been up to and how it fits into his Story. While the Reformation and the Enlightenment have separated theology and ethics, the Covenant of God has always held them together as a way of thinking about what he is doing and then putting one's hand to what he is doing in the world.[64]

Israel

In the twentieth century, the church was exposed, or maybe overexposed, to the idea that Israel is God's time clock. To understand biblical prophecy, we have been told that we must watch what is happening to Israel, a kind of theology informed by news reports. However, in Romans 9-11, Paul provided his readers in Rome some insights on the question of who Israel is. He began chapter 9 by sharing that he had great sorrow and anguish in his heart because Israel had rejected the Messiah (2). In verses 6-8, Paul recalled Old Testament history to prove his point. Even though the family of Esau was the natural descendants of the promise, they were not included in the chosen ones. The fulfillment came through Isaac. Verse 8 demonstrates that the true descendants of Abraham, the true Israel if you please, are determined by the divine election of God not by physical descendants. In short, God can and does choose to do as he wishes. The implication of this for Paul's readers was that not all Jews of his own day could call themselves Israel, only those who emulated the faith of Abraham were the children of promise. He had stated this earlier in Romans (2.28-29). From a New Testament perspective, the church is the new Israel, the new humanity of God.

Learning Objective
Understand the chronological presentation of the Story in the New Testament.

Questions
How does Paul's view of Israel in Romans 9-11 affect the way you have viewed Israel?
If the church is the New Israel, how does that influence the way you view prophecy?

So What?

Prejudice to our own race is epidemic if not pandemic. Paul's thesis is that there is a new race and it was created by God through Jesus and empowered by the Spirit to live in this Present Evil Age in a different way.

Questions
What race are you prejudiced against? How does that cause your new humanity to be less than new?

📖 BOOK READING GUIDE: ROMANS

Introduction 1.1-17

Romans 1-16. TBB. 1559-1576.

Slave to Sin 1.18-3.20

God has created a worldwide family of Jews and Gentiles as the fulfillment of the promise to Abraham. This is marked out by the covenant sign of faith.

Slave to God 3.21-8.39

Slavery to sin, because of Adam, is to be exchanged with slavery to God because of his faithfulness to his Covenant. The power to live a new life in Christ comes only through the Holy Spirit who works in every area of our life to make us just like Jesus.

Act 5: Scenes 1-6

Salvation of Israel 9.1-11.36

It turns out that the failure of Israel to follow God's Covenant is used by God through Jesus to bring about salvation for the whole world. Israel, too, must be saved, not as a nationalistic salvation but an individual one. Every Jew must come to God the same way as every Gentile. While enjoying the benefits of relationship with God, Gentiles are not to become anti-Jewish.

Service to God 12.1-16.24

God has created a new humanity by the death of Jesus. Life, as a newly created human, which includes the coming together of races, heretofore separated, to worship the Creator God. The greetings of the final chapter may be a way of putting this picture together in the Roman church.

Conclusion 16.25-27

 Act 5 Scene 5. The Journey Continues (A.D. '60s)

Reading the StoryLine: Leaving Corinth and Traveling to Caesarea

Acts 20.7-21.16.
TBB. 1490-1491.

Paul left Corinth and retraced his steps through Greece and arrived at Philippi. From there he sailed for Troas. There at an all night meeting of the church, Eutychus fell out of a window during Paul's teaching and was resuscitated (Acts 20.7-12). On the final leg of the mission back to Jerusalem, he stopped in Miletus and spoke to the leaders of the church from Ephesus. He then journeyed to Tyre and Caesarea where he met Agabus (Acts 21.10-16). He ended his Third Church Planting Mission in Jerusalem. This mission took approximately five years.

While in Jerusalem, Paul reported to the church. During this period, he was taking a Jewish vow in the Temple and was seized but rescued by Roman soldiers. After speaking to the Jews, they plotted an ambush of Paul, but Claudius Lysias intervened and sent Paul to Felix in Caesarea. There he stood trial before Felix, Festus, and Agrippa, and after two years, his appeal to go to Rome to stand trial before Caesar was granted.

Reading the StoryLine: Introduction to the Gospels

We will leave Paul for the moment in Caesarea and introduce the Synoptic Gospels.

Synoptic Gospels

The first three Gospels are called Synoptic Gospels. The word synoptic means to *see together*. These three Gospels are similar in order, subject, and language. The Gospels were created with an interchange of materials between their authors. About ninety percent of Mark appears in Matthew and fifty-one percent in Luke.[65] New Testament specialists suggest that Mark was the first of the Gospels written and that Matthew and Luke used Mark as an outline for the writing of their Gospels. There are three reasons for this conclusion:

1. When the order of the material varies, Luke agrees with Mark, if Matthew and Mark differ. Matthew agrees with Mark when Luke and Mark differ.

2. Matthew and Luke never depart from the outline of Mark's presentation.

3. From the 661 verses in Mark, 606 appear in Matthew and 380 appear in Luke without change. There are only thirty-one verses that are found in Mark which do not appear in Matthew or Luke.

Learning Objective
Understand the chronological presentation of the Story in the New Testament.

Materials that are common in Matthew and Luke, but not found in Mark, are believed to originate from a document called "Q" (from the German word *Quelle* which means *source*). The "Q" document has never been discovered in a manuscript. It is a convenient way of indicating a common source for this information and there is disagreement among New Testament specialists about its existence.

There is a third kind of material found in Matthew and Luke but not in Mark. The material in Matthew does not appear in Luke nor does the Luke material appear in Matthew. This set of material is unique to each author and book. Matthew and Luke selected this material in order to tell their stories for their specific audiences.[66]

QUESTIONS
How have you understood the concept of the writing of Scripture in the past? Does the presented view change the way you have viewed the whole of Scripture?

The Synoptic Gospels show the redemptive history of God. They have sometimes been called lopsided biographies, spending most of their time telling the story of the last week of the life of Jesus. Each has a different purpose. Matthew tells his audience of new believers that Jesus is the New Moses for the New Israel, the church. Mark demonstrates how the power of Jesus is stronger than the power of Satan in an evangelistic tract form. Luke portrays the universal appeal of Jesus, a man for all times and places. With the propensity of the Enlightenment to reductionism, the Gospels have found their way into harmonies where they are combined as one written piece. The real difficulty with this approach is that it takes away from the author's intent to write his story to a specific audience for a specific reason, in favor of telling a combined story of the life of Jesus. I often wonder why God didn't think of presenting us with a harmony in the canon of Scripture instead of four different stories about Jesus.

Why Were the Gospels Written?

Two questions are useful to help understand why the Gospels came into existence at this period of the Story. One must remember that the written Story of what had happened in the life of Jesus was written by three writers with specific goals in mind. The first question is: *Why wait for so many years before writing the Gospel?*[67] Some suggest that the cost of writing was too great, or that they had oral tradition and were looking for a quick consummation of the Kingdom, therefore, they did not need writings for future generations.

The second question to consider is: *Why write Gospels?* Some suggest that the apostles were getting older and as eyewitnesses may have had the better recollection of the events surrounding the life of Jesus.[68] Another reason might be that the consummation of the Kingdom had not occurred as had been expected, so they needed to get some material down for the next generation. The church had the Old Testament Story and some of Paul's letters (2 Pet. 3.14) but only oral stories about Jesus.

Dictionary Articles
Read the following Dictionary Articles in *New Bible Dictionary.*
  Gospels

Act 5: Scenes 1-6

Learning Objective
Understand the chronological presentation of the Story in the New Testament.

BOOK
Mark
AUTHOR
Mark
AGE WRITTEN
A.D. '60s
FROM
Rome
TO
Non-Christian and Christian Romans
PROBLEM
How to evangelize the Romans
AUDIENCE
Those who need to understand the claims of the Gospel of Jesus
GEOGRAPHY
✈ Rome

About Mark: An Evangelistic Tract

Mark can be understood as an evangelistic tract used during the first century.[69] The telling of the story of Jesus by Mark resembles the sermons of Peter which are recorded in Acts. Because of this, Mark has often been called the *Gospel According to Peter*. The stories in Mark are presented so that the first century Roman citizen might investigate the claim that Jesus had come into the world to bring the Kingdom of God. The Roman culture loved power, so Mark presented Jesus as a powerful man who did powerful acts. Rome's culture was rich with a history of war. Mark uses this motif to present Jesus' ministry of words and works. The war between Jesus and Satan is played out on the battlefield of earth. Jesus is a powerful man destined to bring the rule of Satan to an end. He was so powerful that he was in control of his own death which would appeal to the Roman reader. Jesus goads the religious establishment. They seek to kill him. For the Roman citizen the concept of buying slaves from the slave market was a common practice. Mark demonstrates that the death of Jesus was not unlike buying slaves and setting them free (the concept of *lutron*, 10.45). There is a pastoral concern in Mark for the converted Romans. Chapter thirteen is one example. Mark shows how Jesus brings hope in the middle of suffering.

Some Beginning Theological Thoughts

The Kingdom of God

The central message of Mark and the Synoptics is the Kingdom of God. The theology of the Kingdom of God, as we have seen, is well rooted in the Old Testament. For the prophets, the Kingdom of God was a day when humankind would live together in peace. When the word *kingdom* is used today, it often means a realm which has a King or Queen as its ruler. When the Bible uses this term, it means the rule or reign of God in the lives of its subjects. The beginning of Mark says that Jesus came preaching that the rule of God was present in his ministry. In the *words* and *works* of Jesus, God's rule had invaded the rule of Satan. The church lives in the tension known as the *now* but *not yet*. The Kingdom of God is present, but we still live in the presence of the Present Evil Age. We are in the world, but not of the world. When you read the New Testament, it is best to understand it within the lens of the Kingdom of God.

The Humanity of Jesus

Jesus portrays his humanity by his refusal to give demonstrable proofs of his claims (8.11-13). He suffered and tasted the bitterness of death (8.31ff.; 9.12; 10.32-34, 45). He admitted to his true humanity in the limitations imposed on his humanity (6.5-6; 13.32; 15.31). It has often been said that the people in the first century had a difficult time accepting Jesus as divine. In our century, it is often the opposite. We have a difficult time understanding the humanity of Jesus.

The Importance of Faith

Faith is the atmosphere in which the miracles of Jesus were accomplished. This appeal to faith marks him out from the pagan wonderworkers of his day (9.14-29). Faith is the decor for many of his miracles like:

- the paralytic: Mark 2.5
- crossing the sea: Mark 4.40
- a woman with a hemorrhage: Mark 5.25
- lack of faith in hometown: Mark 6.6
- a blind man, Bartimaeus: Mark 10.52
- the cursing of the fig tree: Mark 11.22
- disciples' lack of faith: Mark 16.14

Jesus' Messiahship is Incognito

That Jesus is the Messiah is misunderstood by official Judaism (3.20-35). It is hidden from the inattentive onlooker and unrecognized by the disciples who fill the term with a political or worldly content (2.27-9.1). However, the truth of his Messiahship is seen by unlikely characters in the drama of Mark (demons, the woman at Bethany 14.3-9; a pagan centurion at the cross 15.39).

The Son of Man

The often suggested meaning of this phrase is that it refers to the humanity of Jesus, while Son of God refers to the divinity of Jesus. This popularized meaning does not take into consideration the historical development of the phrase in Jewish history. The term has its starting point in the book of Daniel (7.13) and blossoms in the Apocryphal book of Enoch. The middle section of the book of Enoch presents four titles which are found in the New Testament and applied to Jesus: Messiah, the righteous one, the elect one, and the Son of Man. These are all concepts which are in keeping with a divine being. The Son of Man, the Messiah, is seen as a supernatural being, preexistent, a heavenly being who is revealed by God.

Confession

There are two parts to the Gospel of Mark. Each has a confession which concludes the section. The material of 1.1-8.29 has a stress on the miracles of Jesus and leads up to the divinely inspired insight of Peter into the true nature of the man Jesus. The *second* ends with a Roman's assurance that Jesus is truly the Son of God. In the first segment of the Gospel, the people did not know who Jesus was. They had various thoughts, like prophet: John the Baptist back from the dead; Elijah, or a prophet from Isaiah's period. The second part of the Gospel clarified what it means to confess that Jesus is God.

The Death of Jesus

Mark told his audience that the purpose for Jesus dying was to buy the slave from the slave market. He used a Greek word, *lutron*, which was the known currency of buying slaves and giving them their freedom. There was no catch. But often, the purchased slaves would turn and serve the Master who had purchased their freedom. This picture demonstrates that Jesus was in charge of his own demise. No man, Roman or Jew, took his life from him. He gave it freely to produce freedom for those caught in the snares of this Present Evil Age.

QUESTION
How can you live in the concept of *lutron* in your life?

The End of Mark

Mark's Gospel ends at 16.8. The additional verses were probably not a

Act 5: Scenes 1-6

Gospels

Learning Objective
Understand the chronological presentation of the Story in the New Testament.

part of his original writings. They are absent from some of the more important early manuscripts. These concluding verses are unlike the rest of Mark in vocabulary and theology. They most likely were compiled during the second century as a teaching summary about the resurrection. This often brings some bewilderment to believers about the validity of the Bible. But as a reader, consider these points:

1. It was likely accepted by the church from the second century as inspired.
2. If compiled in the second century, it demonstrates a firm belief that the church was still charismatic during that century.[70]

So What?

What if you found a way to hand out Mark to your friends and relatives and asked them to read it, say ten or fifteen times? Then you could have an ongoing conversation with them about how they see the Jesus that Mark presents and how different he is from the Jesus that they have always heard about. Create a way. I think you will like the results.

BOOK READING GUIDE: MARK

Mark 1-16. TBB. 1695-1719.

Preparation of Jesus 1.1-13

These introductory verses summarize the ministry of John the Baptist and the coming ministry of Jesus.

Presentation of Jesus 1.14-8.30

Mark presented the story of Jesus from the call of his disciples to his transfiguration. He tells stories about the healing and teaching ministry of Jesus and his contention with religious leaders. The section begins with a summary of the ministry of Jesus and his Kingdom message. The parables of the Kingdom are told and the revelation of who Jesus really was is given by Peter.

Dictionary Articles
Read the following Dictionary Articles in *New Bible Dictionary*.
  Mark (John)
  Mark, Gospel of
  John the Baptist
  Jesus Christ

Passion of Jesus 8.31-16.8

The last week of the ministry of Jesus comprises almost half of the book of Mark. The story begins with the story of the Temple cleansing. Chapter thirteen is an apocalyptic presentation about the future. The last supper, arrest, crucifixion, death, and resurrection stories are all shared.

Reading the StoryLine: Paul's Journey To Rome

Acts 21.17-28.31.
TBB. 1491-1501.

When we left Paul's story, he was arrested in Jerusalem and was going to be escorted to Caesarea when a plot to assassinate him was discovered. After several years in prison, Paul asked to be sent to Rome for his day before Caesar. He was granted an audience, left Caesarea, and sailed to Sidon and then around Cyprus to the Lycian port of Myra. Paul and his associates changed ships. Sailing around the island of Crete, Paul warned the captain not to sail further. They sailed on into the Mediterranean not heeding the words of Paul. Close to Malta the ship sank, but Paul and his company were saved. This was Paul's fourth shipwreck. They remained on Malta for three months and then sailed to Syracuse and on to Rhegium. After a day's wait, the party sailed to Puteoli. The final leg of his trip was through the Forum of Appius and Three Taverns. Acts closes with Paul preaching the Kingdom of God unhindered in Rome. This trip took approximately two years.

Learning Objective
Understand the
chronological presentation of
the Story in the New
Testament.

BOOK
Philemon
AUTHOR
Paul
AGE WRITTEN
A.D. 60-62
FROM
Rome
TO
Philemon, his family, and
the church in Colossae.
PROBLEM
Handling Societal
Dilemmas (Slavery)
AUDIENCE
Believers who think that
change comes from
political activism
GEOGRAPHY
Rome and Colossae

When Paul arrived in Rome, he was a prisoner of the state under house arrest with the freedom to continue to preach the gospel of the Kingdom (Acts 28.31). During this time, he wrote the following four books: Philemon, Colossians, Ephesians, and Philippians. We now turn to each in that order.

About Philemon: An Appeal For Forgiveness

Paul's letter to Philemon was written in a warm friendly manner because Philemon and Paul were friends. It is a one-of-a-kind letter in the New Testament. Philemon was a believer and a slave owner. One of Philemon's choice slaves, Onesimus, had decided to stay in Rome while there doing business for his owner. Paul and Onesimus meet while in Rome and Onesimus became a follower of Jesus. Paul knew of his status as a run-away-slave. It was right for Paul to return him to his master, Philemon, who had an absolute right over Onesimus. The letter from Paul to his old friend suggested that Philemon redeem, restore, and treat Onesimus as a brother, as a visible model of the redemption of Jesus in his own life and a model of what new humanity is all about. There is neither slave nor free!

Some Beginning Theological Thoughts

Christianity and Slavery

The New Testament is almost completely silent on the social issue of slavery in the Roman Empire. Jesus or Paul never condemned it.[71] Paul and Peter are recorded as encouraging slaves who were Christian converts to obey their masters (Eph. 6.5-8; 1 Pet. 2.18-21). The Greco-Roman world thrived on slavery where between twenty to thirty-three percent of its population were slaves. Recorded history suggests that Roman slave owners gave freedom to a great many slaves at the owner's death. You were born a slave or purchased into slavery. Slavery in the ancient world was not like slavery in our modern era. Slavery was not based on some presumed inferiority of an ethnic group. Slavery was a matter of practicality in handling those who fell prey to conquest, or those who became criminals, or those who defaulted on their debts, or those who were born into a slave family. A slave was considered "living property" and was completely under the power of the owner.[72]

Slaves could be found in all professions. They could work for their freedom and were often better off than free persons. Some of the educated slaves were often used to run errands as trusted agents for their masters, such was the status of Onesimus. On the other hand, a slave owner could legally execute his slaves.[73]

Against this backdrop, Paul had a rare opportunity to condemn his Christian friend for having slaves. Instead he asked Philemon to manumit Onesimus.[74] To show forgiveness to a criminal slave who had escaped was a revolutionary thought. This was nothing less than a subversive paradigm switch which could undermine the slave system. A person valued as a brother or sister could no longer be seen as property. Philemon carried such a strong message about slave freedom that the slave owners in America did not want their slaves exposed to Christianity.[75]

The atmosphere which Paul invited Philemon to enter was the very foundation on which the institution of slavery could die. When a person's

Act 5: Scenes 1-6

Letters

Learning Objective
Understand the chronological presentation of the Story in the New Testament.

Philemon. TBB. 1595-1596.

Dictionary Articles
Read the following Dictionary Articles in *New Bible Dictionary*.
  Onesimus
  Philemon
  Philemon, Epistle of

BOOK
Colossians
AUTHOR
Paul
AGE WRITTEN
A.D. 60-62
FROM
Rome
TO
The Christians at Colossae
PROBLEM
False teaching about the person of Jesus, human philosophy, Judaistic elements, worship of angels, exclusiveness and superiority of groups
AUDIENCE
Believers who wander from the simple teaching found in Scripture about Jesus, angels, exclusiveness, etc.
GEOGRAPHY
Rome and Colossae

heart changes, when a person becomes truly human, his or her attitudes and lifestyle will change. For Paul, this was a real live application of what he had written to the Galatians. There really was only one body in Christ, no slave or free. New humanity lived within a culture differently than old humanity. We might look to this biblical example of Paul and Philemon as a way of dealing with social issues which face the church today. Militant resolution, which is frequent, might be based on a wrongheaded model. Living in God's EPIC Adventure will call for a different way of thinking and living.

So What?

We may not think that we have slavery in today's society, but we may have just that. How does life swirl around your relationships: parent-child; husband-wife; employer-employee? How are you either enslaving or being enslaved? If you begin to act out Paul's words to Philemon, how would that change these relationships?

BOOK READING GUIDE: PHILEMON

Introduction 1-3

Approval of Philemon 4-7

Paul offered a prayer of thanks for his friend Philemon.

Appeal to Philemon 8-14

Based on the fact that Onesimus has become a believer, Paul encouraged Philemon to accept him back.

Assurance for Philemon 15-22

Philemon is assured that the action Paul asked him to participate in would be beneficial for Philemon and his Christian faith.

Conclusion 23-25

About Colossians: How to Deal With Cults

Remember, Paul is under house arrest in Rome when he penned Colossians. The letter was written to counteract the beginning of some hazardous syncretistic teaching within the church and may have been sent to Colossae at the same time Philemon was being sent.[76] New converts to the church brought with them other ideas and philosophies, presenting them as equal with the truth of Christianity. Greeks and Jews coming together into one new community wanted their former beliefs to somehow fit into their new faith. This, of course, was contrary to the message of Paul. He saw the urgency of nipping this tendency in the bud. As an example, it was important for the Jewish person to want to retain some of the boundary markers like circumcision, food laws, and festivals. The Greeks, on the other hand, wanted to retain their dualism, which later developed into ❖ **Gnosticism**. ❖ (See 257)

The book may be a model for helping to deal with false teaching in a community situation. The first chapter of Colossians developed the theology of the supremacy and sufficiency of Christ for the life of these new believers. In chapter 2, Paul attacked the emptiness of pagan religion. One should note that he attacked the religions themselves. He did not attack the people that were participating in the religions, a tendency that

some followers of Jesus have. It is important to note that the group called Jehovah's Witnesses use the Colossians 1.19ff. passage to deny the deity of Jesus, a passage which teaches the very opposite. Apparently the church was being taught that Jesus was not God, and Paul wrote these words to deny that belief, not to support it. Finally, Paul instructed the church how to live out their new humanity in the world.

Some Beginning Theological Thoughts

Firstborn

The very passage in Colossians (1.19ff.), which some cults suggest means that Jesus was created by God, is, in fact, Paul's passage to tell the readers in the Colossian church about the supremacy of Jesus as God.

The Supremacy of Jesus

The teaching of the false teachers in Colossae claimed, for those following it, a special knowledge of spiritual reality, which was thought to be deeper and more perfect than could be found in the simple Gospel of Jesus (Col. 2.4, 8, 18).

Rules for the Household

In Colossians 3.18-4.1, Paul wrote about household codes that had been developed by Aristotle. These codes defined how a male of a house would rule his wives, children, and slaves.[77] Paul put a different trajectory on these codes making them move against the flow of the dominant paradigm of the patriarchal culture. In Paul's view of the new humanity, as much was required of the male as the others in the household. Paul reframed these codes within the message of Christianity. New humanity simply required a different way of living.[78]

So What?

We may have all run across folks with whom we disagree theologically. If you haven't, you most likely will some day. How would living in a different Story about how to deal with those challenges change your responses?

We most likely still live in a household with some kind of rules and regulations. Who do the rules favor? How would you go about changing these codes to Paul's Story paradigm?

📖 BOOK READING GUIDE: COLOSSIANS

Introduction 1.1-14

True Christian Doctrine 1.15-2.23

The Colossians are given instruction about Jesus' relationship to God, creation, and the church.

True Christian Deportment 3.1-4.6

Based on the theological information given the reader in the previous chapters, Paul now turned to the household-codes instructions for how the new humanity in Christ would function in marriage, with children, parents, slaves, and masters.

Conclusion 4.7-18

Learning Objective
Understand the chronological presentation of the Story in the New Testament.

Gnosticism
A fully blown Gnostic belief system did not occur until the close of the second century. However, it had its roots during the '60s of the first century. There was a tremendous influx of Gentiles into the first century church. With the inflow came various elements of a Greek philosophical mindset. Dualism was the basic presupposition of this Greek philosophical system. *Gnosis* is the Greek word for knowledge. The followers of an incipient Gnostic belief system believed that they had superior knowledge which allowed them to understand the Christian faith. Their dualism was played out in the philosophy of humankind. They believed that the spirit in humans was basically good while the body was totally evil. Therefore, one could use his or her body in any fashion desired, because it was evil to the core. The spirit must be kept pure. This idea is refuted by Paul in Colossians.

Colossians. TBB. 1581-1584.

Dictionary Articles
Read the following Dictionary Articles in *New Bible Dictionary.*
 Colossae
 Colossians, Epistle of

Letters

BOOK
Ephesians
AUTHOR
Paul
AGE WRITTEN
A.D. 60-62
FROM
Rome
TO
Christians around Ephesus
PROBLEM
How to understand the
purpose
of God in the Church, in
an individual's life and
lived out
in the church
AUDIENCE
To those who need to
understand what God's
purpose is in
the Church and how that
is
worked out in their lives.
GEOGRAPHY
✈ Rome and Ephesus

QUESTION
How does understanding the
concept of adoption help you
better understand your own
story in Christ?

About Ephesians: The Church

The next book Paul wrote while in Rome was Ephesians, which is one of the greatest books that he wrote.[79] Some suggestion has been made that the recipients of this letter were Gentile converts who had found their way into the church after Paul's departure.[80]

It is a tremendous document that gives a theology of the church and is closely aligned with Colossians.[81] It was likely a circular letter that began at the church in Ephesus and made a round-trip to other churches, forming a circle beginning and ending with Ephesus.[82] The primary purpose of Paul was to instruct these believers about what was involved in their commitment to Christ and his church. Christianity was not something that one could achieve; it was something that God had done on one's behalf.

Some Beginning Theological Thoughts

Adoption

Adoption was a Roman law. The father in Roman law had absolute power over his children as long as they lived, even over their life and death. Children never possessed anything. All possessions were the property of the father. To be adopted was to take a serious step.

The ceremony included trading the person to be adopted two times between the two parties and taking the adopted person back two times. On the third time, the trade was completed.

At that point, the person adopted had all the rights and privileges of the new family and lost all the rights and privileges of the old family. This included all the debts and connection with the previous family. The old family was abolished from the adoptee as if it had never existed.

This adopted position came by grace not by right. The adopted son was heir just the same as the natural son. Adoption occurred because of the love of a parent for a child. Love brought him into the family as a full-fledged member of the family with all rights and privileges.

Sonship implied responsibility. It is inconceivable that we should enjoy a relationship with God as his child without accepting the obligation to imitate the Father and cultivate the family likeness.[83]

The Ministry of the Saints

Paul lists several ministries, apostles, prophets, evangelists, and pastor-teachers, whose responsibility is to "equip his people for works of service." Those in leadership positions in the church should be ever moving away from doing ministry on behalf of the congregation, to teaching the congregants to discover what ministries God has called them to and training them to fulfill that ministry. There are no superstars in the ministry of the church contrary to some models that we are constantly exposed to in church and on TV.

Armor of God

Paul uses a figure of speech in Ephesians 6.11-18 that would have been understood by every Roman. The church is at war with Satan, and God has given her armor which is both offensive and defensive. With the armor provided, the enemy can be defeated. There is a *belt, breastplate, sandals, shield, helmet, and sword of the Spirit.* Each has a specific function in protecting and attacking. Getting dressed appropriately is the wisdom needed by those in a community of faith. On occasion when God is expecting his bride and we show up in full armor, it could be quite a shock!

Learning Objective
Understand the chronological presentation of the Story in the New Testament.

So What?

Does your story tell you that the pastor should do the work of the ministry because that is what he or she is paid to do? Ephesians has a different Story for us to begin to live out in our lives. We are each actors/ministers in God's EPIC Adventure. Tired of being tossed to and fro by everything that you hear in church? Well, change your story.

What to wear? That's a dilemma that some folks go through every day. We often have on the wrong dress at the wrong time. As an equipped actor, you will begin to know when to dress as a bride, for an example, and when to dress as a soldier.

- -

 BOOK READING GUIDE: EPHESIANS

- -

Introduction 1.1-3

Ephesians. TBB. 1587-1592.

Purpose and Plan of God 1.4-23

The purpose of God (to create a new humanity) is accomplished by the Son and applied by the Spirit. Paul prayed for the churches.

Dictionary Articles
Read the following Dictionary Articles in *New Bible Dictionary*.
Ephesus
Ephesians, Epistle to the Church

Purpose Demonstrated in the Church 2.1-22

The church is shown from a theological and historical position with a portrait of before and after God's decisive act in Jesus.

Purpose Demonstrated in Paul 3.1-21

Paul used himself to demonstrate how God creates new humanity.

Gospels

Purpose Lived Out in Community 4.1-6.20

The new humanity—the church—is the focal point for where the purpose of God is lived out. Paul gave household instruction about marriage, parents, slaves, and masters. In addition, he talked about warfare and the armor the community and believer has to use in defense, as well as in taking an offensive stand against the enemy.

Conclusion 6.21.24

BOOK
Luke
AUTHOR
Luke
AGE WRITTEN
A.D. 60
FROM
Rome
TO
Non-Christian Gentiles who are cultured and interested in Christianity.
PROBLEM
An apologetic account of the life of Jesus
AUDIENCE
Those who need to understand the historicity of Jesus, the church, and the ministry of Paul.
GEOGRAPHY
⊙ Rome

- -

Reading the StoryLine: A Pause

- -

We pause again from the story of Paul to visit the writings of his companion Luke.

About Luke: A Defense of the Gospel of Jesus

Luke was converted during Paul's Second Church Planting Mission.[84] When Paul went to Jerusalem the last time, was imprisoned, and sent to Caesarea, Luke was with him. He was with Paul when he was under house arrest in Rome. During this period, Luke wrote the first of his two-part work, the Gospel of Luke.

Act 5: Scenes 1-6

Gospels

Learning Objective
Understand the chronological presentation of the Story in the New Testament.

Luke was written as an apologetic—a defense of the Gospel of Jesus—in three major areas. *First*, from a *cultural* point of view, it is designed to defend the Gospel as being classless in its presentation. The Gospel is for everyone not just the lower class or the upper class. The good news was that Jesus was for everyone, regardless of race, color, or creed. The special stories that Luke told, like the Prodigal Son and the Good Samaritan, display that the Gospel of Jesus is for everyone. *Second*, from a *political* point of view, it is designed to defend Jesus as the founder of the Christian movement. *Third*, from a *practical* point of view, it is designed to defend the Gospel as one that bridges cultural and racial differences.[85]

Luke's Literary Richness

Luke is the longest of the New Testament books. When combined with his second volume, Acts, it comprises about twenty-eight percent of the New Testament. Luke's vocabulary is that of an educated man in the first century. His Greek is refined, which adds a breadth of expression to his work. He records for us four hymns. They all receive their names from the first translated word in the Latin Vulgate. They are:

1. **The Magnificat of Mary** (1:46-55): Magnificent means *glorifies*. It is much like the song of Hannah in the Old Testament book of 1 Samuel (1 Sam. 2.1-10).

2. **The Benedictus of Zacharias** (1.67-79): This hymn is much more like a prophecy than a psalm. Benedictus means *praise be*.

3. **The Gloria in Excelsis Deo of the heavenly host** (2.14): The Latin phrase means *Glory to God in the highest*. The Angelic choir recognized the glory and majesty of God by giving praise to him. *In the highest* is most likely a reference to the sphere where God dwells.

4. **The *Nunc Dimittis*** (nuke DE mit tis) of Simeon (2.28-32): The phrase means *You now dismiss*.[86]

Some Beginning Theological Thoughts

The Holy Spirit

Luke is often called the theologian of the Holy Spirit.[87] The Holy Spirit is clearly prominent in Acts, Luke's second volume, so Luke prepares his readers for this in his Gospel.[88] In the beginning of his book, he suggested that several people were "filled with the Spirit." The language of Luke is identical in Luke 1.42, 67 and Acts 2.4. If language means anything, and surely it does, we must learn to speak about this occurrence in the same way Luke speaks about it. The language used by Luke seems clear and seems to point out that the ministry of the Holy Spirit is not a second gracious work that comes to followers of Jesus after they have experienced new life in Jesus. The Holy Spirit empowers the new humanity created by God to carry out the work of ministry to the world. Being "filled with the Spirit" is another metaphor that has the same overtones as being "born from above."

Special Interests in Luke

Luke shows an interest in special groups of people in his book. Here are some of them:

Social Outcasts. He told stories of an immoral woman (7.36-50), the transformation of Zacchaeus (19.1-10), and the repentance of the robber on the cross (23.26-43).

Women. Luke mentioned and told stories about many women not mentioned anywhere else in the Gospels (1.5-3.29; 7.11-17;7.36-50; 8.1-3; 10.38-42; 21.1-4; 23.26-31; 23.44-49; 23.50-24.11).

Children. He recounts the childhood of John and Jesus. These are found only in Luke.

Social Relations. Jesus socializes with all kinds of people. There are several stories in Luke about social meetings with the Pharisees (5.27-32; 7.36-50; 11.37-53; 14.1-14; 19.1-10).

Prayer. Luke records ten occurrences of Jesus praying:

- ◆ At His Baptism: Story 3.1-22; Focus 3.21-22
- ◆ After a Day of Miracles: Story 5.1-39; Focus 5.15-16
- ◆ Before Choosing the Disciples: Story 6.1-16; Focus 6.12-16
- ◆ Before Instructing: Story 9.1-62; Focus 9.18-20
- ◆ At the Transfiguration: Story 9.1-62; Focus 9.28-29
- ◆ On the Return of the Seventy-Two: Story 10.1-42; Focus 10.17-21
- ◆ Before Teaching Disciples How to Pray: Story 11.1-13; Focus 11.1
- ◆ For Peter and the Disciples: Story 22.1-71; Focus 22.31-32
- ◆ At the Point of Suffering: Story 22.1-71; Focus 22.39-46
- ◆ On the Cross: Story 23.1-56; Focus 23.26-49

In addition, there are two parables about prayer that are only in Luke (11.5-13; 18.1-8). Luke alone informed his readers that Jesus prayed especially for Peter (22.31-32).

Universal Love. Luke also told three parables which demonstrate his concept of how universal the love of Jesus is. *First*, the Good Samaritan (10.25-37) which told the story of a Samaritan. This group was hated by the Jews. This ethnic group was created by the interracial marriages during the Northern Captivity. *Second*, the Prodigal Son (15.11-32) whose important character is the Father, not the son. *Finally*, the story of Lazarus and the Rich Man (16.19-31). For Luke the gospel, as he had learned it from Paul, was for the outsider, of which he was one, as well as the insider.[89]

So What?

Luke's special interests should find plenty of fodder for Story change in our lives. How do we treat social outcasts, women, and children? Who do we party with? Is there a place in your life where you can actually party with those who need to know a different Story in their lives? Luke's small vignettes about prayer could be revolutionary as a change of Story from old ways and forms of prayer.

QUESTION
How does Luke's special interests affect your concept of ministry?

Act 5: Scenes 1-6

Learning Objective
Understand the chronological presentation of the Story in the New Testament.

Luke-Acts. TBB. 1419-1501.

Dictionary Articles
Read the following Dictionary Articles in *New Bible Dictionary*.
Luke
Luke, Gospel of

History

BOOK
Acts
AUTHOR
Luke
AGE WRITTEN
A.D. 61
FROM
Rome
TO
Non-Christian Gentiles –
cultured and interested
in Christianity.
PROBLEM
An apologetic account of
the life of the Church,
and the ministry of Paul
AUDIENCE
Those who need to
understand the historicity
of Jesus, the church,
and the ministry of Paul.
GEOGRAPHY
🌐 Rome

BOOK READING GUIDE: LUKE

Introduction 1.1-4

Luke shared that he has written this book to be an orderly account of the ministry of Jesus.

Life of Jesus - Early accounts 1.5-4.13

Luke recounted the childhood of John the Baptist and Jesus. He told about the ministry of John in the wilderness. The stories of the baptism and wilderness temptation of Jesus are also recorded.

Upper Galilean Ministry 4.14-9.50

In this section of his book, Luke described the beginning of Jesus' public ministry. He included stories about the calling of his first disciples; the various conflicts he had with the religious establishment of the day. He pointed to the *words* and *works* of Jesus by telling miracle stories and sharing the teaching ministry of Jesus. This section ends with Peter's confession of Jesus being the Christ and the story of the transfiguration.

Keen Determination of Jesus 9.51-19.27

Luke shows how determined Jesus was to go to Jerusalem. He sent seventy disciples on a mission after providing them with instruction. He told more miracle stories and shared more of the teaching ministry of Jesus.

Execution of Jesus 19.28-24.53

The final section tells the story of the final week in the earthly life of Jesus. He entered Jerusalem in what is often called the Triumphal Entry. He cleansed the Temple. He took his disciples aside and taught them about the future in an apocalyptic discourse often referred to as the Olivet Discourse. He ate the Passover meal with them. Then he was arrested, tried, crucified, died, and resurrected.

About Acts: A Defense of the Ministry of Paul

The book of Acts is the second volume of Luke's work.[90] Luke-Acts should be read together. Luke-Acts was written to be read as a complete defense of Christianity. Luke continues the story of Jesus from the resurrection to the time of Paul preaching the gospel of the Kingdom unhindered in Rome. There are two main characters around which the stories in Acts are told: Peter and Paul.

The Roman government was always suspicious of any new religious sect which might pose a political problem for Rome. Thus, Luke wanted to write a defense for Paul[91] to prove that his ministry and Christianity, as a new sect, were not a menace to Rome or its government.

We might note that the Gospel of Luke shows the incarnational ministry of Jesus (what could be called Body 1). The book of Acts shows the incarnational ministry of the Church (what could be called Body 2). Both ministries are the same.

Some Beginning Theological Thoughts

The Holy Spirit

Learning Objective
Understand the
chronological presentation of
the Story in the New
Testament.

The theological interest of Luke is dominated by the activity of the Holy Spirit.[92] The book could be rightly titled "The Acts of the Holy Spirit."[93] Luke's main theological interest seems to be to show the activity of the Holy Spirit in the mission of the church. Acts 1.8 identified the mission and Luke closely followed its geographic movement from Jerusalem to Rome. The good news moved from Jerusalem to Rome within a thirty-year period. That's remarkable!

The Mission and Methods of the Church

Luke begins Acts with the following words, "In my former book, Theophilus, I wrote about all that Jesus began to do and to teach...." My own research suggests that the "do and teach" motif is carried forward by Luke in Acts. Along with the verbal proclamation (a supernatural ministry) is the other supernatural ministry of the Spirit which is often overlooked. Here are ten different Spirit activities that occur in Acts.

1. Speaking gifts occur four times (tongues or prophecy: Acts 2.4; 10.44; 13.1; 19.1-17)

2. Visions occur four times (10.1-24 [3, 10-11]; 16.6-10; 18.9-11)

3. Power encounter occurs one time (13.4-12)

4. There are two resuscitations (9.32-43; 20.7-12)

5. There are six specific miracles (5.1-11; 8.26-40; 9.1-19; 13.4-12; 14.8-20; 28.1-10)

6. There are seven specific healings (3.1-10; 6.1-7; 9.1-19; 32-40; 14.8-20; 16.16-40; 28.1-10)

7. Laying on hands occurs four times (6.1-7; 8.9-25; 9.1-19; 13.1-3)

8. Sense phenomena occurs three times (2.1-4; 12.1-18; 16.16-40)

9. Signs and wonders occur nine times (2.42-47; 4.32-36; 5.12-16; 6.1-7; 8.4-6; 11.19-30; 11.24-25; 14.1-7; 19.1-22)

10. Angelic visitations are recorded three times (8.26-40; 12.1-18; 27.13-25)

So What?

On every occasion (ten of them listed above) where teaching and what has been called "signs and wonders" occur together, there is always growth in the church. There seems to be some direct relationship between both "signs and wonders" (do) and teaching (teach) in Acts. One should also note that there is no indication in Scripture that the ministry of the Spirit as demonstrated in Acts (do and teach) has ceased. As newly formed humanity, our role may call us from time to time to become participants in God's "signs and wonders" course.

Several years ago, I was teaching a weekend seminar in Bakersfield, CA. I had taught all day Saturday and had about 150 miles to drive to get home. To say the least, I was tired. I sat in a freeway side restaurant waiting for my food to arrive when, around the corner in the aisle I was in, an older lady come into view pulling an inhalation therapy canister of oxygen behind her. As clear as a bell, I had an impression to stop her and pray for her. I didn't have long to make the decision as the aisle was short

History

Learning Objective
Understand the chronological presentation of the Story in the New Testament.

and she was approaching quickly. When she was in range, I said, "My that looks uncomfortable."

She responded, "It is, but it helps me breathe."

I responded, "Would you mind if I prayed for you?"

She must have thought I meant some other time because she said, "That would be nice."

I returned, "No, I mean right now."

She stopped and looked me straight in the eye, "You mean right here, right now? Aren't we in a restaurant?"

I took by that exchange that she may have thought that prayer could only happen somewhere in private like a church or a home, but surely not here in a very public place.

I said, "Yes, right here."

She acquiesced.

Before I began the oral part of the prayer, I said, "May I touch your hand as I pray?"

She asked, "Do you have to?"

I responded, "No."

She said, "Okay" and put her hand down on the table.

I reached out and placed my hand over hers and prayed a very short prayer telling the lungs what to do, and as I finished I noticed that she was openly weeping.

As I finished the oral prayer, she said, "I am so overwhelmed that God sought me out to be prayed for, he must really love me."

I assured her that he did. And she left.

Was she healed? I don't have any idea. However, I do know that she went away with a different understanding of God than she had when she entered the restaurant that evening.

We've been duped into thinking that folks will think us crazy if we become public actors in his Story. I would take issue with that view.

 **BOOK READING GUIDE: ACTS**

See A Quick Look of Acts above (pp. 228-230) for full reading guide.

Spirit Arrives in Jerusalem 1.1-6.7

Proclamation in Judea-Samaria 6.8-9.31

Dictionary Articles
Read the following Dictionary Articles in *New Bible Dictionary*.
  Miracles
  Acts, Book of the
  Pentecost, Feast of

Inclusion of Gentiles 9.32-12.24

Received Gospel in Asia 12.25-16.5

Involvement of Gospel in Asia Minor and Europe 16.6-19.20

Trials – Appeal – Rome 19.21-28.31

Reading the StoryLine: A Return to Paul

We now return to the concluding written works of Paul in the Story of the New Testament.

About Philippians: Joy Comes When Unity Abides

This is the fourth and last of the letters which Paul wrote while under house arrest in Rome. Philippians carries a deep personal tone.[94] Paul had started many churches, but this was the only one that sent him money and a personal attendant to help him during his difficult days as a prisoner in Rome. Epaphroditus, the Philippian gift, had grown ill while caring for Paul. So, Paul wrote to the church to say thanks for the gifts and share why Epaphroditus was returning to them even though Paul was still in prison.

Some Beginning Theological Thoughts

The so-called Kenosis (ki NOH sis) section in Philippians is probably one of the most famous passages in all of Paul's writings.[95] It is a classic Christian passage about the deity of Jesus. It is one of the most important yet most difficult passages written by Paul. Most likely Paul was quoting a hymn of the early church which taught believers about the nature and work of Christ – preexistence, incarnation, passion, resurrection, and exaltation. In the Philippians context, this passage highlights the humility and selfless service demonstrated by Jesus, whose example the Christian is to follow.

Paul's primary concern was that the proclamation of the gospel would be accomplished. Unity, a passion for the gospel, was needed in the proclamation of the gospel and was a high priority. If disunity in the church continued, unity could not occur. The Kenosis passage may have been written to help the Philippians solve the problem of unity among themselves.

Paul instructed them that a self-centered and self-serving attitude should be ruled out (2.3-4). Those who follow Jesus, follow him in selfless service to others (the Kenosis Passage: 2.6-11). The results of others following the model of Jesus and emptying themselves in ministry would be joy which only comes when unity abides.

So What?

Living in the Story of God will cause us to actually do things differently than living in another story of our own choosing.

When I lived in Southern California, I met a young single Christian man who was a banker by trade. We were having lunch one day and he quietly asked me if I needed any money. I thought he was asking me if I would like to apply for a loan from his bank. I assured him that I did and even told him the exact amount that I needed to meet an unpaid bill. I was not prepared for what he did next. He reached into his coat pocket and pulled out his checkbook and wrote me a check for the exact amount that I had just told him. When he finished writing the check, he handed it to me and said, "God bless you."

For a moment, I was speechless. When I finally found my voice, I wanted to know what the terms were. Was there anything that I needed to

Learning Objective
Understand the chronological presentation of the Story in the New Testament.

BOOK
Philippians
AUTHOR
Paul
AGE WRITTEN
A.D. 60-62
FROM
Rome
TO
Christians at Philippi
PROBLEM
Disunity in the Church
AUDIENCE
Those in the church who thrive on disunity
GEOGRAPHY
⟲ Rome

QUESTIONS
How does thinking theologically help you solve problems like disunity?
How does disunity in your life, family, work, or church cause joy to dissipate in your life?
What can you do to correct your present situation?

Letters

Learning Objective
Understand the chronological presentation of the Story in the New Testament.

sign? How much interest was involved? He smiled and said, "This is God's money; he doesn't charge interest to his kids." Then he told me that if I were ever flush and heard that a brother or sister needed some financial help, that I should "pass along God's money to them," no strings attached.

About a year later, we were having lunch again. He had lost his job at the bank. I asked him how he was doing financially. He told me he was a bit short that month. I remembered his words. I pulled out my checkbook and wrote him a check and handed it to him. He looked and told me that the amount would help him over his financial hump.

Living as a newly created being will cause us to live in a different Story, and that Story needs to be comprehended in its many hues for change to occur. Serving others with God's stuff is what his Story is made of.

 BOOK READING GUIDE: PHILIPPIANS

The outline presented below reveals a pattern in this Paul's writing to the Philippians. He began by telling the church that he cared for them deeply. He wanted them to understand that there are models to follow in order for them to live the life of new humanity to its fullest extent. The ultimate example to follow was the model of Christ. He became a servant in order to provide our redemption. Timothy and Epaphroditus were visual examples of what to do as a follower of Jesus. Paul's ministry among them also gave a pattern to follow. Finally, he thanks them for their interest in him.

Philippians 1-4.
TBB. 1599-1603.

Introduction 1.1-2

Paul's Interest in the Philippian Church 1.3-26

An Exhortation: The Pattern of Christ to Follow 1.27-2.18

Example of Timothy 2.19-24

Dictionary Articles
Read the following Dictionary Articles in *New Bible Dictionary*.
  Philippi
  Philippians, Epistle to the

Example of Epaphroditus 2.25-30

An Exhortation: The Pattern of Paul to Follow 3.1-4.9

Philippian Church's Interest in Paul 4.10-20

Conclusion 4.21-23

BOOK
1 Timothy
AUTHOR
Paul
AGE WRITTEN
A.D. 63
FROM
Macedonia
TO
Timothy in Ephesus
PROBLEM
Organizing a second generation church and dealing with false teaching
AUDIENCE
Those who need to organize and fight against false teaching
GEOGRAPHY
🌏 Macedonia

Reading the StoryLine: First Timothy

There have been lots of discussion about where Paul was when he wrote the letters to Timothy and Titus. Wherever he was, he seemed to know about the problems that were occurring in the church at Ephesus and the churches that had been created on Crete. He wrote these letters to his personal representatives in these areas to help solve the basic problems as he understood them.

About 1 Timothy: Pastoring A Second Generation Church

First Timothy is one of four letters that Paul wrote to three individuals (Timothy, Titus, and Philemon). Timothy was the personal representative of Paul to the church at Ephesus that was founded during Paul's Second Church Planting Mission. When Greeks entered the church in number, the tendency was to bring some of their teachings into the church. Often a set of erroneous information evolved. Paul wrote Timothy to give him advice on some of the pressing practical matters within the church, including the need to teach sound doctrine to offset faulty teaching. In addition, Paul wrote about matters of public worship, the qualifications for the church leaders, and how to handle the widows, slaves, and false teachers within the church. It is important to note that this was a second generation church and there was a need for a different set of qualifications for leadership than there was for the churches under Titus' care which were younger churches. It has often been our tendency for harmony that has led us to combine the leadership lists from First Timothy and Titus. When this occurs, we overlook the uniqueness of each book for its first reader and, to our detriment, miss the uniqueness of each book on the subject.

Letters

Learning Objective
Understand the chronological presentation of the Story in the New Testament.

Some Beginning Theological Thoughts

Women in the Church

Clearly the interpretation of the 1 Timothy 2.11-15 passage hinges on the understanding of the words *to have authority.* The debate over whether women[96] can teach men is argued from this passage. The Greek word that is translated *authority* is found only here in the New Testament. Outside the New Testament, it is a word for *sex* and *murder*. Frankly, it is an erotic word. It is translated as such in the *Wisdom of Solomon* (12.6). The context of the city of Ephesus with its temple prostitutes may lend itself to authority being translated as sexual murder. Paul is disallowing women in orgiastic Ephesus to slaughter men by leading them into cultic fornication by their teaching. Thyatira (Revelation 2.20-25) had this problem. Scripture is not silent on this subject. Proverbs 2.18, 5.5, and 7.27 see prostitution and slaughter as being connected. This interpretation fits the book's context. Women are told to dress modestly and not act like prostitutes (2.9-10). In verses 13 and 14, Paul tells us that Eve was seduced by the devil. The word *deceived* has strong sexual overtones. The good news in all of this is that women are safe because of the birth of the child, i.e., Jesus. It appears that it is unwarranted to use this passage as a global ban on women teaching men and women in the church. Rather, it seems right that it is a global ban on women or men using sexual favors as a way to worship God.[97]

Sound Doctrine

Sound teaching means *healthy teaching*.[98] It is a medical metaphor. Paul's concern was with the content of the doctrine which leads to the bad behavior which comes from its teaching. Healthy instruction leads to proper Christian behavior for God's new humanity as compared to the diseased teaching of the heretics which leads to controversies, arrogance, abusiveness, and strife (1 Tim. 6.3-5).

Elders

As the church grew distinct from Judaism, it retained the principle of elder leadership. The terms *elder, bishop,* and *overseer* are just different names for the same ministry of leadership in the early church. Two things should be noted about elders. First, they must have high personal and moral character. Second, their ministry is pastoral.

Question
How does elders as pastoral compare with the current practice of elder as board members.

So What?

Pastoring a second generation church is not easy, or at least it wasn't

Letters

Learning Objective
Understand the chronological presentation of the Story in the New Testament.

for me. Living in a different Story than the congregation was, was very interesting. They had a traditional view of pastoring, i.e., they paid me to make decisions, as long as they were the decisions that they believed they should be; and do all the work that was needed around the church, like mowing the lawns, watering the shrubs, etc.; do all the other ministry items, like visiting the sick in homes and hospitals; and eat anything that was set before me, regardless of how unhealthy it may have been.

On one occasion, two ladies of the church took my wife and me to a "church gathering" in a different but close city. As we were having lunch, a part of pastoring that I really enjoyed, they asked me when I was going to "start" such a ministry in our church, as we had just witnessed.

I suggested that as women in the church that they did not need to fear any reprisal from me for starting such a ministry if they really thought God was calling them to do so, even if it did include teaching men.

They were shocked at my response. They wanted me to do the work. Yep, living in a different Story and trying to get others to do the same is hard work, but it is great work.

BOOK READING GUIDE: 1 TIMOTHY

1 Timothy 1-6.
TBB. 1607-1611.

Introduction 1.1-2

Teach Sound Doctrine 1.3-20

Paul exhorted Timothy to communicate to certain people that they should not become involved with false doctrine because of the controversies to which it leads. He reminded Timothy of Hymenaeus and Alexander, who shipwrecked their faith and were handed over to Satan so they would understand not to blaspheme.

Edict for Public Worship 2.1-15

Paul taught about the importance of church worship, body language, dress, and submission. More heat than light usually comes from this section on women and teaching (See above for fuller explanation).

Administration – Elders – Deacons 3.1-16

Leadership characteristics for elders, deacons, and deaconesses are defined.

Combat False Teachers 4.1-16

Timothy is reminded that in the last days, of which they were a part, that people would abandon their faith and follow demonic spirits which would deceive them. To avoid this, Timothy should devote his time to the public reading of Scripture, to preaching, and to teaching, so that the church could remain secure in their faith.

Hints on Widows, Elders, and Slaves 5.1-6.2a

The church's responsibility for widows, payment to elders for their work in the church, various other thoughts about ordination, quieting stomach problems, and slavery are offered by Paul.

Conclusion 6.2b-21

Reading the StoryLine: Titus

The pioneer spirit of Paul seems to be deeply embedded in him. He was loyal to help those, who had traveled with him for years, continue to keep the appropriate Story alive in churches that had been created around the Mediterranean world of his day. His writing to Titus may be an example of that spirit.

About Titus: Pastoring a First Generation Church

The church in Crete was much younger than the church at Ephesus. Paul had sent Titus there to help bring the young church to maturity. While some of the characteristics of leadership seem the same, it is the overall group that makes the difference. Titus was warned about the influence of false teachers and their teaching. It seems that Paul was still being plagued by teachers with the same attitude that had plagued his churches beginning with the churches in Galatia. (1.10) Titus was exhorted to encourage believers to live their lives in a very practical way as the new humanity. Because the church had a weakness of leadership which led to weak congregations,[99] Paul gave Titus a list of character traits that he should set as a target when selecting leaders for this young church.

Some Beginning Theological Thoughts

Teaching Sound Doctrine

Paul provided a description of teaching in chapter 2. Teaching is not so much a process of transmitting sound doctrine as it is a process of developing a lifestyle which is in harmony with sound doctrine. Thus, teaching is more than just talking. It is training (2.4), encouraging (2.6), setting an example (2.7), and rebuking (2.15). Teaching sound, healthy doctrine will produce an orthodox life.

False Teacher

Scripture is full of suggestions about how to determine whether teachers are false. You can tell by what they teach and how they live. If their teaching denies that Jesus is God, or if their personal lives are marked by arrogance, a love for money, an antagonism to authority, or they are sexually corrupt, if they are totally inclusive, one can say with confidence that they are false teachers.

So What?

Maybe God has called you to act the part of church planter or church planter encourager. Take the work of Paul to Titus into account if this is the hue of the Story that you are being called to live in presently.

BOOK READING GUIDE: TITUS

Introduction 1.1-4

Appointment of Elders 1.5-9

When choosing leaders for the young church at Crete, Titus was provided with a list of character traits for leaders to aim at.

Learning Objective
Understand the chronological presentation of the Story in the New Testament.

BOOK
Titus

AUTHOR
Paul

AGE WRITTEN
A.D. 63

FROM
Nicopolis

TO
Titus in Crete

PROBLEM
Organizing a first generation church

AUDIENCE
Those who pioneer any kind of a ministry

GEOGRAPHY
⊕ Nicopolis

Titus 1-3. TBB. 1615-1616.

Letters

Learning Objective
Understand the chronological presentation of the Story in the New Testament.

BOOK
2 Timothy
AUTHOR
Paul
AGE WRITTEN
A.D. 64
FROM
Rome
TO
Timothy in Ephesus
PROBLEM
How to pass ministry responsibility to a successor
AUDIENCE
Those who are training and being trained for ministry
GEOGRAPHY
☉ Rome

Against False Teachers 1.10-16

False teachers had invaded the early church. Titus was given instructions about how to fight against them and their teaching.

Advice on Practical Living 2.1-3.11

Believers were to live practical lives of obedience. They should not slander, but show humility and remember what God had done for each of them through Jesus.

Conclusion 3.12-15

Reading the StoryLine: Second Timothy

We now come to Paul's last letter. Befitting, it was written to his long time friend and travel companion, Timothy.

About 2 Timothy: Passing the Torch!

The contents of 2 Timothy suggest that Paul was facing death, but even with that hanging over his head, he had time to encourage Timothy. This letter is a moving good-bye from Paul. He reviewed his history from Damascus to the present time of this writing, a recital of sorts. While struggles and victories had been in his path, he had fought the battles and run the course set before him well. Just ahead, after his death, was his reward. With the final good-bye to Timothy, his pen fell silent for eternity.

Some Beginning Theological Thoughts

Next Generation

Second Timothy follows the same pattern as 1 Timothy with the added focus of passing the gospel on to faithful men and women who would proclaim the Story to the following generations.

Scripture

In the 2 Timothy 3.16 passage, Scripture refers to the Old Testament. One must remember that there was no New Testament when this book was being written. It seems that the church has lost its way in terms of thinking about the Old Testament as its Scripture. The influx of the "law and grace" dichotomy introduced by Luther has had a profound effect on the present church in this area. What if we recaptured the Old Testament as part of the Canon for the so-called New Testament Church? How would that change the understanding of the Story we have been called to live out in this Present Evil Age?

Death

Death in Scripture can be viewed from one of three ways: biologically, morally, and spiritually. Death is a terrible distortion of what God intended for his creation. It was the first of these views that Paul points out in 2 Timothy. While death terminated existence in this realm of life for the follower of Jesus, it is the doorway to continued endless life with God.

So What?

My dad was born in 1893 and lived into the twentieth century until he

Learning Objective
Understand the
chronological presentation of
the Story in the New
Testament.

was seventy-seven years old. My wife Donna and I visited my hometown in Florida for about a month before he died. During that time, we were planning a wedding service to honor my mom and dad's fiftieth wedding anniversary. As we would sit around the living room and openly plan, he was silent, except on occasion when he would simply say, "I'm not going to be here!" We would ask where he was going to be and he would answer the same, "I'm not going to be here!"

On the day that we left to travel to Washington D.C to teach in a local community of faith, we stood in the front yard, car packed and ready to go. As I hugged my dad, he whispered in my ear, "Good-bye, son." I pulled back from him and said "we'll be back in a short bit of time for the wedding anniversary service." He smiled and said, "Good-bye, son." It sounded so final.

Donna and I traveled to Washington D.C. and then to Kansas City, MO. We were to be with a church in North Kansas City for ten days so we decided to spend the night in a motel before settling into wherever the church was going to house us. It was Monday night, so I watched Monday Night Football and thought of my dad, because that was his favorite night of the week during football season.

The next morning as we arrived at the church, the pastor met us and told me that a family member had called and wanted me to return his call. As my brother-in-law answered the phone, I sensed that something was amiss. He spoke very gently and said, "Winn, your dad died early this morning in the hospital." It dawned on me what "Good-bye, son" meant.

We made arrangements to go to Florida for his funeral service. When we arrived, we found out that on his last Sunday in church for both services, he made his way on his walker to the altars in front of the church and knelt and prayed. This was not his custom to do such. When he was leaving the little sanctuary, he hugged each person and told them good-bye. They, like me, had no idea what he was saying.

He left the Sunday morning service and the family drove him to his favorite cafeteria to eat. I had eaten with him hundreds of Sundays in cafeterias. Sunday afternoon he asked to take a ride for about an hour. Dad loved to drive and just look around, even though he had seen these sites for many years. Sunday night came and went. The next day, he simply sat around his home during the day and then watched Monday Night football. He went to bed a little after midnight, but woke up having a difficult time breathing early in the morning on Tuesday. The local hospital was only two blocks away. As he lay in the hospital bed with my oldest brother holding him up, he passed on to the other side with a quiet sigh!

I believe that my dad knew in advance that his day to go home was shortly ahead. Like Paul, he had fought a good fight, he had finished the course, he had kept the faith and in a moment of time that defies description, as a faithful servant he slipped into the arms of Jesus.

What was beautiful about the whole set of circumstances was that he was allowed to say good-bye to everyone he loved, eat at his favorite watering hole, take a sightseeing ride, and watch his final Monday Night football game. Then, he went home.

I share all of this as a way of saying that I believe that Paul knew he

Letters

Learning Objective
Understand the chronological presentation of the Story in the New Testament.

2 Timothy 1-4.
TBB. 1619-1622.

Dictionary Articles
Read the following Dictionary Articles in *New Bible Dictionary.*
  Timothy
  Timothy and Titus, Epistles to
  Titus
  Church Government
  Presbyter, Presbytery
  Ministry

BOOK
1 Peter
AUTHOR
Peter
AGE WRITTEN
A.D. 63
FROM
Rome
TO
Christians in Asia Minor
PROBLEM
How to conduct yourself when suffering
AUDIENCE
Those who suffer and others who deny
GEOGRAPHY
🜨 Rome

was at the end of his life. Somehow in his communication to and from God, he had picked up a signal of some kind that his time was short. My hope for my own life would be that I would have the same grace from God.

One learns to deal with death in a different way as a newly created human.

BOOK READING GUIDE: 2 TIMOTHY

Introduction 1.1-2

Petition for Courage 1.3-2.13

Paul reminded Timothy about who he was: an emotional, faithful, and gifted person. Because of these gifts, he would be able to suffer the hardships that the ministry would throw his way.

Pastoral Responsibilities 2.14-4.5

Timothy is advised once again about the evils of false teaching and that he should stand firm against all of it by being faithful to fulfill the ministry God had given him.

Paul's Final Words 4.6-18

The final words of Paul scream with emotion. Ready to die for his faith, he stood as a model for keeping true to his faith through thick and thin. His final reward awaited him. He longed for a personal word of comfort from his friend during his final lonely days.

Conclusion 4.19-22

Reading the StoryLine: First Peter

Paul has been heard from and now in the remaining Story we hear from Peter, Matthew, Jude, and John and only God knows who wrote the book of Hebrews, as Origen once said.[100]

About 1 Peter: What to Do When The Hard Time Comes

Peter did not know the group to which he writes his first book. He discovered that as believers they were suffering persecution, not from Rome or a local government. History records no specific persecutions outside of Rome during this period of time.[101] Peter wrote to believers who were suffering the normal balderdash that comes with being a follower of Jesus in the hostile world of this Present Evil Age.

Four New Testament authors were in Rome at the same time: Paul, Luke, Mark, and Peter. They were writing their books at approximately the same time. It is reasonable to believe that each was aware of the other's work while being written and that they may have had discussion about the contents of each other's work.

Some Beginning Theological Thoughts

Suffering

Suffering will normally arise as a Christian lives his or her life in a hostile, non-Christian world. Suffering is a part of Christian life and we should not be surprised by it (4.12). Peter told his readers that they should rejoice for having the privilege of sharing in the suffering of Christ

Learning Objective
Understand the chronological presentation of the Story in the New Testament.

(4.13a). The end of one's suffering will be blessing, although it may not be clear to you until Jesus arrives (4.13b). Being insulted for being a follower of Jesus should bring a person to a point of praise (4.14, 16). However, one should not suffer because of wrong actions (4.15). The judgments of God will occur on both the just and the unjust. God will work good for the just and destruction for the unjust (4.18). Peter's final command was to continue to suffer for doing good, and commit to God (4.19).

Descent into Hell

This idea is firmly imbedded in the early Christian creeds first appearing in the fourth century. The passage in 1 Peter 3.19 says nothing about a descent of Christ to Hades or a second chance for unbelievers, or even a first chance for those who had died prior to the first coming of Jesus. What it does say is that Christ is victor. It is a message of a victorious Christ on his way to the Father announcing his victory to the supernatural beings held captive.[102] In this passage, Peter presented a priceless piece of pastoral persuasion.

Holiness

The word *holy* means to be *set apart*. It is not a religious word. Peter suggests in 1 Peter 2 some of the items you should put away from your lifestyle. Doing these do not make a person holy. Putting these life habits away is a response to the new birth and becoming truly human. You are holy, therefore, put away these lifestyles in order to remain holy.

Soul

The idea of *getting souls saved,* is the language of Jonathan Edwards in the First Great Awakening in the eighteenth century. The idea has carried down to the present day as good *evangelical* language and is usually based on a passage in 1 Peter 1.9. George Ladd has suggested that soul designates the vitality of life in humankind. It is the summation of a person's personality. It is equivalent to the meaning of *I myself* or *yourself.* Plato developed the distinction between body and soul. Scripture does not indicate anywhere that man *has* a soul but rather that man *is* a soul. In Scripture, body and spirit would be two different ways which the soul is viewed.[103] If we use the phrase *salvation of the soul* in its biblical context, it would mean the salvation of the complete person.

Born Again

While John 3.3 and 1 Peter 1.23 may appear the same in your English translation, the Greek words are different. In John, the phrase should be translated *born from above*.[104] In Peter, it should be translated *born anew*. Both deal with the experience of regeneration which is the redemptive renewal of humankind on the basis of a restored relationship with God through Jesus.

So What?

Want to be normal as you live out the Story of new humanity? Learn to suffer well, and while you are at it, put away malice, all deceit, hypocrisy, envy, and slander. They are a part of another story, the story of this Present Evil Age. Living in a new Story would mean living completely opposite to these lifestyles.

Letters

Learning Objective
Understand the chronological presentation of the Story in the New Testament.

1 Peter 1-5.
TBB. 1723-1777.

Dictionary Articles
Read the following Dictionary Articles in *New Bible Dictionary.*
  Peter
  Peter, First Epistle of
  Persecution
  Descent into Hades

BOOK
2 Peter
AUTHOR
Peter
AGE WRITTEN
A.D. 63-64
FROM
Rome
TO
Christians in Asia Minor
PROBLEM
A denial of the Second Coming of Jesus
AUDIENCE
Those who suffer and others who deny
GEOGRAPHY
⊕ Rome

📖 BOOK READING GUIDE: 1 PETER

Introduction 1.1-2

Praise to God 1.3-12

A model is provided by Peter of what followers of Jesus should do when suffering. Believers should grasp their hope, joy, confidence, and freedom.

Exhortation to Holy Living 1.13-21

Those who follow Jesus should live a holy life, set apart for God and his work, and avoid sin which has a consequence of obliterating Christian fellowship.

Toward Mutual Love 1.22-2.3

Those following Jesus should move toward mutual love when being purified by obeying the truth.

Elevation to God's People 2.4-10

Peter's exhortation about the church as the people of God being a chosen people, a royal priesthood, and a holy nation.

Responsibilities of Believers 2.11-5.11

Peter told believers what to get rid of in their lives: malice, all deceit, hypocrisy, envy, and slander. In place of the present-evil-age-life responses, they should crave pure spiritual milk which will help them grow toward maturity. They should be responsible to submit to their rulers and masters. More responsibilities of Jesus' followers are addressed: husband and wife daily problems; wives were exhorted to lead their non-believing husbands to a relationship with God by a Godly model, not by preaching to them about their need. Husbands should be cautious about how they treat their wives during their lovemaking. Jesus was portrayed as the model for believers to follow. Suffering can occur even when doing good and believers will suffer. Some closing words were given to elders and the young men of the church.

Conclusion 5.12-14

Reading the StoryLine: Second Peter

The church as a whole is about thirty years old and the idea of the consummation of the Kingdom with the return of Jesus was being questioned. Peter writes to keep the followers of Jesus living in the right Story as they patiently wait for that great day to appear.

About 2 Peter: What Do You Mean He Is Not Coming?

Second Peter[105] is apocalyptic.[106] Peter taught against the evils of teachers who teach error. The book looks a lot like Jude.[107] The greatest desire of Peter was that followers of Jesus would grow in the true knowledge of the Story of God. He wanted all believers to become aware of those who were teaching false doctrine, which were forms of other stories. Specific attention should be given to the teaching and attitude about the denial of the Second Coming.[108] Above all, he wanted his audience to become mature.

Some Beginning Theological Thoughts

Second Coming

Because Jesus had not appeared yet, the false teachers seized the moment to teach that he was not coming, because nothing had changed and everything remained the same (3.4). Peter told the church that everything had not remained the same (3.5-7). God has a purpose in what appears from a human standpoint to be a delay. God is not willing that any of his people should perish, i.e., believers. The delay should not be a matter of complaint, but should be taken as an opportunity to repent (3.9). God will not defer his judgment indefinitely. It will come unexpectedly (3.10a) and with finality (3.10b, the use of apocalyptic language).

Learning Objective
Understand the chronological presentation of the Story in the New Testament.

So What?

It seems that we have the opposite problem than the churches to which Peter wrote. For the last century or more, the church has been inundated with information about the Second Coming of Jesus. Writers have written theological books and fictional books containing a brand of popular theology that has flooded the marketplace. The churches in Peter's day thought he was *not* coming because he had not yet arrived. The churches in our day think he is coming any minute because of the world's condition. The first way of thinking was not helpful for those living in the Story; the second way of thinking is just as insidious to living in the Story. The first may have caused followers to want to return to their former life. The second may cause followers to make poor choices about the present because the world as we know it should end any moment.

 BOOK READING GUIDE: 2 PETER

Introduction 1.1-2

2 Peter 1-3.
TBB. 1731-1733.

True Knowledge 1.3-21

Followers of Jesus must know the truth about God in order to receive power to live an effective life. Knowing this truth about God will help the followers of Jesus to abandon their sin.

Warning Against False Teachers 2.1-22

Political correctness was not Peter's forte. He called a spade a spade. He talked about false teachers in specific and plain language. Their end was sure.

Question
How has political correctness in our speech corrupted our ability to say something that needs to be said for fear that we will offend someone?

Obsolete Doctrine No! 3.1-18

Followers of Christ living in the Story should not believe that the teaching about the Second Coming of Jesus is obsolete and discard it from their belief system, nor think it so imminent that they live life haphazardly. The real reason for the delay is that God wanted folks in the church to have an opportunity to repent and move back into his Story.

Dictionary Articles
Read the following Dictionary Articles in *New Bible Dictionary*. Third Edition. D. R. W.
    Peter, Second Epistle of

Reading the StoryLine: Matthew

The church was about thirty years old in the '60s of the first century. In the first region outside of Jerusalem to which the church spread, there seems to have been a continual stream of new followers of Jesus. Matthew, one of the disciples of Jesus, understood the need for these

Gospels

Act 5: Scenes 1-6

Gospels

Learning Objective
Understand the chronological presentation of the Story in the New Testament.

BOOK
Matthew
AUTHOR
Matthew
AGE WRITTEN
A.D. Mid '60s
FROM
Antioch in Syria
TO
The Church in Syria
PROBLEM
How to train new believers
AUDIENCE
New believers and seasoned believers who need to be trained in the basics
GEOGRAPHY

followers, both new and not-so-new, to be rooted in the Story of Jesus. We turn to the book of Matthew to see how followers of Jesus could be storized.

About Matthew: How To Teach New Converts

During the first years after the resurrection of Jesus, there were thousands of new believers who were born into the church and many new churches started. One of these was the church at Antioch in Syria (Acts 1.19). The result of the ministry of the Holy Spirit there was that many new believers came to faith (Acts 11.21). Barnabas was sent from Jerusalem to Antioch when news arrived about the move of God in the church in Antioch. By himself, he was not able to handle the training of the influx of all these new believers. He sought out Saul in his hometown of Tarsus and brought him back to Antioch to help with the task of training these new believers.

During the following years, the Church at Antioch kept bringing new people to faith in Jesus. Two decades after the birth of the church, Matthew wrote his book to provide a training manual[109] for the ongoing stream of new believers. He wanted these people to understand about Jesus, the new Moses for the new Israel, the church.

At the conclusion of his book, he furnished a clue about his intention. He told the story of the command of Jesus that his disciples *make disciples* by baptizing them and teaching them. Matthew took the teaching part of this story to heart. He produced a book to help new believers and not-so-new believers to understand who Jesus was and how to walk out their new found humanity in their Christian life.

To demonstrate to his readership that Jesus was really the new Moses for the new Israel, the church, he used subtle but very obvious comparisons between Moses and Jesus. He told the story about the attempted murder of Jesus by killing all the infants under the age of two (Exodus 1.22 compared with Matthew 2.16). When Matthew presented Jesus' teaching on the mount, it was a comparison to Moses receiving the Law on Mount Sinai. In Luke, Jesus delivered the same sermon on a plain. The most obvious comparison is the five teaching books in which Matthew structures his book.[110] The reading guide below demonstrates how he did this. The goal of Moses in his five books: to train the children of Israel. Matthew's goal: to train new converts to live as truly human in this Present Evil Age.

Some Beginning Theological Thoughts

There are four great themes in Matthew:

Fulfillment of the Old Testament

He was fond of quoting Old Testament Scripture as pointers to the stories in the Old Testament that found their fulfillment in Jesus.

Righteousness

Matthew's teaching in the Sermon on the Mount demonstrated the lifestyle of a Kingdom person.

Community

The church is the community of the Kingdom of God through which the work of God can be carried out in this Present Evil Age.

Eschatology

The Olivet Discourse (Matt. 24-25) taught about the interaction between this Present Evil Age and the Age to Come.

So What?

Looking for some material to use to train new followers and not-so-new followers of Jesus? Teach through Matthew using it as a guide to understanding the Story of Jesus, as a model for your church as newly created actors in his drama.

BOOK READING GUIDE: MATTHEW

Birth And Infancy: 1.1-2.23

Book One

Narrative. Teaching, Healing and Preaching: 3.1-4.25
Instruction. Sermon On The Mount: 5.1-7.29

Book Two

Narrative. The Works Of The Kingdom: 8.1-9.38
Instruction. The Disciples Sent Out: 10.1-11.1

Book Three

Narrative. What The Kingdom Is Not: 11.2-12.50
Instruction. The Parables Of The Kingdom: 13.1-52

Book Four

Narrative. Suffering, Miracles, Conflict: 13.53-17.27
Instruction. Humility, Forgiveness: 18.1-35

Book Five

Narrative. The Old Age and The Age To Come: 19.1-23.39
Instruction. The Future Kingdom: 24.1-25.45

Death, Resurrection, Instructions: 26.1-28.20

Matthew 1-28.
TBB. 1625-1665.

Dictionary Articles
Read the following Dictionary Articles in *New Bible Dictionary*.
  Matthew, Gospel of
  Jesus Christ, Titles of
  Synagogue
  Sanhedrin
  Sermon on the Mount
  Lord's Prayer

Reading the StoryLine: Hebrews

In addition to new believers being trained to live in God's Story, another need in these early churches became apparent. Some of the Jewish brothers and sisters who had become followers of the Jesus Story were beginning to fall away, back to the former story of Judaism. An unknown author preached a sermon to help these folks understand that the Story of Jesus was superior to any other story including their former one.

About Hebrews: A First Century Sermon

"Only God knows who wrote the book of Hebrews," was the epitaph of Origen an early church leader.[111] Apparently it was written to Jewish believers who were suffering and were tempted to deny Jesus as Messiah.[112] It was most likely an oral presentation (sermon) in its original form (Hebrews 13.22 compare with Acts 13.15). These Jewish believers had been influenced by Greek philosophy. The book defends Christianity in Platonic-like thoughts such as: a contrast between the real that is

BOOK
Hebrews
AUTHOR
Unknown
AGE WRITTEN
Mid A.D. Mid '60s
FROM
Unknown
TO
Jewish Christians in Rome
PROBLEM
Christianity was deficient to Judaism
AUDIENCE
Believers who need to understand that the Jesus Story is superior to all other stories
GEOGRAPHY
✈ Rome

Letters

Learning Objective
Understand the chronological presentation of the Story in the New Testament.

heavenly and eternal with the apparent that is earthly and temporal. Christ is always seen as superior in the book. The author had an excellent knowledge of the Septuagint (LXX). He quotes it frequently, usually as story pointers, and then provides his readers a commentary on the passage quoted.[113] Jesus is seen as the pioneer and perfecter of the faith. He was the one who always remained the same.

Some Beginning Theological Thoughts

Superiority of Jesus and Christianity

Much like Stephen and his defense before the Sanhedrin (Acts 7), the author of Hebrews wants to show that Christianity is superior to Judaism because of Jesus, the Son of God, the Great High Priest, and the author of our salvation. Jesus stands at the peak of God's revelation, superior to angels and to Moses (Heb. 1.1-2.9; 3.1-6). He is the reflection of God's own glory, an exact representation. All the revelations that appeared before the time of Jesus were mere shadows of what appeared in him (Heb. 1-3).

Faith

Hebrews 11 is often called the faith chapter. It begins by stating that faith is being sure of what we hope for and certain of what we do not see. The author then listed men and women whose faith in God was expressed in their actions which came from their beliefs. Each of these cases demonstrates that faith shaped the perspective of the future and made a difference in the choices that were made.

So What?

We have lost the art of being oral. Everything is written including this book, but we also can learn well with our ears. Try this on for size. Read the book of Hebrews orally to yourself or to others and listen for the differing hues of light that will cause you to live in God's Story.

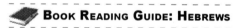

BOOK READING GUIDE: HEBREWS

Hebrews 1-13.
TBB. 1669-1682.

Christ

Superior to the Prophets 1.1-4

Jesus' message is superior to the Old Testament message.

Superior to the Angels 1.5-2.18

Angels are spirits who minister. Jesus was the son whose life and death rendered salvation from our sins.

Superior to Moses-Joshua 3.1-4.13

Moses and Joshua, held in high esteem by followers of Jesus, were inferior to Jesus.

Superior to the Priesthood 4.14-7.28

The Old Testament priest administered sacrifices for the atonement of Israel's sin. Jesus was presented as the perfect High Priest.

Superior Covenant 8.1-10.18

The sacrificial system of the Old Covenant was replaced by a once-for-all sacrifice of Jesus and became a New Covenant.

Faith

Superior Way 10.19-12.29

The faith of past heroes is recited. Believers should now turn to Jesus who is the pioneer and perfecter of their faith.

Conclusion 13.1-25

 Act 5 Scene 6. The Journey Continues (A.D. '70-'90s)

Reading the StoryLine: Jude

We enter a new scene that takes us through the rest of the Story of the New Testament beginning with the book of Jude.

About Jude: Combat Ready!

Jude wanted to write an instruction manual about salvation (3) until he discovered that those whom he had led to salvation[114] had fallen into errors taught by false teachers. Instead, he wrote a stinging assault on the false teachers and their teaching, a bit different than the approach of Paul in Colossians. He neither wasted words nor used the modern concept of tact. Being politically correct in his choice of language did not seem to be a high value on his priority list. Escaping the teaching they had embraced, which was eternally dangerous, was more important than the possible hurt feeling that could come from such a frontal assault. His use of metaphors are some of the most vivid in Scripture. When needed to make a point, he did not hesitate to turn to non-biblical material. He did so more than any other author in the New Testament. He quoted passages from two non-canonical books: *The Assumption of Moses* (9) and *First Enoch* (14-15). Jude told his audience that they would do well to stand firm in what the apostles had taught. It was the safe place to live.

Some Beginning Theological Thoughts

False Teaching

False teaching was a constant enemy of the church in the first century. When Jude wrote to those who have been deceived, he does not take them through a finely tuned point-by-point discussion of the heresies they are involved in. He simply shows the results of living as the false teachers live. He made sure his audience knew that there was nothing new about wrongheaded attitudes about God, which led to wrong ways of living. He pointed back to Israel, the angels, Sodom and Gomorrah, Cain, Balaam, and Korah as examples of ways not to live and the judgment that followed these poor choices.

Gnosticism

Gnosticism was a form of belief that was most dangerous at the close of the second century. It most likely began much earlier than this date. There had been a tremendous influx of Gentiles into the early church. This influx brought with it several elements of the Greek philosophical mindset. The basic presupposition of this philosophy was dualism. This dualism says that spirit was good and material was evil. Salvation was an escape from the realm of matter to spirit via knowledge. This conflict became most acute in the understanding of the person of Jesus. The Gnostic asked the question, "How could infinite pure spirit have anything to do with an

Learning Objective
Understand the chronological presentation of the Story in the New Testament.

Dictionary Articles
Read the following Dictionary Articles in *New Bible Dictionary*.
Hebrews, Epistle to the

BOOK
Jude
AUTHOR
Jude, half brother of Jesus
AGE WRITTEN
A.D. '70s or '80s
FROM
Unknown
TO
Christians everywhere
PROBLEM
False teaching about denying Jesus and immorality
AUDIENCE
Believers who are constantly being pursued by false teaching
GEOGRAPHY
✪ Unknown

Letters

Learning Objective
Understand the
chronological presentation of
the Story in the New
Testament.

evil material body? There were two solutions to this dilemma. Jesus was not really human–he only appeared to be. This was called Docetism which came from the Greek word *dekeo* which is defined as "to seem." This belief made Jesus a ghost, an illusion; he seemed to be a man, but had no real existence. This teaching believed that Jesus' spirit did not inhabit his body until his baptism and his spirit left before his death. This teaching was called Cerinthianism, named such for its leader, Cerinthus. This made Jesus a Dr. Jekyll – Mr. Hyde; one did not know when Jesus was human or when he was divine. The dualism of good and evil may be the background for what Jude says in v. 4a, i.e., *...who changed the grace of our God into a license for immorality and deny Jesus Christ our only Sovereign and Lord.*

So What?

Learning the apostle's teaching might be a way of saying that we should learn a different Story than the one we inhabit.

BOOK READING GUIDE: JUDE

Jude. TBB. 1737-1738.

Introduction 1-2

Contend for the Faith: Why? 3-16

The common salvation that all believers shared was going to be the topic of Jude's letter. However, because of the influence of false teaching which was outright heresy, he wrote to believers to hold on to the firm foundation of "the faith" and not embrace the damnable instructions of the false teachers, which he summarized in verse four. He used illustrations from the Old Testament to support his thesis (5-7), an illustration from non-biblical material (9), additional Old Testament illustrations (11), vivid metaphors (12-13); and, finally, another non-biblical illustration (14-15), to demonstrate why these believers should stand firm in what they had been taught.

QUESTION
How would Jude's
instructions at the end of his
short book allow you to
change stories?

Contend for the Faith: How? 17-23

It is good to know why you should not embrace false teaching. Knowing how to resist would improve the chances of not continuing in deceit. Jude told these followers of Jesus how to defend the faith they had been given. They should remember the teaching of the apostles. They should build themselves up in the most holy faith. They should pray in the Holy Spirit. They should keep themselves in the love of God, wait for mercy, be merciful, snatch away from destruction those who are close to destruction, and finally, continue to have mercy on sinners while not getting involved in their sin.

Dictionary Articles
Read the following
Dictionary Articles in *New
Bible Dictionary.*
  Jude, Epistle of
  Gnosticism

Conclusion 24-25

Reading the StoryLine: The Final Books

We now turn to the corpus of books written by John, the son of Zebedee, who was a fisherman by trade and one of the first disciples. He was the writer of five New Testament books (Gospel of John, 1, 2, 3 John, and Revelation). During the persecution by Domitian, John was exiled to the isle of Patmos off the coast from Ephesus. Upon his return to

Ephesus after his exile, he penned all five of his books. He was probably in his nineties when he wrote these books. We might note that he had waited for almost 60 years before he wrote any of his memories about the ministry of Jesus in his Gospel. Surely, there is hope for older believers to be used by God even toward the end of their lives.

About John: So That You May Continue To Believe

John's[115] Gospel was written much later than the three Synoptic Gospels (Matthew, Mark, and Luke). He wrote with the specific intention that believers should continue to believe in Jesus (see bottom of your TNIV page for 20.31 for an alternative translation). John made explicit what the earlier Gospels made implicit. He viewed the miracles of Jesus as "signs,"[116] revealing Jesus and his mission. It has been said about his Gospel that it "is shallow enough for a child to wade in and deep enough for an elephant to drown in."[117]

John appeared to delight in suggesting to his reader the symbolism found within the stories. As an example, when Judas left the upper room (13.30), it was night, but one can sense John suggesting that Judas was leaving the real light and going into ultimate darkness. John selected only the stories about Jesus that would help him tell the story he wanted to tell his readers (20.30).

Some Beginning Theological Thoughts

Prologue

John 1.1-18 moves from eternity in verse 1, to time in verse 3, to history in verse 6, to the Incarnation in verse 14. John demonstrated that the *logos* is eternal, personal, and divine. Here is a brief look at John 1.1 with added comments:

*In the beginning **was*** (was: an imperfect tense, which means a continuous action in past time with no thought of beginning or ending and it is in the indicative mood, which indicates a simple statement of fact) *the word and the word was with God* (*pros ton theon*: an expression of relationship, being face-to-face with God) *and the word was God* (*logos en theon*: the Greek phrase indicates *word* is deity or divine. The direct article would make absolute equation. God is more than the word, but the word is God).

Paraclete

It is apparent from the way John uses *paraclete* that he intended his readers to understand personality by it. The idea of *paraclete* may be best expressed by the title of *Continuator*. The thought is that the Holy Spirit *continues* the work and ministry of Jesus.[118]

The Seven Signs

Often called signs because these miracles point beyond themselves, they were not seen by John as ends in themselves. These miracles signified that there was transforming power in the ministry of Jesus.

❶ **Turning water into wine: 2.1-12**

This miracle symbolizes the sterility of Judaism and the new wine of the messianic age which was occurring in the ministry of Jesus.

Learning Objective
Understand the chronological presentation of the Story in the New Testament.

BOOK
John
AUTHOR
John
AGE WRITTEN
Late A.D.. '80s - Early '90s
FROM
Ephesus
TO
Christians and/or non-Christians in and around Ephesus
PROBLEM
Weakened Relationships with Jesus
AUDIENCE
Believers who wish to process toward maturity in the Christian Story
GEOGRAPHY
✪ Ephesus

Learning Objective
Understand the chronological presentation of the Story in the New Testament.

❷ **Healing the Official's son: 4.46-54**

The restoration power of the message of Jesus

❸ **Man at the pool healed: 5.1-9**

In God's Kingdom, weakness is replaced by strength.

❹ **Feeding the 5,000: 6.1-14**

This signifies that only Jesus can satisfy spiritual hunger.

❺ **Walking on water: 6.16-21**

The ministry of Jesus is not incapacitated because of realities like gravity and time.

❻ **Healing the man born blind: 9.1-12**

The ministry of Jesus brings individuals from spiritual darkness into light.

❼ **Raising Lazarus from the dead: 11.1-44**

Resurrection power of the Age to Come can bring individuals from death to life.

The spiritual implications of these miracles do not mean that they did not occur in history or that God does not perform such today. Their real significance is that they point to the powerful ministry of Jesus in transforming individuals into God's new humanity.

The Seven "I AM" Sayings

Each of these seven emphatic statements of Jesus suggests an important aspect of the person and ministry of Jesus.

❶ I am the bread of life: 6.35

Jesus is the food which nourishes one's spiritual life. A deliberate echo to manna in the Old Testament Story.[119]

❷ I am the light of the world: 8.12; 9.5

Jesus is the root source of one's illumination. Light gives a choice between darkness and light. There is no light apart from a relationship with him. To have light is to have Jesus.

❸ I am the door of the sheep: 10.7

Jesus is the only passageway. There is only one door to a sheepfold. It was the only entrance for the sheep. There is no other way into God's new humanity, except Jesus.

❹ I am the good shepherd: 10.14

Jesus was a shepherd willing to lay down his life for the lives of his sheep. An echo of Psalm 23.

❺ I am the resurrection and the life: 11.25

Jesus gives resurrection and life to those who believe. He becomes their source of life. The linking of resurrection and life points to the truth that the life Jesus brings is the life of the Age to Come.

❻ I am the way and the truth and the life: 14.6

This statement demonstrates what the others have implied. In contrast to every pursuit of life, only Jesus brings genuine life that comes from God.

❼ I am the true vine: 15.1

Jesus is the root of life.

In addition, there are other "I am" statements (4.25-26; 8.24, 28, 58; 13.19).[120]

The Discourses of Jesus

There are large teaching sections in John that do not seem to be a collection of sayings. They make up the bulk of the body of the Gospel. They are:

Gospels

Learning Objective
Understand the chronological presentation of the Story in the New Testament.

- ◆ New birth: 3.1-21
- ◆ Water of life: 4.4-26
- ◆ Resurrection and life: 5.19-47
- ◆ Bread of life: 6.25-59
- ◆ The deity of Jesus: 8.12-59
- ◆ Good shepherd: 10.1-21
- ◆ The deity of Jesus: 10.22-39
- ◆ The role of Jesus: 12.20-50
- ◆ The departure of Jesus: 13.31-14.31
- ◆ Union with Jesus: 15.1-16.33
- ◆ The glorification of Jesus: 17.1-26

So What?

The Holy Spirit as a Continuator may be a new thought to you. The ministry of Jesus in this Present Evil Age goes on and we are the actors and actresses that he has chosen to send the Holy Spirit to help continue his ministry. What part are you playing in his great drama? What hue of color does the book of John cause you to hear?

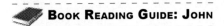

BOOK READING GUIDE: JOHN

Introduction 1.1-18

John 1-21.
TBB. 1741-1771.

From eternity past to eternity present to eternity future, Jesus was presented as God's eternal word. In all of the New Testament, this section is often held as the most profound.

Public Ministry of Jesus 1.19-12.50

John told many stories about the public ministry of Jesus: John the Baptist, the calling of the twelve disciples, the cleansing of the Temple, water turned into wine, the conversation of Nicodemus and the woman at the well, the resuscitation of Lazarus, and the decision of Israel's leaders to destroy Jesus.

Private Ministry of Jesus 13.1-17.26

In this section of his Gospel, John turned to the private ministry of Jesus to his disciples. He told many stories including: the washing of the feet of the disciples and the betrayal prediction. He comforted his disciples and told them that he was the way through which they could relate to the Father. He taught them about the connection they have with him in the story of the vine and the branches. He prayed for himself, for all his disciples, and for all believers.

Gospels

Learning Objective
Understand the
chronological presentation of
the Story in the New
Testament.

Dictionary Articles
Read the following
Dictionary Articles in *New
Bible Dictionary.*
  John, Gospel of
  Incarnation

BOOK
1 John
AUTHOR
John
AGE WRITTEN
Late A.D. '80s, Early '90s
FROM
Ephesus
TO
Christians around Ephesus
PROBLEM
False teaching that
denied that God
had become man in Jesus
Incipient Gnosticism
AUDIENCE
Those who may be
deceived
by a false teacher
GEOGRAPHY
✪ Ephesus

Passover – Crucifixion – Resurrection 18.1-20.31

In the third section of his Gospel, John told the story of the passion week of Jesus. He began with the arrest of Jesus and his series of trials. Peter denied him as Jesus said he would. Pilate, the Roman governor, sentenced Jesus to be crucified. The dark day of the crucifixion, death, and burial are told, followed by the bright day of the resurrection and appearances to Mary Magdalene, his disciples, and Thomas.

Conclusion 21.1-25

Reading the StoryLine: First John

In addition to the Gospel, John wrote three shorter books to help those under his care see the need to continue living in the Story that he and others had shared with them to which they had committed their lives.

About 1 John: Belief Problems With A New Generation

By the end of the first century, Christian teaching was still being corrupted by false teachers in the church. John wrote to followers of Jesus around Ephesus[121] whom he knew intimately[122] who were struggling with a re-statement of information about Jesus that had disrupted the church. He suggested that they test everything that they were being taught. The basic problem which was creeping into the church was incipient Gnosticism. The major point of this aberrant teaching was the belief that you could participate in any form of experience in your body because it did not affect the spirit which had more value than the body. This budding Gnostic belief suggested that Jesus was not really physical, because the physical part of humankind was sinful and God could not live in a physical, sinful form. John reflected in the first few verses that this belief system was wrong. He wrote using vivid contrasts: light and darkness; the love of God and the love of the world; the children of God and the children of the devil; the spirit of God and the spirit of the antichrist; love and hate, to name a few. He also addressed the areas of eternal life, the forgiveness of sins, the Holy Spirit, and fellowship with God and each other. He also wrote about eternal life, forgiveness of sins, the Holy Spirit, and fellowship.

A Beginning Theological Thought

Another Story

False teachers had come in the last decade of the first century to harass the church with its false teachings offering a different story in which to live. John labeled the false prophets (4.1) and counterfeit Christ (2.18 see 4.3). Believers are urged to distinguish the truth from the spurious claims which were being taught. Even though the false teachers had been unmasked (4.4) and expelled (2.19), their influence remained. One can determine the claims of the false teachers by any sentence that begins with, "if any one says...." These teachers boasted of their superior knowledge of God (2.4; 4.8), an incipient form of Gnosticism. Their braggadocio about their love of God (4.20) and fellowship with him (1.6; 2.6, 9) were simply lies in the eyes of John. These false teachers bragged about their unique spiritual experiences (4.1f). They taught a Christology (4.2) that denied the true humanity of Jesus, which in turn cast doubt on the redemptive power of his death. John told his flock that he had heard, seen, and touched Christ (1.1). The Story they had been told to live in was real.

So What?

Do you believe everything that you hear? A lot of folks do without thinking about what they are doing. John's call to the church is to think about what we hear and how we think about it. Would changing our way of thinking about what story we live in cause us to live differently? How?

Learning Objective
Understand the chronological presentation of the Story in the New Testament.

 BOOK READING GUIDE: 1 JOHN

John writes with certain topics in mind. The outline below is to assist the reader in following the flow of the author in his writing. His inspired flow may suggest that complete joy for the believer is the foundation on which conduct, love, and Jesus living in the believer is built. John weaved doctrine and ethics, theology and behavior together in his letter.

1 John 1-5.
TBB. 1775-1779.

> **Complete Joy 1.1-4**
>
> > **Conduct 1.5-2.6**
> >
> > > **Christian Love 2.7-17**
> > >
> > > > **Christian Believer 2.18-27**
> >
> > **Conduct 2.28-3.10**
> >
> > > **Christian Love 3.11-24**
> > >
> > > > **Christian Believer 4.1-6**
> > >
> > > **Christian Love 4.7-5.12**
> >
> > **Conduct 5.13-21**

About 2 John: Undesirable Guest

John wrote this small letter to the "lady chosen by God" and "her children." This is a cryptic way of talking about a house church that John had some influence over.[123] It may be a preview of the way he uses symbolic language in his Revelation. When followers of Jesus believe false teaching, often their love for the Christian community is diminished. John was trying to solve this very problem in this small book. Christians should be alert to what they believe. True love will keep your perspective correct. Love does not accept or condone wrong. Love will segregate itself from heresy and wrong living.

BOOK
2 John
AUTHOR
John
AGE WRITTEN
Late A.D. '80s, Early '90s
FROM
Ephesus
TO
Gaius
PROBLEM
Challenging
spiritual authority
AUDIENCE
Those who challenge
spiritual authority in their
lives
GEOGRAPHY
✈ Ephesus

A Beginning Theological Thought

False Teaching

Itinerant teachers were teaching a denial of the reality of Jesus' human body. While the church should show hospitality to traveling teachers, it should refuse hospitality to these heretics. John instructed this church about showing hospitality to false teachers lest this kindness further the spread of error (7-11). I wonder how that would work today!

So What?

Is there room in your present story to love everyone, brother and sister in the faith as well as fellow humans who are not in the faith? How would a Story adjustment change that?

Gospels

Learning Objective
Understand the chronological presentation of the Story in the New Testament.

2 John. TBB. 1783.

BOOK
3 John
AUTHOR
John
AGE WRITTEN
Late A.D. '80s, Early '90s
FROM
Ephesus
TO
A Church near Ephesus
PROBLEM
Showing hospitality to false teachers
AUDIENCE
Those who may be deceived and support anyone who is a false teacher
GEOGRAPHY
🌍 Ephesus

3 John. TBB. 1787.

Dictionary Articles
Read the following Dictionary Articles in *New Bible Dictionary*.
 John, First
 John, Second
 John, Third

📖 **BOOK READING GUIDE: 2 JOHN**

Introduction 1-3

Love One Another 4-6

Believers were exhorted to love one another.

Look Out For Error 7-11

Followers of Jesus were exhorted to be aware of the errors which false teachers champion.

Conclusion 12-13

About 3 John: Church Discipline Is Important

In this very short letter, John contrasted behavior by looking at the service of Gaius as good behavior and a model to follow, and Diotrephes and his wrong behavior which caused strife in the local church. It is a contrast of living in two different stories. Like many of today's churches, Diotrephes most likely had "an egocentric lust for power, which he had confused with zeal for the gospel."[124] John told the church to remove Diotrephes from the community. It is the only book in the New Testament which told a church to excommunicate a person from its midst and then names him. First Corinthians had a discipline problem and Paul told the church what to do but did not name the individual who was living in sin. Written to an individual (like Philemon), John gives instructions on how to deal with a person who individually decides that he was the authority in the local church.

A Beginning Theological Thought

Good and Bad Behavior

Over the years, John had formulated beliefs about good and bad behavior. In the letter, he contrasts behavior by illustrating good behavior with the life and service of Gaius and the wrong behavior by the strife that Diotrephes had caused. John, like Jude, does not worry about being direct in his confrontation of Diotrephes. He told the church to remove him and imitate the life and service of Gaius.

So What?

Whose story are you living: Gaius or Diotrephes?

 BOOK READING GUIDE: 3 JOHN

Introduction 1

Service of Gaius 2-8

Gaius and his service was exposed to the congregation.

Strife of Diotrephes 9-12

The church was told to excommunicate Diotrephes and not to imitate him.

Conclusion 13-14

Reading the StoryLine: Revelation

Finally, we reach the last of the books in the Story of the New Testament, the book of Revelation, a partial glimpse into how the drama of God will end.

About Revelation: A Book Of Comfort

Interpreting Revelation, a piece of ❖ **apocalyptic** ❖ writing,[125] can bring more heat than light on the subject. A good definition of apocalyptic writing is:

"Apocalypse" is a genre of revelatory literature with a narrative framework, in which a revelation is mediated by an other-worldly being to a human recipient, disclosing a transcendent reality which is both temporal, insofar as it envisages eschatological salvation, and spatial, insofar as it involves another, supernatural world.[126]

The interpretation of Revelation is widely disputed among modern believers. There are only four major ways of interpreting the book that we will look at now.

The Four Views of Revelation

❶ Preterist (In That Time)

This view believes that the book must be understood within the history of the first century. All its prophetic words were fulfilled during the first century and are only good in the following centuries for teaching what happened.

❷ Historical (All of Time)

This view presents history as a timeline which begins in the first century and continues till the end of time. If the readers can discern where on the timeline they are living, then they can discover when the coming of Jesus and the end of time will occur. Today this view is held by Jehovah's Witnesses and the Mormons. This view often sees the Beast as the Roman Papacy and the False Prophet as the Roman Catholic Church.

❸ Idealist (Above Time)

This view suggests that there is a great cosmic conflict occurring between the kingdom of Satan and the Kingdom of God. Time is not an issue. The book simply depicts that good will win over evil. This view may have come into existence in the commentary by Hanns Lilje.[127]

❹ Futurist (End of Time)

There are two basic belief systems within this view.

Dispensationalism

Dispensational Theology interprets the book as a guideline for the future. The seven letters which make up chapters 2 and 3 are seen as seven successive ages within the history of the church. They are:

◆ Apostolic Age: the Ephesus church

◆ Persecution Age: the Smyrna church

◆ Patronage Age: the Pergamum church

Learning Objective
Understand the chronological presentation of the Story in the New Testament.

BOOK
Revelation
AUTHOR
John
AGE WRITTEN
A.D. Mid '90s
FROM
Ephesus
TO
Seven Churches in Asia Minor
PROBLEM
Receiving comfort in times of suffering
AUDIENCE
Those believers who need comfort when it looks like there is no solution to their problems
GEOGRAPHY
⊕ Ephesus

Apocalyptic Writing is a literary report that reveals truths in highly symbolic and poetical terms.

Learning Objective
Understand the chronological presentation of the Story in the New Testament.

Question
Which one of the four views do you presently use to interpret Revelation when you read, study, or teach it? How does knowing the structure help you understand the purpose for which the book was written?

♦ Corruption Age: Thyatira church

♦ Reformation Age: the Sardis church

♦ Evangelism Age: the Philadelphia church

♦ Apostasy Age: Laodicea church

Dispensational Theology believes in a literal seven-year tribulation period before which the church will be raptured.[128] The nation of Israel will be judged by God. The Temple in Jerusalem will be rebuilt. Jesus will come and the final days of this world will play themselves out. Dispensational eschatology has been softened in the recent book *Progressive Dispensationalism*.[129]

Moderate

The Moderate Futurist view does not take the seven letters as a literal representation of seven successive church ages. This view believes that the message of Revelation must be understood within the light of its first hearers, while fulfillment of the seven letters can now happen within any church. God's people are the church, not the Jewish nation. The church will go through the tribulation, but will be saved from destruction by God. The Temple will not be rebuilt and God will not deal with Israel as a nation.[130]

The historic church through the centuries appears to have viewed the book through the lens called the Moderate Futurist View. When seen from this point of view, the book was written within a first century historical context and could have been perfectly understood by its first hearers/ readers. When this view is adopted, it diminishes much of the speculative stargazing that other views indulge in today in books like the *Left Behind* series. The theme of the book is comfort and all its major themes are salted with such an understanding. When being persecuted for the faith, receiving comfort is very important. This is the foundation for a correct understanding of Revelation.

Some Beginning Theological Thoughts

God is in Control

Whatever else is unclear in the presentation of this book, the scene of the Heavenly Throne in Revelation 5.1-11 seems clear. George Ladd puts this succinctly in his commentary on Revelation.[131]

This Revelation will include the destruction of the powers of evil, of Satan, and of death. But before these evil powers are destroyed, they will break forth in a final desperate effort to frustrate the purposes of God by destroying the people of God. However, the terrible conflict that takes place on earth between the Church and the demonic powers embodied in an apostate civilization—Rome in the first century and Antichrist at the end—are in reality expressions in historical form of a fearful conflict in the spiritual world between the Kingdom of God and the kingdom of Satan. Therefore, the Revelation proper begins with the ultimate eternal fact of God is enthroned and ruling in His universe. However fearful or uncontrolled the forces of evil on earth may seem to be, they cannot annul or eclipse the greater fact that behind the scenes God is on His throne governing His universe.

The Rule of God

No other book in the New Testament pictures for the church the sovereignty and rule of God so eloquently as does the book of Revelation (4.1f.). While the historical clash between the church and the emperor cult of Domitian's time was real, it is a picture through which we can view the clash of the kingdom of Satan and the Kingdom of God, between the Dragon, a mythological concept for personified evil, and God. As with Mark 13, the historical fall of Jerusalem provides the immediate foreground behind which the eye of faith can perceive the larger plans of God.

Learning Objective
Understand the chronological presentation of the Story in the New Testament.

Comfort

It appears to me that the main purpose of the book of Revelation is to comfort the church in its struggles against the forces of evil during this Present Evil Age. The symbolic language which breathes life into the book should not be taken with literalness, which often causes its expression of faith to be missed. The battle of this age and the Age to Come is played out in Revelation. The church is the battleground. She can take comfort from its words. God will win! No matter how dark and desolate it looks, God is always in charge.

So What?

Yes, God is in control. The more you hear about the other story, the more it is easy to become fearful and lose the comfort we have in our own Story. Remember, God is in control. Remind yourself often of that as John did to the folks at the end of the first century. Yes, God is in control.

 BOOK READING GUIDE: REVELATION

Introduction 1.1-8

Revelation 1-22.
TBB. 1791-1812.

Vision One 1.9-3.22

John presented a message to each of the seven churches in Asia Minor. There are words of praise, criticism, and promise.

Vision Two 4.1-16.21

Regardless of who one believes is in charge of the world, this vision presented a message that God is ultimately in control of the world (Chapter 4). There is a scroll opened by the Lamb (Chapter 5). The scroll is opened with the breaking of the seals (Chapter 6).

Interlude One 7.1-17

This first break in the action is a literary style that John will use again in Revelation. He gives a small respite of comfort to the reader before continuing the story. This interlude assures the readers/ hearers that no believer will be eternally lost during the tribulation. John presented a before and after view of the church. The 144,000 is the view of the church before the tribulation and the great multitude is the view of the church after the tribulation.

As the Seventh Seal is opened, the picture of the end expands. The Seventh Seal is the Seven Trumpets (Chapter 8, 9).

Act 5: Scenes 1-6

Apocalyptic

Learning Objective
Understand the chronological presentation of the Story in the New Testament.

Dictionary Articles
Read the following Dictionary Articles in *New Bible Dictionary.*
  Apocalyptic
  Revelation, Book of
  Alpha and Omega
  Smyrna
  Pergamum
  Thyatira
  Sardis
  Philadelphia
  Laodicea
  Death
  Hell
  Colors
  Heaven
  Number

Interlude Two 10.1-11.14

John now breaks the story again with a second interlude. In it he tells the story of the angel and the little scroll and the two witnesses. Both stories are to bring comfort to the reader/hearer.

The Seventh Trumpet is blown.

Interlude Three 12.1-14.20

The third interlude told the story of the woman and the dragon, the beast from the sea, the Lamb, the 144,000, the three angels, and the harvest of the earth. All of these stories are told for the comfort of the hearer/reader.

The Seven Bowls of Wrath are now poured out. This was also an extension of the Seventh Trumpet (Chapter 15-16).

Vision Three 17.1-21.8

Chapter 17 tells the story of the mystery of Babylon. Chapters 18-19 record the fall of Babylon. The marriage supper of the Lamb, the coming of Christ, the battle of Christ and the Antichrist, the binding of Satan, the Resurrection, and the millennial kingdom stories are recorded. The final destruction of Satan and death and the story of the new creation is told (Chapter 19.1-21.8).

Vision Four 21.9-22.5

In the fourth and final vision, there was an expansion of the last part of the third vision. This vision shares in more explicit detail the story about the New Jerusalem and a final word about the coming of Jesus.

Conclusion 22.6-21

Reading the StoryLine: To Be Continued...

The Story as presented in the Bible has now found its end. We now move to Act 5 Scene 7, where we presently live and move and have our being, and then on to the Final Scene and look at the question: When will it end?

Act 5: Scene 7

Imagination, Improvisation, and Stories, Final Scene. When Will It End.

In order to do so with integrity and genuine

respect for the whole story of God,

we should thoroughly impregnate ourselves

with the Story of God that has gone before.

Act 5: Scene 7. Imagination, Improvisation, and Stories, Final Scene. When Will It End?

When you finish this session you should be able to:

- ◆ Comprehend that imagination works in living in the Story
- ◆ Understand how others are living in the Story
- ◆ Begin to think of ways to improvise within the Story
- ◆ Comprehend where we are now in the Story

In this lesson, we begin with an overview of imagination Then, we look at several stories of those who are discovering how to live in the Story. Next, we look at the concept of improvisation as it relates to the Story. Then, we will compare Postmodernism and Modernity as they relate to the concept of metanarrative. Then, we look at some glimpses within the Story that point to its consummation. Finally, we point to where we are now in the Story.

Act 5 Scene 7 Imagination, Improvisation, and Stories
    Imagination: An Art and Aid to Story
    Stories of Act 5 Scene 7
        Vineyard Community Church: Shoreline, WA
        Sharon Richards: CEO of the RichardsFam
        Dave Richards: Executive
        Maureen Schuster: Nutritionist
        Diane Ellis: Real Estate Associate
        Nancy Short: School Teacher
        Church of the Savior
        Other Stories
    Improvisation: How We Live in the Story
    Postmodernism or Modernity?
Act 5 Final Scene: When Will it End?
    So, Where Are We Now?

There are millions of actors that

have gone before, some well-known

like Augustine, Luther, and Calvin...some not so

well-known like Jim, Joan, and Susan.

Act 5 Scene 7 Imagination, Improvisation, and Stories

Act 5 Scene 1-6 of God's EPIC Adventure began with Easter and Pentecost as played out in the previous section of this book. It is within Act 5 Scene 7 of God's EPIC Adventure that we *now* live. It is imperative that we act in an appropriate manner in this Act of the Story that is in direct continuity with the previous acts.[1] In order to do so with integrity and genuine respect for the whole story of God, we should thoroughly impregnate ourselves with the Story of God that has gone before. This book has sketched that Story out for you. Therefore, with the guidance of the Spirit, we need to discover ways in which our lives as communities and individuals become the agents for being God's salt and light that bring his redemption to his creation.

We need a life-long immersion in the text of Scripture[2] soaking ourselves in its thought, so that when we lay our Bibles down, we can improvise the concluding act[3] of the play in which we live by acting and speaking in an innovative way that is consistent with the Storyline of the previous Acts. The renewed people of God have new tasks to face. Cloning the past should not continue to be an option.

As God occasionally appoints us to lead or teach, we should seek to be helpers for the people of God to achieve their vocation: to be his people for the sake of the world by learning what it means to "one another" each other in community, thus, becoming the kind of people that can actually carry out our vocation.

Imagination: An Art and Aid to Story

According to the dictionary, imagination is the formation of a mental image of something that is neither perceived as real nor present to the senses. This is what Walter Brueggemann thinks that believers should experience as they read the stories of Scripture.

In his book, *The Prophetic Imagination*, he sets his thesis against the contemporary church that is largely enculturated to consumerism and is so enculturated to that ethos that it has little power to think or act.[4] He asserts, "we [the church] are all children of the royal consciousness,"[5] which I take to mean the bondage to "consumerism" he mentioned. He suggests, "we need to ask if our consciousness and imagination have been so assaulted and co-opted by the royal consciousness that we have been robbed of the courage or power to think an alternative thought,"[6] i.e., to have an imagination or what I call a *theomagination*.[7]

QUESTION
How do you think our consciousness or imagination may have been assaulted by this Present Evil Age?

Brueggeman is a great read, but as with any writer, including the present one, one must be careful of the nuances that are being used. As an example: Brueggeman sees the present postmodern situation as a positive opportunity to help the church in her interpretation of Scripture. At the same time, he places historical criticism[8] within the practice of modernity with the implication that such a practice is to be seen as a negative. We should embrace postmodernity as the context in which the church lives and interprets,[9] but not necessarily wrap our arms around everything it espouses.

The interpretation that he wants to consider is that of a post-Cartesian situation, where knowing consists not in settled certitudes, but in the actual work of imagination. By imagination he means "...the simple

human capacity to picture, portray, receive, and practice in a world in
which things are other than they appear to be at first glance when seen
through a dominant, habitual, unexamined lens." He believes that "the
whole of the human brain-mind-spirit has a capacity for imaginative
construal...."[10] He argues that Christian preaching and proclamation are
essentially an enterprise of imagining the world through the rhetoric of the
text.[11]

His goal is to "fund postmodern imagination," by which he means:

...to provide the pieces, materials, and resources out of which a new
world can be imagined...a place where people come to receive new
materials, or old materials freshly voiced, that will fund, feed,
nurture, nourish, legitimate, and authorize a counter imagination of
the world."[12]

He wonders what it would be like if"

...the clergy accepted as their modest role the voicing of scriptural
material, without excessive accommodating—that is, without
accommodation to what is politically acceptable or morally
conventional, without accommodation to political liberalism or
political reactionism, without accommodation to religious orthodoxy
or critical urbaneness, but only utter the voice of the text boldly, as
it seems to present itself, even though it does not seem to connect to
anything."[13]

I like the idea of "funding" the church with an imagination through
which she can see the recreated life presented in Scripture as her own and
begin to live out what she is imagining. What I have a problem with is
that the Story/text should not be "connected to anything." It seems fruitful
that the text/story is tied to something or it can mean anything that a
reader wants it to mean and usually does while blaming the Holy Spirit
for the resultant meaning. What if we presented the Story set richly in its
historical setting as much as we can determine such without being
dogmatic, and then let the one listening hear another world proposed, a
world that is different than the one presently being lived in so that there is
an opportunity in the telling of the Story for a life change from one story
to another?

I think he is correct when he points out that folks do not change much
because of doctrinal argument or cognitive appeal. Folks don't change
because of moral appeal. Transformation occurs when offered a new
story to live in as we disengage from an old story that we find no longer
to be credible or adequate.[14]

He comes close to N. T. Wright in his proposal that we take Story as a
drama, and that we see the text as a script for that drama, a script that is
fixed and settled but can be rendered in a variety of different ways,[15] what
Wright calls *improvisation*. The drama is the one set in Scripture from
creation through the fall to redemption and new life. Wright believes that
this is what is meant by Hans Frei, a pioneer in the development of
narrative theology[16] when he spoke of "biblical narrative."[17]

Ronald F. Thiemann says, "Scripture, I will argue, presents a
complicated but finally coherent narrative that invites the reader to
consider the world there depicted as the one true reality."[18] I think that
Thiemann is correct and that is the story that Brueggemann and Wright

want the reader/hearer of the Story to enter into and live. The entry for Brueggemann and Wright is via imagination, Brueggeman from "in front of the text" and Wright's entry is from in front of the text while reading also from "behind the text." Brueggeman points out:

Learning Objective
Comprehend that imagination works in living in the Story.

> There is no straight-line communication of data from speaker to listener. There is an open field of speech between the parties that admits to many alternative postures. This means that the listener has nearly as much freedom as the speaker in deciding what is happening. The listener is expected to work as resiliently as the teller. The communication between the two parties is a bonding around images, metaphors, and symbols that are never flattened to coercive instruction. Israel has enormous confidence in its narrative speech, sure that the images and metaphors will work their own way, will reach the listener at the point of his or her experience, and will function with a claiming authority. Such communication is shared practice of the secret which evokes imagination. It includes the listener in the secret, thus forcing the awareness of an insider. And it serves to draw a line on the other side of the listener, distancing the listener from all the outsiders who do not know the secret. That is, once the secret is known, it cannot be not known. The telling of the secret evokes imaginative work in the listener. Thus the practice of imagination moves, on the one hand, with liberation. The listener has freedom to hear and decide, and is expected to decide. On the other hand, however, the story moves with authority to claim people for the inside. The authority that moves through it is not only the authority of the teller, but also the authority of the story. Israel's imagination is liberated and liberating. That does not mean unlimited and undisciplined, as though anything goes. The imagination of Israel is circumscribed by the scope of the stories about which there is consensus. Israel has a covenant with its tongue that the evoking of imagination does not move outside this consensus. We shall see that in the other parts of Israel's canon, there is a breaking beyond this consensus. For the Torah, however, it is enough to accept the consensus and to move around in it fully. It is the consensus on which stories are based that defines the arena for free imagination.[19]

QUESTIONS
What has been your common approach to reading Scripture? From "in front of the text" or "from in front of the text while reading it also from behind the text"? What, if anything, might cause you to change your reading position?

I have quoted Brueggeman at length about imagination because he makes points of which Evangelical readers should take note. However, Wright's position on allowing for the use of history to help the story come alive is also helpful.

Act 5, Scene 7 could be many scenes stretching from the close of the Bible Story at the end of the First Century till the stories of today. There are millions of actors that have gone before, some well-known like Augustine, Luther, and Calvin, etc., some not so well-known like Jim, Joan, and Susan. While technically not part of the Story of the Bible, they are a continuation of the Story of the Bible in praxis.

Here are a few stories to help us imagine what it is like to live today in the Story of God.

Stories of Act 5 Scene 7

Vineyard Community Church Shoreline, WA

The community of storied ones in which I participate is Vineyard Community Church (VCC) in Shoreline, WA. My pastors are Rich and

Rose Swetman. Here is a feel for how story has become important to the ongoing journey of this community of faith.

Rich and Rose Swetman were asked to serve as co-pastors to Vineyard Community Church in late 1999. What they inherited was a Sunday gathering whose style was seeker sensitive, which met in Lynnwood, WA. This dynamic couple are true co-pastors, sharing all points of pastoral ministry including the Sunday teaching time. For them, they have solved the "women in ministry" and "women can't teach men" conundrum.

Over the first three years of their journey they began to understand what VCC's specific calling and purpose was. The seeker style just did not fit what they thought their community of faith should continue to participate in, where attendance at the Sunday morning gathering was the watermark of success.

Their exposure to a greater range of voices in the larger body of Christ began to give them more focus beyond Sunday morning attendance as a success marker. They began to read and hear words like: missional, for the sake of the world, spiritual growth, otherliness (a word usually restricted in theological terms to God, but now being coined to mean ministry to others), spiritual disciplines and practices, and inward and outward journey. These thoughts and words were coming from many different and credible sources within the larger Christian community. They resonated with them.

They began to reevaluate the church story they were living in and what it meant to be a community of faith. They asked questions like: What was the real reason that they existed? They began to use their imagination to think about what it would be like if they quit measuring their success by the three "Bs": buildings, budgets, and butts in their Sunday morning services. Their journey led to a new way of measuring success, which seemed much more in keeping with the biblical Story they were beginning to understand. They now measure success as a community by the three "Cs": conversations, connections, and collaborations. Modernity was being left behind in favor of a more postmodern view of their story.

They began to explore as a community of faith what it meant to be missional, as the agents being sent by God to be "a living, breathing expression of Christ"[20] in a neighborhood.

At this point in their journey, they were meeting in Lynnwood, WA, but began to actively seek God for a specific place in their neighborhood where they could serve people that were economically disadvantaged. They began with a low-income apartment community that was owned by the King County (Seattle, WA) Housing Authority. They asked if they could deliver dinners to its residents. The answer was "yes," but with one restriction. They could not tell the residents, unless asked, where the meals came from. They accepted the condition and delivered thirty-five full Thanksgiving meals to families in the apartment complex. This was the first step that began a four year relationship with that apartment community, which included Christmas parties, gifts, back to school supplies, BBQs, and housecleaning for the elderly. During this time they began to speak of themselves as an "incarnational missional community."

In April of 2004 the community of faith moved into a facility in Shoreline, WA, for the purpose of serving the city of Shoreline. They

Learning Objective
Understand how others are living in the Story.

leased a facility with the primary purpose of serving the community as well as for their Sunday gathering which is no longer seeker sensitive. It now has a much more ancient-future feel with the interactivity of worship stations set up throughout the meeting room to allow congregants to take communion, pray for those that God misses, give gifts to the poor, and pause for personal reflections.

During the first year after their move, they have built and are still working on building trusting relations with each other and the Shoreline community (conversations and connections), which includes families that live in Shoreline, and the many agencies (collaborations) who are also ministering to low-income families. Congregants serve as tutors at a low-income apartment site. Some are on special committees for back to school supplies for the 2000 plus children who live in Shoreline who are on assisted or free lunch programs.

Recently, within the framework of the community of faith, a new ministry has been started called TurningPoint which will serve as the arm to partner with the City of Shoreline to minister to the economically disadvantaged families providing education, coaching, and care.

This community has changed stories from one that preaches a modern success requirement of how big is your building, budget, and how many folks do you have in attendance on any given Sunday. They have changed to a service model: serving God, others in their community, and those in need in the community of Shoreline. This new story, a much more biblically-based model, has them on a journey to continue to discover what it means to be an incarnational missional community to serve others as they improvise by the leading of the Spirit.

The following are stories of congregants whose life stories have been changed by participating with Vineyard Community Church, Shoreline. This is the community of faith with which my family and I participate, so I have chosen to tell some of their stories.

Sharon Richards: CEO of the RichardsFam

Doable acts of ministry are unlimited when one begins to think and live with God's Story. In the community of faith with whom I participate, there are many stories of folks who have been pointed toward living in God's story and find callings in their life. One such person is Sharon Richards. Stuck on an off ramp of one of Seattle's hostile freeways, Sharon began noticing a number of men on the exits holding signs that requested help. I'm sure most of us have had such experiences. Her response was to live within the Story of God and his love for the brokenness of the world of which these men were signs and symbols. So, she drove to Costco and purchased some small bags and food and put together food bags that she would hand out to these men as she would see them on the off ramps. Next, she put a small kiosk in the foyer of the church with these small food bags for others in the community to pick up and hand out. This ministry is solely sponsored by the people who drop in money at the kiosk to replenish the bags of food. How does this happen? The pastors, Rich and Rose Swetman, generously provide an outward looking atmosphere for their congregants who are encouraged to hear God and be sent by him to minister to their neighbors. To put it simply, Sharon lives in a different Story than lots of folks in churches do. She has caught the idea that living in God's story simply means looking for opportunity to minister to the folks God loves.

QUESTION
Do you have a similar story? If so, share it with someone.

Act 5: Scene 7

Learning Objective
Understand how others are living in the Story.

Dave Richards: Executive

Dave Richards, a former executive of RealNetworks®[21] (Real) in Seattle, WA, has opened a new chapter in his ministry in the high tech world to include the world of microfinance. His energy these days is to understand how to best help those who are poor in developing countries around the globe to receive help, not in the form of contributions, but in the form of small loans.

Recently, I asked him the following question: How has your career in software high-tech prepared you to work with microfinance? Here's what he had to say.

I worked in the software industry since my college summer jobs. First, as a programmer, then, as a product manager, next, as new business development manager, then, as a manager in software development, next, as a manager in marketing/P&L software business, then, as a builder and manager of software and [internet] services business unit.

Most of my energy during my career has been figuring out how to build a scalable software product so the software business can make a profit. I discovered that one has to create significant productivity improvements into the software program that allow the end user to do things that they have previously not been able to do, for example: listen to a radio station on your PC from wherever you are in the world while all the time expanding the user base to a large number of people.

QUESTION
Do you have a similar story? If so, share it with someone.

When I joined RealNetworks®, it was a relatively small company with a few million customers using the RealPlayer audio/video software. I led the RealPlayer business to expand dramatically. Today, there are more than 350 million registered RealPlayer users around the world (and continuing at more than one million new installs per day). Today, this product is the foundation of Real's consumer business, which now represents eighty percent of their $350 million in global revenue.

Among the huge number of complex strategic and operational issues you encounter building a scalable software/technology business is the need to create a very crisp and clear plan for both the technology and how you are going to take it to market. The competition is sometimes ferocious. As an example, Microsoft® was threatened by what RealNetworks was doing and spent multiple billions of dollars to stop the RealNetworks from its development.[22]

About two years ago I learned about microfinance from my father, Dick Richards. My dad has been involved in serving on World Vision boards for the last fifteen years, first in Canada, then on the World Vision International board. In a conversation, he told me about this new grassroots movement in certain countries where World Vision was doing development projects. They were experimenting with giving out small loans to women to enable them to start or expand a microbusiness. The results were amazing! At the conclusion of his service to the World Vision board, he was asked to become the chairperson for a new World Vision microfinance fund that is called Vision Fund.[23]

Learning Objective
Understand how others are
living in the Story.

I was really intrigued with the whole idea of using the power of financial services to enable poor people in developing nations to create their own wealth. I had lots of questions which sent me on a new learning curve. Questions like: Would these poor people pay back their loans? Why charge them interest? Why not just give them these small amounts of money instead of making them repay?

I had been a supporter of WV for many years. Our family sponsored a child and helped fund other international development emergencies. I think that I had become pretty much resigned to the fact that the best I could do was help relieve a bit of pain for a few poor people in developing nations. I had very little hope for my donations helping people to actually break out of the generational cycles of poverty.

Then I started reading books on pioneers in microfinance and other people who were investigating alternative ways of thinking about economic approaches to defeating poverty. I wanted to know their stories. I found a few good books.[24] I found it very difficult to easily find resources which gave me the "whole story" on poverty along with what approaches were actually having lasting impact. As a result, I started my own blog, initially as a way to help me collect my thoughts and share with a few friends.

Through my dad's contacts, I was invited to join a five year planning session with World Vision International around the concept of microenterprise development with a focus on microfinance. This was an extremely helpful learning experience for me as I got to see the inside scoop on how microfinance was growing at an amazingly fast pace in more than twenty countries where World Vision was working.[25]

I also learned the little, unhappy secret about development organizations like World Vision, which helps poor people groups with improved water, healthcare, agriculture practices, nutrition, education, etc. It is almost impossible for them to leave an area development project, even after their self-imposed policy limit of 15 years in any one place. Why? The number one reason is that there is not enough local economic activity to continue to support the ongoing maintenance of the infrastructure/services that World Vision has built up. The local economy can't support the maintenance on the water well, pay the teachers in the schools, pay for the medicines and medical staff, to name a few. So World Vision either has to stay on or find another nongovernmental organization to take their place. No real actual economic development has taken place. This system simply sets up dependency welfare. Although well intentioned, they are not creating self-sustainable communities.

Enter microfinance. World Vision is super excited about the potential of microfinance to give them an "exit strategy" for their area development projects. They can actually hope to one day pack up and leave a project area because there will be enough economic activity for ongoing self-sustainability. World Vision can move their resources to the next community in need. Wow!

This was one of the "ah hah" moments for me. It was a road forward for development work from one of lack of hope to one of hope.

Learning Objective
Understand how others are
living in the Story.

Next in my journey into microfinance I was introduced to Unitus[26] and I found an organization (not explicitly Christian, I might add) which had a vision for microfinance which caught my interest. They had identified that the number one issue with microfinance was not whether it "worked" (in defeating poverty – that has long been established, even the stodgy UN declared 2005 the year of microcredit!), but that most poor people didn't have access to microfinance. Today only about sixteen percent of those who needed microfinance have access to it. The growth for access overall was very slow. Why? Because microfinance is primarily being driven by nongovernmental organizations based primarily on donations – public and private.

Unitus has a vision to dramatically accelerate access to microfinance to the people who can benefit from it by connecting up the multi-trillion dollar global capital markets with the microfinance banks. So, instead of a MFI (microfinancial institution) staying at serving a few hundred or a few thousand clients, a MFI could quickly scale to tens and hundreds of thousands of clients. Not only would they then become self-sustainable (a huge benefit as they can continue to operate and serve the poor indefinitely), but they would start to have a major economic impact on whole counties, states and even countries.

An extremely fast growth of an organization (and business) is a very difficult operating challenge. So, the MFIs need partners who can help them not only with raising capital, but also in scaling up their operational capacity. That's where my experience and know-how comes in handy.

Bono, lead singer for U2,[27] has said, "My generation wants to be the generation that ended extreme poverty"[28]. Muhammed Yunus,[29] founder of Grameen Bank (pioneer in microfinance), says that future generations will visit poverty museums to understand what poverty is and wonder why it took us so long to address it. I resonate with both of those visions and I see a path forward that is doable.

I am officially a member of the board of Unitus. I continue to be excited about the opportunity to serve in this role with this organization. I have made and continue to make the move from high tech to microfinance. The skills learned in one are beneficial to the other.

Why do I want to work with the extreme poor on the globe? It is part of the Story of God that I have become sensitized to over the last few years. There are all kinds of innovative ways to live with his Story. This one looks like it is going to be fun as well as a great learning experience.

Here is a story about a recent recipient of microfinance monies. Nazimunisa is forty-eight years old. She has a daughter who is eighteen and lives in Avalahalli, India. She has taken a current loan of $274 and has been a recipient of loans since 1999. With her loans she has created a tailor business and is also a clothing and vegetable shop owner. Here is her story.

Nazimunisa came from a very poor family of daily-wage laborers. Before joining Unitus's MFI partner Grameen Koota (GK), Nazimunisa worked as an incense roller, earning about 22 cents for every 1,000 sticks made; her husband ran a small food shop. When business was good, their family could meet basic needs, but when business slowed they had to pawn family jewelry to stay afloat.

Learning Objective
Understand how others are living in the Story.

Looking for ways to smooth her family's income through rough times, Nazimunisa joined GK in 1999. With her first loan of $91, she bought a sewing machine and started a successful dress-making business. After expenses, Nazimunisa used her profits of $6 to $9 per month to do maintenance on her home and pay for her daughter's education.

By 2004, Nazimunisa was in her fifth loan cycle from GK. She used her subsequent loans (ranging from $136 to $274) to invest in the family's store. They first sold clothing from their shop, but when garment prices fell, Nazimunisa and her husband reopened the store as a vegetable stand. With subsequent loans from GK, they added a new roof to protect their produce during the rainy season and bought a refrigerator so they could sell high-profit perishable goods.

With the help of GK's microfinance services, it took less than one generation for Nazimunisa and her family to lift themselves out of poverty. In the past six years, Nazimunisa has started three successful businesses, and her family's income is comfortable and sustainable. She and her husband hope to open an even larger store and build a new house with their future loans from GK. Nazimunisa also hopes for her daughter to complete school and go to college.[30]

Maureen Schuster: Nutritionist

Maureen is a nutritionist at a hospital in Everett, WA, as well as a house mom and a leader in an international ministry.

Early in the evening of a fall day in 2001, she discovered an important purpose for her life. Without any warning, the story she lived in was about to change. She was attending a mid-week Bible study as good Evangelicals do. At the end of the study, the leader closed with a Lectio Divina scripture meditation. The facilitator read a passage and instructed the participants to insert their own name in the reading. So instead of "I Paul," it was "I Maureen," am called to, then she was to fill in the blank. As she meditated, she clearly heard the following, "I Maureen, am called to the *widow, the orphan, and the unloved.*" She began to weep. It seemed to be so real.

As she drove home, she processed her experience, and then shared it with her husband when she arrived home. Together, they agreed that this idea did not seem far-fetched because they had adopted their two children from Guatemala. Within a week, a friend called her and wanted to introduce her to a nurse practitioner who was planning to take a medical team to Guatemala. The nurse practitioner would be working in a small village with a local doctor along with his wife. She did not know about Maureen's meditation experience at her Bible Study. She thought that she might be interested, since her two children had been adopted from Guatemala and because she worked two days a week as a nutritionist for a local hospital.

QUESTION
Do you have a similar story? If so, share it with someone.

Learning Objective
Understand how others are living in the Story.

She told her friend that she couldn't go on such a trip because of her duties as a wife, mother, and worker outside the home. Her friend persisted by calling her often over the next few days. She finally asked for some information about the medical couple who was going to be working with the medical team. She specifically wanted to know what their passion was that would drive them to go to Guatemala. When she called Maureen back about a week later, she heard the following, "their heart was for *the widow, the orphan, and the unloved.*"

As she shared this story with me, she told me that she got goose bumps all over her body and knew instantly that she was going to Guatemala. That trip caused a story change in her life. She had discovered what she was made to do in the larger Story of God.

When she returned to USAmerica, she helped form a non-profit organization called *Hands of Love*. Today, she spends part of her time fund-raising for the needs of widows and orphans. *Hands of Love* has raised money to build a well that provides water for 400 families, money for the poor to buy goats, and recently finished building a medical and dental clinic for an impoverished village. In addition, she sets up teams to go to minister to poor villages.

Once living in a story which was wife, mom, and worker outside the home, which certainly is a worthy calling, she now finds additional meaning by having her story broadened to include working for the sake of others thousands of miles from the comfort of her home in the state of Washington in USAmerica.

Diane Ellis: Real Estate Associate

Diane is a native of Seattle, WA, and knows the distinctive neighborhoods and the unique small towns and communities that make up the greater Seattle area. She graduated from the University of Washington in pre-law and also has an Associates of Arts degree in interior design.

Diane grew up in a marginally religious Episcopalian home where she attended church on Sundays and lived her life disconnected from the church during the rest of the week. She admits that she never saw any connection nor relevance between what she did on Sunday morning in the church and the rest of her life. She never learned much from the church about the Story of the Bible and knew practically nothing about Jesus except as a swear word. She could not conceive of a living Christ or having a relationship with God. She eventually left the church scene rejecting the whole concept of organized religion. She saw too much hypocrisy and very little authenticity.

QUESTION
Do you have a similar story? If so, share it with someone.

As she has reflected back over her life, she has seen how many places God and her life intersected even though she was not aware of it at the moment of intersection. She has always had an ability to read people and situations which she calls a strong sense of intuition. She told me that she had often been accused of knowing more about people than they knew about themselves, which was a bit scary for her at times. Because it was uncomfortable, she spent many years trying to squash this ability.

She has lately realized that God was continually trying to thrust her into a different story by delivering her from many risky and questionable situations, and just in the nick of time at that.

Learning Objective
Understand how others are
living in the Story.

She recalled to me one specific incident when she was about twenty years old. She, a practicing agnostic, and her college roommate, a practicing Jew, were working on a college philosophy assignment. They were to define and describe their philosophy of life, i.e., what story they were living in. Early in the morning after hours and hours of debate, they felt they had arrived at a theory that would unlock the secret of their life.

The theory fit them well. They sensed they had discovered something significant, the key to life as it was really meant to be. The moment was so profound that this discovery scared them. They called it "the River of Life" theory. As she learned later, there were some uncanny similarities between their theory and the way living in God's Story works, but there were also some obvious and notable differences. Only later did she begin to understand the metaphor of a *river of life* at the conclusion of the Story in Revelation. It was another piece of her story puzzle that was there, but she didn't know where it fit.

Diane married into a large Catholic family which, for her, served as another reminder of the hypocrisy in the church. She knew that there was no room for her in a flock that housed such people. Her focus turned to her marriage and kids and she lived what appeared to be a successful life for the next twenty-five years.

Her storied life came crashing down on her as a series of catastrophies of epic proportions began to take place in her life. Her life story of a *river of life* was taking a pounding. She was no longer able to use her philosophical story to alter what was going on in her world. When her life blew, her *river of life* story didn't hold water: it wasn't enough.

Little did she know that she was about to enter a new story, but first she had to sift through all the stories that she was offered into which to place her life. She looked into eastern philosophies, marginal religions, new age, charkas, energy healings, and on and on. Christianity was not even in her field of vision as she made her search. She was looking for something that would stand the test of time, something that made sense to her shattered world.

She was unknowingly being led to live in a different story, one that she now believes God had always intended for her to live in. She began to realize that God was orchestrating people, events, and leading her down a path toward living in this new way.

In her business venture as a Real Estate Associate, Diane met Leigh Buchan, another Associate in her office. She saw her life was different. There was a glowing calm in troubled times. She wanted to know her story, so she began to ask intense and constant questions. A conversation developed. All of the stories she had tried for life had not passed muster. She would not afford herself another catastrophic event to happen to her. Whatever Leigh's story was, it had to be real and authentic if she was going to embrace it.

Late one evening while she was questioning Leigh about the reality of the Jesus Story, she told me that she was so profoundly touched by God that she could no longer question his existence. She heard God speak to her telling her that he was real and that she could trust him. This was the first of several power encounters that she had as God was drawing her into his Story.

For years even though she had a *river of life* story that kept her life moving forward, Diane had thousands of pieces of a puzzle strewed all over her board of life without knowing how the pieces fit together. But as she began to commit herself to God's Story, she began to see how those pieces formed a new story for her life. As the pieces being put together caused her to see this new story clearer and clearer, she rediscovered her squashed intuition and began to understand God's purpose for its use in her new story.

She has become deeply involved in her community of faith. Her involvement with Global Support *with a mission*[31] fits her like hand and glove. The home group that she leads is a live adventure in learning how to live out this new story of life focused on others in the world. Recently, several of the home group members were baptized as they took a step in their own journey in their story.

Diane loves to give titles to her place in God's story by placing the moments of her life into their own time periods, which helps her focus on the story she's living in. She calls this momentology. From the "Reluctant Christian goes Public" to "Crawling with Other Babies" to "Learning to be a Disciple," she moves forward in this new story as she presses forward toward the calling and ministry of her life.

To equip her she recently took a year training through VCC that took her through the Bible three times, once looking at the background of the Old and New Testament Story, the concepts that are useful to help her understand the contents of the Story, and finally a primer on Old and New Testament theology.

Nancy Short: School Teacher

Nancy Short has been teaching school for over thirty years in the greater Seattle area. I met her several years ago when I was teaching a lay study on the Old Testament. She serves the VCC community of faith by helping the kids in the community understand how to think about living in God's Story.

Nancy believes that kids really matter to God, just as much as adults do, which has led her to also believe that Christian kids should be shown how to live in a different story than their counterparts who are not Christian.

Part of her desire to storize kids is fueled by a quote from the forward of a book by Sue Miller called *Making Your Children's Ministry The Best Hour of Every Kid's Week*.[32] In the forward by George Barna he says, "Did you know that the ideas driving people's behavior are generally acquired and adopted before a person reaches the age of thirteen? Were you aware that the religious beliefs a person develops by the age of thirteen are pretty much the set of beliefs they will maintain until they die? Further, we found that people's major spiritual choices are generally made when they are young, again underscoring the importance of focusing on the development of children."

These words weigh heavy on her and she wants to impact kids so they can impact their communities, neighborhood friends, classmates at school, soccer team members, or their own extended family members. With all this rolling around in her head, Nancy formed a mission statement for the kid's ministry at VCC which reads, *We help kids think, so they can be God's people, reflecting His character, and furthering His purposes.*

She has discovered that finding a suitable curriculum to fit what the mission and values are, became an impossible task. Some materials were great at building character, while others did a good job teaching the Bible. But most used a thematic approach which does not fit the way she wants to train these kids. What was her solution? While taking a year's training from me stressing the value of story, she has continued writing her own curriculum. It's a work in progress. She readily admits that her hopes from the project are greater than her time resources, but she moves along. She is currently seeking an artist to illustrate her vision of a storied Bible for kids; not, she would say, like the story Bibles that are presently available. She rather wants to paint the story on the walls of the classrooms so the kids always know where they are in learning the Story.

Learning Objective
Begin to think of ways to improvise within the Story.

In addition to this focus, she also wants to incorporate meaningful spiritual practices that kids can understand and practice. She has taught the kids to practice the ancient form of Lectio Divina. She encourages them to notice God in their everyday lives as they live in his Story. What is done in the classroom setting on Sunday with kids is breaking out into their lives during the week.

On one Sunday, she told a child that Jesus wanted to have a relationship with him and help him live out the Story of God in his life. He believed her. During the week he and his mom were lying on their couch when the lad asked his mom if she could see Jesus. Somewhat startled, she responded, "No." Then she asked her son what he was seeing. He told her that Jesus was in the room standing by the sliding glass door. Sure, there are ways to interpret this happening. But, isn't it really possible that this could have happened? It surely did in the Story in Scripture. What would be different now? She tells a story about a kid who had a dream from God and another kid in the room who interprets the dream. Sounds somewhat like Joseph, huh? She tells of kids who stand up for their classmates in school when being bullied by others, or comforting them during stressful incidents that happen in their lives. Kids seem to get living in his Story easier than adults.

QUESTION
Do you have a similar story? If so, share it with someone.

The curriculum that Nancy is creating is called *The Bible Eras*. When she first began writing it, she wanted to get her kids through the curriculum in a year. After considering the scope of the project, she has changed her mind. The first emphasis in the curriculum is to tell the stories in the Bible, not with a moral attached to it, but with a basic way of thinking about interpreting each story that a kid can grasp. She wants the kids to grasp the meaning of the Story the same way the first hearers of the Story grasped it.

She uses materials that she creates for the kids during the story telling. On 4½ by 5½ cards there are pictures that relate the events in a Bible story. On the back of the card is a short paragraph with a title. Each card has a different part of the story. The kids lay out the cards and tell the story to each other. As an example of how this works, in the Judges Era, the first lesson shows the Israelites worshiping the Canaanite idols on the cards. The paragraph talks about their actions and how God reacts to their idol worship. By telling the story, the kids learn what these stories say about God and his relationship with people.

On a weekly basis, the kids are told that they are God's people and the stories they tell each other from the Bible are stories that they live during the week.

Act 5: Scene 7

Learning Objective
Begin to think of ways to improvise within the Story.

She also does interactive stuff in the telling of the stories. Again, in the Judges Era, she asked each kid to tell a story about how they had received consequences from their parents for something they had wrongly done. While telling the story, they turned their backs on the rest of the class and then turned to face the class when they tell how the relationship was resolved with their parents. Sometimes they turned away from their classmates more than once in a story, mimicking the cycles found in the stories of the book of Judges. This interactivity makes it easier for the kids to understand the same cycles in their own lives. She has conversations with them about how to face their parents instead of turning their backs on them, because of their need for relationship.

Story has become the driving force behind her passion to pass on these stories, while fitting them into the larger Story of God so the kids can live well in God's Story.

Church of the Savior

Several years ago my wife Donna and I took a trip to Washington D.C. to visit Church of the Savior, founded by Gordon Cosby in 1947 which has become an ecumenical church. We hung out with them for three days learning what they thought a missional church was like. They have hundreds of stories of average folks who have been released to do remarkable things. The one that I tell over and over again is the story of Killian Noe and David Erickson. In 1985, Killian and David, who did not know each other, were attending the morning service of Church of the Savior. On that particular Sunday, Gordon was sharing a story about how many homeless people there were in the D.C. area. By the Spirit, Killian and David imagined what it would be like to serve all those folks that Gordon was talking about. Each of them separately responded to Gordon after the service, wanting to know how they could get involved with the church's ministry to the poor in D.C. They were each informed that Church of the Savior did not have a ministry to the poor in D.C. Though there was no "poor ministry," Gordon introduced Killian and David to each other and suggested to them that they get together and talk about how a ministry to the poor would look. Ministering to the poor was certainly within the Story of God. So they met and together, led by the Spirit with a sense of passion and call, were sent out by Church of the Savior to the homeless, and Samaritan Inns was born. These are two ordinary folks who were called and sent by God to live in his Story in their own neighborhood. The Samaritan Inns ministries continue to provide healing and hope to homeless and addicted men and women.

Other Stories

Years ago, there was a TV program called "The Naked City" in which stories of New York city were told. Each story ended with "There are eight million stories in the naked city. This has been one of them." In the continuing line of stories there are millions, I am sure. I have only told a few of them. Here are some additional short ones. Jim Henderson, co-founder of Off The Map,[33] friend and pioneer, has said that evangelism has too high of a bar to get over for ordinary people to get involved. Jim was tired of living on the map. Maps, by the way, are for people to have, to show places where someone has already been. To be *off the map* is to be living where others may not have been yet by imagining what another way of sharing the good news of the Kingdom could be like. So, in his own words, he says, "I have buried the bar so deep that you can't even find it with a metal detector." He believes that "ordinary Christians" should be participating in "doable" evangelism and has written a book to that focus called, *a.k.a 'LOST:' Discovering Ways to Connect With The People That Jesus Misses Most.*[34] He asked questions like: What If you didn't have to make a speech in order to "witness?" What if you could use everyday experiences to nudge others closer to Jesus? What if the things you are already doing counted as evangelism? Making connections is important to make conversation. What if every "ordinary" Christian lived out this part of the Story in his or her life? Jim has chosen to live in a different story of evangelism.

Learning Objective
Comprehend that there is only one God to serve.

Spenser Burke lived in the American church story for years. He was a pastor at Mariners Church in Irvine, CA, which is a bona-fide mega church with assets of an almost eight million dollar annual budget and twenty-five acres of prime real estate in Southern California. He was daily dealing with great people, great programs, and receiving great pay. But he discovered that he was not a modern evangelical pastor. He had given up on things like a parking lot ministry, three point sermons, the latest steps to evangelism. So in 1998, Spenser started THE**OOZE**,[35] an online conversation about the cultural shift and how followers of Jesus may respond. He was just a guy in his garage with a computer and a new way of imagining the Story.

Years ago, Bill Gates' daring dream was for every desktop to have a personal computer. My dream is to help every follower of Jesus to understand God's Story and begin to live in it. What if every Christian lived out of God's EPIC Adventure instead of other stories in which they may be currently living? How would that change the world in which we live?

Improvisation: How We Live in the Story

As actors in Act 5, Scene 7, we are to improvise as we move forward toward the consummation of the Kingdom. The concept of improvisation is often misunderstood. Improvisation insists that the actors discover their lines and actions by following a general theme and format, in this case the storyline of God's EPIC Adventure. Sometimes improvisation can mean acting spontaneously, but the spontaneity comes within the framework of a structured part. As an example, as an actor you are called on to play a part in a drama which has a scene where someone close to you has just died. How you say your lines within the framework of the larger play is up to you. You improvise the manner in which you speak, emote, and move your body. You may have several takes at doing this same scene and each scene comes out a bit differently because of the response of those in the scene with you. Improvisation does not mean that anything goes. It does not mean that you can change the script and begin reading from another script from another play.

QUESTION
How does improvisation strike you as a way of living in the Story over against fragmented principles that must be applied to your life?

Improvisations can help an actor focus on his or her concentration. As one practices improvisation, she or he must keep their concentration on what is occurring in the scene being performed. "Concentration is a staple of acting classes and workshops."[36] Our responsibility as actors and actresses in God's EPIC Adventure is to "discover, through the help of the Holy Spirit and prayer, the appropriate ways of improvising the script,"[37] in our act of the drama. Using a musical metaphor, N. T. Wright suggests, "No Christian, no church, is free to play out of tune."

He also suggests:

Learning Objective
Comprehend where we are
now in the Story.

...no musician would ever suppose that improvising means playing out of tune or time. On the contrary, it means knowing extremely well where one is in the implicit structure, and listening intently to the other players so that what we all do together, however spontaneously, makes sense as a whole.[38]

With a theatre metaphor he suggests, "...all actors, and all the travelling companies of which they are part (i.e., different churches) are free to improvise their own fresh scenes. No single actor, no company, is free to improvise scenes from another play, or one with a different ending."[39] The fifth Act, Scenes 1-6, then, "remain the standard by which the various improvisations of subsequent scenes are to be judged."[40]

How does all this work, you may ask? Let's take the example of Dave Richards (above). Certainly in the previous Acts of the Story, we are provided with insights about caring for the poor. But, we live in the fifth act. We are not to pick up a previous plan acted out in a previous act and plop it down in our present act. Rather, we are free to improvise how we are to carry out the mandate of caring for the poor. We are free to discover or create new ways of caring for the poor as with the microfinance story. This is not the application of a principle in some exact fashion which comes from a belief system that there is a principle, a proposition, and the application of it fits all occasions. Improvising is an art that the church and individuals must discover and in which they must begin to participate.

Postmodernism or Modernity?

Postmodernism has given us an opportunity to investigate long held views of how we deal with Scripture, but it is not our new home, a place where we make our bed. Part of the task of the church today is to "pioneer a way through postmodernity and out the other side, not back into modernity in its various, even in its Christian guises, but in a new world, a new culture, which nobody else is shaping and which we have a chance to."[41]

QUESTION
How would you describe
your journey in the areas of
self, knowledge, and Story?

We have the opportunity in our Act to put to rights the idea of the all important prideful, self-reliant, knowable, and affirming self. Postmodernity has deconstructed the individual into a "non knowing" place but where "I" is still very important. The last bastion of Descartes seems to have turned out to be a kaleidoscopic mirage. In our Act, God's EPIC Adventure provides for us a vision of becoming a new humanity to replace the Modern Assured Self and the Postmodern Un-assured Self. Truly, if we are in Christ, we are a new creation.

We also have the opportunity to re-image *knowing*. Modernity believed it could know objectively, beyond a shadow of a doubt. Postmodernity showed "objective knowing" as a power play used to control. We are known by what we do.

A final concept is the idea of the great metanarrative. Modernity's metanarrative was that we could progress in our enlightened world. Postmodernity believes that metanarrative is a power play to control other stories. As followers of Jesus, we have a grand metanarrative. We have called it God's EPIC Adventure. It's founder and maker is God who has successfully shown us a new way through the wilderness of our own exile with Jesus and continues to move us forward in the power and presence of the Holy Spirit. This metanarrative also wishes to control. We should allow it to do so for the sake of the world.

So What?

Our task in our Act and Scene is to use *theomagination*, seeing a picture of reality from God's Story that is different from our own present reality and improvising within the guidelines of the overall Story as we move our scene forward toward the consummation of the Kingdom.

Act 5 Final Scene: When Will it End?

We close this book on God's EPIC Adventure with a glance at some of the glimpses of the Last Scene of this drama.

Over the last century, much ink has been spilt in writings, many words have been spoken and recorded, many feet of film have been dedicated to, and many digital 0s and 1s have been created on the topic of the end of time. Despite the consistent writing about *when* the end is going to happen, there are no real hints about *when* in the text of Scripture. However, the text is not completely quiet about the end. We have information from the Olivet Discourse (Matthew, Mark), from Paul in 1 and 2 Thessalonians, from Peter in 2 Peter, and from John in Revelation about the consummation of the Kingdom.

In the last century and continuing into this century, the words "second coming" and to some extent "eschatology" call to mind the term "rapture" because of much of the popularized teaching in this area. Rapture is very embedded into the evangelical and fundamentalist Christian mindset. In USAmerica the *Left Behind* series of books and its brand of theology has further influenced the readers of Scripture to a somewhat mistaken understanding of the end of the Story.

Israel, in this misguided way of thinking about the end of time, is the focal point. It may "actually be deeply un-Jewish, collapsing into a dualism in which the present wicked world is left to stew in its own juice while the saints are snatched up into heaven to watch Armageddon from a ring side seat."[42]

The central text for this rather recent theological insight is 1 Thessalonians 4.16-17. What we discover in Paul is rather different than the popular writers of the day would lead us to believe. Paul shares four important glimpses about the last scene of God's EPIC Adventure. *First*, he speaks of the "Day of the Lord" in 1 Thessalonians (1 Thess. 5.2) and in his follow-up letter to the Thessalonians (2 Thess. 2.2). Contrary to favorite beliefs about this phrase, which is thought to be a metaphor for the time that Jesus will return to earth for the purpose of redeeming the faithful and condemning unbelievers to eternal damnation, it may not mean that at all. It may simply mean a moment of judgment that causes everything to become different. For Paul, could this have been the beginning convulsions of the death of the Roman Empire during the "Year of the Four Emperors" and the destruction of the Temple in Jerusalem (A.D. 70)?[43] Surely there could be many "Days of the Lord" as we live between the times in our own Act.

The *second* concept is *parousia*, which pictures the coming of an earthly king to visit a city within his own kingdom. The king *appears* or is *present* (*parousia*) as opposed to being absent. The word seems to carry the idea of *appearance* rather than returning from a far place. The picture

Act 5: Final Scene

more suitable to the term is "like drawing back a previously unnoticed curtain to reveal what had been there all along." Yes, the appearance of Jesus will be earthshaking, but not necessarily in the way it is "often envisaged in popular presentations."[44]

At the end, we don't go to heaven, rather heaven and earth come to us, i.e., the world as we know it will be transformed. The colonial outpost of "recreation" where we have lived will become the "new heaven and earth." The appearing of Jesus will change the old world to a new one and the old body to a new one.

The *third* concept of Paul is judgment. "Works" for Paul was never something one did to win the favor of God, but was what was done by the followers of Jesus as they focused on their vocation of being new humanity for the sake of the world. The coming judgment will be "in accordance with the entirety of the life that has been led."[45]

The final concept for Paul as he glimpses into the consummation of the Kingdom is that of the renewal of everything. He envisions a world that will be "set free from bondage and decay." Paul's perspective on the end is distant from current popular concepts of the end. Since one can't know when the end is going to be, the words of Jesus recorded in Mark are useful for us, who are living in the present Act, to remember. He said, "Watch," and by that he meant to be prepared. Surely preparation, that is living in his Story, is to include looking outward from ourselves into a needy world and finding our part to play in its recreation.

So Where Are We Now?

Brian McLaren has provided a beginning answer to this question in his book: *The Story We Find Ourselves In*. The title in itself suggests that we live in a story. Living in a story surely goes "beyond the reigning systematic theologies that took shape in the modern world (from, say, 1500 to 1950)—to answer questions and to suit modern tastes."[48] The concept captured in his title encourages a new way of thinking about life and "probably would be less analytical in structure and more rooted in the biblical narrative, less about filling the subpoints of an outline...and more about finding and celebrating meaning from our story."[49] McLaren goes on to tell us:

> ...our whole planet now needs more than ever a good story to live in and to live by. There are a number of stories competing for the hearts and imaginations of humanity as we emerge together into this new century and millennium: the regressive stories of fundamentalist Islam and fundamentalist Christianity, or the progressive stories of secular "scientism" or American consumerism, for example. Once taken to the heart of human culture, each of these stories will produce its own kind of world.[50]

McLaren suggests that if the story that he tells in his book, or another story like it, can get a hearing, a different kind of world can come into being. "The story we believe and live in today has a lot to do with the world we create for our children, our grandchildren, and our descendents one hundred thousand years from now (if?)."[51] We desperately need to discover "a larger story in which the stories of [our] lives can be located.[52]

Learning Objective
Comprehend where we are
now in the Story.

So where are we now? We all live in a story, but which story do we find ourselves in?

As followers of Christ, we should realize that we live in God's EPIC Adventure which is still unfinished. Remember, the first Act was Creation. We don't reside there. God accomplished that in the first Act. However, our present existence is being played out on the stage of his Creation and what he provided for us in the original creation gives us the ability and raw material to continue to create.

Rebellion was the act of humankind in Act 2. We don't live there either, but we do live with the results of that Act. While not living in the Act itself, we may find ourselves from time to time resorting to participating in choosing independence for ourselves over interdependence with God and others, thus producing a world of independence in which we live.

The story of Israel formed Act 3. We don't live there either, although, we may be influenced by how God acted on behalf of his children in that act. His faithfulness to the first Covenant was surely as steadfast as his faithfulness to the second Covenant. Western Christianity has often ignored the whole Story of the Old Testament, opting out for favorite stories within it instead. We may have become the Marcion[46] of our own Act, rejecting Act 3 in favor of Acts 4 and 5.

Act 4 is the great and decisive Act of Jesus. As much fun as it might have been, or maybe not so much fun on occasion, we do not don our sandals and shadow Jesus as he walked the dusty roads of Palestine during his earthly life. However, it should be pointed out that the continuation of the Spirit within the life of the church in its own Act has found her participating in many of the "works" that Jesus did. This was certainly the experience of the earliest version of the church as her story was told by Luke in the book of Acts. We are surely called to act upon that Act in our own Act.

We now return to our opening thought of this Act and Scene. *Act 5 of God's EPIC Adventure began with Easter and Pentecost as played out in this book in the previous section.* Our present time is characterized by two ideas: *First*, our present Act and Scene is based on all that has gone before in this Story beginning with Creation. *Second*, we are to improvise our way forward in our part of the drama as God's agents in forging ahead, creating a better world for the sake of the world.

QUESTION
Do you know what your part
in God's EPIC Adventure is?

So What?

Passages, such as the Paul's Thessalonians text or Mark's chapter 13,[47] contrary to popular books that declare from them a specific pattern of the end, are only glimpses of the end. What held true for the disciples holds true for us today in our Act of the play. The signs of the times, as they are often called, tell us that Jesus has not yet appeared to bring about the consummation of the Kingdom.

What should one learn about the end time? To be content with not knowing, as Jesus rightly and wisely said, "But about that day or hour no one knows, not even the angels in heaven, nor the Son, but only the Father." (Mark 13.32). And, to be content with knowing, as the glimpses consistently conclude that we should be *watching*,

Act 5: Final Scene

Learning Objective
Comprehend where we are now in the Story.

Dictionary Articles
Read the following Dictionary Articles in *New Bible Dictionary*, Third Edition. D. R. W. Wood, A. R. Millard, J. I. Packer, D. J. Wiseman, and I. Howard Marshall (Editors), InterVarsity Press. 1996.
  Day of the Lord
  Eschatology

encouraging one another, and *hoping* in the midst of difficult life situations. These are the watch words of living in God's EPIC Adventure

The Story of Scripture levels the playing field and makes us all part of God's ongoing drama to redeem his whole creation. Remember, this metanarrative also wishes to control our lives, but to do so with the love of the Creator, Jesus, and the Spirit. May it control us as we live in it for the sake of the world.

While God's EPIC Adventure is not yet over, it seems fitting to close the book, God's EPIC Adventure, with the prayer of Paul in First Corinthians, "Maranatha," as translated by *The Message*: "Make room for the Master!"

Epilogue

An epilogue is a literary device that is often found at the end of a piece of literature.
It generally covers the story of how the book came into being,
or how the idea for the book was developed.

...read the Story of God as a story

and not as a fissiparous reading of the text

which seems to be the habit

of so many followers of Christ.

Epilogue

When I started work on this project, I had a vision of its appearance as a book. What I didn't realize was how massive the project was going to become. Small thoughts can sometimes turn into large results. God's EPIC Adventure, as a project, began its seeding process when I read Tom Wight's book, *The New Testament and the People of God*. When I saw his reference to a five-act-play as a way of thinking about Scripture, the light, so to speak, went on. Little did I know how big the bulb was going to become.

I have been teaching Old and New Testament material since the first church I pastored way back in the '70s of the last century. Wow, that makes me sound really old! I had a small class of students from the congregants who had an interest to see a larger view of the text they brought to church every Sunday. From that little experience, my appetite was whetted to offer those who sit Sunday after Sunday and hear topical sermons *ad nauseum* a bigger picture of Scripture in which they could place all those pieces they had gathered over a lifetime.

This passion next grew into two weekend seminars which I entitled "Seeing the Old Testament Live" and "Seeing the New Testament Live." The name represented my desire to have the Bible lived out in the lives of those who might experience the seminar. The material began its growth. Following this season, I went to work for John Wimber and Vineyard Ministries International, where I created a lay training institute to teach perspective pastors the Bible. The material continued to grow. During that time, I finished my first Doctor of Ministry degree and wrote a dissertation called "A Layman's Guide to the Old Testament." I taught this material to hundreds of burgeoning pastors over the years, refining the material as I went. Then, several years ago I entered a second Doctor of Ministry degree program at George Fox University and wrote for my dissertation, what now has become this book: *God's EPIC Adventure*. Len Sweet and my coursemates had a profound influence on me during this educational quest. Len's acrostic for EPIC became embedded into the idea of the book. Of course, if it doesn't work therein, it's my failure, not Len's.

As you might have comprehended from the book, there are several ideas that I wanted to focus on. One is the need to read the Story of God as a story and not as a fissiparous reading of the text which seems to be the habit of so many followers of Christ. It seems to me that there is a possibility that fragmented reading produces a fragmented story in which we live. Another focus is what one does with the Story of God. In the past with the influence of modernity, we have sliced and diced the text and then in the height of its reductionism, we have offered little morsels to be "applied" to our life.

When I was a child, my mom, along with other ladies, used to take fragments of cloth and sew them into quilts. The end result was often pleasing, because the quilt was not just a sum of its fragments but a whole new creation. This seems to work for cloth. But, it seems to me that this is not the purpose of God when he designed Scripture for those who would choose to follow him in the recreation of his universe. But, we, at least for the last 300 years, have persisted in producing "quilted" Christians, or, with another metaphor, a theological mutt. I wondered what it would be like if the followers of Christ were no longer tossed to and fro by every conceivable formation of a story of quilted fragments but became pedigreed by their creator as they learned his Story and how they might discover their part to play in it.

So, the thought of application, a usual one-size-fits-all approach to living out the precepts of Scripture, doesn't seem to be the better of the two approaches. I wondered, what if there was a book that began the process of helping the followers of Christ learn the "whole" story and offered them a way of thinking about the Story that allowed them to actually find wholeness in their lives as the new humanity of the Creator. The result is *God's EPIC Adventure*. Its success won't be known for a period of time. But, I trust that its message finds its way into the lives of many Christ-followers and for the sake of God's world, they play out their part with dignity.

If the story could be told in a really short version, it could sound like this:

Why is the concept of Story important? Because Story is the design God picked to call us to our vocation of partnering with him in the redemption of his creation. Scripture provides God's Story of creation and re-creation. It is within that Story we look to discover how to improvise as we become "truly human" as God intended his human creation to be. We seek to live within the Story that understands the Triune God as Creator and Ruler of all things.

God is the great playwright and he has given us a play for the ages. The drama begins in Act 1 of his play in the Genesis account of creation, "there was a time when God spoke all things into existence." He created humankind and gave them free run of the most beautiful garden, which was his created world. But, in Act 2, as the crown of the Creator's creation, humankind made a decision to worship what God had created rather than worshiping the Creator. What God had created perfect, humankind had flawed and the true humanity of the Garden became distorted and their view of God became dimly lit. The missionary God sought his created beings out and banned them from his Garden.

Act 3 continues the story, which is the content of the rest of the Old Testament, by God's creation of a people whose vocation would be to become the "light of the world" so the pagan societies in which she lived could see what God was really like. Israel's creation came with four great acts of God. He first delivered/redeemed them from their bondage in Egypt in the great act of the Exodus. He took a group of slaves from the slave market of the day and freed them. The next great act of God for his people was the giving of a national charter, a Covenant, so that they would know what it was like to live out their vocation as the people of God. Next, he made them into a kingdom where there vocation moved from nation to individual, which looked forward to a day in which a new kingdom with a truly human being would inaugurate God's Kingdom here on earth. In the last scenes of Act 3, we find Israel in Exile and a short return from Exile. She had all but lost her vocation of being God's "light to the world." In the physical return from Exile, spiritual return did not occur. The Temple rebuilt did not return to its former glory which produced a conception of life that they were continually living in exile waiting for the one promised by the prophets who would bring them their freedom.

Act 4 tells the story of Jesus who stepped into human history, in the fullness of time. In his ministry, he came proclaiming that the Kingdom of God was present in this Present Evil Age. A truly human being, as humans were intended to be, had arrived as God honored his promises to this people. Four different writers tell us four different stories about the events of the life of Jesus. His message: "Repent and Believe!" The first hearers heard him say in this message that they should stop living in their present stories of military means, quietism, or their compromising ways with the present powers and begin living in a different story. He demonstrated for his followers, then and now, in his words what an authentic disciple should be like and demonstrated in his works of healing the sick, casting out demons, and raising the dead what actions his authentic disciples should follow.

Moving into the final act of God's EPIC Adventure (Act 5, Scene 1-6), we find the creation of the church by the Spirit as God's new humanity. Like Israel before her, this new community of the Spirit was and is to be the light to the world by the releasing of gracelets given by the Spirit to help followers of Christ accomplish his mission.

We, as Christ-followers, now live in the scene between the sixth scene of the early church and the final scene yet to be written. Out mission is to discover our part in God's EPIC Adventure and imagine and improvise how we live our part out for his sake, our sake, and the sake of the world. There are some clues about how this grand narrative is going to end, but they are only clues. We are truly God's new humanity, living as followers of Christ, empowered by the Holy Spirit to be effective agents of the Kingdom in this Present Evil Age.

Someone has said that "all good things must come to and end" and someday this Story that we are living in will truly do that very thing. But, until then, may our part in God's EPIC Adventure be thrilling and humbling, mysterious and understandable, and may the beauty of the Trinity be found in our every thought and action.

Out mission is to discover our part

in God's EPIC Adventure and imagine and

improvise how we live our part out for his sake, our

sake, and the sake of the world.

Afterword by Brian McLaren

A short addition or concluding section at the end of a literary work.

"There is so much more to say and do

in helping people get the shape

and meaning of the Biblical narrative."

(Brian McLaren: Afterword)

Afterword

When I was in my late teen years, having just gotten serious about my faith, I wanted to learn the Bible. I had grown up in church, so I knew the Bible in a way - from sermons and Sunday school. But that usually meant knowing points (our preachers were big on alliteration – the Five G's of Revelation 11, the Three P's of Philippians 2, or morals (the story of Samson teaches us not to cut our hair ... or, errr ... not to date girls like Delilah).

I had the feeling that I was missing something; I wanted to get the Biblical story itself, the plotline, if you will, the big picture.

Then I discovered Bible Handbooks, and they helped. I especially liked it when they had timelines of the kings, or when they showed a bookshelf with the books of the Bible in their chronological order. Sometimes they'd give a few paragraphs of historical background so I could relate, say, the story of Moses to what I had learned in school about Egypt under the Pharoahs. And they would often provide an overview of a whole book and maybe even an outline.

What I didn't realize was that each of these handbooks wasn't simply teaching the Bible – it was teaching "the Bible as read by Dispensationalists" or "the Bible as read by Five-Point Calvinists" or "The Bible as read by Charismatics."

What I wished for back then I never really got: an overview of the Bible as a story, not pre-digested or trimmed and stretched to fit nicely into an existing theological system.

I was in my late twenties and a pastor before I decided it was time to fill the gap. I announced to our little church that I was going to teach a one-day seminar called "The Whole Bible in Five Hours" or something like that. I did a lot of research to prepare and I remember feeling, "Why didn't somebody present something like this for me back when I was just learning the Bible? It would have been so much easier if I had started with the big picture."

Of course, I wasn't able to teach that overview of the Bible free of assumptions, giving the Biblical story to the class in pristine objectivity. I brought to the class my perspective, my assumptions, my biases and blind spots. But I remember feeling that whether or not anybody else learned something, that experience had done something for me that I would never lose: it helped me see the big plot line.

Later, when I became an author, I wrote my own attempt to convey the Biblical story in book form: *The Story We Find Ourselves In*. Although I think that book is one of the most important things I've written, I remember feeling when it was finished, "There is so much more to say and do in helping people get the shape and meaning of the Biblical narrative."

That's why I like this book so much. No, Winn Griffin hasn't given us a pristine objective view of the Bible, the final word on the subject; that's simply impossible – and in the end, I'm not sure it's desirable anyway. What this book does is take a lot of the best existing Bible scholarship – and the last few decades have been truly exciting and fertile in this regard – and use it as background for a solid and inspiring presentation of the Biblical storyline.

Afterword by Brian McLaren

Winn has been a pastor deeply involved with "normal" people (if such a thing exists) for decades in local churches. This experience, plus his personal love of learning, uniquely prepares him to write what is in many ways "a new kind of Bible handbook."

But Winn would be the first to say he doesn't mean this book to be used in the way some of the original Bible handbooks were probably intended: to nip any fresh readings of the Bible in the bud and keep all readers in the "fold," so to speak, of a buttoned-down, shrink-wrapped system of interpretation. Instead, this book will give you a running start in reading the Bible afresh and that, I think, is the best way to end this book.

Books like this are like diving boards. Their purpose is not to have you go to the end and bounce, bounce, bounce, bounce, and then walk back.

So, why not plunge into Genesis ... and next time you hear any passage from the Bible quoted in a sermon, why not be sure to mentally place it within the Biblical narrative, even if the preacher fails to do so? Then, after you're refreshed and exercised, get out, dry yourself off, and go live the story in your own home, job, school, neighborhood, social and political context, and world.

Because as Winn has explained, we're still helping write Act 5.

Brian McLaren
Laurel, Maryland
September 2007

Appendix

A collection of supplementary material.

In the throes of the Roman Catholic's teaching

on meritorious works, Luther and Calvin,

in spite of their theological depth,

made a subtle hermeneutical step.

Appendix 1: What Translation Should I Use?

God inspired the original authors to communicate with his children his Story. God's inspiration of those authors produced what we call Scripture. The Holy Spirit illuminates us through informed interpretation to the meaning of the text, so that we can live as characters in God's Story.

Scripture's sixty-six books have come to us originally in three different languages: Hebrew, Aramaic, and Greek. Since most of us will never give time to learning these languages, we need tools to help us in our reading—what we have to help us with this difficulty are good English translations.

One thing we should know about translations is just that: they are translations. They are the product of scholarship working with texts which often have several different renderings. Thus, often a translator has an interpretation within the translation which he or she is also called to interpret. It is useful to use many different translations when reading Scripture. One should be primary, but all should be used or at least as many as you can afford in your library.

Translations

Translating can take many different approaches. We can translate a word-for-word rendering from one language to another, or we can translate an equivalent meaning from one language to another in which the effect of a wording in the source language constructs wording in the receptor language which has the same effect, or we can paraphrase the text completely. I believe a good translation that is translating an equivalent meaning is the most useful.

A good translation will impact a reader in the receptor language the same way the original language would have impacted the reader. A good translation informs and provides feelings that would have been received by the original hearer or reader of the words. There are many things which go into making a good translation whether it is literal, free, or a dynamic equivalent.

A *literal translation* would be an attempt to match words from one language to another. An example would be the New American Standard Bible.[1]

A *free translation* is more like a paraphrase. Recent examples would be the *Living Bible* published in 1971.

A *dynamic equivalent* is an attempt to translate words, idioms, and grammatical constructions of the original language into precise equivalents in the receptor language. Such a translation keeps historical distance on all historical and most factual matters, but "updates" matters of language, grammar, and style. Examples would be the *New International Version, Today's New International Version*, and *New Living Translation*. One might add to this list the *Contemporary English Version*.

As with all translations, it is my opinion that there are problems with both the literal translations and the free translations. The literal translation often makes the English translation ambiguous, while the free translation often updates the original too much.

Appendix

Leviticus 18.6 provides an illustration of the three kinds of translation.

♦ None of you shall approach any blood relative of his to uncover nakedness; I am the Lord (*New American Standard Bible* (NASB): a literal translation).

♦ None of you shall marry a near relative, for I am the Lord (*Living Bible* (LB): a free translation, paraphrase).

♦ No one is to approach any close relative to have sexual relations. I am the Lord (*New International Version* and *Today's New International Version* (NIV/TNIV): a dynamic equivalent translation).

♦ You must never have sexual intercourse with a close relative, for I am the LORD. (*The New Living Translation* (NLT): a dynamic equivalent translation).

♦ Don't have sex with any of your close relatives… (*Contemporary English Version* (CEV): a dynamic equivalent translation).

It is plain that the literal translation of NASB has left the English reader with ambiguity. Does it mean "don't get close to a naked relative?" The *Living Bible* has gone too far by translating and suggesting one should not *marry* a close relative. The NIV/TNIV has left the concept of approach still in its translation which is still cumbersome. The *New Living Translation* omits the "approach" element and simply says "never have sex with a close relative," while the CEV is plain and simple as well "don't have sex with any of your close relatives."

Which Translation Is The Best?

All translations are not equal, not only because of the translation theory being used but also the use of different original texts. As an example, the Greek text which underlies the KJV New Testament is considered by most textual critics to be inferior to the Greek text used in the NIV, NRSV, and NLT. You can see an example of this by referring to the longer ending of Mark as seen in the KJV but not in other translations like the NRSV.

Another illustration would be the text of 1 John 5.7 which reads in the KJV as follows: "For there are three that bear record in heaven, the Father, the Word, and the Holy Ghost: and these three are one." In the New Living translation one finds the following:

So we have these three witnesses[a]—

And in the footnote one reads:

[a] 1 John 5:7 Some very late manuscripts add in heaven—the Father, the Word, and the Holy Spirit, and these three are one. And we have three witnesses on earth.

Which Bible should I read? This is an often asked question by those in search of the "correct" translation. One must remember that every translation of the Bible is an interpretation of the Bible. With that in mind, the question is easy to answer: read every translation that you can find. The first Bible my parents gave me was a *King James Version*. The first Bible I really used for study purposes was the *Revised Standard Version* during my college and seminary days. I now primarily use the New International Version when teaching and am making the switch to the TNIV (when I find a cover and print style I like). I love to read *The

Message, Good News Bible, and *The Promise* and *The Books of The Bible* which is the TNIV with all the additives such as chapters and verses removed.

Translations range from literal word-for-word to freestyle paraphrase. If you drew a line across a page and made the left of the line "literal," the middle of the line "dynamic equivalent, and the right side of the line "free," you could chart the following. On the "literal" end of the line would be *King James Version, New King James Version,* and the *New American Standard Bible.* On the "free" end of the line would be *The Living Bible.* In the middle would be the *New International Version, Today's New International Version,* and the *New Revised Standard Version.* To the right of the middle, but not a "free" translation, would be *The Message, God's Word, The Promise,* and *Good News Bible,* which are also dynamic equivalent translations but a bit freer than NIV/TNIV or NRSV.

The following is a list of Bibles with brief comment about each translation.

Amplified Bible. This version offers nuances of meanings drawn from various translations which are presented in brackets within the text. Difficult and sometimes confusing to read. I call it the multiple choice Bible.

God's Word. This is a natural equivalent translation. The translation expresses in American English ways the style and meaning of the original text.

Good News Bible. This is a dynamic equivalent translation of Scripture and may be the closest in meaning to the Old and New Testament originals, although somewhat dated now.

King James Version (KJV). Often called the Authorized Version which leads some to believe that it is the version that all others should be pitted against. It is written in seventeenth-century English and hundreds of its words are now archaic and not even in current dictionaries. Its authorized status only means that King James authorized its translation for the sake of the common folk in England at the beginning of the seventeenth century. It is not authorized in any other sense.

Living Bible. A paraphrased Bible written by Ken Taylor for his children. It is the most popular of the paraphrases and is very easy to read.

New American Bible (NAB). This is a Catholic version of Scripture. It is the official text of the Catholic Lectionary.

New American Standard Bible (NASB). This translation strives for a literal word-for-word translation of the original text. Useful for study and difficult to read for enjoyment.

New Century Version (NCV). This is written in very simple English, simple enough for children to understand. *The International Children's Bible* uses this text.

New English Bible (NEB). Written for the English reader not for the American English reader.

Appendix

New International Version (NIV). The NIV moves toward a thought-for-thought translation more in line with dynamic equivalency. It is a very readable translation.

New Jerusalem Bible. A modern Catholic translation.

New King James Version (NKJV). If you love the classic English of the seventeenth century but struggle with Elizabethan word usage, NKJV takes care of the archaic words by substituting some modern words for clarity. The publishers took a Public Domain document and replaced archaic words and then copyrighted it.

New Revised Standard Version (NRSV). This new translation of the RSV avoids masculine-oriented language unless the context demands it. It uses inclusive language. This does not include references to God.

The Message. A translation of the Bible which brings out the expressive, earthly flavor of Hebrew and Greek translated by Eugene Peterson. This translation has taken out the added verse markers which makes it easier to read.

New Living Translation (NLT). This translation is based on the most recent scholarship in the theory of translation. The translators accepted the challenge to create a text that would make the same impact in the life of modern readers that the original text had for the original readers. This concept is accomplished by translating entire thoughts (rather than just words) into natural, everyday English. The end result is a translation that is easy to read and understand and that accurately communicates the meaning of the original text. This translation is published by Tyndale House Publishers.

The Promise (The Contemporary English Version). This translation is offered with the listener in mind. More people hear the Bible read aloud than read it for themselves. A contemporary translation must be a text that an inexperienced reader can read aloud without stumbling, that someone unfamiliar with traditional biblical terminology can hear without misunderstanding, and that everyone can listen to with enjoyment because the style is lucid and lyrical.

Today's New International Version. (TNIV). The NIV is now being eclipsed by the inclusive language edition called *Today's New International Version*. The TNIV reflects the most up-to-date biblical scholarship while using the most precise language of any modern English translation. It is the best combination of reliability and readability for today's generation. Its purpose is to reach 18 to 34-year-olds with the Bible. The TNIV update reflects updated language and takes advantage of advances in biblical scholarship. Gender-related changes have been made to update masculine terminology that has generic intent. The TNIV is a gender inclusive translation. References originally intended to be masculine remain masculine in the TNIV.

Here is an example of how NIV and TNIV differ in this area:

NIV *[26]Then God said, "Let us make man in our image, in our* *likeness, and let them rule over the fish of the sea and the birds of the air, over the livestock, over all the earth, and over all the creatures that move along the ground." ²⁷So God created man in his own image, in the image of God he created him; male and female he created them.*

TNIV *²⁶Then God said, "Let us make human beings in our image, in our likeness, so that they may rule over the fish in the sea and the birds in the sky, over the livestock and over all the wild animals, and over all the creatures that move along the ground." ²⁷So God created human beings in his own image, in the image of God he created them; male and female he created them.*

Their new website <http://www.tniv.info> provides an explanation section on some specific passages like: Genesis 1:26-27; 5:2; Psalm 1:1-3, 8:3-8, 34:20; Proverbs 5:21; Matthew 7:3-5; Luke 17:3; John 14:23; Acts 20:28-30; 1 Corinthians 14:28, 15:21; 1 Timothy 2:12; Hebrews 2:17; James 1:12; Revelation 3:20, and Revelation 22:18.

The latest and most readable edition of TNIV is *The Books of The Bible*. This is an edition that has stripped all the additives (i.e., chapters, verses, headings, etc.) out of the text and printed it center column, so it really reads like a book/story. You can see examples at <http://www.thebooksofthebible.info>.

These are some of the prominent Bibles which are on the market for you to buy and use.

One of the easiest distractions that a follower of Jesus can get involved in is to debate which version is best. This topic produces more *heat* than *light*. Often those who do the most arguing have the least insight into how translations work. Legalism here, and anywhere else, can cause frustration, guilt, and anger. One must strive to remain unencumbered with these endless arguments and remember that the purpose of Scripture, regardless of which version you use, is to teach you, correct you, reprove you, and train you to walk the right paths in your Christian life.

So pick any translation or several translations to read and enjoy.

Appendix 2: Figures of Speech for God

Abba (Mark 14.36; Rom. 8.15; Gal. 4.6)
Alpha and Omega (Rev. 1.8)
Architect (Heb. 11.10)
Banner (Ex. 17.14)
Bear Robbed of Her Cubs (Hos. 13.8)
Beginning and End (Rev. 21.6)
Birds Hovering Overhead (Isa. 31.5)
Bridegroom (Isa. 62.5)
Consuming Fire (Deut. 4.24)
Defender (Psa. 68.5)
Dew (Hos. 14.5)
Eagle (Ex. 19.4)
Ever-Present Help (Psa. 46.1)
Father (Deut 1.30; Job 38.28)
Fortress (2 Sam. 22.2)
Gardener (John 15.1)
Green Pine Tree (Hos. 14.8)
Guide (Psa. 48.14)
Hiding Place (Psa. 32.7)
Husband (Isa. 54.5)
Judge (Job. 9.15)
King (Psa. 5.2)
Leopard (Hos. 13.7)
Lion (Isa. 31.4)
Master (Mal. 1.6)
Moth (Hos. 5.12)
Mother (Isa. 49.13)
Portion (Psa. 73.26)
Potter (Isa. 29.16; Isa. 64.8)
Redeemer (Job 19.25)
Refuge (Deut. 33.27)
Rock (Deut. 32.4)
Shade (Psa. 121.5)
Shepherd (Psa. 23.1)
Shield (Gen. 15.1)
Strong Tower (Psa. 61.3)
Woman (Isa. 42.14)

Appendix 3: The Soul

We encounter the word *soul* in the Creation Narrative. The following should help sort out some misconceptions about *soul*. The world of Platonic philosophy is a great hindrance to the modern reader of Scripture. The King James Version (KJV) translation of "living soul" is steeped in problems. The NIV translation is: "living being." The word that is being translated is the Hebrew word *nepes*. The KJV mistranslation mixed with the Greek philosophy of Plato makes the word *nepes* take on a completely different meaning today than the one implied by the Hebrew storyteller.

The range of meaning for *nepes* is much broader and would include words like life, person, self, appetite, and mind. There is a distinct difference between the Hebrew way of thinking about *nepes* (soul in KJV) and the Platonic, or even later Hellenistic, opinions about the human soul.

Early Greek language viewed *nepes* as united with the body and considered it as the inner person. Platonic thought saw *nepes* as preexistent and separated from the body. Thus, one has probably heard or prayed the prayer, "Now I lay me down to sleep, I pray the lord my soul to keep. If I should die before I wake, I pray the Lord my soul to take." This is certainly not a Christian prayer but a Platonic philosophical prayer. The *nepes* was the immaterial core in this way of thinking that would live on after physical life. Salvation for the Platonic Greek was the escape of the soul from the body. Even in the Hellenistic period of the Jews, Philo stood as a proponent of Greek thought and continued the Platonic idea of a bodiless soul. This dualistic dichotomy can also be found in the Jewish Apocrypha and Pseudepigrapha (4 Maccabees 1.20; 26-28; 2 Maccabees 6.30; Wisdom of Solomon 9.15, 15.8).

This Platonic idea of an abstract sense of soul that can and does separate from the body is not a part of the Hebrew thought form. In Genesis 2, man does not possess a *nepes* but rather he becomes a *nepes*. In Leviticus 19.28, one finds the words *nepes mot* which means a dead body that is in contrast with a live body.

The Hebrew word *nepes* is more common than the Hebrew word for spirit. However, in the New Testament, Paul gives priority to spirit over soul (spirit: 146 times and soul: 13 times). In the Hebrew thought, which was Paul's way of thinking, soul is the human life force; while for Paul, spirit has taken on this meaning. It is through spirit that God and humankind have fellowship.

In 1 Thessalonians 5.23, Paul differentiates the soul and body from the spirit. The soul and body constitute the person as a living being, while the spirit indicates the higher capacities of the person in relationship with God. This is not Greek dualism. Paul did not believe that there was a preexistent soul as was believed by Greek philosophy. It is fair to say, from a biblical perspective, that you do not have a soul, you are a soul.[1]

Appendix 4: Behind the Scenes

Here are some words that are of interest that will help you understand the meaning of the storyteller of this Creation story in Genesis 2.

Formed (Shaped). This verb, which is a present participle of *yasar*, means potter. Even though the text says that the first human was created from "the dust of the earth," it may be that the image of potter still lies behind this metaphor in the description of man's creation. The word "formed" is an artistic inventive word that required skill and planning. It suggests that the creation of the first human was not just some afterthought as is described in other creation stories.[2]

Dust. In the stories of creation that come from Egypt and Mesopotamia, man is created from clay sometimes mixed with the blood of a slain god. In the Gilgamesh Epic (1.34), the goddess Aruru created Enkidu from clay. The creation of man from clay was a commonplace idea outside of the Old Testament. Within the Old Testament, man's creation from clay/dust is alluded to many times (Job 10.9; Isa. 29.16; Ps. 90.3; 104.29). It becomes evident that the Genesis 2 storyteller was taking ancient ideas of man's creation and giving these old ideas their own distinctive flavor. The intended meaning of the passage is to suggest that humankind was formed by the Creator-Covenant God and that he was made of a substance that was also created by God, not a substance that was commingled with a god (i.e., blood of a slain god).

Breathed Into His Nostrils the Breath of Life. Humankind is a piece of earth, shaped by God, which has the gift of life given by the breath of God. The word "breath" conveys the idea of being personal and warm. It pictures the face-to-face encounter that God had with his first created human. It is the picture of the intimacy of a kiss. With God's breath, the first man came to life.

Blew (Breathed). This word suggests a large puff of air, not unlike the amount of air that it might take to start a fire. God's breath affirmed that his creation had come to life. Today's English Version translated this phrase as: "and the man began to live." *The Contemporary English Version* says, "and the man started breathing." It is not the possession of the "breath of life" that made the first human different from the animals as is so often posited. Animals are described in the same terms (Gen. 1.29). It is the image of God in which humankind is created that marks humans off from the animals.[3]

Appendix 5: The Tree of the Knowledge of Good and Evil

The story of "the tree of the knowledge of good and evil" is only found in this story (Gen. 2.4b-25). For that reason it becomes very difficult, if not impossible, to discover its significance. The following lists some of the suggestions of how to understand this phrase:

1. The tree is a description of the consequences of obeying or disobeying the commandment of not to eat.

2. The tree means moral discernment. It meant knowing right from wrong.

3. The tree meant sexual knowledge. *First*, this theory believes that because humankind was naked before the disobedience and were unashamed and after the disobedience they were ashamed, the tree should be understood as sexual knowledge. *Second*, the idea that "know" should be understood as sexual is because of its sexual meaning in 4.1. *Third*, an appeal to other Old Testament passages where "to know good and evil" may refer to the sexual urge both before it develops (Deut. 1.39) and after it has faded (2 Sam. 19.35). *Fourth*, it is believed, that in the Gilgamesh Epic that Enkidu, who was created to be Gilgamesh's opponent, acquired wisdom to become "like a god." This "knowledge" came after a week of cohabitation with a harlot. *Finally*, the whole scene is set in a garden that suggests fertility in the ancient mindset.

   Two factors should be taken into consideration before taking this thought as the meaning. *First*, if one is going to be consistent, this theory must apply sexuality to God because 3.22 states, "the man has become like one of us, knowing good and evil." *Second*, if the phrase were to be understood as sexual awareness, then why would God wish to outlaw its possession when the idea of sexual knowledge is already in the garden before the disobedience (2.24)?

4. The tree meant omniscience, the ability to be all knowing. The two trees are a literary device called *merism* that takes a pair of words and puts them together to say something is whole. As an example, the phrase "heaven and earth" could be a *merism* which means "the whole universe."

5. The tree meant wisdom. God revealed his law in the garden by giving the command to not eat of the tree at the pain of death. Since God gave the law, it is reasoned, it cannot be added to my humankind. So when Adam and Eve ate of the tree of knowledge, they gained human wisdom over divine law.

6. The tree suggested moral autonomy. If this view is correct, what is forbidden to humankind is the power to decide for them what may or may not be in their best interest. There are decisions that God has not delegated to humankind. This final interpretation has the benefit of having the best understanding of 3.22 that says, "the man has become like one of us, knowing good and evil." Man indeed has become like God when he makes himself the center and the only frame of reference for life guidelines. When man attempts to act autonomously, he is very much attempting to be godlike.

Appendix 6: The Serpent

The word "satan" is used in a number of ways in the Hebrew Bible. The term refers:

- To the angel of the Lord who may be an adversary (Num. 22.22, 32).
- To another person who may function as an adversary (1 Sam. 29.4; 2 Sam. 19.22; 1 Kings 5.4; 11.14, 23, 25; Psalm 109.8).
- Finally, to an angel in the angelic host as seen in the book of Job.

The word "satan" appears eighteen times in the Hebrew Bible. Out of the eighteen, it appears fourteen times in the first two chapters of Job. We should note with interest that all but one of these eighteen times that "satan" appears (the exception is 1 Chronicles 21.1), the article is attached to the word and it reads "the satan." This form indicates that it is a title not a personal name. The term "satan" does not describe "who" but "what." The term is not a proper name in the Old Testament. We must carefully understand that in the ancient world, not to have a name was to be reduced to nonexistence.

Genesis 3 reveals that the serpent was one of the creatures that the Creator God created. The serpent was not eternal or divine. The storyteller reveals that this creature was "more subtle" than any other animal. This is not a disparaging term. As a matter of fact, the word which is translated "subtle" for us is used in Proverbs several times (12.16, 23; 13.16, 14.8, 15; 18; 22.3) and is translated "the prudent [one, person, man]." This prudent one is contrasted with the "fool," while elsewhere the word is translated as "crafty" which is something that God dislikes (Job 5.12, 15.5). In this story, the storyteller only speaks of the serpent's destiny (Genesis 3.14-15).

Explanations abound about who the serpent was. Some believe that it was a mythological character that had magical powers. Others think that the serpent was a symbol of human curiosity. Still others believe that the serpent was a symbol of some ancient fertility cult. Some see the serpent as symbolic of chaos or evil. Some believe that the voice of the serpent is only the voice of the "inner person." Among Christian and Jewish interpreters, the serpent is often identified as Satan's instrument. Luther, as an example, believed that "the devil was permitted to enter the beast, as he here entered the serpent. For there is no doubt that it was a real serpent in which Satan was and in which he conversed with Eve."[1]

The word "serpent" is the general term for snake. The reptile played a significant role in the ancient world. It was an object of reverence and worship. Serpents are found in ancient myths and represent life, recurring youth, death, chaos, and wisdom. Scripture also possesses the same association for the serpent (the rejuvenating effects of the bronze serpent in the wilderness, Numbers 21.9 is an example).

In the ancient world's Epic of Gilgamesh, the serpent was perceived as the opponent of humankind. Gilgamesh searched for the famed survivor of the flood, the immortal Utnapishtim, so that he could learn how he might obtain eternal life. Utnapishtim revealed to Gilgamesh a secret known only to him and the gods. There was a plant in the deepest part of the sea that could rejuvenate one's life. Gilgamesh obtained the plant and named it "Man Becomes Young in Old Age." However, the plant was stolen by a serpent, who carried it off and shed its own skin (a process of rejuvenation).

In the community that God was creating in the wilderness, the snake was classified as an unclean animal because of its movement on the ground (Lev. 11.41-45). Serpents were associated with the judgment of God for Israel's complaints against God in the wilderness (venomous snakes, Numbers 21.6) as well as being the source of rejuvenation.

So is the serpent in the Garden story Satan? Most likely not, or at least not for the teller of the story.

Appendix 7: God as Father

God the Father in the Old Testament

The concept of the Fatherhood of God has its roots in the Old Testament. Fatherhood is first described in the Covenant relationship between God and Israel. In Exodus, we have these words: *Then say to Pharaoh, 'This is what the LORD says: Israel is my firstborn son,* (Ex. 4.22).

From the beginning of the Old Testament to its conclusion, the Old Testament authors often described God as the Father of Israel. Here are several passages which illustrate this:

Is this the way you repay the LORD,
  You foolish and unwise people?
Is he not your Father, your Creator,
  who made you and formed you? (Deut. 32.6)

Yet you, LORD, you are our Father.
  We are the clay, you are the potter;
  we are all the work of your hand. (Isa. 64.8)

Do we not all have one Father? Did not one God create us? Why do we profane the covenant of our ancestors by being unfaithful to one another? (Mal. 2.10)

While God was viewed as the Father of the whole nation of Israel, when she broke Covenant with him, his Fatherhood was confined to the faithful remnant within Israel. This can be seen in the following two passages:

As a father has compassion on his children,
  so the LORD has compassion on those who fear him;
  (Psalm 103.13)

"On the day when I act," says the LORD Almighty, "they will be my treasured possession. I will spare them, just as a father has compassion and spares his son who serves him. (Mal. 3.17)

With this brief overview, one can see that the Father metaphor for God was used in a nationalistic way between Yahweh and Israel. Later in the life of Israel when she had become unfaithful, he was the Father of the faithful remnant. The personal relationship of a father-child seems to be lacking in the Old Testament.

The Fatherhood of God in Second Temple Judaism

In Jewish literature which appeared between the testaments, often called Intertestamental or Second Temple Judaism literature, the Fatherhood of God was beginning to take on a look and feel of being personal as seen in the following quotes.

*O LORD **Father** and Ruler of my life*
  do not abandon me to their counsel,
and let me not fall because of them! (Sirach 23.1)

We are considered by him as something base,
and he avoids our ways as unclean
  he calls the last end of the righteous happy,
*and boasts that God is his **father*** (Wisdom of Solomon 2.16)

We must remember that these books have not carried any authority in the Church's Canon, but they do give us a window through which we can view how the people in this era of history may have viewed God. These books are designated as Apocryphal Literature. To understand the significance of these two quotes, a brief bit of history is in order.

There are two pieces of Apocryphal Literature in the genre called *wisdom*. The *wisdom* of this literature is like the Wisdom Literature in our own Scripture of which Proverbs is a major example. Wisdom literature is the most unfamiliar to today's Bible readers. You could define *wisdom* as *the discipline of applying to one's life the truth that experience teaches*. Wisdom is personal not theoretical or abstract. Wisdom exists when people think or act according to the truth that they have learned through their own experience. The two books in the Apocryphal Literature which are Wisdom Literature are:

◆ **The Wisdom of Solomon** which was written in the hopes that it would protect the Jews in Egypt from the danger of falling into skepticism and idolatry.

◆ **Ecclesiasticus** which was the oral traditions that were used to teach young men to live piously.

Ecclesiasticus is believed to have been written somewhere between 200 and 175 B.C. in the Greek Period of 330-166 B.C. when Antiochus Epiphanes defeated Egypt (200 B.C.).

Ecclesiasticus is often valued as one of the more important books in the Apocrypha. It is the only book that names its author. Jesus the son of Sirach was most likely a Jewish scribe who taught the Law. He recorded what he taught orally to young men about worthy and pious living. We have in its pages a link to the thoughts of the Jewish people of that era. It may have been the form of material that developed into the schools that produced Pharisees and Sadducees.

The Wisdom of Solomon was written between A.D. 38-41. This was after the Ascension of Jesus and during the period right after Paul's conversion in A.D. 34. Herod Antipas (4 B.C. - A.D. 39) was still the king. The book, while claiming to be written by Solomon (7.1-14), was written by a Greek-speaking Jew.

Along with Ecclesiasticus, it is seen as one of the most, if not the most important book in the Apocrypha. It presents a theological mindset of the Greek way of thinking about theology. It is an attempt to integrate Greek philosophy with biblical theology. It is an endeavor to rekindle a zeal for God in the middle of turmoil.

The important thing to note is that the idea of the Fatherhood of God to the individual was *not* existent during the Old Testament era and mentioned infrequently before the time of Jesus, but was mentioned after the Ascension of Jesus in Jewish Literature. The conclusion: God was not viewed at large in the intimate terms that Fatherhood shares with these two possible exceptions of the Wisdom of Solomon and Ecclesiasticus. The rabbinical literature of the day saw the Fatherhood of God as an ethical relationship between God and Israel (cf. 2 Sam. 7.14; Ps. 68.5; 89.26; Jer. 3.4, 19; Mal. 1.6).

Appendix

The Fatherhood of God in the New Testament

When we open the pages of the New Testament, the Fatherhood of God is the predominant metaphor by which Jesus seeks to reveal God. God's relationship has moved from a national one, as the Father of Israel, to a personal one, as Father to those who are believers. In the New Testament, the Fatherhood of God is seen in three ways.

1. He is the Father of Jesus.
2. He is the Father of the disciples of Jesus.
3. He is the Father of all creation.

It is in the Gospels that we find the predominance of the occurrence of God as Father. The term "father" appears more than twice as many times in the Gospels as it does in the rest of the New Testament. In his conversation with his disciples recorded in John 20.17, *Jesus said, "Do not hold on to me, for I have not yet ascended to the Father. Go instead to my brothers and tell them, 'I am ascending to **my Father** and **your Father**, to **my God** and **your God**.'"*

By the terminology used in John, we can discover two things: *First,* Jesus separated his relationship with God as Father from his disciples relationship with God as Father by the terms "my God" and "your God." *Second,* Jesus saw clearly that his disciples could have an intimate relationship with God as Father.

This is clearly shown in the passage when he teaches his disciples to pray. The Lord's Prayer, better called the Model of Prayer for the Disciples, was never meant to be quoted verbatim. It was meant as a model of how to pray versus a prayer to be prayed. Jesus begins the model by addressing God as Father. It begins with the Greek word *pater* and there is reasonable agreement that *pater* represents the Aramaic *'abbâ*.[1]

The use of this term was as shocking to his disciples as it was to the Jews, in general, who wanted to kill him for speaking of God as Father. While the term brings an intimate concept of God to man, it was never intended to lessen our sense of awe in our approach to God, which is seen by the second phase in the model prayer, "hallowed be your name." No father-child relationship on earth is perfect because no father is perfect, but in God the perfect pattern of Fatherhood can be seen. This simple prayer model was revolutionary to the disciples and to the church.

The early fathers of the church like Chrysostom, Theodore of Mopsuestia, and Theodoret of Cyprus, testified in harmony that *'abbâ* was the address of a small child to his or her father. *'Abbâ* was an everyday word, a family word of intimacy. No Jewish person would have dared to address God in this way. Jesus spoke with God as a child speaks with his father with intimacy and security. He wanted his disciples to experience the same thing.

In Paul, God is seen as the Father of believers as well as a universal Father. We can summarize the teaching of God as Father in the New Testament with: It was a shocking and revolutionary way of identifying with God. No more was he their Father in a national sense; he was now their father in a personal sense.

Why is the Father Metaphor Important?

First, everyone has a father and a mother. For the most part everyone knows who their mother is. However, not everyone knows who his or her father is. It has been said "No man is responsible for his father. That is entirely his mother's affair." This possible broken relationship between father and child provides a basis for humankind to know God in a way that we may not have ever been able to experience on a human plane with a human father.

Second, the metaphor of Father is one that crosses time and culture. Not everyone has a king, not everyone has a Rock, not everyone has a Shepherd, or any of the other hundred plus metaphors for God (see Appendix 2 for a partial list). Nor can anyone identify with these metaphors in a personal way. God chose lots of ways to reveal himself so that his creation could have an intimate relationship with him. The primary one in the New Testament is Father. One must remember that God is not a man but spirit. Scripture uses language of condescension to help us understand and relate to God. He is a personal spirit with whom those who have become his children can be intimate. While the term is not used, God is also revealed as mother and as a woman.

It is the need of our culture to understand the Fatherhood of God because of the number of broken relationships between fathers and children which might affect our understanding of what a true father is like. The parenting aspect of God is often misunderstood. He wants us to experience the freedom to be his children and enter into the intimate relationship with him that awaits us. To know and understand him as Father is the supreme purpose of telling this story. Only at the end of Isaiah does this concept begin to take shape. It seems to have been avoided in the Old Testament before Isaiah.

Remember, that a metaphor, like father, is a metaphor. It represents something, it is not the actual thing. God can be understood as compared to father, but his is more than father. I know it is difficult to put our heads around, but God is not a male-gendered being.

Appendix

Appendix 8: Servant Song

There is a collection of four passages in Isaiah that have been given the name Servant Songs (42.1-4; 49.1-6; 50.4-9; 52.13-53.12). An outline of the four songs could be:

Isaiah 42.1-4

In the first song in Isaiah 42.1-4, there are two points Isaiah makes:

1. The Lord elects the servant (1).
2. The servant's task is to bring justice to the nations (1-4).

Isaiah 49.1-6

The speaker in the second song (49.1-6) is the servant. In these few verses, we can see three points:

1. There are three stages of the development of the servant: election, call, and equipment (1-3).
2. The servant's despondency over apparent failure (4).
3. A new task set before the servant (1-6).

Isaiah 50.4-9

This song gives no clear understanding of who the servant is: nation, prophet, or king.

Two points are made in the third song (50. 4-9):

1. The special tasks of the servant and the results (4-6).
2. The servant's confession of confidence and the certainty of being answered (7-9).

Isaiah 52.13-53.12

There are three distinct parts of the fourth song (52.13-53.12):

1. An opening speech of salvation which includes a contrast of humiliation and exaltation (52.13-15).
2. A confession (53.1-11a) which includes a report of suffering (2-9) and reports of deliverance (10-11a).
3. A closing speech of salvation which includes the success of exaltation.

If we break down the songs, we can see the following:

Call

The servant belongs to the Lord and is chosen by him (42.1) and the servant was called and formed from the womb for a special task (49.1).

Task

The servant is to establish the manner in which life with God should be lived on the earth (42.1-4). He is to bring Israel back to God (49.3f.) and bring salvation to the earth (49.6).

Equipment

The servant has God's Spirit (42.1). He has God's support and strength (49.5). He is depicted as one who is taught by God on a continual basis (50.4-5).

Appendix 9: The Kingdom from Augustine to Wright (An Overview)

From Augustine to the Reformers, the Kingdom and the Church were thought of as the same thing. This view is still common as suggested by our current language. We talk about bringing people into the Kingdom, which is a synonym for church. Augustine believed that as the church grew, so the Kingdom grew. As the church takes the gospel into the world, the Kingdom is extended.[1]

What is usually called the old liberal view that understands the Kingdom of God as the pure prophetic religion taught by Jesus is found in Adolph Von Harnack's *What Is Christianity?* (1901)[2] For him, the Kingdom was reduced to a subjective realm. It was an inner spiritual redemptive blessing (Rom. 14.17). The Kingdom is expressed by the new birth (John 3.3) and is an inward power which enters into the human spirit and takes hold of it. Many scholars have understood the Kingdom primarily in terms of personal religious experience—the reign of God in the individual soul.[3]

Johannes Weiss argued that Jesus' view of the Kingdom was like that of the Jewish apocalypses, although future and eschatological.[4]

Albert Schweitzer picked up Weiss' view and interpreted the entire career of Jesus from an eschatological point of view.[5] The Kingdom is viewed as a place of future blessing which occurs at the Second Coming for the people of God (1 Cor. 15.50; Matt. 8.11; 2 Pet. 1.11; Matt. 25.34). The followers of Jesus enter the Kingdom when he returns. The coming Kingdom would bring about an end to the old order of humanity and begin a new existence in a heavenly order. Thus, the Kingdom is altogether future and supernatural. James Kallas says, "...there was a fatal weakness in Schweitzer's work which threatened from the very beginning to vitiate his contribution to theology. And that weakness was that Schweitzer vindicated the effect and completely bypassed the cause. Schweitzer forcefully demonstrated that eschatology was central in the life of Jesus. But he failed to bring forth the worldview, the basic underlying reasons, which had brought eschatology into being." It was "...a yearn[ing] for the end of the world precisely because they had come to believe that this world was not as it should be."[6]

C. H. Dodd held that the Kingdom of God was realized fully in the ministry of Jesus, hence the name "realized eschatology." The Kingdom of God is an earthly place where there is righteousness, peace, and joy. These are the benefits for those who live yielded lives to the Rule of the Spirit. The Kingdom as a present reality is based on such passages as Matthew 12.28; Romans 14.17; and Isa. 2.4. For Ladd, Dodd was more "platonic than biblical."[7] Kallas says of Dodd, "The central contention of Dodd is that Schweitzer's work was a compromise. That Schweitzer had found two streams of thought in the gospels; one with a forward look to a coming kingdom, and the other positing a kingdom already resent and working. Thus Schweitzer, compromising, insisted that the kingdom was very, very close."[8] Kallas also covers this in his book *Jesus and the Power of Satan.*[9]

If there is a consensus, it is that the Kingdom is in some real sense both present and future. For W. G. Kümmel the primary meaning of the Kingdom is the eschaton…. He holds that the Kingdom is also present, but only in the person of Jesus, not in his disciples.

Appendix

Appendix 9

Jeremias defends a distinctive position. While commending Dodd for achieving a breakthrough in interpretation by his emphasis on the present irruption of the Kingdom, he also criticized him for minimizing the eschatological aspect. He replaces Dodd's "realized eschatology" with "eschatology in process of realization."[10]

In the last century, a rather novel approach to viewing the Kingdom has had a wide influence. This position believes that the Old Testament prophecies to Israel must be literally fulfilled. This is the position of Dispensationalism which has distinguished sharply between the Kingdom of God and the Kingdom of Heaven.[11] This view has been upgraded to what is now being called "Progressive Dispensationalism"[12] in which the authors affirm the dispensationalist's traditional distinctive of a future for ethnic Israel, but also see the need to get past the rigid literalism of the classic dispensationalism of Scofield and Ryrie and work with extra biblical materials in their exegesis and hermeneutics.

Ladd is representative of a moderating interpretation of Jesus' understanding of the Kingdom of God.[13] Ladd believed that "the Kingdom is God's kingly rule. It has two moments: a fulfillment of the Old Testament promises and the historical mission of Jesus and a consummation at the end of the age, inaugurating the Age to Come."[14]

For Kallas the Kingdom was not existential, but "the Kingdom of God meant for them not a psychological experience but an actual event."[15]

Wright believes that this argument by Ladd, i.e., a fulfillment in the present and a consummation in the future was a "linguist trick."[16] Wright asks, "What, then, is central to the understanding of the kingdom? [It was] …the Jewish expectation of the saving sovereignty of the covenant god, exercised in the vindication of Israel and the overthrow of her enemies."[17] Wright also says that the big question which overarches current scholarship since Schweitzer may be: "Is the kingdom present or is the kingdom future or is it somehow both? If so, how both?" Wright continues,

> It depends on what you think the kingdom is. If you think the kingdom is the cessation of the space-time universe and a totally new order all together, then the kingdom is not there in Jesus. If you think that the kingdom is the quiet response on the hearts of those men and women who want to respond to him, then you can make a good case that the kingdom is there in the ministry of Jesus.

Then, Wright poses the question: "Which did Jesus himself think it was, present, future, both, or something else related to those two, but different?" Wright thinks that a better way through the forest of present, future, or compromise is to go back and see what kingdom meant and then we will see better the sense that it might be present or it might be future. Wright believes that what most scholars miss in all of this is that the Jews, when they were using kingdom language, were thinking about Israel being vindicated over the world, i.e., that Israel was going to be placed as top nation in the world who would hold her with respect. A basic solution for Wright is that in one sense, Israel dominating the world is not in the ministry of Jesus. He challenges this concept and denies it and warns Israel that it is not going to be like that. In another sense, it is present because Jesus takes Israel's role on himself, acting it out, so that for which Israel had hoped is present in Jesus. Yet, in another sense, the kingdom is affirmed as being future. Jesus is constantly talking about an inauguration which wasn't yet there.[18]

Appendix 10: Metaphors of Jesus

The Last Adam (1 Cor. 15.45)
Advocate (1 John 2.1)
Alpha and Omega (Rev. 1.8)
Anointed One (Acts 4.25)
Apostle (Heb. 3.1)
Atoning Sacrifice (1 John 2.2)
Author of Faith (Heb. 12.2)
Beginning and End (Rev. 22.13)
Bread of God (John 6.32)
Bread of Life (John 6.35)
Bridegroom (Matt. 9.15)
Capstone (Matt. 21.42)
Chief Shepherd (1 Pet. 5.4)
Cornerstone (Eph. 2.20)
Deliverer (Rom. 11.26)
Firstborn (Rom. 8.29)
Firstfruits (1 Cor. 15.20)
Foundation (1 Cor. 3.11)
Gate (John 10.7)
Head (1 Cor. 11.3)
Hen (Matt. 23.37)
Holy One of God (John 6.69)
Hope of Glory (Col. 1.27)
I Am (John 8.58)
Image of God (2 Cor. 4.4)
Immanuel (Matt. 1.23)
King (John 18.36)
King of Kings (1 Tim. 6.15)
Lamb (of God) (Rev. 6.1)
Life-giving Spirit (1 Cor. 15.45)
Light (John 1.1)
Lord (2 Tim. 4.8)
Mediator (1 Tim. 2.5)
Morning Star (2 Pet. 1.19)
Peace (Eph. 2.14)
Purifier (Matt. 3.12)
Ransom (1 Tim. 2.5)
Savior (John 4.42)
Stone (1 Pet. 2.4-8)
Vine (John 15.1)

Appendix 11: Was Paul An Early Lutheran?

The following is a brief survey on the question stated above.

How Did We Get Here From There?

Luther came into serious conflict with Thomas Aquinas who believed that although grace supplies the ability to act virtuously and comes as a free gift from God and is not the reward of any work, the virtuous action that results can merit eternal life both for oneself and for others.[1] Aquinas was fond of saying that the "primary role of the law...was to terrify the sinner."[2]

In the throes of the Roman Catholic's teaching on meritorious works, Luther and Calvin, in spite of their theological depth, made a subtle hermeneutical step. In the course of discussing the letters of Paul, these two Reformers placed the Roman Church and its hierarchical leadership in the role of first century Judaism. When Paul suggested that justification by faith came apart from the works of the law, they interpreted his statement to be about "the medieval system of salvation by meritorious works.[3] For Luther, however, the works of the Law (Gal. 2.16) became "a cipher for the system of merit that he found in the church's medieval Scholastic writers."[4]

Luther's hermeneutical shift made his understanding of the law "identifiable with the Roman Church's belief that works play a great role in justification. There was no attempt to examine what Paul was opposing and no argument to support the assumption that works of the law in Paul's context were analogous to works of the law in medieval Scholasticism."[5] Luther simply contrasted faith and works of the law.

In the following centuries of Protestant development, the equation of legalism of the Roman Church and Judaism became "a standard feature of Protestant biblical scholarship."[6] Old Testament writers represented Judaism as having fallen away from its strong convictions about nationalism in which the law played a role to a single concern about an individual's relationship with the law.[7] Old Testament specialists like Julius Wellhausen believed that Judaism had "an immense retrogression" while others argued that the religion of Israel spiraled downward to an obsession about the individual's ability to earn a reward from God by keeping the law's commandments.[8]

In the field of New Testament scholarship, the effect of Luther was even more prominent and the knowledge of Judaism was passed on through handbooks such as Ferdinand Weber's *Jewish Theology on the Basis of the Talmud and Related Writings* where he presented a belief in "'legalism' by which he meant the study and fulfilling of the law,"[9] as the primary goal of Israel. God was reduced to becoming a bookkeeper who daily followed each individual keeping track of his or her merits and demerits and then provided rewards of eternal life or punishment accordingly. While Weber's book claimed to be a review of relatively late Jewish writings, interpreters of the New Testament used it as a summation of what Jews believed during the life of Jesus and Paul.[10]

Luther's error has plagued New Testament studies to the present day with additional mixture of German Romanticism and existentialism without expanding energy on comprehending the Judaism of Paul's lifetime on its own terms. With Luther, a new way of thinking about Paul's antithesis between law and grace was established.[11]

When Paul said that believers were not under law but under grace, it was supposed that he was saying that they had been rescued from thinking that they had a duty to follow the law if they were to find salvation.[12]

The protest against the misguided influence of Luther began in the mid 1800s with Claude G. Montefiore, when he concluded that "the law in rabbinic Judaism did not typically produce self-righteous Jews who could think of nothing but earning their way to heaven by means of meritorious works." For them the law was "a benefit and a delight."[13]

The next round of protest came from George Foot Moore who produced a "withering critique" concluding that Weber had imported "the grid of Lutheran dogmatics onto rabbinic material."[14] Even with the clarification of Moore, Protestant scholarship continued to view ancient Judaism as simply a "sixteenth-century Roman Catholicism in different dress."[15]

This view ended with the publication of E. P. Sanders' *Paul and Palestinian Judaism: A Comparison of Patterns of Religion*.[16] Sanders' book is more about Judaism than Paul in which Sanders' compared the pattern of religion in Paul's letters with the patterns of religion in Jewish literature between 200 B.C. and A.D. 200. By "pattern of religion," Sanders meant the way the followers of a specific religion understand "getting in" and "staying in their religion."[17]

Two critical conclusions emerge from Sanders' undertaking. *First*, he concludes that the charges against non-Jewish scholars were correct. *Second*, that Judaism of the period falls into a pattern he called "covenantal nomism,"[18] which is that one's place in God's plan is established on the basis of the Covenant, and the Covenant requires as the proper response of humankind one's obedience to its commandments, while providing atonement for transgressors.

Sanders worked from a paradigm called "Solution to Plight." While Sanders saw that at times "Paul argues from a human plight to the solution in Jesus Christ…these moments in Paul's letters do not mean he arrived at his conviction about Christ by pondering the human dilemma."[19]

Who Are The Major Players?

In any argument/debate or game there are players. Such is the case for this topic. Westerholm's book names Wrede, Schweitzer, Montefiore, Schoeps, Sanders, Kümmel, Stendahl, Bultmann, Wilckens, Drane, Hübner, Räisänen, Wright, Dunn, Donaldson, Cranfield Schreiner, Das, Thielman, Seifrid, Laato, Thurèn, Aletti, Martyn, and Becker.[20] In addition, he suggests that four ancients Augustine, Luther, Calvin, and Wesley may be regarded as a "Lutheran" reader of Paul.[21]

As was suggested above, Sanders' book *Paul and Palestinian Judaism* appears to be the turning point away from the "Lutheran" reading of Paul and was the beginning of the "new perspective on Paul."[22] Two contemporary British scholars, N. T. Wright and James D. G. Dunn, are the proponents of Paul against the Lutherans,[23] while Frank Thielman stands in the Lutheran reading along with Stephen Westerholm.[24] Below we will take a brief look at Luther, Sanders, Wright, Dunn, Thielman, and

Appendix

Westerholm on this subject. First, let's look at a summary of the "new perspective on Paul" and then at the concept of the Old Testament Covenant.

A Summary of the "New Perspective on Paul"

The Lutheran reading of Paul has traditionally been seen as rejecting Judaism of his day because it was believed that it was necessary *to do* the works of the law in order *to be* accepted by God. God's acceptance was based on the merit of a person. If a person could rack up enough merits, these could outweigh his or her sin. The Jewish religion of Paul's day was thought to be legalistic, not in the sense that God had shared the law with his children to show them how to live as his people, but rather that the law was given so that in their human performance of it God would accept them. This view suggested that human works over grace was the order of the day for Judaism and that with such a view one could then contrast Christianity.

Beginning with E. P. Sanders, scholars have reacted against this understanding of Judaism. Sanders demonstrated that much of the literature of Judaism demonstrated that the Jews were accepted as the people of God on the grounds of God's grace in setting up his Covenant with the Jews, and keeping his laws was the response to God's grace and not a meritorious grounds for their entry into relationship with God. Jews kept the law to remain in the Covenant rather than keeping the law in order to enter the Covenant.

Such works were required for the new Gentile followers of Jesus not because they were a way to gain entrance, but because they were signs that they were in fact now in the Covenant with God. For a Gentile, to keep the law allowed him or her to be able to have table fellowship with Jewish Christians. "Works of the law" came to be defined by James D. G. Dunn as those specific things that marked Jews out publicly and acted as boundary markers (circumcision, food laws, festivals).[25]

Debaters find themselves trying to understand where Paul stood in this configuration. I. Howard Marshall, a New Testament specialist, suggests that one possibility has been to see Paul as mistakenly seeing Judaism as a legalistic religion that was based on merit.[26] This, of course, would be quite a leap based on the current understanding of Judaism in Paul's day. Marshall believes that the "traditional understanding is accordingly essentially right and the 'new perspective' must be regarded as flawed."[27]

The Old Testament Covenant

According to Delbert Hillers, an Old Testament specialist, the Mosaic Covenant was given by God to a redeemed people essentially in the form of an elaborate oath.[28] It followed the ancient pattern of a Suzerain Vassal Treaty (often called a Lord-Servant Treaty).[29] These heirs of Abraham were called to be God's light bearers to the ancient world. They were to have no other God. They were to worship no idols. The Covenant was a way in which these redeemed people could relate to God and to each other and demonstrate to the world what being the people of God was really like. The Covenant (Law) was not (as has been thought and taught) a way in which Israel could become God's children. The Covenant was not about "getting in."

Redemption/Exodus came first, then the Covenant (Law). The *law* was never intended to be a system of legal observances by which you could earn God's acceptance, if you obeyed them. The Commandments are the stipulations of the *Covenant relationship* which are rooted in *grace!* They are *basic statements* on the *quality of life* that must characterize those who belong to God. All of Scripture knows only one way of salvation...*the grace of God.* God reveals his redemptive purpose always based on grace, not on man's ability to obligate God to save him because he has kept the law.[30] The Covenant was about "staying in" relationship with God. The Old Testament Story beginning with the giving of the Covenant is told around the concept of Israel's life as they attempted to live in Covenant relationship with God.

Two questions become important: Did Israel continue to understand her relationship with God in this way? And how did scholarship come to replace a "staying in" Covenant with a "getting in" Covenant? Or how did *keeping the stipulations of the Covenant* as loyal obedient Israelites in relationship with God change to *doing the stipulations of the Covenant* in order to "get into" a relationship with God?

What the Players Have Said

Martin Luther

Luther was *not* the first "Lutheran" reader of Paul. Augustine was. Westerholm says, "Whether we should say that Augustine's Paul was 'Lutheran' or that Luther's Paul was Augustinian is a moot point.[31] He also suggests six theses of Luther that are under attack as distorting Paul. They are:

1. In our relationship with God, faith in his goodness rather than the good works we do is decisive.
2. The law, like a mighty hammer, is meant to crush human self-righteousness and to drive human beings, made aware of their sinfulness, to seek mercy from the Savior.
3. We are justified by faith in Jesus Christ, not by the works we do.
4. Though believers are righteous in God's eyes, they remain sinners throughout their earthly lives.
5. The law must be banished from the thinking of believers when their relationship with God is the issue. Yet it must continue its role in identifying and judging their sin.
6. God predestined believers to salvation.[32]

"What Luther means by 'law' is not always transparent.[33] He seems to have three distinct usages: a law of nature; the Mosaic code, divided into two kingdoms, first, temporal and visible and, second, spiritual; and Scripture wherever it places requirements on people.[34] For Luther, the whole of Scripture can be seen under two rubrics; "command and promise...or — in his preferred terminology — law and gospel."[35] The Old Testament shows what one must do or not do and is illustrated by stories of how the laws are broken or kept. The New Testament is the proclamation of the grace given through Jesus. The words "not by works of the Law" for Luther refer to the deeds required by the Mosaic law and imply that nothing one can do can gain justification.

What was the gospel of Christ, according to Luther and all subsequent Protestants?

That man enjoys that acceptance with God called "justification," the beginning and end of salvation, not through his own moral effort even the smallest and slightest degree but entirely and only through the loving mercy of God made available in the merits of Christ and of his saving death on the Cross. This was not a process of gradual ethical improvement but an instantaneous transaction, somewhat like a marriage, in which Christ the bridegroom takes to himself an impoverished and wrenched harlot and confers upon her all the riches which are his. The key to this transaction was faith, defined as a total and trustful commitment of the self to God, and in itself not a human achievement but the pure gift of God. "Faith cometh by hearing and hearing by the word of God": *fides ex auditu*.[36]

Dunn sees the consequences of Luther's rediscovery of justification by faith as dramatic in theology, church, socially and politically. He also sees a negative side to Luther's rediscovery as an "unfortunate strain of anti-Judaism" in which "Paul's teaching on justification was seen as a reaction against and in opposition to Judaism."[37] Luther rejected a medieval church that offered salvation by merit and good works and assumed that this was the same as Paul's rejection of Judaism in his day.[38] Wright suggests that "Luther thought Paul was against the Law."[39]

E. P. Sanders

What scholars call "the Sanders revolution" was precipitated by the writing of his book *Paul and Palestinian Judaism* in 1977, a watershed in Pauline studies. Wright says that Sanders "major point to which everything else is subservient, can be quite simply stated: Judaism in Paul's day was not, as has regularly been supposed, a religion of legalist works-righteousness."[40]

Sanders begins his groundbreaking book by defining what he means by "patterns of religion" which is part of his subtitle. For Sanders, "A pattern of religion defined positively, is the description of how a religion is perceived by its adherents to *function*. 'Perceived to function' has the sense not of what the adherent does on a day-to-day basis, but of how getting in and staying in are understood: the way in which a religion was understood to admit and retain members is considered to be the way it 'functions.'"[41]

For Sanders, there is a single "pattern of religion" that underlies Judaism of the Second Temple period. It is "covenantal nomism" which is "the view that one's place in God's plan is established on the basis of the covenant and that the covenant requires as the proper response of man his obedience to its commandments, while providing means of atonement for transgression."[42] However, he does not believe that "covenantal nomism" is Paul's "pattern of religion," suggesting that Paul "presents an *essentially different type of religiousness from any found in Palestinian Jewish literature*."[43]

For Paul, "Christianity is going to become a new form of covenantal nomism, a covenantal religion which one enters by baptism, membership in which provides salvation, which has a specific set of commandments, obedience to which (or repentance for the transgression of which) keeps one in the covenantal relationship, while repeated or heinous transgression removes one from membership."[44]

Sanders goes on to say:

> The heart of Paul's thought is not that one ratifies and agrees to a covenant offered by God, becoming a member of a group with a covenantal relation with God and remaining in it on the conditions of proper behaviour; but that one dies with Christ, obtaining new life and the initial transformation which leads to the resurrection and ultimate transformation, that one is a member of the body of Christ and one Spirit with him, and that one remains so unless one breaks the participatory union by forming another.[45]

Wright suggests that Sanders has cut the ground from under the majority reading of Paul, especially in mainline Protestantism."[46]

N. T. Wright

Wright was one of the first to espouse the new perspective on Paul in a paper published in the *Tyndale Bulletin* in 1978.[47] For Wright, Paul did not charge the Jews with supposing that they could merit the favor of God by the keeping of Torah. He rather criticized Israel's "relentless pursuit of national, ethnic and territorial identity" working toward becoming like other pagan nations who carried boundary markers.[48]

According to Wright, the concept of justification by faith was not Paul's gospel because Paul was not answering the question of how an individual can be "saved" or enjoy a right relationship with God. Justification was not about how an individual in the first century established a relationship with God. Rather it was about the "eschatological definition" of who was a member of God's people. It was more about ecclesiology than soteriology.[49]

In Galatians, justification is the belief which insists that everyone who follows Jesus belongs at the same table no matter what their race may be.[50] One did not become justified by following a set of legal requirements, but it was about who was included and who was excluded in the people of God.[51]

In Wright's more popular commentary on Galatians[52] in the "for Everyone" series, he says, "we Jews...even though we were born into the covenant family, do not now find our real identity as God's people through the things which mark us out as a distinctive people–that is, through the Jewish law."[53] Being "in" Jesus means that one has lost their previous identity markers because they have become irrelevant. Wright suggests that Paul argues that "we are no longer defined by possession of the law, or by its detailed requirements that set Jews over against Gentiles."[54] The argument with Peter had to do with table fellowship which was one of the identity markers that had to be lost in order to become truly a new creation so that both Jews and Gentiles could sit at the same table as a symbol of this new creation.

As a grammatical note, Wright says (as does Dunn, see below) that "to judaize" describes what the Jewish Christians were doing to the Gentile Christians, i.e., "they were judaizing them" is not strictly the right use of the word. Rather, "judaize" is what pagans do when they become Jews. If you were a pagan and you became a Jew, you are "judaizing." Jewish Christians were not trying to get Galatians to "judaize," but pagans becoming Jews were being judaized.[55]

Appendix

James D. G. Dunn

Dunn's thesis "is that Galatians is Paul's first sustained attempt to deal with the issue of covenantal nomism."[56]

This phrase characterizes the Jewish relationship between God and Israel and its idea is consistently within the corpus of Jewish literature. The law was an integral part of the Covenant "both to show Israel how to live within that covenant...and to make it possible for them to do so (the system of atonement). Thus, in the phrase 'covenantal nomism,' the former word emphasizes God's prevenient grace, the latter can and should not be confused with legalism or with any idea of 'earning' salvation."[57]

Dunn suggests that during the Maccabean period, the retention of national identity and the obligations of covenantal nomism "focused on those features of national and religious life which marked out the distinctives of the Jewish people—circumcision and food laws."[58] For him as for Wright (see above), "the verb 'to judaize' is coined to indicate those Gentiles who choose to live their lives in accord with the ancestral customs and practices distinctive of the Jewish nation."[59] During the Maccabean period, "circumcision and food laws, together with other specific commandments like Sabbath and festivals, remained the clearest identity and boundary markers of Judaism as a whole,..."[60]

What Dunn calls "the social function of the law" is that covenantal nomism was bound up with national and ethnic identity so that the law became a way of understanding the distinctiveness of the Jews *as* God's people and their differences from others, namely Gentiles, who were not God's people.[61]

Dunn admits that the second controversial item in his theology is that "the phrase 'works of the law' was a way of describing the same covenantal-nomistic mindset, that is, 'works of the law' refers to the praxis which the law of the covenant laid upon the covenant member."[62] For him, the boundary markers (circumcision, food laws, and festivals) marked the Jews as a nationalistic entity and were markers that kept the Gentiles and Jewish Christians from being one new creation.

Frank Thielman

Thielman argues against Sanders because Sanders thinks the fundamental difference between (unconverted) Jew and Christian in Paul is Christology, therefore on matters such as sin and grace and forgiveness, Paul is really arguing "from solution to plight": that is, Paul knows the solution, namely Jesus, and then argues back to plight. Thielman argues that when Paul in Galatians and Romans professedly sets out the plight (i.e., sin, or rebellion against God and his law) and then turns to the solution, he is not resorting to a pedagogical device, but is borrowing from a standard pattern in both the Old Testament and in the Judaism of his day.[63]

Thielman is viewed as a "Lutheran Responder,"[64] but he is not seen as representing a return to the Protestant portrayals of Judaism from the pre-Sanders era. Thielman sees the Reformers and their disciples as wrong in not trying to make an attempt to understand Judaism on its own terms and that Paul did not see Judaism as a legalistic religion nor did he attribute to Judaism a doctrine of salvation by works.[65]

Thielman's view of the Pauline argument includes eschatological hope in which the vicious cycle of sin would be broken and the people of God would be transformed to do his will from their hearts.[66] He suggests that Paul appropriated a "plight to solution" pattern that was already established in the Second Temple Judaism period and that membership in the people of God, as it is defined by the Mosaic Covenant, is membership in a people with a plight. Thielman's argument in *From Plight to Solution* is that the common Jewish expectation was that the restored people of God would be enabled by God's Spirit to carry out the law of Moses.

In the final section of his book *Paul and the Law*, Thielman deals with the question: Does the Law Contradict the Gospel? in which he writes about the parallels in the pattern of Judaism in the Mosaic Law and the patterns of Christianity in Paul's letters. Within that framework, his answer is that the Law does not contradict the Gospel.[67] Next, he asks the question: Why, then, the Gospel? For him the Gospel is needed because most of the Jews of Paul's time believed that they lived under the "curses" of the Covenant in this "Present Evil Age." In spite of sacrifices to bring atonement to those "in the Covenant," there was a longing of many Jews in Paul's time who looked forward to the intervention of God on their behalf to recreate hearts and restore their nation. For Thielman, this eschatological redemption was Paul's focus and the Mosaic law had been absorbed by the gospel by the transforming influence of the Holy Spirit.[68] Thielman offers a proposal that "Paul, along with many Jews of his time, adopted the understanding of the relationship between grace and obedience"[69] The basic difference for him between Paul and Judaism was their position within salvation history. The Old Testament and Judaism carried a hope of the restoration of the Covenant in the establishment of a New Covenant while Paul proclaimed that it had been fulfilled.[70]

Stephen Westerholm

Westerholm stands on the Lutheran side of the equation. Thielman assesses his response to Dunn and the "new perspective" as: "Dunn's proposal cannot be correct and...Luther, in spite of his unreliable view of Judaism, is a master when it comes to reading Paul."[71] Westerholm's argument is that "in Paul's letters the term *law* refers most frequently to the Mosaic legislation given to Israel at Mount Sinai so that Israel could 'do' or 'keep' the law. The phrase *works of the law* is most naturally understood as 'the doing of the law'; not as Israel's misuse of the law to limit the people of God to their own national boundaries."[72]

Appendix 12: The Little Apocalypse: Mark 13

BackStory

Chapter 11 of Mark begins on Sunday of the Passion week of Jesus. The conflict with the Jewish leaders was over. Mark 13, often called the Little Apocalypse, occurs on Tuesday afternoon of the last week of the life of Jesus and stands as a bridge between that conflict and the story of the death and resurrection of Jesus. This chapter is prophetic. Prophecy is sometimes like looking at two mountains, but, you cannot see the distance between them. One might see this chapter as the first mountain, a message for the disciples of Jesus played out in their own lives. At the same time there are portions of this story which reveal something about the future without stating a specific time plan for its fulfillment.

Mark 13 is an exhortation regulating the conduct of the disciples in the period when Jesus would no longer be with them. The language of this section is characteristic of a Farewell discourse (Acts 20.17-35). The recurring phrase, "take care" (*blepo*: beware of, see to it: vv. 5, 9, 23, 33) and watch (*gregoreo*: be on guard: in 34, 35, 37), may suggest to the disciples that this is information that will help them in some future crisis. Jesus wanted them not to be disturbed by preliminary signs and that they should not confuse them with the end. With a profound pastoral concern, Jesus prepared his disciples and his church for a future period which would entail both persecution and mission. This would have a profound significance to believers in Rome who were harassed by persecution. It would enable them to fare the crisis of the '60s.

Introduction to the Olivet Discourse (13.1-2)

Mark 13.1

As Jesus was leaving the temple, one of his disciples said to him, "Look, Teacher! What massive stones! What magnificent buildings!"

The Temple was many buildings, enclosures, and porches. In the afternoon sun, it glowed and lit up the whole city of Jerusalem. It comprised one-sixth (1/6) of the city of Jerusalem. Josephus said that the stones that made up the Temple were 36½ feet in length; 11½ feet in height, 16½ feet wide; and weighed one hundred tons each. It was an architectural wonder. The Jewish people had little respect for Herod, but loved his Temple construction. Its construction began in 20-19 B.C. It was still under construction during the life of Jesus (John 2.20). It was completed in A.D. 64, which was only six years, before it was destroyed. The disciples were proud of the size and structure of the Temple.

Mark 13.2

"Do you see all these great buildings?" replied Jesus. "Not one stone here will be left on another; every one will be thrown down."

When Jesus responded to the musing of the disciples, it was emphatic and definite. Titus ordered the whole city and the Temple to be leveled to the ground sometime during A.D. 70, according to the historian Josephus. What Jesus said came to pass in the first century. The prophetic word of Jesus was a continuation of the prophecy of some of the Old Testament prophets (Jeremiah 26.18; Micah 3.12).

The Question of the Disciples (13.3-4)

Mark 13.3-4

As Jesus was sitting on the Mount of Olives opposite the temple, Peter, James, John and Andrew asked him privately, "Tell us, when will these things happen? And what will be the sign that they are all about to be fulfilled?"

Jesus and his disciples had traveled to the Mount of Olives that was opposite the Temple. Four of his disciples asked him privately to tell them when the destruction of the Temple would happen and what would be the sign that it was about to be fulfilled. In Mark, questions from the disciples of Jesus often precede a teaching section (4.10f.; 7.17f.; 9.22; 10.10f.). In verse 4 the disciples asked one question which is in two parts: *When*, which has to do with time, and *what*. The last part of the question, *what*, was answered first. The first part of the question, *when*, was answered last.

Warnings against Deception (13.5-8)

Mark 13.5-6

Jesus said to them: "Watch out that no one deceives you. Many will come in my name, claiming, 'I am he,' and will deceive many."

Jesus pointed out the fact that anyone who says that they have "inside information" on the Second Coming can get a crowd, but the end results is deception. The warning about false *christs* was well suited for Palestine which was plagued with false *christs* prior to the Jewish War (A.D. 66-70). This was one of the principal factors that caused the Romans to destroy Jerusalem. The disciples were told not to be deceived by the course of events into thinking that the end had arrived.

Mark 13.7-8

"When you hear of wars and rumors of wars, do not be alarmed. Such things must happen, but the end is still to come. Nation will rise against nation, and kingdom against kingdom. There will be earthquakes in various places, and famines. These are the beginning of birth pains."

Jesus said that when you hear of disturbances in society (wars and rumors of wars) and nature (earthquakes), that his hearers should not continue to be alarmed. The Roman emperors (Caligula, Claudius, and Nero) kept peace by threatening wars. Between A.D. 30-70 there were four major earthquakes (Crete 46; Rome 51; Apamaia in Phygia 60, and Campania 63). There were four famines during the rule of Claudius (A.D. 41-52). One of them was in Judea in A.D. 44 (Acts 11.28).

The words of Jesus are not to be understood as signs that the end was near. They were to be understood as signs to demonstrate that the end *had not yet arrived*. These signs would help believers not to be deceived into believing that Jesus had returned.

Warnings about Persecution (13.9-13)

Mark 13.9

"You must be on your guard. You will be handed over to the local councils and flogged in the synagogues. On account of me you will stand before governors and kings as witnesses to them."

Appendix

Being handed over to the authorities began as early as Acts 4. Paul recorded in 2 Corinthians 11.2b that he was beaten in the Synagogue with thirty-nine stripes (this was thirteen across the chest and thirteen across the back and often caused the victim of such a beating to die). Jesus himself, not many days from when this event happened, would face Pilate (Mark 15.2) and be beaten. Later in the Story, Paul would face Felix and Festus (Acts 24.1.ff.). Mark wanted to make clear to his readers that the preaching of the gospel would cause offense and public rebuke to his followers. Persecution did not mean that the end had come, nor was it an occasion for the loss of hope. Rather, persecution was and still is an occasion for witness to the nations.

Mark 13.10

"And the gospel must first be preached to all nations."

This saying provided assurance that the Kingdom of God cannot be impeded by any local persecution anywhere. It is important to note that in the interval that comes before the consummation, i.e., the Act of the drama in which we are now living, the church is about her mission, preaching the gospel of the Kingdom to the nations.

Mark 13.11

"Whenever you are arrested and brought to trial, do not worry beforehand about what to say. Just say whatever is given you at the time, for it is not you speaking, but the Holy Spirit."

Jesus spoke of the Holy Spirit who would come to continue his ministry. This can be seen in the story of Peter (Acts 4.7f.); Stephen (Acts 7); and Paul (Acts 24.10f.). The Holy Spirit can take out of a person only what has been placed inside the person. The disciples had been educated and trained by Jesus. The Holy Sprit had lots of information and experience to pull from. When one is not trained and speaks, it is usually *hot air* rather than *holy air* that proceeds from the speaker's mouth. Preaching the gospel of the Kingdom to the whole world will be accomplished through the power of the Holy Spirit, who will give the disciples utterance to proclaim that gospel under the most adverse circumstances.

Mark 13.12-13

"Brother will betray brother to death, and a father his child. Children will rebel against their parents and have them put to death. Everyone will hate you because of me, but those who stand firm to the end will be saved."

Already Jesus had experienced what he was speaking about at the beginning of his ministry, a division within his own family (Mark 2.30f.). The demand for radical commitment that is inherent in the gospel of the Kingdom takes precedence over all other loyalties and may disrupt the deepest ties between families.

Three words are of importance in verse 13. First, *endures* (13b) (*hupomeno*) which means to preserve under misfortunes and trials, to hold fast to one's faith in Christ; to take all the enemy can throw and still have strength to come back and win. Second, *end* (*telos*) refers primarily to the end of the persevering believer's life. Finally, *saved* (*sozo)*, vindicated is another word you can use here, which means to preserve one who is in danger of destruction, to save or rescue. Usually *end* is interpreted as *the end of the world*. But, it seems better to understand it to mean the end of a persevering believer's life. So Jesus has suggested that his followers in their Act of the play should persevere to the end of their life, and, in so doing, be vindicated by God.

The Destruction of Jerusalem 13.14-23

Mark 13.14-23

"When you see 'the abomination that causes desolation standing where it does not belong— let the reader understand—then let those who are in Judea flee to the mountains. Let no one on the housetop go down or enter the house to take anything out. Let no one in the field go back to get their cloak. How dreadful it will be in those days for pregnant women and nursing mothers! Pray that this will not take place in winter, because those will be days of distress unequaled from the beginning, when God created the world, until now—and never to be equaled again. If the Lord had not cut short those days, no one would survive. But for the sake of the elect, whom he has chosen, he has shortened them. At that time if anyone says to you, "Look, here is the Messiah!" or, "Look, there he is!" do not believe it. For false messiahs and false prophets will appear and perform signs and wonders to deceive, if possible, even the elect. So be on your guard; I have told you everything ahead of time."

Jesus now answered the *what* question of the disciples. Earlier in Jewish history (1 Maccabees 1.54), Antiochus Epiphanes had set up an altar to Zeus in the Temple. It was this historical event which every Jewish person would have known about, that Jesus used to talk about another event just like that one. The *abomination that causes desolation* is not the destruction of the Temple in A.D. 70, for then it would be too late to flee. The Zealots had won an impressive victory over Cestius Gallus in November '66. Many in Jerusalem realized that the Zealots would finally lose to Rome and began to leave in droves according to Josephus (Wars 2.20). The Zealots occupied the Temple and allowed criminals to roam freely in the Holy of Holies. In addition, murders took place in the Temple and this all climaxed with a mockery of the High Priest as the town clown (A.D. 67-68). Jesus told his disciples that when they saw these events, it was time to leave Jerusalem.

There should be an urgency to their flight (13.15-16). Jesus wanted his disciples to understand that a concern for life took precedence over possessions. There were possible circumstances that could hinder flight (13.17-18) like pregnancy, younger children, winter (the Jordan River would be swollen and difficult to cross). He told his disciples that there was a reason for flight (13.19-20): it would be a horrendous time. There could be deterrents to flight (13.21-23). This last warning implies clearly a crisis in history and not the end of time when flight will be useless (Rev 6.15-17). He told his disciples not to be deterred by claims that the Messiah was here or there. They should remember the signs to remind them not to be deceived. This last statement is mind boggling. He told them *everything*. I might suggest that there is not anything else that needs to be understood, unlike the words of the doomsday prophets of our time who always have something to add to the message.

The Coming of the Son of Man 13.24-27

Mark 13.24

> *"But in those days, following that distress,*
>
> *'the sun will be darkened*
>   *and the moon will not give its light;*
> *the stars will fall from the sky,*
>   *and the heavenly bodies will be shaken.'"*

The word *but* is to help the reader make a transition: But, as compared to the false *christs*, there would come other days. *In those days* is an expression that was distinctly future of the context into which it fell (Joel 2.28; Jer. 3.16–18, 31.29, 33.15f.; Zech 8.23). This piece of poetry is embedded in Old Testament language which suggests that God was going to appear in history. This imagery language indicates that an important turn in history would occur. In Scripture, this kind of language is a picturesque way of saying that divine judgment would occur (Jude 14f.). We should not take it literally.

Mark 13.26-27

> *"At that time people will see the Son of Man coming in clouds with great power and glory. And he will send his angels and gather his elect from the four winds, from the ends of the earth to the ends of the heavens."*

The elect, the church, will be collected at the end of the age from the whole world (1 Thes. 4.16-17).

The Lesson of the Fig Tree 13.28-31

Mark 13.28-31

> *"Now learn this lesson from the fig tree: As soon as its twigs get tender and its leaves come out, you know that summer is near. Even so, when you see these things happening, you know that it is near, right at the door. Truly I tell you, this generation will certainly not pass away until all these things have happened. Heaven and earth will pass away, but my words will never pass away."*

This paragraph is to be considered in relationship with verses 14-23. The events in verses 24-25 represent the end of the age and can not constitute a previous sign of something else. The fig trees lost their leaves in the winter and the branches became tender with sap. When the leaves began to appear, you would know that summer is near and winter was gone. When you see *these things*, is a reference back to verse 14. The catastrophe of the Temple sacrilege will enable the disciples to know that the destruction of the Temple is near at hand. Just as one knows summer is near when he sees the leaves on a fig tree, a person will know that the destruction of the Temple is near when he sees the *abomination that causes desolation*.

The manner in which Jesus spoke declared the truth he was affirming. *This generation* was the generation of Mark. It clearly designates the contemporaries of Jesus and affirmed that that generation will see the fulfillment of his prophetic word. What is said of God in the OT is said of Jesus in the New. His word will surely happen!

The Call to Vigilance 13.32-36

This is the practical section of the teaching of Jesus.

Mark 13.32

"But about that day or hour no one knows, not even the angels in heaven, nor the Son, but only the Father."

The concept that no one knows is simple to understand. No one knows no matter how many of the current doomsday prophets tell you otherwise, no one knows.

Mark 13.33-36

"Be on guard! Be alert! You do not know when that time will come. It's like a man going away: He leaves his house and puts his servants in charge, each with an assigned task, and tells the one at the door to keep watch. Therefore keep watch because you do not know when the owner of the house will come back—whether in the evening, or at midnight, or when the rooster crows, or at dawn. If he comes suddenly, do not let him find you sleeping. What I say to you, I say to everyone: 'Watch!'"

The disciples were told to be on guard. There were four watches of the night and the watcher should not be caught unexpected when the owner returned. The same is true of the followers of Jesus. Jesus ends this teaching section by telling his disciples to *watch*. To *watch* does not mean to be looking at twenty-first-century newspaper clippings or TV shows so one can discover the latest analysis of the end. To *watch* means to be prepared.

Justification was not about how an

individual in the first century established

a relationship with God.

EndNotes

Reference Information

The stories which characterize the worldview itself

are thus located, on the map of human knowing, at

a more fundamental level than explicitly

formulated beliefs, including theological beliefs.

(N. T. Wright. *The New Testament and the People of God*)

Prologue

1. Story capitalized is a reference to the metanarrative of Scripture while story not capitalized means other stories.

2. George E. Ladd, *New Testament and Criticism* (Grand Rapids, MI: William B. Eerdmans Publishing Company, 1966), 12. The biblical mode of revelation is the revealing acts of God in history, accompanied by the interpreting prophetic word that explains the divine source and character of the divine acts. Acts and words; God acts and God speaks; and the words explain the deeds. The deeds cannot be understood unless they are accompanied by the divine word. The word would be powerless unless accompanied by the mighty acts of God. Scripture is *words-works* revelation.

3. Ibid., 27. God both acts and interprets the meaning of his acts. Scripture is the *works* and *words* of God. This is a *key* concept for understanding Scripture. For us to understand the faithfulness of God, we need to become familiar with how God has acted in faithfulness to his children and what he says those acts mean. *Christ's death* is the act of God. *Christ died for us while we were sinners* is his word of explanation for us.

4. Gordon Fee and Douglas Stuart, *How to Read the Bible for All Its Worth.* Third Edition (Grand Rapids, MI: Zondervan Publishing House, 2003), 89.

5. Ibid., 127.

6. Richard B. Hays, *Echoes of Scripture in the Letters of Paul* (New Haven, CT: Yale UP, 1989), xxiv-xxv.

7. Edward W. Goodrick, *Is My Bible the Inspired Word of God?* (Portland, OR: Multnomah, 1988), 86-88.

8. Leonard I. Sweet, *Out of the Question...Into the Mystery* (Colorado Springs, CO: WaterBrook Press, 2004), 77.

9. N. T. Wright, "How Can the Bible Be Authoritative?," *Vox Evangelica*, no. 21 (1991): 7-32.

10. Tending to break up into parts or break away from a main body.

11. *The Promise: Contemporary English Version* (Nashville, TN: Thomas Nelson, Inc., 1995), vi.

12. Everett Fox, *The Five Books of Moses* (Dallas, TX: Word Publishing, 1995), ix.

13. Susan Niditch, *Oral World and Written Word: Ancient Israelite Literature* (Louisville, KY: Westminster John Knox Press, 1996), 39-41.

14. "The Bible," *The Barna Group* [document online]; available from http://www.barna.org/ FlexPage.aspx?Page=Topic&TopicID=7; Internet; accessed 6 June 2005. "Three-quarters of Americans (75%) believe that the Bible teaches that God helps those who help themselves. (2000)"

15. "A House Divided Against Itself Cannot Stand," *The National Center for Public Policy Research* [document online]; available from http://www.nationalcenter.org/HouseDivided.html; Internet; accessed 7 June 2005. "Lincoln delivered this famous speech, noted for the phrase 'a house divided against itself cannot stand,' when accepting the Republican nomination for U.S. Senate from Illinois in June of 1858. In July of that year he challenged his Democrat opponent, Stephen Douglas to a series of debates over admitting Kansas into the union as a slave state, and, to a large extent, over the future of slavery and of the union itself. Lincoln, of course, represented the anti-slavery position. The skill with which Lincoln debated Douglas helped catapult him to the Republican Party's nomination for president in 1860, a race which he won."

16. Winn Griffin, *Old Testament Interpretation* (Woodinville, WA: Harmon Press, 1996-2005), 8-9.

17. Stanley J. Grenz, *A Primer on Postmodernism* (Grand Rapids, MI: William B. Eerdmans, 1996), 173.

18. Stanley J. Grenz, and John R. Franke, *Beyond Foundationalism: Shaping Theology in a Post Modern Context* (Louisville, KY: Westminster John Knox Press, 2001), 29.

19. Ibid., 28.

20. Ibid., 29.

21. Walter Brueggemann, *Text Under Negotiation: The Bible and Postmodern Imagination* (Minneapolis: Fortress Press, 1993), 3.

22. Grenz and Frank, *Beyond Foundationalism*, 30.

23. Ibid.

24. Ibid., 31.

25. "Empiricism," *Answers.com Fast Facts* [document online]; available from http:// www.answers.com/empiricism; Internet; accessed 30 June 2005. "The view that experience, especially of the senses, is the only source of knowledge."

26. Grenz and Frank, *Beyond Foundationalism*, 32.

27. Brueggemann, *Text Under Negotiation: The Bible and Postmodern Imagination*, 4.

28. Grenz and Frank, *Beyond Foundationalism*, 33.

29. Ibid.

30. Ibid., 34.

31. Ibid.

32. Ibid., 34-35.

33. Wayne Grudem, *Systematic Theology: An Introduction to Biblical Doctrine* (Grand Rapids, MI: Zondervan Publishing House, 1994), 21. This definition of systematic theology was taken from Professor John Frame under whom Grudem studied at Westminster Seminary, Philadelphia.

34. Grenz and Frank, *Beyond Foundationalism*, 37.

35. Ibid., 53-54.

36. "Chapter," *crosswalk.com* [document online]; available from http://www.biblestudytools.net/Dictionaries/EastonBibleDictionary/ebd.cgi?number=T773; Internet; accessed 24 June 2005.

37. N. T. Wright, *Scripture and the Authority of God* (London: SPCK, 2005), 102.

38. Grenz, *Primer*, 172.

39. Ibid., 173.

40. One may look at the *Left Behind* series as an example of cobbling together fragments to produce a wrong-headed conclusion.

41. "General Information: The International Sunday School Lesson Plan," *Smyth & Helwys* [document online]; available online from http://www.helwys.com/curriculum/usgeneral.html; Internet; accessed 22 June 2005.

42. William J. Bausch, *Storytelling: Imagination and Faith* (Mystic, CT: Twenty-Third Publications, 1984), 9.

43. Ibid.

44. Stanley Hauerwas and L. Gregory Jones, *Why Narrative? Readings in Narrative Theology* (Grand Rapids: William B. Eerdmans Publishing Company, 1989), 1.

45. Wright, *Scripture and the Authority of God*, 19.

46. S. E. Porter and C. A. Evans, "Canonical Formation of the New Testament," *Dictionary of New Testament Background: A Compendium of Contemporary Biblical Scholarship* (Electronic Edition. Downers Grove, IL: InterVarsity Press, 2000).

47. Richard L. Morgan, *Saving Our Stories* (Louisville, KY: Geneva Press, 1999), 1.

48. William C. Placher, "Paul Ricoeur and Postliberal Theology: A Conflict of Interpretations?" *Modern Theology* 4, no. 1 (1987): 42.

49. Alister McGrath, *Christian Spirituality: An Introduction* (Oxford: Blackwell Publishers, 1999), 119-120.

50. The classic definition of story is: a narrative with a beginning, middle, and an ending that follows a main character through his or her struggle(s) to achieve a certain goal.

51. Wright, *Scripture and the Authority of God*, 20.

52. N. T. Wright, *Bringing the Church to the World* (Minneapolis, MN: Bethany House Publishers, 1992), 21.

53. Ibid., 152.

54. Bausch, *Storytelling: Imagination and Faith, Storytelling*, 29-80.

55. Ibid., 65-80. These paradoxes are: first, spirituality is rooted in earthiness; second, the absolute is known in the personal; third, freedom is discovered in obedience; fourth, triumph grows out of suffering; fifth, security is found in uncertainty; and sixth, prayer is offered through study.

56. Ibid., 79.

57. Wright, "How Can the Bible Be Authoritative?", 7-32.

58. Ibid., 11.

59. Fee and Stuart, *How to Read the Bible for All Its Worth*, 89.

60. Ibid., 91-92.

61. Ibid., 92-93.

62. Ibid., 106.

63. Gordon Fee, and Douglas Stuart, *How to Read The Bible For All Its Worth*, Second Edition (Grand Rapids, MI: Zondervan Publishing House, 1993), 90-91.

64. Fee and Stuart, *How to Read the Bible for All Its Worth. Third Edition*, 102-106.

65. Hays, *Echoes of Scripture in the letters of Paul*, 14.

66. Kent L. Yinger, *Paul, Judaism, and Judgment According to Deeds* (New York, NY: Cambridge University Press, 1999), 19.

67. Walter Brueggemann, *The Creative Word: Canon as a Model for Biblical Education* (Philadelphia: Fortress Press, 1982), 23, Brueggemann seems to be saying that the characters in the biblical stories are historical but you can read them without any "historical background."

68. Ibid.

69. Ibid., 24.

70. Ibid., 25-26.

71. Ibid., 26-27.

72. Bruce C. Birch, et. al, *A Theological Introduction to the Old Testament* (Nashville, TN: Abingdon Press, 1999), 21-22.

73. Walter Brueggemann, *The Bible Makes Sense* (Atlanta, GA: John Knox Press, 1977), vii-viii.

74. William L. Lane, *The Gospel According to Mark* (Grand Rapids, MI: William B. Eerdmans Publishing Company, 1994), xii. "Only gradually did I come to understand that my primary task as a commentator was to listen to the text, and to the discussion it has prompted over the course of the centuries, as a child who needed to be made wise. The responsibility to discern truth from error has been onerous at times. When a critical or theological decision has been demanded by the text before I was prepared to commit myself, I have adopted the practice of the Puritan commentators in laying the material before the Lord and asking for his guidance. This has made the preparation of the commentary a spiritual as well as an intellectual pilgrimage through the text of the Gospel. In learning to be sensitive to all that the evangelist was pleased to share with me, I have been immeasurably enriched by the disciple of responsible listening."

75. Ellen F. Davis and Richard B. Hays, eds., *The Art of Reading Scripture* (Grand Rapids, MI: William B. Eerdmans Publishing Company, 2003), 2.

76. Ibid., 3.

77. Fee and Stuart, *How to Read the Bible for All Its Worth*. Third Edition, 74.

78. Ibid., 23.

79. N. T. Wright, *Jesus and the Victory of God* (London: SPCK, 1996), 15.

80. Ibid., 199.

81. Ibid., 200.

82. N. T. Wright, *The New Testament and the People of God* (Minneapolis, MN: Fortress Press, 1992), 35. In footnote 12 on page 35 Wright makes the following suggestion for clarity: "We should perhaps note that the adjective 'critical' in the phrase 'critical realism' has a different function to the same adjective in the phrase 'critical reason'. In the latter (as e.g. in Kant) it is active: 'reason *that provides* a critique'. In the former it is passive: 'realism *subject to* critique'".

83. Ibid., 6.

84. Ibid., 13.

85. Ibid., 49.

86. Ibid., 62.

87. Gordon Fee, *Tyndale Lecture Series* (Toronto, Ontario, Canada: Tyndale University College & Seminary)., Tape 1: "The Reader As Interpreter."

88. Wright, *Scripture and the Authority of God*, 6.

89. Ibid., xiii.

90. Ibid., 93-95. By "totally contextually" Wright says that "each word must be understood within its own verse, each verse within its own chapter, each chapter within its own book, and each book within its own historical, cultural and indeed canonical setting." By "incarnational" he says that one should pay "attention to the full humanity both of the text and of its readers."

91. Richard B. Hays, *The Faith of Jesus Christ: The Narrative Substructure of Galatians 3:1-4:11*, Second Edition. (Grand Rapids, MI: William B. Eerdmans Publishing Company, 1999), xxviii. "We have not thought of Paul as a storyteller, for the Jesus stories of the Gospels are absent from his letters. Yet his use of narrative is very important..., because Paul's central concern was to use the narrative to form a moral community.... Paul's most profound bequest to subsequent Christian discourse was his transformation of the reported crucifixion and resurrection of Jesus Christ into a multipurpose metaphor with vast generative and transformative power.... In that gospel story Paul sees revolutionary import for the relationships of power that control human transactions.... Thus Paul's use of the metaphor of the cross resists its translation into simple slogans. Instead he introduces into the moral language of the new movement a way of seeking after resonance in the basic story for all kinds of relationships of disciples with the world and with one another, so that the event-become-metaphor could become the generative center of almost endless new narratives, yet remain a check and control over those narratives." (a quote from W.A. Meeks, *The Origins of Christian Mortality: The First Two Centuries* (New Haven: Yale University Press, 1993), 196-197).

92. Ibid., xxiv-xxv.

93. *George Fox University* [document online]; available from http://www.georgefox.edu/academics/seminary/degrees/dmin/index.html; Internet; accessed 27 June 2005.

94. Leonard I. Sweet, *SoulTsunami: Sink or Swim in the New Millennium Culture* (Grand Rapids, MI: Zondervan Publishing House, 1999), 423

95. Ibid., 424.

96. Ibid., 425.

97. Ibid.

98. Ibid. "People come to worship with problem stories, with painful stories, with jostling narratives and 'narrative dysfunctions,' a condition and process 'by which we lose track of the story ourselves, the story that tells us who we are supposed to be and how we are supposed to act.' Preachers help heal people's narrative dysfunction and help them live out of new, whole stories. Bad stories hurt and impair; good stories heal and help."

99. Leonard I. Sweet, *AQUAchurch* (Loveland, CO: Group Publishing, 1999), 57. These images come from Donna Markova's *No Enemies Within* (Emeryville, CA: Publisher Groups West, 1994) as quoted in Robert Hargrove, *Mastering the Art of Creative Collaboration* (New York: BusinessWeek Books, 1998), 65.

100. Ibid., 59.

101. Leonard I. Sweet, *Summoned to Lead* (Grand Rapids, MI: Zondervan Publishing House, 2004), 133.

102. Ibid., 134. I would suggest that all these kinds of stories may define the overarching Story of Scripture.

103. Sweet, *Out of the Question*, 77.

104. Ibid., 78.

105. Eugene H. Peterson, *Stories of Jesus* (Colorado Springs, CO: NavPress, 1999), 7-8.

106. Stephen Denning, *Squirrel Inc.* (San Francisco, CA: Jossey-Bass, 2004), xiii-xv.

107. Gordon Fee and Douglas Stuart, *How to Read the Bible Book by Book: A Guided Tour* (Grand Rapids, MI: Zondervan Publishing House, 2002), 14-20.

108. Ibid., 216.

109. Craig G. Bartholomew, Michael W. Goheen, *The Drama of Scripture: Finding Our Place in the Biblical Story* (Grand Rapids, MI: Baker Academic, 2005), 12.

110. Ibid., 13.

111. Ibid., 11.

112. *Biblical Theology* [document online]; available from http://www.biblicaltheology.ca/index.htm; Internet; accessed 24 June 2005.

113. C. Marvin Pate, J. Scott Duvall, J. Daniel Hays, E. Randolph Richards, W. Dennis Tucker Jr., and Preben Vang, *The Story of Israel: A Biblical Theology* (Downers Grove, IL: InterVarsity Press, 2004), 9.

114. Ibid.

115. Ibid., 12-15.

116. Ibid., 17, 23.

117. Hans Frei, *The Eclipse of Biblical Narrative: A Study in Eighteenth and Nineteenth Century Hermeneutics* (New Haven, CT: Yale UP, 1974).

118. Paul Ricoeur, *Time and Narrative*, trans. Translation: Kathleen McLaughlin and David Pellauer, vol. 1-3 (Chicago, IL: U of Chicago P, 1984).

119. Hauerwas, *Why Narrative? Readings in Narrative Theology*.

120. Stanley Hauerwas, *Unleashing the Scripture: Free the Bible from Captivity to America* (Nashville, TN: Abingdon Press, 1993), 9.

121. Wright, *People of God*, 140. Fee, *Book by Book*, 14-20.

122. L. Ryken, J. Wilhoit, "King, Kingship," *Dictionary of Biblical Imagery* (Downers Grove, IL: InterVarsity Press, 1998): 476.

123. John Bright, *The Kingdom of God: The Biblical Concept and Its Meaning for the Church* (Nashville: Abingdon-Cokesbury Press, 1953), 18.

124. Ibid., L. Ryken, "King, Kingship," 476.

125. G. E. Ladd, *A Theology of the New Testament* (Grand Rapids, MI: William B. Eerdmans, 1993), 58.

126. Ryken, "King, Kingship," 476. The Hebrew-Aramaic word for king (*melek*) is one of the most commonly used words in the OT appearing about 2,700 times and the Greek word for king (*basileus*) about 175 times in the New Testament. Both terms are applied to human rulers as well as to God as ruler. When the verbal and other noun forms of these and related words are added (i.e., to reign, kingdom, etc.), we find an important biblical motif woven throughout the entire fabric of the Bible's message.

127. Arthur F. Glasser, *Announcing the Kingdom: The Story of God's Mission in the Bible* (Grand Rapids, MI: Baker Book House, 2003), 24. The absolute reign of God over the Kingdom he created and the human beings who care for one another and for the created world depict both the divine ideal and will, as well as the painful truth of the Old Testament. The demand for an earthly king and the behavior of the people under the rule of the earthbound kings set the stage for the new covenant when Jesus would walk among humans and would declare a new covenant in his blood.

128. Wright, *JVG*, 127.

129. Wright, *People of God*, 147.

130. James Kallas, *Jesus and the Power of Satan* (Philadelphia: The Westminster Press, 1968), 119-21. Ladd, *Theology*, 58-59. Ladd also covers some of the same concepts about a Davidic and Apocalyptic Concept.

131. Delbert R. Hillers, *Covenant: The History of a Biblical Idea* (Baltimore and London: The Johns Hopkins University Press, 1969), 28.

132. Ibid., 29-45.

133. W. S. LaSor, et al., *Old Testament Survey: The Message, Form, and Background of the Old Testament. Second Edition* (Grand Rapids, MI: William B. Eerdmans, 1996), 72-75.

134. I heard Tom Wright say this in a presentation.

135. Ladd, *Theology*, 54.

136. Wright, *JVG*, 247.

137. Ibid., 250.

138. Kallas, *JPS*, 119. Herman Ridderbos, *The Coming of the Kingdom* (Philadelphia, PA: The Presbyterian and Reformed Publishing Company, 1962), 3.

139. C. C. Caragounis, "Kingdom of God/Kingdom of Heaven," *Dictionary of Jesus and the Gospels*, (Downers Grove, IL: InterVarsity Press, 1992): Electronic Version.

140. Dr. Kent Yinger, my DMin. mentor (George Fox Evangelical Seminary), pointed out to me that Mark's 'has drawn near [*engiken*]' is debated and ambiguous; Luke 11:20 ["has come" *ephthasen*] is unambiguous already.

141. George Eldon Ladd, *The Presence of the Future* (Grand Rapids, MI: William B. Eerdmans Publishing Company, 1974).

142. Ibid., 218.

143. N. T. Wright, *The Challenge of Jesus: Rediscovering Who Jesus Was and Is* (Downers Grove, IL: InterVarsity Press, 1999), 72-73.

Setting the Stage

1. Margueritte Harmon Bro, *The Book You Always Meant to Read: The Old Testament* (Garden City: Doubleday & Company, 1974).

2. Walter Brueggemann, *The Bible Makes Sense* (Louisville, KY: Westminster John Knox Press, 2001), 23.

3. Ibid., 23-30.

4. D. R. W. Wood and I. Howard Marshall, *New Bible Dictionary*, 3rd ed. (Downers Grove, IL: InterVarsity Press, 1996), 135.

5. "Empiricism," *Answers.com Fast Facts* [document online]; available from http://www.answers.com/empiricism; Internet; accessed 30 June 2005. "The view that experience, especially of the senses, is the only source of knowledge."

6. In the first year of Darius son of Xerxes (a Mede by descent), who was made ruler over the Babylonian kingdom—in the first year of his reign, I, Daniel, understood from the Scriptures, according to the word of the LORD given to Jeremiah the prophet, that the desolation of Jerusalem would last seventy years (Dan. 9.1-2).

7. Onias welcomed the envoy with honor, and received the letter, which contained a clear declaration of alliance and friendship. Therefore, though we have no need of these things, since we have as encouragement the holy books which are in our hands, we have undertaken to send to renew our brotherhood and friendship with you, so that we may not become estranged from you, for considerable time has passed since you sent your letter to us (1 Maccabees 12.8-10 RSV).

8. Wood and Marshall, *New Bible Dictionary*, 1069.

9. Ibid., 136.

10. "All Time Bestselling Books and Authors," *The Internet Public Library* [document online]; available from http://www.ipl.org/div/farq/bestsellerFARQ.html; Internet; accessed 3 September 2005. "No one really knows how many copies of the Bible have been printed, sold, or distributed. The Bible Society's attempt to calculate the number printed between 1816 and 1975 produced the figure of 2,458,000,000. A more recent survey, for the years up to 1992, put it closer to 6,000,000,000 in more than 2,000 languages and dialects. Whatever the precise figure, the Bible is by far the bestselling book of all time." A quote from *The Top 10 of Everything, 1997* (DK Pub., 1996, pp 112-113).

11. W. Musser Fant, Clyde E. Donald, and Mitchell G. Reddish, *An Introduction to the Bible, Revised Edition* (Nashville: Abingdon Press, 2001), 60-62.

12. Ibid., 61.

13. Bruce K. Waltke, "Book Review: Theology of the Old Testament: Testimony, Dispute, Advocacy," *Crux* 41, No. 2 (Summer 2005): 42-44. The idea that historical setting is important is not held by all Old Testament specialists. As an illustration, in Bruce Waltke's review of Walter Brueggemann's book, he suggests that in regard to epistemology, "Brueggemann embraces what he calls a 'post liberal, non

foundational' approach. By this he means that he rejects both historical criticism and the orthodox confessions of the church." 42. I discussed this in the Prologue section on page 20.

14. Bruce K. Waltke, "The Literary Genre of Genesis 1," *Crux* 27 (December 1991): 2-10.

15. J. I. Packer, Merrill C. Tenney, and Jr. William White, *The World of the Old Testament* (Nashville, TN: Thomas Nelson Publishers, 1982), 110-112.

16. I am indebted to David Wollenburg from Concordia Seminary for the following quote from Luther: Martin Luther, *Werke* (Weimar: Böhlau, 1883-), vol. 1, p. 507; from a 1518 sermon on the Ten Commandments.

17. "New American Standard Bible," *BibleGateway.com* [document online]; available from http://bible.gospelcom.net/versions/index.php?action=getVersionInfo&vid=49#books&version=49; Internet; accessed 19 September 2005. "While preserving the literal accuracy of the 1901 ASV, the NASB has sought to render grammar and terminology in contemporary English. Special attention has been given to the rendering of verb tenses to give the English reader a rendering as close as possible to the sense of the original Greek and Hebrew texts. In 1995, the text of the NASB was updated for greater understanding and smoother reading."

Act 1

1. Clyde E. Fant, Donald W. Musser, and Mitchell G. Reddish, *An Introduction to the Bible, Revised Edition* (Nashville, TN: Abingdon Press, 2001), 97.

2. Ibid.

3. W. S. LaSor, et al., *Old Testament Survey: The Message, Form, and Background of the Old Testament. Second Edition* (Grand Rapids, MI: William B. Eerdmans, 1996), 15.

4. Bruce K. Waltke, "The Literary Genre of Genesis 1," *Crux* 27 (1991): 2-10.

5. LaSor, et al., *Old Testament Survey,* 22.

6. Ibid., 75.

7. D. R. W. Wood, A. R. Millard, J. I. Packer, D. J. Wiseman, and I. Howard Marshall, eds., *New Bible Dictionary Third Edition* (Downers Grove, IL: InterVarsity Press, 1996), 467.

8. William Sanford La Sor, David Allan Hubbard, and Frederic William Bush, *Old Testament Survey: The Message, Form, and Background of the Old Testament* (Grand Rapids, MI: William B. Eerdmans, 1982), 73.

9. Walter Brueggemann, *Genesis* (Atlanta, GA: John Knox Press, 1982), 25.

10. Ibid., 26.

11. LaSor, et al., *Old Testament Survey,* 22.

12. "John Donne, Meditation XVII: No man is an island..." *Indiana State University* [document online]; available from http://isu.indstate.edu/ilnprof/ENG451/ISLAND/; Internet; accessed 17 October 2005.

13. Walter A. Elwell, *Evangelical Dictionary of Biblical Theology* (Grand Rapids, MI: Baker Books, 1996), 297.

14. L. Ryken, J. Wilhoit, T. Longman, C. Duriez, D. Penney, and D. G. Reid, *Dictionary of Biblical Imagery* (Downers Grove, IL: InterVarsity Press, 1998), 584.

15. "Leaning on the Everlasting Arms," *Gospel.Hines01.com* [document online]; available from http://gospel.hines01.com/gaithers/Leaning%20on%20the%20everlasting%20arm.htm; Internet; accessed 13 September 2005.

16. Elwell, *Evangelical Dictionary of Biblical Theology,* 297.

17. Leonard I. Sweet, *Out of the Question...Into the Mystery* (Colorado Springs, CO: WaterBrook Press, 2004), 37-87.

18. You can listen to an MP3 of this song at: < http://www.guitarsounds.com/content/mp3/Morning_Has_Broken128k.mp3>. It is the third song on the sample. Move the bar about an inch to the right where "Morning Has Broken" begins.

19. L. Ryken, *Dictionary of Biblical Imagery,* 181.

20. John H. Walton, *The NIV Application Commentary: Genesis* (Grand Rapids, MI: Zondervan Publishing House, 2001), 67.

21. Ibid., 68.

22. Ibid.

23. *TANAKH.* (Philadelphia Jerusalem: The Jewish Publication Society, 1985), 3. This alternative is also found in the Good News Bible in the footnote for Genesis 1.1.

24. Ibid., 70-71.

25. James Barr, *Was Everything That God Created Really Good?,* Walter Brueggemann, Tod Linafelt and Timothy K. Beal, eds., *God in the Fray: A Tribute to Walter Brueggemann* (Minneapolis, MN: Fortress Press, 1998), 62.

26. Brueggemann, *Genesis, 29.*

27. Walton, *The NIV Application Commentary: Genesis,* 74.

28. Victor P. Hamilton, *The Book of Genesis. Chapters 1-17* (Grand Rapids, MI: William B. Eerdmans Publishing Company, 1990), 114.

29. Walton, *The NIV Application Commentary: Genesis,* 74.

30. Ibid., 77.

31. Ibid., 78.

32. Paul R. House, *Old Testament Theology* (Downers Grove, Il: InterVarsity Press, 1998), 59.

33. Victor P. Hamilton, *Handbook on the Pentateuch: Genesis, Exodus, Leviticus, Numbers, Deuteronomy* (Grand Rapids, MI: Baker Book House, 1982), 19.

34. Ibid., 19-20.

35. Conrad Hyers, "Biblical Literalism: Constricting the Cosmic Dance," in *Is God a Creationist? The Religious Case Against Creation-Science,* edited by Roland Mushat Frye (New York, NY: Charles Scribner's Sons, 1983), 101.

36. Walton, *The NIV Application Commentary: Genesis,* 81.

37. N. S. Gill, "Emergence of the Olympian Gods and Goddesses," *about.com* [document online]; available from http://ancienthistory.about.com/library/weekly/aa121598.htm; Internet; accessed 12 September 2005.

38. Gerry Wittig, "Landscape data and complete adaptive system Earth," *c5corp.com* [document online]; available from http://www.c5corp.com/research/complexsystem.shtml; Internet; accessed 12 September 2005.

39. Walton, *The NIV Application Commentary: Genesis,* 130.

40. This illustration comes from my own memory of seeing a Rain Dance in Arizona while traveling with my parents when I was about twelve years old.

Act 2

1. Gordon J. Wenham, *Genesis 1-15* (Waco, TX: Word Books, 1987), 51.

2. Victor P. Hamilton, *The Book of Genesis. Chapters 1-17* (Grand Rapids, MI: William B. Eerdmans Publishing Company, 1990), 192.

3. Wenham, *Genesis 1-15,* 90.

4. See Appendix 6 for clarification.

5. Kenneth A. Mathews, *Genesis 1-11:26, The New American Commentary* (Nashville, TN: Broadman & Holman Publishers, 1996), 183.

6. Ibid., 185.

7. Hamilton, *Genesis 1-17,* 50-51.

8. Mathews, *Genesis 1-11.26,* 52; Wenham, *Genesis 1-15,* 65, 86.

9. Hamilton, *Genesis 1-17 .* 57; See Act 1 "The Names of God."

10. See Appendix 3 for "The Soul."

11. See Appendix 4 for "Behind the Scenes," a fuller description of Formed, Dust, Breathed, and Blew.

12. Victor P. Hamilton, *Handbook on the Pentateuch: Genesis, Exodus, Leviticus, Numbers, Deuteronomy* (Grand Rapids, MI: Baker Book House, 1982), 24.

13. Mathews, *Genesis 1-11.26,* 193-195.

14. Ibid., 200.

15. Dietrich Bonhoeffer, *Creation and Fall: A Theological Interpretation of Genesis 1-3* (New York, NY: Macmillan, 1959), 49.

16. Mathews, *Genesis 1-11.26,* 202.

17. Ibid., 203.

18. Hamilton, *Genesis 1-17* 164.

19. See Appendix 5 for "The Tree of the Knowledge of Good and Evil."

20. Wenham, *Genesis 1-15,* 64.

21. John H. Walton, *The NIV Application Commentary: Genesis* (Grand Rapids, MI: Zondervan Publishing House, 2001), 170.

22. Mathews, *Genesis 1-11.26,* 208.

23. Wenham, *Genesis 1-15,* 67.

24. Hamilton, *Genesis 1-17,* 171.

25. Mathews, *Genesis 1-11.26,* 209.

26. Wenham, *Genesis 1-15*, 67.

27. Mathews, *Genesis 1-11.26*, 211.

28. Ibid., 210.

29. Wenham, *Genesis 1-15*, 67.

30. Hamilton, *Genesis 1-17*, 173.

31. Hamilton, *Handbook*, 28; Matthews, *Genesis 1-11.26*, 212.

32. Mathews, *Genesis 1-11.26*, 212.

33. Hamilton, *Genesis 1-17*, 175.

34. Mathews, *Genesis 1-11.26*, 214.

35. Ibid.

36. Wenham, *Genesis 1-15*, 68.

37. Mathews, *Genesis 1-11.26*, 215.

38. Hamilton, *Genesis 1-17*, 177.

39. Ibid.

40. Wenham, *Genesis 1-15*, 69.

41. Hamilton, *Genesis 1-17*, 179; Matthews, *Genesis 1-11.26*, 218.

42. Mathews, *Genesis 1-11.26*, 218.

43. Ibid.

44. Hamilton, *Handbook*, 29.

45. Mathews, *Genesis 1-11.26*, 219-220.

46. Ibid., 222.

47. Ibid., 222-224.

48. Hamilton, *Genesis 1-17*, 181.

49. Ibid.

50. Mathews, *Genesis 1-11.26*, 224-225.

51. Hamilton, *Handbook*, 42.

52. Ibid., See Appendix 4 "The Satan."

53. Mathews, *Genesis 1-11.26*, 226.

54. Ibid., 227.

55. Ibid., 226.

56. Wenham, *Genesis 1-15*, 72; Matthews, *Genesis 1-11.26*, 232.

57. Matthews, *Genesis 1-11.26*, 232; See Appendix 4 for "The Serpent."

58. Wenham, *Genesis 1-15*, 72.

59. Mathews, *Genesis 1-11.26*, 233.

60. Wenham, *Genesis 1-15*, 72.

61. Hamilton, *Genesis 1-17*, 187.

62. Ibid., 188.

63. Mathews, *Genesis 1-11.26*, 232

64. Ibid.

65. Ibid., 232.

66. Ibid.

67. Ibid., 325.

68. Ibid.

69. Ibid.

70. Hamilton, *Genesis 1-17*, 188.

71. Ibid., 189.

72. Mathews, *Genesis 1-11.26*, 235-236.

73. Hamilton, *Genesis 1-17*, 189.

74. Wenham, *Genesis 1-15*, 73.

75. Mathews, *Genesis 1-11.26*, 236.

76. Ibid., 236.

77. Ibid., 236-237.

78. Ibid., 237; Wenham, *Genesis 1-15*, 73-74.

79. Wenham, *Genesis 1-15*, 74-75.

80. Ibid., 75.

81. Hamilton, *Genesis 1-17*, 190.

82. Ibid.

83. Ibid., 191.

84. Ibid.

85. Mathews, *Genesis 1-11.26*, 239.

86. Ibid.

87. Hamilton, *Genesis 1-17*, 191.

88. Walton, *The NIV Application Commentary: Genesis*, 224.

89. Mathews, *Genesis 1-11.26*, 239.

90. Ibid.

91. Hamilton, *Genesis 1-17*, 192.

92. Wenham, *Genesis 1-15*, 76-77.

93. Hamilton, *Genesis 1-17*, 193.

94. "Memorable Quotes from the Shining," *IMDb* [document online]; available from http://www.imdb.com/title/tt0081505/quotes; Internet; accessed 21 September 2005.

95. Hamilton, *Genesis 1-17*, 193.

96. Wenham, *Genesis 1-15*, 77.

97. Hamilton, *Genesis 1-17*, 194.

98. Ibid.

99. Ibid.

100. Ibid., 196.

101. Mathews, *Genesis 1-11.26*, 343.

102. Ibid.

103. Ibid., 244.

104. Ibid.

105. Hamilton, *Genesis 1-17*, 196.

106. Ibid., 196-197.

107. Ibid., 197.

108. Ibid.

109. Mathews, *Genesis 1-11.26*, 245.

110. Ibid.

111. The footnote in the TNIV for the first translation *crush* says "OR strike."

112. Hamilton, *Genesis 1-17*, 197

113. Mathews, *Genesis 1-11.26*, 246

114. Ibid.

115. Walter C. Kaiser, Jr., *Toward an Old Testament Theology* (Grand Rapids: Zondervan Publishing House, 1978), 36-37.

116. Mathews, *Genesis 1-11.26*, 247-248.

117. Ibid., 248.

118. R. Davidson, "The Theology of Sexuality in the Beginning: Genesis 3," *Andrews University Seminary Studies (AUSS)* 26 (1988): 121-131. (1) Hierarchy was a creation ordinance, but it was distorted by sin. (2) Hierarchy is a creation ordinance and judgment includes a blessing restoring it. (3) There is no subordination before the fall, but Genesis 3.16 is a description, not a permanent prescription for the man-woman relationship. (4) There is no subordination before the fall and Genesis 3.16 prescribes a new pattern. (5) There is no subordination before the fall and "rule" means "like" in 3.16 affirming original equality.

119. Mathews, *Genesis 1-11.26*, 248-249.

120. Ibid., 250.

121. Ibid., 251.

122. Wenham, *Genesis 1-15*, 82.

123. Ibid.

124. Mathews, *Genesis 1-11.26*, 254.

125. Ibid., 247; Hamilton, *Handbook*, 49.

126. Wenham, *Genesis 1-15*, 85.

127. Mathews, *Genesis 1-11.26*, 257-258.

1. Gordon J. Wenham, *Story as Torah* (Grand Rapids: Baker Academic, 2000), 6.

2. W. Brueggemann, *The Bible Makes Sense* (Louisville, KY: Westminster John Knox Press, 2001), 23-30.

3. Gordon D. Fee and Douglas Stuart, *How to Read the Bible for All Its Worth, Second Edition* (Grand Rapids, MI: Zondervan Publishing House, 1993), 78.

4 .W. Brueggemann, *An Introduction to the Old Testament: The Canon and Christian Imagination* (Louisville, KY: Westminster John Knox Press, 2003), 46. Brueggemann makes this suggestion about von Rad.

5. Ibid.

6. W. S. LaSor, D. A. Hubbard, F. W. Bush and L. C. Allen, *Old Testament Survey: The Message, Form, and Background of the Old Testament*, Second Edition, (Grand Rapids, MI: William B. Eerdmans, 1996), 16-17; Bruce K. Waltke, *Genesis: A Commentary* (Grand Rapids: Zondervan Publishing House, 2001), 17-18; Brueggemann, *An Introduction to Old Testament*, 42.

7. Brueggemann, *An Introduction to Old Testament*, 43.

8. Ibid., 76.

9. LaSor, *Old Testament Survey*, 46.

10. John H. Walton, Victor Harold Matthews, Mark W. Chavalas, *The IVP Bible Background Commentary: Old Testament* (Downers Grove, IL: InterVarsity Press, 2000), 47.

11. Ibid., 48.

12. LaSor, et al., *Old Testament Survey*, 47-48.

13. Ibid., 49-51.

14. Bruce C. Birch and Walter Brueggemann, *A Theological Introduction to the Old Testament* (Nashville, TN: Abingdon Press, 1999), 84-85.

15. LaSor, et al., *Old Testament Survey*, 49.

16. Ibid., 50.

17. Wenham, *Story of Torah*, 37.

18. The name Exodus comes from the LXX translation of Exodus 19.1.

19. Raymond B. Dillard and Tremper Longman, *An Introduction to the Old Testament* (Grand Rapids, MI: Zondervan Publishing House, 1994), 64. "This history is called theological or prophetic in recognition of the fact that it is history with a particular intention to reveal the nature of God in his acts."

20. Birch, *A Theological Introduction to the Old Testament*, 103.

21. Ibid., 99.

22. Dillard and Longman, *An Introduction to the Old Testament*, 65.

23. John Goldingay, *Old Testament Theology. Volume One: Israel's Gospel* (Downers Grove, IL: InterVarsity Press, 2003), 288.

24. Ibid.

25. Walton, *The IVP Bible Background Commentary: Old Testament*, 77. The names of the Pharaohs who dealt with Israel in the Book of Exodus are not mentioned.

26. LaSor, et al., *Old Testament Survey*, 64.

27. Ibid., 63-64.

28. Walton, *The IVP Bible Background Commentary: Old Testament*, 80. In the ancient world, names were considered to be intimately connected with the essence of the person. See "Setting the Stage" for a review of the Names of God.

29. Paul R. House, *Old Testament Theology* (Downers Grove, Il: InterVarsity Press, 1998), 97.

30. Dillard and Longman, *An Introduction to the Old Testament*, 63.

31. LaSor, et al., *Old Testament Survey*, 65.

32. Gordon J. Wenham, *Exploring the Old Testament: A Guide to the Pentateuch. Volume One* (Downers Grove: InterVarsity Press, 2003), 58.

33. Ibid., 62. In biblical terminology the heart is sometimes seen as a metaphor for a person's mind and sometimes it is seen as a metaphor for the "whole" of a person. It is not the blood pumping organ within the body.

34. LaSor, et al., *Old Testament Survey*, 68-70. The first nine plagues are set apart from the tenth. They are patterned in sets of three. The first nine have been viewed as "natural phenomena" while the tenth has "no natural" explanation. Brueggemann says, "They are not to be understood "naturalistically" because they make immediate and direct appeal to the hidden and odd power of YHWH, without which they have no force in the story." (Brueggemann, *An Introduction to Old Testament*, 56). The ten plagues are: water turns into blood, frogs leave water and cover the land, land fills with mosquitoes or gnats, land swarms with flies, cattle in the

fields die of a plague, boils cover humankind and animals, hail destroys crops, locusts devour everything that is left, a thick darkness covers the land, and the death of the firstborn.

35. Brueggemann, *Introduction to Old Testament*, 59.

36. Delbert R. Hillers, *Covenant: The History of a Biblical Idea* (Baltimore and London: The Johns Hopkins University Press, 1969), 28.

37. Ibid., 29-45.

38. LaSor, et al., *Old Testament Survey*, 72-75.

39. I am indebted to Tom Wright for this metaphor.

40. LaSor, *Old Testament Survey*, 73.

41. Brueggemann, *Introduction to Old Testament*, 65.

42. LaSor, et al., *Old Testament Survey*, 76.

43. Wenham, *Exploring the Old Testament: A Guide to the Pentateuch. Volume One*, 81.

44. Ibid., 84-89; Dillard and Longman, *Introduction to the Old Testament*, 76-91.

45. Dillard and Longman, *An Introduction to the Old Testament*, 76.

46. Wenham, *Exploring the Old Testament: A Guide to the Pentateuch. Volume One*, 106; LaSor, et al., *Old Testament Survey*, 103-106.

47. Dillard and Longman, *An Introduction to the Old Testament*, 83.

48. LaSor, et al., *Old Testament Survey*, 99.

49. Wenham, *Exploring the Old Testament: A Guide to the Pentateuch. Volume One*, 123.

50. LaSor, et al., *Old Testament Survey*, 112.

51. Brueggemann, *Introduction to Old Testament*, 85.

52. Wenham, *Exploring the Old Testament: A Guide to the Pentateuch. Volume One*, 123

53. Birch, *A Theological Introduction to the Old Testament*, 393.

54. Ernest C. Lucas, *Exploring the Old Testament: A Guide to the Psalms & Wisdom Literature. Volume Three* (Downers Grove: InterVarsity, 2003), 123.

55. LaSor, et al., *Old Testament Survey*, 472.

56. Ibid., 138.

57. Dillard and Longman, *An Introduction to the Old Testament*, 110.

58. Goldingay, *Old Testament Theology. Volume One: Israel's Gospel*, 451.

59. Ibid., 452-453.

60. Brueggemann, *Introduction to Old Testament*, 109.

61. LaSor, et al., *Old Testament Survey*, 144.

62. Dillard and Longman, *An Introduction to the Old Testament*, 114.

63. Brueggemann, *Introduction to Old Testament*, 111.

64. Goldingay, *Old Testament Theology. Volume One: Israel's Gospel*, 531.

65. LaSor, et al., *Old Testament Survey*, 153.

66. Ibid., 160.

67. Ibid., 154.

68. Goldingay, *Old Testament Theology. Volume One: Israel's Gospel*, 601. The book of Ruth follows the book of Judges in the Greek Bible as well as in the Protestant and Catholic versions of the Bible.

69. LaSor, et al., *Old Testament Survey*, 820.

70. Ibid., 430.

71. C. S. Lewis, *Reflections on the Psalms*, (New York, NY: Harcourt, 1958), 3.

72. Clyde E. Fant, Donald W. Musser and Mitchell G. Reddish, *An Introduction to the Bible, Revised Edition* (Nashville: Abingdon Press, 2001), 126-133.

73. Brueggemann, *Introduction to Old Testament*, 131.

74. Fant, *Introduction to the Bible*, 135.

75. Dillard and Longman, *An Introduction to the Old Testament*, 135.

76. Brueggemann, *Introduction to Old Testament*, 145.

77. N. T. Wright, *Bringing the Church to the World* (Minneapolis, MN: Bethany House Publishers, 1992), 60.

78. LaSor, *Old Testament Survey*, 168.

79. Dillard and Longman, *An Introduction to the Old Testament*, 146.

80. LaSor, *Old Testament Survey*, 172-173.

81. Ibid., 176.

82. Fant, *Introduction to the Bible*, 141.145.

83. LaSor, et al., *Old Testament Survey*, 193-196.

84. Ibid., 461.

85. Ibid., 470.

86. Ibid., 498.

87. Ibid., 500.

88. Dillard and Longman, *An Introduction to the Old Testament*, 254.

89. Fant, *Introduction to the Bible*, 155.

90. Ibid., 175.

91. Fee and Stuart, *How to Read the Bible for All Its Worth, Second Edition*, 167-168.

92. "N" stands for Northern Kings.

93. "S" stands for Southern Kings.

94. LaSor, et al., *Old Testament Survey*, 375.

95. Ibid., 377-378.

96. Dillard and Longman, *An Introduction to the Old Testament*, 370.

97. Ibid., 391.

98. LaSor, et al., *Old Testament Survey*, 382-386.

99. Dillard and Longman, *An Introduction to the Old Testament*, 376.

100. Ibid., 267.

101. LaSor, et al., *Old Testament Survey*, 287-288.

102. Ibid., 270.

103. Dillard and Longman, *An Introduction to the Old Testament*, 357-358; 361; LaSor, et al., *Old Testament Survey*, 257-262.

104. Ibid., 406.

105. Dillard and Longman, *An Introduction to the Old Testament*, 319.

106. House, *Old Testament Theology*, 318.

107. I am indebted for this insight to Dr. James Kallas, Thousand Oaks, CA.

108. See footnote in the NIV for this rendering.

109. Wright, *Bringing the Church to the World*, 61.

110. LaSor, et al., *Old Testament Survey*, 528-529.

111. Ibid., 566.

112. Ibid., 574.

113. Brueggemann, *Introduction to Old Testament*, 351.

114. Ibid.

115. LaSor, et al., *Old Testament Survey*, 574.

116. Ibid., 373.

117. Ibid., 193-196.

118. Ibid., 392-396.

119. Ibid., 409-413.

120. Ibid., 545.

121. Ibid., 439-541.

Act 4

1. N. T. Wright, *The New Testament and the People of God* (Minneapolis, MN: Fortress Press, 1992), 147.

2. Ibid., 157.

3. Ralph Earle, *Exploring the New Testament* (Kansas City, MO: Beacon Hill Press, 1955), 17.

4. Wright, *People of God*, 153.

5. James D. G. Dunn, *Romans 1-8*, Volume 38a. (Dallas, TX: Word Books, 1988), 126; Wright, *People of God*, 158.

6. Everett F. Harrison, *Introduction to the New Testament*, Rev. ed. (Grand Rapids, MI: William B. Eerdmans Publishing Company, 1971), 7.

7. Wright, *People of God*, 157.

8. Ibid., 158.

9. Harrison, *Introduction to the New Testament*, 24.

10. Ibid., 227-28.

11. Wright, *People of God* 209.

12. Stephen Westerholm, *Perspectives Old and New on Paul: The Lutheran Paul and His Critics* (Grand Rapids, MI: William B. Eerdmans Publishing Company, 2004), 22.

13. Ibid., 179, 183.

14. James D. G. Dunn, *Jesus, Paul, and the Law: Studies in Mark and Galatians*, 1st American ed. (Louisville, KY: Westminster/John Knox Press, 1990), 201.

15. Stephen Westerholm, "Pharisees," *Dictionary of Jesus and the Gospels* (Downers Grove, IL: InterVarsity Press, 1992): 610.

16. Wright, *People of God*, 186.

17. Ibid., 181-203.

18. D. R. W. Wood, A. R. Millard, J. I. Packer, D. J. Wiseman, and I. Howard Marshall (Eds.), *New Bible Dictionary Third Edition* (Downers Grove, IL: InterVarsity Press, 1996), 1044. Other sources include scattered rabbinic text but of varying value.

19. Walter A. Elwell, *Evangelical Dictionary of Biblical Theology* (Grand Rapids, MI: Baker Books, 1996), 699-700.

20. Wood, *New Bible Dictionary Third Edition*, 1045.

21. Wright, *People of God*, 209-213.

22. Harrison, *Introduction to the New Testament*, 25.

23. Wright, *People of God*, 209.

24. N. T. Wright, *The Challenge of Jesus: Rediscovering Who Jesus Was and Is* (Downers Grove, IL: InterVarsity Press, 1999), 54-55.

25. Wright, *People of God*, 224.

26. Ibid., 226.

27. Ibid., 227.

28. Ibid., 230.

29. Ibid., 231-232.

30. N. T. Wright, *Scripture and the Authority of God* (London: SPCK, 2005), 31, 36.

31. Oscar Cullmann, *Christ and Time: The Primitive Christian Conception of Time and History* (Philadelphia, PA: The Westminster Press, 1964), 145.

32. *Amazon.com* [document online]; available from http://www.amazon.com/gp/search/ref=br_ss_hs/103-8708130-2673442?search-alias=aps&keywords=Harmony%20of%20the%20Gospels; Internet; accessed 19 October 2006. A search on amazon.com revealed approximately 40 such books with the words "Harmony of the Gospels" in some variations in the title.

33. N. T. Wright, *The Original Jesus: The Life and Vision of a Revolutionary* (Grand Rapids, MI: William B. Eerdmans Publishing Company, 1996), 92.

34. Ibid., 106.

35. G. E. Ladd, *A Theology of the New Testament* (Grand Rapids, MI: William B. Eerdmans Publishing Company, 1993), x.

36. Ibid., 4, 9. *Heilsgeschichte* was introduced by J. C. K. Hofmann in 1841 and brought forward by Oscar Cullmann's work called *Christ and Time* (1964) in which he focused on *Heilsgeschichte* as "the unifying center of New Testament Theology."

37. Ibid., 20.

38. Wright, *Scripture and the Authority of God*, 26.

39. N .T. Wright, *Jesus and the Victory of God* (London: SPCK, 1996), 199.

40. Ibid., 245.

41. Ellen F. Davis and Richard B. Hays, eds., *The Art of Reading Scripture* (Grand Rapids, MI: William B. Eerdmans Publishing Company, 2003), 2-3.

42. Cullmann, *Christ and Time*, 147.

43. I realize that the Virgin Birth plays a minor role in the New Testament with minimal occurrences.

44. L. Ryken, J. Wilhoit, "King, Kingship," *Dictionary of Biblical Imagery* (1998): 476.

45. John Bright, *The Kingdom of God: The Biblical Concept and Its Meaning for the Church* (Nashville: Abingdon Press, 1981), 18.

46. Ibid., L. Ryken, "King, Kingship," 476.

47. Ladd, *Theology*, 58.

48. Ryken, "King, Kingship," 476. The Hebrew-Aramaic word for king (*melek*) is one of the most commonly used words in the OT appearing about 2,700 times and the Greek word for king (*basileus*)

about 175 times in the New Testament. Both terms are applied to human rulers as well as to God as ruler. When the verbal and other noun forms of these and related words are added (i.e., to reign, kingdom, etc.), we find an important biblical motif woven throughout the entire fabric of the Bible's message.

49. Arthur F. Glasser, *Announcing the Kingdom: The Story of God's Mission in the Bible* (Grand Rapids, MI: Baker Book House, 2003), 24. The absolute reign of God over the Kingdom he created and the human beings who care for one another and for the created world depicts both the divine ideal and will, as well as the painful truth of the Old Testament. The demand for an earthly king and the behavior of the people under the rule of the earthbound kings set the stage for the new covenant when Jesus would walk among humans and would declare a new covenant in his blood.

50. Wright, *JVG*, 127.

51. James Kallas, *Jesus and the Power of Satan* (Philadelphia, PA: The Westminster Press, 1968), 119-121.

52. Ibid., 119-121. Ladd also covers some of the same concepts about a Davidic and Apocalyptic Concept in *Theology*, 58-59.

53 The words in parentheses reflect the footnotes in TNIV.

54. James D. G. Dunn, *Jesus Remembered*, Volume 1. (Grand Rapids, MI: William .B. Eerdmans Publishing Company, 2003), 345.

55. Ibid., 345-348. He refers several times to Raymond Edward Brown, *The Birth of the Messiah: A Commentary on the Infancy Narratives in Matthew and Luke, 2nd Edition*, (Garden City, NY: Doubleday, 1977, 1993), 517-533, 697-708, concluding that Brown handles this with great sensitivity (Dunn, 347, n. 48).

56. Dunn, *Remembered*, 347.

57. Ibid., 348.

58. H. R. Mackintosh, *The Doctrine of the Person of Jesus Christ* (New York, NY: C. Scribner's and Sons, 1912), 383-385.

59. Ibid.

60. Ibid.

61. Reinhold Niebuhr, *The Nature and Destiny of Man: A Christian Interpretation* (New York, NY: Charles Scribner's and Sons, 1948). A brief summary of Niebuhr's position on Jesus.

62. Karl Barth, *Church Dogmatics* (Edinburgh: T.& T. Clark, 1949), 147-159; 184-212.

63. G. C. Berkouwer, *The Person of Christ* (Grand Rapids: William B. Eerdmans Publishing Company, 1954), 155-235.

64. I am indebted to Tom Wright for this thought which came from his tape series *Jesus & the Kingdom*.

65. Wright, *JVG*, 160.

66. Ibid., 244.

67. N. T. Wright, *The Challenge of Jesus: Rediscovering Who Jesus Was and Is* (Downers Grove, IL: InterVarsity Press, 1999), 34-35.

68. Ibid., 35.

69. Ibid., 37.

70. James Kallas, *The Significance of the Synoptic Miracles* (London: SPCK, 1961), 7-13.

71. Ladd, *Theology*, 54.

72. Wright, *JVG*, 247.

73. Ibid., 250.

74. Wright, *Challenge*, 43-44.

75. Ibid., 39-43.

76. Kallas, *JPS*, 119. Ridderbos says the same thing: Herman Ridderbos, *The Coming of the Kingdom* (Philadelphia, PA: The Presbyterian and Reformed Publishing Company, 1962), 3.

77. Wright, *Challenge*, 53.

78. My mentor Dr. Kent Yinger pointed out to me that Mark's "has drawn near [*engiken*]" is debated and ambiguous; Luke 11:20 ["has come" *ephthasen*] is unambiguous already.

79. See page 161 for a graphic illustration.

80. G. E. Ladd, *The Presence of the Future* (Grand Rapids, MI: William B. Eerdmans Publishing Company, 1974).

81. Ibid., 218. Wright thinks this is a "linguistic trick. N. T. Wright, *Jesus & the Kingdom of God* (Vancouver, BC: Regent Audio). Tape 1, Side 1, and one is not sure if he is jesting or not.

82. Wright, *JVG*, 201.

83. See page 152 for a graphic illustration.

84. James Kallas, *The Satanward View: A Study in Pauline Theology* (Philadelphia, PA: Westminster Press, 1966), 32.

85. Ibid., 24-33.

86. Ibid., 33.

87. See Appendix 9 for an overview of the Kingdom from Augustine of Hippo (A.D. 396) and N. T. Wright (Bishop of Durham, 21st Century).

88. Ladd, *Theology*, 60.

89. Ibid.

90. G. B. Caird and L. D. Hurst, *New Testament Theology* (Oxford; New York, NY: Clarendon Press, Oxford University Press, 1994), 129. And these three are logically so inseparable that it is no surprise to find the New Testament writers moving freely from one sense to another, and even exploiting the ambiguity.

91. Ladd, *Theology*, 68-70.

92. Ibid., 60.

93. Wright, *Jesus & the Kingdom.*, Tape 1 Side 1.

94. Ben Witherington, *Jesus, Paul and the End of the World: A Comparative Study in New Testament Eschatology* (Downers Grove, IL: InterVarsity Press, 1992), 73.

95. James Kallas, *The Real Satan: From Biblical Times to the Present* (Minneapolis, MN: Augsburg, 1975), 60.

96. See 153-158 for fuller development.

97. Ladd, *Theology*, 64.

98. Cullmann, *Christ and Time*, 84. My mentor Dr. Kent Yinger pointed out to me that *deo* can also be used quite literally.

99. A mantra of sorts in the Vineyard Movement of the '80s.

100. Kallas, *Significance*, 77.

101. Ibid., 77.

102. The following insights come largely from the works (*Significance, JPS, Real Satan*) of James Kallas.

103. Edward Langton, *Essentials of Demonology: A Study of Jewish and Christian Doctrine* (London: Epworth Press, 1949), 173.

104. Wendell Willis. (Ed.), *The Kingdom of God in 20th-Century Interpretation* (Peabody, MA: Hendrickson Publishers, 1987), 47.

105. Wright, *JVG*, 690.

106. Ibid., 773.

107. Ladd, *Theology*, x.

108. This insight came from a brief phone conversation with Dr.Kallas in 1998.

109. Wright, *JVG*, 127.

110. Ibid., 127, n. 8.

111. Carey C. Newman, *Jesus & the Restoration of Israel* (Downers Grove, IL: InterVarsity Press, 1999), 244-245.

112. Ladd, *Theology*, 4. A new form of the *Heilsgeschichte* theology has emerged in recent years for there is widespread recognition that revelation has occurred in redemptive history, and that *Heilsgeschichte* is the best key to understand the unity of the Bible. See pages 238-239, 266, 268, 348, 354, 372, 507, 412, 425, 426, 433.

113. N. T. Wright, *The Climax of the Covenant: Christ and the Law in Pauline Theology* (Minneapolis, MN: Fortress Press, 1992), 207, 215, and 205.

114. Dunn, *Remembered*, 698.

115. Ibid., 703.

116. Ibid., 700.

117. Leland Ryken, *The Literature of the Bible* (Grand Rapids, MI: Zondervan Publishing House, 1974), 291.

118. Ibid., 292.

119. Ibid.

120. Dunn, *Remembered*, 698.

121. Wright, *Scripture and the Authority of God*, 13.

122. Wright, *JVG*, 176.

123. Ladd, *Theology*, 93.

124. Ibid., 158-159.

125. Ibid., 69-70.

126. Kallas, *JPS*, 143.

127. Wright, *JVG*, 230.239.

128. Kenneth E Bailey, *Poet and Peasant: A Literary-Cultural Approach to the Parables in Luke* (Grand Rapids, MI: William B. Eerdmans Publishing Company, 1976), 119.

129. Ibid., 124.

130. Ibid., 125.

131. Ibid., 132.

132. Ibid., 119-123.

133. Merrill Chapin Tenney, Gen. Ed. *The Zondervan Pictorial Encyclopedia of the Bible* (Grand Rapids, MI: Zondervan Publishing House, 1975), 5:609-610.

134. See Act 5 Scene 5 for a brief discussion of the outline of Matthew.

135. Wright, *Challenge*, 294.

136. Ibid., 55.

137. Wright, *JVG*, 401.

138. Ibid., 369-442.

139. Wright, *Challenge*, 54-73.

140. Ibid., 294.

141. Margaret Turnbull, *Thinkexists.com* [document online]; available from http://en.thinkexist.com/quotation/no_man_is_responsible_for_his_father-that_was/216579.html; Internet; accessed 20 October 2005.

142. See Appendix 10 for partial list of metaphors for Jesus.

143. Kallas, *Real Satan*, 93.

144. Albert Schweitzer, *The Quest of the Historical Jesus: A Critical Study of Its Progress from Reimarus to Wrede* (New York, NY: The Macmillan Company, 1950), 391 n. 1.

145. Wright, *JVG*, 557.

146. Ibid., 560.

147. Ibid., 609.

148. Ibid., 543.

149. Raymond Edward Brown, *The Death of the Messiah: From Gethsemane to the Grave: A Commentary on the Passion Narratives in the Four Gospels*, 1st ed., 2 vols.(New York, NY: Doubleday, 1994).

150. N. T. Wright, *The Resurrection of the Son of God* (London: SPCK, 2003), 401.

151. Ibid., 605, 405.

152. Ibid., 667.

153. Ladd, *Theology*, 353

154. N. T. Wright "The Resurrection" *The Falls Church* [document online]; available from http://www.thefallschurch.org/templates/custhefalls/details.asp?id=29455&PID=244903&mast=; Internet; accessed 24 October 2005.

155. Wright, *The Resurrection of the Son of God*, 403.

156. Kallas, *Real Satan*, 102.

157. Ladd, *Theology*, 370.

158. Ibid., 371.

159. Kallas, *Real Satan*, 107.

Act 5. Scenes 1-6

1. Luke Timothy Johnson, *The Writings of the New Testament: An Interpretation*, Rev. ed. (Minneapolis, MI: Fortress Press, 1999), 267.

2. Ibid., 164.

3. Ibid., 22.

4. Ibid., 179.

5. Ibid., 183.

6. James D. G. Dunn, *Jesus, Paul, and the Law: Studies in Mark and Galatians* (Louisville, KY: Westminster/John Knox Press, 1990), 201.

7. Westerholm, *Perspectives*, 249.

8. Stephen Westerholm, *Perspectives Old and New on Paul: The Lutheran Paul and His Critics* (Grand Rapids, MI: William B. Eerdmans Publishing Company, 2004), 214.

9. James Kallas, *The Story of Paul* (Minneapolis, MI: Augsburg Publishing House, 1966), 1.

10. Johnson, *Writings of New Testament*, 259.

11. Charles B. Puskas, *An Introduction to the New Testament* (Peabody, MA: Hendrickson Publishers, 1989). A great overview of the chronology of Paul can be found in Chapter 12, 191-203.

12. Kallas, *Paul*, 1.

13. Johnson, *Writings of New Testament*, 217-273.

14. Kallas, *Paul*, 1-2.

15. Ibid., 2.

16. Ibid., 5.

17. Ibid., 27-28.

18. Ibid., 41-42.

19. Ben Witherington, *New Testament History: A Narrative Account* (Grand Rapids, MI: Baker Academic, 2001), 238-240.

20. C. K. Barrett, *The New Testament Background: Selected Documents*, Rev. ed. (San Francisco, CA: Harper & Row, 1989), 27-28.

21. Gordon Fee and Douglas Stuart, *How to Read the Bible for All Its Worth. Third Edition* (Grand Rapids, MI: Zondervan Publishing House, 2003), 58; Johnson, *Writings of New Testament*, 268.

22. Witherington, *New Testament History: A Narrative Account*, 240.

23. Johnson, *Writings of New Testament*, 281. As an example: Luke Timothy Johnson believes that the Thessalonian correspondences were written first while Gundry believes that Galatians was written first, Robert H. Gundry, *A Survey of the New Testament*, 4th ed. (Grand Rapids, MI: Zondervan Publishing House, 2003), 351.

24. Gundry, *A Survey of the New Testament*, 530-31.

25. D. A. DeSilva, *An Introduction to the New Testament: Contexts, Methods & Ministry Formation* (Downers Grove, IL: InterVarsity Press, 2004), 356-358; Gundry, *A Survey of the New Testament*, 304-305; D. A. Carson, Douglas J. Moo and Leon Morris, *An Introduction to the New Testament* (Grand Rapids, MI: Zondervan Publishing Company, 1992), 182-185; David Wenham and Steve Walton, *Exploring the New Testament: A Guide to the Gospels & Acts*, vol. 1 (Downers Grove, IL: InterVarsity Press, 2001), 271-272.

26. Carson, *Introduction to New Testament*, 182.

27. Gundry, *A Survey of the New Testament*, 353-354.

28. Ibid., 351.

29. I. Howard Marshall, Stephen Travis and Ian Paul, *Exploring the New Testament: A Guide to the Letters & Revelation*, vol. 2 (Downers Grove, IL: InterVarsity Press, 2002), 48.

30. Wright, *What Paul Really Said*, 120-122.

31. Wright, *Jesus, Paul and Israel.*, Tape G, Side 1.

32. Marshall, *Letters & Revelation*, 52.

33. Stanley J. Grenz and Roger E. Olson, *Who Needs Theology? An Invitation to the Study of God* (Downers Grove, IL: InterVarsity Press, 1996).

34. Wright, *What Paul Really Said*, 113, 119.

35. Marshall, *Letters & Revelation*, 197-198.

36. George Ladd, *A Theology of the New Testament* (Grand Rapids, MI: William B. Eerdmans Publishing Company, 1993), 556.

37. Carson, *Introduction to New Testament*, 414. There is much debate over the dating of James. Some of the debate suggests that it was written early, during the mid '40s, which would have made it the first book of the New Testament written. Others suggest a later time frame, somewhere before his death in A.D. 62. I am aware that there are problems with dating it right after the Jerusalem Council, but it seems prudent to do so if one sees the book as a response to the council's debate, even though it doesn't mention or allude to the council. It might be possible that we make more of the Jerusalem Council than the folks that were in attendance. So not mentioning the council as a way of dismissing its writing after the council is a non sequitur.

38. Ibid., 410-413.

39. Wenham, *Gospels & Acts*, 248-249.

40. Gundry, *A Survey of the New Testament*, 476. It might have been James' intention to write to *all* believers while focusing on Jewish believers as to how *to live* out this newly found relationship with God as Jews living in a Gentile world. This form of thinking is tied with the above dating (see n. 109 above), but a later date would serve the same.

41. DeSilva, *Introduction to the New Testament*, 822-823.

42. Martin Luther, *Luther's Works*, vol. 35 (Philadelphia, PA: Fortress Press, 1960), 362.

43. Wenham, *Gospels & Acts*, 254.

44. Witherington, *New Testament History: A Narrative Account*, 272.

45. These two questions were offered as a way of thinking about the material of 1 Thessalonians by Dr. James Kallas in a course on Pauline Studies in which I was a student during my days at Fuller Seminary in the 1970s.

46. Gundry, *A Survey of the New Testament*, 363.

47. Craig A. Blaising and Darrell L. Bock, *Progressive Dispensationalism* (Wheaton, IL: BridgePoint, 1993).

48. Gleason Leonard Archer, *Three Views on the Rapture: Pre-, Mid-, or Post-Tribulation?* (Grand Rapids, MI: Zondervan Publishing House, 1996), Three Trinity Evangelical Divinity School professors present their Premillennialist views on when the rapture will occur - before, during, or after the tribulation. Paul D. Feinberg argues the pre-tribulation position. Gleason L. Archer presents the mid-tribulation position. Douglas J. Moo holds the post-tribulation view. In addition, one might also look at Robert G. Clouse, *The Meaning of the Millennium: Four Views* (Downers Grove, IL: InterVarsity Press, 1977). This is an older book but still has value in a discussion of eschatology. While not specific to the pre/mid/post tribulation material, it does give one a position then counter-position assessment of the major views of the Millennium which are: Historic Premillennialism (George Ladd); Dispensational Premillennialism (Herman A. Hoyt); Postmillennialism (Loraine Boettner); and Amillennialism (Anthony A. Hoekema). This book does not take into consideration the softening of Progressive Dispensationalism.

49. Witherington, *New Testament History: A Narrative Account*, 272. There are some discussions among NT specialists that 2 Thessalonians may have been written before 1 Thessalonians and precipitated the writing of 1 Thessalonians.

50. Gundry, *A Survey of the New Testament*, 366-367.

51. John F. Walvoord, *The Rapture Question* (Grand Rapids, MI: Zondervan Publishing House, 1979), 8.

52. Ibid., 152.

53. Clifton J. Allen, *The Broadman Bible Commentary*, vol. 11 (Nashville, TN: Broadman Press, 1969), 29-30.

54. DeSilva, *Introduction to the New Testament*, 575-577.

55. Witherington, *New Testament History: A Narrative Account*, 240.

56. I am indebted to Dr. Russ Spittler, Provost of Vanguard University, Costa Mesa, CA, for this insight.

57. Gordon Fee, *God's Empowering Presence: The Holy Spirit in the Letters of Paul* (Peabody, MA: Hendrickson Publishers, 1994), 730-731.

58. Gundry, *A Survey of the New Testament*, 387-388; Marshall, *Letters & Revelation*, 93-95.

59. There is no textual evidence for the partitioning of 2 Corinthians in this fashion. What one can say is that the scheme above makes some sense out of the texts provided.

60. Witherington, *New Testament History: A Narrative Account*, 407.

61. Marshall, *Letters & Revelation*, 105.

62. Witherington, *New Testament History: A Narrative Account*, 242, 292.

63. Gundry, *A Survey of the New Testament*, 395.

64. Leander E. Keck, ed., *The New Interpreter's Bible: A Commentary in Twelve Volumes (Vol. 10)* (Nashville, TN: Abingdon Press, 1994), 403-404. Volume 10 includes Acts, Romans, and 1 Corinthians. The Romans section is written by N. T. Wright.

65. James Kallas, *Synoptic Gospels Course Notes* (1973).

66. Wenham, *Gospels & Acts*, 61-66. The "Q" theory has some detractors that call for dispensing with the theory. For a very readable view of all the issues surrounding what is often called "the Synoptic Problem," read Chapter 4 "Where Did The Gospels Come From?" of the present book.

67. Kallas, *Synoptic Gospels Course Notes* .

68. Wenham, *Gospels & Acts*, 52-53.

69. William L. Lane, *The Gospel According to Mark* (Grand Rapids, MI: William B. Eerdmans Publishing Company, 1974), 1.

70. I owe this insight to Dr. Russ Spittler, Provost of Vanguard University, Costa Mesa, CA.

71. A. Patzia, "Philemon, Letter To," *Dictionary of Paul and His Letters*, (Downers Grove, IL: InterVarsity Press, 1993): 706.

72. DeSilva, *Introduction to the New Testament*, 672.

73. Craig S. Keener, *The IVP Bible Background Commentary: New Testament* (Downers Grove, IL: InterVarsity Press, 1993), 642-643.

74. Witherington, *New Testament History: A Narrative Account*, 328.

75. Keener, *Bible Background Commentary*, 643.

76. Witherington, *New Testament History: A Narrative Account*, 327.

77. Keener, *Bible Background Commentary*, 580.

78. Witherington, *New Testament History: A Narrative Account*, 327-328.

79. Markus Barth, *Ephesians*, vol. 1 (Garden City, NY: Doubleday & Company, 1974), 3. There is ongoing debate among NT specialists about Paul's authorship of Ephesians. For a discussion see: Ben Witherington, *New Testament History: A Narrative Account*, 326-329; Keener, *Bible Background Commentary*, 538-539.

80. Barth, *Ephesians*, 3-4.

81. Marshall, *Letters & Revelation*, 165.

82. Gundry, *A Survey of the New Testament*, 421-423.

83. William Barclay, *The Letters to the Galatians and Ephesians* (Philadelphia, PA: Westminster Press, 1959), 91-93. See also: F. F. Bruce, *The Epistle to the Ephesians* (London: Pickering & Inglis ltd., 1962), 29.

84. Wenham, *Gospels & Acts*, 279. See the "we" passages that begin at Acts 16.10.

85. Kallas, *Synoptic Gospels Course Notes* .

86. Ralph P. Martin, *New Testament Foundations: A Guide for Christian Students*, vol. 1 (Grand Rapids, MI: William B. Eerdmans Publishing Company, 1975), 250.

87. Gundry, *A Survey of the New Testament*, 211.

88. Wenham, *Gospels & Acts*, 237.

89. Gundry, *A Survey of the New Testament*, 209-211.

90. Wenham, *Gospels & Acts*, 227, 267.

91. Ibid., 295. There are four other reasons provided by the authors as well.

92. Ibid., 292.

93. Carson, *Introduction to New Testament*, 181.

94. Gundry, *A Survey of the New Testament*, 427. There are other thoughts about where Philippians may have originated from discussed in Gundry 427-430.

95. Ibid., 431.

96. The text is translated "wife" instead of "woman" in TNIV. This moves in the right direction. It was not all women that Paul may have had in mind, but that translation still leaves the question about teaching.

97. Keener, *Bible Background Commentary*, 610-61. Keener gives background that leads to a different interpretation than the one offered in this study guide. One might want to also look at Ronald W. Pierce, Rebecca Merrill Groothuis and Gordon Fee, eds., *Discovering Biblical Equality: Complementarity without Hierarchy* (Downers Grove, IL: InterVarsity Press, 2004), 205-223.

98. Keener, *Bible Background Commentary*, 609.

99. Marshall, *Letters & Revelation*, 179.

100. Carson, *Introduction to New Testament*, 395.

102. Marshall, *Letters & Revelation*, 265.

102. Ibid., 268.

103. Ladd, *Theology*, 502. Chapter 34 (499-520) in Ladd/s *Theology* called "The Pauline Psychology" is a great summary of humankind for readers who want a quick overview of the language Paul uses to describe humankind. Does Peter use Paul's language of humankind in the same way? Because Paul's humankind language is closer to Hebrew than to Greek thought, it would be unusual for Peter, who was Jewish, to think differently about the language of "soul" than Paul.

104. See footnote in TNIV for John 3.3.

105. The authorship of 2 Peter is disputed. See Marshall, *Letters & Revelation*, 281-284 for discussion of the problem of authorship.

106. Ladd, *Theology*, 654-655.

107. Marshall, *Letters & Revelation*, 275-287; Gundry, *A Survey of the New Testament*, 488.

108. Marshall, *Letters & Revelation*, 285.

109. Keener, *Bible Background Commentary*, 45.

110. Carson, *Introduction to New Testament*, 61-63. This introduction supplies the reader with a summary of the three "dominant theories" about the structure of Matthew. My choice of theory 3 as presented above seems to me to best fit the overall view of what Matthew was trying to effect in his readers and comes from my own personal research.

111. Ibid., 395. Others who have been favored as possible are: Paul, Barnabas, Luke Apollos; Silas, Philip, Priscilla, and Clement. See Gundry, *A Survey of the New Testament*, 458-459.

112. Marshall, *Letters & Revelation*, 242.

113. Ibid., 233.

114. Jude seems to have a specific audience and circumstances in mind. He called them "dear friends." It is not a far stretch that he knew the church well, may have pastored it and led some of the offenders to

faith. However, it must be said that this is conjecture on my part. The text is not explicit, but implicitly one may find support for such thoughts.

115. One of my mentors in seminary, Dr. James Kallas, told the story of writing his doctoral dissertation on John's Gospel. After writing almost 500 pages about authorship, his advisor asked him if he had made a choice yet about who the author might be. Kallas replied, "Of course, the author is John the Apostle."

116. Carson, *Introduction to New Testament*, 135.

117. Witherington, *New Testament History: A Narrative Account*, 401.

118. D. A. Carson, R. T. France and J. A. Motyer and G. J. Wenham, eds., *New Bible Commentary: 21st Century Edition*, 4th ed. (Downers Grove, IL: InterVarsity Press, 1994), 1023.

119. Johnson, *Writings of New Testament*, 542.

120. Gundry, *A Survey of the New Testament*, 261.

122. Marshall, *Letters & Revelation*, 292.

122. Gundry, *A Survey of the New Testament*, 492-493.

123. Marshall, *Letters & Revelation*, 297.

124. Ibid., 300. A quote by the author from S. S. Smalley's commentary on *1, 2, 3 John* in the Word Biblical Commentary series.

125. Gundry, *A Survey of the New Testament*, 508.

126. Ibid., 307. A quote from J. J. Collins "Introduction: Towards the Morphology of a Genre" in *Semeia* 14, 1979, 9.

127. Hanns Lilje, *The Last Book of the Bible: The Meaning of the Revelation of St. John* (Philadelphia, PA: Fortress Press, 1957).

128. Gundry, *A Survey of the New Testament*, 509-510.

129. Blaising, *Progressive*.

130. Gundry, *A Survey of the New Testament*, 509.

131. George E. Ladd, *A Commentary on the Revelation of John* (Grand Rapids, MI: William B. Eerdmans Publishing Company 1972), 70.

Act 5. Scene 7/Last Scene

1. N. T. Wright, *Scripture and the Authority of God* (London: SPCK, 2005), 90.

2. N. T. Wright, *The New Testament and the People of God* (Minneapolis, MN: Fortress Press, 1992), 140.

3. Wright, *Scripture and the Authority of God*, xiii.

4. Walter Brueggemann, *The Prophetic Imagination* (Fortress Press, 1978), 11.

5. Ibid., 44.

6. Ibid.

7 A word I have coined to mean imagining things from God's point of view.

8. "Criticism," *Answers.com Fast Facts* [document online]; available from http://www.answers.com/historical%20criticism; Internet; accessed 2 December 2005. "Historical criticism is an approach to literature that uses history as a means of understanding a literary work more clearly. Such criticism moves beyond both the facts of an author's personal life and the text itself in order to examine the social and intellectual currents in which the author composed the work."

9. Walter Brueggemann, *Text under Negotiation: The Bible and Postmodern Imagination* (Minneapolis: Fortress Press, 1993), vii-ix.

10. Ibid., 12-13.

11. Ibid., 14.

12. Ibid., 19.

13. Ibid., 20.

14. Ibid., 25.

15. Ibid., 65.

16. "Theology," *Answers.com Fast Facts* [document online]; available from http://www.answers.com/narrative%20theology; Internet; accessed 2 December 2005. "[a] theological development which supported the idea that the Church's use of the Bible should focus on a narrative presentation of the faith, rather than on the development of a systematic theology.

17. Brueggemann, *Text under Negotiation: The Bible and Postmodern Imagination*, 69.

18. Brueggemann quotes Ronald F. Thiemann, *Constructing a Public Theology: The Church in a Pluralistic Culture*, 1st ed. (Louisville, KY: Westminster/John Knox Press, 1991), 51.

19. Walter Brueggemann, *The Creative Word: Canon as a Model for Biblical Education* (Philadelphia: Fortress Press, 1982), 24.

20. Lesslie Newbigin, *The Gospel in a Pluralist Society* (Grand Rapids, MI: William B. Eerdmans, 1989).

21. *RealNetworks* [document online]; available from http://www.real.com; Internet; accessed 22 November 2005.

22. RealNetworks finally settling just a few months ago for more than $800 million in anti-trust settlement fees.

23. "Investing in the Poor," *WorldVision* [document online]; available from http://worldvision.org/med; Internet; accessed 22 November 2005.

24. Dave Richards, "Personalizing Microfinance," Defeating Global Poverty [document online]; available from http://defeatpoverty.com/2006/02/personalizing-microfinance.html; Internet; accessed 22 November 2005. See also "Dave's Defeating Poverty Reading List available at http://povertyreadinglist.blogspot.com; Internet; accessed 22 November 2005.

25. There are more than twenty countries as you read this today.

26. *Untitus* [document online]; available from http://unitus.com; Internet; accessed 22 November 2005.

27. *U2* [document online]; available at http://www.u2.com; Internet; accessed 22 November 2005.

28. *@U2.* [document online]; available from http://www.atu2.com/; Internet; accessed 22 November 2005.

29. "Muhammad Yunus," *Answers.com Fast Facts* [document online]; available from http://www.answers.com/topic/muhammad-yunus?method=8; Internet; accessed 22 November 2005.

30. "Unitus Borrower Success Stories," *Untitus* [document online]; available from http://www.unitus.com/wwd_borrowerprofs.asp; Internet; accessed 22 November 2005.

31. Global Support *with a mission*. During Diane's travels overseas over the last 4 years, she has been exposed to a variety of eye opening, cultural experiences that awakened in her a desire to do something about the plight of others less fortunate. She doesn't believe it was coincidence that brought her across the paths of the poorest of the poor in the world. It seemed those that were the most desperate, the most troublesome to her were the children. The children that she has met had no say about the conditions they were born into, about the injustices they were being subjected to. They had no voice in how they were living, no voice in their future. She realized that she had to help. But how?

She knew she didn't want to just throw money at projects or organizations that she knew little about, and she knew she was not in a position to start her own program in a foreign country. What she needed was to find someone that was already doing the work she would like to do, someone that she could come along side and help support what they were doing. So she began to evaluate what she liked about existing programs, what she thought worked and what didn't. She knew she wanted to stay in a long-term relationship with whatever ministry she decided on. She knew she wanted her efforts to be directed primarily toward children, to help them have a voice in their destiny, in their future. She knew that she wanted to somehow bridge the gap between the resources that are available to her and others and those that had nothing. But how would she do that? Where would she start? There are thousands of worthy causes, millions of marginalized people. How would she choose? Could she really make a difference? She had more questions than answers.

So she continued to refine and define what she valued. She did not want to westernize people, but valued those programs that worked within the existing culture, those that empowered and equipped the people they were serving. She knew she wanted to work with programs designed to become self-sufficient, programs that helped the recipient help him or herself, that enabled him or her to give back and in turn help someone else. That's what she was interested in. She wanted to support programs designed to work helpers out of a job, that did not depend on the helper in the end. And lastly, she knew she valued exposing others to the plight of the marginalized. She wanted, to take teams of people to different cultures to help make an impact and hopefully, in the end, everyone would be changed from the experience.

And so Global Support *with a mission* was launched. It is the non-profit international arm of the Vineyard Community Church, Shoreline, WA. Global Support *with a mission* seeks out those organizations that have self-sustaining programs already serving the poor and that target the marginalized children of the world. It looks for programs that are designed to give not just a hand out, but a hand up, to bring justice and to give a voice where there is none; programs that bring hope to the children, hope for a future that is better than what they have today.

What a difference a story makes.

32. Sue Miller, *Making Your Children's Ministry the Best Hour of Every Kid's Week* (Grand Rapids, MI: Zondervan Publishing House, 2004), 11.

33. See <http://www.off-the-map.org>.

34. ISBN: 1578569141.

35. See <http://www.theooze.com>.

36. "Improvisation," *Wikipedia* [document online]; available from http://en.wikipedia.org/wiki/Improvisation; Internet; accessed 21 November 2005.

EndNotes

37. Wright, *Scripture and the Authority of God*, 93.

38. N. T. Wright, *Paul: Fresh Perspectives* (London: SPCK, 2005), 172.

39. Wright, *Scripture and the Authority of God*, 93.

40. Ibid., 92.

41. Wright, *Paul: Fresh Perspectives*, 173.

42. Ibid., 141.

43. Ibid., 142.

44. Ibid., 143.

45. Ibid.

46. Marcion was an early bishop who rejected the complete Old Testament believing that the God of the Old Testament was not the same God as presented in the New Testament.

47. See Appendix 11.

48. Brian D. McLaren, *The Story We Find Ourselves In : Further Adventures of a New Kind of Christian*, 1st ed. (San Francisco: Jossey-Bass, 2003). xi.

49. Ibid.

50. Ibid., xii

51. Ibid.

52. Ibid.

Appendix

Appendix 1

1. "New American Standard Bible," *BibleGateway.com* [document online]; available from http://www.biblegateway.com/versions/index.php?action=getVersionInfo&vid=49; Internet; accessed 10 August 2005. "While preserving the literal accuracy of the 1901 ASV, the NASB has sought to render grammar and terminology in contemporary English. Special attention has been given to the rendering of verb tenses to give the English reader a rendering as close as possible to the sense of the original Greek and Hebrew texts. In 1995, the text of the NASB was updated for greater understanding and smoother reading."

Appendix 3

1. W. S. LaSor, et al., *Old Testament Survey: The Message, Form, and Background of the Old Testament. Second Edition* (Grand Rapids, MI: William B. Eerdmans, 1996), 16-17; Bruce K. Waltke, *Genesis: A Commentary* (Grand Rapids: Zondervan Publishing House, 2001), 17-18.

2. Kenneth A. Mathews, *Genesis 1-11:26*, The New American Commentary (Nashville, TN: Broadman & Holman Publishers, 1996), 197-199.

3. Victor P. Hamilton, *Handbook on the Pentateuch: Genesis, Exodus, Leviticus, Numbers, Deuteronomy* (Grand Rapids, Mich: Baker Book House, 1982), 27.

Appendix 6

1. Martin Luther, *Luther' Work Lectures on Genesis 1-5*, (St. Louis, MO: Concordia Publishing House, 1986), 151.

Appendix 7

1. The landmark study for *abba* was done by Joachim Jeremias, *New Testament Theology* (New York,: Scribner, 1971), 61-67. Then, a corrective measure by James Barr, "Abba Isn't Daddy, " *Journal of Theological Studies* 39 (1988): 28-47. And another corrective, this time to Barr by Gordon Fee, *God's Empowering Presence: The Holy Spirit in the Letters of Paul* (Peabody, MA: Hendrickson Publishers, 1994), 408-412.

2. John Bright, *The Kingdom of God: The Biblical Concept and Its Meaning for the Church* (Nashville: Abingdon-Cokesbury Press, 1981), 250.

Appendix 9

1. G. E. Ladd, *A Theology of the New Testament* (Grand Rapids, MI: William B. Eerdmans Publishing Company, 1993), 55.

2. Ibid.

3. Ibid.

4. Ibid.

5. Ibid.

6. James Kallas, *The Significance of the Synoptic Miracles* (London: SPCK, 104. See also, James Kallas, *Jesus and the Power of Satan* (Philadelphia, PA: The Westminster Press, 1968), 60-70.

7. Ladd, *Theology*, 56.

8. Kallas, *Significance*, 104.

9. Kallas, *JPS*, 70-75.

10. Ladd, *Theology*, 57-58.

11. Ibid., 57.

12. Craig A. Blaising and Darrell L. Bock, *Progressive Dispensationalism* (Wheaton, IL: BridgePoint, 1993).

13. Wendell Willis, (Ed.), *The Kingdom of God in 20th-Century Interpretation* (Peabody, MA: Hendrickson Publishers, 1987), 46.

14. Ladd, *Theology*, 58.

15. Kallas, *JPS*, 120.

16. N. T. Wright, *Jesus & the Kingdom of God* (Vancouver, BC: Regent Audio), Tape 1, Side 1.

17. N. T. Wright, *Jesus and the Victory of God* (London: SPCK, 1996), 223.

18. Wright, *Jesus & the Kingdom*, Tape 1, Side 1.

Appendix 11

1. Frank Thielman, *Paul & the Law: A Contextual Approach* (Downers Grove, IL: InterVarsity Press, 1994), 17-18.

2. Ibid., 19.

3. Ibid., 22.

4. Ibid., 23.

5. Ibid., 24.

6. Ibid.

7. Ibid.

8. Ibid.

9. Ibid., 25.

10. Ibid.

11. Ibid., 26.

12. Ibid.

13. Ibid., 27.

14. Ibid., 28.

15. Ibid., 29.

16. E. P. Sanders, *Paul and Palestinian Judaism: A Comparison of Patterns of Religion* (Philadelphia, PA: Fortress Press, 1977).

17. Thielman, *Paul & the Law*, 29-30.

18. Ibid., 30.

19. Ibid., 34.

20. Westerholm, *Perspectives*, viii-ix.

21. Ibid., 3-88.

22. Ibid., 178.

23. Ibid.

24. Ibid., 214-215.

25. Dunn, *Jesus, Paul and the Law*, 215-225.

26. I. Howard Marshall, *New Testament Theology: Many Witnesses, One Gospel* (Downers Grove, IL: InterVarsity Press, 2004), 445-46.

27. Ibid., 448.

28. Delbert R. Hillers, *Covenant: The History of a Biblical Idea* (Baltimore and London: The Johns Hopkins University Press, 1969), 28.

29. Ibid., 29-45.

30. W. S. LaSor, D.A. Hubbard, F.W Bush and L.C. Allen, *Old Testament Survey: The Message, Form, and Background of the Old Testament. Second Edition.* (Grand Rapids, MI: William B. Eerdmans, 1996), 72-75.

31. Westerholm, *Perspectives*, 20.

EndNotes

32. Ibid., 22-23.

33. Ibid., 27-29.

34. Ibid.

35. Ibid., 28-29.

36. James D. G. Dunn, *The Theology of Paul the Apostle* (Grand Rapids, MI: William B. Eerdmans Publishing Company, 1998), 336. Dunn quotes in his *Theology of Paul* from Patrick Collinson's response to the question. This quote itself is from "The Late Medieval Church and Its Reformation 1400-1600," in J. McManners, *The Oxford Illustrated History of Christianity* (New York: Oxford, 1990), 255-259.

37. Ibid., 336.

38. Ibid., 30. "Luther made an explicit link: the church was tarnished with 'Jewish legalism'; the Catholics' "rules and regulation remind me of the Jews, and actually very much was borrowed from the Jews"; on faith and works, the doctrine of the church was a variation of the Jewish error that mere acts can win favour in God's sight." n. 7 page 337, cited by M. Saperstein, *Moments of Crisis in Jewish-Christian Relations* (London: SCM/Philadelphia: TPI, 1989).

39. N. T. Wright, *The Climax of the Covenant: Christ and the Law in Pauline Theology* (Minneapolis, MN: Fortress Press, 1992), 137.

40. N. T. Wright, *What Saint Paul Really Said: Was Paul of Tarsus the Real Founder of Christianity?* (Grand Rapids, MI: William B. Eerdmans Publishing Company, 1997), 18-19.

41. Sanders, *Paul and Palestinian Judaism*, 17.

42. Ibid., 75.

43. Ibid., 543.

44. Ibid., 513.

45. Ibid., 514.

46. Wright, *What Paul Really Said*, 19-20.

47. Westerholm, *Perspectives*, 179. "The Paul and History and the Apostle of Faith." *Tyndale Bulletin* 29 (1978): 61-88. This paper was not reviewed in this paper. But according to Westerholm "much of what Wright has written about Paul was anticipated already in that early article." Westerholm. *Perspectives*. 179.

48. Wright, *What Paul Really Said*, 84.

49. Ibid., 119.

50. Ibid., 122.

51 Wright, *Climax*, 137. Wright believes that "Luther thought Paul was against the Law.

52. N. T. Wright, *Paul for Everyone: Galatians and Thessalonians*, 2 vols. (Louisville, KY: Westminster John Knox Press, 2004), 23-27.

53. Ibid., 26.

54. Ibid.

55. N. T. Wright, *Jesus, Paul and Israel* (Vancouver, BC: Regent Audio). Tape G, Side 1.

56. Jouette M. Bassler, David M. Hay and E. Elizabeth Johnson, *Pauline Theology* (Atlanta, GA: Society of Biblical Literature, 2002), 125.

57. Ibid., 126.

58. Ibid.

59. Ibid., 126-127.

60. Ibid., 127.

61. Ibid., 127-128.

62. Ibid., 128.

63. Frank Thielman, *From Plight to Solution: A Jewish Framework for Understanding Paul's View of the Law in Galatians and Romans* (New York, NY: E. J. Brill, 1989), D. A. Carson and Douglas J. Moo, *An Introduction to the New Testament* (Grand Rapids, MI: Zondervan Publishing House, 1992), 299-300.

64. Westerholm, *Perspectives*, 214-218.

65. Thielman, *Paul & the Law*, 27, 239, 188.

66. Thielman, *Plight to Solution*, 36.

67. Thielman, *Paul & the Law*, 240-241.

68. Ibid., 242-243.

69. Ibid., 245.

70. Ibid.

71. Ibid., 43.

72. Ibid.

References Cited

Books and Internet references cited in this book.

...the story of Jesus who stepped into human history, in the fullness of time. In his ministry, he came proclaiming that the Kingdom of God was present in this Present Evil Age.

Allen, Clifton J. *The Broadman Bible Commentary*. Vol. 11. Nashville, TN: Broadman Press, 1969.

Archer, Gleason , ed. *Three Views on the Rapture: Pre-, Mid-, or Post-Tribulation?* Grand Rapids, MI: Zondervan Publishing House, 1996.

Bailey, Kenneth E. *Poet and Peasant: A Literary-Cultural Approach to the Parables in Luke*. Grand Rapids, MI: William B. Eerdmans Publishing Company, 1976.

Barclay, William. *The Letters to the Galatians and Ephesians*. Philadelphia, PA: Westminster Press, 1959.

Barr, James. "Abba Isn't Daddy." *Journal of Theological Studies*, no. 39 (1988): 28-47.

_____. "Was Everything That God Created Really Good?" Walter Brueggemann, Tod Linafelt, and Timothy K. Beal, eds. *God in the Fray: A Tribute to Walter Brueggemann*. Minneapolis, MN: Fortress Press, 1998, 55-65.

Barrett, C. K. *The New Testament Background: Selected Documents*. Revised Edition. San Francisco, CA: Harper & Row, 1989.

Barth, Karl. *Church Dogmatics*. Edinburgh: T. & T. Clark, 1949.

Barth, Markus. *Ephesians*. Vol. 1. Garden City, NY: Doubleday & Company, 1974.

Bartholomew, Craig G., and Michael W. Goheen. *The Drama of Scripture: Finding Our Place in the Biblical Story*. Grand Rapids, MI: Baker Academic, 2005.

Bassler, Jouette M., David M. Hay, and E. Elizabeth Johnson. *Pauline Theology*. Atlanta, GA: Society of Biblical Literature, 2002.

Bausch, William J. *Storytelling: Imagination and Faith*. Mystic, CT: Twenty-Third Publications, 1984.

Berkouwer, G. C. *The Person of Christ*. Grand Rapids: William B. Eerdmans Publishing Company, 1954.

Birch, Bruce C., Walter Brueggemann, Terrence E. Frethem, and David L. Petersen. *A Theological Introduction to the Old Testament*. Nashville, TN: Abingdon Press, 1999.

Blaising, Craig A., and Darrell L. Bock. *Progressive Dispensationalism*. Wheaton, IL: BridgePoint, 1993.

Bonhoeffer, Dietrich. *Creation And Fall: A Theological Interpretation Of Genesis 1-3*. New York, NY: Macmillan, 1959.

Bright, John. *The Kingdom of God: The Biblical Concept and Its Meaning for the Church*. Nashville: Abingdon Press, 1981.

Bro, Margueritte Harmon. *The Book You Always Meant to Read: The Old Testament*. Garden City: Doubleday & Company, 1974.

Bruce, F. F. *The Epistle to the Ephesians*. London: Pickering & Inglis ltd., 1962.

Brueggemann, Walter. *The Bible Makes Sense*. Louisville, KY: Westminster John Knox Press, 2001.

_____. *An Introduction To The Old Testament: The Canon And Christian Imagination*. Louisville, KY: Westminster John Knox Press, 2003.

_____. *The Creative Word: Canon as a Model for Biblical Education*. Philadelphia, PA: Fortress Press, 1982.

_____. *Genesis*. Atlanta, GA: John Knox Press, 1982.

_____. *The Prophetic Imagination*: Minneapolis, MN" Fortress Press, 1978.

_____. *Text under Negotiation: The Bible and Postmodern Imagination*. Minneapolis, MN: Fortress Press, 1993.

Brown, Raymond Edward. *The Birth of the Messiah: A Commentary on the Infancy Narratives in Matthew and Luke, 2nd Edition*. Garden City, NY: Doubleday, 1993.

_____. *The Death of the Messiah: From Gethsemane to the Grave: A Commentary on the Passion Narratives in the Four Gospels*. 2 vols. 1st ed. New York, NY: Doubleday, 1994.

Caird, G. B., and L. D. Hurst. *New Testament Theology*. Oxford; New York, NY: Clarendon Press, Oxford University Press, 1994.

Carson, D. A., Douglas J. Moo, and Leon Morris. *An Introduction to the New Testament*. Grand Rapids, MI: Zondervan Publishing Company, 1992.

Carson, D. A., R. T France, J. A Motyer, and G. J. Wenham, eds. *New Bible Commentary: 21st Century Edition*. 4th ed. Downers Grove, IL: InterVarsity Press, 1994.

Clouse, Robert G. *The Meaning of the Millennium: Four Views*. Downers Grove, IL: InterVarsity Press, 1977.

References Cited

Cullmann, Oscar. *Christ and Time: The Primitive Christian Conception of Time and History.* Philadelphia, PA: The Westminster Press, 1964.

Davis, Ellen F., and Richard B. Hays, eds. *The Art of Reading Scripture.* Grand Rapids, MI: William B. Eerdmans Publishing Company, 2003.

Davis, Ronald G., Douglas Redford, Ronald L Nickelson, and Jonathan Underwood, eds. *The NIV Standard Lesson Commentary 2001-2002.* Vol. Eight, Annual Volume. Cincinnati, OH: Standard Publishing, 1980.

Davidson, R. "The Theology Of Sexuality In The Beginning: Genesis 3." Andrews University Seminary Studies (AUSS) 26 (1988): 121-131.

Denning, Stephen. *Squirrel Inc.* San Francisco, CA: Jossey-Bass, 2004.

DeSilva, D. A. *An Introduction to the New Testament: Contexts, Methods & Ministry Formation.* Downers Grove, IL: InterVarsity Press, 2004.

Dillard, Raymond B., Tremper Longman. *An Introduction To The Old Testament.* Grand Rapids, MI: Zondervan Publishing House, 1994.

Dunn, James D. G. *Jesus Remembered.* Grand Rapids, MI: William B. Eerdmans Publishing Company, 2003.

_____. *Jesus, Paul, and the Law: Studies in Mark and Galatians.* 1st American Edition. Louisville, KY: Westminster/John Knox Press, 1990.

_____. *Romans 1-8.* Volume 38a. Dallas, TX: Word Books, 1988.

_____. *The Theology of Paul the Apostle.* Grand Rapids, MI: William B. Eerdmans Publishing Company, 1998.

Earle, Ralph. *Exploring the New Testament.* Kansas City, MO: Beacon Hill Press, 1955.

Elwell, Walter A. *Evangelical Dictionary of Biblical Theology.* Grand Rapids, MI: Baker Books, 1996.

Fant, Clyde E., Donald W. Musser, and Mitchell G. Reddish. *An Introduction to the Bible,* Revised Edition. Nashville, TN: Abingdon Press, 2001.

Fee, Gordon D. *God's Empowering Presence: The Holy Spirit in the Letters of Paul.* Peabody, MA: Hendrickson Publishers, 1994.

_____. *Tyndale Lecture Series.* Toronto, Ontario, Canada: Tyndale University College & Seminary, 2003.

Fee, Gordon D., and Douglas Stuart. *How to Read the Bible Book by Book: A Guided Tour.* Grand Rapids, MI: Zondervan Publishing House, 2002.

_____. *How To Read The Bible For All Its Worth, Second Edition.* Grand Rapids, MI: Zondervan Publishing House, 1993.

_____. *How to Read the Bible for All Its Worth. Third Edition.* Grand Rapids, MI: Zondervan Publishing House, 2003.

Fox, Everett. *The Five Books of Moses.* Dallas, TX: Word Publishing, 1995.

Frei, Hans. *The Eclipse of Biblical Narrative: A Study in Eighteenth and Nineteenth Century Hermeneutics.* New Haven, CT: Yale UP, 1974.

Glasser, Arthur F. *Announcing the Kingdom: The Story of God's Mission in the Bible.* Grand Rapids, MI: Baker Book House, 2003.

Goldingay, John. *Old Testament Theology. Volume One: Israel's Gospel.* Downers Grove, IL: InterVarsity Press, 2003.

Goodrick, Edward W. *Is My Bible the Inspired Word of God?* Portland, OR: Multnomah, 1988.

Green, Joel B., Scot McKnight, and I. Howard Marshall, ed. *Dictionary of Jesus and the Gospels.* Downers Grove, IL: InterVarsity Press, 1992.

Grenz, Stanley J. *A Primer on Postmodernism.* Grand Rapids, MI: William B. Eerdmans, 1996.

Grenz, Stanley J., and John R. Franke. *Beyond Foundationalism: Shaping Theology in a Post Modern Context.* Louisville, KY: Westminster John Knox Press, 2001.

Grenz, Stanley J., and Roger E. Olson. *Who Needs Theology? An Invitation to the Study of God.* Downers Grove, IL: InterVarsity Press, 1996.

Griffin, Winn. *Old Testament Interpretation.* Woodinville, WA: Harmon Press (Self Publication), 1996-2005.

_____. *Old Testament Survey: A Study Guide*. Woodinville, WA: HarmonPress, 1997.

Grudem, Wayne. *Systematic Theology: An Introduction to Biblical Doctrine*. Grand Rapids, MI: Zondervan Publishing House, 1994.

Gundry, Robert H. *A Survey of the New Testament*. 4th ed. Grand Rapids, MI: Zondervan Publishing House, 2003.

Hamilton, Victor P. *Handbook on the Pentateuch: Genesis, Exodus, Leviticus, Numbers, Deuteronomy*. Grand Rapids, MI: Baker Book House, 1982.

_____. *The Book of Genesis. Chapters 1-17*. Grand Rapids, MI: William B. Eerdmans Publishing Company, 1990.

Harrison, Everett F. *Introduction to the New Testament*. Revised Edition. Grand Rapids, MI: William B. Eerdmans Publishing Company, 1971.

Hauerwas, Stanley. *Unleashing the Scripture: Free the Bible from Captivity to America*. Nashville, TN: Abingdon Press, 1993.

Hauerwas, Stanley, and L. Gregory Jones. *Why Narrative? Readings in Narrative Theology*. Grand Rapids: William B. Eerdmans Publishing Company, 1989.

Hays, Richard B. *Echoes of Scripture in the Letters of Paul*. New Haven, CT: Yale UP, 1989.

_____. *The Faith of Jesus Christ: The Narrative Substructure of Galatians 3.1-4.11*. Grand Rapids, MI: William B. Eerdmans Publishing Company, 2002

Hillers, Delbert R. *Covenant: The History Of A Biblical Idea*. Baltimore, MD and London: The Johns Hopkins University Press, 1969.

House, Paul R. *Old Testament Theology*. Downers Grove, IL: InterVarsity Press, 1998.

Jeremias, Joachim. *New Testament Theology*. New York, NY: Scribner, 1971.

Johnson, Luke Timothy. *The Writings of the New Testament: An Interpretation*. Revised Edition. Minneapolis, MI: Fortress Press, 1999.

Kaiser, Walter C. Jr. *Toward An Old Testament Theology*. Grand Rapids, MI: Zondervan Publishing House, 1978.

Kallas, James. *The Significance of the Synoptic Miracles*. London: SPCK, 1961.

_____. *Synoptic Gospels Course Notes*, 1973.

_____. *The Satanward View: A Study in Pauline Theology*. Philadelphia, PA: Westminster Press, 1966.

_____. *Jesus and the Power of Satan*. Philadelphia, PA: The Westminster Press, 1968.

_____. *The Real Satan: From Biblical Times to the Present*. Minneapolis, MN: Augsburg, 1975.

_____. *The Story of Paul*. Minneapolis, MI: Augsburg Publishing House, 1966.

Keck, Leander E, ed. *The New Interpreter's Bible: A Commentary in Twelve Volumes (Vol. 10)*. Nashville, TN: Abingdon Press, 1994.

Keener, Craig S. *The IVP Bible Background Commentary: New Testament*. Downers Grove, IL: InterVarsity Press, 1993.

Ladd, George Eldon. *A Commentary on the Revelation of John*. Grand Rapids, MI: William B. Eerdmans Publishing Company 1972.

_____. *New Testament and Criticism*. Grand Rapids, MI: William B. Eerdmans Publishing Company, 1966.

_____. *The Presence of the Future*. Grand Rapids, MI: William B. Eerdmans Publishing Company, 1974.

_____. *A Theology of the New Testament*. Revised Edition. Grand Rapids, MI: William B. Eerdmans, 1993.

Lane, William L. *The Gospel According to Mark*. Grand Rapids, MI: William B. Eerdmans Publishing Company, 1994.

Langton, Edward. *Essentials of Demonology: A Study of Jewish and Christian Doctrine*. London: Epworth Press, 1949.

LaSor, W. S., D. A. Hubbard, F. W. Bush, and L. C. Allen. *Old Testament Survey: The Message, Form, and Background of the Old Testament*. Second Edition. Grand Rapids, MI: William B. Eerdmans, 1996.

References Cited

Lewis, C. S. *Reflections On The Psalms*. New York, NY: Harcourt, 1958.

Lilje, Hanns. *The Last Book of the Bible: The Meaning of the Revelation of St. John*. Philadelphia, PA: Fortress Press, 1957.

Lucas, Ernest C. *Exploring The Old Testament: A Guide To The Psalms & Wisdom Literature. Volume Three*. Downers Grove, IL: InterVarsity, 2003.

Luther, Martin. *Luther's Works*. Vol 1. St. Louis, MO: Concordia Publiishing House, 1986.

_____. *Luther's Works*. Vol. 35. St. Louis, MO: Concordia Publiishing House, 1986.

Mackintosh, H. R. *The Doctrine of the Person of Jesus Christ*. New York, NY: C. Scribner's and Sons, 1912.

McLaren, Brian D., and Leadership Network (Dallas Tex.). *The Story We Find Ourselves In : Further Adventures of a New Kind of Christian*. 1st ed. San Francisco: Jossey-Bass, 2003.

McGrath, Alister. *Christian Spirituality: An Introduction*. Oxford: Blackwell Publishers, 1999.

Marshall, I. Howard. *New Testament Theology: Many Witnesses, One Gospel*. Downers Grove, IL: InterVarsity Press, 2004.

Marshall, I. Howard, Stephen Travis, and Ian Paul. *Exploring the New Testament: A Guide to the Letters & Revelation*. Vol. 2. Downers Grove, IL: InterVarsity Press, 2002.

Mathews, Kenneth A. *Genesis 1-11:26 .The New American Commentary*. Nashville, TN: Broadman & Holman Publishers, 1996.

Martin, Ralph P. *New Testament Foundations: A Guide for Christian Students*. Vol. 1. Grand Rapids, MI: William B. Eerdmans Publishing Company, 1975.

Miller, Sue. *Making Your Children's Ministry the Best Hour of Every Kid's Week*. Grand Rapids, MI: Zondervan Publishing House, 2004.

Morgan, Richard L. *Saving Our Stories*. Louisville, KY: Geneva Press, 1999.

Newbigin, Lesslie. *The Gospel in a Pluralist Society*. Grand Rapids, MI: William B. Eerdmans, 1989.

Newman, Carey C., ed. *Jesus & the Restoration of Israel*. Downers Grove, IL: InterVarsity Press, 1999.

Niebuhr, Reinhold. *The Nature and Destiny of Man: A Christian Interpretation*. New York, NY: Charles Scribner's and Sons, 1948.

Niditch, Susan. *Oral World and Written Word: Ancient Israelite Literature*. Louisville, KY: Westminster John Knox Press, 1996.

Packer, J. I., Merrill C. Tenney, and William White, Jr. *The World of the Old Testament*. Nashville, TN: Thomas Nelson Publishers, 1982.

Pate, C. Marvin, J. Scott Duvall, J. Daniel Hays, E. Randolph Richards, W. Dennis Tucker Jr., and Preben Vang. *The Story of Israel: A Biblical Theology*. Downers Grove, IL: InterVarsity Press, 2004.

Patzia, A. "Philemon, Letter To." *Dictionary of Paul and His Letters*, Gerald F. Hawthorne and Ralph P. Martin, ed. Downers Grove, IL: InterVarsity Press, 1993, 702-706.

Peterson, Eugene H. *Stories of Jesus*. Colorado Springs, CO: NavPress, 1999.

Placher, William C. "Paul Ricoeur and Postliberal Theology: A Conflict of Interpretations?" *Modern Theology* 4, no. 1 (1987): 35-52.

Pierce, Ronald W., Rebecca Merrill Groothuis, and Gordon D. Fee, eds. *Discovering Biblical Equality: Complementarity without Hierarchy*. Downers Grove, IL: InterVarsity Press, 2004.

Puskas, Charles B. *An Introduction to the New Testament*. Peabody, MA: Hendrickson Publishers, 1989.

The Promise: Contemporary English Version. Nashville, TN: Thomas Nelson, Inc., 1995.

The Revised Common Lectionary. Nashville, TN: Abingdon Press, 1992.

Ricoeur, Paul. *Time and Narrative*. Translated by Translation: Kathleen McLaughlin and David Pellauer. Vol. 1-3. Chicago, IL: U of Chicago P, 1984.

Ridderbos, Herman. *The Coming of the Kingdom*. Philadelphia, PA: The Presbyterian and Reformed Publishing Company, 1962.

Ryken, Leland. *The Literature of the Bible*. Grand Rapids, MI: Zondervan Publishing House, 1974.

Ryken, L., J. Wilhoit. "King, Kingship." *Dictionary of Biblical Imagery*, Downers Grove, IL: InterVarsity Press, 1998, 476-478.

Ryken, L., J. Wilhoit, T. Longman, C. Duriez, D. Penney, and D. G. Reid. *Dictionary of Biblical Imagery.* Downers Grove, IL: InterVarsity Press, 1998.

Sanders, E. P. *Paul and Palestinian Judaism: A Comparison of Patterns of Religion.* Philadelphia, PA: Fortress Press, 1977.

Schweitzer, Albert. *The Quest of the Historical Jesus: A Critical Study of Its Progress from Reimarus to Wrede.* New York, NY: The Macmillan Company, 1950.

Stringfellow, Alan B. *Through the Bible in One Year.* Tulsa, OK: Hensley Publishing, 1978.

Sweet, Leonard I. *AquaChurch.* Loveland, CO: Group Publishing, 1999.

_____. *SoulTsunami: Sink or Swim in the New Millennium Culture.* Grand Rapids, Mich: Zondervan Publishing House, 1999.

_____. *Out of the Question...Into the Mystery.* Colorado Springs, CO: WaterBrook Press, 2004.

_____. *Summoned to Lead.* Grand Rapids, MI: Zondervan Publishing House, 2004.

Tanakh. Philadelphia Jerusalem: The Jewish Publication Society, 1985

Tarbell, Martha. *Tarbell's Teachers' Guide to the International Sunday-School Lessons for 1917.* New York, Chicago, Toronto, London, Edinburgh: Fleming H. Revell Company, 1916.

Tenney, Merrill Chapin, Gen. Ed. *The Zondervan Pictorial Encyclopedia of the Bible.* Grand Rapids: Zondervan Publishing House, 1975.

Thielman, Frank. *From Plight to Solution: A Jewish Framework for Understanding Paul's View of the Law in Galatians and Romans.* New York, NY: E. J. Brill, 1989.

_____. *Paul & the Law: A Contextual Approach.* Downers Grove, IL: InterVarsity Press, 1994.

Thiemann, Ronald F. *Constructing a Public Theology: The Church in a Pluralistic Culture.* 1st ed. Louisville, KY: Westminster/John Knox Press, 1991.

Waltke, Bruce K. "The Literary Genre of Genesis 1." *Crux* 27 (1991): 2-10.

Walton, John H. *The NIV Application Commentary: Genesis.* Grand Rapids, MI: Zondervan, 2001.

Walton, John H., Victor Harold Matthews, Mark W. Chavalas. *The IVP Bible Background Commentary: Old Testament.* Downers Grove, IL: InterVarsity Press, 2000.

Walvoord, John F. *The Rapture Question.* Grand Rapids, MI: Zondervan Publishing House, 1979.

Wenham, David, and Steve Walton. *Exploring the New Testament: A Guide to the Gospels & Acts.* Volume 1. Downers Grove, IL: InterVarsity Press, 2001.

Wenham, Gordon J. *Exploring The Old Testament: A Guide To The Pentateuch.* Volume One. Downers Grove, IL: InterVarsity Press, 2003.

_____. *Genesis 1-15.* Waco, TX: Word Books, 1987.

_____. *Story As Torah.* Grand Rapids. MI: Baker Academic, 2000.

Westerholm, Stephen. *Perspectives Old and New on Paul: The Lutheran Paul and His Critics.* Grand Rapids, MI: William B. Eerdmans Publishing Company, 2004.

Willis, Wendell, ed. *The Kingdom of God in 20th-Century Interpretation.* Peabody, MA: Hendrickson Publishers, 1987.

Witherington III, Ben. *Jesus, Paul and the End of the World: A Comparative Study in New Testament Eschatology.* Downers Grove, IL: InterVarsity Press, 1992.

_____. *New Testament History: A Narrative Account.* Grand Rapids, MI: Baker Academic, 2001.

Wood, D. R. W., A. R. Millard, J. I. Packer, D. J. Wiseman, and I. Howard Marshall, eds. *New Bible Dictionary Third Edition.* Downers Grove, IL: InterVarsity Press, 1996.

Wright, N. T. "How Can the Bible Be Authoritative?" *Vox Evangelica*, no. 21 (1991): 7-32.

_____. *Bringing the Church to the World.* Minneapolis, MN: Bethany House Publishers, 1992.

_____. *The Challenge of Jesus. Rediscovering Who Jesus Was and Is.* Downers Grove, IL: InterVarsity Press. 1999.

_____. *The Climax of the Covenant: Christ and the Law in Pauline Theology.* Minneapolis, MN: Fortress Press, 1992.

_____. *Jesus & the Kingdom of God.* Vancouver, BC: Regent Audio. 1984.

_____. *Jesus and the Victory of God.* London: SPCK, 1996.

References Cited

_____. *Jesus, Paul and Israel*. Vancouver, BC: Regent Audio, 1986.

_____. *The New Testament and the People of God*. Minneapolis, MN: Fortress Press, 1992.

_____. *The Original Jesus: The Life and Vision of a Revolutionary*. Grand Rapids, MI: William B. Eerdmans Publishing Company, 1996.

_____. *Paul for Everyone: Galatians and Thessalonians*. 2 vols. Louisville, KY: Westminster John Knox Press, 2004.

_____. *Paul: Fresh Perspectives*. London: SPCK, 2005.

_____. *The Resurrection of the Son of God*. London: SPCK, 2003.

_____. *Scripture and the Authority of God*. London: SPCK, 2005.

_____. *What Saint Paul Really Said: Was Paul of Tarsus the Real Founder of Christianity?* Grand Rapids, MI: William B. Eerdmans Publishing Company, 1997.

Yinger, Kent L. *Paul, Judaism, and Judgment According to Deeds*. New York, NY: Cambridge University Press, 1999.

Internet References Cited

"A House Divided Against Itself Cannot Stand." *The National Center for Public Research*. Document online. Available from http://www.nationalcenter.org/HouseDivided.html; Internet; accessed 7 June 2005.

"All-Time Bestselling Books and Authors," *Internet Public Library*. Document online. Available from http://www.ipl.org/div/farq/bestsellerFARQ.html; Internet; accessed 3 September 2005.

Biblical Theology. Document online. Available from http://www.biblicaltheology.ca/index.htm; Internet; accessed 24 June 2005.

Bono, "The Statesman," Document online. Available from http://www.atu2.com/news/article.src?ID=4081&Key=&Year=&Cat=; Internet; accessed 22 November 2005.

"Borrower Success Stories," *Unitus*. Document online. Available from http://www.unitus.com/wwd_borrowerprofs.asp; Internet; accessed 22 November 2005.

"Chapter," *crosswalk.com*. Document online. Available from http://www.biblestudytools.net/Dictionaries/EastonBibleDictionary/ebd.cgi?number=T773; Internet; accessed 24 June 2005.

Eleanor Farjeon, "Morning Has Broken," *GuitarSounds.com*. Document online. Available from http://www.guitarsounds.com/content/mp3/Morning_Has_Broken128k.mp3; Internet; accessed 12 September 2005.

"Empiricism," *Answers.com Fast Facts*. Document online. Available from http://www.answers.com/empiricism; Internet; accessed 30 June 2005.

"General Information: The International Sunday School Lesson Plan," *Smyth & Helwys*. Document online. Available from http://www.helwys.com/curriculum/usgeneral.html; Internet; accessed 22 June 2005.

George Fox University. Document online. Available from http://www.georgefox.edu/academics/seminary/degrees/dmin/index.html; Internet; accessed 27 June 2005.

Gill, N. S., "Emergence of the Olympian Gods and Goddesses," *about.com*. Document online. Available from http://ancienthistory.about.com/library/weekly/aa121598.htm; Internet; accessed 12 September 2005.

"Historical Criticism," *Answers.com Fast Facts*. Document online. Available from http://www.answers.com/historical%20criticism; Internet; accessed 2 December 2005.

"John Donne: Meditation XVII," *Indiana State University*. Document online. Available from http://isu.indstate.edu/ilnprof/ENG451/ISLAND/; Internet; accessed 17 October 2005.

"Leaning on the Everlasting Arms," *Gospel.Hines01.com*. Available from http://gospel.hines01.com/gaithers/Leaning%20on%20the%20everlasting%20arm.htm; Internet; accessed 13 September 2005.

"Memorable Quotes from the Shining," *IMDb*. Document online. Available from http://www.imdb.com/title/tt0081505/quotes; Internet; accessed 21 September 2005.

"Microfinance, " *WorldVision*. Document online. Available from http://worldvision.org/med; Internet; accessed 22 November 2005.

"Microfinance," *Untitus*. Document online. Available from http://unitus.com; Internet; accessed 22 November 2005.

"Muhammad Yunus," *Answers.com Fast Facts*. Document online. Available from http://www.answers.com/topic/muhammad-yunus?method=8; Internet; accessed 22 November 2005.

"Narrative Theology," *Answers.com Fast Facts*. Document online. Available from http://www.answers.com/narrative%20theology; Internet; accessed 2 December 2005.

"New American Standard Bible," *BibleGateway.com*. Document online. Available from http://bible.gospelcom.net/versions/index.php?action=getVersionInfo&vid=49#books&version=49; Internet; accessed 10 August 2007.

Off the Map. Document online. Available from http://www.off-the-map.org; Internet; accessed 22 November 2005.

RealNetworks. Document online. Available from http://www.real.com; Internet; accessed 22 November 2005.

Richards, Dave, "Personalizing Microfinance," *Defeating Global Poverty*. Available from http://defeatpoverty.com/2006/02/personalizing-microfinance.html; Internet; accessed November 22, 2005.

_____, *Dave's Defeating Poverty Reading List*. Document online. Available from http://povertyreadinglist.blogspot.com/; Internet; accessed 22 November 2005.

"The Bible," *The Barna Group*. Document online. Available from http://www.barna.org/FlexPage.aspx?Page=Topic&TopicID=7; Internet; accessed 6 June 2005.

The Ooze. Document online. Available from http://www.theooze.com; Internet; accessed 22 November 2005.

"The Resurrection," *Falls Church*. Document online. Available from http://www.thefallschurch.org/templates/custhefalls/details.asp?id=29455&PID=244903&mast=; Internet; accessed 24 October 2005.

Turnbull, Margaret, *Thinkexists.com*. Document online. Available from http://en.thinkexist.com/quotation/no_man_is_responsible_for_his_father-that_was/216579.html; Internet; accessed 20 October 2005.

Wittig, Gerry, "Landscape date and complete adaptive system Earth," *c5corp.com*. Available from http://www.c5corp.com/research/complexsystem.shtml; Internet; accessed 12 September 2005.

U2. Document online. Available from http://www.u2.com; Internet; accessed 22 November 2005.

Wright, N. T., "The Resurrection" *The Falls Church*. Document online. Available from http://www.thefallschurch.org/templates/custhefalls/details.asp?id=29455&PID=244903&mast=; Interent; accessed 24 October 2005.

Printed in the United States
204964BV00001B/1-22/A